COUNSELING AND PSYCHOTHERAPY TODAY

Theory, Practice, and Research

Carol Shaw Austad

Central Connecticut State University

Mc Graw Hill **Higher Education**

Boston   Burr Ridge, IL   Dubuque, IA   New York   San Francisco   St. Louis
Bangkok   Bogotá   Caracas   Kuala Lumpur   Lisbon   London   Madrid   Mexico City
Milan   Montreal   New Delhi   Santiago   Seoul   Singapore   Sydney   Taipei   Toronto

Higher Education

Published by McGraw-Hill, an imprint of The McGraw-Hill Companies, Inc., 1221 Avenue of the Americas, New York, NY 10020. Copyright © 2009. All rights reserved. No part of this publication may be reproduced or distributed in any form or by any means, or stored in a database or retrieval system, without the prior written consent of The McGraw-Hill Companies, Inc., including, but not limited to, in any network or other electronic storage or transmission, or broadcast for distance learning.

This book is printed on acid-free paper.

1 2 3 4 5 6 7 8 9 0 DOC/DOC 0 9 8

ISBN: 978-0-07-311225-1
MHID: 0-07-311225-9

Editor in Chief: *Michael Ryan*
Director, Editorial: *Beth Mejia*
Sponsoring Editor: *Mike Sugarman*
Marketing Manager: *James Headley*
Production Editor: *David Blatty*
Manuscript Editor: *Jennifer Gordon*
Cover Designer: *Laurie Entringer*
Production Supervisor: *Tandra Jorgensen*
Composition: *10/12 Minion by Aptara®, Inc.*
Printing: *PMS 471 U, 45# New Era Matte, R. R. Donnelley*

Cover Image: *Thinkstock/Getty Images*

Library of Congress Cataloging-in-Publication Data

Austad, Carol Shaw.
    Counselling and psychotherapy today : theory, practice, and research / Carol Shaw Austad.
—1st ed.
        p. ; cm.
    Includes bibliographical references and index.
    ISBN-13: 978-0-07-311225-1 (alk. paper)
    ISBN-10: 0-07-311225-9 (alk. paper)
    1. Psychotherapy—Textbooks. 2. Counselling—Textbooks. I. Title.
        [DNLM: 1. Psychotherapy-methods. 2. Counselling—methods. WM 420 A932c 2009]
    RC480.A848 2009
    616.89'14—dc22   2008029233

The Internet addresses listed in the text were accurate at the time of publication. The inclusion of a Web site does not indicate an endorsement by the authors or McGraw-Hill, and McGraw-Hill does not guarantee the accuracy of the information presented at these sites.

www.mhhe.com

BRIEF CONTENTS

CONTENTS

PREFACE

✦ CHALLENGES IN PSYCHOTHERAPY TODAY

Having taught students enrolled in an introductory psychotherapy and counseling course for nearly two decades, I know today's students face daunting challenges. They must familiarize themselves with an enormous amount of information from a field that is growing and evolving rapidly. The expansive changes in psychotherapy over the last decade have produced a wide range of information that must be learned, mastered, and applied. Let's briefly review some of the major areas of change confronting psychotherapy practitioners today.

The most obvious challenge is the sheer number of therapeutic orientations that are available. Along with this proliferation in approaches has come a vast increase in the clients who can benefit from psychotherapy; the growing client pool has generated greater complexity in the nature of their problems. Psychotherapy today helps with a wide assortment of human struggles, ranging from helping a highly functioning person to achieve greater levels of personal growth, to allaying a person's worries and anxieties, to helping a severely disturbed and gravely disabled psychotic patient maintain himself in society.

The practice setting has also expanded. Today psychotherapists can be found in psychiatric hospitals, college counseling centers, and health maintenance organizations, among other settings. The health care system in the United States has also impacted psychotherapy. For example, many insurance plans cover psychotherapy as a health benefit as long as the client has an appropriate *DSM* diagnosis. As a result, many see psychotherapy as a form of health care to treat the mentally disordered. Yet, psychotherapy is still broad enough to interface with a holistic or complementary health system where it is viewed as a catalyst to the client's own healing.

✦ MY MISSION AND APPROACH

My primary mission in writing this book is to provide students with a comprehensive, balanced, accurate, and insightful introduction to the major contemporary models of psychotherapy. This text discusses psychotherapy in a way that will help undergraduate and graduate students to think about therapy as it is practiced in a real-world context. I give students an overview of what needs to be considered when psychotherapy is practiced in the United States today. I hope to inspire students to further pursue their studies in this area and to help guide them in choosing an area to focus on in their career.

✦ Why This Book?

After practicing psychotherapy for over a decade in a number of diverse settings, I realized that I needed to write this book. My background includes interning in a state hospital for severely disturbed and destitute patients, serving on the staff of a private psychiatric hospital for wealthy and well-insured patients, running a part-time private practice, and assuming a full-time position in a staff-model health maintenance organization.

In 1987, I became a professor at a public university while continuing a part-time psychotherapy practice. In order to teach my students well, I shared my practical experience with them, impressing upon them that psychotherapy is not practiced in a vacuum. I presented material in such a way as to maximize learning so that my students would be better prepared to accommodate their therapy practice in the real world. Although the therapeutic relationship is at the heart of psychotherapy and can transcend any environment, the context in which psychotherapy is practiced must be considered thoughtfully. This means thinking about the most appropriate models to fit clients as well as other factors that impinge upon the therapist–client relationship, such as time constraints, medical conditions, treatment planning, insurance and reimbursement factors, outcome or results, and supporting evidence for what is done. This book addresses these concerns.

Finally, since our health care system is constantly changing, it is important for students to have information on a variety of perspectives so that they can make the best decision for the client. Armed with knowledge on a range of approaches, psychotherapists are in a better position to make these choices.

✦ Innovative Features

I include two chapters that are typically not part of traditional textbooks for psychotherapy. Chapter 13 is devoted to the biopsychosocial therapy with concepts from health psychology and stress management. With the growing acceptance of the biopsychosocial approach and the strong push to integrate mental and physical health, therapies that can be called biopsychosocial therapies are emerging as popular interventions. For example, stress management programs, which use the relaxation response as a mainstay, are increasingly in demand.

The second innovative chapter is dedicated to psychopharmacology. Because often psychotherapists are not prescribing providers, Chapter 14 stresses how the nonprescribing therapist collaborates with the medical provider. It is vital that all psychotherapists have sufficient knowledge of psychotropic medications, so this chapter is necessarily technical to provide that information.

Another innovative feature of this text is the inclusion of the topic of evidence-based mental health (EBMH). I give hands-on instructions in Chapter 1 and in the online Appendix C to give students practice in conducting individual EBMH reviews. Research into psychotherapy develops at such a rapid rate that by the time a summary is published it is often out-of-date. Students who learn the nuts and bolts of performing their own evidence-based reviews will be able to keep current as well as to access a vast store of information.

✦ ORGANIZATION OF THE TEXT

The text is organized to facilitate learning about the theory, practice, and research of psychotherapy and counseling.

Chapter 1 begins with a broad overview of the current state of psychotherapy. I discuss the wide-ranging changes within the field and place psychotherapy in its sociocultural context. I describe the major categories into which therapies are classified and introduce some of the most important issues and controversies related to current theory, practice, and research. I explain the concepts of evidence-based medicine and mental health and give some practical information about evidence-based searches.

Chapter 2 presents a general discussion of the fundamental professional, legal, and ethical issues psychotherapists face today. I overview the major professional organizations, codes of ethics, and multicultural concerns. I touch briefly on professionalism and the ethical and legal issues that students will need to study further if they intend to become professional psychotherapists.

Chapters 3 to 15 constitute the nucleus of the book. From the several hundred therapies in existence today, I include these models of psychotherapy and counseling because mental health professionals consider them to be among the best established, most reputable, and most frequently employed. The text presents a representative model from each major theoretical group of psychotherapies. Most of the chapters describe a single model, but some contain multiple models when appropriate. For example, rational emotive behavior therapy and Beck's cognitive therapy are both cognitive models with overlapping constructs, but a well-informed therapist generally possesses a working knowledge of both.

Chapter Structure

For the most part, each clinical chapter describes the unique features of the psychotherapy model, including its historical context, theory, practice, and research directions. Each is also considered in light of issues of diversity and major criticisms, so that all perspectives undergo the same scrutiny. Where appropriate, I include biographical information on significant therapists and their contribution to the model. Each chapter concludes with these sections: Summary, Resources, and Class Exercises and Activities.

Several chapters do not follow this format, including Chapter 4 on psychodynamic therapy after Freud and Chapter 15 on eclectic and other therapies. These chapters present their information in a summary format.

The following describes some of the recurring features of the book.

- **Historical Context:** This section describes the cultural zeitgeist from when the therapy emerged. This information helps the student get a feel for the sociocultural context that contributed to the acceptance of the therapy. For example, Rogers found a welcome reception for person-centered therapy with the end of World War II. The public was weary of worldwide violence and hungering for the values found in the human potential movement. Today, the economics of health care is a strong force in encouraging the acceptance of short-term models and in demanding evidence of a treatment's usefulness.

- **Biographies:** When appropriate, biographical boxes are included to give students a better understanding of the primary founders of a theory or psychotherapeutic methodology.

- **Theory:** This section describes the most salient ideas of each model. These sections vary in length and detail depending upon the complexity and depth of a given theory. For example, Freudian theory is rich with abstractions that are interconnected within a complex system. Behavior therapy is an amalgam of experimentally based techniques. Humanist-existentialist therapies emphasize basic theory more than specific techniques. The definition and description of normal and abnormal is underscored since it is often the focus of clinical attention.

- **Practice:** In this section, a fictional composite therapist speaks to the student in a narrative style to describe the major components of therapy practice. He or she presents the material in the following chronology: assessment and diagnosis, negotiation of therapeutic relationship and length of treatment, therapeutic techniques, and the process of therapy. This consistent structure allows the student to look at the same elements from multiple therapeutic perspectives.

- **Therapy in Action:** Each clinical chapter examines the case of Jonathan, a young White male who is depressed because his long-term partner Tuti has left him. Jonathan is analyzed from the perspective of each of the therapies presented. The case studies are presented with simulated condensed therapy excerpts of dialogue between Jonathan and the fictional therapist practicing that chapter's particular modality. The treatment plan for each psychotherapy is also presented to encourage students to conceptualize psychotherapy from a pragmatic and goal-oriented perspective regardless of the model employed.

- **Research Directions:** Discussions about research are written to encourage students to adopt a research-friendly attitude so that they will want to use research to enhance the quality of their practice. I begin with a general discussion about how each model stands in relationship to research. For example, while research has been an integral part of behaviorism since its inception, it has not been a high priority for existentialist therapies. Second, I summarize and report on the recent status of cumulative research findings for each model (reviews, meta-analyses, and recent significant studies). Third, each chapter exposes the student to the basic concepts of evidence-based mental health practice. Selected chapters refer students to the online Appendix C to find sample EBMH reviews or examples of quality research.

- **Issues of Diversity:** This section summarizes key information relating to how each model best deals with multicultural issues that can influence the success of therapy.

- **Major Critiques:** The clinical chapters end with this section, which explains major criticisms of the chapter's therapeutic model. The strengths and weaknesses of the theory, research, and practice of each model are discussed.

- **Summary:** This section provides a recap of the major ideas presented in the chapter to help students synthesize the material.

- **Resources:** Here are useful addresses, phone numbers, and websites for relevant sources of information for the chapter. There are also brief annotations describing the resource.

- **Class Exercises and Activities:** Each chapter includes a set of questions pertaining to theory, practice, and research. These can be assigned as either classwork or homework.

- **Appendixes:** There are three appendixes for the text. Appendix A contains the case studies for Jonathan and Tuti. Throughout the book, students are referred to Appendix A so that they can complete the exercises for each chapter. Appendix B provides tables comparing various therapy perspectives. The online Appendix C contains evidence-based reviews and other relevant research information.

✦ SUPPLEMENTS

The following supplements are available to support *Psychotherapy and Counseling Today: Theory, Practice, and Research.*

- **For instructors:** The instructor side of the Online Learning Center (OLC) at http://www.mhhe.com/austad1e contains the Instructor's Manual (authored by Susan Holt at Connecticut State University), Test Bank (authored by Wade Leuwerke at Drake University), and PowerPoint slides to help you design and enhance your course. This site also includes downloadable versions of key forms from the text and the complete copy for Appendix C: Research, Evidence-Based Practice, and Psychotherapy. Ask your local McGraw-Hill representative for your password.

- **For students:** The Online Learning Center at www.mhhe.com/austad1e provides students with access to a variety of learning tools (authored by Anita Rosenfield at Yavapai College) designed to help students test content mastery. These include a chapter outline, key terms glossary, and practice quizzes for each chapter.

✧ Acknowledgments

A career in counseling, psychotherapy, and related professions can be immensely satisfying personally as well as extremely useful to society. Although it is impossible to convey the full picture of such a career, I hope that my approach and techniques will intrigue and entice students to explore further. Throughout the book, I have attempted to achieve a balance of engaging, relevant prose and comprehensive, accurate, and current scholarship. To the extent that I have succeeded in this, I would like to thank all those who helped me to develop the manuscript.

Expert Reviewers

To assure that the information presented is a true representation of each model of therapy, I called upon expert reviewers to review the chapters covering their area of expertise. Each of the following individuals was selected to review the material because he or she is recognized as a leader in the field. I want to express my deep appreciation to them for their time, support, and criticisms, which have improved this textbook in many ways.

Nicholas A. Cummings, *University of Nevada, Reno*
Henry T. Stein, *Alfred Adler Institute of Northwestern Washington*
Michael D. Spiegler, *Providence College*
Robert Elliott, *University of Strathclyde, Glasgow*
Gary Yontef, *Pacific Gestalt Institute*
Kristene A. Doyle, *Albert Ellis Institute*
Robert Wubbolding, *Center for Reality Therapy* and the *William Glasser Institute*
Laura S. Brown, *independent practice in Seattle, Washington*
Carol Enns, *Cornell University*
John Preston, *Alliant International University*

I would also like to thank the following instructors who reviewed the manuscript and suggested many improvements, additions, and ways of making the book more teachable.

Bethanne Bierer, *Metro State College of Denver*
Steven Birchak, *College of Saint Rose*
Charles Boisvert, *Rhode Island College*
Chris Brown, *Southern Connecticut State University*
Eric Bruns, *Campbellsville University*
Wendy Enochs, *Stephen F. Austin State University*
Jeannine Feldman, *San Diego State University*
Lani Fujitsubo, *Southern Oregon University*
Paul Hernandez, *South Texas Community College*
Amy Herstein Gervasio, *University of Wisconsin-Stevens Point*
Wade Leuwerke, *Drake University*

Cheryl McGill, *Florence Darlington Technical College*
Carolyn Oxenford, *Marymount University*
Susan Styles, *Charleston Southern University*
Leslie Travers, *Casper College*

I am grateful to many individuals whose help and encouragement made it possible for me to write this text. I want to thank members of the McGraw-Hill staff for their tireless work. Thanks to the excellent editorial support from Suzanna Ellison and the editorial assistance from Ann Helgerson and Erin O'Conner. I especially want to thank David Blatty, production editor, for consistently and intuitively knowing what was needed as the project unfolded. A very special and heartfelt acknowledgment goes to Jennifer Gordon for her creative talents used in the development of the manuscript as well as her meticulous and patient editing. Her assistance in this project was invaluable. I would also like to acknowledge Steve Rutter, the first editor on the project, for his innovative thinking and sense of discovery. My deepest appreciation goes to Janie Pittendreigh, who was a source of inspiration, and a special mention goes to Laurie McGee. Thanks also to Debbie and the Cape Codder. On the home front, I want to thank my husband, Robert Swarr, for his support. I also wish to acknowledge the many colleagues whose comments and conversation provided valuable feedback and helped me to refine my thinking.

Carol Shaw Austad
Central Connecticut State University

ABOUT THE AUTHOR

Carol Shaw Austad is a licensed clinical psychologist and a professor of psychology at Central Connecticut State University, a thriving public educational facility in New Britain, Connecticut, where she has taught psychology courses since 1987.

Dr. Austad has extensive psychotherapy experience in a variety of clinical settings. These include an internship at Connecticut Valley Hospital, a public facility for the chronically mentally ill; staff psychologist at Hall Brook Hospital, a private psychiatric inpatient facility; outpatient psychotherapist at Community Health Care Plan, a major staff-model health maintenance organization (a high-quality form of managed care) where clients from every walk of life share in the mental health system; and private practice with individuals, groups, families, and the developmentally disabled.

She has published extensively in the area of health care systems and psychotherapy. She is passionate about developing a sociological view of psychotherapy that attends to the interactive power of the environment, the health care system, and practitioner responses in shaping the psychotherapy experience.

Dr. Austad obtained her PhD from the University of North Texas, her MA from Stephen F. Austin State University, and her BA from Carleton University, Ottawa, Canada. She has traveled extensively to examine systems of health care in other countries. She currently lives with her husband, Robert Swarr, and their three minidachshunds—Hoover, Speckle, and Stretch.

CHAPTER 1

THE STATE OF PSYCHOTHERAPY AND COUNSELING TODAY

Changing Theory, Practice, and Research

Open your arms to change, but don't let go of your values.

–Dalai Lama

The goals of this chapter are to help you, the student of psychotherapy, acquire basic information about psychotherapy and its context. The chapter considers the definition of psychotherapy, the role of the psychotherapist, and the environment in which the psychotherapist works. In addition, it provides an overview of changes in the theory, practice, and research of psychotherapy over the last several decades.

We look at specific changes in theory, including how biological research has advanced our ways of considering psychological problems, how interest in the biopsychosocial and complementary medical models has grown, and how the field has moved away from grand theories and toward more concise ones.

We also examine broad changes in psychotherapeutic practice. Today, psychotherapy interfaces with economics and business, with managed care, and with politics. As well, we look at how pharmacological developments have influenced mental health care and the new model of primary behavioral health care. We look at changes in research, including the stormy history of psychotherapeutic research and its impact on practice. In addition, we examine the closing gap between researcher and clinician and consider how the psychotherapist uses the findings from psychotherapy research and evidence-based mental health to enhance practice.

Finally this chapter introduces students to issues outside of theory, practice, and research. Some of these other concerns are diversity awareness; computer technology and psychotherapy, and long-term versus short-term therapy.

✦ PSYCHOTHERAPY AND THE PSYCHOTHERAPIST

The Greek word *psyche* means "spirit, soul, or being," and *therapy* comes from the Greek *therapeutics*, which means "attendant or caretaker." Psychotherapy, then, is generally defined as the activity of caring for the spirit or soul of another (Kleinke, 1994). Finding a single comprehensive definition to cover all psychotherapy models is difficult. With an estimated 400 types in existence today (Garfield, 1998), psychotherapy is an enormously diverse field. Subsequent chapters of this text discuss the most widely recognized and utilized models. Although no definition is perfect, the following broad definition of psychotherapy is used for this text:

> Psychotherapy is a relationship among people. One person (or more) is defined as needing special assistance to improve his or her functioning as a person, and the other person(s) is defined as able to render such special help.

In the United States, psychotherapy is a form of treatment by psychological means. It aims to improve a person's social and emotional functioning, to provide a means to correct deviant behavior, and to facilitate psychological and/or spiritual development or meaningful experience (Orlinsky, Ronnestad, & Willutzki, 2004, p. 311). Psychotherapy is an effort to relieve suffering and disability, involving a personal relationship between a healer and a sufferer (Frank & Frank, 1991). Some types of therapy rely on the healer's ability to mobilize the sufferer's healing forces.

Beginning students frequently ask, "Is there a difference between psychotherapy and counseling?" Disagreement about the answer to this question has historical roots. Traditionally, some claim that counseling has focused on conscious rather than unconscious issues, the present more than the past, and vocational and academic problems. Counseling has been associated with educational settings and with work in guidance clinics, schools, mental health clinics, and pastoral settings. Psychotherapy has been associated with a focus on the unconscious and with serious mental health problems with origins in the past and with more medically oriented settings such as psychiatric hospitals and outpatient clinics. Although traditionally dissimilarities between counseling and psychotherapy have been emphasized, today there is little distinction made between the two. Years of psychotherapy research have found no differences in outcome as a function of the type of counselor (Hill & Nakayama, 2000, pp. 866–867). In this text, the terms *counseling* and *therapy* are used interchangeably—both are activities that help clients or patients (also interchangeable terms) achieve psychological change.

✦ BECOMING A PSYCHOTHERAPIST OR COUNSELOR

To be a professional psychotherapist is to be among the privileged. Sharing the secrets of the human heart in a protected, confidential relationship is rewarding work. The helping and healing that transpires not only transforms the patient or client but also the therapist as he or she serves as a catalyst for positive change. The therapist grows in the knowledge and understanding of life's circumstances and gains greater appreciation of the human condition.

To become a qualified, competent therapist or counselor, you—the student or trainee—must not only possess a sincere desire and motivation to help others but also

- attain an intellectual grasp of the theories and concepts of psychotherapy.
- acquire the practice skills that come from the experience of working with patients, under a skilled and qualified supervisor.
- know the status of research evidence supporting the effectiveness of psychotherapies and be able to justify your choice of interventions.
- understand the sociocultural context that affects practice, such as the health care system, economics, multiculturalism and diversity, business, technology, and even politics.
- choose a profession under which you practice psychotherapy; this could include a career in psychology, psychiatry, social work, counseling, and psychiatric nursing, among others.

Once you decide what kind of professional you want to be and enter a training program, you will be exposed to many different theoretical orientations. You can look at all of the available models and select one or more types of therapy that you believe is best suited to your way of being with clients. Generally, the training institute you attend will have some favored models or specific orientations to a type of psychotherapy.

✦ MAJOR TYPES OF PSYCHOTHERAPY

Professionals generally have an allegiance or preference for specific models of therapy. While hundreds of therapies exist, they generally fall into the following major classifications (Messer, 1992; Stricker & Gold, 1996):

- *Psychoanalytic and psychodynamic models* are based on Sigmund Freud's original theory and focus on intrapsychic conflicts that originate in early childhood and generate anxiety. Uncovering and resolving these unconscious conflicts is the major goal of psychoanalysis and psychodynamic therapies. This text includes classical psychoanalysis and a sample of post-Freudian therapies.
- *Humanist-existential models* emphasize the individual or the person underlying the cognition, emotions, and behaviors. The model assumes human beings have an innate potential to live a meaningful existence, and the goals of therapy focus on discovering one's own true potential and achieving self-actualization. This text includes person-centered therapy, logotherapy, and gestalt therapy.
- *Behavior models* focus on how people acquire adaptive and maladaptive behaviors. Changing maladaptive behavior to adaptive behavior occurs through learning. This text includes a number of behavior therapies based on operant conditioning, classical conditioning, and modeling.

- *Cognitive models* hold that thoughts shape human emotions and behaviors. To achieve good mental health, people need to change their irrational and distorted thinking to more rational and realistic thinking. This text includes Albert Ellis's rational emotive behavior therapy and Aaron Beck's cognitive therapy.
- *Sociocultural or culturally specific models* focus on the social context and the larger social structures within which the person lives. Interpersonal relationships are at the center of their adjustment. The custom of a specific society and culture must be considered in order to understand the person. This text includes feminist therapy as an example of a sociocultural model.
- *Biological models* are based on the idea that mental illness is a function of a physical system gone awry. Biochemical imbalances, structural defects, and faulty genes can cause psychological symptoms. Many biological theories now use the term *biopsychosocial* and stress the importance of the interaction among biological, sociocultural, and psychological variables. The person is an interconnected system, and it is assumed that the person is best treated in a holistic and integrated way through mind–body therapies (Weil, 2004). This text includes psychopharmacology and biopsychosocial therapies such as stress management in this category.
- *Eclectic and integrative models* intermix theories and practices from more than one system of therapy. With no unifying theoretical base, the therapist uses experience and knowledge to choose the most appropriate interventions for a particular client (Norcross & Goldfried, 2005). Therapists may blend two or three theories or may amalgamate specific aspects of theories. They may choose one therapy, believing that it is most helpful for the particular client and the particular problem. They may reason that no single therapy is adequate for all problems, but some therapies are better for treating some specific conditions (Goin, 2005). This text includes the Lazarus BASIC ID therapy. Mixed models incorporate significant theoretical and practice features from major models that have proven useful, such as interpersonal therapy, which combines elements of psychoanalytic and cognitive therapy, or dialectical behavior therapy, which combines elements of cognitive, behavioral, and mind–body therapies.
- *Postmodern or constructivist models* are based on the idea that each person creates his or her personal view of reality. The focus is on the meaning clients attribute to the world and the way it shapes their view of self, interpersonal relationships, and events in their lives (Neimeyer & Bridges, 2003). In this category, this text includes solution-focused therapy and narrative therapy.

Which models are currently most popular? Studies of American psychotherapists over the years reveal that in the last decade over 25 percent of therapists who were surveyed (clinical/counseling psychologists, psychiatrists, social workers, and counselors) identified their primary theoretical orientation as eclectic, a greater percentage than for any other single model of psychotherapy (Bechtoldt, Norcross, Wyckoff, & Pokrywa, 2001; Norcross, Karpiak, & Lister, 2005; Prochaska, DiClemente, & Norcross, 2003). Cognitive therapy was the primary theoretical orientation for over 24 percent of clinical/counseling psychologists but it accounted for less than 10 percent among counselors, social workers, and psychiatrists. Psychodynamic therapy was named as the primary theoretical orientation for 22 percent of social workers, 19 percent of psychiatrists, 27 percent of clinical/counseling psychologists, and 8 percent of counselors (Sharf, 2004, p. 5). While early in the history of psychotherapy, psychodynamic therapy was the most popular, today there is a strong trend to adapt eclecticism. The popularity of theoretical models changes over time and within professions.

As a student of psychotherapy, you will inevitably have preferences among the therapies. Typically, one model will be especially appealing to you, and you will use this model as a way to see your client, develop expertise in this area, and deepen your commitment to this perspective. You will adapt your chosen model to your own style. Eventually, you will have your own unique way of being with the client, which will be derived from your professional training, the perspective gained from a therapy model, and your own personality and personal style. However, when you apply these models in practice, you will discover that you face the realities of the practice environment, with features that influence how you conduct your psychotherapy (Compass & Gotlib, 2002). This practice context is considered next.

✦ EVOLVING THEORY, PRACTICE, AND RESEARCH OF PSYCHOTHERAPY

Psychotherapy takes place in a complex sociocultural environment. Students of psychotherapy face the daunting task of grasping and integrating a large amount of information. Figure 1.1 illustrates the complexity of the environments in which psychotherapy is practiced, including the service delivery system itself and other social institutions, as well as currents of change in the community (Orlinsky et al., 2004, p. 321).

This chapter assembles some practical knowledge about a variety of topics with which the therapist must deal in day-to-day practice. And although this information is very basic, it will be helpful to you as a starting point.

The end of the twentieth century heralded revolutionary changes in the U.S. health care system (Cummings, 2006). As a result, psychotherapy assumed a different trajectory and shape within mental health care (Meyers, 2006). A number of changes in the theory, practice, and research of psychotherapy emerged and yielded major themes that we will discuss throughout this textbook (Austad & Hoyt, 1992); these themes are outlined in Table 1.1.

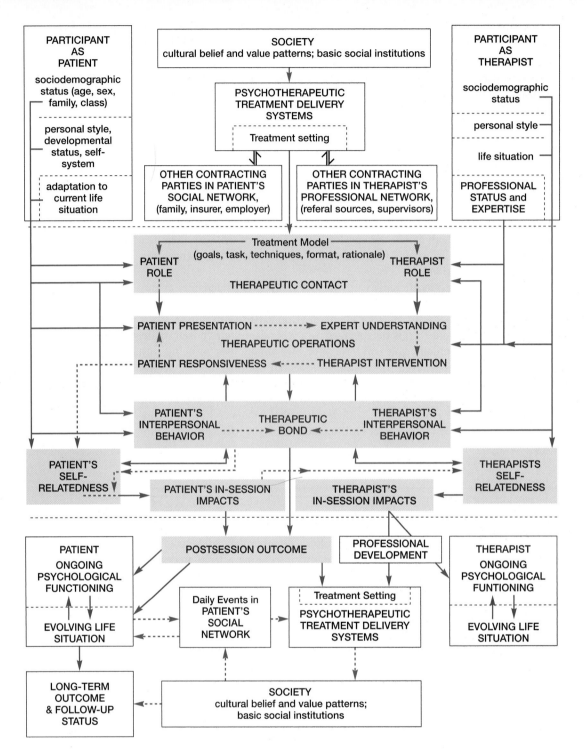

FIGURE 1.1 *Generic Model of Psychotherapy: Integration of Input, Process, and Output Variables.*

Source: From Michael Lambert, *Bergin and Garfield's Handbook of Psychotherapy and Behavior Change* (John Wiley & Sons, 2004). Reprinted with permission of John Wiley & Sons, Inc.

Table 1.1		
Themes in the Evolution of Theory, Practice, and Research of Psychotherapy		
Theory	**Practice**	**Research**
Discoveries about the biology of mental disorders; identification of sources of pathology/abnormal behavior	Provider is accountable for the results of treatment chosen in U.S. health care system; must justify choices and produce outcome	Greater appreciation of value and usefulness of research; researcher/clinician gap narrowing
Biopsychosocial perspective develops; complementary medical mind–body relationship accepted	Elements of business and profession—economics, politics, managed care—affect the practice of psychotherapy and how it is integrated into health care	Search for best therapy is pitted against the common-factors approach to psychotherapy
Psychopharmacology successes increase; efficacy and effectiveness demonstrated	Integration of psychotherapy and psychopharmacology Short-term interventions chosen over long-term ones	Efficacy and effectiveness of psychotherapy defined and studied
Increased use of medical model and *DSM* diagnoses	Emergence of behavioral health/integrated care/primary care model	Methodologies develop from simple to more sophisticated
Theories less grand and less unifying; instead, more inductive and specific; psychotherapies seen as discrete treatments; based in data; evidence-based health care shapes theory	Information technology; use of evidence-based medicine in mental health; individual practitioner can access literature; online practice/coaching	Easy access to research findings through user-friendly information technology; evidence-based practice encourages new standards for professional guidelines and individual providers

✦ CHANGES IN THEORY

Theories of psychotherapy are not sacred or immutable beliefs. They are tools to assist the therapist to help the client. Theories can be shaped by the demand characteristics of the sociocultural environment. Grasping the big picture of how theories change helps the therapist to gain perspective, to be more objective, to be more conscious of options, and to choose wisely. This section examines some of the key environmental events that have influenced the theory underlying current models of psychotherapy.

Emphasis on Biology

Advances in the biological sciences have increased our knowledge of human behavior, both normal and abnormal. For example, brain imaging has helped us explore inside the mind, confirming that mental states and physical states are linked. We can now identify some of the neural correlates of specific mental tasks (Crick & Koch, 2002); and we know a strong connection between genes and behavior exists. For example, the Human Genome Project has demonstrated that part of the infant–mother attachment process is based in biology. In turn, these advances have shaped both the theory and practice of psychotherapy.

As the evidence of the link between mental states and biology grows, so does the belief in the medical model. A cadre of mental health professionals views psychological problems and medical disorders similarly. Mental disorders, like physical disorders, must be diagnosed, treated, and cured. The diagnosis is based upon the American Psychiatric Association's *Diagnostic and Statistical Manual of Mental Disorders*—properly known as the *DSM-IV-TR* for fourth edition with text revision—which was introduced in 1956 (the *DSM-V* is expected to be published in 2011; for simplicity, this text uses the shortened title *DSM*). The *DSM* is the official diagnostic tool used in the United States; it is based upon a multiaxial system of five types of information needed by traditional medical practitioners:

- Axis I—clinical disorders and other conditions that are the focus of clinical attention
- Axis II—personality disorders and mental retardation
- Axis III—general medical conditions
- Axis IV—psychosocial stressors and environmental problems
- Axis V—global assessment of functioning (GAF)

In Axis I are disorders of mood, anxiety, somatoform, dissociation, sexuality and gender, eating, sleeping, impulse control, adjustment, substance abuse, delirium, dementia, and other cognitive disorders, as well as schizophrenia and other psychotic conditions. Axis II contains personality disorders such as antisocial, borderline, narcissistic, histrionic, dependent, paranoid, schizoid, schizotypal, obsessive-compulsive, and mental retardation. Axis III includes any physical conditions that can cause symptoms of mental disorder such as HIV or brain tumors. Axis IV notes any life events that can impact the disorders listed in Axis I and II—for example, death of a loved one or loss of a job. Axis V contains the clinician's rating of the client's level of functioning currently and during the previous year.

Many practitioners use the *DSM;* its medical framework shapes their way of looking at clinical problems and influences their choices for treatment (Follette & Beitz, 2003). However, the *DSM* is only one way to see psychological problems, and the values and assumptions of a particular therapy model may be incompatible with the *DSM* diagnosis. For example, a person-centered therapist may be reluctant to give a client a medicalized label such as borderline personality disorder.

Students may find it useful to review the *DSM* as they consider which models of therapy are most useful for specific diagnoses in abnormal psychology. To find information about which interventions might be most useful for a particular diagnosis, students are encouraged to visit the websites of professional, scientifically reputable organizations, such as the American Psychological Association (APA) Division 12, Society of Clinical Psychology: http://www.apa.org/divisions/div12/cppi.html. This basic diagnostic information is presented to help the student therapist come to grips with the interface between diagnosis and choice of therapy. Keep in mind that to qualify for insurance reimbursement, the therapist must report a *DSM* diagnosis.

While there is strong support and appreciation for the medical view of mental illness, there is also growing dissatisfaction with its limitations. The Western model of medicine is allopathic. It relies heavily upon invasive techniques such as surgery, special treatments, and drugs to restore physical health. Treatment is to produce a condition that is antagonistic to the condition that needs to be cured, and in this view, psychotherapy is seen as an adjunctive aid to psychiatric medications (Weil, 2004).

Many who think the medical model is too limiting point out that progress in the biological sciences has also reinforced a belief in the mind–body connection. For example, rhesus monkeys, which develop behavioral attachment disorders when separated from their natural mothers at birth, show permanently altered levels of the stress hormone ACTH (Champoux, Byrne, DeLizio, & Suomi, 1992). The fearful/anxious temperament is likely to be a relatively stable personality trait involving right frontal brain activity and elevated hormone levels (Kalin, 2002).

It seems safe to conclude that some disorders have primarily psychological causes, others have primarily biological causes, and others are caused by a combination of the two. This belief has produced a kindling of theories—called biopsychosocial—that maintain that the causes of abnormal behavior are a function of the interaction of the biological, psychological, and sociocultural (Goleman, 1995, 2003; Hansell & Damour, 2005). Many psychotherapists now accept the importance of the mind–body connection and hold that the psychotherapist must consider and assess all possible reasonable alternatives in order to provide high-quality mental health treatment (U.S. Department of Health and Human Services, 1999). Psychotherapies tending toward the use of a mind–body approach use tools to train the mind and cultivate a change in inner conditions to achieve balance and happiness (Horrigan & LeTourneau, 2003; Ivker, Anderson, & Trivieri, 1999; Penn & Wilson, 2003).

The biopsychosocial perspective is taking its place in the world of mental health. It incorporates elements of the medical model, complementary medicine (holistic, natural, or integrative treatment), the social psychological, and the sociocultural to provide a more comprehensive slant on human interaction and the ways to deal with problems (Prochaska et al., 2003). From this perspective, the role of the psychotherapist is more like that of a psychological family practitioner who identifies a patient's mental health as well as physical disorders such as depression and anxiety (Cummings, 1995; Khan, Bower, & Rogers, 2007).

Move to More Concise Theories

The trend in psychotherapeutic theorizing is away from grand, all-encompassing models to more specific ones. This is primarily because no one theory has successfully integrated the field (Stricker & Gold, 1996). Early therapists such as Freud, Jung, and Adler created sweeping theories that explained the human personality in its totality. Using a top-down approach, they relied primarily on deductive reasoning.

For example, in his analyses of patients, Freud sifted for evidence to confirm his theoretical reasoning about his model of the unconscious. He found evidence to support the constructs that he made up, but today we know the very act of observing affects observation, and thus bias cannot be avoided. We now recognize this as the *allegiance effect* (explained on page 21).

Today, theorizing tends to be inductive as opposed to deductive, with research findings spawning some theoretical models. For example, James Prochaska and Carlo DiClemente (1984) examined data from thousands of people trying to quit smoking. The data showed clients arrived in therapy at varying levels of readiness to change. The researchers created the stages-of-change model based upon a pattern analysis of patients' reality. They suggested various interventions according to a client's stage of change. In the stages-of-change theory, actual clinical events and occurrences informed theory.

The information explosion of the last decade means that a tremendous amount of scientific information is available about personality, too much to integrate into a single framework (Kenkel, 2006). The use of more focused hypotheses makes it easier to conduct research. Current theories tend to have a more specific focus, like a microtheory. For example, dialectical behavior therapy concentrates on helping the borderline personality (Linehan, 1999), and Beck's cognitive therapy focuses on the thought processes of depressed and anxious clients (Beck, 2001; Passer & Smith, 2007).

✣ CHANGES IN PRACTICE

The psychotherapy practice environment is constantly changing, and a well-informed therapist understands which aspects of theory and research are best integrated into practice to help clients succeed in reaching their therapy goals. This section examines some of the key events that have influenced current psychotherapy practice today.

Business and Psychotherapy

Psychotherapy is both a profession and a business. Being a doctor of the mind is a rewarding and fulfilling profession, but it must also produce sufficient income (London, 1964). Thus, psychotherapy students need to learn about the "business" of conducting psychotherapy, as well as about clinical processes.

Doctors and psychotherapists are professionals, which is differentiated from pure entrepreneurs by the code of ethics they set for their standards of conduct. They are expected to act in the best interest of the client and to rise above commercialism (Austad, 1996). For example, it is assumed that a surgeon will not perform unnecessary operations simply for profit. Similarly, it is expected that a psychotherapist will not maintain a client in therapy unnecessarily. But at times, there is tension between the professional's care ethic and his or her business interest. In addition, changes in the types and numbers of professionals in mental health have made the practice of psychotherapy more market driven and competitive.

Health care and mental health care are growing enterprises. From 1975 to 1990, the ranks of the mental health profession swelled. The number of psychiatrists increased from 26,000 to 36,000; psychologists from 15,000 to 42,000; social workers from 25,000 to 80,000; and marriage and family therapists from 6,000 to 40,000 (Kirk & Kutchins, 1996). In 2004, psychiatrists numbered over 30,000; psychologists who worked in health care, private practice, or consulting came to 107,000; and counselors (including marriage and family, mental health, and substance abuse) added up to 196,000 (U.S. Department of Labor, 2006). As the number of professionals increases, competition for a set number of patients becomes fierce.

The categories of diagnoses are also expanding. The *DSM* has increased from approximately 50 pages to nearly 900 pages, and the number of diagnostic labels has gone from around 100 to over 800 (Follette & Houts, 1996). Some believe that as the number of mental health professionals increases, so does the number of diagnoses and thus the number of eligible patients (Kirk & Kutchins, 1996).

Economics and Psychotherapy

Economic forces now exert such a strong force on mental health care that they have added an element of consumerism to the therapeutic relationship. But, at the same time, a good deal of psychotherapy in the United States is conducted within the framework of the health care system and is a covered benefit in many health insurance plans.

Until the 1970s, the major form of health insurance was indemnity insurance, a system of payment in which the provider billed the payer, and reimbursement was made with no questions asked. Insurers respected the expertise of health professionals, paying out the usual and customary fees as requested. A doctor's judgment was final. However, as medical care costs spun out of control in the 1980s, major purchasers of health care and mental health care—such as employers, the Veterans Administration, and government programs like Medicare and Medicaid—sought a way to control them. Payers no longer trusted providers to independently decide upon the costs and charges of their care, and they turned to the managed-care concept. The result was a profound economic and structural change in medical and, therefore, in mental health and psychotherapy services.

This impact on the profession was profound because both funding and oversight shape practice habits. What is paid for is more likely to be adopted than what is not. For-profit and corporate entities now control much of reimbursement, and they want efficacious and cost effective models of psychotherapy in managed-care settings. Psychotherapists cannot ignore the realities of managed care unless they practice in an entirely out-of-pocket, fee-for-service environment. Students entering practice will find it beneficial to have a grasp of basic managed-care constructs (Cummings & Cummings, 2005; Levinsky, 1998).

Managed Care

Managed care is any health care delivery method in which someone other than the health care provider manages both financial and medical aspects. Based on the premise that providers change their practice habits in response to financial incentives, managed care was created to control the costs, the use, and even the quality of health care by making providers accountable to payers, by promoting competition, and by adopting specific practice standards (Bobbitt, 2006).

Managed care has it roots in prepaid health care, which began in the early twentieth century. Originally, the purpose of prepaid health care was to deliver affordable, accessible care to poor and middle-class farmers and laborers in order to eliminate unexpected medical bills. Doctors agreed to provide a set package of services for a preestablished fee. For example, Dr. Michael Shadid, a crusader for affordable, prepaid health care and founder of the Cooperative Health Federation of America in 1947, staunchly advocated for cooperative ownership of hospitals that employed physicians in a group practice with the focus of preventive medicine (Austad, 1996).

In the 1980s, managed health care proliferated and transformed into a wide variety of techniques that integrated financing and the delivery of health care. Managed-care methods now include review of the medical necessity of services, intensive management of high-cost cases, regulation of inpatient admissions and length of stay, incentives for selecting less costly forms of care, beneficiary cost sharing, and selective contracting with health care providers who agree to hold down costs (Austad & Hoyt, 1992).

Managed-care arrangements are defined according to structural characteristics, the relationship of providers and patients to systems, and financial arrangements. Some of the managed health arrangements that a psychotherapist will encounter include the following:

- *Utilization review and management:* This is the simplest level of management. The reviewer evaluates the medical necessity and appropriateness of the mental health services prospectively, concurrently, or retrospectively. The sentinel effect operates so that a provider is more likely to think about the economics of his or her own health care just by virtue of the fact that he or she is being monitored.
- *Health maintenance organization (HMO):* HMOs offer services to a defined population for a fixed prepaid price (capitation) and provide a basic benefit package to their members. Two fundamental plans are the staff and the group models. Staff models consist of providers who are salaried employees or contractors who work in specific locations. Group-model HMOs contract with groups of providers to devote a specified percentage of practice time to subscribers on a salaried or a capitated basis, usually in a central location. Providers share in the group's profit or loss. HMOs may carve out certain benefit categories, such as mental health, and subcapitate these to a mental health HMO network.
- *Independent practice association (IPA):* Individual providers contract with an HMO to provide care in their own offices. Reimbursement is a prearranged

fee for service, a capitated price, or a percentage of the subscriber's premium. Providers contribute to risk pools, and holdbacks are incentives to control use.

- *Preferred provider organization (PPO):* PPO caregivers must offer cost effective care to a predetermined subscriber group for either discounted rates or a schedule of maximum payments in return for a certain volume of referrals. Consumers can use nonparticipating providers but receive discounts or financial incentives to use PPO providers. An exclusive PPO pays only for services to participating providers.
- *Point of service (POS) plan:* In this open-ended plan, fees are reduced or benefits increased to encourage the use of network providers.
- *Employee assistance plan (EAP):* Mental health services are provided to the employee in the workplace or off-site.

Managed care can also be a hybrid with the characteristics of several models. The specific arrangements may vary in order to meet diverse local and regional requirements, state regulations, and specific statutes. Managed mental health care or behavioral services are often "carved out," meaning separated from a general health plan. For example, if a client is a member of Kaiser Permanente, his health care services may be given by staff members, who are salaried employees. If a client is a Blue Care member, she will seek providers who practice independently but agree to cooperate with the managed-care company and thus, in exchange, are approved by the plan and can take referrals.

Practitioners of psychotherapy are faced with the task of dealing with many managed-care organizations and arrangements depending on the client's medical insurance. These arrangements may affect the choice of treatment models in subtle ways. For example, if a client's insurance will only cover 20 sessions, the therapist is likely to choose a model that can accommodate the client's financial needs. The new practitioner undoubtedly faces many such challenges in a changing behavioral health practice.

Controversies Around Managed Care

What are the advantages and disadvantages of managed care, especially in terms of managed mental health care? Proponents of managed care argue that it emerged because health care professionals failed to police themselves. Some providers of health services abused the system, maximizing patient care and their own profit. They artificially inflated diagnoses, overused services, ignored the big picture of national cost, failed to establish universal standards of care, focused on illness instead of wellness, and protected their own interests through professional guilds at the expense of the consumer.

The financial incentive in private practice is the more care rendered, the more fees charged. There is little motivation to provide less care when the more the care, the larger the profit. Large mental health hospital chains made profits on unnecessary hospitalizations and inpatient overtreatment. Their services were rationed only by the clients' ability to pay (Schlesinger, Gray, & Perriera, 1997). Managed care forced health professions to reexamine appropriate standards of care. Managed care is also partly responsible for stimulating the current wave of integrated behavioral/ primary care that is rapidly gaining momentum, since behavioral health care providers that experienced the managed-care setting are leaders in the field (Cummings, 2006).

Opponents of managed care argue that the financial incentive is to profit by giving less treatment, which, theoretically, curbs medical costs. In reality, managed care denies and limits access to necessary treatment, narrows the patient's choice of provider, disrupts continuity of care, uses less qualified providers to render and review care, and risks patient confidentiality; in essence, managed care follows a business ethic and profit motive at the expense of the appropriate and compassionate patient care. Therapists are forced to do unreasonable amounts of paperwork and must interface with unqualified managed-care personnel in order to obtain authorization and payment.

In reality, managed care has resulted in less accessible services, has closed clinics and eliminated necessary care, has diminished the power and status of the therapist, and has eroded professional autonomy in treatment decision making. Furthermore, managed care has not succeeded in curbing escalating medical costs (Bobbitt, 2006; Schlesinger, Wynia, & Cummins, 2000).

Figure 1.2 shows a typical treatment plan that a clinician must complete to receive reimbursement from an insurer for services. The psychotherapeutic plan expected by many managed-care and insurance companies, which has become a standard in the field, is based on a medical model and reinforces the choice of short-term therapy. Business, economics, and managed care have changed how mental health services are financed and reimbursed and have shaped mental health practice today (Regestein, 2000; Schlesinger et al., 2000).

Integrated Behavioral Health Care

With these trends gaining momentum—acceptance of the biopsychosocial perspective, the demands to render effective care and provide accountability, and the effectiveness of pharmacological intervention—there is a real need for the student of psychotherapy to coordinate and integrate mental and physical health care. Let's look at some powerful reasons for the psychotherapist to develop the skills to interface with the health system.

In 2004, "Americans made more than 1.1 billion visits to doctors' offices and hospital emergency and outpatient departments" (Hing, Cherry, & Woodwell, 2006). The average primary care physician in the United States conducts 120,000 to 160,000 patient interviews in his or her practice lifetime (Frankel & Beckman, 2004, p. 45). A large number of visits to primary care doctors are from patients who have mental health/emotional issues (Strosahl, 1996). Nicholas Cummings (2006) estimates that as much as 85 percent of behavioral health care is currently being provided by primary care physicians and not mental health therapists.

David Satcher, the Surgeon General from 1998 to 2002, pointed out that primary care "offers golden opportunities as a point of first contact with patients and their families" (U.S. Department of Health and Human Services, 2000). The landmark *Mental Health: A Report of the Surgeon General* (U.S. Department of Health and Human Services, 1999), bolstered by the President's New Freedom Commission on Mental Health, recommends collaborative/integrated approaches to health care. Primary care providers, mental health specialists, and consumers can work together using an evidence-based approach. This provides an important practice niche for behavioral specialists (Garcia-Shelton, 2006).

Unfortunately, clinical education has not always kept pace with these changing expectations and practice requirements of our health system. Too few training programs currently educate psychotherapists to acquire sufficient expertise (Kenkel, DeLeon, Mantell, & Steep, 2005). However, some significant organizations have taken initial steps to develop integrated behavioral health programs. For example, the U.S. Air Force has placed psychologists in all of its 167 worldwide primary health care settings. Kaiser Permanente of Northern California now has psychologists in all of its primary care settings. Other major insurers such as United Health Care and Aetna have begun the process of co-location of a psychologist and primary health care professional (Cummings, 2006; Cummings, personal communication).

Psychologists have taken the lead in developing the primary care behavioral model and have developed programs such as health psychology, behavioral medicine, and integrated health care (Creer, Holroyd, Glasgow, & Smith, 2004, p. 697). Some programs have been established to provide certificates in primary behavioral health care for graduate-level therapists from a variety of disciplines (Blount, 1998). In short, psychotherapists of the future will need to incorporate the psychosocial, psychobiological, and psychopharmacological information into practice (Puskar, 2007). The primary care/behavioral health model is ideal since it addresses a majority of personal health care needs, continues over the life span, and provides comprehensive, coordinated, personalized, integrated health and mental health care (Frank, McDaniel, Bray, & Heldring, 2004).

Politics and Health Care

The financing of health care in the United States is a politically charged issue. With 46 million Americans currently uninsured, and many more underinsured, the nation is in a health care—and mental health care—crisis. The informed therapist who understands the political forces—at the federal, state, and local levels—involved in financing health care often has the opportunity to make a social contribution. Psychotherapists are inevitably interacting with clients who are in need of care but cannot afford it. Therapists need to be able to navigate around the mental health and political systems to be patient advocates who can help their clients when possible (Institute of Medicine, 2001). At the very least, psychotherapists can act in a socially responsible manner, be informed about the politics that influence health care and its financing, and be willing and able to take political steps, such as advocating for increased funding of mental health care, writing letters to state legislators, or speaking out in a public forum. Grassroots political activists in various groups, for example, the National Alliance for the Mentally Ill (NAMI), have lobbied successfully to obtain equitable service and increased benefits for the seriously mentally

Managed Care, Inc. Outpatient Treatment Report

Patient/Client's Name: _____

Address: _____

Insurance ID Number: _____

Policyholder's Name: _____ DOB: _____

Employer Group: _____

Primary Care Physician's Name: _____

Presenting Problem/Chief Complaint/Reason for Appointment: _____

Any Previous Treatment for This Diagnosis? _____

Previous Treatment History (x if present)

☐ Outpatient ☐ Mental Health ☐ Substance Abuse Date(s): _____

☐ Inpatient ☐ Mental Health ☐ Substance Abuse Date(s): _____

Medication(s): (list all)

Name: _____ Dates: _____ Dose: _____

Name: _____ Dates: _____ Dose: _____

Name(s) of Treatment Facilities: _____

Name(s) of Treating Providers: _____

Current Risk Assessment

Suicidality: ☐ no ☐ yes plan: _____ means: _____

History of Attempts: _____

Homicidality: ☐ no ☐ yes plan: _____ means: _____

History of Violence: _____

Substance Use/Abuse/Dependency: _____

DSM-IV Diagnosis

	Description
Axis I :	
Axis II :	
Axis III :	
Axis IV :	
Axis V : Current: _____ Highest: _____ Past Year: _____	

Describe any relevant details: _____

Describe Functional Impairment

Use GAF levels (1–100)*

Area	Severity	Duration	Impairment
			Low Moderate High
Work	_____	_____	☐ ☐ ☐
Family	_____	_____	☐ ☐ ☐
Social relationships	_____	_____	☐ ☐ ☐
Other	_____	_____	☐ ☐ ☐
Disabilities: None _____ Mental Health _____ Medical _____			

Symptoms/Problems	Severity	Duration	Impairment
			Low Moderate High
Anxiety	_____	_____	☐ ☐ ☐
Appetite disturbance	_____	_____	☐ ☐ ☐
Assaultive behavior	_____	_____	☐ ☐ ☐
Bizarre behavior	_____	_____	☐ ☐ ☐
Cognitive impairment (disturbed thinking)	_____	_____	☐ ☐ ☐
Depression	_____	_____	☐ ☐ ☐
Impaired judgment	_____	_____	☐ ☐ ☐
Impaired memory	_____	_____	☐ ☐ ☐
Interpersonal problems	_____	_____	☐ ☐ ☐
Obsessions/ compulsions	_____	_____	☐ ☐ ☐
Poor judgment	_____	_____	☐ ☐ ☐
Phobias	_____	_____	☐ ☐ ☐
Paranoia	_____	_____	☐ ☐ ☐
Panic Attacks	_____	_____	☐ ☐ ☐
Sleep disturbance	_____	_____	☐ ☐ ☐
Sexual dysfunction	_____	_____	☐ ☐ ☐
Somatization	_____	_____	☐ ☐ ☐
Self-care/ independent living	_____	_____	☐ ☐ ☐

*Global Assessment of Functioning

16

Outpatient Treatment Report

Patient's name: _____

Problems Presenting problems (DSM-IV symptoms)	Goals/Objectives Goals of treatment and objectives	Interventions List treatment modalities to meet goals and objectives
		☐ Individual 20/30 minutes ☐ Individual 40/50 minutes ☐ Family therapy ☐ Group therapy ☐ Medication management ☐ Case management ☐ Other
		Requested # sessions: _____ Frequency of sessions: _____ Estimated total treatment sessions: _____

Additional information related to authorization request:

_____

_____

_____

_____

_____

_____

FIGURE 1.2 *Typical Treatment Plan Required for Managed Care*

*GAF (Global Assessment of Functioning) ratings: 100–91, superior; 90–81, minimal symptom; 80–71, mild transient symptom; 70–61, mild symptom; 60–51, moderate symptom; 50–41, serious symptom; 40–31, inability to function; 30–21, gross impairment; 20–11, some danger; 10–1, serious danger of hurting self

ill. Other groups, such as the National Mental Health Association (www.nmha. org/state/parity), have lobbied for parity, and many mental health providers have offered their support.

Psychopharmacology and Psychotherapy

Today, mental health treatment relies heavily upon medications (Meyers, 2006). The drug industry now uses direct-to-consumer advertising, which increased drug expenditures from $13.1 million in 1989 to more than $900 million in 1997 (Hollon, 1999). As well, others besides medical doctors can now prescribe drugs in some cases. Psychologists gained prescription privileges in New Mexico in 2002 and in Louisiana in 2004, and they are currently lobbying in a number of other states for the same privileges. Psychiatric nurse practitioners currently prescribe in many settings and states (Kenkel, 2006). The *Physicians' Desk Reference* (*PDR*) continues to increase in size as more and more medications are created. The use and availability of psychotropic medications, herbal remedies, nutritional supplements, and drug abuse are at a peak (Preston, O'Neil, & Talaga, 2005). At the same time, pharmacological researchers are seeking a magic bullet or a psychotropic cure for specific psychiatric conditions (Holmer, 1999).

The majority of mental health treatments are provided today by nonmedical therapists. However, if a medication can alleviate psychological suffering rapidly and effectively, therapists should be able to help clients access appropriate medications (Sochurek, 1988). To practice competently, a capable nonmedical psychotherapist must be able to (Preston et al., 2005)

- identify mental illness with a biological base.
- know when and how a patient can benefit from pharmacological treatment.
- refer patients to a practitioner so they can obtain medication.
- distinguish the physical diseases that have accompanying psychological symptoms and how to refer these cases to a primary care doctor when needed.

✦ CHANGES IN RESEARCH

It is incumbent upon the therapist to know the relevant research that supports the efficacy and effectiveness of psychotherapy. *Accountability* is the new buzzword faced by psychotherapists who must meet demands from third-party payers and consumers to demonstrate that the treatment they provide is useful and cost effective. There is a rich body of research currently available on psychotherapy. The following sections touch on important research-related topics the student can tap into in order to be informed.

Researcher/Clinician Gap

Traditionally, researchers and practicing psychotherapists were polarized. They communicated little with each other, except to criticize and complain. Practitioners accused researchers of being ivory tower academicians who were more preoccupied with achieving perfectly controlled studies than informing real-life practice (Garfield, 1998). Clinicians complained that most research results were unclear or difficult to understand (Gordon, 2000). Typically, these results told clinicians virtually nothing that enhanced the therapist's daily work with patients (Reynolds & Richardson, 2000). On the other hand, researchers saw practitioner concerns as disruptive to the conduct of pure clinical science (Anderson, 2000). They perceived clinicians as frequently biased toward positive findings, as having too much faith in uncontrolled case studies, and as unrealistic in their expectations of research findings. In the past, the practitioner and researcher have had very different goals: While the therapist has attempted to discover methods to help clients in the context of his or her whole life, the researcher has tried to isolate the effects of specific techniques and consider them apart from the patient's life context (Cone, 2001).

Today, both researchers and practitioners are making a concerted effort to integrate psychotherapy research and practice in order to make it meaningful, especially to the client/consumer (Gordon, 2000). Many research projects now serve a practical purpose, and the trend is to integrate theory, practice, and research so that researchers in psychotherapy and practitioners will be in shouting distance of each other (Borckardt et al., 2008). Furthermore, lobbying for relevant research now occurs on a regular basis.

Often, therapists must deal with the problem of integrating research into their practice from researchers who appear to be uninterested in the practice of therapy. Naturally, it is best if the researcher knows what it is like to practice therapy, because knowing what the clinician wants and thinks allows the researcher to ask useful and informed questions about the clinical situation (Soldz & McCullogh, 2000, p. 90). To understand how the field got to this point, let's first review the history of psychotherapy research.

History of Psychotherapy Research

In the days of Freud, therapists relied on the case study for primary research. By the 1940s, researchers launched larger-scale research projects and began to use surveys and other methods. The well-known psychotherapy researcher Hans Eysenck shook the field in 1952 when he called the effectiveness of all psychotherapy into question. He reviewed 24 psychotherapy research articles, which included 8,053 clients, on the outcome measures of hospital discharges and insurance settlements. In the review, he found that two thirds of all neurotics who entered psychotherapy improved within two years, but two thirds of neurotics who did *not* enter therapy likewise improved. Eysenck concluded that psychotherapy with neurotics was no more effective than *no* psychotherapy, which incited controversy and interest in a primary question: Is psychotherapy effective?

Research Methodology

Eysenck's findings aroused closer scrutiny of psychotherapy. The scientific community of psychotherapy researchers wanted to establish standards and produce rigorous scientific assessments in order to validate conclusions about the value of psychotherapy. Researchers have faced, and still face, a number of thorny issues. It has been, and still is, difficult for researchers to

- find a universal, standardized, operational definition of psychotherapy.
- use and devise research designs with sound strategies for measuring outcomes.
- control variables such as the nature of the sample; amount and quality of therapy; nature and onset of duration of pathology; precise definitions of disorders (making cases comparable across studies); duration and rigor of follow-up; and patient, therapist, and process variables.
- incorporate the use of both process and outcome research in a meaningful way.

As a consequence, studies of psychotherapy have been uneven in quality, but over the past 40 years, they have met more stringent scientific criteria. And as scientific methodology has improved, so has confidence in experimental results. Eysenck's data has been reanalyzed and reinterpreted many times.

In the 1980s, the *meta-analyses method*—a statistical quantitative procedure that allowed researchers to examine the size of effects across multiple psychotherapy studies—was developed. Mary Lee Smith and Gene Glass (1977) reviewed 375 psychotherapy studies and found therapy clients better off than 80 percent of those who received no treatment. Other meta-analytic studies led to the confirmation that psychotherapy is helpful and clinically significant and that patients who show an initial change maintain that change (Lambert, 2001).

Critics of the meta-analytic method cite numerous flaws. For example, meta-analyses examine such a diverse group of studies that they compare apples and oranges, often violating the statistical assumption of independent samples. They give as much weight to a poorly designed study as they do to a well-designed one. Furthermore, meta-analyses involve many subjective judgments that are subject to potential bias, such as what studies to include and eliminate, which statistical measure to use, and so on (Wierzbicki, 1993).

Outcome and Process Research

There are two major types of studies in psychotherapy research—outcome and process. *Outcome research* focuses on the assessment of how well clients function, using measures of symptom remission, behavior change, improved social and vocational functioning, and/or personality growth. *Process research* examines specific events that occur within the therapy session between patient and therapist, or "those characteristics of therapists, patients and therapeutic techniques that may account for positive changes in patient functioning" (Compass & Gotlib, 2002, p. 325). The therapist variables studied include verbal responses, facilitative behavior (e.g., empathy), and the tendency to give advice, provide information, or offer interpretations. The client variables studied include level of involvement, type of client statements, emotions during therapy, and identification of "good" moments in therapy that show improvement, such as expressiveness, the therapeutic bond, motivation, and empathic understanding. Carl Rogers pioneered process research when he taped sessions and analyzed how some form of action by the therapist (empathic responding) brought about a predictable outcome, such as increasing the client's feeling statements in a session.

At one time, therapy researchers tended to be staunch supporters of either the process camp or the outcome camp. In a comprehensive review of the literature that scrutinized 279 studies and 42 reviews of studies conducted since 1985, researchers concluded that any responsible account of psychotherapy research must include both process and outcome research (Orlinsky et al., 2004). Indeed, today there is a growing attempt to combine process and outcome research (Trull & Phares, 2001, p. 318).

The Equivalency Effect

By the 1980s it was clear that Eysenck was wrong. Although not everyone benefits from psychotherapy, and a few even suffer from negative or iatrogenic effects, the psychological distress of most clients is relieved through clearly planned, systematic efforts of trained therapists. Accumulated evidence shows that psychotherapy has a positive effect for most recipients.

Once it became obvious that psychotherapy was effective, the next logical question is which therapy is most effective. No definitive evidence proves that one particular theoretical approach is better than another. This is called the *equivalency effect;* it is also referred to as the *dodo bird verdict* from *Alice in Wonderland.* Alice creates a race for the creatures in Wonderland. At the end of the contest, the dodo bird is asked to declare who is the winner. He answers, "All have won and all must have prizes" (Carroll, 1898; Wampold et al., 1997). In other words, there are few notable differences in the outcomes of most psychotherapies.

Some claim that when differences are found, they can often be explained by the *allegiance effect,* meaning that the results are affected by the researcher's alliance to a particular therapy model (Wampold, 2001). The relationship between the researcher's theoretical orientation and the theoretical model being researched has a bearing on the results of the study. In other words, if a psychotherapy researcher favors or has an allegiance to reality therapy, then the results of the study are likely to provide evidence that the reality therapy, the favored therapy, is preferable to another (Lambert, Garfield, & Bergin, 2004). When statistical adjustments correct for the allegiance effect, the differences in outcome between different therapies are generally negligible (Piper, 2004).

Although the equivalency effect is a strong finding that has been replicated over and over, some findings show that specific therapies work better for some specific problems (Bergin & Garfield, 1986). Specific behavioral, cognitive, and some eclectic techniques are particularly helpful in the treatment of circumscribed behaviors, such as stuttering, childhood aggression, and sexual problems. The current research trend is to search for the specific effects of specific interventions by specific therapists on specific patient types.

The major findings from the last 50 years of psychotherapy research have been summarized in Michael J. Lambert's well-known work, *Bergin and Garfield's Handbook of Psychotherapy and Behavior Change.* For an in-depth and detailed analysis, the student can read this edited volume. However, a summary of findings tells us the following:

- A huge body of research shows that most forms of psychotherapy, given by stable and wise therapists, result in appreciable gains for clients, which are clinically meaningful and statistically significant in research studies. Treated patients do better than controls or those who receive a placebo (Lambert & Ogles, 2004, pp. 180–181).
- Little evidence exists to show that one form of therapy is clinically superior to any other. The equivalency effect applies to major models of psychotherapy (Lambert & Ogles, 2004, pp. 180–181).
- Although some forms of therapy (behavioral, cognitive, eclectic) have shown superior outcomes to verbal therapies in a limited number of studies, this is not generally the case. Some studies show that in outpatients diagnosed with moderate disorders (panic, phobias, and compulsiveness), behavior and cognitive therapies do better than other forms of therapy and have had good results for childhood aggression, psychosis, and health-related behaviors (Lambert & Ogles, 2004, pp. 180–181).
- Growing evidence indicates that some specific techniques and some common factors across treatments are effective, and this had led researchers to look at the interaction effects between type of therapy and type of client (Lambert & Ogles, 2004, pp. 180–181).
- Some argue that good research includes a complex but comprehensive view of psychotherapy that deals with a combination of process and outcome variables. Effective therapy is more than a set of technical procedures, and it is more than simply a warm, supportive relationship. Both factors of relationship and specific therapeutic interventions have an impact on outcome (Orlinsky et al., 2004, p. 363).
- Outcome seems to be best understood as a synergistic result of the patient's problems and resources in combination with the therapist's skill and limitations. Relationship variables, intervention procedures, patient participation, and therapist influences contribute jointly and variously to shaping psychotherapy outcome (Orlinsky et al., 2004, p. 363).
- All in all, the best predictor of good therapy outcome is the therapeutic alliance or a positive collaborative relationship between the therapist and the patient (Crits-Cristoph & Barber, 1990; Krupnick et al., 1996; Strupp, 1995).
- Therapy is highly efficient; brief therapies can result in meaningful changes. For clients who are dysfunctional, at least 50 percent can be changed by 21 sessions; 75 percent of clients improve after 50 sessions (Lambert & Ogles, 2004, pp. 180–181).
- It is premature to advocate one therapy over another given the great variation of and difficulty in controlling all the variables involved. More valid research evidence is needed. We await an answer to the specificity question: "What aspects of therapy, and what kinds of therapy, provided how and by what kind of therapist, under what circumstances, for what kinds of patients with what kinds of problems are likely to lead to what kinds of results?" (Orlinsky et al., 2004, p. 362).

Empirically Supported/Validated Therapy

Despite the equivalency effect, researchers are still very interested in determining which therapies are most effective and efficacious. Major professional organizations have devised recommendations or guidelines for practice, based on research findings about various therapies. For example, the American Psychological Association's Division 12 Task Force on the Promotion and Dissemination of Psychological Procedures published a list of empirically validated treatments illustrating that there are efficacious treatments for specific psychological problems (APA, 2008; Chambless & Hollon, 1998). Students can access the detailed findings on the APA website.

Critics argue that the list is premature; the use of the phrase "empirically validated" is inaccurate because it implies that therapies that are not included are not efficacious when, in fact, they may never have been tested. It is also controversial to uphold using randomized control trials (RCTs) as the gold standard. Controlled studies do not necessarily represent real-world therapy. In addition, the list ignores important process variables and is not consistent with the equivalency of findings (Garfield, 1996). Substituting the phrase "empirically supported" for "empirically validated" toned down the controversy somewhat, but philosophical opposition to the idea of empirically supported treatment continues (Woody, Weisz, & McLean, 2005).

Another approach taken by Division 29 of Psychotherapy in the APA research showed that the therapeutic relationship was the active ingredient for successful psychotherapy and that it accounted for as much of the treatment outcome as did any specific treatment method. Furthermore, matching the treatment and the therapy relationship to the individual client, not just his or her diagnosis, was also important (Norcross, Beutler, & Levant, 2005; Wampold, 2001). Division 29 recommended using empirically supported relationships or "therapy relationships that work" as a criterion for effective therapies. In short, researchers need to examine process variables, the therapist–patient relationship, and what works best in the therapy relationships for particular clients; as well, they need to use qualitative methods and well-correlated studies, to encourage therapists to participate in research, and to monitor patients' responses to therapy (Norcross et al., 2005).

Efficacy Versus Effectiveness

A landmark event in the history of psychotherapy research was the publication of a *Consumer Reports* study in 1995 (Seligman, 1995). Thousands of replies from consumers showed that they believed psychotherapy was effective regardless of type. However, they rated therapy with psychologists, psychiatrists, and social workers as more effective than therapy with less well-trained providers, such as marriage and family therapists.

The study called attention to the distinction between *efficacy* and *effectiveness* research. Efficacy studies are ideal because they are tightly controlled experimentally. Effectiveness studies look at therapy as it is practiced in the real world and are subject to limitations because the variables cannot be well controlled. The *Consumer Reports* study provoked widespread debate about methodology and highlighted the

Table 1.2

Efficacy and Effectiveness Psychotherapy Research

	Efficacy	**Effectiveness**
Trials	Trials in laboratory setting	Trials in clinical setting
Validity	High internal validity	High external validity
Controls	Control over multiple variables	Natural clinical setting; little control
Patients	Preselected for treatment	Patients in treatment; not preselected
Therapists	Trained in particular therapy modality	Works in setting; no special training; only original training
	Monitored for adherence to model	No monitoring in setting
	Retrained if lack of adherence	No retraining
	Manualized treatment likely	Manualized treatment not as likely
Dose	Managed dose	No management; attrition minimized
	Random assignment of subjects	No random assignment of subjects
	Blind procedures	No blind procedures
	Demonstrate causal effect between therapy outcome and treatment	Cannot demonstrate causal effect between therapy outcome and treatment

need for researchers to reach out to clinicians to ascertain what type of research would help them make meaningful clinical decisions and for clinicians to understand how research could improve practice. Table 1.2 compares efficacy and effectiveness research.

Evidence-Based Practice

In the last decade, there has been a strong effort to fully integrate practice and research in psychotherapy; to accomplish this synthesis, psychotherapists turned to *evidence-based practice* (EBP). Evidence-based practice is "the conscientious, explicit and judicious use of current best evidence in making decisions about the care of individual patients, based on skills that allow the doctor to evaluate both personal experience and external evidence in a systematic and objective manner" (Sackett, Rosenberg, Gray, Haynes, & Richardson, 1996, p. 71). What this means is that therapists merge their expertise with the best clinical research evidence available (Sackett et al., 1996, p. 71). The APA notes that EBP also considers the patient's characteristics and culture, along with the therapist's practice and research (2006, p. 273). The Centre for Clinical Effectiveness (2006) explains that the best available evidence should be modified by patient circumstances and preferences, and then it should be used to improve the quality of the clinician's judgments.

Evidence-based practice provides a framework for the translation of research into practice and the use of methodological guidelines to evaluate the therapy (Reynolds & Richardson, 2000). Also called *evidence-based medicine* (EBM), EBP dates back to the middle of the nineteenth century in Britain. It begins with knowing what clinical questions to ask, how to find the best practice, and how to critically appraise the evidence for validity and applicability to a particular patient's care. The Cochrane Collaboration (2007), founded in 1993, was inspired by Archie Cochrane, a physician who criticized the medical profession for not having up-to-date, user-friendly summaries of effective interventions. It consists of regularly updated collections of EBP. It gives clinicians the most current information about health care interventions. Public Med (PubMed), another important resource intended for clinicians, is an online accessible version of the MEDLINE database with a search engine that looks for therapy, diagnosis, allergies, and prognosis. PsycINFO is another important search resource for mental health professionals. Given these resources, mental health EBP is becoming more available to every practitioner.

In just 20 years, the field has blossomed in the United States, and technology has made vast amounts of information accessible. Clinicians can access the Internet and make use of worldwide data to inform their individual practice, in essence, effectively linking research and practice. The evidence-based working group of the American Medical Association recommends that all clinicians acquire some skills to evaluate the mounting research evidence available to all (Guyatt, Meade, Jaeschke, Cook, & Haynes, 2000a, p. 1296).

As a result, one of the philosophical objectives of this book is to create a scientific attitude and a mind-set within you, the student of psychotherapy, toward your clinical work. It is important to think about how any form of psychotherapy you choose with your client is supported in research data. I encourage the neophyte to ask, "What can I tell my client about the evidence that is available that will help me to justify my choice of treatment? What kinds of studies and what kinds of data are available to inform my practice that can be explained in a simple and straightforward manner?" (Peterson, 1992). Thus EBP is a welcome tool for using research findings to guide practice; it can be applied as a straightforward approach to decision making in which the clinician uses the best evidence available, in consultation with the patient, to guide treatment decisions.

Box 1.1 shows the steps a student can take to begin using EBP. As the therapist, the student will ask a specific question about the clinical care of a specific patient, find the best evidence for the validity and usefulness of the answer, then apply the results and evaluate the outcome of the therapeutic intervention (Guyatt, Meade, Jaeschke, Cook, & Haynes, 2000b; Reynolds & Richardson, 2000). This is a career skill that will soon be expected of all therapists.

There are a number of general strategies to help psychotherapists implement EBP (Gotham, 2006). Psychotherapists can train themselves or attend training workshops in how to conduct evidence-based reviews (Stout & Hayes, 2005), and they can regularly consult with lists and registries such as the American Psychological Association Division 12 Task Force reports (Chambless, 1996; Chambless & Hollon, 1998); Cochrane library reviews (Cochrane Collaboration, 2007); federal agencies such as the Agency for Healthcare Research and Quality's Evidence Based Practice Center's

BOX 1.1   STEPS RECOMMENDED BY AN EVIDENCE-BASED APPROACH

1. Pose a clinically relevant and specific focused question about the care of a particular patient (e.g., Which is the better treatment for major depression—therapy or medication?).
2. Search on the Internet for the evidence that best answers the question (or ascertain that there is no research available). The literature sources are multiple, but some are evidence-based reviews, such as the Cochrane Collaboration.
3. Select an article (or more) that contains the information that can answer your question.
4. Read:

   Abstract: big picture and an overall summary of the question, method, results

   Methods: assess validity and identify the populations studied

   Results: direction and clinical importance of the outcome

5. Evaluate and bring the research study to the level of direct patient care.

   Validity: Is the study valid? How sure can we be that the results are due to the treatment and not to some other, uncontrolled variable? From most likely to least likely to be valid are systematic reviews and general information about therapy; meta-analysis; randomized controlled studies; cohort studies; cross-control studies; cross-sectional studies; case reports.

   Outcomes: What were the results of the study? Based on outcome measures and rating scales used, can you calculate magnitude of improvement? Did the patient move into normal range of functioning?

   Safety: Is treatment safe?

   Meaningfulness: Are the results clinically meaningful? Can the results of the clinical trial be applied to the individual patient? To decide, use Number Needed to Treat (NNT) to produce one additional good outcome beyond that obtainable with the control or comparison condition.

   Applicability: Is the result applicable to my patient? Is my patient represented in the research sample? How were the outcomes measured? Can I apply the treatment in my practice?

This information is derived from Reynolds and Richardson's (2000) and March's (2002) recommendations.

Report System; and the Substance Abuse and Mental Health Services Administration (SAMHSA) National Registry of Evidence-Based Programs and Practices.

In this text, each chapter will include an exercise to familiarize the student with research on psychotherapy. While I do not expect students to become experts in conducting evidence-based reviews, I encourage students to take on the attitude of the "local clinical scientist" (Messer, 2004). However, the evidence-based approach should *not* be the only tool used to draw conclusions about psychotherapeutic research, as discussed below.

Controversies over EBP

EBP is a controversial topic at this time, so let's examine all sides of the debate (Table 1.3 presents a summary of the arguments).

Opponents of EBP see it as a superficial, cookbook method of classifying therapy. They argue that the quantification of psychotherapy can serve as a political

Table 1.3

Controversies Associated with Evidence-Based Mental Health Practice

Proponents	Opponents
Recall of information you learned in graduate school diminishes.	Graduate school gives the basics; stay current after that on your own.
To deliver quality care, it is mandatory to be aware of current knowledge. New treatment methods are being used, tested, reviewed, discussed, and critiqued.	New treatments have always been publicized in major journals and conferences, and word gets out when an effective treatment is found.
Learning EBP provides you with tools you need to find the information conveniently and quickly.	Mental health care should not be based on a MEDLINE, Cochrane, PsychARTICLES, or PsycINFO search.
Amount of information available grows exponentially; it is impossible to keep up with all of it. Errors will continue; know how to find what is needed, to know when patients need the treatment.	Most professionals can keep up by attending conferences and ordering key journals. They do not have to be researchers themselves.
Total information available in the literature is far more powerful than expert opinion only (from one or from a group of experts).	Clinical expertise is the most important part of treating, diagnosing, or assessing. The clinician is the one expert.
Patient confidence will increase because the clinician can back up judgments with empirical findings in literature.	The patient is an individual who has faith in what the therapist says, not in statistics and articles. The patient expects the therapist to use expert judgment.
The therapist can point to the evidence and use it to justify treatment to payers.	Payers should accept expertise as the bottom line.
Close the gap between research and practice and the false dichotomy between them.	There is a difference between research and practice, and until researchers make the research meaningful, it is not of value to clinicians.
Evidence is not the sole basis of decision making; rather, it should serve to bolster clinical judgment, patient values, and expertise and be integrated into clinical practice.	There is too much reliance on pure research. Clinical judgment and expertise is superior to research findings on paper; the clinician is there, but the researcher is not.
The clinician acquires new skills (computer) and understanding of formal rules of evidence in appraising research.	These tasks are too time-consuming. Clinician time is better spent working with patients.
Keep searching and eventually you will find the most efficacious and effective elements of treatment.	The preponderance of evidence over many years shows no empirical support for the idea that one form of therapy is superior to another. Look for common factors.

tool for cutting costs and as a dehumanizing approach (Woody et al., 2005). EBP deprives the psychotherapist of autonomy, restricts practice by emphasizing randomized control designs and meta-analysis as psychotherapeutic criteria, takes the heart and soul out of therapy, prematurely mandates the use of specific therapies for specific disorders, does not consider variation in the therapeutic skills and quality of therapy among therapists, and ignores the clinical reality that different people who have identical diagnoses possess different traits that affect their therapy differently (Corrie & Callanan, 2002; Norcross et al., 2005; Sackett et al., 1996). These criticisms as well as a lack of training are barriers to the acceptance of evidence-based practices (Pagoto et al., 2007).

Proponents of EBP argue that it integrates clinical expertise with the best available research evidence. It is a young, evolving discipline. Diagnosis is not the only basis for determining which therapy should be chosen; other dimensions can be studied. Research has discovered empirical facts about therapy that the therapist needs to integrate into his or her practice (Katz et al., 2003). Even clinicians who are very busy can practice EBP by devoting scarce reading time to selective, efficient, patient-driven searching, appraisal, and incorporation of the best available evidence into their practice (Sackett et al., 1996, p. 71). External evidence should be used to inform, not replace, clinical judgment. Used appropriately by skilled clinicians, EBP should lower the cost of care.

This text encourages you to explore EBP and to ask whether the evidence justifies the use of any particular therapy. Consider which treatment guidelines and manuals might exist. In the online Appendix C there are some examples of evidence-based mental health (EBMH) searches. This will help you to develop research-based thinking.

Common Factors Versus Specific Techniques

Another significant area of psychotherapy research addresses the question of why psychotherapy works. Some believe there is a specific factor, or one active ingredient, that underlies the cause of the success of a given therapy. Others believe that, since different forms of therapy result in similar outcomes, there are common underlying factors that work for all therapies. Common factors are "those dimensions of the treatment setting (therapist, therapy, client) that are not specific to any technique" (Lambert & Bergin, 1994, p. 156). Rather than ponder why one model is better than another, the common-factors approach tries to identify universal therapeutic variables (Weinberger, 1995).

Researchers have found some evidence for both perspectives, but the results must be interpreted carefully. Specific targeted interventions have added something unique, beyond the effect of common factors but within a context of interactions. For example, if the symptoms are severe, some specific techniques are helpful in the treatment of disorders such as depression, phobias, panic, substance abuse, schizophrenia, and some health-related disorders. Less directive techniques work better with clients who have an internal locus of control; psychodynamic techniques seem to work better with more motivated and better adjusted clients; interpersonally well-adjusted clients do better with brief, focused dynamic treatment; those who are depressed and avoidant may be better off with cognitive therapy while those who are depressed and

Table 1.4

Common Factors of Psychotherapy Associated with Positive Outcomes

Support	Learning	Action
Catharsis	Advice	Behavioral regulation
Identification with therapist	Affective experiencing	Cognitive mastery
Mitigation of isolation	Assimilation of problematic	Encouragement of facing fears
Positive relationship	experiences	Mastery effects modeling
Reassurance	Changing expectations for	Practice
Release of tension	personal effectiveness	Reality testing
Structure	Cognitive learning	Success experience
Therapeutic alliance	Corrective emotional	Taking risks
Therapist–client active	experience	Working through
participation	Exploration of internal frame	
Therapist expertise	of reference	
Therapist warmth, respect,	Feedback	
empathy, acceptance,	Insight	
genuineness	Rationale	
Trust		

Source: From Michael Lambert, *Bergin and Garfield's Handbook of Psychotherapy and Behavior Change* (John Wiley & Sons, 2004). Reprinted with permission of John Wiley & Sons, Inc.

obsessive may react better to interpersonal therapy (Hoglend, 1999). While the common-factors model is supported by evidence, there is also empirical support to show that patient characteristics, the quality of the therapy relationship, the match between patient and therapist, and specific interventions are important variables related to the success of psychotherapies (Beutler, 2002; Wampold, 2001).

The core common factors that are generally considered to be involved in a positive therapy alliance are client exposure to earlier conflicts in imagination or in reality, a corrective emotional experience, expectations of change, therapist qualities of empathy and positive regard, and a new perspective from the therapist to the client to frame his or her life situations (Messer, 1992). Table 1.4 describes a comprehensive summary of the common factors of therapy that are associated with positive outcomes. All in all, there is little solid evidence to show that any one model of therapy is more effective than another. In fact, the outcomes for many different types of therapy have been shown to have fundamentally the same results (Lambert & Ogles, 2004).

✢ OTHER ISSUES RELATED TO THEORY, PRACTICE, AND RESEARCH

There have been major changes in theory, practice, and research, but the context in which psychotherapy is practiced has also changed. Issues of diversity, computer literacy, and the demand for short-term therapy hold important implications for today's psychotherapist.

Diversity Awareness

Although the basic elements of the helping relationship are universal, many aspects are culturally bound, and how this care is delivered varies from culture to culture, ranging from shamanism to today's Western psychotherapy. Over the past several decades, consciousness has been raised about the importance of understanding differing worldviews, alternative realities, and cultural relativism in relationship to theory, practice, and research in psychotherapy (Fukuyama & Sevig, 1999). Diversity has become a topic of concern for psychotherapists because the American population is multicultural, the economy is globalizing, and people are taking pride in their personal heritage rather than blending into a dominant culture. Professionals acknowledge that psychotherapy is a sociopolitical act as well as a helping act.

Derald Wing Sue and David Sue (2003, p. 8) bluntly say that psychotherapy has resulted in great harm to members of culturally diverse groups. Therapy has characterized values from diverse cultures as deviant and pathological and, thus, imposed the values of the dominant Western culture upon members of a minority culture, denying them culturally appropriate care. Derald Wing Sue (2003, p. 137) encourages Caucasian therapists to look at White privilege, or the unearned advantages that Whites have by virtue of belonging to a system that is normed on White experiences, values, and perceptions and awards them dominance. He encourages asking the traditionally invisible, even taboo, question: What does it mean to be White?

The public is constantly exposed to messages about race, ethnicity, gender, sexuality, and class. As a result, we cannot avoid taking on stereotypes and prejudices toward other groups. We all have a role, albeit indirect, in oppression. We want to be aware of the list of harms that have come about in the mental health profession and in society in general because of the *isms*. Informed therapists should watch for these issues if they play out in therapy and critically examine and weed out biases, prejudices, or stereotypes that might affect treatment.

Most professional organizations require that psychotherapists be trained to raise consciousness about how their personal beliefs, attitudes, and biases influence their work with culturally diverse clients (American Psychological Association, 2003). All of the major professional organizations whose members are trained in psychotherapy have ethical guidelines to become educated about diversity by making cultural competence (satisfactory skills in multicultural therapy) an essential part of training and practice. Multicultural therapy (MCT) (discussed in Chapter 2) consists of goals and methods consistent with the cultural values and life experiences of clients, acceptance and use of universal and culture-specific strategies, a balance of individualism and collectivism, and the will to change a system, rather than an individual client, when that is indicated.

Computer Literacy

The development of computer literacy has affected mental health in at least three significant ways: (a) research possibilities have increased tremendously, making large-scale, longer-term projects possible; (b) in-office computers have increased psychotherapists' access to databases and research findings; and (c) Internet therapy has arisen.

Researchers can collect and analyze large amounts of information and achieve a much greater understanding of psychotherapy than we could have imagined 30 years ago. Researchers can access national databases such as the National Ambulatory Medical Care Survey (NAMCS) and the National Institute of Mental Health (NIMH) Epidemiological Catchment Area. Technology has also allowed the use of sophisticated data analyses, including meta-analysis, recalculation, and summarization of old data (Austad, 1996).

Psychotherapists can access research findings and perform a computer search right in their office. Not too many years ago, the researcher had to go to the library and look up information in volumes, spending hours of time out of the office. The therapist now can access whatever he or she wants to know from a desktop computer, as discussed in the evidence-based section above.

The technological revolution has also brought about the e-mail phenomenon, which has potential as both a primary form of therapy or as an integral adjunct to therapy. Of course, this uncharted territory raises questions about ethics, legalities, depersonalization, standards of practice, and privacy, but many practitioners have found safe and ethical applications. Advantages of cyberspace therapy are anonymity, convenience, accessibility, and a unique appropriateness for some diagnoses, such as social phobia.

Length of Treatment

In the past, good therapy meant long-term therapy, but recently this sacred assumption has been challenged. Time, in therapy, is limited and affects significant aspects of treatment (Hoyt, 1988). There are many pressures on the therapist to use short-term therapeutic methods—society's desire for quick results and for a magic cure, the mandate for treatment to be cost effective, and the medicalization of psychotherapy among them. The characteristics of short-term therapy are rapid, prompt intervention; a high level of therapist activity; specific and circumscribed goals; clear time limits; flexibility in approach and technique; and a goal-oriented therapist who rapidly assesses, maintains a clear focus, and uses the client's resources as strengths (Bloom, 1997).

Accumulated data on treatment outcomes have consistently shown that short-term treatment is very effective for a wide range of both health and psychological problems. The trend now is to limit time and goals, to focus on a specific issue, to be active and flexible in scheduling psychotherapy, and to provide an intermittent approach (Cummings, 1991). The reality is that short-term therapy is what people really receive.

⇥ HOW PATIENTS USE PSYCHOTHERAPY

Lakein Phillips (1985a, 1985b), a psychotherapy researcher, studied over a million cases of psychotherapy in international, national, and local databases. He found that regardless of the setting or therapist's orientation, the average number of psychotherapy visits is four to eight. Between one third and one half of clients do not return after a single visit. By session six, 60 to 70 percent of those who began no longer remain. Less than 10 percent continue in therapy beyond 10 or 15 sessions. A consistent pattern, called the *attrition curve,* emerges in which a high proportion of patients make one, two, or three visits to the psychotherapist. There is a gradual drop-off in the number of clients who remain as the number of visits increases from 4 to 10. Only a small concentration of high users, or outliers, exists (15% or less) who account for the bulk of psychotherapy visits and expenditures.

High users fall into four basic subgroups:

- Patients with less serious mental illness who are in long-term, insight-oriented therapy; these patients are often termed the "worried well" by critics who claim that this kind of long-term psychotherapy is a luxury.
- Patients with multiple somatic and mental complaints.
- Patients with chronic mental disorders, who receive both drug maintenance and supportive psychotherapy.
- Patients with serious mental disorders.

Outside of these groups of high users (outliers), the majority of people who seek psychotherapy expect and receive short-term therapy (Bloom, 1997; Koss & Shiang, 1994).

Consistent with Phillip's findings are those of researchers from Northwestern and the University of Chicago who studied the relationship between quantity of psychotherapy and improvement, or the *dose-effect relationship,* similar to that used in the study of drug effects in pharmacology. They calculated the linear relationship between the number of sessions and the percentage of improvement for over 2,400 patients over a 30-year period. The plot of the dosage (number of sessions against a variety of measures of the effectiveness of therapy) showed that most improvement occurred during the early stages of therapy. Ten to 18 percent of patients reported some improvement even before attending the first appointment. Forty-eight to 58 percent of patients showed improvement by the 8th session, and 75 percent of patients showed improvement by the 26th session. Researchers conclude that 8 sessions is the median effective dose of individual therapy, and by 26 sessions an effective dose of 75 percent is attained. Replications of these earlier studies confirm that 76 percent of clients improve by 14 sessions (Anderson & Lambert, 2001).

Despite these facts, many therapists cling to the belief that long-term therapy is the ideal therapy. One reason for this perception is the clinician's illusion, or a tendency to believe that the course of treatment is the same for everyone, even when the attributes of the population receiving therapy are quite different (Cohen & Cohen, 1984). The clinician's illusion can be illustrated with a look at a typical psychotherapy practice.

Pretend you are a therapist who has practiced for 20 years. Reviewing your records for hundreds of clients, you see that the majority of patients left by the 25th session, and only a small percentage, 15 percent or less, remained beyond 25 sessions. So if 100 patients arrived during your first week of practice, after 25 weeks, 85 were no longer in therapy and only 15 remained. Let's say another 100 referrals came your way during the 26th week. After another 25 weeks, only 15 of the second set remained—so a total of 30 long-term patients remained. Repeating this pattern, in two years your practice fills up with 60 long-term patients. Your memory of your short-term patients recedes into the background while the long-term clients remain in the forefront of your clinical practice. You assume that the patients you see in long-term work actually represent the "true patients" or the typical or ideal clients. Although the majority of patients are in therapy for a short time, therapists tend to erroneously assume that the familiar small sample represents the whole population of treated clients (Austad, 1996).

An overwhelming amount of research clearly shows that short-term work is effective, as well as inevitable (Bloom, 1997). However, one important factor is whether short-term therapy is planned or unplanned. Planned short-term therapy is brief by design and not by attrition (Budman & Gurman, 1988). Mary Koss and Julia Shiang (1994) summarize why brief therapy is now an entity in its own right:

- Patients who enter therapy are expecting to resolve specific and focal problems and are not seeking a deep personality change.
- A wide range of severe psychological and health-related problems can be effectively treated with brief interventions; brief therapy is not just appropriate for less severe and minor problems.
- Short-term therapies have encouraged the use of treatment manuals and, thus, have clarified the therapy procedures and allowed for more meaningful comparisons of the effectiveness of therapies.

Given the actual use of psychotherapy by clients as shown by the epidemiological data, the findings from the dose-response research that the early sessions of psychotherapy are the most potent, and the call for cost effectiveness and evidence-based models, it is especially important for student therapists to be trained in brief work modalities.

SUMMARY

- Psychotherapy is a career comprised of helping others; it is a truly satisfying vocation.
- The major types or models of psychotherapy include psychoanalytic and psychodynamic, humanist-existential, behavior, cognitive, sociocultural and culturally specific, biological and biopsychosocial, eclectic or integrative, and postmodern or constructivist.
- While the nature of the therapeutic relationship—one human being helping another—has remained constant over time, the practice environment has changed rapidly and radically.
- Psychotherapy has three important components: theory, practice, and research. And as the field itself has changed significantly over the past 20 years, so have these components.
- Psychotherapeutic theory has changed as biological research discoveries have brought about a reconsideration of the mind–body connection. The medical model, an allopathic view of therapy as treatment of a disease, has been both the object of some discontent as well as a favored model substantiated by numerous biological findings. The biopsychosocial model considers mental conditions as a function of biological, psychological, and social interactions.

This more holistic view considers psychological problems as the result of an imbalance, and treatment is focused to integrate mind and body. Theory also has moved from sweeping, generalized perspectives to more concise and circumscribed models.

- The practice of psychotherapy also has been affected in the past several years by economics, business orientation, managed care, politics and financing of health care, and pharmacology advances. The economics of health care is complicated. Psychotherapy is both a business and a profession. Today, health care and mental health care practice is more entrepreneurial. The number of professionals who perform psychotherapy is increasing, with the exception of psychiatrists. Managed-care entities dominate the reimbursement system. Managed mental health care or behavioral services come in a variety of forms. The integrated care behavioral health model provides new practice opportunities for the psychotherapist to co-locate and work within primary health care settings.

- Finally, psychotherapy research has had a stormy history; this turmoil is reflected in the controversies surrounding the researcher/clinician gap, methodological struggles, differences between process and outcome research, and tensions between efficacy and effectiveness research. Research is advancing as a result of more sophisticated methodology, closing the gap between clinical work and research.

- Psychotherapists who face increased accountability are seeking therapies that are supported by research. Psychotherapy researchers try to identify effective and efficacious forms of psychotherapy and/or discover the common factors underlying all therapies.

- Evidence-based practice is an up-and-coming but controversial method of assessing medical treatment and has more recently been applied to psychotherapy. Pressure is on the therapist to know and understand the research literature. Professional organizations are maintaining practice standards and guidelines to help guide their members. Evidence-based practice can be helpful to the clinician and can close the researcher/clinician gap.

- Understanding diversity is important to psychotherapy today. Psychotherapists must be sensitive to how race, culture, ethnicity, gender, and sexual orientation affect practice and how therapists' own beliefs, attitudes, and biases influence their work with culturally diverse clients.

- Computer literacy is another issue of importance in therapy today. This technology allows researchers to conduct large-scale, longer-term psychotherapy projects and allows psychotherapists to easily access research findings. It also has opened the door to Internet therapy.

- Brief therapy is practiced more today than in the past. The use of long-term therapy has been challenged as evidence has grown that short-term treatment is effective for a wide range of psychological problems. The trend now is to limit time and goals, to work with a focal issue, to be active and flexible in scheduling psychotherapy, and to provide an intermittent therapeutic approach.

RESOURCES

National Center for Health Statistics
Statistics Branch
3311 Toledo Road
Hyattsville, MD 20782-2003
(301) 458-4013
http://www.cdc.gov/nchs

This is the nation's principal health statistics agency, which compiles statistical information to guide actions and policies to improve the overall health of the population. It gathers information from birth, death, and medical records; interview surveys; and clinical data. The center helps to identify and address critical mental health and health problems.

National Institutes of Health
Office of Behavioral and Social Sciences Research
9000 Rockville Pike
Bethesda, MD 20892
(301) 402-1146
http://www.nih.gov

This is the nation's medical research agency. As the primary federal agency for conducting and supporting basic, clinical, medical research, it investigates the causes, treatments, and cures for diseases and applies knowledge to improve health and reduce illness and disability.

CLASS EXERCISES AND ACTIVITIES

Theory

1. What are common factors and what are specific factors within psychotherapy research?
2. Differentiate between empirically validated and empirically supported psychotherapies.
3. How is time an important factor in psychotherapy? What are the differences between long- and short-term psychotherapy?
4. Prescription privileges are a controversial topic. Who do you think should prescribe drugs? Why do you think there is such a controversy over these privileges?
5. What should nonmedical providers know about psychiatric medications and/ or medical illnesses?
6. The President's New Freedom Commission on Mental Health (www .mentalhealthcommission.gov) recommends that we address mental health with the same urgency as physical health. How do you see this affecting the practice of psychotherapy now and in the future?
7. What are the goals of integrated behavioral health care?

Practice

1. Read the case of Jonathan in Appendix A. Look at Figure 1.2, which is the sample of a typical treatment plan required by managed-care companies. Put yourself in the role of the therapist who is assessing Jonathan and fill in the treatment plan. Discuss the information you need to do a thorough job.
2. What is evidence-based practice? Go to the Duke University website (www .mclibrary.duke.edu/subject/ebm?tab=overview) and try an EBM review. Make up a review for a mental health diagnosis or problem. Can you find other tutorials? See the online Appendix C.
3. What is the *Diagnostic and Statistical Manual* of the American Psychiatric Association? Why would a therapist need to know about the *DSM?*
4. Define managed care. Discuss some of the controversies associated with managed care in the health care system in the U.S. today.
5. Define integrated behavioral health care. Look through the literature to find articles that discuss this new and interesting way of delivering psychotherapy.
6. Why is it important for a psychotherapist today to have some basic knowledge about psychopharmacology?

Research

1. Define some important concepts in psychotherapy research: the dodo bird verdict or equivalency effect; empirically supported and validated therapies; efficacy versus effectiveness.
2. Go to the Cochrane Collaboration on the Internet. Look up the *Cochrane Manual* (www.cochrane.org/admin/1Manual3_2007.pdf). Describe the general methodology used to conduct a Cochrane review. What is your opinion? Do you think this is progressive? Discuss the controversies surrounding the use of evidence-based medicine or evidence-based mental health practice in general.
3. Find various websites that contain tutorials or instructions about evidence-based mental health. These are continually updated and are an excellent source of up-to-date information for the student, professional, and practitioner. Here are a few:
   - Centre for Clinical Effectiveness: Monash University: http://www.mihsr .monash.org/cce
   - *British Medical Journal*: http://www.bmj.com/cgi/content/full
   - Center for Health Evidence: University of Alberta combined with other Canadian Universities: http://www.cche.net/usersguides/ebm.asp
   - McMaster University Evidence-Based Practice Center: http://hiru.mcmaster.ca/epc
   - Oxford University Evidence Based Medicine Centre: http://www.cebm.net
   - SUNY Downstate University Evidence Based Medicine Tutorial: http://library.downstate.edu/EBM2/contents.htm

CHAPTER 2

PROFESSIONALISM, ETHICS, AND LEGAL ISSUES IN PSYCHOTHERAPY

The first step in the evolution of ethics is a sense of solidarity with other human beings.

–Albert Schweitzer

The goals of this chapter are to help the student define professionalism, ethics, and legal issues as they relate to psychotherapy. The chapter describes the people and professions performing psychotherapy and discusses professional credentialing, licensing, and certification. Major issues governed by professional ethical codes of conduct are discussed including competence, informed consent, confidentiality, involuntary commitment, dangerousness, duty to warn and protect, multiple or dual relationships, and record keeping and HIPAA. Other issues addressed in the chapter are malpractice, the National Practitioner Data Bank, and multiculturalism and diversity.

✦ HISTORICAL CONTEXT

Complaints about ethical violations and malpractice litigation against mental health professionals are increasing (Bernstein & Hartsell, 2000), and the practice of psychotherapy in today's health care environment is increasingly complicated and challenging (Rychik & Lowenkopf, 2000). To maintain high ethical standards, therapists must adhere to the code of ethics associated with their particular profession.

Ethics, or ethical principles, are conventions that direct professional conduct (Sturmey & Gaubatz, 2003). All therapists, regardless of profession or therapeutic orientation, have a singular and overriding goal—to work in the best interest of the client. The professional, ethical, and legal standards for psychotherapy have evolved over time for pragmatic purposes. Standards protect the public, the individual client, and the therapist. While standards make therapists accountable for their actions and allow clients to seek restitution for any wrongdoing, they also form the basis of reasonable actions to allow for an objective review and evaluation of therapists' behavior (Hixson, 2007).

It is important to understand the terminology describing the profession and the people who perform psychotherapy. Professionals are individuals who work in occupations for which they receive extensive instruction, rigorous training, and continuing education. Mental health professionals include psychologists, psychiatrists, social workers, counselors, and psychiatric nurses, among others. Professionals such as these possess a title (such as psychologist), the use of which is regulated by licensing or certification laws set by the state. The terms *licensed* and *certified* are protected by law, and thus to use these designations people must meet state requirements or distinct rules and regulations to legally and legitimately practice their respective professions.

For example, in the state of Connecticut, in order to call yourself a psychologist, you must complete a doctoral degree, either a PhD or PsyD, from an accredited university, complete a 2,000-hour internship, and work for a year full-time under the supervision of a licensed psychologist before being eligible to take the statewide exam. After passing the exam, you can legally call yourself a licensed psychologist. Thus it is a protected title (Connecticut General Statutes, 2006).

A psychotherapist is a person who practices psychotherapy. The titles "psychotherapist" and "counselor" are, in most states, generally not protected terms, meaning there are few laws that limit their use. In many states, nearly anyone can hang out a shingle and call her- or himself a psychotherapist or a counselor. For example, in Washington State, to become a registered counselor a person need only pay the $40 fee and take a four-hour training course in AIDS awareness. No higher degree, not even a high school diploma, is needed (Berens, 2006).

In reality, competent psychotherapists need to have specialized knowledge and a defined skill set, which, in turn, means significant education and training. An informed public knows that a psychotherapist needs credentials, but an uninformed public can be duped by the unscrupulous. However, because insurance companies will not reimburse providers who lack professional training and licensing or certification, that is one indicator of a psychotherapist's qualifications.

Psychotherapy Practitioners Today

Legitimate psychotherapists generally enter one of the professions that provide education in the theory, practice, and research of psychotherapy. This is step one in obtaining the appropriate credentials. A number of professions are involved in the provision of psychotherapy/counseling, including psychiatrists, psychologists, social workers, professional counselors, and psychiatric nurses. We will briefly review some of the major current practitioners of psychotherapy and describe their areas of expertise.

Clinical Psychologists

Clinical psychologists obtain a doctoral degree. They earn either a PhD, a traditional doctor of philosophy, from an accredited university with training that focuses on clinical treatment and research, or a PsyD, a doctor of psychology, with training that stresses clinical work more than research. Clinical and counseling psychologists who work in independent practice or who render patient care must be licensed or certified and limit their practice to areas in which they have developed professional competence. The use of the professional title "psychologist" is protected and is contingent on licensing as well as one of the doctoral degrees mentioned. Each state has required criteria. These typically include an internship, postdoctoral supervised work under a licensed psychologist, a licensing exam, and (in some states) continuing education requirements.

The professional responsibilities of clinical psychologists include psychotherapy, assessment, and clinical supervision. They work with a wide variety of patients and problems, as well as with the seriously disturbed (Habben, 2005). With additional training, psychologists have gained prescription privileges in two states (New Mexico and Louisiana) and are in the process of obtaining it in other states (U.S. Department of Labor, 2004).

Counseling Psychologists

Counseling psychologists earn a PhD, a PsyD, or an EdD from an accredited university, with a specialization in counseling psychology. Historically, there were specific differences between clinical and counseling psychologists. Counseling psychologists worked with less seriously disturbed clients, focused on vocational counseling, tended to focus on the present and not the past, dealt with vocational issues rather than unconscious issues in therapy, and stressed a developmental perspective across the life span. Today, the distinctions are blurring. Counseling psychologists are licensed in all 50 states and practice independently as health care providers, and they work side-by-side with clinical psychologists performing similar duties (Roger & Stone, 2006).

In 2004, psychologists held 179,000 jobs in the United States. Of these, 20 percent worked in a health care setting, and 40 percent were self-employed in private practice or consulting firms (U.S. Department of Labor, 2004).

Counselors

Counselors earn a master's degree in counseling or a closely related field and generally complete a minimum of two years supervised postmaster's clinical work. Counselor education programs in universities are generally housed in departments of education or psychology. Counselors are professionals who provide a full range of services, including assessment, diagnosis, and psychotherapy, and they work with issues such as addiction and substance abuse, stress management, vocational concerns, marriage and family problems, educational decisions, and parenting, among others. Counseling providers include mental health counselors, substance abuse and behavioral disorder counselors, marriage and family counselors, and gerontological counselors.

They train in a variety of therapy techniques. The Council for Accreditation of Counseling and Related Educational Programs (CACREP) accredits counselor training programs. Attendance in an approved program facilitates state licensing requirements. Counselors also can elect to be nationally certified by the National Board for Certified Counselors (NBCC), which makes it easier to fulfill state requirements. In

2004, the U.S. Department of Labor reported that there were 96,000 mental health counselors, 76,000 substance abuse/behavioral disorder counselors, and 24,000 marriage and family therapists (U.S. Department of Labor, 2004).

Psychiatrists

Psychiatrists are physicians who earn a doctor of medicine (MD), or a doctor of osteopathic medicine (DO) from an accredited university and pass a licensing exam. The use of the professional title "psychiatrist" is protected and is contingent on licensing in all states. To obtain board certification, or specialization in psychiatry, the physician must complete four years of residency training in psychiatry.

Psychiatrists are considered the primary health caregivers in mental health. Generally, they have an understanding of the complex relationship between emotional illness and other medical illnesses and can prescribe medication. They assess and treat mental illness through psychotherapy and psychopharmacology, as well as other biological treatments such as electroconvulsive therapy. In 2004, there were 30,618 psychiatrists in the United States (U.S. Department of Labor, 2004).

Clinical Social Workers

Clinical social workers, or mental health and substance abuse social workers, earn a master's degree in social work (MSW), which is required for clinical work. The MA program is two years, with a minimum of 900 hours of supervised internship. Doctorate degrees in social work, DSWs, are generally necessary for teaching and supervision. The clinical social worker completes a supervised clinical field internship as well as two years of supervised clinical employment at the postgraduate level. All states have licensing or certification requirements that must be met in order to use the professional title. The National Association of Social Workers (NASW) offers credentialing on a voluntary basis, but it is highly recommended for private practice. In 2004, there were 272,000 mental health social workers and 116,000 substance abuse social workers (U.S. Department of Labor, 2004).

Psychiatric Nurses

Psychiatric nurses, or advanced practiced registered nurses (APRNs), have nursing degrees and specialize in psychiatry. They have earned a bachelor of science in nursing (BSN) from a four-year university or an associate degree in nursing (ADN) from a two-year college, and they have passed a licensing exam. Advanced practice nurses must complete the educational and clinical work requirements to work as a clinical nurse specialist (CNS) or as a nurse practitioner (NP). Those who specialize in mental health nursing diagnose and treat individuals or families and must be licensed, which is managed by the state boards of nursing in which the APRN practices.

The psychiatric nurses have prescription privileges in many states. Some programs now focus on training psychiatric nurse practitioners to work in primary care, a new and important role in the changing era of mental health care. For example, some psychiatric primary care nurse practitioner programs offer training in short-term psychotherapy, along with the advanced physical assessment skills and preparation in holistic (medical and psychosocial) adult primary health care with psychiatric clients in a variety of settings. There are an estimated 7,000 psychiatric mental health nurses, credentialed by the American Nurses Credentialing Center, as specialists in mental health in the United States today (American Psychiatric Nurses Association, 2008).

School Psychologists

School psychologists have completed, at minimum, a postmaster's degree program that includes a one-year internship focusing on mental health and child development, school organization, learning styles and processes, behavior, motivation, and effective teaching. About 75 percent are nondoctoral. School psychologists are certified or licensed by the state. They can also obtain National School Psychology Certification from its board (NSPCB). School psychologists work directly with children and collaborate with educators, parents, and other professionals. Most school psychologists work in public and private school systems, but they can also practice in school-based health centers, clinics, hospitals, private practice, universities, community and state agencies, and other institutions. There are an estimated 25,000 school psychologists in the United States (Fagan & Wise, 2000).

Where Psychotherapists Practice

These psychotherapy providers are licensed or certified by the state in which they work. They can practice in a variety of settings: private practice; medical facilities; private and public institutions, such as mental health clinics; community settings (private and public community agencies); child welfare agencies; integrated delivery systems, hospitals, employee assistance programs, in managed or integrated behavioral health care; schools; and substance abuse treatment centers. With the necessary credentials, they can also teach and perform research. Table 2.1 summarizes the qualifications and the requirements for licensing or certification in various professions.

Above and beyond licensing and certification procedures, most professionals voluntarily join a national professional organization such as the National Association of Social Workers (NASW) or the American Counseling Association (ACA). Each of these professions has a professional code of ethics and a process whereby the behavior of its members can be reviewed by peers in the event of an ethics complaint.

Although the professions differ in training requirements and perspectives, they are remarkably single-minded on the key components of their codes of ethics. However, each differs in emphasis according to the profession. The NASW stresses the importance of rights and social justice, whereas the APA (American Psychological Association) code focuses more on the individual client. The public can seek redress from the state licensing board as well as contact the professional organization. For example, Monique's therapist, Dr. X, forces her into a sexual relationship with him. She wants to report his unethical behavior. If Dr. X is a licensed psychiatrist, she can complain to the state board that certifies psychiatrists, and she can further complain to the American Psychiatric Association, assuming that Dr. X

Table 2.1

Psychotherapy Professions

Profession	Degree	State Requirements	Professional Organization	Psychotherapy Practiced (dominant)
Psychologist—clinical or counseling	PhD, PsyD, or EdD	Licensed in state	American Psychological Association	Variety of therapies Limited pharmacotherapy
Psychiatrist	MD or DO	Board certified	American Psychiatric Association	Pharmacotherapy Some insight-oriented, cognitive/behavioral
Social worker	MSW	Licensure by state	National Association of Social Workers	Psychodynamic now changing to cognitive
Counselor (career, college, community, gerontology, family, mental health)	MA or higher in counseling or closely related field	50 out of 54 U.S. states and territories	American Counseling Association	Variety of therapies
School counselor	MA	Certificate or license	American School Counselor Association	Cognitive Variety of therapies
School psychologist	MA	Certificate	National School Psychology Certification Board	Consultation with student, teachers, parents, and school Evaluation Behavior therapy
Addiction counselor, Level I (NCAC I) and Level II (NCAC II)	BA or MA 450 hours of training	Certificate or license	National Association for Addiction Professionals	Substance abuse Relapse prevention
Marriage and family therapist	Master's in behavioral health and/or family therapy	Certificate or license	Association of Marriage and Family Therapists	Family therapy
Advanced practice registered nurse	MA in psychiatric mental health nursing	License varies state to state; certification for American Nurses Credentialing	American Psychiatric Nurses Association	Variety of therapies
Generic psychotherapist	No requirements determined by state	No state license or certification		

is a member. If Monique's therapist is a "psychotherapist" who is not in a profession that is credentialed by the state and does not belong to a professional organization, neither the state nor any profession has jurisdiction over his practice. He cannot be censured by a professional organization, since he does not belong to one. The client's recourse is limited to and determined by whether the actions meet the criteria for a civil or criminal suit.

For interested students, additional resources appear at the end of the chapter as well as Internet addresses where students can readily access the most updated version of each professional code.

✦ ETHICAL ISSUES

Now that we have described the professionals who perform psychotherapy, we can turn to some universal ethical issues all therapists must grapple with regardless of their specific professional affiliations. These issues are generally covered by the ethical code for each profession, which provides a set of standards to cover most clinical situations encountered by psychotherapists. The primary purposes of these codes are to protect the client and the public and to inform and guide therapists in their work with clients. The codes address a broad range of topics including competence, informed consent, confidentiality, commitment, assessing dangerousness, duty to warn and protect, dual or multiple relationships, diagnosis and assessment, and record keeping and HIPAA.

Competence

From a legal and ethical standpoint, professionals must be competent and practice only what they have mastered. For example, the American Psychological Association (APA) code of ethics (2003) states that psychologists should provide services only in areas that are "within the boundaries of their competence, based on their education, training, supervised experience, consultation, study, or professional experience." Psychologists are further obligated to understand the factors that affect the delivery of their services associated with "age, gender, gender identity, race, ethnicity, culture, national origin, religion, sexual orientation, disability, language, or socioeconomic status." If the therapist is not qualified by training and experience to address these issues professionally, he or she must seek consultation and possibly supervision or must refer the patient to another therapist. All the professions ask their members to accurately represent their training and to not present themselves in any way that misrepresents their skills.

Informed Consent

Informed consent means that the patient can fully appreciate and understand the information the therapist provides so that the patient can make a fully informed and voluntary choice to enter treatment. The concept has both legal and ethical components, which are examined below.

Informed consent is the legal standard of care in medical practice. It is based on the idea that each person has the right to determine what he or she wants to do with his or her body. The principle first emerged for surgical procedures, then for general medical ones, then for medication itself, and now it is integral for psychotherapy. The therapist may only obtain informed consent if he or she has provided the information needed for the client to make a rational choice about treatment. According to Laura Weiss Roberts and Allen R. Dyer (2004), this information includes the following:

- goals of therapy
- role of the therapist
- role of the client
- expected outcome
- prognosis
- diagnosis
- benefits and possible harms from treatment
- estimated length of the therapy
- fees and the consequences of not paying the bills
- cancellation policy
- confidentiality agreement, specifically limiting the conditions under which confidentiality may be breached
- third-party relationships, such as with insurance companies, and what information they will want to know about the treatment
- record keeping
- termination
- how to handle disputes or complaints
- notice of any consultations with others
- notice of supervision received
- alternatives to the treatment offered, if there are any

In addition to these minimum information requirements, other information may also be helpful to the client. As a guiding principle, it is recommended that the therapist or counselor provide the patient with information that is relevant to a particular decision. Many therapists believe that more than one session is needed to thoroughly discuss what is essential for the client to participate in informed consent. For example, straightforward issues such as fees, cancellations, and scheduling can be discussed immediately; more complex topics such as goals and treatment planning can extend for weeks (Pomerantz, 2005). The details and depth of discussion vary as a function of the risks and costs of the treatment, whether viable alternatives are available, the level of professional acceptance of the treatment, and whether there are any controversies involved. Good clinical judgment is necessary to ensure that conditions for informed consent are met.

Some therapists do not believe that informed consent is always helpful. These therapists tend to believe that since the client is most likely in a state of uncertainty, the flood of information concerning informed consent can only add to the client's confusion. Despite these objections by some providers, informed consent is a legal and ethical responsibility. A review of the literature showed that informed consent can help to foster a positive treatment outcome because the therapist–client interaction in discussing informed consent stresses patient autonomy and responsibility for the therapeutic work and progress (Beahrs & Guthrie, 2001). Such a conversation decreases the likelihood of regression and provides checks and balances on the therapist's judgments. Ultimately, it decreases the therapist's liability. The downside of informed consent is the possibility of replacing the client's positive expectations with negative suggestions as well as diminishing the clinical nature of the therapeutic alliance by taking a legalistic stance.

Only persons who have the capacity to make a decision are legally empowered to do so. Some individuals may not be capable of giving informed consent. For example, a person who is incapacitated because he or she is under the influence of drugs, in a coma, or in a psychotic state would not be able to give consent.

In addition, children cannot give informed consent since they are minors. Decision making must flow from the parents or legal guardians in conjunction with the therapist to meet the best interests of the child. The older and more responsible the child, the more the therapist should obtain the assent of the child as well as the permission of the parent. Understanding the rights of minors is complicated, and, generally, those who work with children must receive specific training (Committee on Bioethics, 1995).

Confidentiality

Every patient has a legal right to privileged communication, which means that what he or she says in therapy is totally private and cannot be repeated to anyone else without written permission. The client is the holder of the privilege, or the rightful owner of any information. Confidentiality is extremely important to therapy because it provides the groundwork for a psychologically safe environment, which allows people to explore themselves in an honest and unfettered way (Phillips, 2003).

The legal system recognizes that confidentiality is at the heart of the therapeutic relationship. In the Supreme Court case of *Jaffe v. Redmon*, confidentiality between therapist and patient was strengthened. The justices found the therapist–client relationship to be privileged communication in all federal cases and not to be questioned on a case-by-case basis by a judge as to whether it can be breached (Corey, Corey, & Callanan, 2003). However, there are limits to confidentiality. These exceptions include the following:

- If a client is a danger to himself or herself (suicidal), or a danger to others (homicidal), or gravely disabled and must be prevented from bringing harm to himself or others, commitment must occur to preserve the well-being of the client and/or the public.
- If a child (or elderly or disabled person) is being physically or mentally injured, sexually abused or exploited, neglected, or maltreated, the therapist is mandated to report the abuse to an appropriate state agency.
- If the court issues a subpoena, the therapist is ordered to release records or testify.

- If the therapist makes consultations, receives supervision, or gives records to clerks to file, information must be released.
- If the therapist has permission of the client or if there is an emergency, information must be released.
- If the client requests in writing that the information be given to another party, information may be released.

The therapist is obliged to inform the client about these limits of confidentiality as part of informed consent (Fisher, 2008).

Involuntary Commitment

Therapists may have to take action to protect the public or a patient from harming others or him- or herself. State laws regulate involuntary commitment, which is the use of legal means to commit an individual to a mental hospital against his or her own will. Depending upon state law and profession, the procedures vary. Physicians can commit a person single-handedly. Psychologists can commit in some states, provided the client receives a physical examination within a short period of time. Social workers and counselors do not directly commit but seek consultation from medical providers.

There are two basic categories of commitments: emergency commitments and long-term commitments. An emergency commitment is a method used by a physician or psychologist when a person is at risk and needs emergency care and observation for a short time, such as 15 days. In such a case, the clinician assesses that the client is at imminent risk and is a danger to self or others or is so gravely disabled he or she will come into harm's way if not given immediate care. Longer term commitments require a court hearing and more complicated legal proceedings. These commitments provide long-term care for those with very serious and permanent disabilities. For example, the elderly person with advanced Alzheimer's will not be able to care for herself.

For short- or long-term voluntary commitments, clients who do not want to be held in a hospital can ask for a timely hearing. The client pleads her or his case before the court or judge and argues why hospitalization is not necessary. The judge then decides if the client can be released or if an involuntary commitment should prevail. No one can hold a client involuntarily without providing appropriate care for the client.

Dangerousness

Although there is a common perception that mental health providers can predict if and when a disturbed person presents a danger to self or others, determining dangerousness is not an easy task. It is an art, not a science at this time, and it is fraught with many difficulties, uncertainties, and unknowns. The clinician must determine if the person is suicidal or homicidal. To do so, the therapist needs to conduct a thorough assessment, obtain psychosocial and medical history, consult with another professional if possible, contact the authorities and family members, and inform any specific parties who might be the target of harm. Whether the therapist is right or wrong in the clinical assessment is a judgment call. To prevent malpractice, it is best to know how to behave under these situations (Peszke, 1975; Roberts & Dyer, 2004).

Duty to Warn and Protect

Therapists are obligated to protect the public as well as their own clients. Once a client has been assessed as a danger to others, according to many state laws, the clinician has a duty to protect and warn the target of the patient's potential aggression, if it is a specific and identifiable person. *Tarasoff v. Regents of the University of California,* a landmark case, mandated a "duty to protect" in 1976. Prosenjit Poddar, an Indian student at the University of California, Berkeley, dated Tatania (Tanya) Tarasoff. Poddar was in therapy with a psychologist at the university counseling center. Poddar informed his therapist he intended to kill Tarasoff when she came home from an extended trip to South America. The psychologist notified the campus police, who questioned Poddar. Ultimately, the police released him because they did not think he posed a real threat. The psychiatrist who headed the university clinic insisted that the allegations be removed from Poddar's records; as well, he admonished Poddar's therapist for notifying the police, which the psychiatrist considered to be a breach of Poddar's right to confidentiality. Upon Tarasoff's return, Poddar went to her house. She opened the door to him, and he proceeded to stab her to death. Her parents sued the regents of the University of California, and the court ruled that the psychologist had a duty to protect and warn Tarasoff since he specifically knew of the danger, could have located her, and could have informed her about Poddar's intention to kill her.

The *Tarasoff* decision established that therapists in the state of California have a duty to protect members of the public from potential violence on the part of their clients and must fulfill that duty by warning them. While California has made this provision law, not all states have adopted the *Tarasoff* standard. In 1999, the Texas State Supreme Court ruled directly opposite to the *Tarasoff* decision when the justices determined that mental health care practitioners do not have any duty to third parties when a patient divulges an intent to harm another (Grinfeld, 1999).

All states have mandated reporting laws so if a professional mental health provider learns that a child, elder, or a dependent adult is being abused or neglected, the therapist is obligated to make a report to the appropriate authority. Mandated reporters, however, are not legally required to tell the involved parties that they are making the report, but they are free to decide if informing them is therapeutically advisable.

The issue of duty to warn is an evolving area of mental health law, and there are many shades of gray in decision making. For example, in Connecticut, according to state statutes, a broad prohibition exists on disclosure of HIV-related information by any person other than physicians and public health officers (CGSA §19a-581[10]). Thus, considering all state laws, the therapist may be liable for failure to diagnose dangerousness when it could reasonably be done; for failure to warn a potential victim, who may be the target of the dangerous patient; for failure to commit a dangerous client; and for releasing a dangerous client from the hospital when he or she is still dangerous and a reasonable person would have known he or she was. The legal obligations may vary according to state statutes, so a psychotherapist should make every effort to know the state laws governing his or her practice.

As part of competent practice, and from a moral perspective, psychotherapists may be faced with situations when the legal and ethical decision making can be at odds. When there are doubts about the therapist's legal and moral obligations, it is best to consult an attorney or experienced supervisor for advice. Private practitioners almost always carry malpractice insurance to protect themselves from potential liabilities.

Multiple or Dual Relationships

Multiple relationships, also referred to as dual relationships, occur when the psychotherapist and the client relate in more than one way or in more than one role. There are sexual and nonsexual dual relationships. Having sexual relations with a client is clearly unethical, illegal, and unprofessional. However, other forms of dual or multiple relationships are possible and may include situations in which a client is a friend, social acquaintance, fellow church member, business associate, professional colleague, clerk at a store, or family member (Zur, 2007). What constitutes appropriate behavior in these relationships may not be as straightforward.

In many communities and situations, it may not be possible for psychotherapists to avoid social or other nonprofessional contact with patients, clients, students, supervisees, or research participants. However, psychotherapists must always be sensitive to the potential harmful effects of such interactions on their work and on their clients. A psychotherapist should refrain from entering into a personal, scientific, professional, financial, or other relationship with others if it appears likely that such a relationship reasonably might impair the therapist's objectivity, interfere with the effectiveness of the therapy, or harm or exploit the other party in any way (APA, 2003). If there is a preexisting relationship, whenever feasible the psychotherapist should avoid becoming involved in a professional or scientific relationship with those parties to avoid the risk of such harms.

Diagnosis and Assessment

Psychotherapists who are qualified to assess and diagnose should make sure that assessments are performed by those with the necessary skills and competence to do so. When administering an assessment, the tests used must be valid, reliable, accepted by the profession, supported by an appropriate evidence base, and applied properly. In addition, the therapist must recognize the limitations of any evaluation or assessment and be sensitive to issues of diversity (variables such as a person's gender, age, race, ethnicity, national origin, religion, sexual orientation, disability, language, or socioeconomic status) as they might interact with the assessment. Finally, psychotherapists should adequately explain to clients the results of the assessment, along with the strengths and limitations of a test. This is especially important when the validity and reliability of the assessment have not been established.

Record Keeping and HIPAA

State laws govern record keeping among health professionals. All psychotherapists are required to keep adequate records of therapy for many good reasons: ensuring high-quality clinical care; safeguarding the therapist by documenting what has transpired in therapy; informing third parties, such as insurance companies, for reimbursement if approved in writing by the patient; covering liability issues; and meeting legal requirements of the state. Access to records is limited. Patients are the holders (or owners) of the privilege of the information and the records. They have complete access to their own records and also dictate to whom they can be sent. Clients should be told about any of the limits of confidentiality discussed earlier in light of records.

Experienced psychotherapists tend to keep careful records and notes, with the understanding that such information might be in the hands of others in the future. Most records and notes include a minimum of: demographic data; medical information; mental status exams; signed informed consent forms; diagnosis; prognosis; treatment plan; presenting problems; data from tests and any other records; treatment documentation; dates of appointments; summary of treatment during appointments; documents and correspondences; and discharge summaries.

Law standards for record keeping vary from state to state. The rule of thumb in many states is that records should be maintained for seven years. In the absence of state mandates, ethical codes recommend records be maintained and be available for at least three years.

The student of psychotherapy must become knowledgeable about and compliant with the state laws covering record keeping and confidentiality. The Health Insurance Portability and Accountability Act (HIPAA) was enacted in 1996 and is a federal law. It is also named the Kennedy-Kassebaum Bill or Public Law 104-191. If a psychotherapist uses electronic transactions, he or she must be compliant with this law. Part of the HIPAA law guarantees that people can get comparable health insurance coverage when they change their employment. Another part establishes standards for the electronic health transactions or communication of health care data and protects the individual's privacy. HIPAA (2006) specifies which medical and administrative code sets should be used; requires national identification systems for health care patients, providers, plans, payers, and employers; protects patient privacy; and establishes national privacy fair information practices. It protects clients' rights to access their own medical records, restricts access by others, and allows clients to know how their own records have been accessed and by whom. It keeps disclosures of protected health information to the minimum needed for treatment and for business, and it establishes criminal/civil sanctions for inappropriate disclosures. Students can access the HIPAA website and find the full text of the law and explanations about how to use and apply the regulations as they are updated (www.hipaadvisory.com/REGS/HIPAAprimer.htm).

→ MALPRACTICE

Malpractice lawsuits are filed because a client is dissatisfied for some reason. The more informed the psychotherapist is about professional ethical standards, the more likely it is that he or she will be able to prevent malpractice suits. All mental health professionals should understand what malpractice is and how to prevent legal actions and ethical complaints.

Malpractice is a legal concept with four components (Bernstein & Hartsell, 2000):

1. There must be an established professional relationship.
2. The therapist or counselor must perform some inappropriate action, deviate from the standard of care, or be negligent.
3. A definable injury must be inflicted on the client.
4. There must be a clearly demonstrated causal relationship between the therapist's malpractice and the client's injury.

The most common types of malpractice cases include sexual impropriety, completed suicides that were preventable, and incorrect treatment. There are six situations where the therapist is particularly vulnerable and where vigilance is helpful (Corey et al., 2003):

- when the therapist treats the patient with methods that are not standard professional practice
- when treatment is beyond the therapist's area of expertise or competence
- when a more helpful procedure could have been used but was not
- when there is a lack of informed consent
- when the therapist fails to warn a person who may potentially suffer harm from a patient
- when the therapist fails to explain potential consequences of treatment to the patient

It might be useful for therapists to keep a checklist in the office of the items that have particular potential to bring about legal action. These should also be mentioned in an informed consent form and in a sample letter of termination.

✦ THE NATIONAL PRACTITIONER DATA BANK

Recently, the federal government created the National Practitioner Data Bank (NPDB) in the Department of Health and Human Services. According to its website, the NPDB "provides a vast amount of information that is helpful in evaluating the performance of doctors and health care professionals." The bank was created "in response to increasing criticism about the failure of medical licensing authorities to protect patients from incompetent or negligent doctors."

The NPDB contains information about payments to satisfy malpractice claims; adverse disciplinary actions by state licensing boards, hospitals, and professional medical societies; and actions by the federal government, such as revocation of licenses or hospital privileges. Mental health professionals—such as psychologists, psychiatrists, counselors, social workers, and so on—are included in the database. Currently, access to the NPDB is restricted to state licensing boards, medical societies, and specific health organizations such as hospitals and managed care. However, strong lobbying attempts are underway to make this information available to any consumer. General information about the NPDB can be accessed at www.npdb-hipdb.com.

→ MULTICULTURALISM AND DIVERSITY

The 2000 census shows that the U.S. population is rapidly becoming more diverse with more cultural and linguistic variability than ever before (U.S. Census Bureau, 2001). According to the U.S. Census Bureau (2001), the proportion of non-Hispanic Whites in the population is decreasing. By 2050, the population will be less than 53 percent non-Hispanic White; 16 percent Black; 23 percent Hispanic; 10 percent Asian and Pacific Islander; and about 1 percent American Indian, Eskimo, and Aleut. Psychotherapists must be sensitive to a large variety of diversity factors, such as ethnicity, language, race, gender, biracial/multiracial heritage, spiritual/religious orientation, sexual orientation, age, disability, socioeconomic situation, and historical life experience such as immigration and refugee status (APA, 2003; Espin, 1997; Santiago-Rivera & Altarriba, 2002; Sue & Sue, 1987, 2003).

As the United States becomes more pluralistic and psychotherapies serve the needs of diverse groups, psychotherapists from all professions will be expected to have mastered an array of cross-cultural competencies (Zane, Hall, Sue, Young, & Nunez, 2004). All of the professional mental health organizations include cultural competence in their ethical guidelines and require that such training be considered an essential component of their profession (Root, 1985). Cultural competence is more than a set of skills and information. It is a mind-set with a perspective of social justice, the assumption that all people are equal and entitled to quality mental health care, and an understanding about the relationships among race, ethnicity, gender, culture, and medicine. Cultural competence requires that therapists have the knowledge and skills to work effectively in any cross-cultural encounter and that the therapist systematically review and generate hypotheses about how any given culture influences a client's psychological world (Lo & Fung, 2003).

Derald Wing Sue (2001) says the core characteristics of cultural competency consist of three general processes:

1. *Scientific-mindedness, or the ability to form and test hypotheses about clients from diverse cultures and to free the self from ethnocentric biases.* Culturally competent psychotherapists do not fall prey to the myth of sameness or the belief that all client processes are the same across all cultures.
2. *Dynamic sizing or the ability to flexibly generalize.* Culturally competent psychotherapists know when to generalize and be inclusive with clients and when to individualize and be exclusive.
3. *Culture-specific expertise or the ability to understand one's own culture and its perspectives, as well as knowledge of the cultural groups with which these therapists work.* Culturally competent psychotherapists can make interventions that are culturally informed and effective (Sue & Chu, 2003).

Being culturally competent means that one is capable of performing multicultural therapy (MCT). This therapy consists of goals and methods consistent with the cultural values and life experiences of clients, acceptance and use of universal and culture-specific strategies, a balance of individualism and collectivism, and the will to change a system rather than an individual client when indicated.

For example, if racism, prejudice, and discrimination are at the root of the client's problems, the therapist does not try to change the client's self-image.

Derald Wing Sue and David Sue (2003, p. 16) say that acquiring cultural competence involves awareness, knowledge, and skills. In terms of awareness, the culturally competent psychotherapist

- changes from being unaware to being aware, develops sensitivity to his or her own cultural values, and is respectful of differences.
- is conscious of his or her own values and their impact on minority clients.
- is comfortable with differences and does not see those due to race, gender, sexual orientation, and other sociodemographic variables as deviant.
- is aware of his or her own limitations in performing multicultural counseling and refers out when appropriate but does not avoid dealing with the issues.
- faces and deals with his or her own biases, whether racist, sexist, heterosexist, or other.

In terms of knowledge, the culturally competent psychotherapist

- knows specific information about the group with which he or she is working.
- knows how the sociopolitical system treats marginalized groups and how institutional barriers prevent the use of mental health services for some groups.
- knows the inherent values and assumptions of normality and abnormality and how they affect the client.

In terms of skills, the culturally competent psychotherapist

- possesses a wide variety of verbal and nonverbal responses so he or she can send appropriate and accurate verbal and nonverbal messages or communications.
- has the ability to intervene at an institutional level when necessary.
- can acknowledge his or her own limitations and anticipate their impact on clients.
- is flexible to change, to make environmental interventions (e.g., home visits, outreach, collaboration with folk healers, etc).

The following is a summary of the major points contained in two APA guides: the Task Force on the Delivery of Services to Ethnic Minority Populations (1988) and Guidelines on Multicultural Education, Training, Research, Practice, and Organizational Change (2003). These offer suggestions on providing culturally competent services for therapists working with ethnic, linguistic, and culturally diverse populations. Some of the recommendations are paraphrased to summarize very helpful information.

- Consider cultural beliefs and values of the clients and their community in providing intervention.
- Understand the client's ethnic and cultural background, as well as his or her familiarity and comfort with the majority culture.

- Be sensitive to oppression, sexism, elitism, and racism and understand stress levels related to acculturation and recognize their parameters in psychological processes.
- Question how personal cultural background, experiences, attitudes, values, and biases influence psychological processes.
- Increase the client's awareness of personal cultural values and norms and how they affect the client's life and society at large.
- Analyze to clarify if the client is accurately viewing the problems (does a problem stem from racism or bias?).
- Identify resources such as family roles, members, community structures, hierarchies, values, and beliefs within the client's culture.
- Know and respect indigenous beliefs and practices; be willing to consult with traditional healers if helpful to clients and consistent with cultural and belief systems. Respect clients' religious/spiritual beliefs and values, including attributions and taboos.
- Ensure that both therapist and client have a clear and reasonable understanding of expectations of services, roles, and psychological interventions (e.g., goals and expectations in writing and in language understandable to client).
- Match the linguistic skills of the therapist and the client; if not feasible, make an appropriate referral and use a translator with cultural knowledge.
- Match intervention strategies with client's level of need (e.g., low income may be associated with overt conditions; rural residency with inaccessibility of services; refugees with violent treatments by governments).
- Eliminate biases, prejudices, and discriminatory practices affecting the psychological welfare of the population being served.
- Help clients to understand, maintain, and resolve issues around their own sociocultural identification.
- Know the relevant research and practice issues as they are related to the client's culture.
- Seek out education and training about cultural, social, psychological, political, economic, and historical material of the particular ethnic group being served.
- Recognize limits of competency and consult with or make referrals to appropriate experts as needed.
- Be critical of and assess the validity of any intervention or assessment device. Be aware of a test's reference population and its possible limitations; interpret results cautiously and in ways relevant and understandable to the needs of those assessed.
- Consider the impact of adverse social, environmental, and political factors in assessment, interventions, and all past practices.

Unfortunately, there is a lack of rigorous research on the theory, practice, and efficacy and effectiveness of psychotherapy for ethnic minority populations (Zane et al., 2004). Very little baseline information is available because minorities were excluded in early psychotherapy research, and no programmatic research has been conducted (Comas-Diaz & Griffith, 1988). This lack of quality research leaves many unanswered questions. For instance, is psychotherapy effective for ethnic minority populations?

How can therapy be improved and made relevant to the needs of these groups? Are the empirically supported therapies effective with diverse clients (Sue, 1988, 1998)?

As the APA points out, the integration of the psychological constructs of minority group identities into psychological theory, research, and practice is in the early stages. As we increase our understanding of how historical, economic, and sociopolitical forces affect human behavior and develop a deeper knowledge and awareness of minority populations in psychological constructs, we will increase the effectiveness of psychotherapy overall. Acquiring cross-cultural competence can only improve both the practice and the science of psychotherapy (Sue & Sue, 2003).

Cultural competence is a challenge—an essential lifelong task that will inevitably improve the sophistication of research and increase the psychotherapy's generalizability and knowledge base (Heppner, 2006). It will also help psychotherapists to realize, on a deeper level, that counseling occurs in a *cultural* context, and thus it will enhance counseling effectiveness and the profession's ability to address diverse mental health needs across diverse populations worldwide.

Summary

- Client complaints about ethical violations and malpractice litigation are growing in an increasingly complicated psychotherapy practice world.
- Becoming familiar with professional, ethical, and legal aspects of psychotherapy should be a high priority for students. Knowing these features of psychotherapy will help students maintain high practice standards.
- A number of professionals perform psychotherapy including clinical and counseling psychologists, psychiatrists, clinical social workers, counselors, advanced practitioner psychiatric nurses, and school psychologists.
- To be a mental health professional means to undergo extensive instruction, rigorous training, and continuing education.
- Psychotherapists practice in a variety of settings from private practice to integrated behavioral health care to public institutions.
- The terms *licensed* and *certified* are protected by law. To use these designations, persons must meet state requirements to legally practice psychotherapy as members of their respective professions.
- Most professionals are associated with a national professional organization, each of which has a professional code of ethics. The primary purpose of these codes is to protect clients and the public from harm and to inform and guide work with clients.
- Codes of ethics for professional psychotherapists share key components. They deal with matters such as competence, informed consent, confidentiality, involuntary commitment, assessing dangerousness, duty to warn and protect, multiple relationships, diagnosis and assessment, and record keeping.
- Psychotherapists must abide by the Health Insurance Portability and Accountability Act (HIPAA) to ensure that they are in compliance with the laws governing electronic transactions and client data.

- Malpractice is a legal concept, and all mental health professionals need to understand what it is and how to prevent legal and ethical complaints. The most common malpractice complaints for psychotherapists revolve around sexual impropriety, preventable suicides, and incorrect treatment.
- The National Practitioner Data Bank provides evaluative and malpractice information about the performance of health care professionals.
- Ethical codes encourage professional psychotherapists today to acquire cultural competence. Training should enable the therapist to effectively and competently treat clients in any multicultural encounter, to strive to deliver high quality care to all patients equally, and to eliminate disparities in the mental health services delivered to various minority groups.

RESOURCES

American Psychological Association (APA)
Office of Ethics
750 First Street NE
Washington, DC 20002-4242
(202) 336-5930
www.apa.org/ethics

The APA is the oldest and largest professional organization for psychologists in the United States.

American Psychiatric Association (APA)
1000 Wilson Boulevard, Suite 1825
Arlington, VA 22209
(703) 907-7300
http://www.psych.org/psych_pract/ethics/ethics_opinions53101.cfm

The American Psychiatric Association is the largest professional organization for psychiatrists in the United States.

National Association of Social Workers (NASW)
750 First Street NE, Suite 700
Washington, DC 20002-4241
(202) 408-8600
www.ssc.msu.edu/~sw/ethics/nasweth.html

The NASW is the professional organization in the United States for social workers.

American Counseling Association (ACA)
5999 Stevenson Avenue
Alexandria, VA 22304
(800)347-6647 (outside U.S.: +1 (703) 823-9800)
http://www.amhca.org/code

The American Counseling Association promotes the counseling profession through work in advocacy, research, and professional standards.

National Association of School Psychologists (NASP)
4340 East West Highway, Suite 402
Bethesda, MD 20814
(301) 657-0270
http://www.nasponline.org/standards/ethics.aspx

The NASP represents and supports school psychology to enhance children's mental health and educational competence.

American Association for Marriage and Family Therapy (AAMFT)
112 South Alfred Street
Alexandria, VA 22314
(703) 838-9808
http://www.aamft.org/resources/LRMPlan/Ethics/ethicscode2001.asp

The AAMFT is the professional association for the field of marriage and family therapy.

American Nurses Association (ANA)
8515 Georgia Avenue, Suite 400
Silver Spring, MD 20910-3492
(301)-628-5000
http://nursingworld.org/books/pdescr.cfm?cnum=15#07SSPMH

The ANA works to develop policies, set standards, advocate in government and private settings, provide education, and maintain the code of ethics for psychiatric nurses. It has 54 constituent member associations.

National Organization for Human Service Education (NOHSE)
5326 Avery Road
Newport Richey, FL 34652
(813) 929-2915
http://ethics.iit.edu/codes/coe/nat.org.human.services.1996.html

The NOHSE is comprised of a variety of professionals including practitioners in public and private agencies, in private practice, in various religious organizations, and in nonprofit organizations. The ethical guidelines are a set of standards of conduct proposed for all human service professionals and educators to consider in ethical and professional decision making.

CLASS EXERCISES AND ACTIVITIES

Ethics

1. Break into small groups. Each student plays one member from each of six professions: social work, psychiatry, psychology, counseling, school counseling,

and psychiatric nursing. Each of these professions has a code of ethics. Use the links in the Resources section above to access the most updated versions. Compare the codes considering informed consent, sexual involvement with clients, social justice, confidentiality, HIPAA, or other issues of interest.

2. Professional organizations regulate the behavior of their members. However, critics maintain that these professional organizations misuse their power to build a guild, or a turf, that monopolizes the field and that prevents nonprofessionals, laypersons, from access to business arrangements. Formulate an opinion about this. Argue the pros and the cons.

3. Discuss confidentiality, informed consent, cultural competence, duty to warn, and involuntary commitment in relationship to practicing psychotherapy.

Professional Issues

1. Find out what your state requirements are to be licensed or certified as a psychologist, psychiatrist, social worker, or counselor who performs psychotherapy. Is the title "psychotherapist" or "counselor" a protected title in your state?

2. Debate whether or not you think the title "psychotherapist" or "counselor" should be a protected title. Justify your opinion. What are the pros and cons? How complicated would it be to make it a protected term?

3. Suppose you believe the title "psychotherapist" or "counselor" should be protected, and you want your state representative to sponsor a bill. Write out a draft bill to present to the Committee on Health Care Regulation.

4. Choose a profession you would like to join. What are the ethical standards for your chosen profession? Will you be licensed and certified? What are the requirements for the licensing and certification? Do you know where to seek consultation? How will you obtain your ethics training and how will you continue to maintain your ethics education?

5. Pretend you are launching your private practice. Make up an informed consent form for a new client. Help your friend, who has decided to work at a public clinic, make up such a form. Are there any differences between these forms? If so, why? Explain.

6. Create a model file for your private practice. Include all of the necessary forms you need for record keeping that would pass the scrutiny of any ethics committee or state board governing your profession.

CHAPTER 3

FREUD'S CLASSICAL PSYCHOANALYSIS

I sacrificed, unhesitatingly, my budding popularity as a physician and an extensive practice among nervous patients, because I searched directly for the sexual origin of their neurosis. Only the silence that followed my lectures, the space that formed about my person, and the insinuations directed toward me caused me to realize, gradually, that statements about the part played by sexuality in the etiology of neuroses cannot hope to be treated like other communications. I realized that from then on I would belong to those who . . . have disturbed the world's sleep.

–*Sigmund Freud*

The goals of this chapter are to present a general overview of Sigmund Freud's classical model of psychotherapy. The chapter looks at biographical information about Freud, the historical context of Freudian therapy, and the theory, practice, and research of this model. The simulated psychotherapist, Dr. John Garrett, presents a treatment plan and some therapy excerpts for the case of Jonathan. Finally, issues of diversity and major critiques are presented.

✦ HISTORICAL CONTEXT

Sigmund Freud saw himself as an intellectual revolutionary and a visionary. A controversial figure, he is the father of Western psychotherapy and the first to integrate a personality theory with a system of psychotherapy. Freud planted a seed that took firm root and spread branches of psychodynamic psychotherapy throughout the Western world. The golden age of American psychoanalysis lasted from the 1920s to the 1950s; today the numbers of Freudian psychoanalysts are dwindling, with only 3,500 members in the American Psychoanalytic Association (2007). Competition from other therapy models, the expansion of biological psychiatry, and an emphasis on evidence-based medicine have contributed to its decline. However, many of Freud's theoretical constructs and practice techniques have evolved, expanded, and been integrated into other forms of therapy (Magnavita, 2002).

The life of Freud (see About Sigmund Freud box) and the creation of psychoanalysis are inextricably intertwined. The evolution of psychoanalysis and the post-Freudian psychodynamic therapies consist of the history of Freud, his followers,

ABOUT SIGMUND FREUD

Sigmund Freud was born on May 6, 1856, in Freiberg, Moravia (now the Czech Republic), to Jakob and Amalié Freud. Jakob was a wool merchant, twice a widower at the age of 40 when he married Amalié, 20 years his junior. Jakob's adult sons from an earlier marriage lived with Freud in the early years. His half-brothers were closer to his mother's age than his father. Amalié doted on Freud, even after the birth of his five younger sisters. Freud acknowledged that a man who is his mother's indisputable favorite feels like a conqueror for life (Jones, 1953).

After graduating with honors from a prominent secondary school in 1873, Freud attended medical school at the University of Vienna. Here, he was influenced by Ernst von Brucke, a physiologist of great repute, who inspired Freud to envision the psychodynamics of the mind. In 1883, Freud shifted from studies of physiology with Brucke to neurology at the Viennese General Hospital, and he became interested in the medicinal uses of cocaine, which he wrote about in a paper. In a letter in 1884 to then-fiancée Martha Bernays, Freud referred to cocaine and its powerful applications:

> Woe to you my Princess, when I come, I will kiss you quite red and feed you till you are plump. And if you are forward you shall see who is the stronger, a gentle little girl who doesn't eat enough or a big wild man who has cocaine in his body. In my last severe depression I took coca again and a small dose lifted me to the heights in a wonderful fashion. (Jones, 1953, pp. 10–11)

Hoping this was a discovery that would make him famous, he began prescribing cocaine as a panacea for a number of disorders. However, Freud is not credited with one of the few safe medical uses for cocaine, as a local anesthetic, because a colleague was the first to report this usage to a medical society in 1884. Freud stopped advocating cocaine use after his friend, Ernst von Fleischl, to whom Freud had prescribed it, became addicted and later died of an overdose.

In 1885 Freud attended the Saltpetriere Institute in Paris for four months. He was deeply impressed by the neurologist Jean-Martin Charcot who treated the conversion reactions of hysteria with hypnosis. Freud substituted dream analysis and free association in place of hypnosis. Freud also became intensely interested in trauma as the basis for abnormal behavior as he gained firsthand exposure to criminal childhood abuse cases; this information later was integrated into his controversial seduction theory (Masson, 1992). He also worked with Josef Breuer and his patient, Anna O. Suffering from hysterical symptoms, she improved when under hypnosis she talked about emotional and painful memories in a cathartic fashion. From these experiences, Freud began to develop his psychoanalytic theory.

In 1886, Martha Bernays and Freud married and remained together until his death in 1939. In their traditional marriage, Martha raised the six children while Freud worked in his practice. In a letter to her granddaughter, Martha described her 53-year marriage to Sigmund as one in which there was never an unfriendly look or a harsh word, and Sigmund described Martha as an adored sweetheart in youth and as a beloved wife in maturity. Anna, his youngest daughter, continued to develop psychoanalytic thinking.

Although Freud was trained as a neurologist, his intellectual interest continued to be drawn to the psychological realm, even as he worked with other well-known medical practitioners who influenced his thinking. Breuer eventually broke with Freud because he disagreed with Freud's conviction that the origin of hysteria was sexual. From 1887 to 1902, Freud's closest friend and confidant was Wilhelm Fleiss, an eye-nose-throat specialist, who believed that the nose and the sexual organs were deeply connected and were a cause of problematic masturbation. Freud eventually distanced himself from Fleiss due to his eccentric theories. The Fleiss–Freud correspondences are at the heart of a controversy stirred by Jeffrey Masson in the 1980s. Masson, at one time the director of the Freud Archives, accused Freud of succumbing to political pressure when he abandoned his seduction theory—that childhood sexual abuse led to adult neuroses and hysteria—and claimed instead that the abuse was merely a fantasy.

Continued

ABOUT SIGMUND FREUD *Continued*

Freud replaced Fleiss with a growing number of followers. By 1902, young doctors had begun to participate in Freud's famous Wednesday night gathering, during which they discussed the theory and practice of psychoanalysis. As Freud gained fame, he attracted more and more followers as psychoanalysis spread from Europe to the United States (Ellenberger, 1970).

Freud's strong and determined character was both a boon and a bother to the development of psychoanalysis. His attitude toward dissension was stern as he believed that "psychoanalysis is my creation. Even today, when I am no longer the only psychoanalyst, I feel myself justified in assuming that none can know better than myself what psychoanalysis is, wherein it differs from other methods of investigating the psychic life, what its name should cover, or what might better be designated as something else" (Freud, 1914/1917, p. 10). It took firmness, courage, and perseverance to popularize a creative theory in a society that

was resistant to controversy, but it also drove out critics who could have made contributions (Gay, 1988).

In 1923, Freud detected a malignant cancer on his palate. His illness and treatment became all-encompassing. As World War II approached, the Nazis burned Freud's books publicly and prohibited the practice of psychoanalysis. Freud escaped to London in 1937. Anna Freud, his daughter who took over the leadership of psychoanalysis, tended to his medical treatment, a process that was long and arduous. Over a 10-year span, he underwent 33 surgeries and suffered unbearable pain. At the end, he told his physician, Maxim Schur, that his life was nothing but torture and that it made no sense to live any longer. As Freud lay dying, Schur injected him with a dose of morphine strong enough for two. Freud sank into a peaceful sleep and then a coma from which he did not awake. He died on September 23, 1939, from cancer of the jaw and throat at the age of 82 (Gay, 1988).

and their interactions as well as the societal and cultural factors of their era. By 1902 Freud had gained a number of followers; some remained loyal to Freud and his theories, while others rebelled and created their own psychotherapies (Ellenberger, 1970). Freud turned to Alfred Adler to lead and promote the growth of psychoanalysis, but their relationship ended in disagreement. He then selected Carl Jung to be the next proponent of psychoanalysis as he had founded it (Freud, 1914/1917). Jung eventually resigned from the presidency of the International Psychoanalytic Association and developed Jungian analysis.

Freud jealously guarded his ideas and fought to preserve his intellectual property. Convinced that he had found the truth in psychoanalysis, he was intolerant of disagreement. Freud had a well-defined mission: to discover a theory that would explain the psychodynamics of human mental life—the unconscious and conscious forces—as well as the technical procedures for investigating a science of mental process and the treatment of neurosis.

Freud visited the United States when invited by Clark University, where he met with William James, and he lived to see psychoanalysis attract a number of American followers (Green, 2007). Psychoanalysis in the United States was encouraged by recent European immigrants and by others who studied with Freud and then began their own American centers. But psychoanalysis may not have flourished if its strong-willed disciples had not argued, separated, and traveled along independent paths. Each of the groups played different roles: the loyalists, the rebellious dissenters, the new therapists who lived in a pre- and post-Freud world, and the modern analysts. The link among them is that their origins lie in Freud's psychodynamics. His theory was responsible for inspiring many forms of psycho-dynamic psychotherapy; these extensions and permutations of Freud's classical analysis are discussed in Chapter 4.

✦ THEORY OF CLASSICAL PSYCHOANALYSIS

Psychoanalysis, as created by Freud, includes both a theory of personality and a psychotherapy. The *theory of personality* calls upon the concepts of unconscious forces, repression, libidinal drives, infantile sexuality, and a triarchical system of id, ego, and superego. The *psychotherapy* focuses on freeing psychic energy bound up in unconscious conflicts that are a result of repressed unconscious impulses and the resultant anxiety and on dealing with resistance and transference. The method releases the energy to enable the person to work, love, and play in a mature way (Wolitzky, 2003). Freud continually revised his theory and practice throughout his life, and the concepts in this chapter represent Freud's later work.

Key Concepts

The key concepts of psychoanalytic theory include psychodynamics (the study of forces and their interactions within personality), libido or instincts (instinctual energy directed to external objects), levels of consciousness (awareness), personality structures (systems that organize libidinal energy), psychosexual stages of develop-ment (a predictable biodevelopmental sequence of maturation that forms personality), anxiety (fears), resistance (opposition to making the unconscious conscious), repression and defense mechanisms (a forgetting of and relegation of unacceptable materials into the unconscious), and normality/abnormality.

The key concepts in psychoanalytic practice include free association (stream of consciousness), transference (feelings from the past projected onto the therapist), countertransference (therapist's feelings from the past projected onto the patient), dream work (disguising conflicted material in the mind during dreams), and inter-pretations (linking the past with the present to gain insight into symptoms).

Psychodynamics

Classical Freudian psychoanalysis is based upon *psychodynamics,* which governs the way in which the personality forms, grows, and adapts. *Dynamics* implies there is a force or motive that brings about interactions among parts of the human mind. These parts act in harmony or in opposition to one another. Freud saw these forces as generally conflicted and at different levels of awareness. Therefore, a person's personality—comprised of behavior and emotional state—is the product of the interplay and constantly changing balance among conflicting conscious and uncon-scious motives and personality structures (Arlow, 2005). And any change brought about in psychoanalysis is the result of altering the psychodynamic interactions among resistance, defenses, and transference (Freedheim, 1992).

Libidinal Energy and Cathexis

Freud analogized between mental science and physical science. *Libido,* meaning "I desire," is the energy of the personality, which fuels thinking, perception, memory, imagination, sex, and aggression. Libido motivates the person to survive as an individual by seeking food and water, and to survive as a species by seeking reproduction. The libido, or instinct, behaves similarly to physical energy described by Gustav Fechner, a popular psychophysicist in the late nineteenth century. This human energy system is closed and contains a finite amount of energy that cannot be created or destroyed. It is dynamic, constantly moving, and redistributes itself by *cathecting*, attaching, to parts of the personality structure. All humans are born with a natural (genetic) endowment of libidinal energy, and their capacities are shaped by its amount, availability, and distribution.

How libidinal energy is apportioned determines how personality functions. Libido attaches, or cathects, to parts of the personality to energize the areas that predominate as development proceeds and/or to a particular memory or object in the psyche. The more libido that attaches to a particular object, the less energy is available for other parts. Freud's model is a tension reduction model. As energy accumulates, it causes discomfort; pleasure comes from its release. For example, as the infant becomes hungry, more and more tension accumulates. Eating allows the discharge of this energy. Psychosexual activity is gratification of any need (Frager & Fadiman, 1984).

Freud modified his view of libido a number of times. In an effort to explain why people acted in self-destructive ways, he divided libido into *eros,* energy for love and sexuality, and *thanatos,* an instinct for self-destruction and death.

Levels of Consciousness

Freud believed humans have three levels of awareness—conscious, preconscious, and unconscious. The *conscious* mind contains material that is in present awareness. For example, you know you are reading words at this moment. The *preconscious* mind contains what can be voluntarily brought into consciousness. For example, the answers to the questions "Where did you park your car?" and "What is your favorite teacher's name?" are in the preconscious. The *unconscious* mind contains thoughts, feelings, memories, wishes, or impulses of which a person is not aware and that cannot be voluntarily brought into consciousness. Some materials in the unconscious are more easily accessed than others. Deeply repressed thoughts and feelings resist entry into consciousness, thus the true nature of motivation is outside of conscious awareness. When unconscious material begins to surface, the individual perceives a threat, and the ego protects itself from harm by resisting awareness and adapting defenses.

Personality Structures

As the psychosexual stages unfold, the *personality structures*—id, ego, superego—develop simultaneously. At birth, all libidinal energy is concentrated in the id; gradually that energy is infused into the ego and the superego as well. Since the id, ego, and superego compete for libido within the closed energy system, balance is important. If inordinate energy is invested in one structure, too little may be available for others. For example, if the id has most of the libido, the superego and ego will not have enough energy to perform their essential functions. The id is totally unconscious and begins to develop at the oral stage; the ego is both conscious and unconscious and begins to develop during the anal stage; and the superego is both conscious and unconscious and develops during the phallic stage.

The *id* is the reservoir of all libidinal energy; it is primitive, raw, animal instinct. Its aim is self-gratification. Governed by the pleasure principle, the id primarily wants immediate sexual and aggressive satisfaction. The id wants what it wants when it wants it, regardless of the consequences. For example, suppose a person standing on top of the Empire State Building feels uncomfortably warm from the hot summer day. The id's drive for immediate gratification is so intense, and its lack of understanding of the consequences is so feeble, that the id will urge, "The heat is unpleasant. Jump off! The breeze against your face will cool you right now!" If people were only id-driven, society would be in chaos, because the id is irrational, knows no reason, possesses no sense of time, and respects no boundaries.

The *ego* evolves out of the id and acts as a liaison between the id and reality. The ego plays the role of a rider on a wild horse. The ego tells the id to check its raw, primitive, animal instincts. It realizes that the pursuit of pleasure, particularly of a sexual and aggressive nature, must be modulated for individual survival. When the id urges a person to jump off the Empire State Building to obtain the immediate pleasure of cooling down, the ego intervenes and says, "Wait. The consequence is death! Let's be more realistic. Find an air-conditioned building or get a fan!" The reality principle guides the ego as it gains satisfaction without harming itself. It preserves the safety of the organism, respects boundaries, and delays gratification to achieve longer term goals. The ego is part unconscious and part conscious, and it also protects the person from experiencing the overwhelming anxiety of intrapsychic conflicts. Through repression and defense mechanisms, the ego prevents emotionally charged material from reaching awareness. However, although defense mechanisms reduce anxiety, they also distort reality so that the person does not see the world accurately. The ego not only liaisons with the id, it also does so with the superego.

The *superego* is conscience. It is partly conscious and partly unconscious, irrational, and without boundaries. Introjection is the process by which the child internalizes norms into personality. Parents convey their values to the child through conditional love. Approval is given when the child is good, and punishment is meted out when the child is bad. The superego controls the person's behavior by inducing guilt. Based on the particular parental dictates and societal information received and introjected, it can be a harsh or loose morality. Too much guilt underlies neuroses, and too little guilt underlies character disorders. For example, if strictly religious parents teach that all sexual pleasure is bad except for the purpose of propagating children, the superego and the id will be in conflict, with the id wanting to obtain immediate gratification, and the superego fighting against it. This conflict would consume a great deal of the limited supply of libidinal energy, causing the person to invest in neurotic conflict and weakening the ego.

Psychosexual Stages

The human personality matures in an orderly and predictable series of chronological biodevelopmental stages, each with its own challenges. How the individual negotiates these—the oral, anal, phallic (Oedipal/Electra), latency, and genital stages—as well as the nature and quality of parental care deeply affect the vitality of the personality. In a normal personality, libidinal energy is distributed efficiently so that all parts of the personality receive the amount needed to function optimally. In an abnormal personality, one or more elements of an individual's personality are out of balance, producing dysfunctional behavior. For example, a person with a weak ego may not have enough libidinal energy invested in the ego to handle the conflict of competing demands between the id and the superego. Unable to remain emotionally stable in the face of environmental stressors, he may regress into a depression or suffer from symptoms of anxiety.

Each stage of psychosexual development is associated with an erogenous zone. These zones are parts of the body that experience pleasure when tension is released and libidinal energy becomes available to them.

Oral Stage

At birth the child's libidinal energy is concentrated in the id. In the *oral stage* of development, between birth and approximately 18 months, libido cathects in the oral zones. The newborn explores the world through his or her mouth. Chewing, sucking, eating, biting, and crying discharge tension and, thus, bring about gratification. The mother's breast is the object that pleases and satisfies.

The quality of parental care at this stage lays the groundwork for future positive mental health or for psychopathology. For example, if a child receives sensitive and loving care, a positive image of self and others ensues. If a child is severely deprived of oral gratification, his or her libidinal energy will be bound up in the oral stage because of an unfulfilled craving and will seek to compensate for lost pleasure. When oral needs are unmet and the breast is withheld, the child may have a low frustration tolerance and be easily overwhelmed by anxiety, rage, helplessness, and depression as an adult. When a child's oral needs are overindulged, there is a risk of narcissism, with the adult feeling entitled to all that he or she demands in the world. Many adult psychopathologies can come from oral fixations, including dependency, distrustfulness, and an inability to provide tender care to others.

Anal Stage

In the *anal stage* of development, between 18 and 36 months, libido cathects in the anal zone. Discharging bowels and bladder, or letting go, is pleasurable. When parents begin potty training, the child suffers discomfort due to the tension of holding urine and feces. If the right discipline and guidance is given, the child will be able to negotiate the many adult responsibilities that lie ahead. Toilet training that is too strict or too lenient can cause adult problems. If parents are too forceful, the child may resist external control and hold on to his or her feces, becoming stubborn, resistant, and rebellious or overly compliant. If parents are too lax, the child may not develop enough control and frustration tolerance, and he or she will feel overwhelmed with anxiety, rage, or helplessness. As adults, these individuals may become anal-retentive (stubborn, stingy) and passive-aggressive, or anal-expulsive (tending to be messy but generous).

Phallic Stage

In the *phallic stage* of development, between 3 and 5 years, stimulation of the genitals discharges sexual tension, which brings pleasure. Freud intended this to mean a broad pleasurable feeling, not necessarily intercourse. Relationships with the parents take on great significance. Normal sexual functioning in adulthood is dependent on successful identification with the parent with the appropriate gender. While both sexes are looking for sexual gratification, the psychodynamics differ for females and males.

The *Oedipal conflict* describes the boy's tasks in this stage. The boy desires his mother as a source of pleasure and satisfaction. However, on an unconscious level, the boy fears that Dad will mete out a punishment that fits his crime. The boy develops castration anxiety. Imagine the anxiety of a 4-foot, 40-pound 5-year-old boy vying with his adult father for the affections of his mother. While the child's id pushes for sexual gratification, the developing ego, governed by the reality principle, realizes the boy is no match for a 180-pound adult male competitor. Since the ego must find an adaptive way to handle his fears, sexual wishes are repressed and transformed into a socially acceptable channel through identification with the aggressor and sublimation. This means the child introjects, or takes on, the father's characteristics. He behaves like his father and understands that he and his father can have a different relationship with the mother. In the long run, he will develop normal sexual behavior in adulthood.

A parallel experience, the *Electra conflict*, affects girls. The 3- to 5-year-old girl competes with her father for her mother's undivided attention. When she notices that she does not possess a penis, she concludes that she has been castrated in retaliation for her forbidden sexual longings. She develops penis envy or a jealousy of boys who possess the penis, which can be seen as the feminine counterpart of castration anxiety. When the girl discovers that her mother also lacks the organ, she blames her for this sad state of affairs. Resentment toward her mother and continued incestuous urges toward her father add to her feelings of inferiority. This motivates her to attach to her father as she realizes she will never have her own penis, but the way to get one temporarily is through intercourse with a male. Her incestuous feelings are repressed, and she identifies with and introjects her mother's characteristics. If she acts like her, she can find a man like Dad. She displaces her feeling for her father to other eligible males, and resentment toward her mother dissolves.

The psychodynamics of the phallic stage of development form the basis for normal sexual identification. Successful negotiation of the phallic stage means the adult personality is able to give and take and can appreciate a partner's perspective. Through successfully negotiating the phallic stage, the individual acquires and maintains a positive self-image. As well, these psychodynamics enable the completion of superego development. For a boy, the superego incorporates the ideals and prohibitions of the father, which allows him to control his aggressive and sexual urges.

However, since the Electra complex is longer and since girls retain some of the attachment to their fathers, their desires are less strongly repressed. Therefore, a girl has a weaker superego than a boy (Hall & Lindzey, 1985).

Latency Stage

Upon the completion of the phallic stage of development, the *latency stage* begins and lasts until puberty (ages 6–12). Libido is channeled into school, sports, and other external activities. Sexual impulses are repressed, and oral, anal, and phallic activities are inhibited.

Genital Stage

The *genital stage* begins in early adolescence and continues throughout life. Libido cathects to members of the opposite sex. Pleasure is found in heterosexual activity. The greater the libidinal energy cathected in the genital stage and the less energy fixated in earlier stages, the more likely it is that individuals will develop the skills needed to form and maintain heterosexual relationships and pursue lives free of neurosis.

Fixation

If a fixation occurs at any stage of development, some of the libidinal energy needed to negotiate the next stage remains cathected at this earlier stage. Energy needed for maturation is bound up, causing a neuroses or a more serious abnormality. Freud believed every current pathological experience is built upon an earlier event that imbued it with a pathological quality (Freud, 1914/1917). Thus, the distribution of libidinal energy in parts of the personality in different stages of development, during traumas, and when anxiety-provoking stimuli are confronted can impair the formation of normal personality. Fixations impede development and increase the possibility that an individual will regress to an earlier stage of development when confronted with stress. The stage at which the fixation occurs determines the type and the severity of the abnormal behavior.

 Anxiety comes in three forms: real, neurotic, and moral. Anxiety signals the ego that danger is near and could overpower it if the danger is not heeded. *Real anxiety* is a realistic fear of a genuine threat to safety in the environment. For example, the news of an approaching hurricane results in a person experiencing great fear that motivates her to take action to protect herself and her property. She first boards up the windows of the house and then leaves for a safe area. *Neurotic anxiety* is an unrealistic fear of punishment for gratifying forbidden libidinal impulses. For example, an adult male avoids sexual contact with women because he has an unconscious fear that he will suffer some horrible consequence. This stems from an unconscious dread that his father will punish him for cuddling with his mother, a childhood trauma from the past. *Moral anxiety* is an unrealistic fear that emerges when a person violates the parental standards incorporated during childhood and fears that he or she will be punished by the superego. For example, if a person with a strong superego steals a cigarette lighter, he might develop a fear that a blood clot will develop in the hand that he used to steal it.

Resistance is intrapsychic opposition that protects a person from the unpleasant experience of remembering past traumas or the uncertainty of developing new ways of adapting. Psychic functions block the unpleasant feelings that accompany unconscious conflicts by preventing unconscious material from surfacing (Alexander, 1956).

The most common form of resistance is *repression*—or amnesia for the emotionally charged event. The ego forces anxiety-producing memories, thoughts, wishes, and feelings out of consciousness. When repression fails and unconscious material surfaces, the ego uses other defenses such as transference, symptoms, and dreams. Resistance also takes the form of conflicts over competing drives, a weak ego, uncontrolled libido, connection to unconscious guilt, repetition compulsion, castration anxiety, passive/homosexual wishes in men, and penis envy in women.

Resistance is like a protective parent who tries to shield her child from the pain of the awful. For example, a 4-year-old boy's dog is hit by a car. The body lies in the front yard. A mother will protect her child from psychological pain by preventing him from seeing the sad sight of the beloved pet (or *traumata*). She may distract the child and say, "Let's go to the store." She carries her son through the back door to the car while the father removes the pet. Later she tells the child the dog has disappeared. The boy searches for his dog, hoping for his return. Mom does not understand that in the long run, her child is better off facing painful reality now rather than later. An important part of the analyst's work is to break through resistance to make the unconscious conscious. If this child were in psychoanalysis as an adult, the analyst might help him to become aware of the content of the repressed material.

Repression and Defense Mechanisms

The theory of repression is the cornerstone on which the whole of psychoanalysis rests (Freud, 1914, p. 16). Amnesia underlies each of the defense mechanisms, which act like reflexes to repel anxiety and to deal with unacceptable thoughts, feelings, wishes, urges, and impulses that represent a conflict between personality structures. Thus, repression is a purposeful but unconscious forgetting. The most common defense mechanisms include the following:

- *Denial* is a refusal to acknowledge a painful aspect of reality or a protection from an unpleasant reality by not perceiving it. For example, the alcoholic whose family confronts him about his drinking says "I do not drink too much. And, I can stop any time that I want." His family asks him to stop immediately, and he agrees to do so. When he lapses into drunkenness again, his family confronts him, accusing him of breaking his promise; he adamantly insists that he did not break his promise and says "I did not *want* to stop." Or the mother who is informed that her son was killed in the war in Iraq says, "No. It is not true. You are mistaken."
- *Displacement* is a shifting of unacceptable thoughts, feelings, wishes, urges, and impulses from the real target to a less threatening object, replacing the original object with a substitute. For example, an employee whose boss screamed at her arrives home and yells at her husband and children because they do not have the power to dismiss her.

- *Projection* is attributing one's own unacceptable thoughts, feelings, wishes, urges, and impulses onto someone else to protect the ego from recognizing distasteful personal characteristics. Curtis wants to kill his political adversary, but instead of owning his aggression, he becomes fearful because he believes that his opponent is out to get him or, more specifically, wants to kill him.
- *Reaction formation* is thinking, feeling, or acting in a way that is exactly the opposite of a person's true inner thoughts, feelings, wishes, urges, or impulses. Megan is sexually attracted to Brad, but he is taboo. She will see Brad as very unattractive. Since she yearns to act out sexually, Megan protects herself from her own unacceptable impulses by burning pornography in front of City Hall.
- *Undoing* is a making up for a transgression by neutralizing the unacceptable thought, feeling, wish, urge, or impulse that the person regrets. Deborah compliments her friend after not recommending her for a job in her company.
- *Introjection* is a taking in or incorporation of an object to make it into oneself. Identification with the aggressor constitutes the manner in which the child defends against castration anxiety in the Oedipal phase. Another example is that Lisa's mother, a devoted nurse, dies unexpectedly. The following year, Lisa decides to change her major from journalism to nursing with no conscious awareness that it is related to the loss of her mother.
- *Rationalization* is an intellectual justification for unacceptable thoughts, wishes, or behaviors—such as concealing true motivations by offering reassuring explanations. For example, Jennifer is not selected to be a member of her high school band. Instead of dealing with the painful feelings associated with rejection, Jennifer tells herself she really did not want to associate herself with such a second-rate orchestra anyway.
- *Regression* is a return to a less mature or childish level of functioning. Michael argued with John over a minor matter and rushed off to his bedroom, placed his head under the covers, and waited until someone came to soothe his hurt feelings.
- *Sublimation* is channeling unacceptable thoughts, feelings, and urges into a socially acceptable activity. Freud believed it was the only truly healthy defense mechanism. David channeled his angry feelings toward his father, who always beat him at every game, into a single-minded drive to become the best debater in his college.

Which particular defenses will a person develop? It depends upon the intensity of the anxiety, developmental history, and maturity. A defense mechanism can be primitive or sophisticated, brittle or robust, rigid or flexible. The least destructive defenses are those that least distort reality (Wenar & Kerig, 2000). Some defenses can be helpful if they prevent a person from being temporarily incapacitated. For example, temporary denial of a loved one's death can help a grieving person to function rather than fall apart and become incapacitated.

Normal and Abnormal Behavior

The person whose behavior is normal is one who is free of intrapsychic conflicts. Although intrapsychic conflict is inevitable, the normal ego is strong enough to deal with the demands of the real world. It can mediate between the id and the superego so that the individual is not overwhelmed by guilt, shame, or nervous anxiety. The ego transforms impulses that could produce neurotic and moral anxiety into socially acceptable behavior, ideally through sublimation. The person experiences more pleasure than pain. To be in such a state of positive mental health, the person has, within reason, successfully negotiated all the hurdles as he or she passed through the psychosexual stages. Libidinal energy was attached to objects appropriate for each stage.

Abnormal and normal behaviors are quantitatively, not qualitatively, different. The person who behaves abnormally has an impaired capacity to love and to work. This means that the individual has more pain than pleasure, is in significant inter-personal conflict, or is excessively anxious, depressed, or guilty. There are generally three circumstances that provide the conditions for the development of abnormal behavior (Arlow, 2005):

- A person is unable to cope with the stress of normal development. The developmental tasks involved in maturing are too difficult for the person to attain.
- Losses (loss of object, loss of an object's love, castration anxiety, and guilt) can bring about the reactivation of childhood conflicts, particularly those associated with Oedipal fantasies. Symptoms are formed that are regressions to an earlier level of functioning where libido may have been fixated.
- A person's current situation is so much like a past unresolved conflict or trauma that he or she distorts reality in terms of childhood conflict and acts as he or she did in childhood by forming symptoms.

Adult abnormal behavior is the result of an imbalance between the drives and the ego defenses. When a person perceives a threat, internal or external, anxiety emerges; how it is handled is at the root of all abnormal behavior. When the ego comes face-to-face with an idea that arouses distress or when the id or superego challenges the idea, the ego tries to control the intrapsychic conflict and develops defenses against psychological pain and anxiety.

The form that mental illness takes is a function of abnormal drifts of libido beginning in some early stage of development (Freud, 1910); that is, as individuals pass through psychosexual stages, they fail to successfully negotiate a developmental hurdle. Depending upon what stage, different forms of adult pathology form. For example, at birth, any environmental danger could bring about unresolved global feelings of helplessness and distress. In the oral phase, the mother's absence produces a fear of loss of love. In the phallic stage, impending castration (which then translates into any bodily injury) produces anxiety. In the post-Oedipal phase, negative self-evaluation and self-statements cause fears after parental standards have been internalized into the superego (Monte, 1987).

Neurotic anxiety, the fear of punishment from an imaginary outside source, can overwhelm a person. Two opposing forces are in conflict—one governed by the id or pleasure principle and the other governed by the ego or reality principle. These forces compete for instant gratification versus a delay and a redirection into socially acceptable channels (Rennison, 2001).

When the id is in constant conflict with the realism of the ego and/or the moral mandates of the superego, much libido is used just to maintain a psychodynamic balance. Little is available to invest in healthy living. For example, when the id's urge to "kill the opposition" clashes with the superego's mandate to "be a pacifist," the ego scrambles to find a way to balance these opposing demands. If the superego is very harsh, and the ego is weak, individuals may be unable to enjoy even the simplest of harmless pleasures because their energy is consumed with hiding, protecting themselves, and expelling mental content from awareness. The greater the fixation and the weaker the ego, the more psychic energy is necessary to fight with the id or superego. If a patient cannot resolve the contradiction, he or she "forgets." If the ego is weak and cannot balance the unbridled demands of the id with the strict, moral concerns of the superego (Rennison, 2001), then the dynamic balance that maximizes pleasure and minimizes tension is upset. The result is pathology or mental illness.

The ego ideal is the image of the perfect self. The closer a person is to becoming the ego ideal, the greater the self-esteem; and the further away the person is from becoming the ego ideal, the lower the self-esteem. If a person does not reach the ideal, it may result in a libidinal regression so that he or she behaves in a childish, immature, narcissistic, immoral, or destructive manner. For example, if aggressive id urges come to consciousness, and the ego is so weak that it becomes overwhelmed by anxiety, the person displays symptoms of emotional and/or physical paralysis. If the internalized superego is harsh and punishes the person, then shame or guilt may emerge.

It is unresolved fears from early development, and the anxieties accompanying them, that lay the groundwork for adult pathologies. Abnormal behavior—neurosis and psychosis—is caused by a number of factors, and adult symptoms must be traced to their sources through psychoanalysis.

Transference and Countertransference

Transference is the process whereby a person projects his or her experiences, impulses, feelings, fantasies, attitudes, conflicts, and defenses arising from relationships with childhood authority figures onto current relationships. Unaware, the person finds her- or himself acting out these indiscriminate, nonselective repetitions of the past and coloring or ignoring reality. The degree to which a person distorts reality reflects the intensity of the pathology (Eagle & Wolitzky, 1992). Thus early childhood experience shapes future emotional health. A patient reacts to the analyst as she did to her parents. If she was afraid of her abusive father when she was 5 years old, then she will also fear the current authority figure (the analyst). If the patient is afraid of the analyst, it is not because of any action on the part of the analyst; it is because the fear has been transferred from the early childhood situation to the analyst in the present.

Countertransference is the unresolved feeling that the analyst transfers onto a patient, as a result of having unresolved conflicts with his or her own significant others in the past. For example, an analyst who continues to harbor resentment toward his abusive father may find it difficult to deal with an angry, abusive client. The analyst may react in a number of ways and find himself bored, impatient, afraid, uninterested, or even overly interested in what the client says during sessions. In actuality, the analyst is defending against anxiety from his own unconscious fear of retribution from past unresolved Oedipal issues. The analyst must examine his own emotions to see if they interfere with treatment. If so, the right thing for the analyst to do is to seek supervision and to find a way to work through his own unresolved issues. A training analysis during the therapist's education is intended to take care of any unresolved issues to maximize the therapist's ability to work with the largest variety of patients. However, no analysis is perfect, so the analyst must maintain a lifelong vigilance of his or her own countertransference.

Dream Analysis

Dream analysis is a useful tool to unlock the secrets of the unconscious. Freud called dreams the royal road to the unconscious. During sleep, the ego relaxes its censorship, making it easier for unconscious, repressed wishes, thoughts, feelings, urges, and impulses to emerge into consciousness. Dreams, like symptoms of abnormal behavior and defense mechanisms, represent a form of inner dishonesty, since they distort inner conflict. Once the patient describes the manifest dream, or the superficial meaning, the analyst coaxes out the hidden and repressed ideas, or the latent, hidden meaning. Although Freud believed in some universal dream symbols, he interpreted them within the context of the specific patient's life.

✦ PRACTICE OF CLASSICAL PSYCHOANALYSIS

Now that we have examined the basic theoretical concepts that underlie psychoanalysis, we will explore its practice. Dr. John Garrett, a composite fictional psychotherapist, provides a firsthand perspective of how he integrates theory with practice and applies the techniques of classical psychoanalysis.

Assessment and Diagnosis

The first time I see a patient, I conduct a face-to-face interview. In the initial assessment, which can last from one to several sessions, I ask the following:

Is this person a suitable candidate for analysis?
Will he or she be able to endure the lengthy, intense, arduous, emotionally
  painful, and financially expensive process of treatment?
Does he or she have the ego strength to tolerate the anxiety that will emerge?
Can he or she fully participate and use interpretations to make the unconscious
  conscious?
Can analysis make his or her life more enjoyable and active?

If the answer to each of these questions is yes, I accept the person into treatment. My ideal patient is one who is not severely disturbed, but moderately neurotic, Oedipally conflicted with a developmental lag from the phallic stage. The Oedipal and Electra conflicts show themselves in three forms—symptoms, work inhibition, and self-punishing character patterns. I understand that I will be discovering more about the answers to these questions as the therapy goes on, but I make the best assessment possible to begin analysis (Cartwright, 2004).

If the risk of harm is too great, so that the patient might be overcome by anxiety to the point of regression or even psychosis, I refer him or her to supportive therapy where treatment will be less stressful and more reassuring. More serious problems that disqualify patients originate in the pre-Oedipal phase and may have been so devastating to normal development that the person may not be able to respond to psychoanalysis.

To understand the patient's clinical problem or pathology, I take a detailed and careful history, gathering enough verbal and nonverbal clinical information about the patient's psychodynamics to make decisions about suitability for treatment. However, I will only discover the complete answers to my questions as therapy progresses:

How and where is libidinal energy distributed?
How well are the id, ego, and superego functioning, especially the ego's ability to
  handle anxiety related to sex and aggression?
What is the balance of the conscious, unconscious, preconscious?
How has the development of the psychosexual stages proceeded, and what are the
  fixations?
What are the unconscious conflicts, defense mechanisms, and forms of resistance?
What are the nature, effects, and meanings of the patient's symptoms?

Although patients present with a wide variety of symptoms, they commonly present with an anxiety, a phobia, an obsession, or depression. I do not accept any symptom at face value. It is the tip of the iceberg, a symbol of an underlying, unresolved, unconscious conflict that protects a vulnerable area of the patient's emotional life and defends against the pain experienced from a traumata (an impressed but forgotten scene). When dangerous and threatening thoughts, wishes, urges, or fantasies are pushed into unconsciousness, they have undischarged sums of energy or excitement attached to them (conversion). When they press to come into awareness, anxiety is created; if not handled by a sufficiently strong ego, a symptom arises.

Negotiation of Therapeutic Relationship and Length of Treatment

Once I accept the candidate as the analysand, we negotiate a contract. We must agree upon the structure of the analytic situation, which includes dates, times, and fees and the number of sessions per week (e.g., 4–5 weekly for a range of 4–7 years). I inform my patient that the average number of sessions is 835 over four or more years (Garfield & Bergen, 1994). I also tell the patient about the benefits and risks of entering treatment and summarize the scientific information available about the effectiveness and efficacy of the therapy. After settling the pragmatics, we agree on the clinical responsibilities.

My role as therapist is that of an authority figure. I listen with therapeutic neutrality, or a nonjudgmental attitude. I build a therapeutic alliance and guide the analysand by using my expertise gained from years of training and my own personal analysis. I see myself as a mental health detective and the symptom as a clue to understanding the patient's psychodynamics. My task it is to help the patient to understand the symptom's unconscious meaning. I find relevant associations, trace them back to repressed affects, and free up and release the repressed affect to rid the patient of the abnormality. To do so I must fight the resistance.

The patient's fundamental clinical responsibility is to free-associate. Simply put, he or she must say anything that comes to mind and report each and every thought, feeling, experience, fantasy, or dream with absolutely no censorship.

The long-term goal of classical analysis is to free the patient from neurotic tendencies, to increase his or her capacity to live an active and enjoyable life, and to resolve the conflicts that are causing symptoms, inhibitions, or self-punishment. Ultimately, this means character reconstruction by strengthening the functioning of the ego so it can control unconscious sexual and aggressive drives. I achieve this by using techniques created by Freud to discover the unconscious meaning of repressed memories, feelings, thoughts, or wishes that underlie unconscious conflicts and their relationship to the rest of the personality (Eagle & Wolitzky, 1992). Successful psychoanalysis results in the patient having greater stability, generalizability, resistance to new stressors, and, of course, the disappearance of presenting symptoms (Wallerstein, 1988).

Therapeutic Techniques

A number of techniques help me achieve my therapeutic goals throughout the psychoanalytic process. I confront, clarify, and interpret repeated patterns of thinking, feeling, and behaving, which Freud called *repetition compulsion*. My patient becomes more aware of how his or her early relationships affect his or her current functioning. I use the patient's resistance as a road map to unconscious conflict. Resistance takes many forms—symptoms, simple repression, transference, dreams, and defenses. Concrete examples of resistance during the sessions include editing or talking about irrelevant material, forgetting important material, failing to gain insight, blocking or inability to free-associate, evoking sympathy or approval, doubting the usefulness of therapy, forgetting, tardiness, missing appointments, dropping out of therapy, refusing to accept interpretations, externalizing and blaming others, and acting out conflicts in and outside of treatment (Greenson, 1965, 1967).

I break through resistance by making correct *interpretations*. I begin with *clarification* statements that help the patient to be aware of unconscious feelings, thoughts, impulses, or actions that cause anxiety as they surface. Then, I clarify how and what the patient is resisting and explain the nature and function of resistance. I trace back the symptoms to their source in the patient's life history. I may *confront* or point out inconsistencies in speech or behaviors to the patient with "You seem to laugh when you discuss these sad issues," followed by a clarification of "Your laughter seems to mask your sadness. Is laughter your way to avoid unpleasant feelings?" These preparatory statements lead up to a tripartite interpretation when I link the patient's behavior in the moment (transference), with the recent past (significant figures), and with the childhood past. "Your laughter helps you to avoid facing your hurt. You laugh at me and are afraid to show me your disappointment when you think I let you down, just as you laughed when your husband was unfaithful and just as you laughed when your father beat you when you were 5."

Acceptance of the interpretation discharges psychic energy, freeing up resources to gain insight. To determine if my interpretation is correct, I observe the patient's reaction. If resistance is conscious, the patient may lie or deliberately withhold information. If resistance is preconscious, the patient generally acknowledges my interpretation by admitting that he or she was beating around the bush and escaping from the emotional discomfort. If resistance is unconscious, the patient defends against anxiety, guilt, and other unpleasant feelings as they emerge into consciousness (Wachtel, 1982).

A single interpretation seldom eliminates symptoms. It is more likely to bring about a mobilization of anxiety and an increase in defending, such as denial, rationalization, derision, or laughing off of the interpretation. I must repeat interpretations to effectively break through the associations being kept unconscious by inner affective resistance.

I interpret various forms of resistance, such as symptoms, simple repression, transference, dreams, and defenses. Transference interpretations are particularly important because I can make use of the strong feelings, both positive and negative, my analysand develops for me. I become his or her mother, father, or other significant authority figures from the past, providing a particularly powerful opportunity to work through unconscious material.

Therapeutic neutrality is important to assure that the feelings arise out of the analysand's dynamics and not from my interactions, allowing me to make interpretations. My patients resist giving up symptoms, and I do not blame them. If a person has been walking with the aid of a crutch, there is a strong tendency to hold onto the crutch, even if it is no longer needed (Basch, 1982). It is my job to find a way to break through resistance and motivate the client to walk normally in order to outweigh the fear of putting aside the crutch.

As the analyst, I must observe my own self so that any countertransference will not detract from the analysis. If there is any suspicion that my own unresolved conflict is detrimental to the patient, I seek consultation. I must be sure that I do not have a blind spot that gets in the way of my working with the patient.

The Process of Therapy

In the *initial phase* of therapy, I sit upright in a chair behind the patient, observing his or her every verbal and nonverbal behavior, taking notes and gathering materials so I can formulate my understanding of this patient's psychodynamics to prepare my interpretations. My patient lies on the couch, free-associating and disclosing conscious or unconscious memories, thoughts, feelings, experiences, fantasies, and dreams. I encourage my patient to say whatever comes to mind. Since the patient and I agreed in the assessment to free-associate, I instruct my patients using Freud's exact wording in his "fundamental rule" (1913, pp. 134–135). I say,

> You will notice that as you relate things various thoughts will occur to you which
> you would like to put aside on the ground of certain criticisms and objections.
> You will be tempted to say to yourself that this or that is irrelevant here or is
> quite unimportant, so that there is no need to say it. You must never give in to
> those criticisms, but must say it in spite of them. Indeed, you must say it precisely
> because you have an aversion to doing so. . . . Never forget that you have
> promised to be absolutely honest, and never leave anything out because . . . it is
> unpleasant to tell it.

As I listen to the patient's stream of consciousness, I link each word with one idea, then with another, then with one word or image suggesting another, tracing the connections between the patient's spoken free associations and repressed unconscious content. I do not give advice or sympathy. By saying little and remaining neutral, I encourage transference. I stimulate the conflicts and fantasies to help the patient to project his or her wishes, thoughts, feelings, and perceptions onto me. When the patient actually relives core conflicts, reacting toward me as he or she did toward mother and father, my interpretations will help the patient understand these repetitious patterns more consciously. I link what is happening between the patient and me with similar feelings from the past and the conflicts of early childhood.

Timing is important in making unconscious material conscious. My interpretations mobilize an appropriate amount of anxiety that can be *decathected* or *catharted* (released). I am cautious about the pacing of the analysis. Proceeding too quickly can create too much anxiety, which means the ego will be flooded by fear, creating more resistance. The risk is that the analysand will escape and avoid dealing with the conflict by dropping out of therapy or by decompensating. Too little anxiety means the patient will not be challenged enough to increase awareness and integrate it into consciousness.

In the *middle phase* of therapy, working through resistance is a slow, continual, lengthy, tedious, and evolving process. As my patient's transference to me deepens and as my understanding of the patient's personality dynamics increase, I continue to make penetrating interpretations. As each incidence of transference is worked through, it stimulates the recall of another significant event and provides another opportunity to make the unconscious conscious. My patient gains increasing awareness of his or her own unconscious conflicts. I must break through all of the patient's opposition to get at repressed material.

Termination occurs when the patient finally works through his or her major conflicts. I set a definite date for termination. The patient now understands more about his or her self-defeating habits and immature defenses, has freed up cathected libido, and can channel anxiety into a more mature character structure. At the prospect of leaving me, the patient acts out. Often, new memories emerge. I help the patient work through any fantasies he or she might have about his or her condition after leaving therapy. If the patient has a neurotic attachment to me, I must help the person to work through any dependencies and reluctance to give up the analysis. Once this last crisis is resolved, the patient terminates psychoanalysis.

How do I measure a successful outcome? There is structural character change, so that "Where id was, there shall ego be" (Freud, 1914/1917). The analysand will have insight into what went wrong and should be able to use the libidinal energy that was inappropriately cathected to pregenital conflicts to function in a healthier and more mature manner. The finished product will be a patient who is free of symptoms, work inhibitions, or self-defeating character patterns.

Some pitfalls can occur in psychoanalysis. The patient can fail to improve or can worsen. He or she may not be suitable for the intensity of psychoanalysis, in which case I know my initial assessment was not accurate. Countertransference is a serious problem if it takes the form of nonempathetic responsiveness. I must make certain that I do not let my own issues interfere with any patient's integrity, autonomy, and progress (Wolitzky, 2003).

THERAPY IN ACTION: DR. JOHN GARRETT AND THE CASE OF JONATHAN

To illustrate the application of psychoanalysis, we examine a treatment plan for Jonathan, followed by excerpts from therapy sessions with our fictional psychotherapist, Dr. Garrett. Keep in mind the case excerpts are simulated interviews and represent the ideal of psychotherapy. In real life, clients may take much longer to meet therapeutic goals. Table 3.1 provides a summary of Dr. Garrett's treatment plan.

Case Excerpts

Dr. Garrett conducted an initial assessment and diagnosis of Jonathan. The following excerpts are from sessions based on that assessment and psychoanalytic case formulation.

Session 1

Dr. Garrett: Jonathan, we will begin the process of analysis as discussed. We have agreed that your four sessions a week will be on Tuesday through Friday at 1:00 P.M. My role is to listen to you carefully, using all of my expertise and training to help you to become aware of your internal conflicts. Your role is to free-associate, or say whatever comes into your mind with no censorship whatsoever. Lying on this couch during sessions will facilitate this process. Are you ready to begin?

Jonathan: Well . . . I feel a little awkward lying here on this couch not looking you in the eye. What am I supposed to talk about—my past? I already did that with you a few weeks ago . . . well . . . OK . . . I am not sure what to talk about. But coming

Table 3.1	
Classical Psychoanalytic Treatment Plan for Jonathan	
Assessment and Formulation	• Presenting problem: Symptoms of depression, self-punishment, work inhibition represent intrapsychic conflicts that appear to be unresolved issues (castration anxiety) from the Oedipal phase • J. ideal candidate due to ego strength; neurotic not psychotic, motivated, intelligent, verbal, psychological minded • Able to accept and work with trial interpretations
Therapeutic Relationship	• Analyst is an authority figure • Therapeutic neutrality • Working alliance—J. feels safe and accepts transference interpretations and works through resistance
Contract, Goals, and Treatment Plan	• Free client from neurotic behaviors • Decrease or free J. from symptoms of depression, work inhibitions, self-punishment, and self-degradation • Increase J.'s capacity to work and love • Time: Agree to meet 5 times a week; able to devote time and able to afford therapy
Techniques	• Free association for J. • Clarification and confrontation • Interpretations of resistance and of transference
Process of Therapy	• Initial phase: free association, building good working alliance, building transference • History taking is ongoing • Interpretations delivered for tolerance of anxiety • Defenses: denial, undoing, obsessions • Interpretations: rage at mother for neglecting him; rage at father for frustrating him from Mom's affection • Middle phase: continue to work through resistance, make deeper levels of interpretation, especially with patterns of anxiety when J. expresses anger at analyst, Tuti (his significant other), father/mother • Guilt from conflict between id's desire to destroy Tuti/Darren and superego's mandate against anger • Neurotic anxiety from fantasies of revenge stirring up his deep-seated fear of retaliation • Anxiety causes J. to defend through reaction formation and desire "not to hurt" Tuti and Darren (analyst, or father)
Termination and Outcome	• J. gained insight into nature of intrapsychic conflicts • Greater ego strength/better ego control over id and superego • Intrapsychic conflicts resolved Oedipal issues (castration anxiety) from the Oedipal phase • Temporary regression and symptoms interpreted and resolved • J. better able to work and love

here makes me think of my parents. [*laughs*] My father died five years ago at the age of 68. I was sad but I also felt relief because it stopped his dreadful suffering so much with his cancer. My mother died two years before him, and I think she died an early death because he treated her so badly. She was only 60. It's sad to be without my parents . . . alone . . . no support. Here I am an adult with no one to care for me . . . nobody cares. Oh . . . what am I saying . . . I feel silly talking about these things, yet I can feel that they still bother me. I am surprised. Should I go on? [*looks toward the analyst, almost straining to get up*] Can't you tell me what I ought to do?

Dr. Garrett: Go on.

Jonathan: OK . . . It simply isn't right that she is gone, and he is, too. He was eight years older than Mom . . . my dad was eight years older than my mom. My mother—a woman who did not really want to have me . . . not a warm, loving mother. [*laughs, then sighs*] When I asked for a hug she'd say "you are nearly a man; you need to grow up." I felt alone. [*tears edge down his face*] Like my father . . . he was cold, and too strict. He'd hit me once for no good reason. If he drank, he was a "mean drunk." [*long pause*] I remember. I was four or five years old. I tried to hit him back. He threw me on the floor . . . knocked the wind out of me. I couldn't breathe. I thought he was killing me. [*tears stream down his face; he cries loudly, then laughs*] I was a pathetic kid. No one cared. That made me not want to be near either of them. I stayed away after that. [*long pause*] My sister . . . she was loving. [*stares off into space for a minute and obviously is editing his thoughts*]

Dr. Garrett: Please, you need to say what comes into your mind and not edit what you are saying to me.

Jonathan: Oh . . . yeah . . . OK. My sister would bundle me up and take me to visit friends. One time, my mom dumped me off at my aunt's for a long time. Auntie did not really want me. My sister was the only one who really cared. Dad and I did start getting along, but that was for only a couple of years before he died. Damn. Fat chance. Too little too late. That's the way that things go . . . just as we are getting close he dies on me.

Session 200

Jonathan: I just don't think I can come up with anything else. I cannot free-associate. Plus, I don't think you care. I think you are demanding too much from me.

Dr. Garrett: Say anything . . . anything that comes into your mind.

Jonathan: Nothing. Nothing comes to mind.

Dr. Garrett: Thoughts will come to you that you would like to put aside. Say it in spite of your feelings. Because you have an aversion to doing so they may be important. You promised to be absolutely honest, and never leave anything out because . . . it is unpleasant to tell it.

Jonathan: I am angry that you say nothing. [*long pause*] Oh I am so sorry. I did not mean that. I know you are helping me.

[*Comment: This is a pattern. Jonathan is enthused, disappointed, enraged, afraid of his rage, and profusely apologetic. I made a number of interpretations connecting J.'s anger with his defense of undoing or apologizing and feeling guilty after he became angry. I connected his anger at me with his anger at Tuti and Darren with his anger at his mother and sister for abandonment or not taking care of him in the way that he wanted. His fear of his own anger made him "undo" it or take it back after he expressed it.*]

Session 600

[*Comment: Jonathan began to appear late for appointments. His fear of expressing his rage at me for neglecting him remained repressed.*]

Jonathan: I am tired of therapy. It is not pleasant. It is going sour. I think I am "falling apart," and I am not able to perform for you. I don't think this free association stuff works.

Dr. Garrett: Please try.

Jonathan: I have been dating Susan for a year now. The time was right for sex. It just came naturally. Then, bam, I go impotent. I am coming here to get better, and here I am impotent. You are not helping me! Can you help me or not? I am paying you lots of money.

Jonathan: [*blurts out*] I am sorry! I did not mean to get angry at you. You are trying to help me. I am so sorry. I never should have said those things.

Dr. Garrett: Continue saying what comes to your mind.

Jonathan: OK . . . but please forgive me. [*long pause*] I guess, just before, I had a flash of a memory. Walking with Tuti at the mall, a man grabbed his kid who was having a temper tantrum and shook him. The child screamed, "Stop, Daddy, stop." Tuti laughed and said "The child deserved it. He was being a brat!" She sided with the dad . . . what about me? [*laughs*]

Dr. Garrett: Did you feel angry at Tuti for not protecting the child from its father? Just as you felt angry at me for not protecting you from Susan's anger about your impotency? As you were angry with your mother for not protecting you from your father?

Jonathan: [*long silence; begins to sob*] Yes . . . I needed protection. Someone should have helped me. I was left alone to fend for myself all the time. It's not right. No one protected me. And you are right. You are not protecting me either. My mom did not protect me. I recalled times when I tried to talk with my mother in her bedroom. Dad would interrupt, pick me up, and forcefully shake me, screaming "get the hell out of this bedroom!" Mom laughed.

Dr. Garrett: Did Dad's attacking you, and mom's deriding you, cause you to feel rage and anger that was difficult to express to them?

Jonathan: Yes!

Dr. Garrett: You seem to be afraid of talking to me about certain issues and the fear toward me seems to mask your anger at me. When you are fearful you come late for sessions and wonder whether you should be here at all. Are you running away from telling me that you are angry at me?

[*Comment: These preparatory statements lead up to an interpretation in which Jonathan's behavior in therapy (transference) was linked with the recent past (impotency with girlfriend) and with the parental behaviors in childhood.*]

Dr. Garrett: Your fear helps you to avoid facing your anger. Is being late for appointments the way you protect yourself from experiencing your rage toward me when you think I treat you in an unfair, arbitrary, and unpredictable way?

Jonathan: Perhaps this is the case.

Dr. Garrett: Is this what happens within you with your girlfriend? When you feel she is treating you in an unfair, arbitrary, and unpredictable way and will reject you, you show her your rage by being impotent. And that goes back to the feelings of rage you felt at your father for his unfair, arbitrary, and unpredictable punishments and your fear of expressing your rage toward him. And you fear he would punish you for your love of your mother. This made you defend yourself by acting in a helpless, impotent, and weak way.

Jonathan: [*after some silence*] You should be helping me more. I feel as if you also do nothing for me.

Dr. Garrett: After you express anger at me, you get apologetic. Could you see me as the person to fear? You are angry at me, but afraid that if I see your anger, I will hurt or abandon you. Thus you behave like a helpless victim, weak and incapable of fighting back. Isn't that what you did with Tuti, especially when she prevented you from defending that child? Instead of telling her that you were angry, you went impotent?

Case Comment

Jonathan's symptoms of anxiety and depression over Tuti's loss resulted from the emergence of repressed rage into consciousness. Loss of Tuti brought back the childhood conflicts of feelings of anger at his mother for her neglect and abandonment. His ego, defending against the discomfort of anxiety, transformed the rage into anger turned inward, resulting in feelings of depression and self-hate. Unresolved Oedipal issues emerged, where Jonathan felt anxious when he got close to his mother, unconsciously fearing retaliation from his father. Identification with his father meant Jonathan acted in a way to repress his anger—opposite to his true feelings—being overly compliant, seeking approval from authority sources, and reluctant to disagree. His resistance takes the form of dawdling, procrastinating, inefficiency, helplessness, and generalized anxiety. Whenever his rage or sexual desires emerged into consciousness, Jonathan felt anxious due to past overly harsh and unpredictable punishments. While his superego told him no, his id urged him to say yes. His ego defenses repressed his rage and sexual appetite.

Dr. Garrett reported that Jonathan's five-year analysis was successful. He recognized the connections between his anger and his fear and his repetition of a pattern of events from childhood in his current intimate relationships, and with Dr. Garrett. The long-term goals—to help Jonathan gain insight into and modify his self-defeating way of handling relationships—were achieved. He became more confident in his relationships and married Susan. The core conflicts apparent with the loss of Tuti and Darren changed. From regression, rationalization, denial, and reaction formation as defenses, he moved to levels of sublimation through work and love of his new wife. He gained ego strength and an understanding of his anger and fears of abandonment. Jonathan was no longer, sad, depressed or impotent and was able to use libidinal energy to live a better, more functional life in which he was freer to love and live.

✦ Research Directions of Classical Psychoanalysis

The evidence base supporting the use of classical Freudian psychoanalysis is sparse. Currently, there is no compelling evidence to show that psychoanalysis is uniquely efficacious and effective (Magnavita, 2002). Even Sheila Gray, president of the American Academy of Psychoanalysis in 2002, says that psychoanalysis is particularly challenged because it has been based on conviction alone rather than scientific data (2002, p. 90).

Early research conducted by Freud relied upon case studies. While Freud approached the practice of psychoanalysis from an experimental mind-set, he relied upon the observations of a trained analyst as the mainstay of data by which to evaluate treatment and outcome. While case studies serve as good examples, the case study method is subject to the biases that derive from theoretical allegiances, from the analyst's investment in the success of a model, and from the desire to protect one's domain (Jahoda, 1977). Questions arise about how analysts choose to direct their observations, how they interpret what they see in their cases, and how they select the information that they use to support their theories. Furthermore, without verbatim records, how do analysts know that their notes reconstructed after the session are accurate? Strong reliance on case studies reinforces doubts about the scientific validity of psychoanalysis.

Freud's research was also limited by the technology and methodology of his time (Meninger & Nemiah, 2000). Even the well-established allegiance bias, which we now know results in more optimistic reports of effectiveness, was not something that early Freudian psychoanalysts were aware of (Hollon, 1999; Luborsky et al., 1999).

In addition to case studies, there have been some large-scale and longitudinal studies of psychoanalysis, with some positive findings. In 1941, a cross-cultural survey of 543 analytic clients showed that 60 percent of patients consistently claimed that they were cured or much improved (Knight, 1941). In addition, the Meninger Psychotherapy Research Project Study, begun in 1952, followed a small sample of 42 patients for 30 years. Recently, the International Psychoanalytic Association conducted a scientific review of 26 more current studies of psychoanalytic treatment in Europe and North America.

Some interpret the evidence from a number of pre- and postinvestigations to indicate that psychoanalysis may be consistently helpful to patients with milder disorders and somewhat less consistently so for more severely disturbed groups (Gabbard, Gunderson, & Fonagy, 2002). Overall, differences between treatment outcomes in classical psychoanalysis and in other forms of psychoanalytic psychotherapy have shown that psychoanalysis can have a positive effect (Anderson & Lambert, 1995; Sloane, Staples, Cristol, Yorkston, & Whipple, 1975; Wallerstein, 1989, 2002).

However, there are many limitations associated with this research (Ablon, 2004). The small number of large-scale and longitudinal investigations of psychoanalysis means it is difficult to make valid comparisons. The studies that have been done contain a number of serious methodological flaws including poor designs or nonexistent experimental controls, placebo control, or randomized trials; a lack of standardized procedures for selection of therapist and patient; differing levels of training, expertise, experience, and maturity among analysts; few, if any, standards to assure that therapist, patient, and therapy situations are equivalent; deficient statistical analyses; a lack of standardized diagnostic procedures and independent outcome assessments; client samples that lack diversity and, thus, external validity; inadequately specified procedures; no baseline measures; and no follow-up for dropouts (Kazdin, 1994). Thus, none of the outcome studies used a methodology that would satisfy modern-day evidence based criteria.

Some proponents of psychoanalytic therapy argue that substantial evidence for the effectiveness of psychoanalysis has accumulated for over a century, but it often goes unrecognized and unexamined, or has been neglected or ignored because the information is scattered throughout the psychological literature (Aveline, 2005). What is needed is a coherent and cohesive view of the current state of psychoanalytic work (Safran, 2001). The International Psychoanalytic Association (2008) points out that the methods required by an evidence-based approach are not suitable for the study of psychoanalysis, so more appropriate ways to research psychoanalysis are needed (Paris, 2005; Robertson & Perry, 2004); Others point out that sources of biases among evaluators may account for a poor research record (Almond, 2006; Leichsenring, Biskup, & Kreische, 2005).

Despite a variety of views about the role of research and psychoanalysis, many analysts now acknowledge that the survival of psychoanalysis depends on the production of high quality psychoanalytic research (Hauser, 2006; Sandell, 2001; Vaughan et al., 2000). This would reassure the public about the effectiveness of psychoanalysis, strengthen relationships with the academic and clinical world, and prevent psychoanalytic therapies from being discarded by the health care system (Kernberg, 2004, 2006).

Gray (2002) believes the techniques that will provide the kind of evidence needed for psychoanalysis to establish its credibility as an empirically based treatment are soon coming. The Academy of Psychoanalysis is sponsoring a research project that examines characteristics of current psychoanalytic patients and treatment procedures (Friedman, Bucci, Christian, Drucker, & Garrison, 1998). Psychoanalysts are participating in the Quality Care 2000 national study in which depressed patients receive analytic therapy (Gray, 1996, 2002). The Department of Psychotherapy at the University of Ulm, Germany, has a large collection with over 15 million transcribed words of recorded psychotherapies and psychoanalyses, stored in computer files with programs that assist researchers in accessing and using them. The University of Zurich, Switzerland, has JAKOB, a database with 5,000 hours of videotaped and audiotaped psychoanalyses and psychotherapies that are accessible, fully indexed, and in many cases transcribed (Holt, 1989). A visit to the International Psychoanalytic Association (IPA) website (http://www.ipa.org.uk) lists current or ongoing studies. The IPA sponsors annual research training programs to train analysts in empirical and conceptual approaches including longitudinal, biopsychosocial, and intergenerational research; psychotherapeutic process and outcome work; research into attachment; personality and psychopathology; emotion; psychotherapy; and qualitative research methods (Gottdiener, 2007). Methodologically sound studies with control groups are being planned (Hale, 2000). Furthermore, many analysts want to provide systematic clinical evidence for outcomes of psychoanalysis in the future (Bachrach, Galatzer-Levy, Skolinoff, & Waldron, 1991).

Drew Westen (1998) advocates taking a broad view of research and psychoanalysis. Admittedly, for psychoanalysis to become an evidence-based therapy, much work needs to be done. However, with the newer generations of psychoanalytically oriented clinicians showing an appreciation for empirical work, psychoanalysis should not be judged so harshly. Criticisms about the lack of valid psychoanalytic research often pertain to obsolete versions of psychodynamic theory that do not represent today's models (as we will see in Chapter 4); in fact, psychodynamic therapies have evolved and should not all be lumped together.

It is important to consider the strides analysis has made, such as the revisions of libido theory that stress human needs for relationship and self-esteem. Psychoanalysis has moved into other areas such as the cognitive and neurosciences, and much research supports the concepts of developmental dynamics; the origins of personality; social dispositions in childhood; mental representations of the self, others, and relationships; unconscious cognitive, affective, and motivational processes; ambivalence and the tendency for affective and motivational dynamics to operate in parallel and produce compromise solutions. We should view psychoanalysis as a clinically tested therapy that is recognizing the need for a research base and is in the process of obtaining it.

What can a therapist say to a client to justify the use of psychoanalysis? The therapist can explain to the client that psychoanalytic psychotherapy has limited scientific data to support it, but currently psychoanalysts are attempting to establish that empirical evidence. Undertaking this research task is daunting and arduous because, by its very nature, analysis is lengthy, complicated, and based on complex theoretical ideas. This equates to research that is difficult, expensive, time-consuming, and longitudinal with valid outcome measures. It is also difficult to convert the current accumulated research findings into relevant guidelines that are meaningful for practice. On the other hand, the absence of studies is not definitive evidence that psychoanalysis is *not* helpful. Sufficient evidence for the efficacy and effectiveness of classical psychoanalysis has not been affirmed *at this time.*

The therapist can say he or she chooses to use psychoanalysis based upon a combination of factors—clinical expertise, clinical experience, and a study of the research on psychoanalysis that does exist. Psychoanalysis has withstood the test of time. It has been used for over a century and continues to be endorsed by a substantial number of supporters, both clinicians and clients alike, as a credible and effective method of treating mental illnesses. The therapist who performs this therapy is continuously challenged to be thoughtful, careful, and analytic while evaluating what is happening in treatment. Finally, if we invoke the equivalency effect, we can say that any of the major tested psychotherapies show a larger treatment effect relative to controls.

→ ISSUES OF DIVERSITY

Classical psychoanalysis—theory, practice, and research—is a product of Western culture and aimed at those with that worldview. Even today, the psychoanalyst is generally White, Western European, and male. Freud perceived a gap between the European psyche and the non-Western psyche, arguing that the mind of the "primitive" is less evolved, less conscious, and less differentiated but more mystical and more in harmony with nature, although in a state of a childlike timelessness (Richards, 1997). Early on, Freud (1905) predicted it would be necessary to modify psychoanalysis to treat people who were not suited for traditional analysis, which was based on treating the moderately neurotic, Oedipally conflicted patient.

In reality, though, Freud and his adherents have not been as responsive as they could be to the needs of diverse patient populations. In general, classical psychoanalysis has not paid enough attention to issues of gender, ethnicity, religion, socioeconomic status, educational background, profession or career, and life experiences. And how customs and values differ across cultures, engendering the formation of personality and abnormal behaviors, is an area that psychoanalysis has yet to examine (Wohl, 1995).On the positive side, psychoanalysis provides a theoretical framework for analyzing the psychological effects of cultural phenomena such as childrearing, but generalization of Western theories to other cultures is difficult, and too little has been done to adapt psychoanalysis to the needs of diverse populations.

❧ Freud's views on women are an intricate amalgam of accepted commonplaces, tentative explorations, and unconventional insights. After researching the feminine personality for 30 years, Freud claimed he had little to show for it. In his own words, early female development was uncertain and unsatisfactory, and the sexual life of the adult woman remained a dark continent to him (Gay, 1988). For a man who admitted he knew little about women, Freud made many sweeping generalizations about them. Using male sexuality as the standard for normal sexual behavior, female sexuality is pathological to the degree that it deviates from a male convention. Since a boy's superego develops after the threat of castration eliminates his desire for his mother, Freud believed that men develop a greater sense of justice and objectivity. A girl's disappointment in her lack of a male organ is accompanied by feelings of inferiority and jealousy. Thus a sense of justice that comes from feelings of inferiority or from a fear of losing love must be less principled than that of the male's sense of justice. A female superego is never independent of emotions. Thus, to Freud, a woman is a failed man.

Freud's view that anatomy is destiny is a form of stereotyping with negative connotations for the mental health of women. Feminists severely criticized Freud's conception of female sexuality. Karen Horney (1950), a neo-Freudian (see Chapter 4), was the first feminist to challenge him publicly by creating her own form of psychoanalysis. Accusing Freud of misunderstanding women, she dismissed the legitimacy of the Oedipal conflict. She argued that the whole notion of penis envy was based on inadequate evidence from a biased sample of neurotic women. The cause of abnormal behavior was attributable more to basic anxiety and hostility within interpersonal relationships than to early childhood trauma. Horney injected a number of important issues into her form of psychoanalysis, including the capacity for personal growth and an open, optimistic, and self-actualizing view of patients and therapy goals.

Modern feminists Nancy Chodorow and Jean Baker Miller (1979) formed a working group of theory-building feminine analysts. The members argued that Freud's choice of a male norm as the ideal for sexual functioning, rather than a female norm, was arbitrary, capricious, biased, and based upon unproven and false assumptions. They contended it is just as legitimate to say that womb envy, or breast envy, or lack of emotional intelligence are deficits in male functioning.

They also took Freud to task for his belief that dependence is pathological. They argue that interdependence is the ideal for normal, healthy functioning and should be included in psychoanalytic goals and outcomes. The feminists have raised consciousness, resulting in an awareness of the significance of gender issues in psychoanalytic work.

In terms of socioeconomics, psychoanalysis is more readily available to those who can afford large fees. People with limited finances are not likely to have the option of engaging in long-term analysis. The original patients for whom psychoanalysis was created were well-off and well-educated White Europeans. Woody Allen represents the quintessential analysand of modern culture. Thus, it is largely unknown how helpful psychoanalysis would be for those of other socioeconomic classes.

→ MAJOR CRITIQUES OF CLASSICAL PSYCHOANALYSIS

Psychoanalysis has been and continues to be a controversial model of therapy. Criticisms of psychoanalytic theory, practice, and research have been numerous, but praise has been plentiful as well. Let's summarize the most significant areas of criticism.

Critics of psychoanalytic theory contend that its concepts are so flexible that the theory can explain everything, and therefore, explains nothing. The theory fails to provide a set of relational rules that allows the therapist to predict what will happen if certain events occur or to detect the cause by tracing back a set of events that are causal. Furthermore, the same overt abnormal behavior can have very different roots (Hall & Lindzey, 1985). For example, if Sara is overly indulged or deprived during the oral stage, as an adult she may become an overeater. The same event can produce different pathologies. If Sara is overly indulged or deprived of food during the oral stage, as an adult she may become an anorexic (and not an overeater). John's unconscious rage at his father can show itself as an overt behavior that is functional or dysfunctional, depending upon which specific defense his unconscious selects. If he uses projection, he might attack and retaliate. If he uses reaction formation, he might become obsequious and overly friendly.

Vague theoretical constructs in psychoanalytic theory are often reified. Terms such as *id*, *ego*, and *superego* have taken on a life of their own, and they are often treated as if they are as real as a liver or a spleen. Imagine what an id or superego looks like. These constructs are difficult to operationalize and nearly impossible to validate scientifically, making the theory of psychoanalysis less than scientific and very subjective.

The theory of classical psychoanalysis depicts an extremely mechanistic, deterministic view of human nature that can be very limiting. By reducing all of human motivation to libidinal urges, the theory neglects the humanistic and spiritual side of human nature.

Critics also say psychoanalysis is a "one size fits all" treatment. The same techniques are used for all patients regardless of diagnosis. Since Freud believed that psychoanalysis should be limited to the treatment of phobias, hysteria, obsessional neurosis, and the abnormalities of character that replaced these mental disorders, its scope of practice is limited (Cummings, 1991; Frager & Fadiman, 1984). Patients with narcissism and psychotic conditions could not be treated successfully (until post-Freud developments when more and more pathologies were thought to be treatable).

Since the patient cannot know his or her own unconscious, the practice of psychoanalysis lies on the assumption that the therapist is authoritarian and nearly infallible in the analysis of the patient's psychodynamics. The analyst always has the upper hand since he or she has greater objectivity and knowledge of the patient's unconscious. If the patient and therapist disagree, the patient's objections are labeled resistance. There is no way to know for certain whether the analyst's clinical impressions are valid and accurate unless long-term studies corroborate.

Freudian analysis is lengthy, making measuring therapeutic success difficult, especially since the expected psychoanalytic outcome is a change in character structure and a strengthening of the ego, which are reified and hard to measure as constructs. Since analysis takes years, many variables could account for change, such as simple maturity, experience, and relationships outside of analysis. Until the analyst can say with certainty that patients are responding to the treatment and not to attention or expectancies (of their own, the analyst's, or an outsider's), and until the analyst can say with confidence which interventions were responsible for the change, the therapy lacks construct validity. The concept of cure is difficult to define, and the criteria by which to judge success are vague and nebulous.

Psychoanalysts have tended to claim that classical analysis is the purest of the psychotherapies, but they have not kept pace with modern research techniques or the demands of the health care environment for empirically supported therapies. Psychoanalysts need to stop depending on their own word and conduct sufficient systematic studies (Garfield & Bergen, 1994).

Psychoanalysis must become much more scientific and demonstrate that the principles upon which it is based are accurate. An evidence-based practice approach must be in the future of psychoanalysis if it is going to bridge the gap between research and practice and move out of its theoretical box into an era of integrated practice (Cone, 2001). Despite the difficulty and expense of conducting such research (Schacter & Luborsky, 1998), it will hopefully provide sufficient data to confirm the effectiveness of psychoanalysis. It is fortuitous that techniques to study outcomes and the internal processes of analysis are currently being created (Sexton, 1996).

Finally, some believe that psychoanalysis is a dying practice and that it has been largely replaced by biological psychiatry, which has dominated mental health over the last 20 years (Bornstein, 2001, 2005). In addition, some have cast some doubt on Freud's intellectual integrity. There have been controversies over Freud's professional and personal behavior, such as those described by Masson (1990, 1992), who accused Freud of modifying his theories for political expediency. Only time will tell if classical psychoanalysis will survive and flourish in its present form.

SUMMARY

- Freud created psychoanalysis, both a theory of personality and a psychotherapy, which has exerted a tremendous influence on the development of modern psychotherapy.
- There are three levels of human awareness: conscious, preconscious, and unconscious. Personality is based upon psychodynamics, the way in which libidinal energy moves, redistributes itself, cathects, and is balanced among conflicting conscious and unconscious motives and personality structures. The major personality structures are the id, ego, and superego.
- Development proceeds through biodevelopmental stages, which are psychosexual in nature and include the oral, anal, phallic, latency, and genital stages, each with its own erogenous zone and built-in challenges. How successfully the child negotiates these psychosexual stages influences his or her future mental health and determines if adult pathologies, neuroses, and more serious abnormalities are present. The Oedipal conflict and Electra conflict at the phallic stage of development are of particular importance for adult sexual adjustment.
- Anxiety alerts the ego to threats. Neurotic anxiety comes from unconscious forbidden id impulses, and moral anxiety comes from conflicts between the id and the superego. To deal with anxiety and painful affect, the person defends himself through repression, or resistance to remembering past traumas. Repression forms the basis of all defense mechanisms.
- The most common defense mechanisms include denial, displacement, projection, reaction formation, undoing, introjection, rationalization, regression, and sublimation. The ego also uses transference, symptoms, and dreams to deal with conflicts.
- Adult abnormal behavior is the result of an imbalance between the drives and the ego defenses. Abnormal and normal behaviors are quantitatively, not qualitatively, different. The causes of abnormal behavior include an inability to cope with current stress, losses, or unresolved childhood conflicts.
- In the practice of psychoanalysis, assessment and diagnosis aims at determining if a person has sufficient ego strength to tolerate therapy as well as the capacity to benefit from the therapy. The psychoanalyst is a neutral authority figure. Therapeutic techniques include free association and interpretations of resistance, transference, defenses and symptoms, and dream analysis.
- The process of therapy (from 5 to 7 years) consists of an initial phase in which resistance is first challenged, a middle phase in which the client's transference deepens and repressed material is confronted, and termination, in which the patient is free of symptoms, work inhibitions, or self-defeating character patterns.
- There is a lack of evidence-based research in psychoanalysis; the research that does exist relies on case studies. For psychoanalysis to survive, it must generate relevant research, although such studies are arduous.

- Psychoanalysis has been criticized for a lack of attention to diversity in theory, practice, and research and for insufficient efforts to adapt and apply psychoanalysis to members of diverse populations. Critics of the theory say the concepts are too vague, too flexible, too difficult to test, and nearly impossible to validate scientifically. As well, psychoanalysis has an overly mechanistic and deterministic view of human nature.

Resources

American Psychoanalytic Association (APsaA)
309 East 49th Street
New York, NY 10017
(212) 593-0571
http://apsa.org

This organization of approximately 3,500 members focuses on education, research, and development. It is a component of the International Psychoanalytical Association. The APsaA publishes the *Journal of the American Psychoanalytic Association* quarterly.

New York Psychoanalytic Society and Institute
247 E. 82nd Street
New York, NY 10028
(212) 879-6900
http://www.psychoanalysis.org

This organization provides training, treatment, and workshops in psychoanalysis.

International Psychoanalytical Association
Broomhills
Woodside Lane
London N12 8UD
United Kingdom
http://www.ipa.org.uk

This group is the largest worldwide psychoanalytic organization and accrediting body for psychoanalysis. It has 70 constituent organizations in 33 countries and 11,500 members; it focuses on debate, research, and training. The association interfaces with other groups to coordinate for worldwide activity. It conducts a biennial congress that is open to all.

Class Exercises and Activities

Theory

1. Do you think Freud's defense mechanisms are effective coping methods? Provide a rationale for your opinion. Do you think Jonathan's defenses are effective? Explain.

2. Critique Freud's theory in light of today's modern society. Do you think his theoretical constructs are applicable to mental health problems as diagnosed today?
3. What do you think is the future for Freud's theory? Will psychotherapists continue to use it? If so, in what way?

Practice

1. Bring a tape recorder to class. Pair up into teams of two. One student should play the role of Jonathan, and the other play the analyst. The analyst will formulate three interventions (clarification, confrontation, interpretation) for Jonathan. Then reverse roles.
2. Transcribe the simulated sessions recorded in exercise 1 above and analyze them. Take note of the speech patterns of both client and analyst. Comment on how the analytic dyad and the process transpired. What are the difficulties involved in "just listening"? Is it difficult to be an objective observing ego? Why?
3. Set up a tape recorder in a private place where you can recline comfortably. Lie down and pretend you are an analysand. Free-associate for 50 minutes. Analyze how you feel. Play back the tape recording and analyze your own reactions.
4. Look at the sample treatment plan in Chapter 1 (Figure 1.2). Use it to fill out a sample treatment plan for Tuti for psychoanalysis. (Both Jonathan's and Tuti's case histories are in Appendix A.)

Research

1. What is the evidence to show that psychoanalysis is efficacious or effective? What kind of research articles are available regarding psychoanalysis?
2. Taking a quick overview of the articles, describe and discuss the nature of the articles and the kind of evidence they contain to support their efficacy and effectiveness.
3. Perform your own evidence-based literature review. Record the key words you have used to search. What have your found? Do you believe the case studies are of any value to the psychoanalytic therapist? Why? Why not?

CHAPTER 4

PSYCHODYNAMIC THERAPY AFTER FREUD

. . . any line of investigation which recognizes these two facts [transference and resistance] and takes them as the starting-point of its work has a right to call itself psycho-analysis even though it arrives at results other than my own. But anyone who takes up other sides of the problem while avoiding these two hypotheses will hardly escape a charge of misappropriation of property by attempted impersonation, if he persists in calling himself a psycho-analyst.

–Sigmund Freud

The goal of this chapter is to present models of psychodynamic therapy that evolved after Freud's death. The chapter looks at the five major types of post-Freudians: (a) dissidents; (b) second-generation sociocultural analysts or neo-Freudians; (c) ego, object relations, and self psychologists; (d) short-term psychodynamic therapists, and (e) relational psychoanalysts. The chapter briefly describes salient features of the theory, practice, and research of these psychodynamic models.

✦ HISTORICAL CONTEXT

Psychoanalysis is the origin of modern Western psychotherapy. Its early history consists of a series of successive reactions to Freud's classical drive theory and his insistence that the major motives for behavior were libidinal and aggressive wishes (Eagle & Wolitzky, 1992). The rich legacy of Freud's psychoanalysis is difficult to capture in a single chapter because there are subtle distinctions among the many offshoots of his theory (Ellenberger, 1970). We will start with asking what happened to psychoanalysis immediately after Freud died.

Although it is difficult to categorize all the therapies that derived from Freud's classical psychoanalysis, for the purposes of this chapter these are organized into five different types. First are the therapies that represent those who openly disputed Freud's theoretical constructs. Two of these rebels—Alfred Adler and Carl Jung—pioneered their own therapies (Robbins, 1989). Jung's analytical therapy is discussed in this chapter, and Adler's psychotherapy is covered in Chapter 5.

The second group of therapies adapted Freud's basic psychodynamic theory to address social, cultural, and wider interpersonal factors. Karen Horney and Harry Stack Sullivan are two proponents of these therapies.

The third offshoot of Freud's theory consists of mainstream theorists who believe they represent the evolution of Freud's psychoanalysis. In other words, if Freud were alive today, his thinking would have developed in this direction. These therapies include ego analysis, object relations, and self psychology (Lachman, 1993).

Another group of psychodynamic therapists believe time, or length of psychoanalysis is an important variable that must be addressed to make psychoanalysis more useful and practical. Peter Sifneos, James Mann, David Malan, and Habib Davanloo have created models of short-term, or brief, dynamic therapy.

The final group of therapies derived from Freud is based on the relational model. These therapists believe they represent the future of psychodynamic therapy and the paradigm shift for psychoanalysis.

✦ ANALYTICAL PSYCHOLOGY

Carl Jung's major theoretical divergence from Freud initially concerned their differing concepts of the unconscious (see About Carl Jung box). Jung believed that Freud's view of the unconscious was negative and incomplete. He developed the notion of the *personal unconscious,* which was like Freud's unconscious, but Jung also believed in the *collective unconscious,* which housed *archetypes.*

ABOUT CARL JUNG

Carl Jung (1875–1961) was born in Switzerland. He was the fourth but only surviving child of Paul and Emilie Jung. His father was a rural minister. His mother, from a wealthy Swiss family, battled mental illness throughout her life.

After graduating from the medical school at the University of Basel, Jung worked in a psychiatric hospital in Zurich. He married Emma Rauschenbach in 1903, and the couple had five children (Hall & Lindzey, 1985).

From 1906 to 1914, Jung and Freud related on a professional and personal level. Jung was drawn to Freud's psychoanalysis after reading his works on interpreting dreams. Jung wrote to Freud, and after a series of intellectually stimulating correspondences, they met in Vienna and spent over 12 hours in conversation. This meeting of the minds prompted Freud to choose Jung as his crown prince and successor. Jung became the first president of the International Psychoanalytic Association. However, as Jung began to disagree with elements of Freud's theory, their relationship deteriorated and ended in a dramatic breakup.

After Jung resigned from the association, Jung and Freud never interacted again (Hall & Lindzey, 1985). Jung eventually created his own system of therapy called *individual analysis.* He traveled worldwide, visiting Africa, America, and India and incorporating many foreign ideas into his theoretical thinking. Jung's view of human nature became very different from Freud's. He saw human nature as teleological, with people motivated by their future aims and aspirations as well as driven by their past experience. He also believed in the importance of racial and ancestral origins. He saw the importance of myths, religion, symbols, spirituality, rebirth, and primitive functions to human personality. He died on June 6, 1961, in Zurich.

Jung also emphasized the mystical, spiritual side of life. Humans are motivated by a drive to develop a wholeness and unity over the life span. The psyche consists of all thinking, feeling, and behaving. It contains the conscious mind (ego, persona, attitudes, and functions) and the unconscious mind (the collective and personal unconscious). The ego is at the center of the conscious mind and monitors experiences for admission to the conscious.

The personal unconscious contains suppressed and rejected experiences and material that can be made conscious. The collective unconscious contains archetypes, which are primordial images from our racial and animal past. Four important archetypes exist. The *persona* is a mask, or a façade, that a person shows to the world. In the *anima/animus* archetype, the anima is the feminine side of the male, and the animus is the masculine side of the female. The *shadow* archetype reflects the animal instincts from lower forms of evolution within humanity. Although the shadow represents the dark side and strong emotion, it also houses creative urges and spontaneity. When the ego harnesses the shadow, the person is energized and creative; but without proper outlets, the person can be destructive of others and self. The self moves the person toward wholeness and is the center point, or the totality, of the personality (Douglas, 2005).

Jung created a psychological typology consisting of functions and attitudes. The two major attitudes, which are defined by the direction in which the energy or libido moves, are extroversion and introversion. *Extroversion* is an orientation toward subjective experiences, so extraverts are outgoing and energized by interpersonal relationships. *Introversion* is an orientation toward objective experiences, so introverts are energized by being alone, practicing introspection, and focusing on the inner world. All individuals have both opposing attitudes, but one tends to dominate in the individual's personality, so the less pronounced attitude becomes unconscious. The unconscious of the introvert is extraverted, and vice versa.

The four functions by which people take in and then understand internal and external stimuli are *thinking, feeling, sensing, intuiting*. One function is generally dominant and conscious, while the others are unconscious. Thinking and feeling are classified as rational functions because they involve making a judgment. Thinking emphasizes intellectual processes, so the thinking person tries to connect ideas, solve problems, and understand the world. Feeling is judgmental because it is the basis for accepting or rejecting stimuli based upon like or dislike and pleasure or displeasure. The feeling person reacts emotionally and focuses on emotions. Sensing means the operation of the sense organs. The sensing person looks for concrete evidence that he or she can see, taste, feel, touch, or hear. "Intuiting" means perceiving subliminally or at an unconscious level. Intuitive people use hunches to guide them. Sensation and intuition are not rational functions because the response to the stimuli is direct, without any form of evaluation.

Everyone possesses all four functions, but generally one is dominant. Attitudes and functions combine so that they create eight psychological types—introverted/thinking; introverted/feeling; introverted/sensing; introverted/intuitive and extroverted/thinking; extroverted/feeling; extroverted/sensing; extroverted/intuitive. Although people fall into these basic categories, every person is unique and possesses his or her own distinct combination and interaction of attitudes and functions.

Jung also emphasized that human development continues across the life span. He disagreed with Freud that the early years are the most important for personality development. Jung described four stages of life—early childhood, youth and young adulthood, middle age, and old age—and he stressed the importance of the third stage, in which a person turns to spiritual concerns over material matters.

Balance is a key concept in Jung's theory. Thus the goal in the practice of Jungian therapy is to achieve a harmonious balance and integration, to "consolidate the ego and let the psyche heal and responsibly enlarge itself so that all parts of the self can develop, reintegrate, and maintain a more balanced and less egocentric relationship with each other" (Douglas, 2005 p. 125).

Jungian Practice

By making the unconscious conscious and resolving inner conflicts, the Jungian therapist helps the client to fully access all parts of the personality and thus facilitates individuation and self-realization. There are four basic stages of therapy, which are not necessarily chronological:

- *Confession/catharsis:* the client shares secrets both intellectually and emotionally, discharges intense emotions, and the therapeutic alliance is initiated
- *Elucidation, or interpretation:* clarification of the meaning of symptoms, the archetypes, and the client's problems; transference and countertransference develop, are explored, and guide therapy
- *Education:* address any gaps in the client's development
- *Transformation:* bringing about the emergence of the self, an understanding of the client's unique personalities or self, and individuation and self-realization (self-actualization)

Jungian practice techniques include transference and countertransference, dream analysis or interpretation, active imagination, word association, and symbolism and rituals.

Transference and Countertransference

The therapist interprets and analyzes transference in four stages. In stage one the client sees the subjective value of the images that cause problems. In stage two, the client learns to differentiate what belongs to his or her own psyche from what belongs to the collective realm of culture and archetype. In stage three, the client grasps the personal reality of the analyst and is able to compare this to his or her internalized image of a therapist. Finally, the client acquires a realistic evaluation of the therapist and has formed a genuine, empathic connection (Douglas, 2005).

In Jungian practice, the therapeutic relationship is a fundamental tool that provides a safe place in which clients can explore their archetypal and personal unconscious within a supportive and healing dyad. The therapeutic alliance is a reciprocal process that affects both client and therapist. One person's healing and growth helps both client and therapist.

Dream Analysis or Interpretation

Dream interpretation allows the analyst and client to glimpse the client's unconscious. Jung believed dreams were the clearest expression of the unconscious and that they compensate for the neglected aspects of the client's psyche. Furthermore, he believed dreams provide insights into solutions to problems and help to outline future plans. Using a series method, Jung looked for a coherent pattern of dreams and searched for their meaning.

Other Jungian Techniques

In Jungian practice, *amplification* means the client and analyst give multiple associations to a particular dream element to clarify its symbolic meaning. Another dream analysis technique is *active imagination* in which clients are asked to focus on a visual image they spontaneously produced or to focus on a dream image. The *word association test* is a method of tapping into the unconscious, studying emotional content, and obtaining clues to complexes. The therapist reads a standard list of words and asks the client to respond with the first word that comes to mind. If a word elicits a delay in verbal response or some form of physiological arousal, it is thought to have tapped into a complex.

There is very little therapy outcome research on Jung's analytical psychology. His theoretical constructs are difficult to quantify, and thus comparisons are difficult to obtain. Jungians rely on clinical observation and case studies and use evidence from dreams, myths, fairy tales, religions, alchemy, and parapsychology and continue to do so today. Currently there are over 2,500 certified Jungian analysts who are members of the International Association for Analytical Psychology worldwide, with training from a variety of institutes (Richards, 1997).

✦ NEO-FREUDIAN PSYCHOANALYSIS

A second generation of neo-Freudians acknowledged Freud's concepts as significant in the formation of their own theories; however, these theorists strongly incorporated social, cultural, and interpersonal factors into their views of personality (Gilman, 2001). Two of the best known of these neo-Freudians are Karen Horney and Harry Stack Sullivan.

Karen Horney's Psychoanalysis

Horney's (1939, 1942, 1945, 1950) theory was a major challenge to Freud's notion of female sexuality (see About Karen Horney box). She claimed that female psychology should not be based on the notion of penis envy but on the need for equal status, power, and opportunity. Horney proposed that every human suffers from the basic anxiety of knowing he or she is helpless and vulnerable in the face of nature's vast and

ABOUT KAREN HORNEY

Karen Danielson Horney (1885–1952) was born near Hamburg, Germany, on September 16, 1885; she was the second child of four born to Clotilde and Berndt Danielson. Even as a child, Karen dealt with depression. She described her father as a strict disciplinarian and was very close to her brother Berndt. When she felt rejected by her brother, her depression worsened.

Karen devoted herself to schoolwork; because she felt unattractive, she saw academic achievement as her means to happiness. She earned a medical degree at the University of Berlin and trained as a psychoanalyst; she was analyzed by Karl Abraham, a colleague of Freud's (Hitchcock, 2004). In 1909, Karen married Oscar Horney, a law student, and the couple had three daughters. The marriage ended with Karen leaving Oscar in 1926 and formally divorcing him in 1937. She remained single for the rest of her life. In 1923, Horney's brother Berndt died as a result of lung disease, which led her into more depression, with intermittent thoughts of suicide.

Horney moved from Berlin to Chicago to be the associate director of the Chicago Psychoanalytic Institute in 1932. In 1934, she taught at the New York Psychoanalytic Institute, where she exchanged ideas about psychoanalysis with Eric Fromm, Harry Stack Sullivan, Abraham Maslow, and Medard Boss, among others (Quinn, 1987). Horney considered her theory and therapy to be consistent with the framework of psychoanalysis but a challenge to some of the ideas. In 1923, Horney presented a theoretical paper that defied Freud's notion of penis envy. She disagreed with Freud about the role of anxiety—how it arose and was handled—as well as his ideas about the interaction of id, ego, and superego and masochism. She believed psychoanalysis needed to shed instinct theory and saw human motivation as a way to protect basic security. Gaining a reputation as a maverick and a nonconformist with radical Freudian ideas, she was formally expelled from the New York Psychoanalytic Institute in 1941. She and other like-minded psychoanalysts organized the Association for the Advancement of Psychoanalysis and the American Institute for Psychoanalysis, where she was dean until she died (Gilman, 2001). Horney's stress on cultural, societal, and family influences as well as her optimistic view of human nature as it relates to change at all ages and stages influenced the field of psychotherapy and marriage and family therapy (Hyatt, 1977). She died of cancer in 1952 at the age of 67.

---

powerful forces. Good parenting in early years provides the child with the security to develop the strength to cope with these feelings. A lack of good parenting can result in neurotic distress. Parental mistreatment in early childhood results in the formation of basic anxiety and basic hostility. Basic anxiety or the "all pervading feeling of being lonely and helpless in a hostile world" (Horney, 1937, p. 89) is accompanied by basic hostility or the expectation of harm from others, resulting in guardedness and suspiciousness. Hostile feelings are repressed because the child fears that expressing them may invoke punishment and withdrawal of love from parents.

This puts in process the vicious circle: Basic anxiety leads to excessive need for affection; when these demands are not met, the child feels rejected and becomes even more hostile but must repress the hostility or lose the love he or she has. Not dealing with these intense emotions and suppressing them creates a diffuse rage, followed by an increased need for more affection. The circle is repeated.

The *real self,* which is a positive growth force that underlies self-realization in non-neurotics, fails to develop adequately. Individuals who suffer from basic anxiety and hostility deal with conflict poorly and develop neuroses. Their coping attempts involve the idealized self-image (unconscious image of self as powerful), the search for glory (attempt to be and live up to the idealized self-image), neurotic pride (false pride supporting the idealized self-image) and sources of self-hate (self criticism), the tyranny of the shoulds (impossible, rigid demands), and externalization (denial of thoughts and feelings and imputing them to others) (Hall & Lindzey, 1985). Soon they acquire self-hate, and eventually they are alienated from the self.

In the neurotic, the tyranny of the shoulds operates when the person fails to reach the goal of being the idealized self. The shoulds tell a person what he or she ought to do. Neurotics are ill prepared to deal with conflict, however, and because they use rigid ways of dealing with others, they block themselves from having satisfying relationships and diminish personal development. Horney theorizes that neurotics avoid conflict in three major, rigid, and unhelpful ways. They relate to others by

1. *Self-effacement,* which includes moving toward other people, seeking affection, or attempting to find safety by looking for the protection of others. This person acts in a way that is compliant and self-effacing.
2. *Expansion,* which is characterized by moving against people with a desire to dominate and exploit them and achieve their own way at any cost. This person acts in an arrogant, vindictive fashion and feels superior to others.
3. *Resignation,* which is characterized by moving away from and avoiding contact with others, withdrawing from interpersonal relationships and even from life itself. The person behaves in a way that lacks commitment and is despairing and anxious.

Practice of Horney's Therapy

The practice of Horney's therapy emphasizes that the therapist–patient relationship is mutual, cooperative, and democratic. Therapists continually analyze themselves while helping their patients and handling countertransference. Unlike an expert Freudian therapist, Horney believed the therapist must act like a real human being who is able to reveal who he or she is, with real faults and strengths, and who has a sincere respect for clients and a genuine interest in their well-being. Therapists should use all of their faculties—including reason, knowledge, intuition, and emotion—and almost forget about themselves while still maintaining a level of objectivity in reacting to the patient. Interpretations should be tentative, with truthfulness about the degree of certainty.

Therapists help clients give up defenses and replace a search for glory with self-realization; therapists also assuage clients' anxiety, reinforce their healthy drives, and encourage their struggle to change and to accept the self. While clients may not resolve all conflicts between healthy and neurotic forces, it is helpful if there is enough of a shift in the balance of power for clients to strive for growth and to continue to self-analyze. Thus healthy clients gain insight into their behavior, acquire self-confidence, and escape from the vicious circle to find new ways to behave. If therapy goes well, the central inner conflict is resolved. The client gives up the search for glory, tolerates uncertainty, and accepts limits.

ABOUT HARRY STACK SULLIVAN

Harry Stack Sullivan (1892–1949) was born in Norwich, New York, to immigrant Irish parents. He earned his medical degree from the Chicago College of Medicine in 1917. He served in the army in World War I as a major, and when he died in 1949, was buried in Arlington National Cemetery (Arlington National Cemetery, 2008).

He trained as a psychiatrist and worked with schizophrenics and other severely disturbed patients in St. Elizabeth's Hospital in Washington, DC. From 1922 to 1930 Sullivan worked at the Sheppard and Enoch Pratt Hospital in Towson, Maryland (Wake, 2007), where he set up a ward for male schizophrenic patients. He specialized in working with severely disturbed, psychotic patients, advocating that they were not hopeless cases and should not be forgotten in the back wards of mental institutions (Hall & Lindzey, 1985).

In 1931, Sullivan moved to New York to open a private practice, and he, Karen Horney, and Erich Fromm became friends. In 1936, Sullivan moved back to Washington, DC, and along with Horney and others founded the Washington School of Psychiatry. Sullivan also founded the journal *Psychiatry* and the William Allison White Institute of Psychiatry in New York (Rioch, 1986).

Details of Sullivan's personal life remain obscure. He advocated a liberal approach to working with homosexuality. He never married or had biological children, but lived with another man, whom he called his foster son, for 22 years (Allen, 1995). Rumors of his being homosexual were widespread but never confirmed (Wake, 2007). Sullivan said his theoretical thinking was influenced by Freud, Adolf Meyer, and William Alanson White. His form of psychodynamic therapy is called *interpersonal psychoanalysis*. He disagreed with Freud about the nature of the parent–child relationship, seeing it as the child's quest for security. His emphasis on the social-psychological view and interpersonal relations is the precursor to the emerging relational psychoanalysis of today. Sullivan died in Paris on January 19, 1949, of a brain hemorrhage (Perry, 1982).

Research on Horney's Therapy

Little research has been conducted by Horney or by the few who practice her work today. There is no controlled systematic research program. Currently, there is a small International Karen Horney Society with the goal of encouraging communication, research, practice, and exchange of information among people interested in Karen Horney's work.

Harry Stack Sullivan's Interpersonal Psychoanalysis

Sullivan believed psychiatry was the study of what occurs in interpersonal relationships between two people—and one of the persons might even be imaginary or only present in the mind (1953). He developed the interpersonal theory of psychiatry, which deviated from Freud's theory by stressing the dynamics of what goes on *between* people rather than what goes on *within* one person (see About Harry Stack Sullivan box). Personality exists, and can be understood, only within the context of interpersonal interactions.

The person is motivated to reduce tension and fulfill bodily needs, but the person also wants to minimize the insecurity that arises from trying to fulfill social and cultural needs, and that can cause the experience of anxiety. Anxiety, a tension that is the result of real or imagined threats to one's security within interpersonal relations, increases the need for security. The major motivation of personality is to avoid and reduce anxiety.

Thus anxiety is the motor of the personality and an educative influence. Anxiety is initially transmitted from the *mothering one,* the primary caretaker, to the infant through her behavior toward the infant, and influences personality development. According to Sullivan, there are three relatively stable personality characteristics:

- *Personifications* are internal mental images of the self and of others, pictures in the mind's eye that are the result of a complex of attitudes, feelings, and concepts. For example, a satisfying interpersonal relationship will produce a series of positive mental images of the mother as good; negative experiences will produce a series of negative mental images of the mother as bad.
- *Dynamisms* are behaviors or relatively enduring patterns of energy transformation, such as talking or fantasizing, that characterize interpersonal relations.
- The *self system* consists of two parts: the security system, which allows a person to defend against anxiety; and the personified self, which is how the person integrates how others perceive the person. The self system can form the good-me, consisting of positive feelings from the mothering one; the bad-me, which consists of feelings of disapproval from a punishing mother; and the not-me, the parts that were ignored or neglected.

Sullivan described three types of cognitive functioning: *prototaxic* (undifferentiated thinking or simple images, feelings, and sensations), *parataxic* (associational thinking or seeing causal relationships between events), and *syntaxic* (logical, realistic thinking allowing people to communicate). *Consensual validation* means logical thinking and learning, arriving at agreement, and validating it.

In Sullivan's theory, personality in Western European societies develops through stages: infancy, childhood, juvenile era, preadolescence, early adolescence, and late adolescence (Chapman, 1978; Hall & Lindzey, 1985). Infancy, from birth until speech occurs, lays down the fundamental experience with interpersonal interactions based on the infant's feeding experiences with mother. Childhood, from the learning of language to the need for playmates, begins the formation of personifications in the self system such as gender identification. The juvenile stage, lasting through grade school years, brings about an orientation in living so the person adapts to adjust to the demands of the real world. Preadolescence is a brief period in which peer relationships are formed and a need for a chum of the same sex emerges. Early adolescence is the time in which heterosexual activity occurs and ends when the person finds a way to satisfy his or her genital strivings. The person also struggles with conflicts produced among the need for sexual gratification, intimacy, and security. Late adolescence is a period in which the person transitions into adulthood.

Practice of Sullivan's Interpersonal Psychoanalysis

Sullivan's therapy practice focuses on correcting a person's harmful perceptions through the interpersonal therapeutic process (Seligman, 2005). When he worked with schizophrenics, and found free association increased anxiety, he stressed the role of communication between the therapist and patient. He saw the role of the therapist as that of a participant observer, skilled interviewer, and expert in interpersonal relations in order to draw out the patient's underlying thoughts and feelings. The therapist establishes a good respectful relationship, with an emphasis on nonverbal communication, keeping levels of anxiety at a controllable level, and reciprocity between therapist and client. Therapy is a learning process. Interpretations are simple and to the point. Therapy is complete and successful when the client's understanding of her- or himself is consistent with the consensually validated viewpoints.

Research on Sullivan's Interpersonal Psychoanalysis

Sullivan's research publications were few, but his lectures, especially those at Chestnut Lodge—an asylum for the mentally ill in Rockville, Maryland—and notes have been published by his descendants. Sullivan's major contribution to dynamic therapy is his stimulation about interpersonal relationships within psychoanalytic thinking and his application of psychoanalytic work to very disturbed clients (Chapman, 1978). He encouraged other psychiatrists to engage in research and founded the journal *Psychiatry* (Hall & Lindzey, 1985). Sullivan's ideas and work have been underappreciated by the psychotherapy community until recently with the revival of interest in relational psychoanalysis, but his writings were published posthumously by Helen Swick Perry, who also published a biography of Sullivan in 1982 (Perry, 1982).

✦ Ego Analysis and Object Relations/ Self Psychology

Ego analysis or psychology, object relations therapy, and self psychology are offshoots of Freud's psychoanalysis. They are psychoanalytically oriented psychotherapies created by followers of psychoanalysis. These followers extended Freud's theory in a way that Freud himself would have, had he lived long enough to see psychoanalysis mature and evolve.

Each of the three approaches—ego analysis, object relations theory, and self psychology—assesses different aspects of the person and his or her life conflicts and their consequences for treatment. Each of the three derivatives of Freud's psychoanalytic theory shares some commonalities and some distinctions in the theory and practice of psychotherapy. They vary primarily in how they conceptualize the formation of personality, pathology, client selection, the nature of the therapeutic relationship, the subgoals of therapy, and how the practice of psychotherapy is conducted—specifically, which techniques are used (St. Clair, 2004).

Ego Analysis

The best-known ego analysts are Anna Freud, Heinz Hartmann, Ernst Kris, Rudolf Loewenstein, David Rapaport, Erik Erikson, Edith Jacobson, Robert White, and

Margaret Mahler (who is also an important figure in object relations). This section briefly highlights some of the most notable work of Anna Freud, Heinz Hartmann and Erik Erikson.

Anna Freud (1895–1982), Freud's daughter and successor, was an ego analyst and the founder of child psychoanalysis. She worked directly with hundreds of children at Hampstead Clinic in London (her father saw only one child in analysis). She believed that normal development proceeded from an egocentric focus to an other-centered focus. Anna modified her father's view of drive theory to include the idea that the ego had the capacity to synthesize, integrate, and adapt to living.

In her book *The Ego and the Mechanisms of Defense* (1936), she expanded on Freud's original defense mechanisms and theorized that external factors play a role in how they her views dominated American psychoanalysis from the 1940s to the 1960s (Sandler, 1996).

Heinz Hartmann (1894–1970) left Vienna for the United States, and together with Ernst Kris and Rudolf Loewenstein, among others, created a broad-based ego psychology that was popular within academic psychology (Hale, 2000). Hartmann graduated from the University of Vienna with a medical degree and underwent analysis with Sigmund Freud. Fleeing the Nazis, he arrived in New York in 1941. He became a member of the New York Psychoanalytic Society and the president of the International Psychological Association in the 1950s. His theorizing about the independence of ego over drive theory, the role of external reality, and the average expectable environment made him an important contributor to the development of ego psychology.

Erik Erikson (1902–1994) was born in Germany. He developed a keen interest in psychoanalysis, graduated from the Vienna Psychoanalytic Institute in 1933, and was analyzed by Freud's daughter, Anna. He left Germany when the Nazis took over and settled in the United States, where he taught at several universities and worked as a clinician in a number of settings such as Austen Riggs in Massachusetts. He taught for 10 years at Harvard until he retired in the 1970s.

Erikson made a significant contribution to ego psychology in his book *Childhood and Society* (Erikson, 1950). A post-Freudian, he believed that development continued in psychosocial stages across the entire life span, including old age.

Theory of Ego Analysis

Although the ego analysts have fought theoretical battles with one another, they agree on a number of issues. In contrast to Sigmund Freud's view of the significance of drive theory or the role of the id in his early classical analysis, the ego analysts emphasize the importance of the ego. Followers who embraced this idea emphasized the role of the ego (as opposed to the id) in human personality functioning; they called themselves *ego psychoanalysts* rather than *id psychoanalysts*. They pointed out that as Freud reached the end of his life, he himself stressed the importance of the ego and, at the time of his death, was on his way to becoming an ego analyst.

Ego analysts generally believe that the ego has roots of its own, can function independently, master life's tasks, and obtain gratification apart from the id. The ego is a mediator of, but not necessarily at odds with, the id, the superego, and the reality of the outside world (Hartmann, 1939). As an integrator, the ego brings about harmony and equilibrium in a conflict-free sphere of functioning (Hartmann, Kris, & Loewenstein, 1964). The ego regulates human motivation and interpersonal relationships, and its adaptive functions include basic activities such as thinking, perceiving, remembering, and building ego strength as well as object relations and a sense of self and others (Liff, 1992). Ego analysts see human development occurring over the entire life span, with pre-Oedipal and later-in-life growth being as important as Oedipal development. Defense mechanisms, resistance, levels of consciousness, and the meanings of symptoms are seen similarly to how they are viewed by classical analysts.

Erikson (1950) is considered to be the ego analyst who extended Freud's notion of developmental stages. Each person faces psychosocial crises, or internal challenges, which are a part of life's key stages and govern growth and personality. Each crisis is a conflict between two opposing emotional pressures. In each stage of biodevelopment, the child negotiates with social forces, which interact with the physical and psychological forces. These psychosocial tasks must be negotiated successfully in order for normal development to take place. Erikson's eight stages are as follows with those of Freud indicated in parentheses in the following list (1950, 1968):

1. *Trust vs. mistrust* (oral: infancy): the child begins to learn to trust others. A failure to negotiate this stage makes one more likely to distrust others.

2. *Autonomy vs. shame and doubt* (anal: early childhood): the child begins developing a sense of autonomy. A failure to negotiate this stage makes one more likely to feel shame and insecurity.

3. *Initiative vs. guilt* (phallic: preschool age): the child begins taking on challenges and learning new skills. A failure to negotiate this stage makes one less purposeful, less likely to assume responsibility for tasks, and more likely to feel guilty.

4. *Industry vs. inferiority* (latency: school age): the child learns to master the tasks involved in constructive work, attends school, and develops social skills. A failure to negotiate this stage makes one feel inferior and socially awkward.

5. *Identity vs. role confusion* (genital: adolescence): the child learns who she is and how she fits into society. A failure to negotiate this stage causes one to suffer identity confusion and uncertainty about one's place in the world.

6. *Intimacy vs. isolation* (genital: young adulthood): the child is able to be close to others—friends, spouse, lover—and develops a clear sense of identity. A failure to negotiate this stage makes one less able to make a commitment to another and leaves the person feeling alone.

7. *Generativity vs. stagnation* (genital: middle age): the person is concerned with the next generation, and future generations, and produces children or work creations. A failure to negotiate this stage leaves one in a state of stagnation, without creativity.

8. *Integrity vs. despair* (genital: later life): the person comes to terms with life and the end of life. A failure to negotiate this stage makes one despair over how one has lived one's life.

Erikson's biodevelopmental theory asserts that if a stage is well negotiated, the person develops sufficient strength to navigate through the next psychosocial stage of life. However, if a stage is not successfully negotiated, maladaptations (too much of the positive and too little of the negative) and malignancies (too little of the positive, too much of the negative) arise and jeopardize mental health.

Practice of Ego Analysis

Like classical Freudians, the ego analysts initially assess clients by taking a detailed, careful history, delving as far into the past as possible. In general, assessment focuses on the ego and how it is functioning in relationship to the id and superego, but the ego analyst is most concerned with how the ego itself is working. The ego analyst appraises the client for anxiety, self-control, and levels of consciousness and how stages of development proceeded. He or she tries to identify the dynamic basis of the patient's problems by examining the quality of and conflicts occurring within current relationships.

The ego analyst is more of a collaborator than an authority in the treatment process. The ego analyst can play the role of an auxiliary ego and a role model and takes on a more supportive function to the client than does the classical Freudian analyst. The therapist can even act as a borrowed ego until the client can develop a stronger ego of his or her own (Blanck & Blanck, 1986).

The ego analyst's treatment goal is ego strength. To reach that goal, the analyst creates a conflict-free zone in which the patient can think, perceive, and remember. As the patient's ego functioning is widened, he or she develops a strong identity that will improve the client's ability to create intimate interpersonal relationships (Blanck & Blanck, 1986).

The ego analyst uses techniques similar to those of classical analysis, including free association and transference, and interpretations similar to those of psychodynamic therapy. The ego analyst can make interpretations about pre-Oedipal issues such as early mothering and feelings of loss and ego weakness. Therapy can center on reparative work that strengthens those areas where the psychosocial developmental stages were not well negotiated. The ego analyst focuses more on current problems as opposed to past fixations and is more likely to accept statements at face value and less likely to probe the client for deeper meanings, as did Freud.

Object Relations and Self Psychology

Therapists who can be loosely grouped as object relations theorists include Margaret Mahler, Melanie Klein (1975), W. Ronald D. Fairbairn (1952a, 1952b), D. W. Winnicott, Otto Kernberg (1976), John Bowlby (1973), Edith Jacobson, and James Masterson. Here we will highlight the work of Margaret Mahler as an example of an object relations theorist. The self psychologist we will study is Heinz Kohut.

Margaret Schönberger Mahler (1897–1985) attended medical school in Budapest, Hungary, where she met Sandor Ferenczi, an analyst, who sparked her interest in Freud's theory of the unconscious. She and her husband Paul Mahler immigrated to the United States in 1938 and settled in New York City where she founded a therapeutic nursery at the Masters Children's Centre. She worked with a large variety of children, ranging from normal to severely disturbed, conducting research on the effects of the mother–child interaction. Her major contribution to psychoanalytic theory was developing the separation-individuation theory. Her research observations of the attachment behaviors of mother and children in various stages of development changed both object relations and ego psychology and greatly increased understanding of how child development proceeded (Russo & O'Connell, 1992).

The basic constructs underlying both object relations and self psychology (see below) are complex, and it is helpful to be familiar with their vocabulary since it differs sharply from Freudian terms (St. Clair, 2004). In these theories, *object* is a technical psychoanalytic term. It refers to a person (or a thing) toward whom an action is directed. A human fulfills his or her drives with an object. For example, the hunger drive is satisfied by food or the breast, for the infant. *Representation* refers to how the person psychologically represents an object. There are external, observable objects, and there are internal mental representations of objects or mental images of the external world. Of particular interest are the inner representations of the self and others that influence and help to determine current perceptions and relationships or object relatedness. *Self-representation* is the "mental expression of the self as it is experienced in relationship with the objects (significant figures) in the environment" (St. Clair, 2004, p. 7). As the infant develops, he or she determines if an object is good or bad based on its ability to gratify or frustrate. Representations can also be parts rather than the whole object, as when the infant sees only the mother's breast and not her as a whole.

Structures are the parts of the personality or the psychological processes and functions that are stable and organized. These constructs are inferred through the person's behavior or inner experience. Different theorists have different views of the structure of the personality. *Splitting* is a mechanism of normal and defensive development processes. At birth, infants are dealing with so much stimuli that they are not capable of integrating their experiences into stable images. Splitting is used to separate the good and bad aspects of mother. *Projective identification* means a process in which parts of the self are split off and projected onto an external object (Malin, 1966).

Although there are a number of differences and subtle distinctions among the object relations theorists and the self theorists, they all reconceptualize specific instances of Freud's theory in four core areas: (a) the nature of objects, (b) the formation of psychic structures, (c) the developmental stages in relationship to objects, and (d) the formation of attachments (St. Clair, 2004, pp. 10–12).

Objects and Interpersonal Relationships

Object relations/self theorists believe humans seek interpersonal relationships naturally. Attaching to objects is an inborn, preordained mechanism. Libido seeks objects, not simply pleasure (Eagle & Wolitsky, 1992). This breaks from Freud's belief that biological drives are the basis of human motivations. The most important motivator of human behavior is striving for interpersonal relationships and not libidinal sexual and aggressive drives (St. Clair, 2004, p. 25).

Psychic Structures

For object relations/self therapists, the infant forms personality primarily from internalizing external objects through early interactions with the caretaker. Objects act as a guiding principle for the self, and they are the major organizers of personality. The child transforms interactions with external objects into part of his or her own self-regulation system, or psychic structures. Thus persons are shaped according to their relationships with significant others surrounding them. They focus on maintaining relations with others, but at the same time, they also attempt to differentiate themselves from others. People make internal representations of the self during childhood that are played out in adult relations, and they continue to act as they did in old object relationships as a way to master them and also to become free of them.

Developmental Stages

While object relations/self therapists differ in how they view the developmental stages and formation of personality structures, all of them see the pre-Oedipal phases of development as crucial. Most important is the child's move from fusion with the caretaker and dependence on the caretaker to independence and differentiation. The self emerges as relationships mature. The psychic structures form, and the quality of the relationship between the self and significant other differs at various stages of development. Development proceeds from the fused, undifferentiated self to the separated and independent self.

Attachment

Attachment, described by Bowlby, is a need to form intimate emotional bonds. The child and the caretaker form an attachment system. Their reciprocal behaviors help them to shape a close emotional bond. As the caretaker touches, feeds, comforts, and soothes the infant, the infant responds by smiling, clinging, and clutching. These attachment behaviors lay the groundwork for relationships later in developmental stages. The degree to which the caretaker can provide the child with a secure base brings about normal development. Infant responses can be categorized into secure, anxious/avoidant, anxious/resistant, or disorganized/disoriented attachment (Ainsworth, 1962; Ainsworth, Blehar, Waters, & Wall, 1978).

Margaret Mahler's (1968) research observations of the attachment behaviors of mother and children in various stages of development led her to theorize that the mother–infant relationship is the prototype that forms the basis for all future relationships. Internal objects modify and are modified by life experience, from early childhood to old age (Russo & O'Connell, 1992).

Focusing on the child's process of separation-individuation and object constancy, she described three phases of infant development. *Normal autism,* from birth to about a month, is the phase in which the infant sleeps and is in a state of primitive, hallucinatory disorientation and is objectless. *Normal symbiosis* (1 to 4 months) is the phase in which the child cannot differentiate self from environment since they are not seen as independent from each other. The *separation-individuation* phase is the period in which the child practices rapprochement, or separating from the caretaker and returning after exploration. It includes the following subphases: differentiation (5–10 months), practicing (10–16 months), rapprochement (16–24 months), individuation (5–10 months), and object constancy (24–36 months).

Self Psychology

The proponent of self psychology that we will feature here is Heinz Kohut (1913–1981). Kohut received his MD from the University of Vienna and moved to Chicago in 1940. He trained further in neurology and psychiatry at the University of Chicago, and he became a member of the Chicago Institute of Psychoanalysis.

Kohut's work, *The Analysis of the Self: A Systematic Analysis of the Treatment of Narcissistic Personality Disorders* (1971), introduced a new variant of psychodynamic therapy, called psychoanalytic self psychology, which expanded views of Freud's theory of narcissism. Kohut identified empathy as the essential way of knowing in psychoanalysis, and his work made him a pivotal figure in postmodern theories of psychoanalysis and self psychology (Strozier, 2001).

Self psychology has been described variously as a subcategory of object relations, as an advanced technique, or as its own model. Kohut's expansion of classical Freudian theory includes a nuclear self, a personality construct that stimulates empathic understanding, interpersonal interactions, self-esteem, and healthy adaptation. In the self psychology model, experiences during early developmental relationships (self–object experiences) form the core of the personality. Positive early self–object experiences can result in the formation of a strong, cohesive self with a healthy narcissism. Negative early self–object experiences bring about personality deficiencies such as narcissistic rage, which is a way to protect the self against fear and shore up the vulnerable self with a false sense of strength and self-esteem.

Kohut reframed Freud's concept of narcissism to be a part of normal development. It is distributed on a continuum and imparts self-esteem and self-confidence to the person. To the developing child, other people need gratifying. The child must identify with the idealized competence of figures who reflect back their self-worth and mirror empathic caregiving. This is how a child develops self-soothing skills as well, and this helps to grow a cohesive sense of self. Narcissistic disorders will generally develop when there is a lack of parental empathy.

The analyst must have empathic immersion in these subjective experiences. Interpretations, understanding, and explanation are offered after consideration of the client's subjective experience (Kohut & Wolf, 1978). While Kohut specializes in assessing for narcissistic personality disorders, Otto Kernberg is the analyst who specializes in borderline personality disorders.

Object Relations and Self Psychology Practice

Whereas Freud centered his attention on the neurotic personality and repression, the object relations and self theorists concentrate on deficits in the structure of personality that bring about difficulties within relationships. The Freudian analyst tries to uncover the cause of neurotic symptoms formed from conflicts among the id-ego-superego and from the unresolved unconscious childhood issues that emerge in adulthood with the ego defensively responding to libidinal urges.

The object relations and self theorists try to uncover the causes of pre-Oedipal problems (e.g., narcissism or borderline personality characteristics). Among them are a damaged self structure and/or deficits in the development of a healthy cohesive self that prevent the integration of psychic structures. Object relations and self psychotherapists look at the nature and quality of the mother–child relationship. Since they see personality as a function of self–object formation, they focus on how relationships were internalized and transformed into a sense of self throughout the stages of development, particularly in the early relationships.

Object relations and self theorists focus on the client's relationships as part of the diagnostic and healing processes. If the client has not integrated the various split-off parts of his or her personality and has deficits, he or she has not dealt with the primitive feelings or the chaotic, contradictory feelings that came about from poor interpersonal relationships (St. Clair, 2004). Object relations therapists assess how the child perceives the internalization of the relationship with the mother (or caretaker) and its effects on the adult personality. They assess for motivation that can come from both internal drives and from the outside world. Self psychologists assess self–object development and narcissism, or the weak vulnerable self, and damage to the structures of the self.

Whereas Freud emphasized transference, object relations and self theorists focus on relationships as part of the diagnostic and healing process (Summers, 1999).Therapists provide an immediate relationship to encourage clients to integrate the various split-off parts of their personalities, as well as to heal the personality deficits. By dealing with chaotic, contradictory feelings with the therapist, the client is able to manage all feelings in a more mature fashion. In addition, the therapist can serve as a borrowed ego until the client learns to handle these feelings productively (St. Clair, 2004). While the object relations therapist listens with empathy and becomes a good object to the patient, the self psychologist provides extreme empathy to the client. The client's fundamental clinical responsibility is to bring the important issues to the session. While the transference relationship is significant, there is more emphasis on empathy and collaboration. Sessions can range from once a week to four to five times a week.

Object relations and self therapists' goals are to help patients modify their inner object world or mental representations and to develop more mature interpersonal relations. Object relations therapists work to help the client replace the bad objects with good objects, which will improve interpersonal relationships outside of therapy with others and with the self. It will also increase the clients' self-esteem and allow them to improve their self-image. Self psychologists help clients to work through the failures of empathy that have occurred in the past by providing extreme empathy in the therapy relationship. This helps clients to achieve healthy narcissism— that is, a cohesive, strong, vital self, heading toward the self-realization of skills and talents and the development of an autonomous self with adequate self-esteem.

Many of the basic techniques used in classical analysis are used and adapted by object relations and self analysts. Countertransference is a necessary part of treatment, which is monitored by the therapist as an emotional barometer to identify the precise nature of the patient's projective identification. The therapist's response to the patient (countertransference) helps to identify and treat pathology (Cashdan, 1988).

The object relations analyst uses emotional linking to convey empathic understanding (Cashdan, 1988). The therapist transforms the conversation from a factual dialogue to an emotional one, shows the client he or she is on the client's side, and in order to bond may offer suggestions that will succeed. Interpreting transference is important in object relations practice but not the central activity. Interpretations revolve around early mothering, internalized objects, separation-individuation, loss, dependency, control, sexuality, and ingratiation. The therapist attends to the manner in which a client projects previous object relationships into the interactions with the therapist and helps to resolve pathology within the patient by helping him or her experience a real relationship with the therapist.

Self psychologists use empathic immersion or vicarious introspection, mirroring, and internalization of the therapist as a good object. These are ways to develop the extreme amount of empathy needed to help the client to confront feeling states on a feeling level. Since the client learned within a relationship, the way to unlearn is within a corrective relationship. The therapist is verbally and behaviorally firm and lets the client know the therapist will not participate in any pathological behavior. Mirroring transference is a way to give the client what was missed as well as an opportunity to see how these early relationships lead to problems. Empathy is an essential ingredient. The therapist becomes the idealized parent and listens, accepts, regards, understands, and explains.

What happens in ego analysis, object relations, and self psychology therapy that differs from classical analysis? Table 4.1 compares some of the major concepts of these theories and their practice, along with Freud's classical psychoanalysis.

Ego Analyis and Object Relations/Self Psychology Research

There are no long-term, randomized controlled outcome studies of ego analysis, object relations, and self psychology theories. Research on both efficacy and effectiveness of these therapies is sparse. The research that is available is based primarily on case studies. However, there is a great deal of general and related research (beyond the scope of this chapter) that demonstrates that attachment behavior is an important component of human adult behaviors and that developmental changes occur over the lifespan. Erikson (1974) is also noted for psychohistory research that took the form of in-depth study of the person using both psychoanalytic and historical research methods. For example, he wrote about the lives of historical figures such as Adolph Hitler and Mahatma Gandhi, offering rich hypotheses about how they became what they became.

Table 4.1			

Comparison of Classical Psychoanalysis with Ego Analysis, Object Relations, and Self Psychology Therapies

	Classical Psychoanalysis	Ego Analysis	Object Relations	Self Psychology
Human Motivation	Instinctual drives: sex and aggression	Ego itself and its functions independent of drives	Interpersonal relationships with others	Interpersonal relationships with others
Role of Therapist	Neutral	Auxiliary ego and role model	Is the good object	Provides extreme empathy
Emphasis on Issues in Treatment	Oedipal issues	Pre-Oedipal issues	Pre-Oedipal issues	Pre-Oedipal issues
Goals of Therapy	Control of libidinal drives Transform id into ego Insight into behavior that expelled defensive part of self again	Strengthen ego Develop conflict-free spheres of ego autonomy Understand ego defenses to adapt to world in positive ways	Replace bad objects with good objects Enhance interpersonal relationships with self and others Rework self-image	Attain adaptive ideal self Work through failures of empathy in therapeutic relationship
Well-Known Theorists	Sigmund Freud	Heinz Hartman Anna Freud Erik Erikson Margaret Mahler*	Melanie Klein W. R. D. Fairbairn Margaret Mahler* Donald Winnicott Otto Kernberg James Masterson	Heinz Kohut

*Mahler made contributions to both object relations and ego analysis.

✦ SHORT-TERM DYNAMIC THERAPY

Short-term therapy is another offshoot of Freud's psychoanalysis that alters the length of psychotherapy and thus limits the goals of the psychotherapeutic encounter. Short-term therapy, also called brief therapy, was part of the community mental health movement of the 1960s. The earliest clinicians who wrote about short-term therapy were psychoanalytically oriented (Bloom, 1997). Freud did not create psychoanalysis with a consideration of time as a variable of great importance, and he himself worked with some of his analysands on a short-term basis. For example, he worked with Little Hans in only several sessions. He treated the great composer and conductor Gustav Mahler for impotency and obsessions in a single four-hour session. However, as Freud aged and as his energy level and health declined, he saw fewer patients for longer periods of time—some for up to six years.

As psychoanalysis evolved and became more complex, its treatment goals became more inclusive; the acceptable length of treatment extended and became customary (Budman, 1981). Research did not play a role in determining the appropriate length of psychoanalysis or psychodynamic psychotherapy (Budman & Gurman, 1988).

Eventually, some psychoanalysts recommended reducing the number of sessions in an effort to make therapy more efficient and effective. Franz Alexander, in the Chicago Psychoanalytic Institute, was one of the first to shorten classical psychoanalytic procedures in the 1940s but met with resistance from the medical community (Lipsitt, 2001). Sandor Ferenczi (1873–1933), a Hungarian psychiatrist, advocated a more active role for the analyst. Hans Strupp and Lester Luborsky studied the effects of shortened psychodynamic therapies in the academic setting at the University of Nashville (Messer & Warren, 1995).

Sociological demands continued to pressure psychotherapists to develop effective brief interventions. World War II created a need for short-term treatment for shell-shocked soldiers so they could return to battle or regain their mental health after the war. Franz Alexander and Thomas French's work on short-term treatment was published in 1946, which challenged some of the assumptions of long-term therapy. They discussed the corrective emotional experience, meaning that patients were helped if they experienced an emotional response with therapists in a safe relationship that allowed patients to handle situations more positively. They claimed that the changes that they observed in their patients after short-term treatment were not necessarily less stable, less profound, or less permanent than long-term work.

Other social forces also spurred interest in short-term work. Long waiting lists at clinics concerned clinicians. The Coconut Grove nightclub fire in Boston in November 1942 claimed 492 lives. The event encouraged Erich Lindemann, a psychoanalytic therapist, to design a crisis intervention therapy to treat those among the 500 survivors suffering from posttraumatic stress disorder who wanted therapy. The community mental health movement of the 1960s reached out to a diverse client pool; the current managed-care system in the United States has created additional pressure for brief treatment.

Bernard Bloom (1997) sees three generations of short-term therapists. First, as mentioned, Freud himself conducted short-term therapy. The second generation of short-term therapists consisted of the psychodynamic therapists, described earlier. The third generation of short-term therapists consists of today's cognitive, solution-based, and interpersonal clinicians, among others (Austad, 1996). Four well-known individuals who developed short-term dynamic therapies are Peter Sifneos (1992), Habib Davanloo (1990, 2001), David Malan (1976), and James Mann (1973). The following discussion draws heavily from their original works.

Sifneos founded *short-term anxiety provoking therapy,* which has a psychodynamic focus on problems of unresolved Oedipal issues, separation, or grief. He actively uses anxiety-provoking confrontation and clarification and deals with transference clearly and directly. He terminates the treatment when there has been a change in the client's neurotic behavior. His selection criteria are restrictive and include clients who have circumscribed symptoms, have Oedipal issues, and are reasonably mentally healthy and motivated for treatment. Clients must be psychological minded and flexible in their abilities to interact with the therapist (Sifneos, 1992).

Malan created the *Tavistock system of short-term dynamic psychotherapy.* He discusses client resistance using two triangles that Davanloo later named and adopted in his own work. The *triangle of conflict* consists of the impulse, the defense, and the anxiety, as in symptom formation in the psychoanalytic theory. These feelings originate in the client's past, and when they emerge into consciousness, the client feels anxious. To handle and decrease the anxiety, the patient uses defenses, which push the feelings back into the unconscious. The therapist interprets conflicts by linking impulse, defense, and anxiety in order to help the client face his or her fears and reduce the need for further defenses. The *triangle of person* represents significant people from the past (e.g., primary caretakers, parents, significant others), current relationships, and the therapist. The client's emotions from the past can be set off in current relationships and also in the therapy relationship. The therapist interprets the triangle of person to the client and develops useful connections between the patient's past and transference in the present. Meaningful interpretations can link any of these components.

From the 1960s to the 1990s, Davanloo—a psychiatrist born and schooled in Canada—developed his therapy, called *intensive short-term dynamic psychotherapy.* He was dissatisfied with the length of time it took for clients to undergo psychoanalysis but wanted to remain faithful to the tenets of traditional psychoanalytic theory. In his form of psychodynamic psychotherapy, he uses techniques that he believes are the most efficient in breaking through the client's resistance. The major primary goal of intensive short-term dynamic psychotherapy is to help patients overcome unconscious resistance to experiencing feelings that have been repressed because facing them is painful and frightening. Davanloo presses the client for material, relentlessly challenging any defenses. He asks the client to experience the feelings to the maximum degree possible as quickly as possible. Davanloo claims that rapid character change can occur if the therapist assists the patient to break through and give up his or her defenses against emotional experience (Schubmehl, 1996). His techniques mobilize clients' unconscious therapeutic alliance so they reveal their core feelings and conflicts underlying character problems. Davanloo adopted Malan's triangles of conflict and person in his therapy (Davis, 1990).

Mann created *time-limited psychotherapy.* In this form of therapy, time is of the essence as an ingredient within psychotherapy. Mann limits the psychotherapy to exactly 12 hours of treatment. The end date is determined from the first session. By specifying a limited time, the client and therapist are confronted with the reality of the work to be done and the limits that must be faced. Since life consists of many separations from people, this therapy provides an opportunity to work through the feelings that accompany these comings and goings. Mann also focuses on four major central issues: independence versus dependence, activity versus passivity, adequate self-esteem versus diminished self-esteem, and unresolved grief.

Short-Term Dynamic Therapy Practice

Assessment

Short-term psychotherapists perform an initial assessment in a face-to-face interview. History taking is limited to what is needed to appropriately assess how well the patient will respond to the treatment. Sifneos and Malan avoid treating any pre-Oedipal problems, whereas Davanloo and Mann are not as exclusive and will assess the client's ability to tolerate the intensity of therapeutic interventions. Sifneos and Malan accept highly motivated clients with sufficient ego strength and a specific chief complaint or problem focus. Davanloo accepts clients who can tolerate his relentless interpretations. Mann selects clients who have a negative self-image as a result of separations, loss, or feelings of regret.

Therapeutic Relationship

For Sifneos, the therapist is an educator and a friend; for Davanloo, the therapist is emotionally neutral and able to accept intense transference, because inevitably, the client will soon be irritable and angry at the therapist. For Malan, the therapist makes simple initial formulations and has intuitive understanding. For Mann, the therapist is the timekeeper who is working with a client who is motivated and adheres to the 12-session limit imposed by the therapy.

Presenting Problem

All four therapists believe that presenting problems are symptoms of unconscious forces. Sifneos, Davanloos, and Malan look for and select clients based upon Oedipal issues in the presenting problems as well as unresolved grief and separation issues. Davanloo and Malan interpret the client's anxiety to be generated as a function of impulse, or defense anxiety. Davanloo expands his eligibility and feels that those with severe disturbances—such as obsess ional neurosis, phobias, and other severe forms of conflict—qualify. Mann looks for central foci that take the form of independence, activity level, self-esteem, and grief.

Goals and Treatment Plans

The goals of these four therapists are short term but are intended to effect permanent change. For Sifneos, emotional reeducation and improving problem-solving skills is the intended goal of therapy. For Davanloo and Malan, the goal is to resolve the central problems in the triangle of conflict and triangle of person by raising consciousness and the patient's experiencing of the conflict in the therapeutic dyad. Mann's goal is to help the client to reduce the negative self-images he or she acquired as a function of the losses and separations life brings, to counteract the nontherapeutic effects of time, and to focus.

Therapeutic Techniques

As in all analytically based therapies, many techniques from classical analysis are, but the emphasis differs as a function of theoretical orientation. All four therapists use confrontation, clarification, and exploration. However, all of them challenge defenses with much more vigor than the classical analyst. For example, Malan has challenged the wisdom of passivity in dealing with resistance. He interprets conflicts by linking the impulse, the defense, and the anxiety. He also uses interpretation to develop useful connections between the patient's past and the transference in the present. Davanloo uses these same techniques, but he uses repetition and will not allow the patient to avoid experiencing anxiety. He nearly implodes the patient with anxiety by not preventing any resistance or avoidance. He relentlessly pursues until the defense is broken down. He inquires into the problem, focuses on the problem, labels defenses, and interprets as the client gets more uncomfortable, increases resistance, and challenges defenses. The client becomes angry, and these impulses break through defenses. The unconscious material is more accessible, and the client experiences relief, sadness, grief, and, ultimately, freedom from the bound-up emotions. The client is able to resolve conflicts as the unconscious material becomes conscious. Sifneos uses early repeated interpretations of resistance, ambivalence, and negative transference. Mann uses the time limit of 12 sessions to bring about the therapeutic change (Bloom, 1997).

Course of Therapy

The therapies of Sifneos, Davanloo, and Malan range from 10 to 25 sessions with once-a-week attendance. Mann is very specific about the 12-session limit. For Sifneos, the beginning of therapy is the patient–therapist encounter and the height of treatment occurs when it is clear there is evidence of real change. For Davanloo, the beginning of therapy is the patient–therapist inquiry into the problem followed by an agreement about the focus and the labeling of the patient's defenses. Complete symptom relief is at the end of therapy. For Mann, therapy is divided into thirds. In the beginning third, the patient has rapid symptomatic improvement. During the second third, the patient's enthusiasm wanes. In the final third, termination occurs.

Outcome

In successful short-term therapy, patients emerge with stronger egos, have better internalized object relations, or have a better sense of self. For Sifneos, the successful outcome is tangible evidence of a change in neurotic behavior. The client has a clear understanding of the conflicts that caused the problems. The symptoms are absent. There are improved relationships with others and an increase in problem-solving, self-esteem, and adaptive skills. For Davanloo, outcome measures are freedom, relief from sadness, and grief as unconscious material becomes conscious. For Malan and for Mann, outcome success is the ability to solve new emotional problems long after treatment has terminated.

Short-Term Dynamic Therapy Research

Psychodynamic therapy has received a great deal of research attention. A number of meta-analyses have been conducted, beginning with Mary Lee Smith, Gene Glass, and Thomas Miller (1980). Through the years, many more meta-analytic studies have been conducted with the results showing that psychodynamic therapy usually brings about improvement in significantly more clients than untreated controls and is generally just as effective as other therapies to which psychodynamic therapy is compared. Although some authors report that behavior therapy and cognitive therapy are consistently superior to psychodynamic models in some studies, the differences are small, and the allegiance effect can account for that.

Short-term psychodynamic therapy has also received quite a bit of research attention (Anderson & Lambert, 1995). Some studies found psychodynamic therapy to be less effective than behaviorally oriented therapies. However, defenders of psychodynamic models argue that the differences were small and could be caused by an allegiance effect (Crits-Christoph, 1992). The findings about short-term psychodynamic therapy are similar to those of psychodynamic psychotherapy in general. The accumulation of evidence indicates that short-term psychodynamic psychotherapy is superior to no-treatment controls and to treatment as usual (Leichsenring & Leibing, 2003; Leichsenring, Rabung, & Leibing, 2004).

Other researchers have pointed out that since four of the published meta-analyses of short-term psychodynamic psychotherapies found conflicting results, an evidence-based review for short-term dynamic psychotherapies for common mental disorders was in order (Abbass, 2006; Abbass, Hancock, Henderson, & Kisely, 2006). The authors evaluated the efficacy of short-term psychodynamic psychotherapies in comparison to minimally treated and untreated controls. They searched for all randomized controlled studies of clients, with common mental disorders, who received short-term psychodynamic therapy for 40 sessions or less. They interpreted the results of 23 studies representing a total of 1,431 clients. For general somatic, anxiety, and depressive symptom reduction, as well as social adjustment, there was greater improvement in the psychodynamically treated group over the control groups, and in medium and long-term follow-ups, these improvements were maintained. The authors concluded that short-term psychodynamic psychotherapy shows promise. Of course, the limitations of studies from the past are the heterogeneity between studies, variability in treatment delivery, and the vicissitudes of treatment quality. (The Abbass et al., 2006, study is an excellent example of a well-conducted Cochrane evidence-based review. A summary of it and the abstract can be found in the online Appendix C.

Today, models of short-term therapy are no longer limited to shortened versions of psychoanalysis. There are many forms of short-term work that are not psychodynamic. Short-term therapies can be classified into five broad orientations: (a) psychoanalytic; (b) behavioral, cognitive, and cognitive behavioral; (c) eclectic; (d) crisis intervention; and (e) other verbal therapies. Short-term therapy is now defined as a therapy in which the clinician intentionally limits the length and the goals of treatment. It ranges from a minimum of 1 session to a maximum of approximately 20 sessions. When compared to long-term therapy, the goals and the length of treatment are intentionally limited. Table 4.2 compares the fundamental differences and characteristics of long- and short-term therapies (Budman & Gurman, 1988; Koss & Shiang, 1994).

Table 4.2	
Characteristics of Long-Term and Short-Term Therapy	
Long-Term Therapy	**Short-Term Therapy**
Goal is change in core of personality or character change.	Goal is to help patient function as well as possible.
Presenting problem is tip of iceberg.	Presenting problem taken at face value.
Therapy has no time limits and will take however long it takes.	Therapy should have definite time limits.
More is always better.	Shorter is better and more efficient.
Emphasis on pathology of early childhood.	Emphasis on current developmental period and life span development.
Beginning, middle, end have distinct tasks such as building rapport and interpretations.	Specific focus.
Therapist activity low.	Therapist activity high.
Emphasis on what happens in therapy.	Emphasis on what happens outside of therapy, homework, support groups, significant others.
Patient selection restricted.	Patient selection less restrictive.

Short-term psychotherapy has evolved over the past 20 years, and it is increasingly regarded as an appropriate and effective intervention. In their extensive reviews of the literature, Mary Koss and Julia Shiang (1994) point out that the era has ended in which short-term therapy is considered to be a separate category from "real" psychotherapy.

The overall conclusions about short-term therapy from the extensive research have yielded the following conclusions. When short-term therapy is a treatment of choice, it can be effective and can bring about positive changes for a wide range of problems and for specific populations such as those who present with poor interpersonal relations, grief, loss, depression, job stresses (chronic, severe, and health), if treatment goals are kept within reason. Short-term techniques have reported the same success rates as longer term treatment. Nearly 75 percent of clients who benefit from therapy do so within the initial 6 months of treatment. It is generally recognized that clients expect a focused treatment with focal problem resolution when they enter therapy. Comparative studies of short-term and time-unlimited therapies show similar results for a number of problems. Currently, clients who have had long-term follow-up show improvement for several years after treatment.

Research also indicates that in short-term therapy the therapeutic alliance is important for success. Furthermore, therapy received on an intermittent basis is becoming more accepted. The research reviewed suggests that both long- and short-term therapies are similar in their effectiveness, yet thorny problems must be faced when trying to compare long-term and short-term therapy. Multiple layers of variables are involved, so differentiating between long- and short-term therapy can be complicated. In many studies, no distinction has been made between different types of long-term or short-term therapy. As mentioned earlier, the length of short-term therapy can vary from 1 session to 20 sessions with a large variance in how the pattern of sessions is distributed; 20-session therapy over a 2-year period may differ from 20-consecutive-weeks therapy. Furthermore, other issues—such as the client's psychological health and the chronic nature and severity of the client's symptoms—have a bearing on the success of therapy.

All these factors should be considered when designing and interpreting research. It will come as no surprise that research shows that some types of clinical populations may need longer-term psychotherapy. For example, in the dose-effect studies, borderline clients seem to need more therapy to show improvement than other groups of psychiatric patients (Howard, Kopta, Krause, & Orlinsky, 1986; Howard, Moras, Brill, Martinovich, & Lutz, 1996).

✦ RELATIONAL PSYCHOANALYSIS

Jay R. Greenberg and Stephen A. Mitchell published *Object Relations in Psychoanalytic Theory*, the first major work representing relational psychoanalysis, in 1983. Unfortunately, Mitchell died an untimely death in December of 2000. At the time of their book's publication, Greenberg and Mitchell (1983) viewed psychoanalysis as a changing field about to undergo a paradigm shift (Greenberg, 2001). They believed that for psychoanalysis to survive, it must change—that it would be better to discard out-of-date Freudian concepts than to become an outdated therapy that did not meet the needs of today's patients.

In Mitchell and Greenberg's view, psychoanalysis is divided into two broad perspectives—the drive model (expressed in classical Freudian theory) and the relational model, or the evolving new trends. At the time of his death, Mitchell was exploring therapies within the relational model and was attempting to integrate them into a comprehensive interpersonal perspective. The major concepts of relational psychoanalysis are discussed next (Masling, 2003).

Relational psychoanalysis is a form of psychotherapy that concentrates on relationships. The *relational matrix*—which includes the self, the object, and interpersonal transactions—is the organizing principle and a perspective for interpreting clinical data. Early formative relationships with caretakers and other significant figures form personality.

Relational analysis differs from other forms of psychoanalysis in several ways. It recognizes the personal influence that the psychoanalyst exerts on the client. The relationship is *intersubjective,* meaning that both parties influence it. Two people are involved in the therapeutic relationship, and every therapist–patient relationship has distinct characteristics. What transpires between the two is not predictable and is a function of the unique combination of a particular therapist interacting with a particular patient. The detached neutrality that Freud insisted upon cannot exist because the analyst is a subjective, not an objective, observer and participant. Both analyst and patient influence each other. This recognition is moving psychoanalysis from a traditional one-person psychology to a two-person analysis and psychology.

Relational psychoanalysts believe the primary motivation of humans is to be in relationships with others. Early relationships with primary caretakers mold the child's expectations about future relationships and how to go about meeting needs. Thus motivation is affected by the systemic interaction of a person and his or her relational world. People try to satisfy their needs as they did in early relationships and re-create these early learned relationships in current relationships that may have little or nothing to do with those early relationships. This re-creation is called *enactment.*

In addition to facilitating insight, the therapeutic relationship stresses a healing relationship to help clients break harmful or self-defeating patterns of relating to others. The relationship between client and analyst is one of active involvement. The techniques used by relational psychoanalysts include insight and the corrective emotional experience.

There are a variety of therapeutic styles, some stressing a mixture of waiting and authentic spontaneity, and some using more traditional techniques. Others emphasize the importance of a genuine relationship with the patient, and still others are far more restrained and rely upon well-formulated interpretations with good timing.

The relational model includes concepts from object relations, interpersonal psychoanalysis, and self psychology. The belief is that psychoanalysis should let go of drive theory; the analyst should have greater involvement in the therapeutic relationship and should trust the self-correction of psychoanalysis (Masling, 2003). The relational model represents what many therapists believe is the future for psychoanalysis.

SUMMARY

- Psychoanalysis spun off a number of new therapies after Freud's death. Post-Freudian models of psychodynamic therapy were created by dissidents from Freud's group; neo-Freudians; ego, object relations, and self psychologists; short-term psychodynamic therapists; and relational psychoanalysts.

- Direct followers of Freud who broke with him include Jung, whose analytical psychology contained unique concepts such as the collective unconscious, archetypes, attitudes, and functions. Jung's therapy goals are to help the client to achieve integration, individuation, and self-realization with techniques of transference, countertransference, dream interpretation, and word association. Jungian research is based on case studies.
- Neo-Freudians added the social, cultural, and interpersonal to psychoanalysis. Horney's female psychology is based on the need for equal status and not on penis envy. Therapy practice emphasizes a genuine, mutual, respectful therapeutic relationship.
- Sullivan's interpersonal psychoanalysis sees the person within an interpersonal context. In practice, the therapy relationship is one of respect. Therapy goals are to correct harmful perceptions and control anxiety. Research was limited, with few publications.
- Ego analysis or ego psychology deemphasizes drive theory, underscores an autonomous ego, with development over the life span. The therapist acts as collaborator and auxiliary ego. Goals of treatment are to foster ego strength in a conflict-free zone, strengthen identity, and improve interpersonal relationships. Techniques consist of interpretations of pre-Oedipal issues, repair of psychosocial development, and an emphasis on current problems.
- Theories of object relations and self psychology emphasize the nature of objects, psychic structures, developmental stages, and attachment. Therapeutic relationships are immediate, encouraging, and deal with feelings. The object relations therapist is a good object. The self psychologist provides extreme empathy. Therapy goals are to change mental representations. Techniques vary for object relations and self psychology. Research is based primarily on case studies.
- Short-term dynamic therapies arose as a result of social, economic, and practical demands. Assessment is for appropriate patient selection. Therapeutic relationships are active with focused goals and treatment plans. Therapy techniques include traditional analytic methods, but defenses are challenged with more vigor. Therapy lasts from 10 to 25 sessions.
- In Sifneos's short-term anxiety-provoking therapy, the therapist is an educator and a friend. The focus is on resolving Oedipal issues, separation, or grief. In Malan's Tavistock system, the therapist makes simple initial formulations. The goal is to resolve the central problems in the triangle of conflict and triangle of person. In Davanloo's intensive psychotherapy, the therapist handles intense transference through relentless interpretations. The goal of therapy is to effect rapid character change. In Mann's time-limited psychotherapy, the therapist is the timekeeper. The goal of therapy is to reduce negative self-images, to counteract nontherapeutic effects of time, and to focus on independence, activity levels, self-esteem, and grief.
- Research evidence for short-term psychodynamic psychotherapy shows it is superior to no-treatment controls and to treatment as usual.
- Short-term therapy not only includes psychodynamic therapy, but also behavioral, cognitive, eclectic; crisis intervention, and other therapies.

- Relational psychoanalysis may be the model that represents a future paradigm shift for psychoanalysis.

RESOURCES

International Association for Analytical Psychology (IAAP)
http://iaap.org

The International Association for Analytical Psychology (IAAP) is based in Zurich, Switzerland. Founded in 1955, it is an international association of those who practice psychology in the tradition of Jung.

The Karen Horney Clinic
329 East 62nd Street
New York, NY 10021
(212) 838-4333
http://www.karenhorneyclinic.org

The Karen Horney Clinic offers a variety of treatment programs as well as training programs and internships for mental health professionals and students of social work and psychology.

Object Relations Institute for Psychotherapy & Psychoanalysis
511 Avenue of the Americas, #52
New York, NY 10011
(212) 268-8638
http://www.orinyc.org

The institute provides training in object relations psychotherapy from theorists and authors contributing to the current and growing psychoanalytic literature. It also sponsors an annual workshop series and other educational activities.

Los Angeles Institute and Society for Psychoanalytic Studies (LAISPS)
12011 San Vicente Boulevard, Suite 310
Los Angeles, CA 90049
(310) 440-0333
http://www.laisps.org

The LAISPS offers in-depth instruction in the theory and methods of psychoanalysis. The institute provides training to many types of clinicians such as physicians, marriage and family therapists, social workers, and psychologists. The student can learn about ego psychology, object relations, self psychology, intersubjectivity and relational theory.

Davanloo's Intensive Short-Term Dynamic Psychotherapy (IS-TDP)
http://www.is-tdp.eu

This is the official European website, which provides information facilitating contact with individuals or groups interested in Davanloo's work. The site lists source material in the form of textbooks and articles. There are also referrals to training in Davanloo's IS-TDP offered.

CLASS EXERCISES AND ACTIVITIES

Theory

1. Discuss the major differences among the ego analysts and object relations and self psychologists. How would you explain Jonathan's symptoms from each of these perspectives? (Use the case study of Jonathan in Appendix A.)
2. Pretend you are Carl Jung, Karen Horney, and Harry Stack Sullivan. Sigmund Freud asks you, "Why did you change my theory?" How would you explain your theoretical differences?
3. Does relational psychoanalysis represent a dramatic shift in thinking from classical psychoanalysis? Why or why not?

Practice

1. Which of the post-Freudian therapy techniques do you favor? Why?
2. Think about the differences between Freud's view of personality development and Erikson's view. Which do you think is more meaningful? Why?
3. Look at the sample treatment plan in Chapter 1 (Figure 1.2). Choose two psychodynamic therapies and use them to fill out the treatment plan for Tuti. (Both Jonathan and Tuti's case histories are in Appendix A.)

Research

1. Conduct a review of ego analytic therapies using the following key words in PubMed: *ego analytic* and *ego psychology*. What did you find? Limit your search to *ego analysis randomized control*. What did you find? Conduct a review of self psychology therapies using the following key words in PubMed: *self psychology*. What kind of articles did you find looking at the review? Now limit your search to *self psychology randomized control*. What did you find?
2. Conduct the same literature search using PsycINFO if it is available to you.
3. What kinds of articles about any of the post-Freudian therapies are currently available? Making a quick overview of the articles, describe and discuss the nature of the articles and the evidence upon which they are based.

CHAPTER 5

Adler's Individual Psychology

Those of you who really understand individual psychology and have learned to apply it carry a heavy responsibility.

–Alfred Adler

The goal of this chapter is to present a general overview of Alfred Adler's model of individual psychology. The chapter looks at biographical information about Adler, the historical context of Adlerian therapy, and the theory, practice, and research of this model. The simulated psychotherapist, Dr. Mary Allan, presents a treatment plan and some excerpts from therapy sessions for the case of Jonathan. Issues of diversity and major critiques are also included.

← Historical Context

Alfred Adler (see About Alfred Adler box) was influenced by a number of philosophical, political, and social factors in the formation and development of individual psychology. The most important influences are psychoanalysis, Vaihinger's philosophy, feminism and social justice, holism, and prevention.

Psychoanalysis

Adler's contact with Freud's psychoanalytic circle from 1902 until 1911 helped stimulate Adler's thinking about his own theory and therapy. He agreed with Freud's basic idea of psychodynamics and that personality is formed at an early age (Von Sassen, 1967). But as Adler argued with Freud, Adler strengthened his theoretical emphasis on a holistic, teleological view of humans and the importance of family constellation, community, and society (Cushman, 1992). He envisioned psychotherapy to be a means to help the client develop social interest, not just a way to gain insights into childhood conflicts (Vande Kemp, 2003).

While Freud certainly influenced Adler, some contend Adler's effect on modern psychoanalytic thinking is substantial and that it is Adler who laid the foundation for later theoretical developments in psychoanalysis (Freedheim, 1992). There are even those that argue that "neo-Freudians might more appropriately be called the neo-Adlerians" (Ansbacher & Ansbacher, 1967, p. 17).

ABOUT ALFRED ADLER

Alfred Adler was born on February 7, 1870, in Austria. Third in a family of six siblings, Alder described his childhood as unhappy as he competed with his older brother for his mother's attention (Mosak & Maniacci, 1999). Adler had a good relationship with his father, a middle-class Jewish grain merchant. Adler's early memories are of walking through the woods with his dad, who told Alfred not to believe anything, giving him early training in intellectual skepticism. When Alfred was failing mathematics in school, his father scoffed at a teacher who advised that Alfred should be a cobbler, but he also challenged Alfred to change his ways. Alfred lived up to his father's expectations and earned the highest grade in the class in math (Alfred Adler Institute, 2007).

Illness played a decisive role in Adler's life, as he suffered from a mild spasm of the vocal cords, had awkward physical movements, and did not walk until he was 4 years old due to rickets. His younger brother died of pneumonia in bed next to him when Adler was 4. When Adler also contracted pneumonia at age 5, he overheard his doctor say he was so ill he might die, and he vowed at that moment to become a physician (Grey, 1998). True to his promise, Adler completed his medical degree at the University of Vienna in 1895.

In 1897, Adler married Raissa Timofeyewna Epstein, a member of the wealthy Russian intelligentsia. Raissa was an irreligious political revolutionary and an ardent feminist, who would influence Adler to be sensitive to feminist issues as well (Hoffman, 1996). The couple had four children: Valentine, Alexandra, Kurt, and Cornelia. Alexandra and Kurt, both psychiatrists, actively maintained an interest in modern Adlerian therapy (Kaiser, 1995).

Adler began his medical practice as an ophthalmologist but soon turned to general practice, serving a lower-class clientele in Vienna. Adler's medical practice included waiters, acrobats, and artists who worked at the Prater, a circus and amusement park. He was interested in those individuals' unique strengths and weaknesses and feelings of inferiority and overcompensation. Adler's interests turned him to study psychiatry and mind-body interactions.

In 1902, Adler was a part of Freud's inner circle and intellectual heir. As time went on, Adler disagreed with Freud's theoretical emphases and argued that neurosis was caused by inferiority feelings and overcompensation. Freud was infuriated. After considerable conflict, their personal falling out was complete and irrevocable. In 1911, Freud told his followers that if they associated with the aberrant Adler, they would be dismissed from Freud's Psychoanalytic Association. In 1912, Adler formally started the Society for Individual Psychology.

His psychiatric career was interrupted when he served as a doctor with the Austrian army in 1915 in World War I. He worked on the Russian front, experiencing the horrors of war firsthand. Concerned about the survival of humanity, he stressed the importance of social justice to the survival of humankind and staunchly advocated preventative medicine (Maniacci & Sackett-Maniacci, 2002).

He developed into an ardent child advocate and founded a number of child guidance clinics in Austria that stressed early childhood intervention. He became a sought-after speaker in Europe and the United States, instructing large audiences about childrearing and spoke ardently against using physical punishment with children. But as anti-Semitism grew in Austria, Adler's clinics were closed (Ellenberger, 1970), and in1929, he became a visiting lecturer at Columbia University. Not wanting to leave her own political work, Raissa remained in Vienna. After being jailed for her political activities, she reluctantly left Austria and joined Adler in New York. The Adlers permanently resided at the Gramercy Park Hotel, and in 1932, he took a position at Long Island College of Medicine (Kaiser, 1995).

On May 27, 1937, Adler was on a lecture tour in Scotland at the University of Aberdeen. Taking a walk alone on a street close to the university, he suffered a fatal heart attack and died before the ambulance arrived at the hospital (Alfred Adler Institute, 2007). Many mourned his premature death. The *New York Herald Tribune*'s obituary lauded Adler as the father of the concept of the inferiority complex and one of the three figures besides Jung and Freud who remade the "mental surfaces of their times and leave an impression on civilization fairly comparable . . . to that with which Charles Darwin had devastated a preceding generation" (Hoffman, 1996, p. 323).

Vaihinger's "As If" Concept

Adler was deeply influenced by the work of Hans Vaihinger, a German philosopher who wrote *The Philosophy of "As If"* in 1911. Vaihinger (1952) posited that humans create partial truths, or fictional ideals, which guide them to handle life's demands. These beliefs are not always accurate, although some are closer to objective reality than others. However, people act "as if" what they think is true so a construct can become its creator's reality. For example, a very religious person may believe a religious construct such as "all good people go to heaven" and thus, live a life governed by this belief. A paranoid person may hold onto a hostile construct such as "vicious terrorists are everywhere trying to kill us." In order to gain insight into a person's lifestyle, the therapist must consider each client's relative reality or phenomenology. Adler's emphasis on the idea that humans live in the realm of meanings anticipated the social constructivists' view of human nature that is popular today (Mahoney, 1988; Mosak & Dreikurs, 1967).

Social Justice and Feminism

Adler lived in a time of tremendous global conflict in Europe, spanning two world wars. He was concerned about collective violence, and he saw politics as a struggle for significance. An advocate of social equality, Adler argued that the only suitable relationship among races, classes, sexes, or any human group was one of equality. He insisted that best antidote for social unrest was to cultivate true social interest and that "Only in socialism does social interest remain as an end" (quoted in Ansbacher & Ansbacher, 1967, p. 456). Living in a culture that overvalued men and undervalued women, Adler was an ardent feminist and believed sexism prevented both men and women from reaching their true potential (Stein & Edwards, 1998). He ultimately envisioned an ideal world of unfettered human relationships, and this idealism is expressed in his work.

Adler's integration of politically sensitive ideas about racism, sexism, and classism into his theory and practice was not without controversy. The psychoanalytic group accused Adler of muddying the waters of scientific empiricism by including philosophy and social values in his psychology. Advocates of Adler counter that such a practical and values-based approach is needed in times of global conflict (Hoffman, 1996).

Holism: The Undivided Self

From his training as a physician and his experience as a primary care doctor, Adler developed the idea of organ inferiority. And as he matured, he adopted a psychological perspective with a fully integrated view of the human being. He theorized that each person is a unique combination of physical, intellectual, emotional, social, psychological, and environmental characteristics who interprets the world in an idiosyncratic way. Each person, with his or her unique genetic inheritance, is a product of the interaction of environment and intrapsychic mechanisms (Britzman & Henkin, 1992). Thus Adler advocated the concepts of holistic and psychosomatic medicine.

Adler named his system *individual psychology*. The term *individual* comes from the Latin root meaning "undivided," and he meant to envision a whole person with all of his or her component parts. Ironically, the meaning of *individual psychology* is generally not interpreted as Adler intended. Many take the individual aspect to mean the right to pursue one's own interests above those of collective society. Adler saw the individual as an undivided entity, one where body and mind—or social, emotional, cognitive, and environmental aspects—are interdependent. The integration of individual and group welfare is essential to the well-being of both if the group and the individual are to be healthy (Ferguson, 1989, 2001).

Prevention

Adler theorized that the prevention of mental disorders would be more effective than either counseling or psychotherapy after the fact (Ansbacher, 1990). Education is a tool to foster prevention. He expanded his psychotherapy to include workshops in which he educated general audiences, parents, teachers, and administrators. Emphasizing the power of the teacher–student relationship, Adler advocated for teachers to be altruistic and constructive (Dreikurs, Grey, & Oxford, 1968). The school board in Vienna asked Adler to establish child guidance clinics within school settings, and he sponsored training for teachers and parents in 30 clinics in the Austrian school system (Dreikurs & Grey, 1968). Unfortunately, with the rise of fascism, the breakdown of the Austrian Republic collapsed and the clinics were closed.

If prevention failed, Adler turned to a rich set of methods to help the troubled person. Time-limited counseling could address minor problems, and longer term psychotherapy could deal with more serious predicaments. Anthony Bruck, a follower of Adler, developed brief psychoeducational models of Adlerian counseling to teach people about bettering their parenting, marital relationships, and careers. Another early proponent of Adler's therapy is American Rudolf Dreikurs, who promoted individual therapy in guidance clinics, school settings, and group settings (Dreikurs & Soltz, 1964). Adler's pioneering preventative methods foreshadowed the current fields of prevention, psychoeducation, brief counseling and psychotherapy, and family therapy as proposed by Nathan Ackerman, Murray Bowen, and Care Whitaker, as well as constructivist therapy (Ansbacher, 1990; Carich & Willingham, 1987).

Trends in Adlerian Therapy

Two major streams of Adlerian therapy exist today. The first is classical Adlerian *depth therapy*, which stresses strict adherence to Adler's original teachings and treatment with its original core values of social responsibility, a socially useful lifestyle, cooperation, equality, and democratic living (Stein & Edwards, 2003). Adherents of classical Adlerian depth therapy contend that other adaptations of Adler's theory have moved too far from his original ideas. For example, they criticize some methods of lifestyle analysis that tend to use superficial approaches in which the therapist plays a very active role. Well known among those who have advanced classical Adlerian depth theory are Alfred Adler's son Kurt, Lydia Sicher, Alexander Müller, Sophia de Vries, Anthony Bruck, and Henry Stein (Alfred Adler Institute, 2007).

The second major stream of therapy based on Adlerian individual psychology is *Dreikurian therapy,* which extends and simplifies Adler's work to make it easier for both clinicians and clients to use. The approach emphasizes that mental health and positive self-regard depend upon the individual's belief and perception that he or she is equal to all others (Dreikurs, Cassel, & Ferguson, 2004; Dreikurs, & Soltz, 2005; Marcus, 1998). Advocates argue that since Dreikurs worked closely with Adler for years, he was able to accurately anticipate Adler's direction. Furthermore, Dreikurs's push to train teachers and counselors to be effective professionals makes the therapy more accessible to more people, which has helped to promulgate Adler's beliefs (Ferguson, 2001).Well-known proponents of the Dreikurian form of Adlerian therapy include Eva Dreikurs Ferguson, Donald Dinkmeyer, Linda Albert, and more recently Jon Carlson and Michael Maniacci.

The classical Adlerians and the Dreikurians also differ in their use of vocabulary. For example, Dreikurs popularized the phrase "basic mistake," which he defined as a person's use of a faulty myth such as thinking of oneself as special rather than belonging to a group. This term is not used by the classical Adlerians since it was not an original Adlerian concept.

Adler's ideas permeate modern psychotherapeutic thinking, but he has never received the credit commensurate with his level of intellectual and creative contributions. Heinz and Rowena Ansbacher's translations and reinterpretations of Adler's original works, as well as the Adlerian Translation Project, make more of Adler's original works available in English, which has prompted new appreciation for his ideas (1956, 1967). The Adlerian Translation Project, sponsored by classical Adlerians, has a mission to accurately translate the works of Adler from German to English, especially because the persecution of the Jews by the Nazis in Europe effectively brought Adler's work to a standstill.

Various Adlerian institutes exist all over the world today. Students who wish to know more about classical Adlerian therapy and other current forms of Adlerian therapy can refer to the Resources section at the end of the chapter.

✦ THEORY OF INDIVIDUAL PSYCHOLOGY

The individual psychology of Adler includes a theory of personality, a model of psychopathology, and a philosophy of living. It also includes a strategy for preventative education and psychotherapy techniques and encourages people to develop good health through cooperation, courage, and a feeling of community (Carlson, Watts, & Maniacci, 2005). It aims to improve not only the client's quality of life, but life for everyone else in the client's world and for society in general. It helps "normal" individuals develop themselves to the maximum by setting a possible and inspiring ideal of mental health and by identifying the necessary steps to reach that ideal (Stein & Edwards, 1998).

Key Concepts

Individual psychology is complex and includes many key concepts, both theoretical and practical. Among those concepts we will discuss are striving for significance, inferiority complex, social interest and feeling of community, fictional final goal and style of life, birth order and family constellation, and normal and abnormal behavior. This section also discusses Dreikurs's concept of basic mistake, which is not included in classical Adlerian theory.

Striving for Significance

Adler's *striving for significance* and security is similar to Jung's transcendence and Rogers's self-actualization. For example, a person who feels inferior because he is clumsy may prevail over his disadvantage by practicing to be a skilled dancer. Everyone, from birth until death, strives to overcome imperfection and to attain security, growth, and completion. The goal is not to be superior to others in a competitive or materialistic way, although some may understand the drive in this way, which is detrimental to their optimal development and mental health (Stein & Edwards, 1998).

Inferiority Complex

Adler believed that within each individual, some bodily organs were weaker than others, making the person more vulnerable to particular forms of illness. People overcompensated for these inferior organs by engaging in activities to help themselves rise above this felt inferiority. For example, Demosthenes was a stutterer who placed pebbles in his mouth to overcome his speech impediment and became one of the world's greatest orators. Adler applied his thoughts about physical organ inferiority to overcoming psychological feelings of inferiority.

Subjective feelings of inferiority are normal. All individuals enter life as tiny, helpless babies. It is impossible for an infant to avoid feeling weak and vulnerable. As development proceeds, children are faced with vital tasks. If they feel they lack the skills to succeed, they may feel inferior. It is not the actual physical sense of smallness that matters as much as the personal and subjective sense of it. Although these sentiments can result in feelings of inferiority, they can also act as catalysts or motivators to improve individuals' situations and help them to achieve a sense of strength.

Adler describes a sense of *inferiority* as one that "finally culminates in a never-ceasing, always exaggerated feeling of being slighted, producing a Cinderella fantasy with its longing of redemption and triumph. Children's ideas about their royal or princely origin and temporary banishment from their 'real' home are of this kind" (Ansbacher & Ansbacher, 1967, p. 53). If feelings of inferiority are severe, an *inferiority complex* can result, making the individual feel that he or she is too weak to solve problems in a socially useful manner (Ansbacher & Ansbacher, 1956). To compensate, the person develops a *superiority complex,* a way to hide and conceal the inferiority complex. The person is usually dimly aware of this process, so it remains largely unknown and not fully understood. This unknown portion of the goal is Adler's definition of the unconscious (Dreikurs & Grey, 1968).

Social Interest and Feeling of Community

Adler (1929, p. 31) believed *social interest* was "the true and inevitable compensation for all the natural weakness of individual human beings." It is essential for biological as well as social survival. Although it is an innate human ability, it needs to be nurtured and cultivated. Because the individual lives in a society, social interest is crucial for normal adjustment and a well-balanced life (Ansbacher & Ansbacher, 1967, p. 2).

Social interest, or *gemeinschaftsgefühl,* is difficult to translate precisely from German to English. It has also been called social feeling, community feeling, and social sense. Adler's favorite translation was a "feeling of community," which is actually a broad conception with a meaning much deeper than just social interaction (Ansbacher & Ansbacher 1956, p. 134). A *feeling of community* is a multilevel concept, with a profound and spiritual aspect and a perspective as wide as the cosmos. It is the ideal of social evolution and the development of an attitude that is embedded in a mystical mission, or the feeling one is a part of something greater and all have a role to play and a mission to fulfill (Johnson, Smith, & Nelson, 2003; Stein, 2006). It is a striving for perfection of society, but it is possible to develop some levels and neglect others simultaneously.

Individuals with high levels of social interest have feelings of belongingness to the human race. They empathize, sympathize, make friends, cooperate with and love others. They realize that the good of any one individual ultimately depends on the good of everyone, and they behave in ways that promote self-development, cooperation, and helpfulness toward others. People with high levels of social interest can accept both the comforts and discomforts of life, and they acknowledge the interconnectedness of all people—understanding that what they do to others, they do to themselves (Ansbacher & Ansbacher, 1956).

Adler believed that if people understood social interest and lived according to its tenets, social problems such as war, violence, racism, and genocide would be eliminated. Adler questioned others to obtain a good measure of the level of a person's social interest: "What will be your contribution to life? Will it be on the useful or useless side of living?" (Stein & Edwards, 1998).

Fictional Final Goal and Style of Life

Each individual has his or her own subjective, fictional view of what he or she wishes to achieve in life. The *fictional final goal* is the internalized, personal view of the future. The wish or goal can be realistic or unrealistic, and it is an important part of lifestyle. The fictional final goal helps to form, direct, and organize an individual's life although it is generally unconscious.

People set goals they believe they can ideally attain. For example, Mahatma Gandhi chose as his mission to free India from British rule through nonviolent means, and he achieved this complex and difficult goal (Ansbacher & Ansbacher, 1967). Healthy people who have developed social interest have goals that serve others, whereas unhealthy people adapt fictional goals that serve them and their own well-being.

Style of life, or lifestyle, is a person's characteristic approach to life; it characterizes how an individual approaches or avoids the main tasks of life and attains his or her fictional final goal. A person's lifestyle organizes and regulates his or her behavior, thoughts, and feelings around a goal and guides the person through life's tasks; it is a personal master plan with a set of core beliefs and a strategy that moves the person toward success and away from failure (Slavic, Carlson, & Sperry, 1995). Each person's unique genetic inheritance and specific environmental conditions interact in the lifestyle so the person interprets the world in an idiosyncratic way.

There are as many lifestyles as there are people in the world. A person develops the basic foundations of a lifestyle by age 5 or 6 and continues with it from then on. If it is a self-defeating lifestyle, it will be perpetuated unless the person makes an effort to change it (Ansbacher & Ansbacher, 1967). A healthy person deals with the tasks of life with flexibility. The disturbed individual insists on rigidly sticking to a specific way of handling things. The style of life is the self, the ego, the personality, individuality, the unity of the person, an individual form of creative activity, the method of facing problems, one's opinion about oneself and the problems of life, or one's whole attitude toward life (Ansbacher & Ansbacher, 1956).

Birth Order and Family Constellation

A person's position or *birth order* within the *family constellation* can significantly affect development (Adler, 1992, pp. 126–132). The actual physical position matters less than the psychological place and the meaning assigned to it. If the child believes he or she is in a disadvantageous situation, discouragement can arise. Much depends upon how the parents handle the child's perceptions and situation. They can encourage their children and foster cooperation rather than competition among them. For example, if John is the firstborn, and Mom has Mary on the way, it is important to make John feel that he is a part of the new situation. During the pregnancy, John can be taught to help others and to play a role in caring for and nurturing his new sibling.

Birth ordinal position can provide the conditions for some common experiences. If a person is born a middle child but feels as if he or she is the oldest, then the perception of being the oldest is more salient than the reality. Each place in any family provides the opportunity for a different set of encounters and circumstances. For example, the universal experience for an only child is that of living in a family environment in which parents attend to only one offspring, and there is no forced sharing with siblings. Every first child, followed by a sibling, lives through a loss of the status of only child or a "dethroning" and a forced sharing of assets that at one time belonged solely to the older child. Dethroning can bring about a wish to regain lost power. A childhood behavior pattern of striving for preeminence can become a lifestyle and pattern in interpersonal relationships.

Other variables such as gender can moderate the experience of birth order. For example, a male child may be competitive with a slightly younger brother, but he may feel more protective of a younger sister. If a child is 6 years old when he is dethroned, he is likely to have a more firmly established attitude and lifestyle than if he were 1 year old when the new baby arrived. Thus every ordinal position provides a different vantage point from which to see the world (Ansbacher & Ansbacher, 1967), and influences, both favorable and unfavorable, can be triggered by birth order (Hall & Lindzey, 1985). Only children, never dethroned, are accustomed to being the center of attention and may lack social interest. They want to be close to the mother and may resist competition. Firstborn and oldest children have the monopoly until the second child provides a dethroning. They can be responsible and assume responsibility for others or be anxious, fearing a reversal of fortune. Second-born children (middle children) have always had to share and are never dethroned. They may be ambitious and pacemakers, since they always must catch up, or they can be rebellious, envious, poor followers, and very competitive. Last-born or youngest children have had to share with several others from birth. They often outdo their siblings, are competitive, feel inferior, and have a high probability of being the spoiled babies.

Other Adlerian Concepts

Other key concepts in Adlerian theory are encouragement, scheme of apperception, safeguarding, private logic, conscious and unconscious, and life tasks and personality types.

Encouragement

Encouragement, in Adler's, view is the activation of social interest within an individual. It fosters courageous and creative activity, helps a person to navigate life's difficulties, and develop a sense of contribution to the community, which in turn decreases feelings of inferiority and increases feelings of competency (Bird, 2005). It is used as a primary technique to create a good relationship between client and therapist in order for the therapist to help the client to build strength (Watts & Pietrzak, 2000).

Scheme of Apperception

Beginning in childhood, each person adopts a set of lenses through which he or she sees the self and the world; through this *scheme of apperception,* the person classifies the self, others, the environment, and experiences. Adler believed children have had sufficient experience during the first five years of life to form this scheme.

Perceptions are categorized into simple concepts, based upon the whether the person judges a stimulus to be good or bad. In normal development, children eventually discern the subtle gradations of qualities in themselves and others. However, discouraged persons remain stuck at primitive levels of development. In their "antithetical" scheme of apperception, they see things in black and white. For example, if everyone does not totally love and accept them, they feel humiliated or neglected.

An antithetical scheme of apperception can function to protect and defend the person's choice of a final goal and lifestyle. It is a rigid perception of self, others, and experiences seen from a very narrow perspective. It diminishes a person's ability to think and reason realistically. The greater the degree of discrepancy between reality and the perception of reality, the greater is the psychological disturbance. If a person wants to overcome feelings of helplessness, he may use his private logic to justify manipulation of others to get what he can from them, because it is adaptive to do so, even if his actions harm others.

Safeguarding

Safeguarding is an unconscious way of protecting the self from hidden and exaggerated feelings of inferiority. For example, safeguarding strategies include depreciating or criticizing others in order to feel superior; accusing others to make them responsible for what the person him- or herself has done; making self-accusations in order to fend off criticism, to avoid confrontation, and even to evoke sympathy (e.g., you can't hit a man when he is down); maintaining a holier than thou attitude; distancing one's self through procrastination, being noncommittal, changing states of consciousness through drug use, and even committing suicide; and developing and using specific symptoms as an excuse to opt out of responsibilities (Stein & Edwards, 1998).

Private Logic

Private logic is the cognitive process or the underlying reasoning each person uses to interpret the world. Each person has a unique perceptual process and a private, subjective way in which to interpret incoming stimuli and guide actions. When the outside world, or the consensual view of others, conflicts with the individual, he or she may cling to the private view or logic since it is more familiar and allows the person to maintain psychological comfort (Ansbacher & Ansbacher, 1967).

Conscious and Unconscious

Adler believed in the *unconscious,* but he defined it as that which the person has been unable to formulate into clear concepts (Adler, 1935). The unconscious is a part of consciousness that a person does not understand at the current moment. The unconscious and conscious cooperate for the good of the personality.

Life Tasks and Personality Types

According to Adler, there are three major *life tasks:* to work, to love, and to form and maintain a community. All humans encounter and learn to adjust to these life tasks in their own individual ways. Adler did not want to pigeonhole people in any definitive and rigid manner, but he recognized that energy level and degree of social interest served as a useful framework from which to conceptualize attitudes and behavior. The four personality types that he identified vary as a function of levels of social interest and activity:

- The *socially useful type* is a healthy person who cooperates and engages in socially useful activity that benefits others and contributes positively to life and the evolution of humanity.

- The *ruling type* has a high activity level and low social interest. When she is asked to make a socially useful contribution, she acts in an unsocial way. Because of her high energy level, the ruling type may attack others directly. She may assume the lifestyle of a delinquent, a tyrant, or a sadist. Ruling types with lower activity levels may aggress indirectly and take on the role of the suicidal or the addict, who attack themselves in order to hurt others.
- The *getting type* counts on receiving whatever he needs from others. He is dependent and leans on others to provide for his wants and needs.
- The *avoiding type* avoids solving problems. She will not exert herself or struggle to solve difficulties or remove obstacles to success. Instead, she circumvents concern in an effort to avoid failure.

The three latter types struggle to solve life's social problems, have a common unwillingness to cooperate and contribute, have lifestyles lacking in social interest, and clash with the demands of the outside world that require altruism. They react to difficult situations with shock, which then leads to failure, which is labeled as a form of maladjustment, such as neurosis or psychosis.

Normal and Abnormal Behavior

In Adler's theory, the best measure of good mental health is a feeling of community or connectedness (Stein & Edwards, 1998). The person who is healthy has high social interest and lives a socially useful lifestyle.

Many people do not develop optimally but are average or "normal." The person is reasonably cooperative, does just enough in work and in interpersonal relationships to get by, but does not reach maximum potential. The person does not have significant emotional or physical symptoms but may be somewhat bored, with chronic tension or stress. However, experiencing a stressor—such as a work layoff, illness, marriage, having children, divorce, or retirement—triggers psychological symptoms (Stein & Edwards, 2003).

Rather than pathologize the person's behavior, Adler chose the term *discouraged* to describe behaviors that many other theorists label abnormal. Discouragement has two major causes: insufficiently developed feelings of community and exaggerated feelings of inferiority. Adler believed that in all human failure—including neurosis, psychosis, crime, suicide, alcoholism, drug addiction, and sexual perversion—there is a lack of the proper degree of social feeling (quoted in Ansbacher & Ansbacher, 1956, p. 156). The discouraged person, with inferiority feelings and weak social interest, wants to achieve personal significance and security, but his or her lifestyle lacks cooperation. He relies upon private logic to solve problems in a self-centered way rather than a task-centered way. Problems are approached or avoided, and fictional goals of personal superiority are pursued, yielding imagined triumphs or defeats that have only private meaning and value (Ansbacher & Ansbacher, 1967).

Three basic causes of abnormality or exaggerated feelings of inferiority are (a) physical handicaps, (b) family dynamics, and (c) societal influences (Adler, 1992).

Physical Handicaps

Children with physical handicaps are more vulnerable to discouragement as a result of a lack of community feeling or social interest. If they are pampered or receive too much attention, they form an expectation that others should treat them with special care and avoid facing problems. After they develop dramatic feelings of inferiority, they have more pervasive, subjective feelings of inferiority and live in a psychological state of feeling inferior.

Family Dynamics

Family dynamics include both parenting style and birth order. The effects of parental pampering, or parental neglect and abuse, and the order of birth can strongly influence personality formation and lifestyle.

- *Pampering:* Children who are pampered by their parents develop an expectation that they should be the focus of attention, presume others ought to serve them, and often become takers, not givers. Dependent on others, unsure of themselves, and unable to face the tasks of life, they insist on receiving help and attention. The tactics they use to get their way include aggressively ordering, demanding, and commanding others; indirectly claiming their wishes through weaknesses or by being shy or obsequious; not taking no for an answer; using charm or flattery; or throwing a temper tantrum. They do not know how to face and resolve problems independently. As adults, if others do not help them, they interpret it as aggression. Angry, they may take revenge on these others.
- *Neglect and abuse:* If children do not experience love and cooperation firsthand, if parents neglect, reject, or abuse children, they do not positively connect to others. They tend to be isolated, suspicious, easily discouraged, and exaggerate their problems, and they underestimate their own abilities to solve difficulties. A sense of entitlement permeates their lifestyle so they expect to be compensated for their early deficits by receiving special consideration. While they demand to be treated well, they treat others badly.

Adults who received either pampering or neglect and/or abuse can arrive at similar expectations. The pampered child expects that the pampering will continue into adulthood. The neglected or abused child demands to be pampered to make up for past losses. Both the pampered and the neglected and abused think they are entitled to receive everything, with no obligation to provide anything back. For example, a woman who was a pampered child is chronically depressed, gives up easily, and depends on her husband to take care of her. Although she feels powerful when she controls her husband-caretaker, she pays for her dependency because she does not develop her own unique proficiencies. A man who was abused by his father chooses to despise all men in authority. Thus he never works in a rewarding occupation. He feels morally superior to persons in authority. He prefers to be angry at all of these men rather than overcome his fear and develop his own competence to work well.

For optimal development, parents gain the cooperation of their children and guide them to minimize their inferiority by contributing to others, being active, and seeing that they are a part of the whole. They assist the children in becoming cooperative, productive, and satisfied adults who sense their interdependence with others and who are guided by universal values of justice and truth.

Societal Influences

Societal factors outside the family also influence attitudes and mental well-being. School is especially important. For teachers to make a significant, positive impact on a child's self-image, sufficient encouragement and understanding is necessary. When a society allows discrimination on the basis of class, ethnicity, gender, religion, or even academic accomplishment, the results are feelings of inferiority and a lowered sense of self-worth. Those with overwhelming inferiority feelings have a low sense of social interest (Ansbacher & Ansbacher, 1956, pp. 263–280).

Adler believed a number of individuals can influence social adjustment. In early development, mother, father, siblings, and teachers, in that order, have the potential to elicit cooperation from a child and to correct earlier mistakes as the child matures. In later development, friends, love partners, work colleagues, spiritual community, and a psychotherapist may be able to contribute to the individual developing mutually respectful cooperation.

Thus Adler's concept of discouragement is a process in which a person lacks fully developed feelings of community, possesses a deeply felt sense of inferiority, and fights it with a goal of personal superiority. Such individuals are uncooperative and self-centered and fail to accept human interrelatedness. They take on a mistaken opinion of themselves and the world, which they translate into mistaken goals and a mistaken style of life in which they engage in maladaptive behaviors.

Dreikurs's Basic Mistake

One theoretical construct unique to Dreikurs's theory, which is not a part of Adler's original theory or current depth therapy, is the construct of the *basic mistake*. In Adler's discussion of mistakes, the real mistake is in being self-centered rather than being interrelatedness-centered. This person has a mistaken opinion of him- or herself and the world, and thus has mistaken goals and a mistaken style of life. But according to Dreikurs, basic mistakes are a part of a person's lifestyle, which is self-defeating because it contains faulty myths that diminish social interest. Each person has his or her own idiosyncratic version, but here are some common basic mistakes (Mosak, 2005, p. 71):

- *Overgeneralization:* A person erroneously draws a general conclusion from a particular case. For example, one teacher treats John unfairly so he concludes all teachers are unfair.
- *False or impossible goals of security:* A person believes that if she never displeases anyone, everyone will like her, and no one will hurt her. Thus she feels safe.

- *Misperception of life and life's demands:* The person believes that life is hard or unfair and that his suffering is particularly unfair.
- *Minimization or denial of one's worth:* A person believes that she is inferior and unworthy because she is not a successful actress, when in fact, she is successful in many other aspects of her life such as teaching schoolchildren.
- *Faulty values:* A person adopts values that lack social interest and integrity, such as "the end means justifies the means" or "revenge is sweet."

✦ PRACTICE OF INDIVIDUAL PSYCHOLOGY

Now that we have examined the major theoretical concepts of Adlerian therapy, we will explore its practice. Dr. Mary Allan is our composite, fictional Adlerian psychotherapist who provides a firsthand perspective of how she integrates theory with practice and applies the techniques of Adler's individual psychology.

Assessment and Diagnosis

I initiate therapy by searching out the information that will allow me to make an accurate and meaningful lifestyle analysis of my client. My treatment plan will include using the client's strengths, developing what is missing, reducing inferiority feelings, dissolving the unsatisfactory style of life, tracing the mistaken prototype, and using encouragement. Every Adlerian therapist assesses the client in his or her unique way, but the following basic information is included as a standard (Maniacci & Sackett-Maniacci, 2002).

- *Informal assessment:* I observe the client's nonverbal behavior because body language is a useful indicator in helping me understand the client. I observe how the client approaches me in the waiting room, posture, eye contact, and any other relevant nonverbal information.
- *Formal assessment:* From the start, I involve the client actively in the assessment process, by asking the client to answer many questions in detail. In the initial interview, I obtain standard background history (symptoms; situation; love relationships; family and friends; school and work; health problems, medication, alcohol, and drug use; previous therapy). It is efficient for me to use questionnaires, standardized interviews, projectives, and/or an Adlerian client questionnaire. It helps me to pool both verbal and written information (Stein, 1991).
- *Early recollections:* I ask the client to recall and describe his or her earliest memory and its associated circumstances, feelings, and thoughts to identify the client's views of self, the world, inferiority feelings, goals, scheme of apperception, activity levels, courage, and feeling of community. I use them as a barometer of progress since a memory may change as a function of how the client grows. For example, initially my client reports his earliest memory of mother dropping him on the floor, a reflection of his feelings of inferiority and a lack of safety and trust. As the client changes, he recalls

another early memory, of his mom guiding him up a sand pile, with an accompanying surge of joy as he reaches its pinnacle. The shift in memory shows the client's feelings of inferiority, fear, and discouragement are decreasing; the early prototype of the client's discouraged and fearful lifestyle is changing to one with more hope and optimism.

- *Family constellations and dynamics:* I obtain standard demographic information and as much information as possible about the client's place, subjective and objective, in the family. I may use a genogram to trace family heritage and family relationships across generations as they relate to the present. The genogram is dynamic and can be adjusted to the discovery process within therapy.

- *Strengths:* It is important to identify the client's strengths so the person can draw on inner resources and reinforce them. Since most people possess several strong points, it is relatively easy to point them out, especially if they have performed socially useful tasks.

- *Lifestyle analysis:* The client and I cooperatively develop a picture of his or her lifestyle during the first three stages of treatment. The process of discovery is gradual and is not a simple procedure; it is used to guide progress in therapy. I integrate the information given to me by the client in time lines with important positive and negative events, inferiority feelings, compensatory fictional goals, symptoms and what they may mean, the influence they exert upon the client, degree of social interest, private logic, and maps of future treatment plans. A lifestyle assessment must be thorough and detailed, or the plan will not touch the client's problems in sufficient depth (Stein, 2006). I must use it creatively and diplomatically, with sensitive timing and gentleness, within the context of the client's symptoms and presenting difficulties, in order not to cause pain or to overwhelm or discourage the client. It is a consistent guideline to encourage the client to move in a healthy direction a little at a time (Stein, 1988, 1991, 2006).

Together we assess the accuracy of the lifestyle analysis. We gauge how helpful the client's plan has been in the past and will be in the future for guiding therapy goals. As a classical Adlerian depth therapist, I know it takes experience, strong cognitive skills of analysis and synthesis, artistic empathy, and intuition to arrive at an appropriate plan.

Negotiation of Therapeutic Relationship and Length of Treatment

I am a collaborator—warm and friendly—and I offer and expect mutual respect. I adjust the therapeutic relationship to suit the needs of each client and invent personalized strategies (Stein, 1988). I am tactful, friendly, alert, and interested, with the cool-headed feeling that I am facing a sick person with whom I must not fight but who is always ready to start a fight (Adler quoted in Ansbacher & Ansbacher, 1967, p. 338). I speak to the client in his or her vocabulary.

My client agrees to take responsibility for the treatment and to actively collaborate with me. The client discusses lifestyle, memories, dreams, family history, relationships, and any topic that needs to be addressed honestly and openly. We use a blueprint, based upon our ongoing assessment, which is a one- or two-page summary of the treatment plan, to help us keep track of where we are going.

The length of treatment is individualized, depending on a client's level of social interest, cooperation, and understanding of his or her own lifestyle. I use Adler's suggested way to discuss time in the first session by saying "If you are not convinced in one or two weeks that we are on the right path, I will stop the treatment" (Ansbacher & Ansbacher, 1967, p. 344). Practicalities of everyday life, such as finances, motivation, or interest, determine the time limits of therapy. Clients may terminate at the fourth stage of treatment (a time when the client is encouraged to think differently and take small steps in a constructive direction). Others may wish to deal with philosophical and spiritual issues and complete all 12 stages (Alfred Adler Institute, 2007).

The overall goal of Adlerian therapy is to develop social interest, which is the antidote to worry, anxiety, and suffering. This will improve my client's life and the quality of life for everyone in his or her circle of contact, and thus enhance society (Slavik, Carlson, & Sperry, 1995, p. 168). I expect a deeper change from my clients in classical Adlerian therapy than from those in counseling, which is shorter term (Stein & Edwards, 1998).

Therapeutic Techniques

I use a number of Adlerian techniques, adjusting my style to match the unique needs of each client. But I also use my less scientific, more intuitive side in therapy and employ empathy and intuition (Maniacci & Sackett-Maniacci, 2002). Specific therapeutic techniques I use follow.

Socratic Dialogue

The Socratic dialogue uses questions to lead a person to a particular insight. This age-old philosophical technique is intended to bring out the truth, or latent knowledge, that is contained within every rational being. It helps to increase insight and understanding of personal meanings and underlying emotions. (Ansbacher & Ansbacher, 1967). As a co-thinker and helper to the client in finding a new lifestyle, I begin with gentle probes to search out relevant information and to clarify meaning and then aim to uncover deeper structures of private logic, hidden feelings, and unconscious goals. I help to generate new options and assist the client in making wise choices toward common sense and social interest. Next, I help the client to adapt a suitable philosophy of life and to evaluate his or her new course of action, emphasizing that the client is responsible for his or her own decisions (Stein, 1990, 1991).

Interpretation

To make an interpretation means to explain the client's behavior in a way that makes sense to the client within his or her style of life; interpretation helps clients see that their behavior is a choice. Insight is "understanding translated into constructive action" (Mosak, 2005, p. 73). Spending years in therapy without making any real change is not an effective use of this precious resource (Ansbacher & Ansbacher, 1967). Energy should be put into living a socially useful life.

Early Recollections and Earliest Memory

I use memories, and *early recollections,* even the earliest memory, to help me to see the client's early ways of meeting his or her world. Memories are projective devices that are purely subjective and not necessarily accurate. They can be somewhat distorted or complete inventions. As clients change, so do early memories. Whether they are accurate or fictional, they indicate individuals' feelings and beliefs about themselves and the world. They reveal what the client wants and what the client wants to avoid. They reflect the client's inner world, basic attitudes, style of life, morals, interests, feelings of inferiority, overall attitude, and social interest (Adler, 1937, p. 203).

No chance memories exist. From the enormous number of impressions that could be encoded into long-term memory, clients recall those with personal significance. For example, if an early memory centers around abandonment and feelings of insecurity, it may indicate past parental neglect; if it focuses on a sudden reversal of fortune, it may reflect pampering and dethroning (Ansbacher & Ansbacher, 1967). Thus I use memories as a barometer of change and tools to guide me in assessing progress in therapy (Adler, 1933; Ansbacher & Ansbacher, 1967).

The Question

I ask variants on Adler's basic question, "What would be different if you were well?" The answer to this question can enable a client to recognize the significance and usefulness of his or her symptoms in the client's life. When the answer to this question brings forth an understanding of the meaning of the symptoms, the client gains self-understanding (Mosak, 1989).

Spitting in the Client's Soup

"Spitting in the client's soup" means once clients identify the function of a symptom, it becomes difficult or impossible for them to be unaware of their self-defeating behavior. It ruins the utility and value of the symptom (Monte, 1987). For example, once I tell a client that he is an alcoholic and that the alcohol is in charge of him, his consciousness has been raised, and the armor of denial is penetrated. With each drink comes the thought that this behavior is self-destructive. When the alcoholic says, "I can stop drinking any time I want. I do not see the need to do it now. What's wrong with a little relaxation on the weekend?" I counter with, "Stop now, you are hurting your family. Your wife was here last week and said she would divorce you if you continued to drink." Such an intervention increases his awareness that he is using denial when he says he can stop but has decided he "won't stop" because he chooses not to.

Dream Analysis

I interpret dreams as expressions of style of life and have unique meanings to help the client access and understand private logic, create a mood, or reveal a significant experience. I do not believe in a secret code or universal symbolism of dreams. The intention of the dream is more important than its meaning. I am also curious about why dreams are forgotten, and the answer may hold some interesting information worthy of exploration (Bird, 2005).

Acting "As If"

I encourage a client to play the part of a person who has reached a goal the client wishes to attain. For example, if a client wants to become a scholar, I ask the client to act as if she were on the honor roll this month. If the client wants to lose weight, I ask him to act as if he were a naturally thin person. The client can break down the behaviors of a slender person, part by part, and reenact them. This provides a behavioral road map. By practicing the ideal behaviors, the client increases experience and, thus, self-confidence. There is an old saying: If you whistle in the dark, no one will know you are afraid. Adlerian therapy endorses this logic. The perceptions of other people that the client is unafraid will help the person to be the way others perceive him or her to be—unafraid and courageous (Patterson, 1986).

Bibliotherapy and Homework

I assign topical readings to address specific needs or problems to assist clients to develop better problem-solving skills, to advance critical thinking, and to increase insight into how to help themselves. If clients report back that they have learned to help themselves, this technique is effective (Edwards & Gfroerer, 2001; Riordan & Wilson, 1989).

Homework assignments help clients practice useful actions that increase social interest. I choose homework assignments that are appropriate for the needs of clients and that help them gain insight into problems and rehearse solutions.

The Process of Therapy

There are 12 stages in classical Adlerian psychotherapy. If all are completed, the client can attain optimal levels of functioning (Stein & Edwards, 1998). These phases are not precise; instead, they represent a loose set of guidelines to estimate each person's progress in therapy.

Stage 1. Empathy relationship: I establish a collaborative, cooperative relationship with my client. I promote co-thinking, co-feeling, and cooperating. I try to contact the healthy part of the client and help him or her to realize that life circumstances can be different. In this early stage of therapy, I allow the client to vent. My task is to listen.

Stage 2. Information: I allow the client to speak freely for approximately 5 to 10 sessions. I gather as much information as possible. I explore early childhood memories and dreams. I use the clinical material to integrate a preliminary hypothesis about lifestyle and goals. I very gradually make sensible interpretations.

Stage 3. Clarification: I use Socratic questioning to help the client to examine and assess the quality of his or her own thinking. If I have reservations about the client's beliefs, I correct them. I confront my client's tendency to shift blame to others. I guide the client to move away from any form of mistaken thinking and reinforce a more logical and commonsense approach.

Stage 4. Encouragement: I encourage my client to think outside of the box and to take small steps in an untried, positive direction. I help to clarify the client's reactions about these changes.

Stage 5. Interpretation and recognition: I interpret the dynamics of striving for significance and feelings of inferiority in light of style of life. I work with a fictional final goal of significance and security, birth order, earliest recollections, and dreams. The client accepts my interpretations thoughtfully.

Stage 6. Knowing: The client is able to make interpretations about his or her life and problems and accept what he or she needs to do; but the client may be blocked from approaching his or her goal.

Stage 7. Emotional breakthrough: To promote emotional breakthroughs, I use role playing, imagery, or even group therapy. I help make up for the client's missing experiences in order to correct past errors.

Stage 8. Doing differently: I help the client transform insight into action. Creative solutions can move the client into healthier behaviors, such as spitting in the client's soup or spoiling the fun of the negative behavior.

Stage 9. Reinforcement: I encourage and reinforce changes in a positive direction—in thinking, deciding, and acting. I encourage the client to develop better feelings about the self, to coach the client to develop appropriate emotions, to accompany the change, to reinforce positive feelings and positive results.

Stage 10. Social interest: I promote more cooperation between the client and myself. I use the positive feelings of the client, such as sharing with others and helping others, to increase cooperation outside of our therapy situation. By moving from self-centered activities to outwardly focused endeavors, the client awakens deeper feelings of social interest and community feelings of equality.

Stage 11. Goal redirection: I challenge the client to let go of his or her old style of life, to be more open, and to set a new goal of being socially useful and self-actualized. The client discovers a new psychological perspective and sets this new goal. The client begins to understand that past habits served to help to overcome feelings of inferiority. At this stage, he or she possesses a more secure sense of self and a genuine appreciation of others.

Stage 12. Support and launching: I help the client to reach out, to evaluate him- or herself accurately, and to be encouraged about overcoming difficulties as well as look toward to the unexpected. I want the client to feel equal with me and to promote his or her own personal growth as well as that of others.

When my client has reached a satisfactory goal and made sufficient changes, we terminate. If a client does not want to be involved in full in-depth therapy, he or she may participate in therapy up to stages 4 to 6. Of course, clients who only accomplish the goals in these earlier stages have a more limited cognitive and behavioral change than if they participated in all 12 stages.

Successful therapy means that the client has made at least one positive change in one area. The client has altered his or her lifestyle significantly enough and corrected his or her faulty picture of the world and is on a new and socially interested track with sufficient social interest to feel satisfied.

If the therapist lacks social interest, pitfalls can arise. However, this is a rare. Classical Adlerian depth therapists seek out and receive appropriate training. Ideally, the therapist elicits the client's cooperation. If a therapist feels negatively toward a particular client and his or her feelings are getting in the way, the therapist must seek and obtain supervision or consultation from a peer to do what is in the best interest of the client (Strumpfel & Goldman, 2002).

THERAPY IN ACTION: DR. MARY ALLAN AND THE CASE OF JONATHAN

To illustrate the application of Adlerian therapy, we examine a treatment plan for Jonathan, followed by excerpts from therapy sessions with our fictional psychotherapist, Dr. Allan. Keep in mind the case excerpts are simulated interviews and represent the ideal of therapy. In real life, clients may take much longer to meet therapeutic goals. Table 5.1 provides a summary of Dr. Allan's treatment plan.

Case Excerpts

Dr. Allan conducted an initial assessment and diagnosis of Jonathan. The following excerpts are from sessions based on that assessment and Adlerian case formulation.

Session 1

Dr. Allan: From all that you have told me in the last half hour, I understand you have experienced a great sadness. You want my support and help.

Jonathan: That is why I am here—to find help.

Dr. Allan: Jonathan, what has happened in the past that reminds you of your situation today?

Jonathan: It makes me think about when my sister Annie left home. She was more like my mom than my real mother. She made me feel good about myself when she was around. When she left, I felt lost, and as if I was nothing [*long pause*] for a long time.

Dr. Allan: Did you feel strong when you were with Annie and other important people in your life?

Jonathan: I had not thought about it in quite this way, but perhaps it is true. When Annie left, I fell apart, and now with Tuti leaving with Darren, I am falling apart again.

Dr. Allan: How do you understand their leaving?

Jonathan: Annie got married. But I was left behind. I was only 10, and she was 18. I remember calling her up crying, saying I could not help myself or stop crying, and she'd come over to visit me. That calmed me down.

Table 5.1

Adlerian Treatment Plan for Jonathan

Assessment and Formulation	• Presenting problem: loss of relationships with Tuti and Darren • J.'s low social interest • Lifestyle analysis: J. wishes to be loved more than to love; puts own needs before others, Tuti's
Therapeutic Relationship	• Patient and therapist are equals and collaborators • Dr. A. provides encouragement, collaboration • J. provides a sincere effort and honest reporting
Contract, Goals, and Treatment Plan	• Increase/activate J's social interest: responsibility, cooperation, prosocial attitudes, behaviors (e.g., volunteerism) • Replace self-indulgence with self-transcendence (power, mutual relationship) • Increase awareness of thinking, feeling, behaving • Time: meet weekly and assess progress
Techniques	• Encouragement (verbal/nonverbal, interpretations, etc.) • Socratic inquiry • Examination of J.'s private logic • Question: What happens if J. gives up symptoms of depression? • Imagery for missing elements • Clarification of J.'s responsibility for problems in relationship
Process of Therapy	• J. discusses family, dreams, memories, self • J. encouraged to take on lifestyle with increased social interest; relationships of equals • Insight into his family constellation (e.g., parental indifference, sister's loss), recognition of childhood feelings of inferiority • Therapeutic relationship replaces the missing through interpretations of earliest memory and dreams • Insight into his relationship with Tuti and Darren and choice not to have children • J. volunteers to help underprivileged; changes his work
Termination and Outcome	• Lifestyle convictions more in tune with social interest; in community, work, and love (job in helping profession) • Connects self with others, with equality and cooperation • Corrects faulty logic and picture of the world, accepts more mature view of the world; modifies sexism, controlling, and selfish tendencies • Desires to return to therapy to achieve ideal mental health

Dr. Allan: So your crying brought your sister back! Did you find your helplessness can be very powerful?

Jonathan: [*slight smile*] You may be on to something. I want to think about it. It was not that way with my parents. No matter what, they did not respond to me even if I cried for hours.

[*Comment: J.'s insight early in therapy was a good indicator that he is willing to work if encouraged.*]

Dr. Allan: How else did you manage to cope when Annie left?

Jonathan: I studied hard. I was on the honor roll. I also got involved in tutoring the kids in special classes. I like the outdoors and the kids. Then in college, I threw myself more into schoolwork. I dated a lot of girls, but when I met Tuti, she was right for me. [*pause*] How could she just leave?

Dr. Allan: [*leaning forward in her chair and using a very gentle, but probing tone of voice*] Tell me, what caused Tuti to leave?

Jonathan: [*visibly shaken, tears roll down his cheeks*] I know she always wanted children. I could not do it. I do not want a family. Not at all. She always wanted kids. But she does not understand what our lives would be. I don't like waking up at 2 A.M. to a crying kid. Knowing Tuti, she would be pissed off at me for not helping her.

Dr. Allan: You do not see children as part of your life's plan?

Jonathan: No, not mine. Hers. I want too many things out of life, and children get in the way. Kids cost. They'll put a drain on my career. I tried to convince Tuti that she was being foolish.

Dr. Allan: How do you think Tuti felt when you had such different visions for your lives?

Comment: I assess J.'s ability to empathize with and to care for others close to him.]

Dr. Allan: Jonathan, I am wondering, how do you think they feel about this?

Jonathan: I don't care! How can I even think about it? [*long pause*] Darren won't face me. Tuti, she probably feels guilty and cruel.

Dr. Allan: What is your evidence for this?

[*Comment: Using Socratic dialogue, I try to get at his private logic and assess J.'s ability to see the world with objectivity.*]

Jonathan: [*long pause*] She was mad at me. Maybe she was afraid to hurt me face-to-face. Tuti knows how depressed I become. She led me down the path of this depression. She kicked me when I was down.

[*Comment: J. has learned to use his weakness to avoid responsibility for his own state. He is using safeguarding.*]

Dr. Allan: When you say you are a victim and "Tuti led you down the path," did you play any role in that?

Jonathan: No, I just get depressed. [*nonverbal cues: smiles, fidgets, shows he indicates that he is responsible for his affective state on a non-conscious level*]

Dr. Allan: Jonathan, is it possible that you are trying to control her through depression?

Jonathan: No. I cannot help my depression. It is not my fault. I just fall apart. [*long pause*] Well, I suppose. I suppose it could be that way.

Dr. Allan: Is it possible depression seems to give you some power? Do you think, in the past, it helped to bring back your sister?

Jonathan: I hadn't thought about this before. . . .

Dr. Allan: Jonathan, if you no longer had your depression, what would you do?

Jonathan: [*long pause*] I do not know.

Dr. Allan: This is a very important question so I encourage you to take the time to think and answer it for your own sake. If you are no longer depressed, what would you do?

Jonathan: I would be out, meeting friends, getting my life together, figuring out my plans for the future. I would even explore better, higher-level job possibilities.

Dr. Allan: Then, why do you need to be depressed?

Jonathan: [*surprised*] I do not need to be.

Dr. Allan: [*very gently*] Is it possible depression allows you to avoid responsibilities, even to yourself?

Jonathan: Not really. [*pause*] Or not likely.

Dr. Allan: Just think about your answer, and we can discuss it when you are ready to do so.

Session 2

Dr. Allan: Can you describe your earliest memory to me?

Jonathan: Oh . . . yes. I have set up a lemonade stand, and a man walks by. I am too afraid to ask him to buy lemonade, so I yell to my mother, and she won't come out of the house to help me. And then along comes Annie. She runs down the street and tugs at the man's coat. My brother wants to sell you some lemonade, sir. The man stops in his tracks, smiles at Annie, and comes back and buys a bunch of glasses of lemonade! Boy, did I ever strike it rich.

Dr. Allan: How did you feel?

Jonathan: What an adrenaline rush. She rescued me. I was happy.

Dr. Allan: Let's look at the meaning of your memory. You wanted to do something for yourself to feel significant. But you believed you could not do it alone. How did you feel about being alone?

Jonathan: Scared. That's why I tried to get my mother.

Dr. Allan: You go to retrieve your mom for help. She is not there. But another powerful person takes her place. Does this help you feel big and strong?

Jonathan: Yes, yes . . . that feels right. It does make me feel powerful.

Session 3

Dr. Allan: Together, we have been working on understanding your lifestyle. Can we spend some of our time talking about it?

Jonathan: Yes.

Dr. Allan: I wonder what you are trying to achieve by doing what you have been doing with Tuti. Let's figure out a homework assignment to help understand what we call a lifestyle, the way of life each person chooses. Often we get into the habit of acting without asking why. When we focus and become more aware of the meaning of our actions, we are freer to make choices and not be on automatic pilot.

Jonathan: I used to keep a diary when I was younger, but now I stopped. Maybe I could do that.

Dr. Allan: Let's agree to that. Your homework is to keep a diary.

Session 10

Dr. Allan: I wonder how your life would be different if you had put your needs aside and given Tuti what she wanted.

Jonathan: Yes, I would have her—and I would also have children, traded for some of my professional ambitions. Perhaps that would be better than what I have now. I wanted all her attention. I didn't want to share her with a child.

Dr. Allan: Raising children means giving and giving. You chose not to do this for your own reasons, so you tried to convince Tuti to change her lifestyle rather than change yours.

Jonathan: Yeah . . . I did. Well, you know how we have been talking about avoidance? I think I figured out that my fear of having children is because I want to avoid so much responsibility.

Dr. Allan: Do you think that you are reluctant to take care of others because when you demanded that others take care of you, they did not?

Jonathan: I think you might be right.

Dr. Allan: Many people find if they help other people, they feel much happier.

[*Comment: I say these things because I now have a genuine human therapeutic relationship with Jonathan. I provide basic social interest for him so he can transfer it to others.*]

Session 24

Jonathan: I now really understand what we have talked about. I want to go back to working with needy kids who can use my help. This time, I can use my professional marketing skills. Maybe I'd better worry less about being rich and concentrate on involving myself helping others. Growing up, I was very involved in Boy Scouts. Then I was a Big Brother. I volunteered tutoring. I liked myself much more when I did those kinds of things.

Dr. Allan: Interesting. Let me encourage you to go ahead and work on this project.

Case Comment

Jonathan's therapy continued for one year. Upon termination, he intended to return for more in-depth analysis. He had explored the structures of private logic, hidden feelings, and unconscious goals. His early childhood feelings of inferiority emerged. Pampered by his sister, he had felt neglected by both parents. Feeling abandoned, he felt weak and inferior. His unconscious goal was to punish his neglectful parents for their lack of care and his sister for her abandonment. The situation with Tuti brought out his self-centeredness, interfering with his relationship. His attempts to have others take care of him succeeded only intermittently. Gradually realizing he could care for himself, he matured. He gained insight into his use of self-accusations to evoke sympathy as a way of safeguarding. He beat his accusers to the punch, thinking no one can hit a man when he is down. To avoid responsibility, he distanced himself from his decision not to have children by being noncommittal, and working hard, and pursuing material goods.

Jonathan was encouraged by Dr. Allan and was able to reduce inferiority feelings and increase social interest, helping him to funnel his striving for significance, security, and completion into tasks that promoted equality and encouraged him to make meaningful social contributions. He learned to cope with feelings of inferiority and corrected his false goal of security. He became interpersonally courageous and decreased his helplessness and his self-centeredness, as he cultivated social interest. He contacted Tuti and Darren, and they reached an understanding.

Jonathan later dated and married a woman whose goals were similar to his new revised goals. The couple planned to open a nonprofit organization for underprivileged children. Jonathan generated new options and made choices, found a new course of action, and adapted a more altruistic and satisfying philosophy of life and lifestyle.

✦ RESEARCH DIRECTIONS OF INDIVIDUAL PSYCHOLOGY

As is the case with psychoanalysis, to date, there is little research of any kind, especially psychotherapy outcome studies, to support the efficacy and effectiveness of Adlerian psychotherapy. No major randomized control studies have been performed, and no program of systematized research exists. Dedicated Adlerians make broad claims that Adlerian analysis is a worthwhile investment of time and energy and that it can change people for the better, but there is no strong evidence base to back these assertions (Slavik & Carlson, 2005). Adlerians have not kept up with the demand for an evidence-based individual psychology practice.

Like psychoanalysts, early Adlerians relied upon case studies and qualitative data to support their therapy. And like Freud, Adler was an astute observer of human nature who valued research but who chose to invest his energies in creating and building his theory as well as expanding its practice. This legacy has meant Adlerian therapists have tended to depend more on beliefs than research.

Of the limited amount of research that has been done, little is methodologically sound. No study of Adlerian therapy has used designs that are sufficiently sophisticated to consider and control for a number of relevant and important factors. This small number of studies has many flaws, including lack of standardized procedures and controls, inadequate statistical analyses, no baseline measures, and no follow-up for dropouts. The online Appendix C contains a sample review of Adlerian psychotherapy.

There are some general research findings that do offer some support and credibility to a number of Adler's broad concepts, such as family constellation dynamics, the origins of personality and social dispositions in childhood, and the value of prevention. However, these findings are scattered; they are not only in the psychological literature but also in other disciplines such as sociology and medicine.

One area of Adler's theory of personality development that has spawned much interest centers around birth order (Freese, Powell, & Steelman, 1999). Frank Sulloway (1996) reviewed 26 years of research on birth order. This included quantitative and historical data from a total of 6,566 participants. After controlling for background influences that confounded previous research results (e.g., size of sibship, class, etc.), Sulloway argued that the influence of birth order across all eras and cultures is systematically related to personality and is a better predictor of social attitudes than gender, class, or race. Firstborn adults are more conservative, supportive of authority, and tough-minded than later-borns. In contradiction, however, other researchers analyzed social attitudes from the General Social Survey (GSS) and concluded gender, race, social class, and family size were all more strongly linked to social attitudes than birth order (Freese et al., 1999). They argued birth-order theories are better understood in terms of modest effects in limited domains in particular societies. Thus it is still not clear whether information about birth order can be used to inform clinical practice.

Adlerian psychotherapists are faced with a daunting task to try to produce evidence-based research because Adlerian therapy is time-consuming and expensive.

But there is a movement underway to create a research agenda making it easier to empirically validate and verify Adlerian constructs—applying a scientific approach to analyze its logic and generating new programmatic research (Oberst & Stewart, 2002). Measuring therapeutic success means finding a valid way to quantify social interest and to empirically demonstrate that the individual with social interest is a happier, mentally healthier person than one without it; the next step is to produce solid evidence showing that the techniques used in Adlerian therapies are effective and efficacious in producing these outcomes (Sexton, 1996).

What can the therapist say to justify the use of Adlerian psychotherapy? The therapist can openly discuss the dearth of empirically based evidence but argue that he or she chooses to use Adlerian therapy based upon a combination of factors—clinical expertise, clinical experience, expert opinions from Adlerians, and the research (case studies) on Adlerian work that does exist.

Like psychoanalytic therapies, Adlerian therapy has withstood the test of time. It has been used for over a century and continues to be endorsed by a substantial number of supporters, both clinicians and clients alike, as a credible and effective method of treating mental illnesses. Writings from Adlerians tend to be thoughtful, analytic, and very vigilant regarding what is happening in treatment. Many people report that Adlerian therapy has been directly responsible for enhancing their psychological well-being and has helped them to face problems. Of course, the therapist can fall back on the robust equivalency effect, pointing out that the major psychotherapies are superior to no treatment when provided by a skillful, wise, and stable therapist (Lambert, Bergin, & Garfield, 2004). However, before the therapist chooses Adlerian therapy, he or she should first determine if there is an empirically supported match between the client's disorder and another therapy (Lambert & Ogles, 2004, p. 180). If none is available, the therapist can then choose Adlerian therapy to help the client live a healthy lifestyle (Kopp, 2003).

✦ ISSUES OF DIVERSITY

Its strong emphasis on social justice and advocacy makes Adlerian therapy able to address issues of diversity (Watts, 2003). Adler's views about feminism were far ahead of his time, and even today, his thinking is at the cutting edge of the advancement of equity for diverse groups (Vande Kemp, 2003). But despite this feminist perspective, Adlerian theory and practice are still an invention of Western culture. Although Adler, unlike Freud, worked with the poor and the middle class, the sample was still not very diverse. And although Adler did appreciate the different needs of various populations, his work was primarily with White Europeans.

However, today Adlerian therapy begins with a consideration of the client's unique worldview. Ethnicity, class, race, and gender are carefully considered in order to understand how they affect the client's development and status as a human being. Adlerians honor and respect uniqueness, differences, personal meaning, interpretations, perceptions, and values. The therapy is shaped to fit the idiosyncratic cultural needs of the client through multicultural views of individual clients

(Carlson & Carlson, 2000). The therapist acts only as a guide and does not expect or force the client to adopt any specific values and beliefs other than those of community feeling or social interest.

Adler was a strong advocate for the equality of men and women, which he believed was a way to bring about a higher level of cooperation between them interpersonally and societally (Adler, 1980). Adler believed women had exaggerated feelings of inferiority because the culture reinforced these feelings, preventing them from living full and satisfying lives. At the same time, he saw that culture also overvalued men, giving them inflated and unrealistic expectations (Ferguson, 2001). When they did not attain these expectations, men inevitably experienced increased inferiority feelings. Adler advocated for radical reforms to the debilitating gender roles within various societies. His recommendations are useful in a contemporary world where women are re-negotiating the boundaries of their relationships with men and society. Adler also emphasized the importance of the role of the father in childrearing, of particular interest today since so many men are taking on single parenthood (Watts, 1998, 2000).

Finally, Adlerian techniques encourage the client to bring any problem to the surface and discuss it in a nonjudgmental environment, including the thoughts, feelings, and behaviors associated with issues of diversity, no matter how controversial or difficult to tackle. Such openness promotes a welcoming attitude and an acceptance and valuing of diversity.

✦ MAJOR CRITIQUES OF INDIVIDUAL PSYCHOLOGY

Critics of individual psychology assert that many of its basic ideas are vague, difficult to define operationally, and complicated to study scientifically. Some of the theoretical concepts are so flexible that they can explain everything, and, therefore, they explain little. An Adlerian therapist cannot predict the consequences of certain events, although he or she can trace events back to the cause or its unique and specific origins. For example, the pampered child, the neglected child, and the abused child may all exhibit the same symptoms as an adult. The pampered child expects the familiar pampering to continue; the neglected child or the abused child demands to be pampered in order to be compensated for his or her early losses. The three very different experiences during childhood produce similar adult expectations—as grownups, they feel entitled to everything but obligated to nothing. Therefore, the same, even identical, overt abnormal behavior in these adults arises from very different roots, making prediction and control, an essential part of a good theory, very difficult if not impossible (Monte, 1987).

Critics argue that the terms such as *feeling of community, social interest, striving for significance,* and *feelings of inferiority* are subjective, fictitious hypothetical constructs that pertain to philosophical concerns and values. They have no true empirical standing. They are difficult to operationally define and to standardize. The goal of social interest is unrealistic, unfeasible, impractical, and even unattainable given what we know about human nature. It is the search for the mystical Shangri-la, an earthly paradise that does not exist, rather than a psychotherapy.

While Adler's theory moves away from mechanistic, deterministic, and negative views of human personality, its emphasis on humanism and spiritualism is better addressed by religion and philosophy. The goals of therapy are value driven. If a client improves, the expected outcome is a change in feeling of community and social interest. These outcomes are not only difficult to define but vague and nebulous.

Critics add that the practice methods and techniques of Adlerian therapy have not been validated through any evidence-based research. Some of the techniques even seem theatrical, such as those that direct the client to act "as if." It is difficult to know which particular interventions are most effective in bringing about change. Are clients responding to specific Adlerian treatment methods, or are they responding to something else?

Currently, there are subtle and significant differences in the attitudes and techniques of therapists trained in classical Adlerian therapy and Dreikurs's model. There is not a single standard of practice for all forms of Adlerian therapy, and different training programs can differ enormously in how they interpret Adler's work. The quality of training and the supervision may differ substantially between and within various centers. In short, all therapies called Adlerian are not the same. There are no studies that examine the effects of therapist training and allegiance to a particular model of Adlerian therapy (classical versus Dreikurian). Different trainings can lead therapists to entirely different interpretations of Adler's work. Thus there is no way to guide the client in choosing a therapist that best suits his or her needs. Future researchers should be aware of the differences and adjust the design of their research studies accordingly. Educating clients about the type of Adlerian therapy before they choose a therapist will make them more informed about their own treatment.

A final criticism of Adlerian therapy is that it can create conflicts within the individual. The client can become confused at times when the individual's needs are pitted against those of society, making the client unsure how to resolve competing demands. The balance between the individual and the society needs to be more clearly delineated in discussion with clients.

SUMMARY

- Adler was influenced by psychoanalysis, Vaihinger's philosophy, feminism and social justice, holism, and prevention in his creation of the theory and practice of individual psychology. His individual psychology has given rise to two major styles of psychotherapy. Classical Adlerian depth therapy strictly adheres to Adler's original constructs. The Dreikurian style of therapy extends and simplifies Adler's theory to make it easier to use by clients, clinicians, and educators.
- Individual psychology is complex and includes major key concepts of striving for significance, inferiority complex, social interest and feeling of community, fictional final goal, style of life, birth order and family constellation, and

normal and abnormal behavior. Other key concepts in Adlerian theory are encouragement, dreams, scheme of apperception, safeguarding, private logic, conscious and unconscious, life tasks and personality types.

- Good mental health (normal behavior) is a feeling of community or connectedness. Adler believes all human failures are caused by a lack of the proper degree of social feeling. Adler believes these behaviors arise from discouragement. The basic cause of a lack of social interest or exaggerated feelings of inferiority are physical handicaps, family dynamics (e.g., pampering, abuse, and neglect), and societal influences. Dreikurs's basic mistake is a construct he applied to Adler's individual psychology.

- Assessment, in the practice of individual psychology (classical depth therapy) helps the therapist and client to make a meaningful lifestyle analysis of the client through early recollections, family constellations and dynamics, and strengths, among other information.

- In the therapeutic relationship, the therapist is a collaborator who offers mutual respect. The client's responsibility is to actively collaborate with the therapist. The length of treatment varies for each individual as a function of social interest, cooperation, and understanding of his or her own lifestyle and motivation and means for depth therapy or counseling.

- Therapeutic techniques of individual psychology include the Socratic dialogue, which uses questions to lead a person to a particular insight; interpretation of the client's behavior that makes sense to the client; analysis of early recollections and earliest memory; asking the question—What would be different if you were well?; spitting in the client's soup or identifying the gains derived from a symptom; dream analysis; acting "as if" or playing a role; bibliotherapy and homework.

- The process of classical depth therapy occurs in 12 stages. Clients who participate up to stages 4 to 6 have a limited cognitive and behavioral change. Successful therapy means that the client has made at least one positive change and altered the lifestyle significantly enough to be on a new and socially interested track and feels satisfied.

- Research supporting the efficacy and effectiveness of individual psychology has been scant, especially outcome studies. Of the research that has been done, little has been methodologically sound, and most are qualitative case studies. Some general findings support Adler's broad concepts, such as family constellation dynamics, the origins of personality and social dispositions in childhood, and the value of prevention. Research on birth order yields controversial results and cannot reliably inform clinical practice.

- Individual psychology has a strong emphasis on social justice and advocacy and addresses issues of diversity. It is still an invention of Western culture used primarily with White people of European descent.

- Criticisms of individual psychology are that the theoretical and practice constructs are vague and difficult to define operationally, as well to study scientifically. There are no universal standards of practice for all forms of Adlerian therapy, and training programs can differ enormously in how they interpret and teach Adler's work.

RESOURCES

Alfred Adler Institutes of San Francisco and Northwestern Washington
Alfred Adler Institute of San Francisco
266 Bemis Street
San Francisco, CA 94131
(415) 584-3833
Alfred Adler Institute of Northwestern Washington
2565 Mayflower Lane
Bellingham, WA 98226
(360) 647-5670
http://ourworld.compuserve.com/homepages/hstein

The institute provides training in classical Adlerian therapy. It recently published the first 10 volumes of the 12-volume set of *The Collected Clinical Works of Alfred Adler,* edited by Henry T. Stein, covering Adler's writings from 1898 to 1937.

Adler School of Professional Psychology
65 East Wacker Place
Chicago, IL 60601
http://www.adler.edu

This school was founded in 1952 under Rudolf Dreikurs. It has campuses in Chicago and Vancouver. Social responsibility is a primary focus, with a recently launched program on social exclusion.

CLASS EXERCISES AND ACTIVITIES

Theory

1. Describe the theoretical differences and similarities between the early Adlerian therapists who emerged during the time of Freud and current Adlerian therapists. How would Adler himself view the changes?
2. Discuss your birth order in your nuclear family. How do you think your siblings (or lack thereof) affected your personality development? Do you think you would be different if you were born in a different ordinal position? How? Why? Compare your ideas about birth order with those of Adler. Do they ring true?
3. What are the unique elements of Adler's individual psychology?

Practice

1. Choose a partner in the class. One person plays Alfred Adler, and the other plays a client plagued with feelings of inferiority. Describe the dialogue. Switch therapist and client roles, and concentrate on the different feelings each role generates.

2. Make up a homework assignment for a client in order to promote social interest. What are some of the tasks that can help to increase awareness of how social interest may improve the quality of your client's life?
3. Look at the sample treatment plan in Chapter 1 (Figure 1.2). Fill out the plan for Tuti for Adlerian therapy. (Both Jonathan's and Tuti's case histories are in Appendix A.)

Research

1. A patient asks you, "Why are you using Adlerian therapy to treat me? How did you choose this particular therapy model for me?" Justify your choice.
2. Conduct a review of Adlerian therapies using the following key words in PubMed: *Adlerian therapy, individual therapy.* What did you find? Limit your search to *Adlerian therapy and randomized control.* What did you find? Conduct your own literature review of Adlerian psychotherapy. Which key words would you use to expand the search? Compare your review with the one in the online Appendix C.
3. What recommendations would you give to an Adlerian therapist about improving the status of research?

CHAPTER 6

ROGERS'S CLIENT-CENTERED THERAPY

[T]he most basic learning for anyone who hopes to establish any kind of helping relationship is that it is safe to be transparently real. . . . if I can be sensitively aware of and accepting toward my own feelings then the likelihood is great that I can form a helping relationship toward another.

–Carl Rogers

The goals of this chapter are to present a general overview of Carl Rogers's client-centered therapy. The chapter looks at biographical information about Rogers, the historical context of client-centered therapy, and the theory, practice, and research of this model. The simulated psychotherapist, Dr. John Roberts, will present a treatment plan and some excerpts from therapy sessions for the case of Jonathan. Issues of diversity and major critiques are also included.

✦ HISTORICAL CONTEXT

Extraordinary changes swept through American society in the 1950s and 1960s. In an emerging cultural zeitgeist, key concepts from humanist and existential philosophies found their way into the mainstream of the American psyche, behavioral sciences, and psychotherapy. This so-called Third Force (Maslow, 1969) was formed in opposition to the dominance of behaviorist (First Force) and psychoanalytic (Second Force) ideologies. Behaviorism focused on rigorous scientific objectivity and empirical methodology; radical behaviorism even excluded mental process as a legitimate area of study. Psychoanalysis envisioned the unconscious process as the controller of human behavior. Although polar opposites in content, both behaviorism and psychoanalysis approached the study of human behavior from a reductionistic, mechanistic, and deterministic perspective (Association for Humanistic Psychology, 2005).

Psychotherapists complained that these earlier models neglected the study of vital human elements, such as values, intentions, and meaning (Rogers & Skinner, 1956). The leaders of the Third Force countered these rigid mechanistic views of human beings with themes of humanism, existentialism, and experiential therapy; their humanist and existentialist theorists included Abraham Maslow, Carl Rogers, and Rollo May, among others (Aanstoos, Serlin, & Greening, 2000). Existential therapy and gestalt therapy (discussed in Chapters 7 and 8) emerged in this era as well (Warmoth, 1998).

We begin by looking at the philosophical roots of this Third Force. While concepts from both humanism and existentialism have common and overlapping concepts, there are also differences. This chapter describes and discusses the concepts that inspired humanist psychotherapy.

Philosophical Roots of Humanism

Humanism originally came from the Greek philosophic tradition of knowing oneself (Schneider, 1998). A variety of forms of humanism have emerged throughout history (*Humanist Manifesto*, 1933, 1973). Whether secular, religious, or educational humanism, they all uphold the same core values and beliefs (Schulz, 2002):

- the positive nature of self
- the directive capacity of humans
- a universal morality base
- a connection between the personal and social worlds and an intense faith in a future of peace and conflict resolution
- the transformation of society begins with personal and interpersonal values (Wilson, 1995)

Students who want to learn more about humanism as a philosophy should investigate the website of the American Humanist Association (www.americanhumanist.org).

Humanist psychotherapies incorporate these humanist values in the therapeutic relationship and practice, including a genuine client–therapist relationship, emphasis on knowing oneself and on thinking and becoming, respect for the human being, and appreciation of creativity and purpose in life (Bracke & Bugental, 2002). Humanist psychotherapies reject the objectification of the human being that is so entrenched in Western thinking (May, 1951). A person is a unique, determined, free entity (Aanstoos et al., 2000).

Humanist therapy sees self-actualization as the natural default condition for humans. When this actualization has not been achieved, it has been blocked through environmental variables, which humanist therapy focuses on removing. The therapy adopts a phenomenological approach so that the client and only the client (not the therapist), who knows his or her private world, understands his or her own perceptual field and is an expert on his or her own experiences (Raskin & Rogers, 2005).

It is within this zeitgeist that Carl Rogers (see About Carol Rogers box) developed the first well-articulated form of humanist psychotherapy. He did so in four major and overlapping phases (Kirschenbaum, 2004). First, Rogers emphasized individual work that stressed clarification of the client's feelings and insight and coping or acting positively. Second, in 1942, Rogers stressed faith in the person's capability, the actualizing tendency as the source of change for the client, and the necessary and sufficient conditions for therapeutic change. Third, Rogers established that the final goal of therapy was becoming "one's own experiencing," with an emphasis on *experiencing* (this later led to the development of more existential techniques). Fourth, in the 1970s, Rogers extended his individual psychotherapy to

ABOUT CARL ROGERS

Born on January 8, 1902, the fourth of six children, Carl Rogers grew up in Oak Park, Illinois. His father Walter, an engineer, valued hard work. His mother, Julia Cushing, was a strict, fundamentalist Christian. The family moved to a farm when Carl was 12, and he became fascinated by the growing process of plants and animals; he was very curious about how to facilitate growth, which became a lifelong passion for Rogers (Bohart, 2003).

In college, Rogers majored in religion and intended to enter the ministry. In 1922, however, after he traveled to Asia to attend a World Student Christian Federation Conference, he questioned his religious beliefs and changed his future goals. After graduating from the University of Wisconsin in 1924 with a BA in history, he married Helen Elliott and enrolled in Union Theological Seminary in New York City, where the couple's two children, David and Natalie, were born. Graduating with an MA in 1927 from Columbia Teachers College, Carl worked as a child psychologist at the Rochester Society for the Prevention of Cruelty to Children. After receiving a doctorate from Columbia in 1931, he published prolifically on the nature of the therapeutic relationship, on the constructive forces within each person, and on the importance of feelings and empathy (Rice & Greenberg, 1992).

His ideas about therapy differed greatly from Freud's and the neo-Freudians, so much so that he was even called the person who destroyed the unity of psychoanalysis (Gendlin, 2002). Rebelling against the role of the therapist as an all-knowing authority and an expert on others, Rogers believed the therapist should provide warmth, empathy, and respect to initiate positive change in the client (Lambert, Bergin, & Garfield, 2004). His insight gave him the reputation of a pioneer and "quiet revolutionary"; he is also considered the father of psychotherapy research (Bohart, 2003).

Rogers worked at Ohio State University, the University of Chicago, and the University of Wisconsin. He was active in the American Psychological Association and served as president of the APA in 1946–47. He was also a productive writer, completing numerous books and over 200 articles. By 1963, disillusioned with academic institutions, he moved to La Jolla, California; there he eventually formed the Center for Studies of the Person, where he worked for the remainder of his life. In his latter years, Rogers traveled around the globe to facilitate international conflict resolution. Thus his work evolved from a person and group emphasis to a universal system for obtaining inner and outer peace, and he was nominated for the Nobel Peace Prize in 1987. On February 4, 1987, Rogers died at the age of 85 after suffering a heart attack (Hall & Lindzey, 1985).

other arenas such as encounter groups, industry, educational settings, and national and international peace and conflict resolution (Moss, 1999).

Rogers first called his therapy *nondirective therapy,* and then *client-centered therapy.* The *person-centered approach* refers to the extension of the person-centered relationship of client-centered therapy to nontherapy encounters (such as encounter groups and psychoeducation) (Patterson, 2000). For clarity, this chapter refers to Rogers's therapy as *client-centered therapy.*

Humanistic Therapy Today

Today's humanist psychotherapies continue to be based on the essential components of Rogers's client-centered therapy. Client-centered therapy is considered to be one of the experiential therapies. These therapies are united by the assumptions that human nature is growth oriented, guided by choice, and inherently trustworthy.

They focus on promoting *experiencing* in therapy, as well as stressing a phenomeno-logical approach in which people create their own meaning. Other approaches in this experiential family are gestalt therapy, existential therapy, psychodrama, emotion-focused expressive therapies, body-oriented therapies, and experiential interpersonal views (Elliott, Greenberg, & Lietaer, 2004).

Another recent trend is to combine client-centered therapy with other mod-els. For example, one *process-experiential (PE) therapy,* which is called an *emotion-focused therapy,* combines elements of client-centered and gestalt therapies (Kirschenbaum & Jourdan, 2005); this approach integrates the therapy relationship with reflection on aroused emotion (Greenberg, Watson, & Lietaer, 1998). Some of the other PE approaches are Eugene Gendlin's (2002) focusing-oriented mode, dia-logical gestalt, and integrated forms of client-centered/experiential psychotherapy.

How these therapies are categorized has important implications, particularly for research reviews (Elliott, 2000a, 2000b; Elliott & Greenberg, 2002). For example, psychodrama has a very limited evidence base. However, if psychodrama is classi-fied as an experiential therapy, it is easier to obtain more supporting data for both psychodrama specifically and for experiential therapies in general. Humanist-existential therapies are discussed further in Chapters 7 and 8; The World Association for Person Centered and Experiential Psychotherapy and Counseling (WAPCEPC), an international organization founded in 1999, and the Division of Humanistic Psychology of the American Psychological Association, founded in 1971, are two major organizations representing humanistic therapy today.

← Theory of Client-Centered Therapy

Client-centered therapy, a form of humanistic and experiential therapy, is based on the assumption that all human beings possess a self-directed growth process that activates in the context of an appropriate interpersonal environment, namely, a genuine, caring, empathic, nonjudgmental relationship. Humans have the necessary resources for self-actualization, which can be tapped into and used effectively (Raskin & Rogers, 1989). It is a phenomenological approach; only the client is an expert on his or her own experiences and has the privilege of knowing his or her inner self. Reality is the person's perceptual field.

Key Concepts

The key concepts of client-centered therapy include self-actualization, the self (including the real self and the ideal self), congruence and incongruence, uncondi-tional positive regard, and conditions of worth. Some of the key features of the therapy are genuineness, empathy, and being a fully functioning person.

Self-Actualization

When free, a person naturally progresses toward healthy growth, much like a seed planted in fertile soil and properly nourished grows, blossoms, and becomes a beautiful flower. Just as biological functions unfold in a predictable pattern, so does personality development proceed in an expected direction toward *self-actualization.*

At the heart of human motivation is the self-actualizing tendency, an inner force that moves to "expand, extend, develop, mature . . . express and activate all of the capacities of the organism, or the self" (Rogers, 1961, p. 351). People have a need to survive, maintain, and enhance their lives and to move toward maturation, greater independence, and self-responsibility (Monte, 1987). The person tends to become his or her potentiality. Humans can extend their skills by becoming competent in the use of cultural tools (Rogers, 1977).

The Self

The *self* (also called the *self-structure* or the *self-concept*) is an organized configuration, a differentiated part of the person's phenomenological field (Hall & Lindzey, 1985). It is a kind of conceptual map categorizing information about ourselves in our environment. It is the "I" or the "me," the perceptions of the "I" or "me" in relationship to others, to the world, and to the values that the person attaches to his or her perceptions (Rogers, 1959). The self is the experience of the person as oneself, as the entire person at any given moment in time (Bohart, 2003).

The self is not a permanent structure but an ever-changing experience of one's self at any given moment (Rogers, 1961). The self is fluid and able to incorporate new experiences; it needs to be flexible as the person matures so that it can absorb and assimilate life experiences.

Self is what the person allows into awareness. Self or self-concept develops through social interactions, the earliest of which are usually parental. As the person goes through events in life, he or she processes them in various ways, which include (a) perceiving, organizing, and symbolizing them; (b) ignoring them if they do not seem to relate to self structure; or (c) denying or distorting them.

In order for a healthy self to form, the proper conditions must be met (Rogers, 1951, p. 501). There are two manifestations of the self: the real self and the ideal self.

The Real or Actual Self

The *real* or *actual self* is how the person really is, or who the person is in reality. The real self is what the person strives to be as he or she moves toward self-actualization. Suppose the child has a real self that is gentle and noncompetitive. He wants to relax, enjoy life, and avoid pressures, even though that goes against what his parents want—namely for him to be a great baseball player. He finds it is threatening when his real self and ideal self clash.

The Ideal Self

The *ideal self* is an internalized concept of who the person thinks he or she *should* be. The ideal self is often formed as a function of pressures from outside sources, such as parents and significant loved ones. It comes from what others say the person should be. If parents place conditions of worth on a child, such as expectations that he become a skilled baseball player, the child feels good about himself only if he performs as a high achiever. There is a discrepancy between the ideal and the real self. When the boy strikes out at the plate, he feels threatened and anxious because his real self (the boy who just struck out and is unmotivated to compete) and his ideal self (the boy who wants to excel at baseball to meet his parents' expectations) are discrepant. His real self is gentle and noncompetitive, but his ideal self is an ambitious athlete. When the ideal self and the real self are in conflict, a person is in the state of incongruence.

Congruence and Incongruence

Congruence means that a person is experiencing feelings that "are available to him, available to his awareness, and he is able to live these feelings; be them and able to communicate them if appropriate. . . . No one is perfectly congruent, but the more congruent is the person, the more healthy" (Rogers, 1961, p. 61). Congruence occurs when the real or actual self and the ideal self are in alignment and no inconsistencies exist.

Incongruence is a discrepancy between how an experience ought to be and how it really is, which leads to anxiety and emotional or psychological discomfort. To avoid the distress caused by these feelings, the person defends against anxiety by distorting experience. He will use denial and as a result will misinterpret his environment, which leads to unhealthy behavior. For example, the child who performs poorly at baseball may conclude that he is an unworthy or bad person, resulting in low self-esteem. His self-concept is too rigid to incorporate an image of himself that is not perfect. It is not acceptable to make mistakes. The ideal self and the real self are in conflict.

Symbolization is a process by which the person becomes aware of his or her experiences and then symbolizes them internally. For example, if a child is punished by a parent for being angry, anger could become a symbol of the bad girl. How he or she becomes conscious is a function of how the experience fits in with the self, meaning whether it is consistent with or inconsistent with the self (Rogers, 1959, p. 200).

Subception is a process by which the person senses or receives a stimulus from the environment but does not allow this perception to reach full awareness. The person is able to discriminate an event that is below the threshold of conscious awareness. If the material is threatening to the self, the person blocks the material from becoming conscious, defending the self from anxiety and, thus distorts reality; for example, the person uses denial, projection, rationalization, and so on, which are unhealthy ways of dealing with problems similar to Freud's defense mechanisms (Rogers, 1959, p. 200).

Unconditional Positive Regard

Unconditional positive regard is also called warmth, acceptance, caring, receiving, or respect (Raskin & Rogers, 1989). It is an attitude that emanates from one person to another (therapist, parent, friend) and not a specific technique. The person is accepted as a whole with no conditions placed upon him or her. The giver separates the person's behavior from the person. Thus, one can love and support another but still object to and not reinforce self-defeating and unhealthy behaviors. For example, a parent can completely accept a child as a whole person but can also know and understand that some of the child's behaviors are negative or undesirable. The person must know of the genuine caring so that communication of unconditional regard is essential (Rogers, 1986a).

Conditions of Worth

Conditions of worth are a particular set of specific standards imposed on a person when his or her value is judged by others such as parents, family, loved ones, teachers, and persons in authority. For example, if a parent tells a child he is good because he achieves high academic performance, the child is likely to incorporate these specific shoulds into his image of what makes him a good person and what makes him a bad person. What are the consequences to the self, then, when the child earns low grades? Does this make him less of a valued being? Is the self-image diminished? Such conditions of worth can wreak havoc with mental health and personality functioning.

For example, the *locus of evaluation* is how a person judges her- or himself and can be external or internal. If a person's locus is external, then he is dependent upon others for his values and judges himself on them. If the locus is internal, the person's judgment is based upon internal values, and she is free from the imposition of the standards of others (Raskin, 1952).

Genuineness and Empathy

Genuineness means a person (generally the therapist) is able to be herself fully and completely. She is conscious of her own feelings and is willing to express them openly and honestly. Since openness to experience is complete, the person who is genuine has little or no subception and defensiveness. For example, part of being genuine for a parent is to accept all feelings related to his or her child, including negative feelings toward the child's undesirable behavior. When a therapist is genuine, he or she self-discloses openly when it is beneficial for the client's welfare.

Empathy and *empathic listening* are based on respect for and understanding of the person as well as the ability to sense feelings and to grasp another's meaning and experiencing from moment to moment (Rogers, 1961, pp. 62–63). To listen empathically means to fully participate in the client's inner world and phenomenological field. The therapist gains empathy when he or she attends to the client's feelings in an intense, continuous fashion. Empathy is the therapist's tool to develop a relationship in which the client is understood in depth (Rogers, 1951).

Empathy is an interpersonal process central to the psychotherapy relationship. It is not a specific behavior, but an attitude toward and an experiencing of the client, which is intertwined with the congruence and unconditional positive regard of the therapist (Bozarth, 1997).

Normal and Abnormal Behavior

The *fully functioning person* embodies the ideal of mental health. Rogers (1951) describes the fully functioning person as an individual who is completely open to experience, judges the environment realistically, does not distort inner or outer events, listens to his or her own physical and psychological demands, is assertive, is resilient, expresses genuine and true feelings, lives each moment fully, allows the self to emerge spontaneously, is undeterred by anxiety, is unafraid of feelings, trusts in his or her own organism, is creative and nonconforming, does what he or she feels is right, is decisive, and is independent but can relate well to others. The fully functioning person has a self-structure that is congruent, with no discrepancy between the actual self and the ideal self. The perceived self and the actual self are one and the same (Monte, 1987, p. 522). Examples of fully functioning people are Buddha, Jesus, and Muhammad. Most people never reach this level of adjustment. However, since personality is a process, each person is always becoming a unique combination of biological, psychological, environmental, and cultural variables, striving to reach to the level of fully functioning person.

Abnormality is a function of incongruence. Rogers (1947) describes it as the organized concept of self that is available to conscious awareness but is not in accord with the perceptions the person actually experiences. How the person handles this discrepancy determines how well he or she is adjusted.

As described above, incongruence distorts reality, which in turn creates disorganization within the personality and produces clinical symptoms. The more serious the incongruence, the greater the distortion, and the more serious the symptoms. For example, a girl perceives herself as incompetent because she earns a low grade on an exam. This is because in the past her internalized conditions of worth included earning high grades in order to be a worthy human being. As a result, she feels anxious because earning the low grade results in her holding a perception of incompetence, which is not consistent with the self as able and competent. To deal with the anxiety, she defends herself. She denies the part of herself that feels incompetent, which in turn causes more incongruence. This threat makes her even more anxious. The more anxious she becomes, the more threatened she feels. The anxiety destabilizes her, and a vicious cycle ensues.

All people experience some discrepancies between the real self and the ideal self regularly. How these discrepancies are handled results in a healthy integration of self or symptoms such as overwhelming anxiety or other psychological disturbances.

The major cause of incongruence is placing conditions of worth on a developing child. Judgmental parents make their love conditional upon behavior. Children of such parents introject the parents' attitudes into their own self-image, creating fertile soil for the growth of incongruence. These children develop in a way so that they value positive regard from others more than they value following their own inner self (Rogers, 1961).

To be loved, the children of judgmental parents must be the way their parents want them to be. For example, Joan is very angry. When she expresses her rage, her parents show total disapproval. Thus to be loved, she cannot harbor anger and consequently learns to suppress her surging anger. Eventually, she is unaware that anger is a part of herself. When she experiences anger, which truly is a part of her actual self, she defends against it because if she acknowledges it is a part of her, she fears she will lose her parents' love. Experiencing her anger as bad, she denies her actual or real self. Joan is not her own experiences. Her adult self is formed upon false information, causing incongruence between her sensory and visceral experiences and her self-concept (Rogers, 1977). As her defenses become more rigid, she is confused and harbors self-doubt. She defends her own perceptions and further distorts reality. Gaining approval is so important that she is not becoming her own self, thus thwarting her movement toward self-actualization. Abnormal behaviors—such as neurosis, psychosis, and other clinical symptoms—are the result of a lack of unconditional positive regard; this is the necessary and sufficient condition for healthy growth toward self-actualization (Rowan, 2001). The more the personality structure is based upon evaluations and the approval of others, the more negative is the self-image. For Rogers (1957), the therapy relationship heals, and it is the most important variable in the success of person-centered psychotherapy.

✦ PRACTICE OF CLIENT-CENTERED THERAPY

Now that the basic concepts that underlie client-centered therapy have been examined, we will explore its practice. Dr. John Roberts is our composite, fictional client-centered psychotherapist who provides a firsthand perspective of how he integrates theory and practice and applies the techniques of person-centered psychotherapy.

Assessment and Diagnosis

My assessment and diagnosis are process oriented; thus I use them as a part of the therapy. Since the client is the ultimate expert on the self, my assessment is geared to help me to enter into the client's inner world, his internal frame of reference to help me to understand why he is as he is so I can help to set off the process of self-exploration within my client (Bohart, 2003). I look for blocks that prevent the client from solving problems and moving toward self-actualization. I assess markers (problematic reaction points) or a way in which the client acts that puzzles him.

I assess the client's stage of change (Rogers, 1961, pp. 155–156). I can use a technique called the Q-sort: 100 descriptor statements that are sorted into whether they are "most like or least like me." This allows my client and me to have descriptions from the client pre- and posttherapy between the perceived self and ideal self that are based upon the client's phenomenology (Raskin & Rogers, 2005). Recently, other measures such as the SCL-90 (Symptom Checklist-90) are replacing the Q-sort.

External assessments are value judgments, inconsistent with the very essence of person-centered therapy. If I use them, I must be careful not to risk denying my client's individualism, disrespecting her unique phenomenology, and treating her as a member of a group rather than as a unique person. As a modern experiential therapist, I may use the SCL-90 based upon the *DSM*. I do not find traditional assessments or a formal *DSM* diagnosis to be useful in helping my clients.

If my client and I agree, I tape sessions so I can review, study, and understand the process of my client's becoming the person he can be. If the client requests a copy of the session, she can have it.

Negotiation of Therapeutic Relationship and Length of Treatment

I try to establish a therapeutic relationship that provides the best possible conditions in which clients can explore themselves in an atmosphere of safety (Bozarth, 2001). People have the ability to be mature, healthy, and self-actualized, but I must provide the specific conditions that are necessary and sufficient to do so.

Specifically, I "enter into an intensely personal and subjective relationship with the client—relating not as a scientist to an object of study, not as a physician expecting to diagnose and cure, but as a person to person" (Rogers, 1961, p.184). I provide my client with my unconditional self-worth, and I feel he is of value no matter what he is doing or feeling or thinking (Rogers, 1961, 2000; Sharf, 2004).

My focus is to aid the client in identifying and clarifying her own inner experience to help her explore herself. I set this process in motion, and I produce what Carl Rogers considered to be the following necessary and sufficient conditions (Rogers, 1957, 1961):

- *Psychological contact* must be made between the client and me so that we are participants in a relationship that affects each other.
- *Incongruence* is present in the client so he is in a state of distress and vulnerability, and I am *congruent* in regard to this issue.
- *Genuineness* is present in me, the therapist. I must be in the state of congruence in the area that is of importance to the therapy.
- *Unconditional positive regard* is given to the client. I do not have to approve of all of my client's behaviors, but I do accept and care about the client as an individual, accepting every aspect of her humanness regardless of how hurtful, strange, eccentric, good, bad, or abominable her behavior may be.
- *Accurate empathy* is offered by me to the client. Not only do I enter into the client's private world, but I am comfortable within it.
- *Communication of my empathy and unconditional positive regard* to the client is essential. It is not enough to be empathic. I must let the client experience my true caring, understanding, and acceptance of him as a human being.

My clients' part is simply to be themselves; they need to express themselves freely and discuss anything they choose to discuss. As they grow in the environment created by my unconditional positive regard and accurate empathy, the opening up will unfold in the direction of self-actualization.

Meeting once per week for a 50-minute session is typical, but a client and I can plan any schedule of appointments that fits his or her needs. There is no specific time course for the therapy. I can see a client for a single session or for hundreds. A minimum of several sessions is helpful. The client decides what she needs since she is the expert on herself.

The goal of therapy is to facilitate the *inherent growth principle* that is present in my client and in all other living things. I tap into the self that a person truly is. I cannot and will not provide answers to clients because I trust in their own process. I help my clients identify and clarify their own inner experience, be self-directed, reach into their own self, and get at their own inner wisdom (Rogers, 1961).

Therapeutic Techniques

The most important treatment technique is the therapeutic relationship itself. I strive to establish the best possible conditions to assist my client to participate in inner exploration (Brodly, 2006). Once I set up the necessary conditions described earlier and remove any blocks, the client will move toward self-actualization. I rely on the relationship between me and the client to produce change.

It is difficult to give exact directions for and descriptions of what I do, but as a person-centered therapist, I use some specific techniques (Bohart, 2003; Bozarth, 1997). I use reflection as a way to help the client gain insight and understanding, and to communicate that I am in the same internal frame of reference and understand his or her inner world or phenomenological field (Monte, 1987).

To produce empathy, I am responsive to the client's meanings, feelings, and experiences. I communicate my sense of the client's world and frequently check with the client to get feedback to guide my responses. I act as a companion, pointing out the possible meanings in the flow of his or her experience (Rogers, 1961, p. 4).

I am sensitive at every single moment to the

> changing felt meanings which flow in this other person, to the fear or rage or tenderness or confusion or whatever he or she is experiencing. It means temporarily living in his/her life, moving about it delicately without making judgments, sensing, meanings of which he or she is scarcely aware, but not trying to uncover feelings of which the person is totally unaware, since this would be too threatening. It includes communicating your sensing of his/her world as you look with fresh and unfrightened eyes at elements of which the individual is fearful. It means frequently checking with him/her as to the accuracy of your sensing, and being guided by the responses you receive. You are a confident companion to the person in his/her inner world. By pointing to the possible meanings in the flow of his/her experience you help the person to focus on this useful type of referent, to experience the meanings more fully, and to move toward the experiencing. (Rogers, 1961, p. 4)

I self-disclose and share the experiences we have in common in order to communicate empathy and show that I deeply understand my client. I also adapt techniques from any other therapy if it will deepen the therapeutic relationship.

I am genuine and therefore spontaneous in responding to my client. I am in the moment in each session (Bozarth, 2001).

The Process of Therapy

In the initial phase of therapy, to paraphrase the words of Rogers (1961), I enter into a relationship with a person who is in a state of congruence and who wants to change in a positive direction. Once I provide an environment that makes the client feel "received welcomed, and understood," learning and growth begin (Rogers, 1961, p. 156).

My subgoals for the middle and end of therapy are not easily separated. They blend together because the relationship between the client and me is the essential ingredient.

The course of client-centered therapy differs for each unique client and for the goals the client chooses. Clients enter therapy at different stages of development. Their changes will come sooner or later depending on their unique pace. The time required to reach therapy goals depends upon the particular stage in which each client begins. I see the process of client growth in different threads that intertwine. These include (Rogers, 1961, pp. 155–156)

- unwillingness to communicate and little verbal discourse
- feelings—flowing from remote and unowned to the acceptance of continually changing emotions
- experiencing—from remote and fixed to increasingly accurate meanings and the ability to live freely and acceptingly
- incongruence—from no recognition of contradictions to short temporary incongruences between awareness and experience
- cognitive mapping of experience—moving from rigid, with experience as fact, to experience that changes with personal meaning
- problems—from initially unrecognized with no desire to change to complete responsibility
- relationships—from avoiding closeness to living openly and freely in relationship to the therapist and others

At first the threads are distinct and separable, but they move toward unity. Overall, the process shifts from fixed single strands to "flowing peak moments of therapy in which all of these threads become inseparably woven together" (Rogers, 1961, p. 158). The client changes and becomes an interrelated process of changingness (Rogers, 1961). These stages in the flow of the process of change are defined in detail by Rogers in *On Becoming a Person* (1961). Termination occurs when the client decides she is ready; she also determines the outcome.

In the ideal termination, which is theoretical, the outcome is that the person has become self-actualized and is completely open, fluid, congruent, accepting of self, genuine, integrated, authentic, self-aware, and self-accepting. Defenses are discarded, facades are dropped, and the person is open to be what he truly is. He changes from wanting to be a finished product to being a person in process. The therapist also becomes part of the client's experience (Zimring & Raskin, 1992, pp. 642–643). How far and to what end stage the client aspires is his or her decision. Progress is made as long as the client is satisfied. The client's self-report is the most important indicator of success in therapy.

If so desired by the client, a Q-sort can illustrate objectively the client's subjective view of his or her change. It is way to measure change both qualitatively and quantitatively. I measure and verify changes in the perceived self in sortings before therapy, in the middle, at termination, and at the first and second follow-up interviews (Rogers, 1961). As a modern experiential therapist, I may use the SCL-90.

THERAPY IN ACTION: DR. JOHN ROBERTS AND THE CASE OF JONATHAN

To illustrate the application of client-centered therapy, we examine a treatment plan for Jonathan followed by excerpts from therapy sessions with our fictional psychotherapist, Dr. Roberts. Keep in mind the case excerpts are simulated interviews and represent the ideal of therapy. In real life, clients may take much longer to meet therapeutic goals. Table 6.1 provides a summary of Dr. Roberts's treatment plan.

Case Excerpts

The following excerpts are based on phrasing from Rogers's original interviews (Rogers, 1961, pp. 64–65).

Session 1

Dr. Roberts: If you would like, tell me something about what brought you here.

Jonathan: [*shares background of losing Tuti and his consequent depression*]

Dr. Roberts: My job is to provide you with a relationship without pretense. I offer you my openness. I will tell you frankly the feelings that flow in myself any time it is helpful to you.

Jonathan: OK . . . but I feel I just want to give up.

Dr. Roberts: I can sense that you're in deep despair.

Jonathan: Aahh . . . um. [*tears well up, cries*]

Dr. Roberts: [*gently and sincerely*] I can see how really painful this is for you.

Jonathan: [*crying, he begins to talk*] Thanks . . . I appreciate that. I feel so alone. I never cry. I am falling apart; it's like a kick in the stomach. It hurts so much. Tuti was my friend. She reassured me when I felt shaky or lost my grounding. I hurt inside.

Dr. Roberts: Can you stay with the hurt? It seems really important just to let yourself feel how bad it is.

Jonathan: Yes perhaps . . . but then I'm worried I'll fall apart.

Dr. Roberts: Am I correct in sensing you are frightened, fearful, even terrified?

Table 6.1

Client-Centered Treatment Plan for Jonathan

Assessment and Formulation	• Presenting problem: loss of relationship and incongruence for J. • Ideal self is calm, loving, anger free • Real self is enraged, hateful, agitated • Conditions of worth were placed on J. by parents to never be angry, always be loving
Therapeutic Relationship	• Provide proper environment of good therapeutic relationship • Client in state of incongruence • Communicate to J. that therapist provides necessary and sufficient conditions of psychological contact, accurate empathy, unconditional positive regard, genuine and congruent in the area of relationships
Contract, Goals, and Treatment Plan	• Unblock path to self-actualization • Self-healing of client will be released • Agree to what is beneficial for client • Weekly meetings
Techniques	• Provide the proper therapeutic relationship • Reflect feelings and experience
Process of Therapy	• Move through stages: feelings shown but not owned; experience is bound by past; rigid personal constructs to freer flow of expression of self as an object; feelings shown and recognized as feelings; recognition of contradiction in experiences; and personal choices as ineffective
Termination and Outcome	• J. expressed feelings in present, directly, immediately, with less denial and fear struggling; experiences new way of being • Client is satisfied with progress • Q-sort or SCL-90 shows improved self-image and symptoms

Jonathan: Exactly. Without her I'm adrift . . . lost . . . moving in circles. I need her to make it worth my while to go on. I wish I were dead . . . but I must go on. What will happen to me? I should be ashamed. Maybe I did something to deserve it. I must be pretty rotten inside. Can you see how bad I am? I have screwed things up badly.

Dr. Roberts: And so I guess you find yourself turning to me for some kind of expert evaluation of what kind of a person you are. And I find myself wanting to say to you that I really do not know you very well yet, but I sure don't find it in me to judge you badly for how you've handled this.

Jonathan: I am surprised at how upset I am. I put everything I had into the relationship. She threw me away, not caring. I can never trust again. They did not have to be so rotten to me. I can't get rid of these feelings. And how can I let myself feel so bad, so incapacitated?

Dr. Roberts: Your feelings seem more powerful than you thought. Does it make you anxious when you cannot predict your feelings and know yourself for certain?

Jonathan: Yes. You are right on target. I am afraid that I'll do something wrong. [*silence*] I worry. Do you think I am a bad person?

Dr. Roberts: What are *you* feeling, Jonathan, to ask me that question?

Jonathan: I'm not sure. Am I being punished for hating them? For being mad? [*sobbing*] I am not a violent person. How can I be sure I won't get so mad and do something terrible?

Dr. Roberts: You are asking me to reassure you that your feelings will not get out of control. And I want to comfort you and say it will be OK, but I do not know what you feel and will do. I want to help you and support you.

Jonathan: Maybe it is me, but a part of me I thought I had overcome. When I was in sixth grade I beat up a kid who was stealing stuff from my locker. I found myself on top of him hitting him in the face with my fist. Suddenly, I stopped myself and asked, What am I doing? Blood was running down his nose. I was afraid I had hurt him. He ran off and we never spoke about it again. I don't want that now.

Dr. Roberts: You are frightened your feelings of anger could get out of control now . . . the way they did when you were in sixth grade?

Jonathan: [*crying*] Yes . . . yes . . . yes. I never want to do that again. I had not thought about it, but I am so mad [*clenches his fists*] that if I see them, I might do something I would later regret. It wouldn't be me.

Dr. Roberts: So your behavior in the past and the emotions you are feeling right now, do they belong to you? Is it part of yourself and how you see yourself?

Jonathan: I never thought of it quite this way before. I pride myself on being a calm, kind, and rational guy, not one who flies off the handle. I solve problems if you give me the time.

Dr. Roberts: So you want time to work on these feelings that seem as if they are problem to you, that seem to be so scary to you? Is that right?

Jonathan: Yes. I need to learn to control my feelings. And I can't believe I loved them. And now it has turned to hate.

Dr. Roberts: So it is confusing. At this time you feel fury toward them, and not long ago you loved them. So you are really questioning who the person was that loved and now is so angry.

Jonathan: Yes. Acknowledging this fury feels strange, even foreign. I feel just in talking this way so far I am getting more upset. I am beginning to see that I love Tuti and Darren, but I am surprised at how love changed to hate. The feeling comes from here, like alum inside my throat. Is it me? I don't like this, your bringing it up to the surface, but I need to work on this and begin to experience what I really am. I feel pretty comfortable with you. You seem to accept me and what I am experiencing. I sense I can trust you.

Dr. Roberts: And now I sense a willingness to go on and explore and understand yourself.

Jonathan: Yes, I'd like to see you a couple times a week at first, please.

Session 20

Jonathan: I have been grappling with how surprised I was that I had such anger. I think I have been suppressing it for many years. I am an angry person. I can see myself clearly—and am several different selves! The angry Jonathan, the loving Jonathan, the not jealous Jonathan.

Dr. Roberts: You recognize that you have many contradictions within you.

Jonathan: Yes. Exactly. I didn't know it, but I suppose we all have contradictions. For example, I am heartbroken, but there is a part of me that says I can start a new life all over again. I have bits and pieces of myself all around, and I have to pick them up and put them back together, and how I rearrange the pieces is important. Almost as though I am physically putting myself back together and that maybe I can be a better person than I am now or was with Tuti.

Dr. Roberts: So your process is becoming but there is a sense of wanting to be a different self . . . that your self is not good enough, and you are putting conditions on your value and worth.

Jonathan: Yes . . . and then may be I can be the person I want to be. And then I might stop being the person she needed me to be.

Session 40

Jonathan: I couldn't wait to see you today. You are my safe place. This may sound silly, but at times I think I was not the person I wanted to be. I was trying to fit myself into a mold so that everything I did would be right for my relationship. I don't want to blame anyone else. I did it to myself. I was uncomfortable with some of the things I did and thought. Talking with you makes me feel accepted. I am who I am. OK. The real truth is that I knew Tuti wanted kids, but I thought I'd convince her not to. I was very self-centered.

Dr. Roberts: You feel safe enough so your anger and your selfishness are accepted here and you can be who you really are.

Jonathan: I know I am a good person at the core. But I am too selfish to give what you have to give to be a good dad. What is wrong with that?

Dr. Roberts: Does it make it easier to accept it yourself if you are accepted here?

Jonathan: Yeah. I wish Tuti had also accepted me.

Dr. Roberts: So you are exploring yourself . . . and you are feeling more comfortable. It's difficult to put it into words, into concrete terms, but here with me you are really able to experience it and discuss it and that makes it less scary. And you are better able to accept it is you.

Termination

Jonathan: I feel much more like a whole person. I believe now I can understand that all of this is me. All of us continue to change as long as we are alive!

Dr. Roberts: I'd like to see if I can capture what it means to you. You know yourself much more intimately and have touched the core of yourself. You know this core as something that is good. No one can take it from you, and you really know how valuable it is to you.

Jonathan: Strange that you say it, but you do understand where I am—learning to respect myself and to give and receive love. And I feel so much more open. I understand more about how Tuti felt and how she could not be who she really was, and that maybe it is time for each of us to do what we needed to grow as humans. She was doing what she needed to do, and now I am free to be myself and explore my options. I may be a different person without her. But it is important to become my best. I will have new and different life experiences now. I am better off because I just accept myself for who I am. I understand now, and I can go it alone until I need a recharging.

Case Comment

Jonathan responded well to the relationship I was able to provide for him. I tried to make him feel received, welcomed, and understood. I saw that Jonathan learned and grew and moved toward becoming more self-actualized. At first, Jonathan did not see rage as belonging to him, but the intensity of his feelings jarred him into a recognition that rage is a part of him. Jonathan thinks, "I love Tuti and Darren, so it is incongruous that I can feel this enraged toward them." He was motivated to continue working through his pain. I continued to use nonjudgmental, unconditional acceptance to begin the process of building a relationship and a safe environment in which he could explore his incongruity.

We reached into Jonathan's past experiences where the incongruity was formed. He began to realize he can be all of his own experience. As he explored and experienced the anxiety accompanying the incongruity without the defensiveness of subception, I offered him warmth, genuineness, and unconditional positive regard. I used accurate empathy and reflection during the interviews, reflecting back his own feelings to him, allowing him to feel understood.

Termination occurred when Jonathan truly accepted anger as a part of himself, resulting in greater congruence. He is in balance in that he is aware of and accepts the intensity of his emotions. As therapy progressed, Jonathan's expressions about self flowed more freely. He accepted communications about his anger from his inner self and broke through subception of emotions when he was afraid of his anger because it disorganized him and felt shameful; he recognized his fears of being alone and abandoned. He opened up to his self and became less evaluative and critical. Finally, he accepted his own feelings and others' as well. He increased self-esteem, reached levels of congruence sufficient for himself, and trusted more in his own self.

← RESEARCH DIRECTIONS OF CLIENT-CENTERED THERAPY

The evidence base associated with Rogers's client-centered therapy is large, complex, involved, and fraught with controversy. More than half a century old, it contains an extensive body of research that includes theoretical writings, qualitative studies, process and outcome studies, meta-analyses, and those that look at person-centered therapies as part of a matrix of experiential therapies. Differences of opinion about how to interpret the accumulated results abound.

The field of psychotherapy owes a debt to Rogers for his early pioneering work. He encouraged scientific scrutiny, analysis, critique, replication, and validation of psychotherapy (Orlinsky, Ronnestad, & Willutski, 2004). Rogers (1961, 1986b) was the first to audio-record and transcribe sessions to create a permanent database of verbatim accounts. Rogers (1957) adapted statistician William Stephenson's Q-sort technique to measure perceived changes in the self over the course of therapy (Brown, 1996). Comparing the change in self-image scores of clients with no-treatment controls allowed Rogers to objectively study the subjective self.

Rogers's research was of two types: (a) process studies, which attempted to find the necessary and sufficient conditions for psychotherapeutic change, and (b) outcome studies to confirm the effectiveness of client-centered therapy (Hill &

Lambert, 2004). Accurate empathy, genuineness, and acceptance, among other therapist characteristics, were seen as both necessary and sufficient conditions for the success of therapy (Rogers, 1961, pp. 127, 225). Effectiveness researchers indicated that the outcomes for clients who received Rogerian therapy was that they were more congruent and thus better adjusted psychologically (Patterson, 1984; Rogers & Dymond, 1954).

Critics have argued that these conclusions are not sound because these studies contained serious methodological flaws. For example, evaluations were based on the rater's, not the client's, view. Rated segments of therapy were too brief, and nonverbal communications were left unrated. These studies also used vague rating scales, self-reports, and lack of appropriate controls (Beutler, Crago, & Arezmendi, 1986). Disbelievers also argued that college students, who were the primary people with whom Rogers worked, had only mild psychological problems (Prochaska & Norcross, 2003). However, Rogers did a study of hospitalized schizophrenics and found that those who experienced higher levels of empathy, warmth, and genuineness spent the fewest days in the hospital, though they did not make significant gains on other outcome measures (Rogers, Gendlin, Kiesler, & Truax, 1967). Critics also argued that alternative explanations—for example, cognitive restructuring—might enhance the quality of the therapeutic relationship and thus be responsible for changes in the client rather than the necessary and sufficient conditions of personality changes described by Rogers (Bozarth, 1998, 1999; Gordon, 2000).

In the 1970s, the practice of pure client-centered therapy declined in the United States, although its practice remained popular in Europe. With that decline in practice came a halt to the research on most forms of experiential therapies (Greenberg, Elliott, & Lietaer, 1994). However, the advent of meta-analytic methods in the 1980s revived interest in Rogerian research. The results of meta-analyses in general showed that the outcome effects of client-centered therapy exceeded those of no-treatment and placebo groups. Thus the equivalency effect applied to client-centered therapies (Smith & Glass, 1977; Smith, Glass, & Miller, 1980).

More recently, proponents have looked at client-centered therapy together with other experiential therapies collectively. These researchers (Elliott et al., 2004) reviewed 112 studies of 6,569 clients, categorizing the studies into client-centered only (52), nondirective (11), PE therapies that were task focused and integrative experiential (18), gestalt (10), encounter/sensitivity (11), and others (15). The data were analyzed with current methodologies (Chambless & Hollon, 1998). The results indicated that clients treated with experiential therapies were better off than untreated clients and "clients maintained or perhaps even increased their post-treatment gains over the post-therapy period" (Elliott et al., 2004, p. 494).

In a review of 32 studies comparing outcomes of client-centered or nondirective/supportive therapies to cognitive behavior therapy (CBT), experiential therapies were as helpful as CBT in the treatment of depression, anxiety, trauma and interpersonal difficulties, marital problems, schizophrenia, and personality disorders. They may be efficacious in the treatment of aggression and health-related conditions (Chambless & Hollon, 1998).

In the 1990s, interest grew in finding empirically supported therapies. Professional groups (such as the APA) identified therapies with proven track records of outcome research as empirically supported therapies. Client-centered therapy was not on the list. Compared to CBT, client-centered therapy had fewer outcome studies. Insurance companies supported therapies with a strong outcome evidence base. As a result, therapy practice and training programs moved toward the use of directive, empirically validated interventions and away from nondirective techniques (Lambert et al., 2004, p. 811).

However, client-centered advocates noted that client-centered principles were used by many, if not most practicing therapists. Furthermore, more and more schools of psychotherapy were recognizing the significance of the therapeutic relationship "as a means to, if not a core aspect, of therapeutic change" (Kirschenbaum & Jourdan, 2005, p. 10). While only a small number of therapists call themselves pure client centered , more than a third of eclectic therapists integrate methods from these models into their therapies (Bohart & Greenberg, 1997). Thus it is just as important to consider empirically supported *relationships* as it is to study empirically supported therapies (Norcross, 2001, 2002).

A number of studies have focused on the relationship components of client-centered therapy—such as empathic understanding, positive regard, and congruence. Other meta-analytic research has examined the components of client-centered therapy that have been integrated into other forms of therapy (Bohart, O'Hara, & Leitner, 1998; Elliott, 2000a, 2000b). Client-centered proponents claim that empathy, unconditional positive regard, and probably congruence are core conditions that are essential to effective psychotherapy (Bohart, Elliott, Greenberg, & Watson, 2002).

Others say that accurate empathy, warmth, and genuineness do facilitate therapeutic success but may not be necessary and/or sufficient variables (Orlinsky & Howard, 1986). Michael Lambert (2004) cautions that the large effects found in meta-analyses should be tempered with the knowledge that "innovative therapists . . . whose allegiance to the viewpoint is strong" conducted the research reviews (Lambert et al., 2004, p. 812). A strong allegiance can produce a greater effect for a favored model (Luborsky et al., 1999). No one denies that experiential therapies have made substantial contributions to a body of research on therapeutic process and relationship, but a more conservative interpretation says the data do not justify the strong claim that they are unconditionally supported (Beutler et al., 2004).

Countercriticisms are that much of the research on core conditions does not actually evaluate client-centered therapy because the therapy is not treated holistically, which means that the researchers are not studying the therapy as proposed and created by Rogers. Valid conclusions cannot be drawn when there are differences in the definitions and operationalizing of concepts (Raskin, Rogers, & Witty, 2008).

Experiential research findings have been used to shape practices. There is evidence that, if experiential components are added to client-centered therapy, outcomes are improved (Greenberg & Pascual-Leone, 2006). The *pure, nondirective client-centered approach* calls for the therapist to *be* with the client. It views the therapy relationship as the ingredient that is necessary and sufficient for change. The *process-directive experiential approach* is more active, directs process, and attempts to deepen the experience within the context of a client-centered relationship. It calls for the therapist to *do* something with the client (Lambert et al., 2004, p. 812).

Process-experiential (PE) therapy is a developing form of humanist-existential psychotherapy that integrates elements of client-centered and gestalt therapies by combining techniques from the therapeutic relationship and reflection on aroused emotions to create new meaning for the client (Greenberg, Rice, & Elliott, 1993). Research shows that process-directive therapies seem to be slightly superior to nondirective experiential therapies. It appears that it is not the traditional nondirective, client-centered aspect of experiential therapy that is producing the largest effect, but the action-oriented directive interventions. These effects rival those of behavioral and cognitive interventions.

Experiential therapists have challenged the assumption that empirically validated therapies are truly more worthwhile than other therapies (Western, Novotny, & Thompson-Brenner, 2004); they argue that the methods used to determine outcome may be dehumanizing and may be an ineffective way to test the usefulness of a therapy that is looking at the bigger questions in life. Experiential therapists recognize that it is important to produce an evidence base, but they point out that the nature of experiential therapy itself makes it difficult to empirically validate (King et al., 2000). They argue that other therapies have been shown to be effective in so many studies because they are easier to measure and research. For example, keeping track of negative thoughts in CBT is much simpler than quantifying the attainment of self-actualization. However, outcome measures that are short term, that implicitly endorse the medical model, and that depend on the manualization of treatments are inconsistent with the holistic and longer term values of experiential therapies (Bohart, 2003). It is inherently unfair to say one therapy is better than another based on the nature of outcome measures.

Humanist-existential proponents ask that mainstream empiricism adopt psychotherapy research that respects qualitative methods and provides rigorous inquiry into the experiential world, guides the development of relevant hypotheses, renders insights into psychological processes, and provides rigorous research into everyday situations (Schneider, 1998). They remind others that since the major therapies that have been studied are uniformly beneficial, this should not be discounted for the client-centered approach (Wampold, 2006).

What can the therapist say to the client to justify his or her use of client-centered therapy? The therapist can explain to the client that over a 50-year span, research into client-centered therapy has produced a substantial number of studies that lend some level of support that it is effective (Bohart, 1996). Although the experts sometimes disagree about how to interpret many of these findings, they do agree that the equivalency effect applies, so experiential therapies are as effective as nonexperiential therapies (Purton, 2002). Clients who participate in client-centered therapies improve more than those who receive no therapy (Wampold, 2001).

In addition, research shows that the client-centered relationship as developed in client-centered therapy—including unconditional positive regard and genuineness or congruence as described by Rogers and authenticity as upheld by existential psychotherapists—is important in the success of therapy. Once a genuine therapy relationship is established, the therapist integrates aspects of the various therapies that fit the client's and therapist's individual personalities (Hill & Nakayama, 2000).

The therapist should decide to use client-centered therapy based upon a combination of factors—clinical expertise, clinical experience, and the research on client-centered and other experiential therapies that exists. Person-centered therapy has an established track record as a useful therapy. Although some experts disagree about the nature of some of the findings, one central finding is that the therapeutic relationship is a most important ingredient to the success of therapy. Client-centered therapy is the relationship that has been tested.

← ISSUES OF DIVERSITY

One criticism aimed at the very heart of client-centered and other experiential therapies is that "the emphasis on a separate bounded, autonomous self that self actualizes" is based on Western values of individualism, along with White, male ideals (Bohart, 1996). The very concept of self is a function of culture, with different conceptions of boundaries in various cultures. In Western society, boundaries are firm and well established. Causes are located inside the individual, not outside. But in some non-Western societies, the boundary of self does not stop at the skin of one client but extends to members of a significant reference group, such as family or kin. Fluid boundaries are valued over firm self-boundaries. In Asian American and Hispanic cultures, the psychosocial unit of operation is the group, and the individual is not always first. For example, Westerners ask "How are you today?" and Asians and Hispanics ask "How is your family today?"

The nondirectiveness of client-centered therapy is not equally valued and respected by all cultures (Poyrazli, 2003). In hierarchical cultures, the client will tend to defer to the therapist as an expert. These clients may have problems with the nonauthoritative stance of the client-centered therapist and may even feel misunderstood. The expectations of how and what an expert ought to communicate to others differs for various cultures. What seems like empathic caring in the West may be perceived as uncaring by other cultures. The communication style of the client-centered therapist may not be well tolerated for those who do not like ambiguity. Many who seek advice from an authority figure may expect to receive specific information. Some minorities group members have a more positive response to the influencing skills than others (Wong, 2003). For example, "American Indians, Asian Americans, Black Americans, and Hispanic Americans prefer more active directive forms of helping than nondirective ones" (Sue & Sue, 2003, p. 144).

Another issue to consider is that the basic philosophical belief that clients have the resources to solve their own problems if the therapist gives them unconditional positive regard seems to dismiss or minimize the importance of the social maladies that contribute to human misery. In this way of thinking, the client's problems reside "within the individual rather than society" (Sue & Sue, 2003, p. 147). Some contend that experiential psychotherapy actually supports the social and political status quo unintentionally because its proponents have remained fairly silent about social change (Prilleltensky, 1992). Others complain that client-centered therapy fails to consistently and proactively address structural violence caused by the inequalities in access to resources that are a function of race, gender, and class. Client-centered therapists need to address these dimensions of structural difference in power in order to be helpful to the client (Chantler, 2005, 2006).

In defense of Carl Rogers and his psychotherapy, his intent was to extend client-centered values of respect, love, and empathy to all cultures and oppressed persons (Rogers, 1977). A genuine and authentic therapist is positive when it enables the therapist to openly share and explore thoughts and feelings about racism. An effective way to handle issues such as prejudice, discrimination, and oppression is to discuss them openly and honestly and to admit what the therapist does not know about others, either as individuals or as a member of a group. Direct engagement with these variables could enhance client-centered therapy and practice (Chantler, 2005).

The values of humanistic psychotherapy are skewed in the direction of supporting culturally competent practice. For example, these therapies have overtly encouraged gender equity and a feminist perspective with sympathetic components such as the ability to tolerate silence, to listen well, to respect the client, and to be open-minded and nonjudgmental (Black, 2005). Client-centered therapy is not bound by any time constraints in theory, only by the pragmatic life circumstances of the client. Since the client is the expert on the self, he or she decides what is needed in therapy, when satisfactory goals have been accomplished, and when therapy ends. He or she is in control of the process and is not dependent upon the authority of others.

← MAJOR CRITIQUES OF CLIENT-CENTERED THERAPY

Critics say that the theoretical constructs and concepts of client-centered therapy are vague, unclear, and lack construct validity. For example, Rogers adapted a number of biological concepts, such as an innate drive toward self-actualization, that have no basis in evidence (Rowan, 2001). Rogers's notion of a self-actualizing tendency is as obtuse as Freud's notion of the id. How does the researcher quantify self-actualization? Or the self construct? This lack of operationally defined constructs leaves client-centered theories without empirical measures. The result is that little prediction or control is possible, making it difficult both to test the theories and to make predictions about future behavior.

Humanists see the human condition from a more optimistic, even naive, perspective. They trust in the goodness of humankind if left to its own devices. But how do they account for evil in the world? How can they deal with the dark and dangerous side of humanity? Have they turned a blind eye to wars, genocides, and oppression? There does not seem to be an in-depth discussion of these very real matters and the social problems that arise from them.

Critics claim that a vague theory means that practice must also be poorly defined. How do therapists know they are practicing congruence, unconditional regard, and empathic understanding with scientific precision? A tremendous degree of uncontrolled variability is within each client's self. It is difficult to be certain that two people are conducting the same therapy. Some manuals have been developed, but it is difficult to standardize empathy. Is it realistic to expect a therapist to give any client true unconditional love and be totally empathic? Will learning in the therapy session generalize to the harsh realities of the real world? Critics also claim that the practice of client-centered therapy encourages self-centeredness, even to the point of self-worship (Vitz, 1977).

Others counter that if a client is encouraged to attain self-actualization, he or she will be altruistic. Rowan (2001) says that although these suspicions are understandable, it is clear that humanistic psychotherapy is not intended to promote narcissism, selfishness, or egotism. Rather, it encourages movement toward a fuller sense of self. The tendency of popular culture to associate humanistic discourse with narcissistic and overly optimistic worldviews is highly unfortunate (Bohart & Greening, 2001). Rogers's work is more consistent with the Eastern view of self and selflessness. Self-actualization can be seen as similar to nirvana, where people ultimately strive to become self-*less*.

Others say it is difficult to train someone to be a client-centered therapist. How can a supervisor teach a supervisee to be genuine? One can verbally instruct a person, but how can the supervisor know with certainty that the trainee is using his or her real self?

No one has contributed more to understanding the role of the therapeutic relationship than Carl Rogers. Yet critics continue to claim that experiential psychotherapies, including client-centered therapy, lack a systematized, coherent empirical base of methodologically sound outcome research; as well, the process studies tend to be piecemeal, are not sufficiently outcome-oriented, and do not answer the questions about efficacy and effectiveness. Critics say that client-centered, and all experiential therapists, rely too much on subjective and self-reporting. Furthermore, the emphasis on the therapeutic relationship may de-emphasize the need for the therapist to acquire a skills-based training in psychotherapeutic techniques. These therapists may actually miss opportunities to help clients since they do not emphasize action and education in the therapy.

Regardless of the criticisms, Rogers contributed invaluably to psychotherapy by emphasizing the importance of research. We can reasonably assume that Rogers would continue to advocate for research today, although he might offer some ethical objections to the emphasis on outcome research and the political and economic motivations behind it. But his early research programs produced a number of therapist-researchers whose descendants continue to conduct numerous studies today.

Summary

- Historically, client-centered therapy emerged from a cultural zeitgeist in which humanist and existential philosophies became popular in the mainstream of American culture and the behavioral sciences.

- The major theoretical assumption of client-centered therapy is that all humans possess a drive toward self-actualization, or a growth process that activates in the context of a genuine, caring, empathic, nonjudgmental relationship.
- The individual possesses a self (a real self, and an ideal self) that can be in congruence (if healthy) or in incongruence, when there is discrepancy between the real and ideal self, which leads to anxiety.
- Unconditional positive regard is an attitude of warmth, acceptance, caring, and respect that emanates from one person to another. Conditions of worth, or standards imposed on a person when being judged by others, can result in subception, which distorts reality.
- Genuineness means a person is able to be herself fully and completely. Empathy and empathic listening are based on respect for and understanding of the person and an ability to sense feelings and to grasp another's meaning and experiencing in the moment.
- Abnormality is a function of incongruence, which in turn creates disorganization within the personality and produces clinical symptoms. The fully functioning person embodies ideal mental health.
- The practice of client-centered therapy is based on the therapeutic relationship, which involves psychological contact between the client and therapist; the therapist must be congruent for the client and must communicate genuineness, unconditional positive regard, and empathy to the client. The goal of therapy is to facilitate the inherent growth principle. There is no specific time course for the therapy.
- Therapeutic techniques include the therapeutic relationship itself, reflection, self-disclosure, and sharing experiences. The process of therapy brings a person from a state of incongruence to congruence. Termination occurs when the client decides he or she is ready, as only the client determines the outcome.
- Rogers is the father of psychotherapy research; he initiated tape-recording sessions and the Q-sort method in psychotherapy. The evidence base for client-centered therapy is large and complex. Critics argue that some conclusions are not sound because studies contained serious methodological flaws. In the 1990s, client-centered therapy was not on the list of empirically validated therapies, but there is data to call it an empirically supported relationship. New therapies—process-directive experiential approach and process-experiential therapy—show promise. Experiential therapists argue that mainstream empiricism should adopt qualitative methods to evaluate psychotherapy research.
- Members of non-Western cultures may have values that clash with self-actualizing, individualistic values of client-centered therapy. The indirect style of helping may also be unfamiliar to people from non-Western cultures.
- Major criticisms of client-centered therapy are that its constructs are vague, and its research lacks validity. A vague theory means that practice may also be poorly defined. Self-centeredness may also be encouraged, because popular culture associates humanism with narcissism. Overly optimistic worldviews may be naive.

RESOURCES

World Association for Person-Centered and Experiential Psychotherapy and Counseling (WAPCEPC)
P. O. Box 142
Ross-on-Wye
HR9 9AG
United Kingdom
http://www.pce-world.org/idxjournal.htm

The WAPCEPC is for therapists working within the client-centered and the experiential paradigms. It fosters and encourages communication, research, and improvement of practice across language groups and cultures. It publishes *Person-Centered and Experiential Psychotherapies.*

Rogerian Training Institutes
Center for Studies of the Person
1150 Silverado Street, Suite 112
La Jolla, CA 92037
(858) 459-3861
http://www.centerfortheperson.org

The Center for Studies of the Person is an excellent resource center offering website listings, papers, DVDs, and other information about Carl Rogers.

Association for Humanistic Psychology (AHP)
1516 Oak Street, #320A
Alameda, CA 94501-2947
(510) 769-6495
http://www.ahpweb.org

The AHP is an organization formed in 1962 by Abraham Maslow, Carl Rogers, Rollo May, and others to support contact and communication among persons who share the values of humanism and want to express their maximum potential as human beings. Membership is open to anyone. The AHP offers workshops and publications to accomplish their mission.

Person Centered Expressive Therapy Institute (PCETI)
726 Mendocino Avenue
Santa Rosa, CA 95401
http://www.pceti.org

The PCETI is an organization run by Natalie Rogers, an expressive art therapist and daughter of Carl Rogers. The work is based on her father's philosophy. The institute provides psychotherapist training, personal growth, and communication.

CLASS EXERCISES AND ACTIVITIES

Theory

1. The origins of humanistic psychotherapy are embedded in a social and cultural context. Trace the origins.
2. How are the core concepts of humanism present in American psychotherapy and society today? Why would a client choose a therapist based upon the underlying core values of client-centered therapy?
3. Access these websites for humanistic psychotherapies: http://www.ahpweb.org/aboutahp/whatis.html; http://www.pce-world.org/idxjournal.htm. Compare contemporary humanism with ideas about humanism from history.

Practice

1. Play the role of Carl Rogers. Explain your therapeutic practice with a client. Compare and contrast the major practices that are at the core of humanistic psychotherapy.
2. What are the differences and similarities between the practices of client-centered therapy and psychoanalysis? Mention goals, techniques, and measurable outcomes. Compare the goals of self-actualization with insight or social interest as a goal of psychotherapy. Which do you think is more important in working with clients? Why? What cultural values affect your judgment?
3. Look at the sample treatment plan in Chapter 1 (Figure 1.2). Fill out the plan for Tuti for client-centered or experiential therapy. (Both Jonathan's and Tuti's case histories are in Appendix A.)

Research

1. Outcome research is like a snapshot since it captures one moment in time. Process research is like a movie or video since it records over a longer time period. Explain the differences between the two types of research in experiential psychotherapy. Comment on the unique contribution of each to an understanding of psychotherapy. Which type of research is more helpful to the practicing clinician?
2. A patient asks you, "Why are you using client-centered or any form of experiential therapy to treat me? How did you choose this particular model for me?" Justify your choice.
3. Conduct a review of client-centered therapies using the following key words in PubMed: *client-centered therapy*. What did you find? Limit your search to *client-centered therapy and randomized control*. What did you find? What kinds of articles are available about research into client-centered therapy? Taking a quick overview of the articles, describe and discuss the nature of the articles and what evidence they contain to support the efficacy and effectiveness of client-centered/experiential therapies.

CHAPTER 7

EXISTENTIAL THERAPY

Ultimately, man should not ask what the meaning of his life is, but rather must recognize that it is he *who is asked. In a word, each man is questioned by life; and he can only answer to life by* answering for *his own life.*

–Viktor Frankl

The goal of this chapter is to present a general overview of existential therapy and an overview of one specific model, Viktor Frankl's logotherapy. The chapter will look at biographical information about Frankl, the historical context of existential therapy and logotherapy, and the theory, practice, and research of these models. The simulated therapist, Dr. Francine Victor, presents a treatment plan and some excerpts from logotherapy sessions for the case of Jonathan. Issues of diversity and major critiques are also included.

✦ HISTORICAL CONTEXT

Existential therapies arose out of a popular movement that developed in Europe in the 1950s and made their way into American psychotherapy in the zeitgeist of the 1950s and the 1960s (as described in Chapter 6). Existential and humanistic therapies are often grouped together because both share similar beliefs and values. For example, both schools of thought agree that vital aspects of human behavior—such as values, intentions, and meaning—were ignored by psychoanalysis and behaviorism and are central to psychotherapy (Aanstoos, Serlin, & Greening, 2000).

However, there are differences historically between these two therapy families, which are narrowing today since they are being grouped together in the family of *experiential psychotherapies*. Early existential therapists and early humanists lived very different experiences. The early European existential therapists directly encountered the horrors of war and genocide in their homeland (Monte, 1987). Dealing with the dark side of human nature, they attempted to reconcile it with a coherent view of humanity. On the other hand, Americans tended to be more optimistic and positive, since their experience with war and its horrors was less immediate.

Historically, the earliest models of humanist therapy and existential therapy hold similar theories about human nature. Both see the human being as a unique, whole person, free to choose and to move toward fulfilling his or her human potential. Both highly value freedom and choice. There are some differences, however, in the themes that each psychotherapy emphasizes in theory and practice (Aanstoos, Serlin, & Greening, 2000).

In existential therapy, there is a strong focus on the responsibility that comes with the freedom to choose. In humanist therapy, there is an emphasis on self-fulfillment that involves cultivating the many positive characteristics of the self-actualized person. In existential therapy, there is a focus on how the self transcends and makes meaning out of the inevitable suffering, death, and alienation that must be confronted as a person interfaces with the world. Existential therapy deals more directly with the painful, negative facets of life than does humanist therapy.

The humanistic psychotherapist sees the causes of abnormal behavior as coming from the world and blocking the innate drive toward self-actualization. The existential psychotherapist sees the causes of dysfunctional behavior as deriving from a lack of authenticity or meaning, which can come from avoiding responsibility. Both psychotherapies see the therapy relationship as central. The humanist therapist serves as a catalyst who provides the necessary and sufficient conditions of growth to set off the client's natural healing process. The existential therapist provides authenticity and confronts issues more directly and firmly.

The goal of humanist therapy is self-actualization, congruence, genuineness, experiencing self, and removing blocks toward these goals. The goal of existential therapy is transcendence and authenticity, responsibility, meaning, and experiencing with a focus on moral, ethical, and spiritual issues. Self-actualization is not an end in itself. Proponents of both models are concerned that traditional and evidence-based practice has the potential to objectify human beings. Their goal is to perform research that enhances the human condition, not dehumanizes it.

There is a current trend to blend existential and humanist therapies (E-H) under the umbrella term *experiential therapy* (Elliott & Greenberg, 2002). For example, Leslie Greenberg has combined features of gestalt therapy and person-centered therapy into experiential therapy, or *emotion-focused therapy*. Thus the future of existential-humanist therapies seems to be headed in the experiential therapy direction, which has at its center a deep, personal, or intimate search process for meaning (Schneider, 2003).

Origins of Existential Therapy

Existentialism comes from the Latin root *existare*, which means "to become" (Schneider, 1998, 2003). It is a philosophy that examines the experience of the individual as a unique and isolated being in a universe that is indifferent, even hostile. Human existence is inexplicable. Humans, free to choose, are responsible for and are the consequences of their own actions. Modern existentialism began in Europe, with the work of Kierkegaard, Nietzsche, Heidegger, Husserl, Sartre, and Buber, among others. We will briefly review some of these philosophical underpinnings as they relate to existential therapy.

Soren Kierkegaard (1813–1855), the Danish father of existentialism, explored the topics of anxiety, despair, the importance of the individual, and subjectivity and truth. His major works are centered around the concepts of dread, fear, and anxiety.

Friedrich Nietzsche (1844–1900), a German philosopher, advocated honest inquiry into any accepted doctrines and a questioning of authority. He delved into power as a motivator for and an explanation of human behavior. In his major works, he discusses how people can be driven to a will to power, resentment, and a desire to be a self-determining superhuman.

Martin Heidegger (1889–1976) asserted that humans, after being thrown into an existence, live in an indifferent, ambiguous, even absurd universe. Each person has a unique way of being in the world. Edmund Husserl (1859–1938), the father of phenomenology, encouraged the study of immediate experience as the source of all knowledge by which humans can understand the experience of life. Phenomena, or shining forth of immediate reality, is understood only through subjective experience. Individuals should free themselves of their preconceptions in order to grasp what they are actually intuiting and experiencing. This phenomenological method was broadly accepted by existential psychotherapists (Hall & Lindzey, 1985).

Jean Paul Sartre (1905–1980) and Simone de Beauvoir (1908–1986), French existentialists, stressed that from the moment a person is born, he or she is destined to die. Existence precedes essence. Valuing authenticity and a conscious examination of the self, they asserted that we are who we are because we make ourselves. Martin Buber (1878–1965) emphasized the I–Thou relationship in which two people have a dialogic, or a truly mutual, relationship (Bugental & Kleiner, 1993; Yalom, 1989).

Existential Therapists

Two early existential psychotherapists were Ludwig Binswanger (1881–1996) and Medard Boss (1903–1990), both of whom lived and practiced in Switzerland. Binswanger (1958) and Boss (1962, 1963) were psychoanalytically trained psychiatrists who drew from Heidegger's and Husserl's work. Binswanger (1963) integrated the concepts of being in the world, the importance of phenomenology, and the clients' internal experience as a means of understanding their own selves through psychotherapy. Boss encouraged openness and clearness in relationships and stressed how emotion shapes the way in which people relate to others and the world, particularly the effects of guilt on choice. Since every choice means giving up endless alternatives, choice symbolizes the many losses that people endure throughout life.

Rollo May (1953, 1955) and Viktor Frankl are the best-known contemporary existential psychotherapists. May, a practicing psychoanalyst who studied with Alfred Adler in Vienna, was an important influence in bridging the gap from the European existentialists to American theorists. May's early work focused on the meaning of anxiety, in which all humans grapple with issues of aloneness in the world, dread about dying, growth, and the pursuit of independence. *Existence,* published in 1958, presented the basics of existential psychology. May's prolific and profound writings earned him the reputation of being the major representative of existential psychotherapy in the United States until he died in October 1994 in Tiburon, California.

Viktor Frankl (see About Victor Frankl box) emigrated from Austria to the United States after World War II and promulgated his logotherapy, a form of existential therapy that emphasizes the will to meaning. There has been a revival of

ABOUT VIKTOR FRANKL

Born in Vienna on March 26, 1905, Viktor was the middle child of three children. His father was the minister of social services, and his mother was a kind, religious woman. Growing up, Frankl demonstrated a keen intellectual curiosity. By age 19, he was attending night classes in psychoanalysis and corresponding with Sigmund Freud; he had also published an article in the *International Journal of Psychoanalysis*.

Although Frankl trained and practiced as a psychoanalyst, he eventually objected to its mechanistic view of the human mind. He later criticized the psychoanalyst's role for being too much of a technician who viewed the patient as a diseased machine, rather than as a whole human being. Frankl advocated that medicine be more "psychologized" and that psychiatry be more "humanized" (1959, p. 213). After he obtained his medical degree in 1930, he worked at a university clinic, organized free mental health clinics, and opened a private neurology/psychiatry clinic.

During World War II, Frankl faced a choice—either emigrate to a country where he could be safe or stay and protect his parents in Austria. Frankl asked for a sign from God to help him decide. While visiting his father, he saw a piece of marble with a gilded Hebrew letter on it that his father explained represented the Fourth Commandment—honor thy father and thy mother that thy days may be long upon the land. His father had rescued it from a Viennese synagogue that had burned to the ground. Frankl chose to remain with his family (Frankl, 1992). In 1938, Austria was invaded by Hitler. Frankl was working in the neurology unit at Rothschild Hospital and writing his now-classic book *The Doctor and the Soul* (Frankl, 1965). He, his wife, his parents, and his brother were sent to a concentration camp in Bohemia. Frankl faced the utter horrors of the three camps he survived (see Box 7.1). By the time of his release in 1945, Frankl had lost every member of his family except his sister.

After his release, Frankl transformed his suffering and channeled it into helping others through the development of logotherapy. He worked as the director of the Neurological Division of the Vienna Policlinic for 25 years, and he remarried. His book describing logotherapy, *Man's Search for Meaning* (Frankl, 1959), became a best seller, translated into almost 40 languages. His logotherapy promoted an attitude of love and forgiveness. In an interview given at the age of 90, Frankl addressed criticisms for never using the word *Jew* in his books and for being too much of a reconciling spirit. He replied that his calling was to heal souls and to appeal to the higher part of man (Scully, 1995). For Frankl, maintaining an attitude of hate interfered with his core belief that a person's only real freedom lies in choosing an attitude toward circumstances (Frankl, 1959). Frankl died in 1997 after having lived the days that were "long upon the land" (Längle & Sykes, 2006).

---

interest in logotherapy recently. Because it calls upon the human capacity for inner transformation and the ability to rise above adverse and painful circumstances to emerge stronger and more fulfilled, it is a way to help people cope with the inevitability of illness, aging, suffering, and death (Mattes, 2005).

The most influential contemporary existential therapists are Irvin Yalom (1980, 1996) and James Bugental (1964, 1990). Both have published extensively about their existential models of psychotherapy. Yalom is known for his clarification of the concepts of existential therapy and group therapy. Among his well-known works are *Love's Executioner and Other Tales of Psychotherapy* (1989). Bugental has published *The Art of the Psychotherapist* (1987) and *Existential–Humanistic Psychotherapy* (1990). Another therapist, Clemmont Vontress, has raised consciousness about issues of diversity in existential psychotherapy (2003).

✦ THEORY OF EXISTENTIAL PSYCHOTHERAPY

Existential psychotherapy is a frame of reference, a perspective, and an inquiry into human existence (May & Yalom, 2005). Founded in philosophy, it inspires an attitude toward living and poses deep questions about life and the human condition (Lukas & Hirsch, 2002). It includes looking at awareness of self, being and nonbeing, suffering as a condition of living, responsibility, and the need for others (Breitbart, Gibson, Poppito, & Berg, 2004). Certain themes run throughout all forms of existential therapies, including such abstract issues as human freedom, isolation, anxiety, death, meaningfulness, and a realistic view of self, the world, and interpersonal relationships.

Although experts differ about how to accurately define existential psychotherapy, these ongoing debates are advantageous because they encourage constant questioning and reexamination of the tenets and worldviews associated with the therapies (van Deurzen-Smith, 1990a, 1990b, 1998; Mahrer, 1996, 2005). There is no clear distinction among subtypes of existential psychotherapies, but among existentialist psychotherapists, there is considerable difference of opinion about how to find answers to life's questions.

For example, theorists differ in regard to the philosophical implications of experiencing in the therapeutic dyad. All existential therapists believe that clients must confront what underlies their ultimate concerns, but the specific nature of those concerns differs for each individual. May focuses on themes such as the disintegration of cultural mores, loneliness, anxiety, and isolation. Yalom (1980) focuses on the need to confront death. Bugental focuses on the need for clients to confront embodiment-change, finitude-contingency, action-responsibility, choice-relinquishment, separation-apartness, or relation-being. Frankl focuses on meaning, freedom, and responsibility as well as noogenic neuroses, or those that result from existential frustration.

Some of the core principles that all the existential therapies share are listed here:

- Understanding life cannot be done solely from a scientific rational or objective perspective.
- Raising consciousness and human awareness is highly valued.
- Phenomenology, or the subjective experience of the person, is the most important method for exploring the truth.
- Meaning is understood from within.
- People create their own purpose through their own actions and interpretations.
- People are free, but responsible, for their own lives.
- How people struggle with living an authentic life is a significant issue in the therapeutic dyad.

Key Concepts

The following are the key concepts underlying most existential therapies: being in the world; the I-am experience; the four existential realities, including death, freedom and responsibility, isolation, and meaninglessness; anxiety and choice; time; and authenticity.

Being in the World

Being in the world, translated into German *dasein,* is overall human existence. To be in the world *is* existence. A human being is part of the world, and the world is part of the human being. One cannot be understood without the other as they are intimately connected, inseparable, and interdependent. Separating the inside from the outside, or the objective from the subjective, is unreal (Schneider, 2003, p.170). Thus to be in the world means to have an awareness of the world and also to be creating the world though personal perceptions.

Understanding each individual human as he or she exists in the world is accomplished by studying immediate experience. The emphasis is upon how the individual perceives his or her own world uniquely and using the phenomenological method to do so. Many existentialists have created a language of being in the world based upon German concepts created primarily by Binswanger (1958). These are as follows:

- *Umwelt* is the natural world. It consists of the physical world, the biological world, and our physical surroundings such as the landscape or the terrain into which a person is placed. It follows the natural laws.
- *Mitwelt* is the interpersonal world and how we relate to other humans (Binswanger, 1963). It consists of the individual's relationships with others or a person's fellow human beings.
- *Eigenwelt* is our own subjective world. It consists of the individual's relationship with his or her psychological self as the physical self. Our relationship with the psychological self is the thought-world, and with our physical self the body-world. It is the world of self-awareness, self-relatedness, and personal meaning.
- *Uberwelt,* or our beliefs about world, is a more current existential concept, not originally considered by Binswanger. It consists of spiritual values or what a person believes the world ought to be (van Deurzen-Smith, 1998).

The I-Am Experience

The *I-am experience* is the recognition that "I am" or that "I exist." It is the actual experience of being, of realizing that I am alive, which includes the recognition that at some time, I will *not* be alive. In being, the person works out the question of existence. Being is an activity that is preconceptual; that is, if it occurs, any logic, theory, or specific ontology develops (Heidegger, 1996). When we grasp what it is to be, we clarify the meaning of being. The I-am event is what determines a being *as* a being. It is an ontological experience or an explanation of the understanding of being and a look at the person becoming. Existential therapy rejects the notion that the person and the environment are separate (May & Yalom, 2005).

Four Existential Realities

Yalom (1980) depicts themes or givens that are central to human experience and underlie most psychological problems. These are *death, freedom and responsibility, isolation,* and *meaninglessness.*

Death

Death anxiety is at the very core of human existence. Ultimately, all people are concerned with death, and the fear of death is a source of anxiety for everyone from an early age. All people know that they will age and grow old. They possess limited time. Each person has a will to live, a desire to continue to exist, but also the realization that he or she will die. Thus, humans are torn by the will to live and the knowledge that they will die.

Part of the human dilemma is to deal with the haunting specter of death, which is omnipresent. To manage it, humans create and use defense mechanisms, particularly denial. If the fear of death or annihilation grows great enough, the individual can develop symptoms. Some forms of abnormal behavior, then, represent a failure of the individual to transcend death (May & Yalom, 2005). Self-deception comes when humans do not face up to their own mortality and fundamental nothingness. By facing the truth, the individual becomes more aware of the human capability to choose to live in a deliberate and conscious way (van Deurzen, 2007).

Freedom and Responsibility

All individuals are the authors of their own lives, the products of their own choices, and need to take responsibility for who and what they are. Since everyone is free to create their own self, they in turn are responsible for the product, or who they are. Just as all successes can be attributed to the free choices people make, so, too, are any failures attributed to them. Thus freedom can be very frightening, especially when people know they are responsible for what they are.

The degree to which the person accepts responsibility for his or her own life varies. Some people accept responsibility squarely. Others tend to blame authority figures or the environment for any problems. Some take on the role of a mentally ill person in order to avoid accountability.

The capacity to confront limits is also part of freedom. When a person is free (and existential psychotherapy's purpose is to set people free), the person is able to say, I can, or I will (May, 1967).

Isolation

Isolation comes in three forms—interpersonal, intrapersonal, and existential. *Interpersonal isolation* is the result of poor social skills and is simply the gulf that arises between the self and others. *Intrapersonal isolation* means separation from parts of the self. For example, dissociations occur between our feelings and our thoughts. However, *existential isolation* is a function of the uniqueness of each individual. No one can ever share another person's consciousness completely. We are all born into this world alone, and we will depart alone. Although the fear of isolation may drive us to seek out others and to involve ourselves in interpersonal relationships, to use others, to attempt to relate to another, to even fuse with another, we are only denying that that we are isolated in human existence. Admitting this isolation makes it possible to reach out in a truthful acknowledgment; if the person does not admit this separation, he or she may want to get involved superficially with others to avoid the isolation. The result may be troubled interpersonal relationships (May & Yalom, 2005).

Meaninglessness

Why do we live? What is the meaning of our individual existence? What activities make our futures of value? How can we find meaning in a seemingly meaningless universe? Do we make our own meaning? And if so, how do we know any meaning is the right one?

Human beings seem to require some meaning in their lives, even to the point where the nervous system is preprogrammed to process incoming stimuli in a meaningful manner. When we choose our values, and everyone does, we are assembling our own unique meaning (Yalom, 1980).

Anxiety and Choice

Anxiety is seen from a wide-ranging perspective. It differs from fear and is part of a person's vitality. May defines *anxiety* as the "apprehension cued off by a threat to some value which the individual holds essential to his existence as a self" (1967, p. 72). This includes the person's fear of death or dissolving into nothingness.

Anxiety surrounds *choice*, because every time we make a choice, we eliminate other opportunities. Each choice means we relinquish another. Our potential to choose has limits in our cosmic, cultural, genetic, and circumstantial destinies.

Normal anxiety is appropriate for the situation, and if it is not repressed, it can serve as a tool to handle existential dilemmas. Neurotic anxiety, however, is out of proportion for the situation. Its influence can be destructive. To deal with neurotic anxiety, the person must have the strength to face the existential issues that are causing it. Existential anxiety comes from having to confront the world, deal with its unknown forces, and find a place in it.

If individuals are anxious in the right way, it can help them to be reflective, and it can foster movement toward an existence that is meaningful. Anxiety can serve as a good starting point to explore what may be wrong with the person's life, and thus anxiety can help a person to map the course of his or her life (May & Yalom, 2005).

Time

Time is a central issue in life and death, and thus it is of particular significance to the existential therapist. While every person knows he or she will die, no one knows when. Within existential therapy, time can be grist for the mill. The existential psychotherapist is not bound by time constraints as part of a rigid therapy plan but may integrate time-related issues into the therapy itself. Whether a person has time or does not have time to perform a task or achieve a goal is significant in his or her own life plan. The person can expand or contract time to include or exclude the past or future. For example, being aware that I am going to graduate from a doctoral program expands time into the future. Realizing I have only a minute to finish a task shrinks the concept of time (Hall & Lindzey, 1985).

Authenticity

The *authentic* person actualizes his or her potentialities and the grounds of his or her existence. The *inauthentic* person shuts the self off from that grounding. Authentic people are aware of the self and their relationship with the world, make choices knowing that the decisions are the consequences of responsibility, and take responsibility for their choices. Authentic individuals have values and goals that are their own. Inauthentic people have values and goals based upon what others think of them. The authentic person knows that his or her awareness is far from perfect and strives to increase it (Bugental, 1965, 1990).

Therapy Relationship

The existential therapist's role is to be in the therapeutic relationship—that is, to be in an authentic I–Thou encounter. Thus the work of the therapist is to "cultivate presence or attention, choice and freedom and responsibility to that presence" (Schneider, 2003, p. 169). The I–Thou dialogic approach is a primary vehicle for conducting existential psychotherapy.

There is no particular, specific way to perform existential psychotherapy. Any techniques are acceptable if they enhance the therapeutic relationship and help the client to deal in the here and now with basic existential themes. Existential therapy is performed with great sensitivity to the unique needs of the individual without any preconceptions or set ways of proceeding.

The therapist becomes familiar with and scrutinizes the client's unique experience, situation, and stance in the world. As much as is humanly possible within the confines of the limits of knowing another, the therapist strives to understand the client's worldview, state of mind, meaning, values, and beliefs and helps put the client's life into perspective, clarifying his or her issues and contradictions. The therapist tries to recognize what tensions are affecting the client's life (van Deurzen, 2007).

Although many existential psychotherapists have been trained in other therapies, they have a similar way of looking at the person that can be used within these other therapeutic systems. For example, Albert Ellis integrated existential elements into his cognitive behavior therapy because it helped some clients to more deeply examine life's purpose (Hutchinson, 2005).

Normal and Abnormal Behavior

The well-adjusted person is an "existing, immediate person" and is in the process of becoming completely human and authentic (May & Yalom, 2005, p. 296). To be mentally healthy means to make wise choices, to be in balance with one's self and the world in which one exists, and to be free to choose within the limits of destiny—cosmic, genetic, cultural, and circumstantial (May, 1955). The normal person lives a fulfilled existence while struggling to examine and deal with freedom, destiny, meaning, isolation, and inevitably death (Yalom, 1980). This person acknowledges his or her freedoms and transcends the past and present in order to reach the future.

The unhealthy person fails in one or more of these tasks. He or she may not address the inevitable concerns of being authentically human and its conditions, the fundamental realities of the world, or the networks of relationships and feelings. He or she may not become a unique autonomous individual and may fail to transcend past and present in order to shape the future (May & Yalom, 2005, p. 274). The unhealthy person lives an inauthentic life, develops a dysfunctional identification with some limitation, and as a result dampens his or her true potential. Anxiety, fear, depression, despair, alienation, loneliness, guilt, meaninglessness, boredom, and unhappiness follow and are the result of unwise choices, the failure to be authentic, and/or a refusal to come to grips with death or nonexistence (Wong, 2004).

These are the basic themes and core ideas underlying most forms of existential therapies. The following section of this chapter discusses Frankl's logotherapy, giving us a look at a specific type of existential psychotherapy in theory and practice.

✦ THEORY OF LOGOTHERAPY

Frankl's logotherapy is a form of existential therapy and a philosophical/psychological system that deals primarily with the theme of meaning. *Logos* is a Greek word that means "meaning" and also "spirit" (Frankl, 1959, p. 160). *Logotherapy* concentrates on finding the meaning of human existence in life and "moves between the boundaries of medicine and philosophy, psychology and religion" (Lukas & Hirsch, 2002, p. 349). Frankl's system has a unique perspective, since he incorporated into his work his personal experience of enduring the horrors of the Nazi death camps (Rice & Greenberg, 1992).

Key Concepts

It is difficult to clearly and succinctly define the key concepts of logotherapy, because like all forms of existential therapy, it is a perspective and an attitude more than a technique. Box 7.1 illustrates how Frankl's background is inextricably integrated into the development of logotherapy.

Aside from the general attitude Frankl proposed, some of logotherapy's key concepts are will to meaning and values, freedom, noeticism and noodynamics, and self-transcendence. Frankl uses the term *existential* in three ways: (a) human existence itself, (b) the meaning of existence, and (c) a striving to discover the concrete meaning in the individual's existence, or the will to meaning (Frankl, 1959, p. 159).

Will to Meaning and Values

The *will to meaning* is a primary motivation to find significance in one's own life. Each unique individual has a specific meaning that only he or she can fulfill. A person does not invent the meaning of his or her own existence, but rather detects it. For Frankl, *values* "do not drive or push a man, but rather pull him" (Frankl, 1959, p. 157).

BOX 7.1 THE INSPIRATION FOR LOGOTHERAPY

The nature of the experience that helped to inform and inspire the development of logotherapy is so outside the range of normal human experience it deserves highlighting. In his autobiographical work, *Man's Search for Meaning* (1959), Frankl wrote about the three concentration camps he endured in World War II.

The prisoners looked like living skeletons, and as they died, their corpses were piled up all around the camp. They lived in a chronic state of enormous mental stress, not knowing where their loved ones were and with the threat of death looming over them every second. Rations were one and a half ounces of bread and some thin soup. There were brutal beatings daily by the guards, unpredictable attacks, the constant threat of physical injury or mortal wounding, forced labor, near starvation, and inhumane punishments such as standing for hours. Frankl recalls the plight of a young man, forced to stand with no shoes in the snow, until his toes, rotten from frostbite, were removed with tweezers one by one. He had a sudden and striking realization:

> . . . my body is really a corpse already. What has become of me? I am but a small portion of a great mass of human flesh . . . behind barbed wire, crowded into a few earthen huts; a mass of which a certain portion begins to rot because it is lifeless. (Frankl, 1959, p. 48)

As prisoner 119,104, Frankl dealt with both the most primitive and the most transcending experiences a human may confront. Observing the psychological reactions or stages victims experienced, he admired the way in which the average prisoner coped with the conditions in the camp and how the human spirit stood up to the severest of sufferings.

Frankl described adaptation to these inhumane conditions. Initially, a great shock comes with the horror of being arrested, transported, and processed into a concentration camp as a prisoner. The person who did not immediately go to the gas chambers suddenly understood that all of his former life was negated. To stay alive, a person had to look fit and act capable of working or be killed by the guards and withstand the overwhelming torture of painful emotions such as longing for family and home and disgust with the surrounding ugliness. Next, the prisoners experienced an apathy—detachment or numbing of feelings and nonresponsiveness to the suffering around them and a blunting of emotions and insensitivity to daily beatings—and the development of a protective shell. This loss of meaning and detachment were devastating.

To counteract this, the prisoner had to develop a sense of purpose, a reason to survive by finding a meaning in his existence. For example, Frankl found meaning in writing a manuscript. When it was confiscated, he developed a desire to write the manuscript anew. His will to complete the manuscripts helped him when he was in grave danger of collapse.

Frankl identified three types of prisoners and what he perceived to be their reactions to these extreme conditions. First, capos were selected by the SS for their characterological ruthlessness and their ability to carry out the brutal mission of the camp. They used any means to survive, gave up their scruples, and were morally and mentally hardened. Many were sadistic, with deadened feelings to humanity, but surprisingly, some also showed they were capable of showing human kindness. Frankl speaks of one capo who risked his own well-being to give him some extra bread. Second, some prisoners lost their will to find meaning. Believing that they had nothing left to expect from life, they gave up and died. Third, the survivors, including Frankl, possessed and maintained a will to meaning, a mission to accomplish, and a reason to survive. Suffering and death were seen as part of a wider circle of life.

Frankl was able to cope with living in these conditions for three years because he used his experiences to forge the core concepts of his logotherapy. Frankl faced the ultimate in human cruelty as he existed in the concentration camps and saw all that he loved destroyed. His ability to practice what he preached, to maintain an existential perspective on life, and to uphold a positive attitude in the face of horror bolsters faith in the belief that people are free to choose their attitudes, even in the most heinous of life's conditions.

Freedom

Freedom, as discussed earlier, means that a person has free will. It is always a factor in choosing values. Individuals are not driven to moral behavior but make a cognizant decision to behave with integrity. An individual chooses to commit him- or herself in the interest of a cause, for the benefit of a loved one, or for the sake of a higher power.

Noeticism and Noodynamics

Noetic refers to "beings of spirit." *Noos,* a Greek word for "mind," pertains to the spiritual core of the human personality. Whereas many animals have somatic and even psychological aspects to their being, only humans have the noetic or spiritual side, which allows them to transcend the physical and the psychological. The noetic part of a person remains intact in the face of any adversity. It cannot become ill or disabled. It includes a person's life plan, expectations, and goals—and their implementation—as well as commitments, responsibilities, and freedom to choose. It includes morality, ethos, religious experiences, artistic visions, culture, and inspiration.

Noodynamics is spiritual energy. The will to meaning is fulfilled or not fulfilled through noodynamics. Spiritual energy occurs in a polar field of tension. One end of the pole is represented by a meaning to be fulfilled, and the other end is represented by the person who must fulfill it. If individuals do not fulfill their meaning, problems arise. Conflicts can emerge among various values.

Through noodynamics, a frustrated will to meaning can transform into an unhealthy *will to power,* where the person is trying to find his or her meaning in power, or *will to pleasure,* where the person tries to find his or her meaning in pleasure (Frankl, 1959, 1965).

Self-Transcendence

Frankl clarifies an important conceptual aspect of existential therapy when he states that the true aim of human existence is *self-transcendence,* not self-actualization:

> . . . only to the extent to which man commits himself to the fulfillment of his life's meaning, to this extent he also actualizes himself. In other words, self actualization can not be attained if it is made an end in itself, but only as a side effect of transcendence. The world must not be regarded as a mere extension of one's self. Nor must the world be considered a mere instrument, or as a means to the end of one's self actualization. (Frankl, 1972, pp. 175–176)

Normal and Abnormal Behavior

The transcendant person is one who lives a life with meaning. Tension is inherent in people; the mentally healthy person has a certain level of tension between what he or she has already achieved and what he or she should become. Striving and struggling for some worthy goal represents potential meaning waiting to be fulfilled.

Abnormal behavior, or emotional disturbance, is generally a function of not exercising a will to meaning. If people do not fulfill their meaning, they can become neurotic and self-centered and spend their efforts trying to escape the awareness of their life mission. Isolation, alienation, disconnection with others, and the absence of meaning are forms of abnormal behavior (Dubois, 2006).

Existential frustration is at the basis of all abnormal behavior. It occurs when the will to meaning is frustrated. It plays a large role in the *noogenic neurosis*. This neurosis is rooted in the noological, not the psychological. A noogenic neurosis results from conflicts that emerge among various values that conflict, either morally or spiritually (Frankl, 1959, p. 160). This neurosis is a will to meaning gone awry.

The *existential vacuum* is a loss of the feeling that life is meaningful, which manifests itself in a state of boredom. The person experiences a state similar to the so-called Sunday neurosis, which occurs when people stop the rush of their busy lives and become more aware that something is missing (Frankl, 1959, p. 169). It is a widespread phenomenon of modern life and may reflect the weakening or loss of traditional belief systems.

Frankl (1959; 1963) describes specific forms of pathology. In noogenic neurosis, the frustrated will to meaning shows itself through depression, phobia, anger, and chronic boredom. Those with little or no purpose have no tension between existence and need. *Psychogenic neurosis* and psychosomatic illness are the result of personal insecurity. The person lacks trust and self-confidence and expects the negative out of life; such individuals are preoccupied with bodily functions such as sleeping, eating, and sexual functioning, almost to the point of compulsion. Shame and embarrassment are easily experienced. *Endogenous psychoses* such as schizophrenia and bipolar disorders are organically based and cause a great deal of suffering. The person realizes he or she has an illness that must be tolerated.

The inability to make up one's mind, combined with a sense of hopelessness that comes from low frustration tolerance, results in what Frankl calls *existential frustration and valued ambivalence*. Finally, *pathology of spirit and collective neurosis* can affect an entire society. With global threats and crises looming, and the inequitable distribution of planetary resources, not all citizens of the world can expect to attain a dignified future. The result is the prevalence of a negative attitude that is difficult to bear and transcend.

Suffering is not necessarily the result an abnormal process or a symptom of neurosis. Existential frustration is not pathological in itself but may represent spiritual distress. For example, a man who entered psychoanalysis because his job duties conflicted with his ethical values spent five years struggling to resolve Oedipal issues. After transferring to Frankl for logotherapy, with the encouragement of his therapist, he found a new vocation and became quite happy within several sessions. Treatment in psychoanalysis resulted in a neglect of spiritual issues. By addressing the moral dimension in logotherapy, however, the client solved his problem. Frankl points out that moral and spiritual struggles are not diseases but can cause significant suffering if not dealt with appropriately.

✦ Practice of Logotherapy

Now that we have examined the basic theoretical concepts that underlie both existential psychotherapy and logotherapy, we will explore its practice. Dr. Francine Victor is our composite, fictional existential logotherapist who provides a firsthand perspective of how she integrates theory with practice and applies the techniques of Frankl's existential logotherapy.

Assessment and Diagnosis

Therapy begins with the assessment and diagnostic phase. In this assessment phase, I interview thoroughly and gather background information. I avoid the question "What is wrong?" because it can mislead the client and even foster an iatrogenic neurosis—that is, a neurosis in which the patient is made worse by the treatment. If I emphasize what is wrong in my questioning, the patient may hyperreflect on "wrong." I gather information from past medical records to rule out neurological problems.

Negotiation of Therapeutic Relationship and Length of Treatment

The client and I co-participate in a relationship to explore and deepen the client's understanding. The therapy relationship is the central component of existential therapy. It is phenomenological, experiential, and relational.

I involve myself maximally in the relationship process as it unfolds and develops and put great effort into being emotionally present and available at all times. I emphasize authenticity and awareness. The client and I face each other, and we focus our vision in the same direction. I am not directive, but I am not passive. I am active in that I keep my thinking as clear as possible, am engaged in my own self-reflection, and continue to stay on the path with the client. I can be confrontational when needed. For the client, experiencing the genuine relationship is the most important component to healing.

My relationship with my client is authentic. I assist him or her to discover the unique meaning of his or her life as well as to discover the meaning in the moment. I rely on my intuition to apply the correct techniques. I actively try to uncover the client's point of view. I will point out, analyze, and identify issues. I look at the physical, psychological, and specifically the noetic dimensions of the patient's personality, especially since it is so neglected in today's culture (Lukas & Hirsch, 2002). My client's role is to fully participate in our co-relationship. Existential therapy is, at its heart, a very collaborative approach.

After the initial assessment, we do not plan a set number of sessions, and we meet for as long as it takes. Generally sessions last the traditional 50 minutes, but I am not rigid about time. and I will do what is needed to assist the patient. While time is of particular significance to the existential therapist and it can be an important issue in the sessions, I am not bound by time constraints. I integrate time-related issues into the therapy itself.

As an existential therapist, I believe healing occurs through a variety of processes. The ultimate goal is transcendence, becoming authentic, and dealing well with responsibility, meaning, experiencing, and moral, ethical, and spiritual issues as well as being able to cope with suffering, alienation, and isolation through awareness and consciousness raising.

In particular, as a logotherapist, my goal is to help patients find meaning in their lives, to actualize values, and to help fill the existential vacuum. I believe that the physical and psychological parts of the human being are susceptible to illness, and they must be treated with appropriate methods. For example, diabetes is treated with insulin, and mania is treated with lithium and talking cure. However, the noetic part of the person cannot be ill. I help the patient access this dimension. I do not use psychotherapy in general, but logotherapy, because I enter the spiritual dimension of human existence. I deal with any blockage to finding meaning in spiritual terms.

Each individual has a unique treatment plan. I use any techniques that are appropriate to help patients to reach their goals and to acquire healthy meaning in life.

Therapeutic Techniques

I use a variety of techniques to help the client find meaning. Some of the specific methods are those that Frankl described in relation to specific conditions (1959). I help my clients to find meaning and to help themselves by asking them to perform one or more of the following exercises:

- *Do a deed or take action.* For example, a person who has suffered a great loss can give something to someone in need or help others who are in need.
- *Experience a value.* For example, an anxious person can appreciate nature or art, or experience another person by loving him or her. Love, not equated with sex, allows a person to experience togetherness, to see the essential traits and features of another, to appreciate his or her potential, and to help actualize those potentials.
- *Endure suffering.* For example, a man who has lost his wife can learn to tolerate his suffering if he understands that he has saved his beloved wife from suffering his loss because he is the one left behind to face life alone.

Some other techniques that I use are described in the following.

Socratic Dialogue
In this method, used also by cognitive behaviorists, I dialogue with the patient. We work together to grapple with the client's questions and challenges.

Attitudinal Adjustment
I help the patient to assimilate an attitude that is meaningful and helpful regardless of the problems she or he is facing in the current life situation. I encourage the

patient to assume an attitude that is positive and healthy and enhances meaningfulness and well-being. I assist the client in doing away with any negative attitudes at the root of unpleasantness and stress.

Dereflection

I ask clients to forget themselves and to focus on others. In this way, I help clients to diminish excessive self-observation, to detach from self-absorption, and to distract themselves from their symptoms. Clients learn to channel their energy and attention to areas of life that are more positive.

Paradoxical Intention

At times I instruct patients to do the opposite of what they fear or want. In this way I am dealing with the underlying problem and not with just the symptom. I might tell a person who cannot tolerate a mess to live in a filthy room for a week. Or I might ask a person who feels guilty about something, such as not studying, to try to feel even guiltier by not studying at all for a week.

I do not fight resistance with resistance. For example, if the patient with insomnia focuses on trying to sleep to the degree that she develops anticipatory anxiety about not sleeping, it is more likely that she will not sleep. Rather, I prescribe the symptom. I say, "I want you to stay awake tonight. Under no circumstances can you fall asleep." The patient often does the opposite of my command. If I see an anxious compulsive who wants to stop unlocking a door or checking an iron, I instruct him to check continually; no stopping is permissible for several hours. Often, the fear will diminish. If I say, "Don't think of the color green," what is the general reaction? I find the technique is useful in conditions in which anticipatory anxiety exists. Paradoxical intention can help the patient to stop avoiding.

Appealing

I teach clients to relax by speaking calmly and softly; I encourage clients to experience a state of willingness in which they will become and stay well. Based on the power of suggestion, I help patients to prepare to be calm, to distance from problems, to master anxieties. Once patients are calm, they are more prepared to hear what I have to say through Socratic dialogue (Lukas & Hirsch, 2002).

Confrontation

I use confrontation in a direct way as Frankl described it (1972, p. 152). I differentiate between psychoanalysis and logotherapy by saying that in psychoanalysis, the patient "lies down on the couch and tells the analyst things that may be disagreeable to hear," whereas in logotherapy, the patient "sits erect but must hear things that may be very disagreeable to hear!"

Dealing with Specific Problem Behaviors and Attitudes

There are specific techniques that I use to address neurotic and negative behaviors:

- *Noogenic neurosis and depression:* I encourage patients to search the past for meaning. I ask them to revive old meaning and to think of a goal to achieve that would make the world a worse place if it did not happen (Lukas & Hirsch, 2002).

- *Psychogenic neurosis and psychosomatic illness:* I know the insecure neurotic person, in particular, is in need of noetic or spiritual strength so I strengthen the noos, or part of person that cannot be damaged, and the logos or unconditional meaningfulness. I try to use humor to help my patients make choices, distance themselves from their own mixed feelings, and laugh at their negative expectations. I make light of and joke about their threatened fears. In this way I encourage them to break up the self-defeating cycle, allowing them to decrease anticipatory anxiety and regain some self-confidence. They ignore their symptoms and stop focusing on them. Then I am able to guide patients to dereflect on personal needs and reflect on others' needs. In this way, they begin to forget about themselves and are able to find more meaning in their existence (Frankl, 1963, 1992).

- *Endogenous psychoses and incurable illness:* I believe that medications are appropriate for conditions such as schizophrenia, bipolar disorders, and endogenous depression because these conditions have a biological basis. Individuals with physical disabilities and incurable critical illnesses face unavoidable suffering (Frankl, 1978). I help them to cope with their emotional disturbances by searching for some meaning in their suffering. As Frankl advises, I see that the client can use the opportunities provided by suffering to realize his or her values, activate potentialities, and thus fulfill meaning: "The innermost core of the patient's personality is not even touched by psychosis," and the psychotic still maintains dignity (Frankl, 1959, p. 212).

- *Existential frustration and value ambivalence:* To stabilize patients, I teach the tenets of responsibility and respect for others. The undue influence of others coupled with a low frustration tolerance can cause a patient to give up or to surrender to the struggle. The inability to make a decision and stay on the path can result in a descent into hopelessness and the existential vacuum (Frankl, 1959).

- *Pathology of the spirit of the times and collective neurosis:* Some patients develop negative attitudes from the state of the world today, such as wars and genocide and environmental disasters. I treat these patients by using the relationship and my dialogue to actively oppose negative attitudes with a meaning-oriented philosophy (Frankl, 1959).

The Process of Therapy

Logotherapy has three phases—diagnostic, therapeutic, and follow-up (Lukas & Hirsch, 2002). Initially, in the diagnostic stage, my most important goal is to develop a genuine and authentic relationship with my client, a key element to the success of the therapy. I keep the session in the here and now. I empathize with the client and I attempt to understand the client's phenomenological field. Once I begin the authentic relationship, I assess the nature of the problem and look for pathology of spirit. I assess the client's noodynamics and look for themes with which the client is dealing—isolation, alienation, anxiety, depression—that question and challenge the meaning of his or her life. We explore this noetic part of life and move to the therapeutic phase.

In the middle of therapy, I continue to deepen the authentic relationship. Together, the client and I search for meaning, explore values, activate the client's potential, and help the client face what he or she has been avoiding. The client takes responsibility for life choices and moves toward finding new meaning in life or reevaluates the current meaning though acting or experiencing a value. In this stage of therapy, I use tools such as the Socratic dialogue. I help the client to cope with his or her feelings of alienation, aloneness, lack of connection, loss of meaning, and broken relationships; and I help the client to search the past to revive his or her meaning.

We terminate therapy when the expected outcome occurs—that is, when the client has detected his or her will to meaning and has transcended suffering. As a result, the client has a will to meaning, or a reason to be, feels more spiritually satisfied, and is working toward spiritual fulfillment. I accept the patient's verbal report as the indicator of treatment success. The symptoms with which the client came to therapy will be resolved. We may have some follow-up sessions if the client needs them.

Therapy in Action: Dr. Francine Victor and the Case of Jonathan

To illustrate the application of logotherapy, we examine a treatment plan for Jonathan, followed by excerpts from therapy sessions with our fictional therapist, Dr. Victor. Keep in mind these are simulated interviews and represent the ideal of therapy. In real life, clients may take much longer to meet therapeutic goals. Table 7.1 provides a summary of Dr. Victor's treatment plan.

Case Excerpts

The following excerpts are from sessions based on Dr. Victor's logotherapy case formulation.

Session 1

Dr. Victor: If I understand what you said, you believe you have truly failed?
Jonathan: Definitely. I am a failure. Look at what happened. I can't stand the hurt.
Dr. Victor: And what are you worried about at this moment?
Jonathan: I was deserted. I will be alone. My best friends left. What am I to do?
Dr. Victor: What have you done so far about your aloneness?
Jonathan: Right now, nothing. I need to get over the shock.

Table 7.1	
Logotherapy Treatment Plan for Jonathan	
Assessment and Formulation	• Presenting problem: loss of relationship • Depression stems from J.'s loss of meaning • J. is experiencing noogenic neurosis/existential vacuum
Therapeutic Relationship	• Client and therapist strive for authenticity in relationship • Co-participants explore/deepen the client's understanding
Contract, Goals, and Treatment Plan	• Help J. find meaning in his life • Encourage will to meaning • Encourage J. to do a deed, experience a value • Time—meet as needed
Techniques	• Develop authentic relationship • Cope with feelings of alienation, aloneness • Search past to revive meaning • Socratic dialogue and problem solving to find meaning • Paradoxical intention for sleeplessness
Process of Therapy	• Authentic relationship maintained, deepened • Question why meaning in life was focused on Tuti • Cope with feelings of alienation, aloneness, lack of connection and relationship • Search past to revive meaning • Problem solve to find meaning
Termination and Outcome	• Resolve depression/noogenic neurosis • Find new meaning and potential • Escape from anxiety, lack of connectedness

Dr. Victor: How long ago did they leave?

Jonathan: It's been about two and a half months, but I just cannot snap out of this state, and I feel sick physically.

Dr. Victor: What are you afraid of for your own self?

Jonathan: I'll never be happy again. And I should not need anyone, yet aloneness is horrid.

Dr. Victor: So you have fears and a sense of isolation?

Jonathan: I don't know if I'll ever get what I need, the way Tuti gave it to me.

Dr. Victor: Together, let's try to find the reason for the problem and to find some solutions so you will feel differently.

Jonathan: That is why I am here.

Dr. Victor: What does their leaving mean to you?

Jonathan: Why me? Why did this happen to me? Am I not any good? Well, I wonder. What did I do? I must have done something wrong for them to treat me this way. Am I doing what I am supposed to be doing?

[Comment: I listen intently, building an authentic relationship. I take the opportunity to dialogue in a way that shows I understand J.'s unique situation, his stance, worldview, state of mind, meaning, values, and beliefs.]

Dr. Victor: Do you think life is questioning you? Is life challenging you to face up to something?

Jonathan: I don't know. Maybe it is telling me I must be a pretty wretched person for my lover to run off with my best friend. I deserve a horrible existence.

Dr. Victor: What is horrible about your existence?

Jonathan: I hate them. But I do not want to be an angry person. I don't like what is happening to me. I should not have to go through this or be angry.

Dr. Victor: Why can't you be angry?

Jonathan: When I get mad, my stomach gets tight. I ask what is the point of all this? What is the reason to continue?

Dr. Victor: What can you do to give yourself some reason to be?

Jonathan: [*long pause*] Without her, there is no reason.

Dr. Victor: *Before* you loved her, was there a reason?

Jonathan: [*long pause*] I don't remember. [*long pause*] I guess there was something. [*tearing up*] My sister Annie. I loved her and when she left for college, she left me alone. She abandoned me. [*tears fill J.'s eyes*] Well, I abandoned others, too. I was a volunteer—a Big Brother. It was hard, and I thought I never wanted to do that again. But it kind of haunts me. All these kids in the ghetto. Don't get what they need. I just left to go to college, like Annie.

Dr. Victor: So you loved your sister. And your work with Big Brothers gave you special meaning. You were productive and did worthwhile deeds. Did these activities make you feel needed?

Jonathan: Well, yes. I had not thought of it quite that way before. I did feel like there was a purpose in the work. That is what attracted me to Tuti. She was so into helping her community. She opened my eyes to social inequities toward the indigenous people of Hawaii, and she helped lots of underserved kids and homeless people. I left that work and went for the bucks. I did not like to see all that suffering around me. It made me feel helpless.

Dr. Victor: Suffering is inevitable and part of human existence. We all have pain, but we have the freedom to choose our reactions to it. We can never avoid suffering completely, but we can decide how we respond. That is what makes us uniquely human.

Jonathan: Yes. I suppose.

Dr. Victor: Does this situation have you really questioning what is important in life?

Jonathan: I suppose.

Dr. Victor: Can I ask you to forget yourself for the moment while you are here with me? Can you focus on Tuti and Darren and what you think they are feeling?

[*Comment: I attempt to decrease J.'s self-absorption and channel his energy to increase his awareness and compassion.*]

Jonathan: That's too much to ask. Yes, I love her and want her to be happy, but I am not a saint.

Dr. Victor: What question has this loss placed in front of you?

Jonathan: Like what the hell am I supposed to do now? How am I supposed to feel?

Dr. Victor: Sometimes suffering opens us up to greater experience. We might have to answer a question—what does life want from me rather than what do I want from life?

Jonathan: [*long pause*] I don't know the answer.

Session 6

Jonathan: I've been doing well. I know that I'm not special. I am not alone, and everyone suffers. But this week I had a very hard time. I've tried, but I can't sleep or stop thinking about them.

Dr. Victor: I can tell you are very sad today. I can see it on your face.

Jonathan: Remember how I told you that when I was a little boy that I depended on my sister so much? I realized how very hurt I was when suddenly she left for college. I was very sick on the day after she left. My temperature was so high that they thought I might die. I was out of school for weeks. My sister did not call, and I thought I'd die without her. Later I found out that my mother did not want to upset her at college so she did not tell her I was sick. I thought my sister didn't care about me, but I later understood they were trying to protect her.

Dr. Victor: So in your mind, did you think she could protect you from death if she was there?

Jonathan: I think in my child's mind I did. Even now, I worry about dying. When I'm alone at night, I can't fall asleep because I am concerned I won't make it to the morning, and who will know it if I'm no longer alive and here?

Dr. Victor: Oh, so when you are alone, you, perhaps, do not feel safe?

Jonathan: I do feel a little edgy, unsafe. It scares me. What can I do?

Dr. Victor: I think almost all of us are anxious when we think about facing death, but your fears are strong at this point. How do you think this affects your life now?

Jonathan: It may have limited me from doing some things.

Dr. Victor: How do you think it may have limited the choices that you have made?

Jonathan: I would be more open and self-confident in my relationships, and perhaps I would have been more open and receptive to her ideas.

Dr. Victor: Could your anxiety propel you to do things differently? Perhaps made it difficult for you to see any value in having children?

Jonathan: The less confident I feel, then the less open I am to the other person. I see why I may have problems sleeping. I thought it might be Tuti's leaving. Yes it is, but I can see it was her presence that kept me feeling safe. How can I get rid of this—perhaps it is—fear of death?

Dr. Victor: Staying awake may be a way you use to protect yourself from harm you think might come about if you let down your guard and relax. I want you to stay awake tonight. Under no circumstances should you sleep.

Jonathan: What if I get sleepy?

Dr. Victor: Fight it off. This way you will be less fearful of being alone, if staying awake is a way to protect yourself, then do this. Under no circumstances should you sleep.

Jonathan: OK. I'll give it a try.

[Comment: When J. returned the next day, he had fallen asleep fighting not to succumb. It was the first good night's sleep he had experienced in four months.]

Session at Six Months

Jonathan: I see what you mean about having a goal that is meaningful. Once I started sleeping better, I was able to make some plans. Once I started doing something that was useful, I started feeling better. I am still hurt, but I put it into perspective. Now I know I can be sad, but at the same time, feel OK because I am doing something that puts my troubles into perspective. I spend 15 hours a week now volunteering at the evening camp for kids with AIDS. I have some purpose.

Dr. Victor: So you do not see yourself as the helpless victim that you felt like when you first came in to see me?

Jonathan: Yes, I found I was less depressed and angry. And I actually drink a lot less alcohol. Oh and I am exercising more. [*long pause*] And I must say, you have really helped me to open my eyes.

Dr. Victor: I am here to support you. Since we have been working together, I see how you have taken small steps and now larger ones and have made some changes and commitments to others. You are accepting responsibilities. You know you always have choices, even if they are choices about what attitude you take on.

Jonathan: Yes, you are right again. I am developing a better attitude about my life and my personal tragedies. I thought the loss of Tuti was unbearable, but now the pain is becoming manageable. I am not alone, and I want to keep going.

Dr. Victor: Remember, the real freedom you have is to choose your own attitude in the given set of circumstances.

Jonathan: Yes, I have gone from a rather hateful and bitter attitude to one of understanding and acceptance. It feels better.

Case Comment

This was a satisfactory treatment of depression. I encouraged Jonathan to search his past for personal meaning and to think of a goal he wanted to achieve. Jonathan and I developed an authentic relationship that helped him to heal. He came with his feelings of alienation and lack of connection between himself and the people in his world.

Paradoxical intention was helpful. Jonathan's focus on trying to sleep had resulted in his symptoms worsening and the development of anticipatory anxiety. To him, sleep seemed to represent a loss of control and a symbolic fear of death. I addressed this by telling Jonathan to do the opposite of sleep—stay awake rather than sleep—to deal with the underlying problem—his fear of loss, death, alienation—and not with just the symptom. He returned to normal sleep patterns.

Jonathan searched for meaning in the suffering he was enduring as a result of the loss of his significant others. He increased his awareness of how his past experience changed the meaning of his current life. His relationship with me deepened over time, and it will continue to deepen as he continues in therapy. He increased awareness of and faced his death anxiety, and his symptoms of depression decreased. At termination, he is better able to deal with anxiety. He is moving toward new meaning in life through his sense of connection with worthwhile projects.

Jonathan has been in therapy for approximately two years and wants to continue to see me intermittently.

✦ RESEARCH DIRECTIONS IN EXISTENTIAL THERAPY

The evidence base supporting the efficacy and effectiveness of existential therapy, including logotherapy, is sparse. Meta-analytic reviews of psychotherapy outcome studies generally do not include pure models of existential therapies (Smith & Glass, 1977; Smith, Glass, & Miller, 1980). Most claims of the success of existential therapies rely primarily upon case studies and clinical expertise.

Psychotherapy researchers have grouped some Third Force therapies together under the category of experiential psychotherapies and conducted research reviews on the combined models. Included among them are existential, gestalt, and client-centered models. These psychotherapies fit together because they share important common features—that human emotions act as an organizing power in human lives and that experiencing is at the core of change. They also embrace similar values and attitudes about how experiential psychotherapies and research ought to interact (Grawe, Donati, & Bernauer, 1998). As a result, our discussion about research for client-centered, existential, and gestalt therapies (Chapters 6, 7, and 8) overlap to some degree. The assumption here is that the results of these reviews can be applied to existential therapies, since existential therapy is considered to be an experiential psychotherapy and thus an empirically supported relationship.

As discussed in Chapter 6, Robert Elliott, Leslie Greenberg, & Germain Lietaer (2004) reviewed 112 studies of experiential psychotherapies. Clients treated with experiential therapies were better off than untreated clients. The equivalency effect, with which the student is now quite familiar, is alive and well for these experiential therapies. Also, as the student knows, there is evidence that the therapeutic relationship as practiced in experiential therapies facilitates change (Greenberg & Pascual-Leone, 2006). Thus, supporters of existential psychotherapy contend that since the existential psychotherapies cultivate the therapeutic relationship, it is possible to conclude that they are likely to be effective (Mendelowitz & Schneider, 2008).

Regarding logotherapy in particular, the specific intervention—paradoxical intention—has been the focus of three meta-analytic studies. When compared, paradoxical interventions were consistently more effective that nonparadoxical interventions in a meta-analysis of 15 outcome studies (Hill, 1987). Other researchers looked at 12 data sets with group designs and with randomly assigned subjects in individual therapy (Shoham-Salomon & Rosenthal, 1987). They concluded that paradoxical interventions are at least of average therapeutic effectiveness in the typical treatment situation and were more effective than other interventions when compared a month after termination and with clients with greater severity of symptoms. A review of 29 outcome studies showed paradoxical treatment was superior to other treatments at posttest and at follow-up (Hampton and Hulgus, 1993). From these small-scale meta-analyses, proponents say that this research may foreshadow positive results that substantiate the usefulness of existential therapies in the future.

Experiential psychotherapists also embrace similar values and attitudes about how experiential therapies and research ought to interact (Grawe et al., 1998). Existential therapists complain that mainstream clinical research and evidence-based practice clearly favors empirically based psychotherapies at the expense of experiential and other insight-oriented psychotherapies (Quintana & Minami, 2006). They worry that those models that aim to help human beings deal with big life issues (death, freedom, isolation, and meaningfulness) are being shoved aside for therapies that can be empirically validated and assessed and that the push for evidence-based therapies is driven more by economics than scientific ideals. Existential psychotherapists are not deeply concerned about traditional scientific validation or randomized controlled trials. Furthermore, they dislike standardization and structure since these are incompatible with the spirit of existential therapy. They frown on using numbers to judge human beings since such actions objectify and dehumanize (Bohart, O'Hara, & Leitner, 1998). They resist formalizing and fabricating methods that can be re-created by every therapist with every new client (van Deurzen, 2007). Thus there is a fundamental clash of values between advocates of evidence-based practice and proponents of existential psychotherapy (Beutler et al., 2004).

Despite this philosophical opposition, many existential psychotherapists acknowledge that a more research-friendly approach could increase the acceptance of existential therapy among practitioners. So, let's look at how humanist-existential researchers are bridging the gap between practice and research.

Some existential therapists are attempting to transcend what they consider to be the restrictive criteria of evidence-based therapies and create a new research paradigm (Elliott, 2000a, 2000c). They are designing innovative research methods that rely on a mixture of both qualitative and quantitative information that will improve the performance of the therapist and help clients to derive more from their therapy (Schneider, 2001). One example is the hermeneutic single-case efficacy design (Elliott, 2001, 2002). The psychotherapist and researcher use a case record that contains both positive and negative data. Once a potential cause of change is identified, it is assessed and analyzed, and researchers look for all possible explanations for changes, which are scrutinized in depth (Elliott & Greenberg, 2002). This type of study encourages the use of "experience-near" research, which means using research methods that are true to clinical events as practiced in the real world (Klein & Elliott, 2006; Schneider; 2001).

Another method suitable for studying experiential therapy is multiple-case depth research. It calls on a combination of case-study method linked with depth–experiential therapy principles. It takes into consideration factors such as whether the data from cases are linked to the theory in a believable way and they can be generalized and whether the conclusions can be disconfirmed (Gurman & Messer, 2003).

In order to enhance communication and facilitate collaborative research, a number of experiential therapists are creating networks of evidence (Klein & Elliott, 2006). In the Netherlands, the Humanism: Meanings of Life Project is run by researchers who value humanistic qualitative and phenomenological approaches to research. They point out that there already exists a good deal of empirical evidence to show that personal meaning is important to human health and survival. The information needs to be collated and communicated in a meaningful way. An example of research into existential psychotherapy, with a more traditional bent, is Aaron Keshen's development of a succinct, well-defined model of existential psychotherapy with its own manual (2006). The success of his prototype remains to be tested. In any case, experiential researchers are trying to fulfill the need for an evidence base that offers support for experiential psychotherapies, but they are creatively adapting the research and finding methods that are compatible with the values associated with their psychotherapies.

What can a therapist say to justify use of existential therapy or logotherapy? The therapist can candidly inform clients that there is a weak empirical evidence base for existential therapy (as defined by the current standards of quality research). The very nature of existential therapy makes it difficult to perform meaningful research, but existential therapists are currently searching for appropriate methods to demonstrate that it is helpful to the client. Existential therapists (like client-centered and other experiential therapists) highly value the client–therapist relationship, which research shows is one of the common factors underlying therapeutic success. Much of the work in therapy has to do with how the client and the therapist work together in a truly authentic, honest, and open relationship, an activity that is difficult to quantify and measure. A therapist can choose to use existential psychotherapy, or logotherapy in particular, based primarily on clinical expertise, judgment, and experience. Clients will benefit from the consistent framework that allows them to probe concerns dealing with meaningfulness, spirituality, and adversity or suffering.

➔ ISSUES OF DIVERSITY

Not all cultures value the phenomenological world and the needs of the individual over the needs of the group. Being nondirective, placing the responsibility for progress in therapy upon the individual, and putting aside the needs of others (family included) so that personal freedom can be treasured is primarily a Western point of view.

As discussed in Chapter 6, the concept of a separate, autonomous self that is able to transcend derives from a Western, White, male perspective. In many other cultures, there is a different view of self–other boundaries, so the therapist must be sensitive to different sociocultural values on this issue.

In addition, nondirective therapists are not universally valued by all cultures. Some patients desire concrete advice from an expert and do not want the therapist to try to foster the patient's own abilities (Wong, 2004). The client from hierarchical cultures may not be able to grasp covert cues; this could even result in the client feeling misunderstood because the therapist has not met his or her expectations and assumed the role of the authority or the role that is consistent with his or her cultural values.

May (1967) points out that in the Western scientific tradition, there is a great emphasis on gaining power over nature as well as over ourselves; this may mean that we treat ourselves as objects to be manipulated. Such an attitude detracts from a meaningful life, and it invalidates the self. Others believe that existential therapists are too passive in the face of the social injustices. Remaining silent about the importance of social injustice can be construed as existential psychotherapy actually supporting the status quo (Prilleltensky, 1992). As well, the therapy may indirectly hold the client responsible for all and any problems, attributing their cause as coming from within the individual and not society. This can foster a "blame the victim" attitude that can result in harm to clients (Sue & Sue, 2003, p. 147).

On the other hand, there are some aspects of existential psychotherapy that promote culturally competent practice. Since the client is free to discuss prejudice, discrimination, and oppression freely, existential therapy can be seen as providing an open environment where this can happen without any negative judgment. Experiential therapies endorse the ability to tolerate silence, to listen well, to respect the client, and to be open-minded and nonjudgmental (Black, 2005).

Empathy, or the ability to put oneself in the other's position, is universally valued in existential therapy, as are discussions about the meaning of life, death, isolation, suffering, and love (Vontress, 2003). However, the existential therapist needs to avoid the assumption that all clients share the same concern about the fear of death and isolation, when these may be Western cultural issues rather than universal ones. Patients from other cultural backgrounds, those with more open attitudes about death and greater support and value on the extended family, may not have these same concerns. All in all, existential therapies attempt to rise above the Aristotelian concept of cause and effect and help clients to accept their personal experiences within the framework of their personal cultural values (Bauman & Waldo, 1998).

✦ Major Critiques of Existential Psychotherapy

As is the case with person-centered and other humanist-experiential psychotherapies, critics say that the theory and concepts of existential therapy are vague, obtuse, and unclear (Keshen, 2006). The lack of operationally defined constructs leaves experiential theories with serious limitations about how to measure concepts objectively (Rowan, 2001). Specifically, for example, Frankl's construct of the will to meaning is loose and fictional. How can a researcher empirically and objectively measure a will to meaning or a way of being in the world? Little prediction and control are possible. Existential theories, with their emphasis on phenomenology, contend the only reality ever known is the person's subjective world. So how can outside observers understand anything outside of their own phenomenological field?

Some believe existential psychotherapies are merely philosophies masquerading as psychotherapies. They are belief systems similar to religions posing as social sciences with underlying assumption that are naive. Sensitive clients might construe the adamant belief in individual responsibility as blame. Furthermore, the theory is fatalistic in that there really are no solutions to suffering; it is inevitable that we suffer, so the best we can hope for is an attitude adjustment. But this belief deemphasizes and discourages individuals to take social action.

Again, as is the case with other experiential psychotherapies, if the underlying theory of existential therapy is vague, then its practice and research is likely to be poorly defined as well. The therapist's activities are discussed loosely and are idiosyncratic for each client. The style of the therapist is so individual that it is difficult to be certain that two people are conducting the same therapy. How does the therapist intervene to alleviate existential anxiety and noogenic neurosis and help to shift the client's phenomenological field, with scientific precision? Practice is based upon intuition with little critical appraisal.

Critics such as Thomas Szasz (2005) complain that existential therapists have assumed a self-congratulatory attitude and tone when they discuss the definitions and scope of their practice. He argues that even though existential therapists claim they do not support the medical model, they do apply a metaphor of mental illness to the normal human condition. Since human existence is not an illness, it should not be treated as a sickness. Psychotherapy has nothing to do with illness, treatment, and medicine. Existential therapists, in particular, should commit themselves to rejecting the medical model and its economic and professional benefits, rather than operate under vague and romantic philosophical notions.

On a positive note, sociocultural conditions have sparked renewed interest in addressing spiritual, religious, and philosophical dimensions through such issues as end-of-life care, experiencing a good death, the hospice movement (Zaser, 2006), suffering with chronic disease, and health directives (Lantz, 2006). Existential therapies provide excellent tools with which therapists can address issues that are typically difficult to discuss with clients (Schneider-Berti, 2004).

SUMMARY

- Existential and humanistic therapies entered American psychotherapy in the1950s and are often grouped together because they share similar values.
- Existential therapy is based in modern existential philosophical thought. It is an inquiry into the nature of human existence, posing questions about life's significance. The core principles include that life cannot be understood wholly from a rational or scientific perspective, that meaning is understood from within, that how people *are* in the world is significant, that human awareness is highly valued, that phenomenology is an important method for exploring truth, that people create their own purpose, that people are free but responsible for their lives, and that people struggle with living an authentic life.
- The four existential realities include death, freedom and responsibility, isolation, and meaninglessness. Existential therapy rejects the notion that the person and the environment are separate. The different worlds in which we exist are *umwelt, mitwelt, eigenwelt, uberwelt.*
- The I-am experience is the recognition that "I exist," which includes the understanding that I will *not* be alive. Anxiety occurs when a person faces a threat to an essential value. Choice produces anxiety because each choice means relinquishing another. Time is a central issue in life and death, and thus it is of particular significance to the existential therapist. The existential therapist's role in the therapeutic relationship is to provide an authentic I–Thou encounter in which the client can participate.
- An authentic person actualizes his or her potentialities. The well-adjusted person is an immediate person in the process of becoming completely human and authentic. The unhealthy person is inauthentic and does not adequately address being human.
- Frankl's logotherapy is a form of existential therapy that deals with the meaning of human existence. Key concepts include will to meaning, noodynamics, self-transcendence or fulfilling life's meaning, existential frustration, and existential vacuum.

- In the practice of logotherapy, assessment and diagnosis include gathering background. The therapeutic relationship emphasizes authenticity, awareness, and a collaborative approach. The length of treatment is individualized according to need. The goal is to help clients find meaning in their lives, to actualize values, and to fill an existential vacuum.
- Therapeutic techniques include doing a deed, experiencing a value, enduring suffering, Socratic dialogue, attitudinal adjustment, dereflection, paradoxical intention, and dealing with specific problem behaviors and attitudes.
- The evidence base for models of pure existential therapy is sparse and relies primarily on case studies. Since the nature of existential therapy makes it difficult to research, existential psychotherapists advocate the development of appropriate research designs for existential therapies such as the hermeneutic single-case efficacy design and multiple-case depth research.
- Existential values are based on a Western, White, male perspective and may not be accepted by members of diverse cultures who do not place the needs of the individual over the group. These populations may not accept the idea of a separate, autonomous self and may not have the same value for the phenomenological world.
- Criticisms of existential psychotherapy are that theoretical concepts and techniques are vague. It deals with an overly subjective world that is difficult to study and understand and exudes a self-congratulatory attitude and tone.

Resources

Viktor Frankl Institute of Logotherapy
P. O. Box 15221
Abilene, TX 79698-5211
http://www.logotherapyinstitute.org

Founded in 1977 in Berkeley, California, this institute offers education, credentialing, and publications for Frankl's psychology. The institute serves to educate the public and provide workshops for professionals.

International Society for Existential Psychology and Psychotherapy (ISEPP)
c/o Trinity Western University
Graduate Counseling Psychology Department
7600 Glover Road
Langley, BC
V2Y 1Y1
Canada
1-604-0513-2056
http://www.existentialpsychology.org

The ISEPP is an interdisciplinary organization promoting existential psychotherapy. The focus is on finding meaning in the lives of real people in real situations. Its mission is to advance existential psychotherapy into the mainstream of psychology.

Society for Humanistic Psychology
Division 32, American Psychological Association
750 First Street, NE
Washington, DC 20002-4242
(800) 374-2721 or (202) 336-5500
http://www.apa.org/divisions/div32/homepage.html

The society's mission stresses healing the fragmentary nature of contemporary psychology, bringing about a more comprehensive and integrative approach, and developing systematic and rigorous methods of studying human beings compatible with humanistic-existential values.

CLASS EXERCISES AND ACTIVITIES

Theory

1. Name and describe some of the early philosophical influences in the development of existential psychotherapy. Which resonate with you personally and why?
2. Describe the underlying core values of logotherapy and discuss what types of clients might want this form of therapy.
3. Divide into three groups: the existentialists, the psychoanalysts, and the behaviorists. Which view of the world is preferable to you? Debate and discuss why you prefer the model you choose.

Practice

1. Break into groups. Select one person to play the role of Viktor Frankl and another to play the client. The remainder of the group members can coach or help Dr. Frankl by adding observations about what is going on between the client and therapist. How would you, as Dr. Frankl, explain your therapeutic practice to a client? Compare this explanation with how you would explain another type of therapy (of your choosing).
2. What are the differences and similarities between the practices of Rogers's client-centered therapy and logotherapy? Compare self-actualization and the will to meaning. What cultural values affect your judgment?
3. Look at the sample treatment plan in Chapter 1 (Figure 1.2). Use it to fill out a treatment plan for Tuti for existential therapy or logotherapy. (Both Jonathan's and Tuti's case histories are in Appendix A.)

Research

1. Comment on why there is a limited evidence base of research for existential psychotherapies. Is there a principle involved? If so, what is it?
2. Describe an argument between a managed-care company that is asking for a justification for payment and the existential logotherapist who is treating a client who has terminal pancreatic cancer. The managed-care company claims there is no justification for using logotherapy with this client.
3. A client asks you "Why are you using existential therapy to treat me? How did you choose this particular model for me?" How would you answer the client?

CHAPTER 8

GESTALT THERAPY

Our dependency makes slaves out of us, especially if this dependency is a dependency of our self-esteem. If you need encouragement, praise, pats on the back from everybody, then you make everybody your judge.

–Fritz Perls

The goal of this chapter is to present an overview of gestalt therapy. The chapter looks at biographical information about Fritz and Laura Perls, the historical context of gestalt therapy, and the theory, practice, and research of gestalt therapy. The simulated therapist, Jennifer Pert, MSW, presents a treatment plan and some excerpts of gestalt therapy sessions for the case of Jonathan. Issues of diversity and major critiques are also included.

✦ HISTORICAL CONTEXT

Gestalt therapy, part of the Third Force, presented a very different approach to psychotherapy from the reductionist models of psychoanalysis and behaviorism. Gestalt therapy values awareness, trust in self-regulation, contact between the therapist and client, and existential dialogue and experimentation (Yontef & Jacobs, 2008). It emerged at the same time as client-centered psychotherapy in the cultural zeitgeist that was receptive to humanism and existentialism discussed in Chapters 6 and 7.

Because the lives of Fritz and Laura Perls spanned nearly 100 years and carried them across several continents—from Europe to Africa to the United States—they were able to be in contact with a diverse array of extraordinary intellectuals (see About Fritz Perls and Laura Posner Perls box). This made it possible for them to create an exciting new psychotherapy, interwoven with rich information from a wide variety of cultures. Some of the major historical influences on the development of gestalt therapy include psychoanalysis, gestalt psychology, field theory, humanism, existentialism, holism, phenomenology, Goldstein's organismic theory, and homeostasis (Latner, 1992; Rosenfeld, 1977; Yontef & Jacobs, 2008).

Psychoanalysis

At a time when Freud's theory was thriving and growing internationally, both Fritz and Laura Perls were well grounded in psychoanalysis (Wulf, 1996). However, like many psychoanalysts at the time, they began to revise analytic theory.

ABOUT FRITZ PERLS AND LAURA POSNER PERLS

Frederick (Fritz) Salomon Perls was born in Berlin, Germany, on July 8, 1893. His mother, Amelia, and his father, Nathan, were middle-class Jews whose relationship deteriorated after several years of marriage. Fritz was a troublesome and difficult child and was expelled from school for behavior problems.

Despite these early years of rebellion, Fritz earned his MD from Friedrich Wilhelm University in 1920. He studied at the Vienna and Berlin Institutes of Psychoanalysis with Wilhelm Reich as a training analyst. He was also very intrigued by the theater and acting. He served as a medic in the German army during World War 1, and he worked for a short time at the Institute for Brain-Injured Veterans in 1926, where he became interested in the theory of organismic functioning, as proposed by neuropsychiatrist Kurt Goldstein. This is where he met Laura Posner.

Laura Posner Perls was born in Pforzheim, Germany, in 1905. She was musically gifted, dancing and playing piano from childhood into her old age. A brilliant and versatile woman, Laura earned her DSc in psychology at Frankfurt-am-Main University. She studied gestalt psychology and trained in psychoanalysis. Her early educational mentors included Goldstein and the philosophers Paul Tillich and Martin Buber.

Fritz and Laura married in 1930, and they had two children—Renata, born in 1931, and Steven, born in 1935. The Nazis' oppression caused Fritz and Laura to flee Germany for Amsterdam in 1933. They later moved to South Africa, where they opened the South African Psychoanalytic Institute and developed the core ideas of gestalt therapy. They also cultivated a friendship with Jan Smuts, a prominent holistic thinker.

With the rise of apartheid, Fritz left South Africa in 1946 to open up a psychoanalytic practice in New York. Laura joined him 1947. In 1952, they founded the New York Institute for Gestalt Therapy where they collaborated with prominent American intellectuals, informed about psychoanalysis, who contributed theoretical and practical insights to gestalt therapy. Some of these contributors were Paul Goodman, Isadore From, Ralph Hefferline, and Paul Weisz.

Perls became a major attraction at the New York institute when he conducted therapy training sessions and workshops. Fritz was a charismatic and fascinating presenter. His therapeutic interventions dazzled novice therapists. His tone at workshops and demonstrations was dramatic, memorable, and often confrontational. He was skilled at arousing strong feelings within clients, and he incorporated some of the theatrics he learned early in his life into his therapy. (Woldt & Toman, 2005).

Initially, Fritz Perls received recognition for the creation of gestalt therapy, but in the 1970s, Laura Perls claimed appropriate credit for her share of the work. She contributed to the writing of *Ego, Hunger and Aggression* (1942/1992), a seminal work, and was integral to the organization and running of the New York Gestalt Institute (Rosenfeld, 1977). Laura was an expert therapist, theorist, and consultant. When Fritz decided to settle at the Esalen Institute in Big Sur, California, as the resident psychiatrist where he conducted workshops and therapy sessions from 1964 until 1969, Laura remained at the New York Institute. In the last 15 years of Fritz's life, the couple did not live together but remained married and in contact.

In 1970, Fritz died shortly after he had moved to Vancouver Island in British Columbia to set up a gestalt community. Laura died in 1990, having remained active in gestalt therapy in New York throughout her life. Their son Steven wrote about his relationship with his father (Perls, S. 1993), and the interested student can also learn more about the Perls from Fritz's book *In and Out of the Garbage Pail* (1969b).

They came to disagree with Freud's view of the neutral analyst; their conception of the role of the psychotherapist was that of a co-director and an active participant in a mutual relationship.

Fritz Perls approved of and integrated into gestalt therapy a number of post-Freudian ideas such as constructs of human attachment, self-satisfaction, and a personal sense of the self. He also liked Wilhelm Reich's concept of *character armor*—that the body was tied to the mind and psychic life and so a person's physical body posture and overt behavior could be a gauge of inner well-being or psychological conflict (Latner, 2005b). Fritz agreed with post-Freudian psychoanalyst Otto Rank that it was important to focus on the immediate moment in the psychotherapy relationship (Yontef & Jacobs, 2008).

By the 1950s, both Fritz and Laura Perls had diverged significantly from Freud's classical psychoanalysis. They had also developed their own therapeutic approach, which Fritz named *gestalt therapy* (Rosenfeld, 1977).

Gestalt Psychology

Gestalt psychology was developed in the early 1900s by academic psychologists Max Wertheimer, Wolfgang Köhler, and Kurt Koffka as a method of studying perception. Laura Perls introduced Fritz to the work of the gestalt psychologists, which he later integrated into his therapy. The gestalt psychologists believed that perception is an active, not passive, act. Humans organize their percepts into a meaningful whole, so that the whole is different than the sum of its parts (Feldman, 2005). A person organizes perceptual stimuli into a central figure (what stands out) and a background (the backdrop that recedes) (Passer & Smith, 2004).

While the gestalt *psychologists* studied cognitive processing in experimental, academic settings, the gestalt *therapists* extended this framework to psychotherapeutic situations in imaginative and useful ways (Patterson, 1986). For example, Perls applied the concept of perceptual figure and ground to mean a person's met and unmet emotional needs, which is central to an understanding of emotional functioning in gestalt therapy.

Fritz Perls's application of academic gestalt to clinical gestalt stirred some controversy. Some believed he was stretching gestalt psychology too far (Henle, 1975). Others credit his expansion of gestalt psychology, with its narrow interpretation of the outside world, to an understanding of perception as reflective of the person's internal physical and emotional state as a remarkable achievement (Rosner, Beutler, & Daldrup, 2000; Sherrill, 1986). Fritz Perls himself admitted, "The academic Gestaltists of course, never accepted me. I certainly was not a pure Gestaltist" (1969a, p. 62).

Humanism, Existentialism, and Phenomenology

Both Fritz and Laura Perls incorporated concepts from existential philosophy into gestalt therapy. For example, gestalt therapy sees the person as Heidegger did, as a being thrown into the world who is free to choose from among all possibilities at any given moment. People construct who they are through their choices. Gestalt stresses the importance, as did Kierkegaard, of exploring the nature of existence, what it means to be a single individual, and the truth of subjectivity. People who lack truthfulness about the self in the world may experience anxiety and dread. To be authentic, a person must be responsible for self (Wulf, 1996).

Gestalt therapy taps into phenomenology, an existential philosophical value that encourages awareness and an understanding of a person's subjective perception of reality; it is also a method to study consciousness in its subjective meaningful structure and function (Heidegger, 1927/1975).

Martin Buber's phenomenological view of the I–Thou encounter permeates the gestalt therapist–client relationship. The I–Thou relationship means that two people are meeting each other in their authentic existences, creating a mutual and very real encounter without any qualification or objectification of each other. Awareness of "the other" is central (Friedman, 1985). Integrating Buber's I–Thou into gestalt therapy made it a relational approach, far different than the early Freudian view that therapeutic neutrality and transference were fundamental to early models of psychotherapy. Interestingly, today psychoanalysis is also moving toward a relational approach, and some gestaltists are joining forces with relational psychoanalysts to produce relational psychoanalysis (see Chapter 4).

Other Influences on Gestalt Therapy

Several other theoretical perspectives came together in the development of gestalt therapy. These include holism, organismic theory, field theory, and homeostasis.

Jan Smuts was the South African prime minister who created the concept of *holism.* When Fritz and Laura fled to South Africa, they became friends with Smuts and became familiar with this intellectual trend. The person is a unified self-regulating creature, who thinks, feels, and acts as an integrated whole. All parts are interdependent, including body, mind, and soul. The gestalt approach of looking at the whole person, which contains its past and much of its future in the present, is an adaptation of Smut's holistic theory (Wulf, 1996).

Laura Perls was familiar with the classic book *The Organism,* in which Goldstein's *organismic theory* hypothesized that living beings possess a master drive toward self-actualization. To achieve their goals, humans organize their perceptions into figure and background fields. If a need is pressing, they respond by perceiving it, or making it the figure in the figure–background relationship. What causes one figure to grab attention over another is the requirement of the task at hand (Perls, 1969a, 1973/1976). For example, if the task at hand is to watch a movie, the person must attend to the screen and not to the audience around her. If a friend sitting next to her at the movie begins speaking to her, her attention will be focused on the friend's voice and not the screen.

Field theory, described by Kurt Lewin, was based upon the physics of the day and incorporated into gestalt therapy by Fritz Perls. The field consists of the complete environment of the person. Behavior is a function of the tensions that occur between the person's self-perceptions and the environment she encounters. The total environment of the person and interactions with others must be understood in order to comprehend behavior. People participate in a variety of life spaces (e.g., family, work, sports) that have both positive and negative influences on the person, which are affected by the person's perceptions and underlying psychological needs. In this contextualist worldview a person "exists in a field and cannot be understood outside of it" (Perls, Hefferline, & Goodman, 1951/1994).

Walter Canon (1932) described *homeostasis,* a process by which every living organism strives to maintain its internal balance in a changing environment. Situations upset a person's internal and external balance. To arrive at a balanced state, the organism makes changes of equal size in an opposite direction, through a process of interdependent regulations. In psychological homeostasis, a person meets his or her needs, discharges tension, and achieves balance once again.

Trends in Gestalt Therapy

With the book *Gestalt Therapy* in 1951, the new form of psychotherapy was established (Perls et al., 1951/1994). The New York Institute of Gestalt Therapy opened in 1952, and Laura and Fritz also began to conduct regular workshops and trainings. Those trained at the New York Institute founded other institutes throughout the United States, and gestalt therapy acquired a wide audience in the 1960s.

As gestalt therapy evolved over the years, a number of modern therapists, such as Erving and Miriam Polster wrote extensively, expanding its theory and practice (Polster, 1987). Part of gestalt's popularity and rapid growth in the United States was due to Fritz's charismatic personality and his electrifying, provocative, and entertaining style as a therapist (Perls, 1969b).

After Fritz's death, gestalt therapists shifted their practice slightly to make the psychotherapy relationship softer, more supportive, and much less directly confrontational than the style used by Perls. The current trend in gestalt therapy emphasizes attachment theory and how relationships shape and define the person's life. This means specifically addressing actual life events and developmental traumas, such as child abuse (Yontef & Jacobs, 2008). In addition, there is close consideration of how the therapist's attitude, behavior, and meta-messages affect the client in psychotherapy. The reasons for disruptions in the therapeutic relationship and their effects on the client are explored. For example, the therapist and client might consider how shame has been created in interpersonal relationships and its current impact in psychotherapy, and the possible negative effects or iatrogenic triggering (Jacobs, 1996; Yontef, 1999).

✦ THEORY OF GESTALT THERAPY

Gestalt therapy has many sources, as we reviewed above. It proposes the uniqueness of the individual and personal responsibility above all. The person is an integrated whole who possesses the innate potential of growth and mature self-expression; the person is never reduced to parts and structural ends. Of crucial importance is the interplay among biological maturation and environmental influences interacting with the individual and creative adjustment (Friedman, 1985, p. 89).

The emphasis in gestalt therapy is on process (what is happening) more than on content (what is being discussed). Clients and therapists in gestalt therapy communicate their phenomenological perspectives through dialogue and these differences in perspective become the focus of continued dialogue and experimentation in psychotherapy (Yontef, 1993). Gestalt therapy encourages clients to accept responsibility for who they are and for what they are doing and to learn to distinguish perceiving, feeling, and acting from other intellectual functions and attitudes (Association for the Advancement of Gestalt Therapy, 2005; Yontef, 1993).

Key Concepts

Key theoretical concepts in gestalt therapy include holism, field theory, gestalt, and figure–ground relationship, contact and contact boundary, awareness, and the paradoxical theory of change. Other concepts of gestalt therapy are present centeredness, the dialectical principle, unfinished business, and creative adjustment.

Holism, Field Theory, Gestalt, and Figure–Ground Relationship

Gestalt therapy embraces holism, as described by Smuts, and sees the person as a self-regulating entity, composed of physical, cognitive, emotional, and spiritual components (Perls, 1973/1976). The person is trying to shape his or her life into a harmonious whole and move toward positive growth or self-actualization, which is the primary or master motivation (Perls, 1969a).

Drawing from field theory, Perls said the person exists in a field, or dwells in and interacts with the environment. Thus, the self cannot be understood outside of its context, just like day cannot be understood without contact with the night. Every person–environment interaction is unique (Perls et al., 1951/1994). The same event will be experienced differently by different people based on the different points of observation and the nature of the different aspects of the field as the person perceives it (Jacobs, 1998). Thus, in field theory, any occurrence can be interpreted from multiple perspectives.

An important part of a person's environment is his interpersonal relationships. The self is dependent upon others for existence. No self exists without "the other." "The person *is* an interaction," with fluidity, continual contact, and communication with his or her world (Bohart, 2003, p. 124). However, there are boundaries, and these boundaries exist between the self and the other and also define how the person relates to the world (see discussion of contact boundary).

A *gestalt*, German for "whole" or "configuration," is a perception that is formed from the interaction between all environmental possibilities and a person's needs (Yontef & Jacobs, 2008). Each person arranges or organizes his or her perceptions into a gestalt. It is the *organization* of perceptions, and not the individual perceptions, that gives a given perception its specific meaning (Perls, 1973/1976). Thus each person's world is organized by the subjective reality of his or her perceptions (Polster & Polster, 1990).

Needs organize a person's perceptions and actions. When a need emerges, the need comes out of a background and becomes a figure. The dominant need takes the foreground as other needs recede into the background. This is where Cannon's idea of homeostasis comes in. The person, who wants stability, begins the process of restoring equilibrium by satisfying the need (Barlowe, 1981). When the need is fulfilled, it ceases to be a figure and recedes to the background in a never-ending pattern of consciousness (Perls et al., 1951/1994; Yontef, 1993). Although a person's prevailing need at any moment partly determines what is figure and what is ground, all parts are interrelated and responsive to one another. For example, a mother is engrossed in her favorite television show. The show is the figure, and the surroundings are background. If suddenly her newborn infant cries out, the cry becomes the figure, and the television becomes the background. Only one figure can be of interest at a particular time, but the figure of importance can change rapidly.

There are three ways in which a person can satisfy needs: (a) equalizing processes or tension; (b) getting what they want in the world; and (c) becoming self-actualized (Perls, 1969a, 1973/1976). The person's ego has the important function of structuring the figure–ground in a way that will fulfill his or her needs. The person, or the self, is a system of contacts, and there are boundaries between the self and the other (Perls, 1973/1976).

Contact and Contact Boundary

Contact is the "awareness of, and the behavior toward, the assimilable, and the rejection of the unassimilable novelty" (Perls et al., 1951/1994, p. 230). Contact means being in touch with what is up-and-coming. Through contact (and contact boundaries), people connect to and separate from others, changing themselves and their experience of the world.

A *contact boundary* is the point of interaction between the person and the environment (Perls, 1973/1976). It is where psychological events—thoughts, actions, behaviors, and emotions—happen. An example is the beach, a boundary between water and sand that brings about both separation and union. The beach is always an encounter between saltwater and sand, yet each wave is unique and impermanent and encounters the sand only once. Yet, both water and sand exert an effect upon each other and produce a mutual, or dialectic, relationship. Although there is no *thing* between the water and the sand, everyone recognizes the boundary that makes up the seashore (Latner, 1992). Like the sand and water at the beach, people contact each other, and, thus, meet their psychological, emotional, and physical needs. People also withdraw from contact in order to maintain their own identity and to regulate how much stimulation is received (Polster & Polster, 1973).

There are several types of boundaries. An *I-boundary* differentiates one person from another. It is a part of a responsive meeting with others and facilitates the assimilation and integration of experience (Kirchner, 2000). It is a way to change the self (Polster & Polster, 1973). For example, if a student hears an inspiring lecturer in class and is so impressed that she decides to enter the same profession, this event (or series of events) has been assimilated.

Body boundaries define the sensations that are acceptable or not to the person; *value boundaries* inform the person about the values he or she holds; *familiarity boundaries* set up conditions and events and are usually taken for granted and seldom talked about; and *expressive boundaries* represent the behaviors that are permissible, such as when to cry or touch (Polster & Polster, 1973).

Awareness and Present Centeredness

Awareness in gestalt therapy is similar to the mindfulness described in Zen. It focuses the energies of the mind in the moment (Kabat-Zinn, 1990). Awareness is important for self-regulation, and falls along a continuum. Individuals who are fully aware know what they are doing and experiencing; they own it, take responsibility for it, and respond in an adaptive way, understanding that they are choosing their actions among alternatives (Yontef, 1993).

Present centeredness in gestalt therapy means that the person is thinking about what he is doing and how he is doing it by focusing on the tiniest details of the action. For example, when eating, a person is aware that this act involves procuring, chewing, swallowing, and assimilating food. The person tastes it, feels its texture, and decides if he wants to take in more or not. The person is conscious of what he is doing and how he is doing it and how it is it organized (Latner, 1992). Being present centered means that no energy is given to the past or projected into the future, because that detracts from the now, which needs full energy to live life to the fullest (Perls et al., 1951/1994).

Other Gestalt Therapy Concepts

There are many other concepts that are important to gestalt therapy, some of which are briefly discussed here.

Phenomenology

Based on Martin Buber's idea of the dialogic relationship, phenomenology is an integral part of gestalt therapy. Reality is subjective, a function of the client's perception, and the dialogue between the observed and the observer defines the nature of the relationship (Yontef & Jacobs, 2008). The relationship is the vehicle that brings about a heightened awareness—in conjunction with creative and active experimentation. The client feels confirmed as a person and moves toward fulfilling his or her potential, freer to be accepting and nonjudgmental of all, including self (Jacobs, 1998; McCall, 1983). The speediest path to change is by fully embracing the person that we are (Beisser, 1970).

Paradoxical Theory of Change

Gestalt therapists adhere to the *paradoxical theory of change* with its basic assumption that "change occurs when one becomes what he is, not when he tries to become what he is not" (Beisser, 1970, p. 2). Change cannot occur by coercing, manipulating, persuading, or interpreting but happens when the client wants to be who he or she is. Clients can be invited to communicate, to dialogue, to be aware of the roles they assume and play, and thus to identify with the alienated parts of themselves and re-own and integrate these fragments. Thus gestalt therapy does not try to change clients as much as it encourages them to be whatever they are experiencing at the moment (Lampert, 2006).

Dialectical Principle and Polarities

People experience conflicts among behaviors, thoughts, feelings, or values that are polar opposites. These polarities within the person may result in feeling pulled apart. For example, if a person is torn between what he considers to be good and bad (e.g., faithfulness to spouse versus having an affair), self-regulation may be disrupted. Recognizing only one aspect of one's self (faithful and honest) may result in its polar opposite (unfaithful and dishonest) becoming strong enough to come out of the background and become a figure, pulling the person in two directions. This creates imbalance in the person. To regain balance, the person will strive to integrate these polarities through experiencing full awareness of them (Perls, 1976).

Responsibility

Responsibility means that a person is the principal agent of her own life and is responsible for what she chooses to do. People confuse blame and responsibility. When they blame external factors for the choices they make (e.g., "It is because my parents mistreated me when I was a child that I am a failure"), they may torture themselves with shoulds, oughts, and musts. They may ignore their true needs and wants and lack spontaneity. A person displays responsibility when she accepts the consequences of his or her own choices (Perls, 1973/1976).

Anxiety

Perls sees stage fright as the paradigm for all human anxiety. Just as the curtain is about to go up, the actor becomes anxious, fearful, and at odds with himself. So although the actor values acting, the actor must grapple with anticipatory anxiety (Association for the Advancement of Gestalt Therapy, 2005). Anxiety is the fear of one's own daring. It is the conflict that arises when people are caught between their interest in something and their fear of it (Perls et al., 1951/1994). For example, George is deeply in love with Alyson and wants to ask her to marry him, but he is afraid to propose because he dreads rejection.

Unfinished Business

Unmet and unsatisfied needs result in incomplete gestalts or *unfinished business*. These can cause a person to be polarized and alienated from parts of his or her own self. All experience "hangs around" until closure is reached. There is a push-and-pull for it to seek completion.

Unfinished business can manifest itself in symptoms, dreams, diminished energy, diminished control, and nonverbal behaviors. If the force becomes powerful enough, the person may become wary, obsessive, or preoccupied with an issue and engage in self-defeating behaviors. The person is living partly in the past, preventing or blocking him from living in the moment. Where growth should be, there is either stagnation or regression (Kirchner, 2000). The person uses avoidance as a way to prevent the self from completing unfinished business. Closure is reached by becoming aware of the unfinished business and revisiting and resolving it (Polster & Polster, 1973).

Normal and Abnormal Behavior

Creative adjustment is the process by which a person is able to be in her environment and, adjust to it (Spagnuolo Lobb, 2006). The healthy individual is able to strike a balance between the self and the world and adjust to challenges (Spagnuolo Lobb & Amendt-Lyon, 2003). Life is a series of needs, contacts with the environment to fulfill the needs, followed by need fulfillment through assimilation from the environment (Perls, 1969a, 1973/1976). When a person completes one situation, another one develops, and he or she needs to deal with the new situation. Meeting a need completes a gestalt, which then dissolves, and so on in the figure–ground relationship (Patterson, 1986). The healthy person is able to structure the figure-ground in a way that allows satisfactory, respectful, and dignified contact with others. The person grows and matures as each incomplete situation is completed.

Pathology is disrupted contact and/or awareness with boundary disturbances (Latner, 2005a). It can be a function of a creative adjustment that was successful in the past but did not change as the field changed. Thus an inflexible habit forms that is not adaptive or constructive. For example, a young woman who was sexually abused by her brother stays at the library until late in the evening to avoid being alone with him. However, as an adult, she continues to avoid all interpersonal conflicts, even those that she could successfully resolve. Her method of avoiding unresolvable conflict was effective in her earlier situation, but it is ineffective in the present. There is much unfinished business to finish, which causes her to be cut off from I–Thou potential. The person is so defensive and self-protective that a nonjudgmental acceptance of self and others is unlikely, and the person feels deadened and inhuman (Jacobs, 1998). When normal boundary functions are interrupted, boundary disturbances can occur, of which there are five major patterns (Polster & Polster, 1973; Sharf, 2004):

1. *Introjection* means psychologically swallowing the whole—hook, line, and sinker—without critical evaluation. The person accepts another person's

views as her own. For example, a child may take in his mother's view of the world as a dangerous place without analyzing the real threat of harm. This belief becomes a part of the person from childhood on. The person may not know what he believes and may show compliance or dependency (Perls, 1973/1976).

2. *Projection* occurs when a person attributes responsibility for something to someone or something other than the self inappropriately relocating a boundary. Part of the self is assigned to someone else. For example, a wife is angry at her husband and is not aware of her own feelings. When her husband arrives home after work, she interprets his tiredness as his anger at her. She moved the boundary of herself (her anger) and placed it onto her husband (Latner, 1992). The woman is unaware of the split between her thoughts and feelings and her awareness of them (Polster & Polster, 1973).

3. *Retroflection* occurs when a person does to himself what he desires to do to someone else, or he does to someone else what he wants done for himself. For example, enraged at her lover for his infidelity, a woman attempts suicide. Thus her anger is directed away from her lover and placed onto herself. Or a man wants his lover to gratify his every whim, so he tells her "Your wish is my command!" The person using retroflection uses energy to block the feelings from being released, making that energy unavailable for creative spontaneity (Polster & Polster, 1973).

4. *Deflection* is used to avoid contact. A person discusses his feelings as if they did not belong to him, speaking vaguely and including irrelevant details. Individuals also avoid contact by jumping around from one task or topic to another or by moving from one place to another (Perls, 1973/1976).

5. *Confluence* occurs when there is little to no boundary between the self and the environment. The individual cannot make a good contact or withdraw from contact, or cannot tolerate differences in others. The individual does not know what he or she really feels or thinks. Individuals believe they have the same feelings as others, but in actuality, they may give up their own true feelings in order to be accepted or may insist that others be like them. Parents who consider their children as extensions of themselves and who try to control their every move have a boundary disturbance of confluence (Perls, 1973/1976).

Unhealthy and healthy development begin in childhood. In proper maturation, the child learns to handle frustration by mobilizing internal resources. If the child believes frustrations are overwhelming, or if the child is spoiled and deprived of the opportunity to "do for himself," psychopathology (neurosis) follows. The person may manipulate the environment by using inauthentic and phony behavior such as role playing or taking control to ensure that these intolerable frustrations will not occur again. He may disown parts of himself rather than accept who he is (Perls, 1973/1976).

✦ Practice of Gestalt Therapy

Now that we have examined the basic theoretical concepts of gestalt therapy, we will explore its practice. Jennifer Pert, MSW, is our composite, fictional gestalt therapist who provides a firsthand perspective of how she integrates theory with practice and applies the techniques of gestalt therapy.

Assessment and Diagnosis

As a gestalt therapist, assessment is part of the ongoing, constantly changing relationship between client and therapist and is performed in the moment-to-moment interaction. I notice the client's body movements, feelings, and sensations. I assess the client's level of awareness, contact boundaries, and any disturbances.

Diagnosis is part of traditional assessment. As a gestalt therapist, I acknowledge that the use of traditional diagnosis is necessary for medical purposes and insurance reimbursement, but I am free to choose not to work in or adhere to the medical model. I may or may not use any formal *DSM* diagnosis. This is an individual decision, based upon the authenticity of each person.

Negotiation of Therapeutic Relationship and Length of Treatment

The therapy relationship is dialogic (Jacobs, 1998). My major goal is to establish and maintain a dialogue with my client and to emphasize client awareness. I have no script or manualized treatment or set techniques (Bohart, 2003). I trust in the ability of the client to self-regulate. I possess my own unique therapeutic style, which depends partly on my life experiences and skills. I do not have access to a higher or more accurate truth than my client (L. Perls, 1976). My client's role is to engage in dialogue with me, to agree to take on responsibility for her- or himself, to participate in experiments, and to maximize adjustment to his or her environment as well as to take on a new perspective (Polster, 1987).

The simple goal of gestalt therapy is to increase awareness, which will stimulate the client to grow, mature, be self-responsible, and move toward autonomy and self-actualization (Perls, 1969a). Because gestalt therapy is relational, both therapist and client co-construct the psychotherapy. There is no specific length for treatment. It is based on the unique client's need.

Therapeutic Techniques

To accomplish the goal of awareness. I use experiments that emphasize direct experience, such as the here and now, emotional process, awareness, and choice (Fiebert, 1983; Rosenfeld, 1977). My primary technique is the dialogic relationship. I use inclusion, presence, and commitment to the dialogue.

Dialogic Relationship

The dialogic relationship is the most fundamental gestalt experiment. It involves these qualities:

- *Inclusion:* Inclusion is what most people call *empathy.* I put myself into the client's existence so I feel it within my own self, as a sensation within my body. I try to "take the client's eyes, glue them to my forehead, and look at life, and especially look at our relationship through these new eyeballs" (Jacobs, 1998). This is not a merging of two people, because at all times I continue with my own sense of self. However, I will be changed because I can now see in a different way.
- *Presence:* I am authentic, congruent, self-disclosing, and transparent to the client. I share my perspective, feelings, preferences, personal experience, and thoughts through my own phenomenological reporting to help my client to do the same. I do not manipulate my image to the client in any way. I let my presence show and let the client know who I am.
- *Commitment to dialogue:* I allow contact to occur between me and the client by letting the interpersonal process transpire. I yield and I do not control the interchange. I am committed to our dialogue even when the conversations are difficult. I try to meet clients where they are, without any attempt to change them (Jacobs, 1998).

My contact with the client is authentic. I listen, paying close attention to what is transpiring. I create a safe therapeutic atmosphere and prepare the ground for the I–Thou experience so clients can increase their awareness. I validate my clients' subjective experiences and offer them honest feedback. I provide an opportunity for a healing experience (Jacobs, 1998).

Other Experiments and Gestalt Techniques

Experiments offer an opportunity to help the client explore her- or himself. The data of these experiments are the phenomenological experiences of the client (Yontef & Jacobs, 2008). The experiments flow spontaneously from the interaction between my client and me and can take many forms. I choose an experiment that fits the client and that fosters clear awareness, full energy, and an expression (Zinker, 1977). I might introduce it with, "Try this experiment to see what you become aware of."

Some of the many experiments and techniques used in gestalt therapy are listed below. The focus in on helping the client pay attention to something out of the ordinary so that the client notices his or her own attention.

- *Focusing:* I ask clients to focus their awareness. I ask questions that bring their attention to the immediate situation such as, "What are you experiencing, here at this moment?" and I observe how awareness changes from moment to moment on a continuum of awareness.
- *Language patterns:* I bring attention to the use of language to increase client's awareness of conflicts that they can resolve (Patterson, 1986). For

example, I recommend the use of the word *I,* or a personal pronoun, instead of the word *it,* in order to raise consciousness about responsibility and self-empowerment. I might ask the client who says "It is hard for me to get up in the morning" to restate the issue as "I have a problem rising early." I might point out that saying "I won't" rather than "I can't" affects a person's sense of power. The words "I can't" imply helplessness, but the words "I won't" indicate free will and choice. Clients can be asked to turn their questions into statements to encourage taking responsibility for who they are (Polster & Polster, 1990).

- *Nonverbal behavior:* I bring attention to the client's body language (Glinnwater, 2000). I point out discrepancies between body posture and verbal behavior. For example, a person who says he is very open may have his arms folded tightly across his chest, appearing as if he is protecting himself. His body language shows his true feelings, that he is feeling suspicious and anxious (Kepner, 1987). I may ask a client who is tapping her foot, "What is your foot doing?" in order to increase her awareness of her feelings.

- *The here and now:* To encourage the client to focus on the present, I may ask the client "What?" and "How?" or "Of what are you aware now?" In this way, the client notices his or her attention (Yontef & Simkin, 1989). I avoid asking why rather than how because asking why leads to intellectualization.

- *Dialogue:* I encourage dialogue between parts of the self if a client is thinking in a dichotomous fashion. This helps clients be aware of all sides of an issue and free themselves when they are stuck between two forces or poles.

- *Enactment:* I encourage the client to turn feelings and thoughts into some form of action through three enactment techniques: role playing, empty chair, and creative expression (Yontef, 1995).

- *Role playing:* The client plays a role that represents some part of a conflict. For example, if my client is fighting with his mother, I ask him to play the role of his mother. If he is obsessed with a goal, like making money, I might ask him to play the role of the acquired money, to be the wealth.

- *Role reversal:* The client acts in the opposite way of some person, place, thing, symptom, characteristic, or personality trait. If a client is shy, I ask her to play the role of the assertive, demanding self.

- *Empty chair technique:* I ask the client to place a significant other (or any entity with whom the client has conflict) on a chair and enact a dialogue between them. The client speaks directly to the imagined person (or entity) in the empty chair. The client plays each role. As the client alternates roles, she changes her seat, facing whoever is appropriate (Kellogg, 2004).

- *Confrontation:* I use any method that allows me to gently point out that clients are avoiding responsibility or denying their feelings. My style of confrontation is not belligerent, but it does invite clients to look at their inconsistencies (Polster, 1987).

- *Finishing unfinished business:* I encourage clients to face and resolve unexpressed feelings, which may unconsciously cause them to behave in a self-defeating way if unaddressed. For example, if a person felt abandoned by his mother, he will look for what he did not receive in others. He may depend on women for his self-worth and may be overly needy. If he addresses his feelings and resolves this impasse to finish his unfinished business, he can clear away the baggage of the past and engage in other fulfilling relationships (Polster & Polster, 1973).

- *Dream analysis:* I help clients understand the meaning of their dreams by treating each item in the dream as an extension of the dreamer, as a projection of a part of the self that is contradictory, inconsistent, and polarized. I ask clients to relive their dreams, to describe them in first person, chronologically, as though they were dreaming, to play the role of each part of the dream, and to carry on a dialogue among all of the parts. As a client plays each part, he or she may recognize and resolve unfinished business (Polster, 1987). For example, a client dreamed she was walking down a road and saw a beautiful tree. Underneath the tree was a stranger sitting on a large black rock. I ask her to play the role of each object in the dream. I instruct her to "Be the road. What is the road doing, saying, thinking, feeling?" I ask the road to dialogue with the other parts of the dream. "The road can talk to the stranger on the rock." By having this dialogue, my client will learn about her feelings and her contradictions, and, I hope, resolve them. I avoid actual dream interpretation because I do not want to introject myself into the client's discovery of the meaning of the dream for him- or herself (Latner, 2005c).

- *Homework:* Assignments flow naturally from the psychotherapy session. For example, I may collaborate with the client to finish dreamwork by writing out the parts of the dream. We may decide that keeping a journal is helpful. Homework can be from any experiment or exercise that is appropriate for the present and focuses responsibility onto the client (Yontef, 1998).

The Process of Therapy

Rather than seeing it within a timeline, I see gestalt therapy as a process that includes discovery, accommodation, and assimilation (Polster, 1987). In *discovery,* the client is aware of the self and the situation she wishes to change. The major concern is to solve problems. In *accommodation,* the realization that she is free and can choose, my client explores and tries out different ways of acting. In *assimilation,* the client actually makes changes in his or her behavior and satisfies his or her needs.

I relate to clients through five levels of contact. The process is like peeling an onion, shedding neuroses or symptoms to become a mature person. Each client reaches his or her core at his or her own pace and can vacillate. Just as a layer peels away, so too can it be put back on again. These layers of personality include (Perls, 1969a, 1970)

- *Phony layer:* Individuals often react to other people in an inauthentic manner. For example, many people ask "How are you?" They do not, however, expect to get a truthful answer.
- *Phobic layer:* A person feels fear and anxiety, but the urge to avoid pain is strong, and so the person covers up these feelings.
- *Impasse:* Fearful of change, people feel as if they are stuck and cannot get out of the situation. They frequently ask for help at this stage.
- *Implosive:* Feelings have been repressed to the degree that the person feels cut off from a part of her- or himself and even feels dead inside.
- *Explosive:* Feelings are authentic and have no pretext. The person's energy is freed up because he or she has let go of the old self that was so repressed.

Throughout the therapy process, we explore blockages to growth and impasses to problem solving. A person may need to negotiate the impasse by obtaining appropriate external support until he or she can support him- or herself sufficiently (Perls, 1970; Yontef, 1993).

Termination occurs when clients are aware and will be able to use this awareness to know themselves, to know their environment, to accept themselves, to take responsibility for their own choices, and to solve their own problems.

Therapy in Action: Jennifer Pert and the Case of Jonathan

To illustrate the application of gestalt therapy, we examine a treatment plan for Jonathan, followed by excerpts from therapy sessions with our fictional gestalt therapist, Jennifer Pert, MSW. Keep in mind that the case excerpts are simulated interviews and represent the ideal of therapy. In real life, clients may take much longer to meet therapeutic goals. Table 8.1 provides a summary of Pert's treatment plan.

Case Excerpts

The following excerpts are from sessions based on Jennifer Pert's gestalt therapy case formulation.

Session 1

Jonathan: [*looks sad and agitated*]
J. Pert: Of what are you aware at this moment?
Jonathan: Nothing. I am just upset.
J. Pert: I see you are moving in your chair.
Jonathan: Yes, I cannot sit still. I can't help it. I came here to have you help me.

Table 8.1

Gestalt Therapy Treatment Plan for Jonathan

Assessment and Formulation	• Presenting problem: loss of relationship with Tuti and Darren • Low level of awareness, bodily and psychological • Contact boundary between self and Tuti is disturbed • Unfinished business interfering with equilibrium and growth • Feelings of dread, anxiety, anger • Unable to meet needs for intimacy • Lack of external and internal support • Impasse—external support is withdrawn, and J. believes he cannot take care of self
Therapeutic Relationship	• J. Pert provides authentic relationship, inclusion, presence, and commitment • J. has direct engagement through contact
Contract, Goals, and Treatment Plan	• Increase awareness of awareness in all elements of thinking, feeling, behaving • J. experiences emotional pain he is avoiding; peels off layers and gets through impasse, moving toward wholeness • Completes unfinished business • Time: meet as needed; twice weekly at first
Techniques	• Presence of therapist, dialogue, self-disclosure • Contact between J. and J. Pert in every moment and over time • Appropriate self-disclosure • Experiments to show how J. has blocked his awareness • Enactment techniques: empty chair, role playing, etc. • Homework • Dreamwork
Process of Therapy	• J.'s energy is freed; lets go of the old self that was so repressed • J. integrates all of the parts of himself
Termination and Outcome	• Awareness of awareness • Better integrated • Finished business with sister, Tuti, and Darren

J. Pert: Can I ask, how does it feel to ask for help?

Jonathan: Like I am not myself. I don't know why they did it and why I feel so angry.

J. Pert: Who is responsible for your feelings?

Jonathan: Them. I wouldn't feel like this if they hadn't done this to me.

J. Pert: Of what are you aware at this moment sitting here with me?

Jonathan: I feel terrible. Like I don't want to feel this way. I want to feel good, not like a miserable piece of crap.

J. Pert: How does a piece of crap feel?

Jonathan: [*smiles and almost laughs*] I don't know. I guess crap doesn't feel.

[*Comment: Listening intently, I give J. every bit of energy I possess in this moment to build our relationship and help him to be aware of himself and his experiencing with me in the moment.*]

J. Pert: But *you* feel. Can you describe the experience?

Jonathan: It's pain, deep in my gut like I'm gonna explode if I don't have her. [*tears fall*] I am hurt. I do not want to be dependent on someone else.

J. Pert: Does being dependent make you feel vulnerable?

Jonathan: Yes. I feel unsafe. I worry my feelings will get out of control. I won't be able to work.

J. Pert: Would you be willing to try a little experiment?

Jonathan: I suppose if it would help me to feel better.

[*Comment: I can sense J. needs to understand some of his own internal forces that are pulling him in so many directions and polarizing him. I use my presence to let him know I am here with him.*]

J. Pert: Use these two chairs to play the role of you and Tuti. Look at this chair. Tuti is sitting there, ready to talk to you. What does she want to say to you?

Jonathan: I can't even begin to imagine.

J. Pert: OK, Jonathan. Play yourself. Pretend Tuti is sitting in the chair in front of you. Now what do you want to say to her?

Jonathan: Look at what you have done to me. I'm falling apart. You have taken away everything. I can't eat, sleep, function at work. You've done this to me. I'm up at 2:00 A.M., and then I have a cigarette. Then I stare at the TV. I don't really watch it. I try to go back to sleep but can't, and then I have to get up at 6:30. I drag myself out of bed. You are not there anymore. You left me alone. And on top of it, you took away my best friend. Wasn't it enough that you ruined my life by leaving? Did you have to steal my buddy too? [*cries, tears streaming down his face*] I hate you! [*cries*]

[*Comment: I am saying very little, yet my presence is in the session to support J. From his nonverbal behavior, the empty chair technique has increased his awareness, helping him to come into contact with some of the rage and hurt he has avoided facing.*]

J. Pert: Jonathan, please sit in the other chair. Play Tuti. What does she say back to you?

Jonathan: I can't do it.

J. Pert: Is it possible you're avoiding the pain that comes with this experience? Please try.

Jonathan: [*gets into other chair hesitantly, but then speaks as Tuti*] Ha. I finally got you, didn't I? I warned you. I told you I wanted children. I told you if you said no you would be sorry. You deprived me of what I wanted the most from you. You tried to fool me and to convince me that I did not want children. You tried to make me into something I am not.

J. Pert: Be yourself again. Answer Tuti. Change chairs. Can you risk feeling these feelings?

Jonathan: [*as self*] So I did not want to have kids. It was for your own good. You don't know how hard it would be to devote all of your time and energy to them. We wanted to travel, to get rich, to live the good life. If you were smart, you would appreciate what I was trying to do. To protect you from your silly self. How could you ever take care of kids? I would have wound up doing it. No, you didn't love me enough to give up your silly ideas. And on top of it, you couldn't just leave me. You had to turn to my best friend. You can't do anything. [*angrily shouts at her*] Nothing on your own. You were so dependent on me that I wanted to run away half the time anyway.

J. Pert: You let her know how you feel. Now, change seats. But make the tone of your voice even more convincing.

Jonathan: [*playing Tuti*] You were always trying to make me into something I was not. I put everything I had into our relationship, and you won't give me the one thing I always wanted. You hurt me. How could you treat me like this? How could you do this to me? I wasted my time with you. You are a liar. And I'm feeling much more like a woman with him than I ever did with you.

J. Pert: [*seeing J.'s reaction*] Now you are in control. You write the script. What do you want to say back to her? Be yourself again and talk back to Tuti.

Jonathan: [*looks shaken, but becoming organized, more integrated, tearfully looking at the empty chair*] That is not true. We loved each other. We are angry and disappointed with one another because we are both very powerful people, and we want to have our own way. I feel very sad that we have to split up on this issue. I know how much you want children, and I know how much I do not want them. You know I loved you, and you know I'll do anything for you up to the point of having children. But that I can't do. I just can't.

J. Pert: You are being you and talking from your heart. I suggest you continue this heart-to-heart discussion. Take Tuti's seat.

[*Comment: J. was shaken and found it painful to face his feelings; they are more integrated now. Session continues with J. understanding his ambivalence and polarities.*]

Session 2

J. Pert: What are you experiencing at this moment, here and now?

Jonathan: I'm confused.

J. Pert: I see you clenching your fists and with tears in your eyes. What are you experiencing?

Jonathan: I am really hurt, so hurt.

J. Pert: When you do allow yourself to feel that hurt, how do you tolerate it?

Jonathan: No, I can't . . . and I will not do so.

 J. Pert: Can you stay with the "not wanting to hurt"?

Jonathan: Yes . . . I can do that. I feel so embarrassed. A grown man crying when I ought to hunt them down and kill them. My friends are laughing at me. I am embarrassed. I feel like I am a joke!

J. Pert: What is that like for you?

Jonathan: [*tears now streaming down his face*] What a fool I am. Look at what I did not notice. I did not see the signs of this affair. How long were they were carrying on behind my back? What kind of an idiot am I? I am a joke! A bad joke.

J. Pert: Of what are you aware now, right here?

Jonathan: I feel small—like a little kid. I remember in second grade, I brought some flowers in for Lucy. I really liked her. I told a couple of friends my plans. They got together to play a joke on me. When I brought the flowers, Lucy was sitting on the bench in the schoolyard. I presented her with my bouquet. Right then, Jerry the schoolyard bully punched me. He told me to stay away from Lucy. He took the flowers and started throwing them to the other kids. He picked out each one and went "loves me" and threw it, "loves me not" and threw it. All the kids were jumping up and down and laughing, grabbing for one of the flowers. When he got to the last flower, he said "loves me not" and threw it at me. Lucy kind of smiled as he did it. All morning I saw somebody holding one of the flowers like a reminder. My dad hears about this and came into school. That was even more embarrassing.

J. Pert: Jonathan, I wonder if we can go through this step by step. Close your eyes. Imagine it is happening now.

[*Comment: Here we are using focusing and guided imagery to help J. to resolve this unfinished business from the past that plays itself out in his relationship today.*]

Session 9

J. Pert: I see two opposites. One part wants to be free, and another wants to be with Tuti. They do not seem to listen to each other.

Jonathan: I have been thinking about what these two parts have to say.

J. Pert: Can you share your thoughts?

Jonathan: Yes. There is the part of me that wants Tuti, and the part of me that wants to be free and not make concessions. I feel pulled apart. But what I am beginning to realize is that everything is not going to be "all right," not as I expected. I can't have everything the way I want it. I need to make changes. I have my own wants and needs. I can't live for others. But also, I must learn to accept people for who they are and stop trying to make them fit the mold I want for them. I will stop being dishonest with myself. I'll take responsibility for what I am doing. I am making a choice. If I do not want to have children, am I willing to give up my relationship in order to have a child-free life? I think I am. So now I am really aware of what issues I must face and am willing to go ahead and do what I need to do to feel happy—and I'll get over Tuti's leaving me and Darren's betrayal. I do not want to let it be unfinished business and drain me of my energy. I will write them a letter telling them what I feel and then let go of it. There are many possibilities for me in this world, and I am willing to take my chances of living a different life where I can really be myself and do what I know I must do.

Session 21

Jonathan: I know I can take responsibility for my life again.

J. Pert: I agree.

Jonathan: Thanks. Can I drop in if I feel I am slipping back? Can you hear my changes just by listening to the quality of my voice? I am aware of who I am ever so much more. I am grateful to you. Thanks.

Case Comment

As my relationship deepened with Jonathan and authentic dialogue transpired, he increased his awareness, becoming aware of his awareness. He was able to be authentic and honest with himself. He could tolerate feeling the fear, anxiety, and intense anger in the breakup of his relationship. He stopped avoiding his feelings and faced his pain. Jonathan became more aware of his polarized self, an internal split between being the responsible father and the playful kid. He had suppressed the playful kid because he feared he would do the wrong thing and lose Tuti. In short, he had what Perls would call stage fright or anticipatory dread of losing Tuti. As a result, he was not fully available to her because he was not being authentic with her and was manipulating her by convincing her not to have children.

His unfinished business with his mother and sister and his deep feelings of rejection and abandonment interfered with his present life. I used phenomenological focusing skills and dialogic contact over about 20 sessions until Jonathan knew he was ready to get on with his life. He increased awareness, his clarity of perception of himself and his world, creative adjustment, and self-acceptance. He was able to make an honest self-appraisal, increase his self-respect, and venture out into the world without Tuti, ready to make challenging choices.

✦ RESEARCH DIRECTIONS IN GESTALT THERAPY

Gestalt therapy has limited empirical support. Not many methodologically sound studies have been published. In meta-analyses and outcome studies, gestalt is usually classified and analyzed as a form of experiential psychotherapy. Like existential and client-centered psychotherapy, gestalt therapy was included in reviews of experiential psychotherapies as we discussed in Chapter 7 (Elliott, Greenberg, & Lietaer, 2004). The review of over 100 studies showed that clients treated with experiential therapies were better off than untreated clients.

Gestalt therapy has been the subject of more research as part of a developing model—process-experiential (PE) psychotherapy or emotion-focused therapy—which integrates person-centered and gestalt therapy into a single format. Leslie Greenberg and his group have researched this experiential therapy for over two decades (Greenberg & Paivio, 1997; Greenberg & Pascual-Leone, 2006). Supporters of gestalt therapy use the same arguments as other experiential researchers (as discussed in Chapters 6 and 7) regarding the value of the therapy. Because gestalt therapy emphasizes the therapeutic relationship, which has been shown to be a common factor that facilitates change, it is logical to conclude that gestalt therapies are effective (Norcross, 2001, 2002).

Research on specific, circumscribed gestalt interventions shows promising results. The empty chair technique in particular has garnered some empirical support. In a review of outcome studies for trauma and abuse, the empty chair technique resulted in greater improvement over a longer time than psychoeducational interventions and cognitive interventions. The empty chair work resulted in some clients satisfactorily resolving unfinished issues with significant others (Elliott et al., 2004). In a number of studies, clients who experienced trauma and abuse and had unresolved feelings, and who received experiential therapy, showed greater improvement than a psychoeducational group, or control groups, or wait-list comparisons. Overall, the empty chair technique decreased self-criticism, increased self-understanding, and facilitated conflict resolution when compared to cognitive behavioral techniques (Paivio & Greenberg, 1995). While it is convenient to study the specific techniques used in gestalt, it may not be possible to generalize from using parts of the therapy out of the context with its complex relational aspects (Cain & Seeman, 2001).

Uwe Strumpfel (2006), a German proponent of Gestalt therapy, attempted to document the evidence base for gestalt therapy. He looked at 74 process and/or outcome studies (and a re-analysis of 10 meta-analyses), covering approximately 3,000 clients with varying diagnoses treated in gestalt therapy (as well as other clients who served as controls or were treated with other therapies). Seventy-five percent of the studies looked at classical gestalt therapy in at least one treatment condition, or at gestalt therapy that was combined with other approaches such as process-experiential therapy. The review included both published and unpublished studies, single-case reports, outcome studies, and both individual and group therapies. Strumpfel concluded that gestalt therapy, especially when it includes other experiential therapies, reduces symptoms at the same or even a better rate than behavior therapies, shows good treatment outcomes in specific areas of change, and is, thus, efficacious and effective (Strumpfel & Goldman, 2001). Critics say the studies Strumpfel included did not meet stringent criteria. Serious methodological flaws included lack of randomization, varying baselines for the intervention and the control groups, loss of participants, insufficient follow-up, small samples, and unpublished studies that did not undergo peer scrutiny.

To contrast Strumpfel's all-inclusive review with an evidence-based review, we turn to one conducted by the Centre for Clinical Effectiveness-Monash (Hender, 2001). The research question posed was: Is gestalt therapy more effective than other therapies? While they looked at hundreds of studies, only seven met their inclusion criteria for sound methodology. Six out of seven of the qualified studies showed gestalt therapy had some positive outcome. However, based on the small number, the reviewers could not arrive at any firm conclusion about the effectiveness of gestalt therapy, especially since there was a variation in the quality of methodology of the research studies. (A summary of this evidence-based literature review can be found in the online Appendix C with a link to the entire study.) This is a good illustration of the different criteria that EBM researchers and experiential researchers use to interpret study results.

What can a therapist say to justify use of gestalt therapy? The therapist can make statements similar to those made about other experiential therapies discussed in previous chapters. The empirical evidence base for gestalt therapy is, at best, spotty, and researchers interpret the body of literature differently. It can be assumed that the equivalency effect holds for gestalt therapy, so it is likely to be as effective as any therapy that has been researched more thoroughly when it has been tested. The gestalt therapist cultivates an authentic and genuine therapy relationship that fits the client's unique needs and stresses the importance of the therapeutic relationship; thus it is most likely an empirically supported relationship. Like other experiential therapists, gestalt therapists agree that the evidence-based perspective may be dehumanizing to clients. The nature of gestalt therapy makes it difficult to research from an evidence-based empirical approach. A therapist would choose to use gestalt based on clinical expertise, clinical experience, and the research on gestalt that is available. Clients will likely benefit from the task of increasing their conscious awareness, which allows them to probe concerns dealing with being who they are.

➔ Issues of Diversity

Similar arguments apply to gestalt therapy as pertain to the other experiential therapies. Gestalt therapy values the phenomenal field, individual freedom, fulfilling the needs of the individual, and the ability to tolerate silence, to express emotions freely, and to be nondirective. Those with different cultural expectations may not be comfortable with these parameters. As discussed in previous chapters (person-centered and existential therapies), all of these values are predominantly Western and not necessarily held in high regard in all cultures. Like all experiential therapies, gestalt, done well, is sensitive to cultural issues. It welcomes dialogue about any and all topics, whether taboo, politically incorrect, or shocking, and discusses them in a totally nonjudgmental environment.

Some gestalt techniques, such as the empty chair technique, emphasize the expression of strong feelings. When using such emotive methods, the therapist should take particular care to keep cultural mores in mind. For example, a young Islamic woman who is encouraged to express her rage at her father for insisting she wear traditional clothing may find family discord to be too large a price to pay; it may not be a battle worth fighting. Each therapeutic incidence needs to be judged with sensitivity on a case-by-case basis.

✦ MAJOR CRITIQUES OF GESTALT THERAPY

Criticisms that were made of all experiential models (as discussed in Chapters 6 and 7) apply to gestalt therapy. The theoretical constructs are difficult to operationally define, to quantify, to measure, to test, and to determine if they are the elements that lead to change.

Criticisms unique to gestalt therapy are that the Perls adapted ideas from scientific theories popular in their era and created an illusion of scientific validity. While gestalt appears to based on scientific reasoning, in actuality it is simply a pretentious hodge-podge of constructs encountered by the Perls and conveniently strung together.

One criticism is that some gestalt trainees are not adequately prepared for the responsibilities that come with being a psychotherapist. When Fritz Perls founded Esalen, it became a major gestalt training center. A wide variety of people received training, some of whom were trying to find theatrical therapeutic gimmicks and quick fixes for clients (Woldt & Toman, 2005). Techniques used out of context by those with minimal, even poor, training and credentials can be harmful. Gestalt therapy misapplied has the potential to hurt because it seems to strike people at a deep emotional level, leaving clients vulnerable to outside influences. Abuse of power is possible (Brown, 1988).

Responsible gestalt therapists are addressing these issues. For example, the European Association for Gestalt Therapy (EAGT), founded in 1985, has established minimum training standards for gestalt therapy in order to increase the professionalism of practice and the credibility of the therapy. The consumer of gestalt therapy needs to ensure that he or she is receiving treatment that helps from a trained professional, one who has a strong grounding in the ethics of a professional organization.

SUMMARY

- Fritz and Laura Perls created gestalt therapy, drawing on information from diverse sources including psychoanalysis, gestalt psychology, field theory, humanism, existentialism, holism, phenomenology, organismic theory, and homeostasis.
- Some of the key theoretical concepts include field theory or the self that cannot be understood outside of a context of interpersonal relationships; gestalts formed from the interaction among all environmental possibilities and a person's needs; a person's world is organized by subjective reality; and

heightened awareness with creative and active experimentation. Life is a series of needs and contacts with the environment to fulfill the needs. Needs come out of a background and become a figure. Unfinished business consists of unsatisfied needs due to incomplete gestalts.

- Contact is being in touch with what is; a contact boundary is the point of interaction between the person and the environment. Awareness and present centeredness involve paying attention in the present moment.
- Paradoxical theory of change says change occurs when one becomes what one is, not when one tries to become what one is not. Polarities are conflicts among behaviors, thoughts, feelings, or values. Each person is responsible for his or her own choices; anxiety is the fear of one's own daring.
- Normal and abnormal behavior are a function of creative adjustment. Pathology is disrupted contact with boundary disturbances. The major patterns of contact-boundary disturbances are introjection, projection, retroflection, and deflection.
- In the practice of gestalt therapy, assessment and diagnosis are part of the ongoing relationship; the therapeutic relationship is dialogic between the client and the therapist. In the I–Thou moment, there is growth through awareness, a willingness to accept, and no need to change what is found.
- Therapeutic techniques include the dialogic relationship with inclusion, presence, and commitment to dialogue. Experiments include focusing, language patterns, nonverbal behavior, here and now, dialogue, enactment, role playing, the empty chair technique, finishing unfinished business, dream analysis, and homework. The process of therapy is like peeling an onion uncovering various layers—phony, phobic, impasse, implosive, explosive.
- Research in gestalt therapy has produced a limited evidence base. While proponents of gestalt claim there is support for its effectiveness, reviewers who use an evidence-based approach claim it is not possible to make any firm conclusions due to the variation in the methods and quality of research studies. The empty chair technique has some consistent empirical support.
- Criticisms about issues of diversity and the theory and practice of gestalt are those that apply to all experiential therapies. Unique to gestalt is that the training has been variable, and the informed consumer should check the credentials and qualifications of gestalt therapists.

Resources

European Association for Gestalt Therapy (EAGT)
EAGT Office
c/o Marga Berends
Noorderdiep 304
9521 BL Nieuw Buinen
The Netherlands
http://www.eagt.org

Founded in 1985, the EAGT is a resource for individual gestalt therapists, training institutes, and national associations. The association fosters high professional standards for gestalt therapy and has 300 members (institutional and individual) from more than 20 European nations.

Association for the Advancement of Gestalt Therapy (AAGT)
400 East 58th Street
New York, NY 10022
(212) 486-1581
http://www.aagt.org

AAGT supports forums to preserve and advance the philosophy, theory, practice, and research of gestalt therapy. AAGT has a wide international membership that includes mental health professionals from diverse professions as well as teachers, academics, writers, artists, performers, organizational consultants, political and social analysts, activists, and students.

CLASS EXERCISES AND ACTIVITIES

Theory

1. Fritz and Laura Perls created gestalt psychotherapy by drawing from a wide variety of intellectual roots. Choose one theoretical concept that appeals to you from gestalt therapy. Trace its roots and discuss how it evolved and became part of gestalt therapy (e.g., holism, gestalt, organismic functioning, etc.).
2. Define the therapeutic relationship in gestalt therapy.
3. How applicable is the theory of gestalt therapy to the current mental health problems we are experiencing in American culture? Is gestalt therapy dated? Can it flourish today?

Practice

1. Break up into dyads. One person should play the role of the therapist and the other the client. The therapist rejects the role of "changer" and encourages the client to be what he or she is. How would you do this?
2. Discuss how a gestalt therapist can develop an authentic relationship with a client. What are some of the thoughts, feelings, and actions that help you to cultivate such a relationship?
3. Fill out the sample treatment plan in Chapter 1 (Figure 1.2) for Tuti for gestalt therapy. (Both Jonathan's and Tuti's case histories are in Appendix A.) What are the difficulties in formulating a concrete plan? How could you explain your choice of using gestalt to treat her?

Research

1. Is evidence-based research compatible with the values of gestalt therapy? Describe research that could be helpful to the practicing gestalt therapist.

2. Review the Monash evidence-based review study with highlights contained in the online Appendix C. Practice performing an EBM review by adding on to the study from the last date that was searched by the Monash Institute. Compare that with the Monash review findings. Plug in the key words used by the Monash Institute and see if you come up with similar findings.

3. Conduct a review of gestalt therapies by using the following key words in PubMed and PsycINFO: *gestalt therapy, gestalt psychotherapy.* What did you find? Limit your search to *gestalt and randomized control.* What did you find? What kinds of articles are available about gestalt therapy? Taking a quick overview of the articles, describe the nature of the articles and the kind of evidence they contain.

CHAPTER 9

BEHAVIOR THERAPY

Education is what survives when what has been learned has been forgotten.

–B. F. Skinner

The goal of this chapter is to present a general overview of behavior therapy. The chapter looks at biographical information about B. F. Skinner and Joseph Wolpe, the historical context of behavior therapy, and the theory, practice, and research of behavior therapy models. The simulated therapist, Dr. Carl Wilson, presents a treatment plan and some excerpts from behavior therapy for the case of Jonathan. Issues of diversity and major critiques are also included.

✦ HISTORICAL CONTEXT

Unlike psychoanalysis, behavior therapy was not originated by a specific charismatic leader but evolved from a variety of sources, theorists, and therapists (Antony & Roemer, 2003). Initially, behaviorism was launched by John Watson as a purely objective branch of the natural sciences, and it served as a vehicle with which to counter the mentalism of psychoanalysis. By the 1970s principles of behaviorism were well integrated into clinical practice and now have laid the foundation for the development and success of today's cognitive behavior therapies (Fishman & Franks, 1992). We will review some of the notable historical forces that formed the basis for modern behavior therapy.

Ivan Pavlov and Classical Conditioning

Ivan Pavlov was a Russian physiologist who won the Nobel Prize in 1904 for his study of digestive processes. A perceptive scientist, Pavlov looked beyond physiological responses to learning in laboratory animals. Noticing that his dogs salivated as he delivered their meals, he surmised that they made a temporal association between the sound of his footsteps and the arrival of food. His consequent experiments shed light on a type of learning called *Pavlovian* or *classical conditioning*.

According to Pavlov, an unconditioned stimulus (US), or a stimulus such as food, evokes an unconditioned response (UR), or a natural response. Thus his experiments pairing a neutral stimulus, such as a tone, with an unconditioned stimulus showed that the dogs salivated at the sound of the tone; the tone evoked a conditioned response (CR). The tone became a conditioned stimulus (CS) that elicited a conditioned response. Pavlov's discovery of classical conditioning prompted a new line of scientific inquiry into the behavior of humans and animals by J. B. Watson, an American psychologist who admired the work of Pavlov.

J. B. Watson and Behaviorism

J. B. Watson (1913), the father of behaviorism, advocated the study of overt behavior, or observable variables that can be collected, counted, and analyzed. He wanted psychology to move away from introspection and to foster a paradigm of radical behaviorism (Fishman & Franks, 1992; Watson, 1913).

In one of his best-known experiments, Watson applied classical conditioning to produce a phobia in a young child, Little Albert. Initially, Albert showed no fear of a white rat, but when a loud sound (striking a steel bar) was paired with the rat, he developed an intense fear of the rat. In 1924, Watson's student, Mary Cover Jones, treated a young child with rabbit phobia using behavioral techniques. These events led Watson to face off with the Freudians, arguing that strong scientific evidence showed that human emotions, such as fear, could be conditioned and that phobias and other psychopathological conditions are caused by conditioned emotional reactions and not unconscious conflicts (Hunt, 1993; Monte, 1987; Watson, 1913; Watson & Rayner, 1920).

Other behaviorists, such as Orval Hobart Mowrer (Mowrer & Mowrer, 1938), applied Pavlovian principles to clinical problems. For example, in the 1930s, children who wet the bed (enuretics) were treated with a bell-and-pad device. When the child urinated in bed, a loud sound woke the child. Eventually, bladder tension alone was sufficient cause to wake the child (Collins, 1976; Houts, Liebert, & Padawer, 1983). This simple conditioning alarm system is still considered to be the most effective therapy for enuresis. The Canadian Pediatric Society (2005) used a recent evidence-based review to make this recommendation (see the online Appendix C).

B. F. Skinner and Operant Conditioning

B. F. Skinner, the most well-known contemporary behaviorist, created the experimental analysis of behavior (see About B. F. Skinner box). Using a recording device called a *cumulative recorder,* Skinner showed that an organism's response was dependent on what happened *after* the behavior was performed. He identified how reinforcement controlled—shaped, established, maintained, and extinguished—behavior through its consequences (Skinner, 1953; 1974).

Skinner's experimental analyses of behavior laid the groundwork for *applied behavior analysis,* or the application of learning principles to clinical work. Clinicians adapted *operant conditioning* to successfully modify the behavior of seriously disturbed psychiatric clients, using *contingency management* and token economies to encourage social interactions in the wards of mental hospitals (Lindsley, 1956; Lindsley, Skinner, & Solomon, 1953).

ABOUT B. F. SKINNER

Born in 1904, Burrhus Frederic Skinner had a stable childhood with his younger brother and parents in Susquehanna, Pennsylvania. He was a curious, creative, and enterprising child who invented a machine to separate berries and a dust remover for dirty shoes. Reading Francis Bacon's works inspired Skinner's use of inductive reasoning and experimentation in his psychology of behaviorism.

After earning a BA in English from Hamilton College, he moved to New York to be a writer but turned his interest to understanding behavior. He studied the works of Pavlov and Watson. He earned a PhD from Harvard in 1931 and published his first book, *The Behavior of Organisms,* in 1938. He joined the faculty at the University of Minnesota, married Yvonne Blue, and the couple had two daughters—Julie, born in 1938, and Deborah, born in 1940 (Skinner, 1976).

Skinner gained notoriety for some of his inventions. For example, during World War II, the U.S. Office of Scientific Research and Development (OSRD) provided funding for Project Pigeon in which Skinner trained pigeons to help guide missiles to accurately bomb targets. With the invention of radar, the project was discontinued (Glines, 2005). Another project was Skinner's Baby in a Box—a heated crib that enclosed the infant in Plexiglas to avoid having the baby get caught in the bars of a traditional crib. Skinner's daughter Julie later denied that she was raised in a giant Skinner box in the biography she wrote about her father.

In 1945, Skinner joined the faculty at the University of Indiana and then accepted an appointment at Harvard where he remained for his academic career. Here he created programmed instruction, using a teaching machine that presents material broken into small steps with careful sequencing. Many of Skinner's ideas have been incorporated into educational programming so that learners gain feedback on their performance before moving to the next item. Skinner also wrote about the philosophical and moral issues associated with behavioral science's influence on society.

Despite having leukemia, Skinner remained active professionally until his death in 1990. He received a standing ovation for his keynote address at the American Psychological Association only 10 days before he died. Even at that late date, Skinner severely criticized the emerging cognitive science movement and pejoratively called it the "creationism of psychology" (Skinner, 1990). B. F. Skinner was a prolific researcher, writer, and philosopher. His influence has been described in these terms: "there are few areas of psychology that have not been affected by his penetrating analysis of behavior" (London, 1964, p. 250).

John Dollard and Neal Miller

John Dollard and Neal Miller (1950) reinterpreted psychoanalytic concepts with a stimulus-response perspective (Zimring & Raskin, 1992). These researchers hypothesized that anxiety and guilt were difficult to extinguish because a person persistently escapes and avoids the situations that incite these feelings (Dollard & Miller, 1950). If cues are associated with the situation, they may also elicit fear and become conditioned anxiety responses. Anxiety can be transferred to increasingly remote stimuli and events, and at some point the originally feared stimulus may even be forgotten, or what psychoanalysts call *repressed* (Dollard & Miller, 1950; Mowrer & Mowrer, 1938). Psychoanalysis may help because a fearful client who avoids facing a painful event is offered an environment in which he is free to talk about an unpleasant situation or express taboo thoughts and feelings, with no negative consequences. The therapist deliberately exposes clients to cues that evoke fear, and fear extinguishes in the absence of any negative consequences. With reduced fear, the

ABOUT JOSEPH WOLPE

Joseph Wolpe, born to parents Michael and Sarah in 1915, grew up in Johannesburg, South Africa. Wolpe earned an MD from the University of Witwatersrand in Johannesburg in 1948 and went on to practice psychoanalytic psychiatry. He became interested in the work of Pavlov and Clark Hull, learning theorists who inspired him to study animal neurosis and to write a dissertation on conditioning and counterconditioning; they also motivated his interest in reciprocal inhibition (London, 1964, p. 85).

During World War II, as a medical officer in the South African army, Wolpe worked with soldiers with war neurosis. He developed desensitization and the unlearning of maladaptive behaviors through gradual exposure to feared objects. In addition, he used counterconditioning—producing a pleasurable response to an aversive stimulus—from his experimental work with cats as a way to reduce anxiety. Years later, Wolpe claimed he treated 200 or so behavioral disorders with such a therapy and achieved a success rate of 90 percent (Wolpe, 1958).

After the war, Wolpe studied and worked at various institutions in the United States. He was at Stanford University's Center for Advanced Study in the Behavioral Sciences (1956–1957) and at the University of Virginia's Department of Psychiatry (1960–1965). He spent many years at Temple University Medical School (1965–1988) and became Distinguished Professor at Pepperdine University in London (1989–1997).

Joseph Wolpe died in 1997 after a protracted bout with lung cancer. He is survived by his two sons, David and Allan, from his first marriage (Poppen, 1998; Rachman, 2000). Perry London writes that Wolpe's "willingness to expose his work to actuarial evaluation sets a model of intellectual good faith that all other pretenders to innovations in psychotherapy must finally emulate" (London, 1964, p. 94).

client is better able to use higher mental processes and face even more fundamental conflicts resulting in a decrease of symptoms (London, 1964). The client unlearns old, ineffective habits and substitutes more adaptive behaviors. This attempt to reconcile psychoanalytic thinking with behavior theory helped to advance behavior therapy among practicing psychotherapists.

Joseph Wolpe and Counterconditioning

Joseph Wolpe (see About Joseph Wolpe box) used Pavlov's principles of counterconditioning to produce and cure experimental neuroses in cats (Wolpe, 1987, 1997). By pairing a buzzer with a shock, Wolpe's cats became so anxious when the buzzer rang they stopped eating. To reverse the fear conditioning, Wolpe used counterconditioning: He stopped pairing anxiety stimuli with eating by feeding the cats in cages dissimilar to the cages with the buzzers, which allowed the cats to discriminate and to decrease their generalization of the fear response. Once the cats were eating in the dissimilar cages, Wolpe placed them in cages that were more similar to the cages in which the fear response was learned. Eventually, he extinguished the fear and anxiety.

Counterconditioning, or producing a pleasurable response in the presence of an aversive stimulus, successfully reduced anxiety. Wolpe's (1990) application of what he called *reciprocal inhibition* to people suffering from neurosis prompted many mental health professionals to integrate behavioral interventions into forms of eclectic therapy (Lazarus, 1963, 1971; Wolpe, 1958).

Cognition and Behavior Therapy

While Watson, a radical behaviorist, adamantly opposed the inclusion of any mental constructs within behaviorism, cognition eventually was accepted into many forms of behavior therapy to the extent that today we use the terms *cognitive therapy* and *cognitive behavior therapy* interchangeably (Bandura & Walters, 1969) (see Chapter 10). In 1974, Donald Meichenbaum published a case in which impulsive children learned to talk to themselves in order to develop self-control (Meichenbaum & Goodman, 1971). This *self-instructional training* teaches appropriate behavior through modeling. Meichenbaum also developed *stress inoculation training,* a specific form of self-management for dealing with stressors (Meichenbaum, 1985, 1993). New forms of cognitive therapies are emerging that also incorporate mindfulness and acceptance-based interventions where clients are encouraged to face and control internal events.

The above describes some of the most important historical developments that led up to behavior therapy becoming a major treatment psychotherapeutic modality. The principles of behavior therapy are not only used in the field of mental health, but in organizational management, child development, marketing, and education (Hayes, Strosahl, & Wilson, 1999; Linehan, 1993).

✦ THEORY OF BEHAVIOR THERAPY

Behavior therapy is not a single form of therapy but consists of a diverse array of interventions and strategies that bring about behavioral change in a desired and predictable direction. Reference works list more than 150 forms of behavior therapy (Bellack & Hersen, 1985), and all of them are derived from empirically based learning theories, principles, and/or research (Krasner, 1971, 1990).

The term *behavior therapy* can be interpreted in different ways. For example, *behavior therapy, behavior modification,* and *applied behavior analysis* are often used interchangeably. Some argue that *behavior modification* should be the umbrella term because it envelops the use of learning principles for all types of behaviors, whereas *behavior therapy* is a more limited term in that it refers to changing maladaptive behavior in a clinical venue (Martin & Pear, 2007). Furthermore, it is not easy to find pure behavioral or pure cognitive therapies since many features overlap (Kazdin, 2003). Most cognitive methods use behavioral techniques, and most behavioral procedures contain cognitive elements (Emmelkamp, 2004).

Key Concepts

The following are some of the basic concepts of behavior therapy: behavior or what organisms do, the scientific approach, classical conditioning, operant conditioning, and observational learning. After the discussion of the key concepts, we will present some of the different models of behavior therapy.

Behavior

Behavior is defined as what the person (or animal) does, or actions performed in response to stimuli, either external or internal. Human behavior is viewed as complex behavioral sequences created and maintained by combinations of operant and respondent conditioning (see below discussion) and cognitive activity. Behavior can be *overt,* or visible, such as walking, talking, or running, making it easily observable. Behavior also can be *covert,* or performed within the skin, such as thinking, feeling, self-talk, and attitude. Covert activity is not easily observed but can be measured (Martin & Pear, 2007).

While radical behaviorists rejected the study of covert behaviors, most behavior therapists today consider attitudes, beliefs, and expectations to be important to the well-being of the client. The bottom line for behavior therapists is that people are what they do (Spiegler & Guevremont, 2003).

Scientific Approach

All behavior therapy models emphasize the scientific approach: rigorous, ongoing assessment, active treatment methods based on science, strict evaluation of outcomes, and generalization of learning from treatment to everyday life. A synopsis of basic learning principles underlying the fundamentals of behavior therapy is provided in Table 9.1 (classical conditioning), Table 9.2 (operant conditioning), and Table 9.3 (observational learning or modeling). Elements of the scientific approach to behavior therapy are outlined as follows (Martin & Pear, 2007; O'Leary & Wilson, 1987):

- *All behaviors, both normal and abnormal, are acquired, maintained, and changed in the same way through principles of learning and within genetic limitations.* What is usually called *personality,* or the person, is seen as a behavioral repertoire, consisting of specific behaviors or what the individual does, thinks, and feels.
- *Assessment of the client and his or her behavior is rigorous, ongoing, and specific.* It focuses on actions in particular situations and the current determinants of behavior rather than past history.

  Behavior therapists use some form of functional assessment of a presenting problem (such as observation, questionnaires, functional analysis) to identify the variables that control the underlying behaviors. In the past, many behavior therapists avoided the terms *diagnosis, treatment,* or *pathology* because those are medical terms that imply that abnormal behavior is a disease.

  Today, some behavior therapists recognize that the realities of clinical practice require the use of diagnoses based on the *DSM* in order to obtain insurance reimbursements (Antony & Roemer, 2003). Furthermore, the fourth edition of the *DSM* is more compatible with behavior therapies than earlier editions since diagnoses are based upon categories of problem behaviors or symptoms (Martin & Pear, 2007). Many of the studies of behavior therapy, which support that behavior therapies are evidence-based interventions, classify clients and conditions according to specific *DSM* disorders. Ideally, the behavior therapist integrates information from the behavioral model and the *DSM* clinically oriented diagnoses into a comprehensive treatment plan (Western, 2001).

- *Treatments, based on a solid empirical foundation, are objective, precise, scientific, replicable, and individualized to meet the needs of patients and problems.* Behavior therapy and cognitive behavior therapies have more empirical support than any other treatment models. The client actively collaborates in treatment, and behavior therapy goals are mutually contracted between therapist and client. The process is individualized for each patient and each problem, and intervention procedures are clearly defined and contained in a manual if possible.
- *Outcome and progress assessment is ongoing, with specific, measurable, and objective goals.* The client's behavior is analyzed methodologically. Behavior therapists use objective measures of change to assess the progress of treatment and its outcome.

  Ideally, the behavior therapist sees each client's individual treatment as a case study, and frames it within a rigorous experimental framework (within the confines of ethical guidelines so that a withdrawal of treatment would not place the client in jeopardy). For example, the *ABA reversal design* consists of three components: baseline (A), treatment (B), and reversal to baseline (A). The treatment plan begins with gathering data as a baseline, followed by specified periods of time in which treatment is applied and then withdrawn. Data are recorded on the target behavior for all segments of the plan, and the client's performance is compared across all of the conditions. If the target behavior systematically varies when the intervention is applied and removed, the therapist assumes the intervention successfully changed behavior.

  In the *ABAB reversal design*, there are at least three demonstrations of the effects of treatment at three different times. In multiple-baseline designs, two or more target behaviors are monitored, or measures are taken for two or more clients (Todman & Dugard, 2001).

- *Intervention produces learning, generalization, and maintenance of behaviors from therapy to real-life situations.* Behavior therapists work toward generalizing from therapy to the client's everyday life. If a phobia is resolved in the therapy room, it must also be extinguished outside of it. Homework provides opportunities to rehearse outside the session and increase the probability that the behaviors are permanently learned and generalized appropriately.

Classical Conditioning

The basic concepts of classical conditioning are summarized in Table 9.1. Classical conditioning is a learning process in which a neutral stimulus takes on the eliciting properties of an unconditioned stimulus by pairing the unconditioned stimulus with a neutral stimulus (Mallott, Whalley, & Mallott, 1997). Some models of behavior therapy that involve classical conditioning (among other learning components) include exposure therapies such as systematic desensitization, assertiveness training, flooding, implosive therapy, and eye movement desensitization.

Table 9.1
Basic Concepts of Classical Conditioning

respondent: an elicited unlearned, reflexive behavior made to a stimulus. For example, salivating at the taste of lemon juice.

unconditioned stimulus: an event that elicits a natural or reflexive response with no learning. For example, a lemon causing salivation or delicious food causing a hungry person to salivate.

unconditioned response: an unlearned response elicited by an unconditioned stimulus. For example, salivating to lemon juice or to food when hungry and being startled at a loud noise.

conditioned stimulus: a previously neutral stimulus paired with an unconditioned stimulus until the neutral stimulus elicits a response similar to the unconditioned stimulus.

conditioned response: a learned response that occurs or is elicited because of its association with an unconditioned stimulus.

respondent conditioning: also called classical and Pavlovian conditioning, produced by presenting a new stimulus and pairing it with another stimulus that elicits that particular response. After sufficient pairings, the organism reacts to the previously neutral stimulus in the same way it did to the original stimulus.

higher order conditioning: a repeated pairing of a stimulus that elicits an unconditioned response with alternative variables. The unconditioned stimuli elicit the same response as the stimulus with which it was originally paired so that another neutral stimulus can be conditioned to the conditioned stimulus, and so on, allowing a chain of conditioned responses.

conditioned emotional response: an emotional response that results from conditioning.

neurosis: a conditioning of emotions that results in maladaptive behaviors. If a feeling is transferred to a new stimuli, it elicits that emotion as well.

avoidance: a problematic behavior that develops from reinforcement. Removing aversive stimuli alleviates anxiety, which is reinforcing and increases the probability that avoidance will occur. Because the feared object is never confronted, the organism is not able to learn that there is nothing to fear, and the behavior perpetuates itself.

stimulus generalization: increased response to one stimulus due to reinforcement in the presence of another stimulus or a response to a stimulus that is transferred to another. For example, if a child learns to fear one teacher who has punished her, she may learn to fear all teachers and perhaps all other authority figures if the stimuli seem similar.

stimulus discrimination: a response to a stimulus that does not transfer to another or responding differently to differing cues.

response generalization: reinforcement of one response increases the probability of a similar response occurring.

response prevention: an organism faces the feared situation and is prevented from performing any escape or avoidance behavior that could decrease anxiety.

Sources: Cooper, Heron, & Heward, 2007; Kazdin, 2001; Mallott et al, 1997; Martin & Pear, 2007; Spiegler & Guevremont, 2003.

Operant Conditioning

The basic concepts of operant conditioning are summarized in Table 9.2. Operant conditioning is a learning process in which reinforcing consequences immediately following a response increase its future likelihood. Aversive consequences immediately following a response decrease its future likelihood (Mallott et al., 1997). Some

---

Table 9.2

Basic Concepts of Operant Conditioning

operant conditioning, Skinnerian conditioning: strengthening a behavior by reinforcing it; weakening a behavior by punishing it.

operant behavior: behavior that is emitted and influenced by its consequences.

antecedent: an event that precedes a behavior.

consequent: an event that follows a behavior.

reinforcer: an event, object, or incentive that increases the operant that was performed just before it, making it more likely that the person will repeat this particular behavior in the future.

primary reinforcer: a naturally pleasurable event, object, or incentive that, when applied, increases the probability of a behavior. An example is food or water.

secondary reinforcer: a stimulus that has no reinforcing value until paired with a primary reinforcer. By association, it acquires the reinforcing properties of a primary reinforcer. For example, money is reinforcing only by virtue of its pairing with primary reinforcers such as food, water, and safety.

positive reinforcement: applying a pleasant stimulus to increase the probability a response will occur. For example, if a child sings and the parent rewards her with a candy bar (primary reinforcer) or praises her (secondary reinforcer), the child will be more likely to sing in the future.

negative reinforcement: removing an aversive stimulus to increase the probability that a response will occur. For example, a child is confined to his room in isolation because he did not do his homework. He does his work and is immediately removed from time-out. The removal of time-out, the aversive, is reinforcing and increases the probability that the child will do his homework in the future.

punishment: decreasing the probability that a behavior will occur. It is the mirror image of reinforcement.

punisher: an aversive stimulus that when presented decreases the probability that a response will occur. Punishment takes two forms.

- **application of an aversive stimulus:** For example, if a child does her homework, and a parent slaps or verbally scolds her for doing homework instead of housework, the child is less likely to do her homework in the future.

- **removal of a positive reinforcer:** For example, if a child screams at her mother and is placed in time-out, this is a punisher because all the positive reinforcers (social contact, toys, games) are removed; this decreases the probability that she will scream at her mother in the future.

time: an important factor in reinforcement and punishment; reinforcers and punishers produce the greatest learning when delivered immediately after the operant is performed.

shaping: teaching or learning a new behavior by applying reinforcement through successive approximations until the more complex behavior is established.

generalization: a response to one stimulus is made to another because the stimuli resemble each other. For example, pigeons who peck circles for a reward learn to peck ovals.

discrimination: a stimulus does not elicit the same response as another stimulus because the stimuli are not similar enough. For example, a pigeon respond to circles but not to ellipses or flat lines.

stimulus control: a behavior is rewarded (or punished) in one setting and not another.

extinction: a reinforcement is stopped completely, and the response rate decreases to prelearning levels.

spontaneous recovery: a temporary, usually short-lived, recovery of an extinguished behavior.

escape: running from a noxious stimulus after it is applied.

avoidance: getting away from a feared stimulus before it occurs based upon a cue with which it is associated. Avoidance continues indefinitely because escaping anxiety is self-reinforcing.

schedules of reinforcement: used to receive and deliver reinforcers as a function of time or number of responses. Each schedule elicits a unique response pattern and resistance to extinction. There are a number of major schedules:

- **continuous reinforcement:** the application of reinforcement each time a correct response occurs. This schedule is used for establishing new behaviors.
- **partial or intermittent reinforcement:** the application of reinforcement for only some occurrences of the behavior.
- **interval schedule:** reinforcement occurs as a function of amount of time that elapses.
- **fixed interval:** reinforcement occurs for first performance of the target response. The person responds with a slow rate after receiving the reinforcer and increases responding as time to receive a reinforcer is close. For example, students spend more time studying as the exam date approaches; after the exam, students' studying drops off.
- **variable interval schedule:** reinforcement occurs as responses are correctly performed at varying time periods. The time interval changes. The person has a steady rate of responding because he or she cannot predict the time between behavior and the reward. For example, students who receive pop quizzes are likely to study at a steadier rate than those on a fixed interval schedule.
- **ratio schedule:** reinforcement occurs based upon the number of responses performed.
- **fixed ratio schedule:** reinforcement occurs as responses are correctly performed after an unvarying number of responses. An example is piecework in a factory, where for every 10 buttons spray-painted, the pay is five dollars.
- **variable ratio schedule:** the application of reinforcement as responses are correctly performed after a varied number of responses. Responding is highly resistant to extinction. For example, casino slot machines produce winnings on a variable ratio schedule.

Sources: Cooper et al., 2007; Goldfried & Davison, 1994; Kazdin, 2001; Mallott et al., 1997; Martin & Pear, 2007; Spiegler & Guevremont, 2003.

Table 9.3

Basic Concepts of Observational Learning or Modeling

imitation, observational learning, modeling: performing a behavior as a consequence of observing another person performing the behavior. There are four major components to learning and performing any behavior:

1. **attentional processes**: observer characteristics (perceptual/cognitive capacities, arousal level, and past performance) and event characteristics (relevance, affective valence, complexity, functional value, model's characteristics, and intrinsic rewards).
2. **retentional processes**: observer characteristics (cognitive skills) and event characteristics (cognitive organization and cognitive rehearsal).
3. **motor reproduction processes**: observer characteristics (physical capabilities and subskill mastery) and event characteristics (selection and organization of responses and feedback).
4. **motivational processes**: observer characteristics (incentive preference, social bias, and internal standards) and event characteristics (external reinforcement, self-reinforcement, and vivacious reinforcement).

Sources: Bandura, 1977, 2000.

---

models of behavior therapy that involve operant procedures (among other learning components) include contingency management, self-direction and control, token economies, aversive therapy, and time-out.

Observational Learning or Modeling

The basic concepts of observational learning or modeling are summarized in Table 9.3. Observational learning, or modeling, is a process in which a new behavior is learned by watching a model. Learning can take place even without the performance of behavior (Bandura, 1997). Some models of behavior therapy that use observational learning (among other learning procedures) include problem solving, self-instructional training, stress inoculation, and social skills training.

Normal and Abnormal Behavior

What others label mental illness, psychopathology, emotional disturbance, or psychological disorder, behavior therapists call *maladaptive* or *faulty learning*. Normal behavior is adaptive, and abnormal behavior is maladaptive. If a behavior is maladaptive, it falls into one of three general categories (Alloy, Riskind, & Manos, 2004):

1. *Behavioral excess* means a person (or other organism) performs too much of a specific behavior; it is too frequent, too intense, or too lengthy. For example, a person who talks nonstop, spends money extravagantly, drives recklessly, and sleeps less than 3 hours a night could be considered behaving excessively.

2. *Behavioral deficit* means a person (or other organism) shows too little of a specific behavior; it is not frequent enough, not intense enough, or not long enough. For example, a person who has no social contacts, stays at home for weeks at a time, lounges in bed, sleeps irregularly, frowns, cries, and has no appetite could be considered behaving deficiently.

3. *Inappropriate stimulus control* means a person (or other organism) performs a behavior in the wrong place or at the wrong time. For example, the child who masturbates in public is doing so in a badly chosen place. Although masturbation is normal, it is inappropriate in public, and the child is showing inappropriate stimulus control.

✧ MODELS OF BEHAVIOR THERAPY

Behavior therapies combine the building blocks of the principles of behavior to create many different models of treatment. Contemporary behavior therapy consists of a large number and variety of forms of interventions that blend these key elements for specific interventions for specific problem behaviors. We divide these behavior models into three basic categories:

1. *Exposure therapies:* based on exposure to a feared stimulus or situation, such as systematic desensitization, assertiveness training, implosive therapy, and eye movement desensitization and reprocessing (EMDR).

2. *Contingency management and behavior modification therapies:* based on operant conditioning principles, these are generally conducted in institutions and in special training settings, such as self-direction, self-control, token economies, and aversive conditioning.

3. *Observational and modeling therapies:* based on a combination of behavioral and cognitive elements, these are generally used in clinical settings, such as modeling, stress inoculation, problem solving, and social skills training.

Therapies that emphasize cognition, such as rational emotive behavior therapy (REBT) and Beck's cognitive therapies, are described in Chapter 10.

Exposure Therapies

Exposure therapies are used to treat anxiety disorders and other negative affective responses through exposure to the situation that creates the negative emotion (Spiegler & Guevremont, 2003). In exposure therapy, the client's clinical condition is seen in terms of conditioned fear or anxiety responses reinforced by avoidance behaviors. Avoidance is a particular problem because when an aversive is removed and anxiety is alleviated, it is very reinforcing and sustains maladaptive behavior. Thus avoidance provides immediate reinforcement, which increases the probability that the avoidance will occur again.

These therapies expose the client to the stimulus or situation that brings out the negative emotional responses, but in a safe environment and while eliminating escape and avoidance responses (Mowrer & Mowrer, 1938). Anxiety diminishes after the person has had sufficient contact with the source of the fear and suffers no harm.

Exposure can occur in two ways: (a) gradual exposure to anxiety-producing situations, such as systematic desensitization and in vivo exposure therapy, and (b) immediate exposure to highly anxiety-provoking stimuli for a prolonged period, or flooding, coupled with response prevention. Exposure therapies also occur in at least four different formats:

- *In vivo exposure* means the client faces the feared object or situation in the real world.
- In *imaginal exposure*, an imagery-based technique, the client imagines being in the presence of the fearful stimuli.
- In *interoceptive exposure*, the client is exposed to feared sensations such as the physical sensations of a panic attack like a pounding heart, dizziness, and light-headedness.
- In *virtual reality exposure*, the client faces his or her feared stimulus in the form of a computer-generated image in much the same way as in vivo exposure (Antony & Barlow, 2002).

Wolpe's Systematic Desensitization

Wolpe's *systematic desensitization* is a method of treating fear-based conditions or phobic behaviors that exposes the client in reality or imaginally to the anxiety-provoking situations. The technique is based on the construction of a hierarchy of anxiety-producing stimuli followed by the gradual presentation of stimuli so the person no longer feels anxious in their presence.

Wolpe saw human phobias as classically conditioned fear habits. Just as his experimental cats that had been shocked showed persistent escape and avoidance of the conditioned anxiety-provoking stimuli, Wolpe realized that people could react similarly. Classically conditioned cues associated with the frightening stimulus could produce avoidance responses that could be generalized to increasingly remote stimuli.

Wolpe used counterconditioning to antagonize the maladaptive response and replace the old habits through *reciprocal inhibition* (London, 1964, p. 85). Fear is replaced with the incompatible response of relaxation. A person cannot be relaxed and anxious at the same time, and so one of the behaviors will predominate. In successful treatment, the client is gradually introduced to the fear-producing stimuli either through in vivo exposure or imagined scenes. Relaxation dominates and anxiety dissipates. Wolpe's (1990) systematic desensitization has three distinct parts: development of the anxiety hierarchy, relaxation training, and desensitization.

Anxiety Hierarchies   First, the therapist teaches the client to rate his or her level of fear according to *subjective units of discomfort* (SUD), a fear rating from 0 to 10 (or 0 to 100) with 0 indicating total relaxation and 10 indicating an anxiety level as high as can be experienced. The client rates the level of anxiety associated with a given stimulus and describes the parameters of the fear-inducing situation with the

Table 9.4	
Anxiety Hierarchy with Subjective Units of Discomfort	
Anxiety Scenes	**Subjective Units of Discomfort**
Airplane angles down and descends for final landing	100
Airplane landing gear goes down	95
Airplane approaches landing field	90
Pilot announces final descent is beginning	85
Airplane begins to descend for landing	80
Airplane shakes in turbulence	75
Pilot announces some turbulence	70
Plane is in air at flying altitude	65
Airplane ascends into sky	60
Captain announces altitude of 10,000	55
Airplane takes off for flight	50
Putting on seat belt	45
Boarding the plane	40
Checking luggage	35
Walking up to counter	30
Saying good-bye to relatives	25
Arriving at airport	20
Driving to airport	15
Calling and purchasing ticket 2 months before flying	10
Making decision to travel by air in a month	5

therapist. For example, if the problem is fear of flying, the therapist obtains very specific information: When and where does this occur? What thoughts occur to you about flying? What physical reactions occur when you think of flying? Describe your reactions when you have flown (or think about flying). Do you know why this fear developed? The therapist can also administer tests or questionnaires to help better understand the fear.

The therapist and patient then work together to design an anxiety hierarchy, ranking scenes that produce the fear from very anxiety provoking to least anxiety provoking. A person with a fear of flying might identify the most frightening scene, level 10, as the plane angling down and descending for its final landing. The least anxiety-provoking scene, or level 1, might be a preliminary behavior to flying, deciding to take a plane trip. Scenes are devised so the client can experience graduated exposure to the fear-provoking situation. See Table 9.4 for an example of a typical anxiety hierarchy.

Relaxation Training   The second part of Wolpe's systematic desensitization occurs simultaneously with the development of the anxiety hierarchy. Here, the client learns an adaptive, competing response to the fear or to any negative emotion. If the maladaptive response is anxiety, the competing response is relaxation. They are incompatible because it is impossible for a person to be relaxed and anxious at the same time.

The therapist can select from a variety of relaxation training techniques, but behavior therapists often choose some variant of Edmund Jacobson's (1938) deep muscle relaxation technique developed in the 1930s. Clients first learn to relax and tense each major muscle group of the face, arms, neck, shoulders, and chest and then compare the sensations of tenseness and relaxation. Initial sessions are conducted in the office, and the client is assigned the homework of practicing for a minimum of 15 minutes a day twice a week. Often the technique is used with a tape guiding the exercise (Davis, Eshelman, & Mckay, 2000).

Desensitization   Desensitization, the third segment of the treatment, begins after the hierarchies have been constructed, and the client has learned the relaxation exercises. The session begins with the therapist asking the client to become deeply relaxed. Once this successfully occurs, the therapist asks the client to imagine the least anxiety-provoking scene from the hierarchy that elicits a mild fear reaction or anxiety reaction. The client imagines the scene while relaxing. The therapist continues to present the scene to the client until he or she is relaxed so that the fear is inhibited. The therapist gradually introduces more anxiety-producing scenes as the client demonstrates relaxation, and fear is inhibited for each step of the hierarchy. By counterposing the relaxation response with a hierarchy of fear-inducing stimuli arranged from least to most fear provoking, the relaxation response replaces anxiety. The anxiety is extinguished.

After the imaginal work is complete, the client must face the feared event in the real world in order to consider treatment as successful. Although anxiety is the most common condition treated by systematic desensitization, it can also be used to deal with anger, insomnia, sexual problems, and shyness, among other negative emotions.

Wolpe's Assertiveness Training

Wolpe also developed *assertiveness training,* another counterconditioning technique that became very popular and has generated many variants used today. Wolpe defines assertive behavior as the "proper expression of any emotions other than anxiety toward another person" (1973, p. 81) and the appropriate expression of personal rights and feelings in a way that does not violate the rights of others. Based on the principles of counterconditioning, assertiveness training, in group or individual therapy, can be learned by anyone (Lazarus, 1973).

When clients lack assertiveness, their anxieties or fears block them from making appropriate responses in interpersonal situations. Clients may also respond aggressively due to lack of assertiveness. Clients who are nonassertive may have difficulty accepting positive responses from others and may feel embarrassed when others express praise or admiration. Nonassertive people also tend to be afraid to express anger.

With Wolpe's assertiveness training, counterconditioning increases the probability of appropriate responses. Clients are taught effective verbal responses by learning to substitute assertive behaviors: feeling talk, appropriate facial expressions, I-talk, body posture, body gestures, voice training, direct eye contact, refusal of unreasonable requests, acceptance of compliments, and requesting favors. The therapist and client develop a hierarchy of assertive behaviors so the client will be able to practice them in a graduated fashion in role-play situations with the therapist. After rehearsal, the client is asked to practice in real-life situations.

Operant and cognitive techniques are also used in assertiveness training. Inappropriate behaviors are counterconditioned, and appropriate responses are positively reinforced in behavior rehearsal in reality and in role-play situations. The therapist provides instruction, modeling, and feedback. Wolpe's assertiveness training has also been used to teach a wide variety of social skills for clients who have developmental disorders or chronic mental illness.

Flooding

Flooding is an exposure therapy in which the client is exposed to a high-intensity anxiety-provoking situation until the fear response is extinguished. At the same time, the client is not permitted to perform any escape or avoidance behaviors. Repeated, prolonged exposure to the stimulus results in fear dissipating completely (Spiegler & Guevremont, 2003).

In vivo flooding—exposing the client to the real, fear-provoking stimulus—is, for example, placing a client who has a flying phobia directly on an airplane. *Imaginal flooding* means exposing the client to an imagined version of the real fear-provoking stimulus. Just as in desensitization, the client is asked to imagine the fear-provoking scenes and to indicate the subjective unit of discomfort (SUD) level. However, in flooding, exposure to the anxiety hierarchy begins with highly anxiety-provoking scenes, even a level 10. For example, a client with a plane phobia visualizes or imagines the worst fear first, the airplane angling down, descending for its final landing. With each engagement of the scene, the client indicates the SUD, which should continually diminish as the scene is repeated. When the SUD rating of 2 or less is permanent, treatment is successfully completed.

There are obvious practical advantages to imaginal flooding over in vivo flooding. In addition, the client can face a worst-case scenario at the top of the anxiety hierarchy, which may be even more fear provoking than reality.

Implosive Therapy

Devised by Thomas Stampfl, *implosive therapy* is a form of exposure therapy based on flooding and response prevention. Its unique feature is the incorporation of cues, based on psychoanalytic themes, into the conditioning (Stampfl & Levis, 1967). Through the use of imagined stimuli, the therapist tries to induce the maximum amount of anxiety in the patient at any one session to illustrate that the unpleasant anxiety is not unbearable. From cues the patient provides, the therapist develops the scenes for the patient to face. Therapists use their judgment in changing the imaginal scenes, based on the client's answers to questions such as, "What are you thinking and feeling?" as the client experiences the hierarchal scenes (Spiegler & Guevremont, 2003).

Eye Movement Desensitization Therapy

Francine Shapiro (1999, 2001) developed *eye movement desensitization reprocessing* (EMDR) for clients with posttraumatic stress disorders and other anxiety-related conditions. EMDR combines imaginal flooding, counterconditioning of eye movements (or some other disruptive movement), and cognitive restructuring. The following describes the phases of EMDR treatment (Shapiro, 1999; Shapiro, Snyker, & Maxfield, 2002; Soderlund, 2007):

1. *Client history and treatment planning:* The client's ability to tolerate EMDR is assessed and the therapist designs the treatment plan—goals, potential problem areas, and specific skills needed, such as relaxation techniques.
2. *Preparation for EMDR:* The therapist educates the client about EMDR, teaches self-control techniques, and assigns self-study materials.
3. *Assessment of the target:* The client identifies a specific distressing memory—a visual image and the thoughts and feelings that come with it (e.g., a memory of an assault) and identifies a current negative cognition related to the memory (e.g., I am weak and defeated). The client then selects a positive image to replace the negative image (I am strong and victorious). The client rates the accuracy of this positive belief using the Validity of Cognition (VoC) Scale of 1 (completely false) to 7 (completely true) and rates the distress level of the emotions that accompany the visual image when it is combined with the negative belief from 1 (calm) to 10 (most distress) on SUD. It is common for a client to rate the positive belief as unlikely (1–3).
4. *Desensitization and reprogramming:* While the client holds the traumatic visual image, the negative cognition, and accompanying feelings, the therapist asks the client to perform a set of eye movements, rapidly, simultaneously moving his or her eyes from side to side for 15 or more seconds, thus disrupting the memory. The therapist then gives bilateral stimulation in the form of moving a finger across the client's visual field, or making a noise, or tapping a finger in repeated, dosed exposures. The purpose is to activate information processing. The client is asked to relate what material arose during the process and to describe a scene such as "I see the attacker coming after me." This subject becomes the focus of the next set of eye movements. The cycle of alternating focused exposure and client feedback is repeated several times until the SUD level is 0 or 1.
5. *Cognitive installation of the positive self-statement:* The therapist tells the client to pair the original traumatic image with the positive self-statement and hold it in mind, while encouraging more bilateral stimulation or eye movements until the VoC level is at least 6.
6. *Body scan:* The client scans for all tension and bodily sensations as he or she thinks about the image; the client looks for signs of emotional distress

manifested physiologically. Processing is successful when the client remembers the traumatic memory without feeling any body tension.

7.   *Closure:* Once the memory does not interfere with functioning, closure begins.
8.   *Reevaluation:* At the beginning of every session, assessments are made to determine whether gains have been maintained.

Successful treatment means the client has processed the traumatic life events in a way that allows the information to be unlocked from memory without triggering unpleasant associations.

Contingency Management and Behavior Modification Therapies

Contingency management, also called *applied behavior analysis,* stresses operant learning and determines the relationship among antecedants and a behavior or response to be changed (Kazdin, 2001). The therapist identifies *antecedents,* the environmental events that precede a behavior, and *consequents,* the environmental events that follow a behavior, which are reinforcers or punishers.

For example, Sarah's parents say they want to eliminate their daughter's frequent temper tantrums. The therapist asks the parents to record, count, and classify each of the tantrums and what happens just before the tantrums (antecedants), during, and directly after the tantrums (consequents) for a week.

They return to the therapist with a week of data collection. The therapist and parents graph the data and perform *a functional analysis.* They identify the *contingencies* (causes) that initiate, maintain, and end behaviors. They discover the antecedent is Sarah being alone in her room. The operant (screaming loudly) is reinforced by the consequent (attention from a parent), which is a reinforcer (comfort and escaping being alone). Furthermore, the reinforcement is delivered on an intermittent schedule. Both parents respond inconsistently. Sometimes Mom reacts with caresses; other times mom scolds or ignores Sarah. Sarah cries for varying intervals before she receives a response. One night the parents tried to let Sarah "cry it out," but Dad's frustration level peaked, and after 20 minutes, he intervened, thus reinforcing Sarah. They tried spanking Sarah but were inconsistent in how spankings were administered.

The functional analysis showed that variable interval and variable ratio schedules of reinforcement and punishment were making the temper tantrums more resistant to extinction. By their inconsistent delivery of reinforcers and punishers, the parents were inadvertently reinforcing the tantrums they did not want.

The therapist and parents collaborated on a contingency management program, tailoring the plan according to Sarah's unique needs (Haynes, Leisen, & Blaine, 1997). Often the therapist and client sign a *contingency contract,* a written agreement specifying the target behavior, the behavior the client wants to change, the consequences (rewards or punishments) for performing or not performing the behavior, and the rewards or costs that will follow. A contingency contract can also be made between a person who wishes behavior to be changed (such as a parent) and the person whose behavior is to be changed (such as a child) so that it clearly specifies the relationship between the behavior and its consequences.

Reinforcement contingencies were chosen to increase wanted and decrease unwanted behaviors. Effective reinforcers generally fall under specific categories. For example, they could be consumable items such as food and drink; pleasurable activities such as watching a movie; enjoying a possession such as wearing a favorite outfit or playing with a favorite toy or computer game; or forms of social reinforcement such as praise or smiling.

In Sarah's case, the parents use extinction and thus completely ignore her tantrum behaviors until they stop. At the moment Sarah stops crying, they enter her room and visit her for a moment, giving her social reinforcement such as praise, smiles, and say "Good girl, sleep well." If spontaneous recovery occurs (that is, the maladaptive response reappears seemingly spontaneously), they continue to completely ignore the tantrums, using extinction. Within two weeks, the temper tantrums are extinguished completely, illustrating the effectiveness of contingency management therapy.

Self-Direction

Contingency planning for one's self is the essence of *self-directed behavior modification*. The client obtains directions (such as a book) on self-modification and self-administers his or her own program, or can collaborate with a therapist to implement the plan as part of formal behavior therapy, with the therapist acting like a coach. The features of a high-quality self-help plan include rules that clarify the techniques, precisely spelled out goals and subgoals, feedback about behavior based on self-observations, evaluation of progress through feedback about goals and subgoals, and fine-tuning of the plan as conditions change (Watson & Tharp, 2002).

The basic steps of self-directed behavior modification parallel those of contingency management: (a) select a goal and translate it into target behaviors; (b) specify a target behavior to change and make it simple, attainable, and realistic; (c) anticipate obstacles to progress; (d) self-monitor; and (e) evaluate the action plan and make changes as necessary (Cormier & Nurius, 2003, pp. 586–589; Watson & Tharp, 2002). People who are trying to stop smoking or lose weight frequently use a self-modification program. Table 9.5 provides an example of a self-directed behavior modification plan.

Self-Control

Self-control behavior modification means the client intentionally undertakes self-selected outcomes by manipulating antecedents and consequents. Clients must learn the fundamentals of behavior therapy and then practice on themselves, administering their own reinforcement and punishment. Clients play an active role in administering interventions to change behavior. Thus they act as their own therapist. *Self-control* means clients can postpone gratification by performing a response that results in a delayed reward rather than a response that produces a smaller but more immediate reward (Cooper et al., 2007).

Table 9.5

Self-Directed Management Plan

Step 1.   *Selecting my goal:* My doctor told me I was "prediabetic." Unless I eat healthier, I will become diabetic. My goal is to change my lifestyle to maintain an ideal weight of 140 pounds.

Step 2.   *Identifying my target behavior:* My target behavior is to eat healthy foods. I will consume 1,500 calories per day six days per week and 1,900 calories on Sunday. I will eat only the foods from a list of healthy, low-fat, low-carbohydrate foods.

Step 3.   *Establishing a baseline:* I will record all that I eat and drink for one week. I will weigh myself daily. I will determine antecedents and consequents to help me design a good plan.

Step 4.   *Assessing my baseline:* After a week of recording, my baseline showed that I eat on average 2,800 to 4,000 calories per day. To reach 140 pounds from my current weight of 197 pounds, I must lose 57 pounds.

Step 5.   *Monitoring my behavior:* I will monitor my food intake and calories per day, keeping accurate records.

Step 6.   *Anticipating obstacles:* I will completely empty my refrigerator of extremely tempting foods and have only nutritious foods easily available.

Step 7.   *Establishing contingencies:* My contingencies are that for every day I stay at 1,500 calories, I will deposit five dollars in a healthy eating jar. I can afford to do this because I am saving money usually spent on junk food. At the end of a month, I will cash in the money and purchase new clothing.

Step 8.   *Evaluating progress:* I will evaluate as I work on the plan and change whatever needs to be changed.

Step 9.   *Reporting to others:* I will go public with my therapist, and I will relate my progress to my best friend. He has agreed to be a management partner.

Alan Kazdin (2002, p. 330) describes a number of self-control interventions. First is *self-assessment* in which clients determine if they are in need of help. In *self-monitoring*, clients keep careful records of the behavior they want to change. Using *stimulus control*, clients manage their own behavior by changing the situational events that act as behavior cues. With *self-reinforcement* and *self-punishment* clients apply certain events to themselves after a specific behavior has occurred. Clients are free to partake of the reinforcement or to not apply the punisher. With *alternate response training*, clients perform a response that interferes with or replaces the response clients want to control. *Self-help resources* are techniques clients can use to implement their own treatment interventions, determining when and how to apply them.

Self-control has been used for a variety of problems including anxiety, depression, sexual dysfunction, weight control, addiction, disease management, and home and school behaviors.

Token Economy

Token economy is a system of reinforcement generally used for a group of participants within an institutional setting. Tokens are earned for various behaviors and are used to buy backup reinforcers. Tokens are secondary reinforcers (like money) that the client earns and exchanges for primary reinforcement. The clients earn conditioned reinforcers such as points, tokens, or stars as an immediate consequence for performing desirable behaviors, which they can later cash in for rewards.

Usually this type of behavior modification therapy is used for people confined to psychiatric hospitals, juvenile halls, or prisons; also, teachers sometimes use this method to control classroom behavior. For example, a token economy could be set up in a hospital schizophrenia ward with the goal of increasing levels of self-care (Ayllon & Azrin, 1965).

The objective is to teach clients specific behaviors. To set up a program, the therapist selects exact target behaviors for the participants to learn. The behaviors are carefully specified. The rules that govern earning tokens and the value of performing the target behaviors are very precise, because there are typically numerous staff members involved in administering the program. The tokens can be cashed in for backup reinforcers or desirable items, such as food, beverages, recreational activities, games, movies, and even time away from the institution. If participants misbehave or do not follow the guidelines, tokens can be taken away; thus behaviors have a *response cost* or a punishment in which a positive reinforcer is taken away due to the client's undesirable behavior (Kazdin, 1977).

Aversive Conditioning and Punishment

Punishment is the application of an aversive stimulus or removal of a positive stimulus following a behavior, causing the behavior to decrease. When applied immediately, punishment is very effective in suppressing the target behavior that precedes it. Punishment can be used to make a desirable reinforcer—such as a cigarette, alcoholic drink, or an unhealthy food—less attractive by its association with unpleasantness.

Behavior therapists are reluctant to use therapies based upon punishment due to ethical and practical considerations. For example, punishment can generalize to the punisher (often the therapist), and typically the client responds to punishment with avoidance behaviors, such as running away or lying. The client might avoid therapy altogether. Clients also sometimes react to punishment with lack of response or physical aggression. Clients observing punitive behaviors may model such behaviors. Punishment is reserved for last-resort situations, and the justification of its use must outweigh the risks. It is generally used for chronic or life-threatening self-injurious behavior (SIB) such as head banging, self-mutilation, and substance abuse (Mallott et al., 1997).

Despite these concerns, if therapies based on punishment are performed safely and humanely, with strong oversight, they can be effective. Various forms of therapies that use punishment are described next.

Physical Aversion Therapy   In *aversion therapy,* an unpleasant or noxious stimulus is counterconditioned to the behavior to be eliminated. Physical aversion therapy involves applying a physically painful or unpleasant stimulus, like a shock or a spanking, to a maladaptive behavior. As the undesirable behavior decreases, the unpleasant stimulus does as well, until termination of the undesirable behavior is achieved. In physical aversion therapy, clients receive an aversive stimulus (painful or unpleasant) at the time he or she performs the maladaptive behavior. Thus clients associate the performance of the behavior with the unpleasant consequence (classical conditioning).

Physical aversion therapy can be a helpful treatment with seriously harmful behaviors. For example, an autistic child who persists in banging her head against the wall can receive mild electric shocks to stop the dangerous self-harm. For the client who drinks excessively, it is necessary to counteract the reinforcing power of alcohol. The client is given a drug (such as Antabuse) that makes her nauseated immediately after she takes a drink of alcohol. The alcohol and nausea are repeatedly paired until the alcohol by itself elicits the nauseated reaction.

Covert Aversion Therapy Covert aversion therapy uses covert conditioning or sensitization to change behavior. Clients imagine both unwanted behaviors and the specific consequences of those behaviors. For example, a client imagines himself doing an unwanted behavior, such as smoking, and then imagines negative or punishing consequences that will aversively condition the behavior and decrease the smoking (Cautela, 1967) The following is a typical sample script used in covert sensitization to aversively and imaginally condition a person to stop smoking:

> Imagine that you have smoked a cigarette. As you put the cigarette out in the ashtray, you see the black tar and nicotine at the end of the filter. Imagine that black tar and nicotine in your lungs. They are filling up with the black tar, the same substance used to pave driveways. Your lungs are completely coated with a thick layer of black tar. There is a pool of black tar that stagnates at the bottom of your lungs. In that black tar there are thousands of cancer cells waiting to rush into the rest of your body and take over. They cannot wait to overcome your other precious organs and make you ill, terminally ill.

Covert aversion therapy is the work of Joseph Cautela; it combines cognitive behaviors with overt behaviors and is responsible for opening up the field of behavior therapy to the use of cognitive and behavioral interventions, blending operant conditioning, respondent conditioning, and cognitive techniques (Glass & Arnkoff, 1992).

Time-Out and Response Cost *Time-out,* or time-out from positive reinforcement, is a milder form of negative punishment that is used in short doses. It is based on extinction and the removal of positive reinforcers. The client is placed in a location where he or she has no access to reinforcement and thus cannot earn positive reinforcers. The time-out period needs to be very clearly specified and is usually kept very brief (15 minutes or less). Absolutely no escape or avoidance responses are allowed during time-out.

Response cost is a form of punishment in which a specified amount of a reinforcer is removed from the client for performing a behavior, either for a limited time or permanently. It is the contingent loss of a reinforcer and is similar to a fine. An example is the suspension of computer privileges for a child if he does not do his homework and watches TV instead. This should increase the rate of homework and decrease the amount of television viewing. The child will want to "remove the removal" and gain back the computer, resulting in an increase in the target behavior.

Observational Learning and Modeling Therapies

Observational learning, also called *modeling,* is a cognitive behavioral technique that can be used alone or that can be integrated into other forms of behavior therapy. Modeling occurs when a client observes a model displaying a behavior and then imitates that behavior. Clients are more likely to respond to future situations in the same way if the consequences observed are positive than if they are negative.

The basic functions of modeling are teaching, prompting, motivating, reducing anxiety, and discouraging behaviors (Spiegler & Guevremont, 2003). For example, a therapist can model (teach) an assertive or appropriate response that the client can repeat. Let's say a client is is learning to say no. The therapist models a polite refusal, worded tactfully, such as, "I would love to accept your invitation and join you, but it is not possible for me to be there at that time."

Modeling as a social prompt and motivator occurs when the therapist initiates and motivates similar behavior in the client; for example, the client is prompted to discuss specific problems by the therapist beginning the conversation. Modeling can also be used to reduce anxiety for the client, simply through observation, such as when a client with an insect phobia watches her therapist calmly handling a bug.

Finally, modeling can be used to discourage inappropriate behavior. For example, the addicted client can watch videos of a person on cocaine or graphic illustrations of the suffering of a person who is experiencing the physical effects associated with alcoholism, such as heart disease and cirrhosis.

Self-Efficacy

Albert Bandura's constructs are helpful to bolster a client's belief in his or her self-efficacy (1997, 2000). Bandura describes perceived *self-efficacy* as the person's belief that he or she can perform the behaviors needed to produce a particular outcome (2000). A person's level of self-efficacy influences his or her choice of behavior, the quality of the performance, and the degree of persistence.

- *Those who have a weak belief in their self-efficacy tend to shy away from difficult tasks.* They have low aspirations and weak commitment to their goals. They tend to dwell on personal deficiencies, obstacles, and adverse outcomes. They attribute failures to weakness in their abilities, give up quickly, recover slowly after failures or setbacks, and are prone to stress and depression. They maintain a self-diagnostic focus rather than a centering on how to perform.
- *Those who have a strong belief in their self-efficacy tend to set challenging goals.* They have strong commitments to their objectives and see difficult tasks as challenges rather than as threats. They view failures as a result of insufficient effort, so they try harder in the face of difficulties, quickly recover after failure or setback, and display low vulnerability to stress and depression. They maintain a task-diagnostic focus.

The processes of self-efficacy are based on four areas: cognition, motivation, emotion, and selection. The behavior therapist can help a client to develop a strong sense of efficacy by several means. First, the therapist can encourage the performance of successful behaviors because experiencing success increases a person's belief in his own personal efficacy whereas failures undermine it. Second, the therapist can show the client competent models that perform successful behaviors and thus teach the client-observer effective skills and strategies for managing environmental demands through observation and vicarious reinforcement. Third, the therapist can persuade the client verbally that she has what it takes to succeed and structure situations to help her succeed. Finally, the therapist can reduce stress reactions in the client and help the person see his state of arousal as potentially energizing his performance, rather than debilitating it.

Problem-Solving Therapy

Problem-solving therapy teaches clients to understand and effectively solve problems, using both cognitive and behavioral interventions. The goal is to educate clients to deal with immediate problems as well as to teach those skills that can generalize to future ones.

Problem-solving models share some basic characteristics, including breaking down any problem into its component parts and identifying the various steps of the solution; choosing and implementing the solution; and performing a cost-benefit analysis of the solution. Problem-solving therapies have been applied to people of all ages for issues such as marital discord, depression, stress relief, anger management, assertiveness training, and school adjustment (Kazdin, 2002; Miklowitz, 2001; Nezu, 1986; Spiegler & Guevremont, 1993, 2003).

Self-Instruction and Stress Inoculation

Donald Meichenbaum's work on self-instruction training and stress inoculation firmly integrated cognitive material into behavior therapy. *Self-instruction training* shows people how to learn to deal with problematic situations (Meichenbaum, 1974; Rokke & Rehm, 2001). In Meichenbaum's work with impulsive children to help them develop self-control, he describes using cognitions or instructional training (Meichenbaum & Goodman, 1971). For example, first the adult demonstrates self-instruction to the child by modeling the behavior, saying "I'll draw a straight line and then a circle next to it," followed by a reinforcing statement such as "I did a good job." The child then performs the action (draws the figures), and the adult verbalizes. Next, the child performs the task while verbalizing. Gradually, the overt self-instruction fades, and the child is encouraged to repeat both the task and the instructions and to praise himself. Finally, the adult prompts the child to repeat the instructions and the praise to himself silently.

Meichenbaum also developed stress inoculation training, a specific form of self-management of stress (Meichenbaum, 1985, 1993). The client learns to recognize that it is not the stressor itself that is the problem but the way in which he or she is interpreting the stressor. This technique involves various coping skills to deal with stressful situations such as relaxation, self-talk, self-instruction, and self-reinforcement. In the application phase, clients rehearse their coping skills imaginally and in vivo (Meichenbaum & Deffenbacher, 1988). This model is discussed in Chapter 13.

Social Skills Training

Social skills training is a behavioral intervention that helps clients acquire a skill in which they are deficient, such as how to interact appropriately in social situations. People can have inadequate social skills for many reasons, including insufficient practice, ignorance, lack of motivation, or insensitivity to situations. Training methods for social skills include reinforcement, shaping, behavioral rehearsal, corrective feedback, and direct instruction.

There are also techniques to apply such as making flowcharts, writing scripts, making videos, and giving self and others verbal and visual feedback. The acquisition of the skill is the target behavior, and an individualized contingency management program is designed to help the client acquire it. For example, anger management programs often reinforce the performance of prosocial behaviors by ensuring that group members and leaders give group reinforcements (Lochman & Wells, 2002; Spiegler & Guevremont).

✦ PRACTICE OF BEHAVIOR THERAPY

Now that we have examined the theoretical concepts underlying behavior therapy and several models of intervention, we will explore its practice. Dr. Carl Wilson, our composite fictional behavior therapist, provides a firsthand perspective of how he integrates theory with practice and applies the techniques of behavior therapy.

Assessment and Diagnosis

In the initial interview, I begin a functional assessment, which includes a variety of approaches to identify the antecedents and consequences of a behavior and to help me to determine what kind of behavioral techniques are needed (Watson & Tharp, 2002). As I assess, I educate my clients about basic behavioral principles, teaching them that so-called problem behaviors can be changed through the principles of learning. I deemphasize labeling because I want to focus on behaviors.

The assessment involves the following:

- *Identify the problem, define the target behaviors to be modified, and prioritize.* Define the final goals clearly. Specify the nature and the levels of behavior change desired. For example, if the target behaviors are temper tantrums, the goal is to decrease the frequency and ultimately eliminate them.
- *Educate the client and others involved about behavior therapy to gather appropriate information.*
- *Gather baseline data.* Select the recording procedures and determine how the target behavior, its antecedents, and its consequences will be tracked and recorded to assess what is maintaining it and how it is currently under stimulus control.
- *Specify the details of the client's program.* Identify all components of the operant and respondent conditioning procedures, such as type and

schedules of reinforcement, stimulus generalization, construction of anxiety hierarchies, competing behaviors, application of exposure, training in any skill that will help, and so on.

- *Design and describe how the programming will be implemented.*
- *Designate who is responsible for each part of the plan.* Identify who records, administers reinforcement, learns relaxation, and so forth to all parties involved. Specify dates and time lines.
- *Arrange for data collection and accurate recording and analysis of information.*
- *Monitor and review events on a specific schedule and revise when necessary if any part of treatment is not working.*
- *Arrange for observation of the target behavior in the setting in which it occurs.* I can choose from self-observations, diaries, self-report measures, and physiological monitors. I may use problem checklists, survey schedules, questionnaires, and stimulus-organism-response-consequence (SORC), and information from significant others in order to clearly identify target behaviors, record the frequency and intensity properly, and graph the data if appropriate (Martin & Pear, 2007). The more accurate the behavioral assessment, the more likely the treatment plan will be successful (Nelson & Hayes, 1986).
- *Determine the best strategy for changing the behavior from among the available interventions already applied.*
- *Create an individualized treatment plan in consultation with the client.* If the target behavior is anxiety driven, I ask questions that will allow me to construct a future hierarchy.
- *Correlate DSM diagnosis with my behavioral assessment.* (Not every behavior therapist agrees with this tactic, but this is how I prefer to operate.)

Negotiation of Therapeutic Relationship and Length of Treatment

My role is as an expert, and advisor, and a problem solver; I am directive but open in offering effective behavioral interventions. Because research shows the quality of the therapeutic relationship contributes to the success of the treatment, I am careful to be empathetic and supportive, or what behaviorists call *positively reinforcing.* I nurture a strong therapeutic alliance. The client is an active and cooperative participant in treatment and agrees to accept my expertise, instruction, and advice to guide him or her in learning adaptive behaviors and unlearning maladaptive behaviors.

There is no specified length of treatment for behavior therapy; this is based on achieving the goals. The client and I plan a schedule of appointments that fits his or her needs, and we revise the plan to accommodate outcomes. Termination occurs when we reach the mutually agreed upon goal. I accept presenting problems at face value rather than looking for hidden meanings.

The goals of treatment are to change the client's specified maladaptive target behavior to adaptive behavior through interventions based on empirical learning principles. I stress effectiveness and efficiency and accomplish the goals as quickly as possible.

Therapeutic Techniques

I choose from the numerous techniques and models of behavior therapy (described earlier in the chapter). I attempt to match the client, method, and problem behavior with the best intervention based on the evidence of research findings.

The nature of the client's problem determines the choice of the specific technique. For example, if the target behavior is to acquire self-care skills in a developmentally delayed client, I review the literature and find that contingency management is an optimal choice. I arrange the best schedules of reinforcement to reach the desired behavioral changes. Each therapy plan is unique and tailored to meet the needs of each client.

The Process of Therapy

Initially, behavior therapy begins with some form of functional assessment that extends from the first session until sufficient data have been gathered to create the appropriate treatment plan. The plan is then implemented. Behavioral outcome measures are recorded and analyzed and objectively demonstrate the changes in relationship to the interventions. Termination occurs once the client achieves the goals clearly outlined in the assessment. I implement a follow-up to ascertain that changes are permanent.

No matter how masterful a behavior therapy plan is, treatment is difficult when clients are unwilling participants, such as people who are involuntarily committed to an institution or who are compelled by others to seek treatment. Inaccuracy in data gathering can be a significant problem, as measurement is essential in planning, implementing, and assessing the outcome of treatment. Another problem is inadequate control over the treatment conditions. Token economy programs are particularly vulnerable to this pitfall. Reinforcement that the client receives from an unregulated source that is not a part of planned treatment, or bootleg reinforcement, can unhinge the contingencies.

THERAPY IN ACTION: DR. CARL WILSON AND THE CASE OF JONATHAN

To illustrate the application of behavior therapy, we examine a treatment plan for Jonathan, followed by excerpts from therapy sessions with our fictional behavior therapist, Dr. Wilson. Keep in mind the case excerpts are simulated interviews and represent the ideal of therapy. In reality, clients may take much longer to meet therapeutic goals. Table 9.6 provides a summary of Dr. Wilson's treatment plan.

Table 9.6

Behavior Therapy Treatment Plan for Jonathan

Assessment and Formulation	• Presenting problem: loss of relationship with Tuti and Darren; abrupt withdrawal of reinforcement • Behavior deficits: low rates in activity at work, self-care, social interactions • Behavior excesses: ruminating, crying over loss • Inappropriate stimulus control: crying at work • Escape and avoidance of aversive situations (e.g., situations that remind Jonathan of earlier losses and activate conditioned emotional responses)
Therapeutic Relationship	• Dr. W. is consultant, expert in behavior management, and source of positive reinforcement • J. is recipient of expertise and consultee and active participant who contracts with therapist
Contract, Goals, and Treatment Plan	• Change maladaptive learning to adaptive learning • Address behavior deficits: increase rate of responding at work, self-care, social interactions • Address depressive behaviors: withdrawal, lack of sleep • Gain appropriate stimulus control of J.'s behaviors: crying, ruminating, sleeping, eating
Techniques	• Contingency management for work, social, self-care at home, and physical exercise • Stimulus control: decrease escape and avoidance through response • Psychological education about behavior management • Therapist models appropriate behaviors
Process of Therapy	• Antecedent events: physical reminders of Tuti and Darren • Response: withdrawal (e.g., watch TV, stay in bed) • Consequent: relief of anxiety and escape from unpleasant emotions • Generalize responses from home to office and social settings • Therapy relationship: reinforce J. through positive verbal reinforcers • Education of J. about behavior therapy • Contingency contracting: identify sources of reinforcement (e.g., watch sports in social setting), homework to encourage higher rate of response, self-rewards; higher rate of response cost • Positive verbal reinforcement; implement program and change according to J.'s needs
Termination and Outcome	• Successful change from maladaptive behavior to adaptive behavior • Found effective reinforcers: appropriate social contact, exercise • Identified antecedent events, consequents, pleasurable social interactions • J. views therapeutic relationship as warm and supportive, approximately 15 sessions over 3 months • Mastered tools of self-modification • Total frequency counts of behaviors and changes • Increased positive behaviors (social encounters, phone conversations, etc.) • Decreased/eliminated depressive behaviors

Case Excerpts

The following excerpts are from sessions based on Dr. Wilson's behavior therapy case formulation.

Session 1

Dr. Wilson: First, I want to say I am so glad you are here today because coming here can make a difference. It takes courage to come to seek help. I firmly believe if we work together, your life can be better. [*warm, caring smile and positive statements serve as reinforcers*]

Jonathan: My boss insisted I see a shrink and sent me to the employees' assistance program where I was told I had a major depression. It's why I am not functioning on the job.

Dr. Wilson: What do those words *major depression* mean to you?

Jonathan: I have something really wrong with me. What if I can't control this?

Dr. Wilson: Words like *major depression* are labels that mental health professionals use as an official diagnosis. What is important is to look at how you are acting.

Jonathan: OK.

Dr. Wilson: What are you doing, or how are you behaving, that makes you call yourself depressed?

Jonathan: [*describes Tuti's loss*] I know I am depressed, and I just can't stand feeling this way anymore. I hate it.

Dr. Wilson: I think it's important for you to have some immediate relief from these feelings of sadness. Let's talk about what can help you to feel less sad and more satisfied. We can work together to set some specific goals for you immediately.

Jonathan: Yes. I want to do that. The situation is rough. I think about it all the time.

Dr. Wilson: How frequently do you think "about it" or the situation?

Jonathan: All the time.

Dr. Wilson: When you say all the time, is there ever a time when you are not thinking about it?

Jonathan: [*pauses*] It feels like most of the time. Maybe it's 90 percent of the time.

Dr. Wilson: But what's going on the other 10 percent of the time?

Jonathan: I am just OK. But I am not happy. I just sit there and feel little or nothing. But what bothers me is I cry at times. I go into the men's room so no one will see me. I'm not going to lunch or hanging out with anyone. I don't want to talk to people, not even to make casual conversation.

Dr. Wilson: Are you avoiding something?

Jonathan: I am pretty embarrassed. I don't want anyone to know what happened. I am avoiding people I guess.

Dr. Wilson: So if you change some of these behaviors, like crying and avoiding people, do you think you will feel better?

Jonathan: I suppose.

Dr. Wilson: Yes. Let's also look at other behaviors that you might want to change. May I ask you to describe a typical day? Please tell me what you do.

Jonathan: Well, I wake up at 2 or 3 A.M., and I worry about what Tuti did to me. I get up, light up a cigarette, turn on the TV, and stare at it. I don't really watch it. I get tired and try to go back to sleep. Most of the time I do not get to sleep till about 5 A.M. Then I have to get up at 6:30. I hear the alarm and drag myself out of bed. Before she left, Tuti woke me up and made coffee, and we would have a cup together and then discuss our day. Now I am alone.

Dr. Wilson: So Tuti's company during your morning coffee is gone! And it used to be a major source of pleasure. What do you do to replace these enjoyable moments? [*rewards*]

Jonathan: Not much. I skip coffee now. Coffee drinking makes me feel too lonely, too empty. I drive to work early. I shuffle my papers around and wait for lunch. Lately, no one has asked me to go to lunch so I go out and have a cigarette and then come back to my desk with a sandwich.

Dr. Wilson: And then?

Jonathan: I go home and watch TV. I don't want to go out and do anything. It's a waste of time.

Dr. Wilson: Is there anything that you do for enjoyment?

Jonathan: Not really. I am a strong guy, and now I want to be alone to nurse my wounds.

Dr. Wilson: Let's look at what is happening. It seems as if you are not receiving very much of a reward or pleasure for yourself. Looking at the history you wrote in your application, Tuti and your friend Darren really were your social support. Am I right?

Jonathan: Yes . . . and they are gone.

Dr. Wilson: Exactly! So you need to find other supports and activities that give you some pleasure.

Jonathan: And I don't want anyone else. I don't trust anyone. But I suppose you are right. I guess I am upset because I put everything I had into the relationship. It hurts. I've got to change my habits.

Dr. Wilson: Absolutely. We can learn new behaviors that help us to be more content and replace the old behaviors that are causing us pain and are not working for us. It will be easier to control our own lives and circumstances.

[*Comment: Here I explain some of the principles of behavior therapy to Jonathan; after explaining, I will describe how learning applies to his depression.*]

Dr. Wilson: What happens when we don't receive enough reinforcement?

Jonathan: I guess we become discouraged, and not want to do anything because we aren't getting what we are expecting.

Dr. Wilson: Exactly. So let's work together to change the circumstances in your life so that you maximize your enjoyment. What is pleasurable to you besides being in the company of Tuti and Darren?

Jonathan: I like to go out to a sports bar where I work. It is mostly guys there, and we watch the game. We make small talk. I drink a beer and then just seltzer. It's the company I like. And I can talk sports and nothing else there.

Dr. Wilson: Great. Think you might be able to do this?

Jonathan: Maybe.

Dr. Wilson: OK . . . exactly when? Could you do it one night this week? At 7 P.M.?

Jonathan: I think that I might be able to try to do it.

Dr. Wilson: Let's write up a contract between us. This way we can be very specific and figure out exactly what we need to do. It tells us what will happen if you do what we agree on or if you don't. What is a good motivator for you, or reward?

Jonathan: I like certain TV programs. I also like videogames.

Dr. Wilson: OK. Let's discuss this. [*determines specific parameters*] If you make one social contact a day, you can play one videogame at the arcade. If you do not make any contacts, you will have no videogames.

Jonathan: [*smiles while signing the contract, shown in Figure 9.1*] Pretty good incentive . . .

CONTRACT

Who: Jonathan   **Who:** Therapist
What: Make one social contact per day   **What:** Will report to therapist weekly
        with written record
When: By 9 P.M.
Reward: Can play one videogame for 1 hour
Response cost: No videogame if social contact not completed by 9 P.M.

Sign here:_____

Sign here:_____

SOCIAL CONTACTS

Date of Contact

	M	T	W	Th	F	S	S
Contact (Describe) Events before and after							
Name of videogame							

FIGURE 9.1   *Jonathan's Contingency Contract*

Dr. Wilson: We can also work on one other behavior this week. You tell me that you wake up at 2 or 3 A.M. and worry, have a cigarette, watch TV, stay awake until 5, and then avoid breakfast and coffee because it is associated with Tuti. Can you see any problem here?

Jonathan: Hmm . . . I guess it's obvious. I see the problem now.

Dr. Wilson: What is it, and how can we change this?

Jonathan: I suppose I should not smoke. It is a stimulant. And the TV does not help.

Dr. Wilson: You're right. So let's figure out how to change home conditions to maximize getting sleep. Can you come up with some possible solutions here?

Jonathan: Well, I could make sure that I try to relax and stop thinking about Tuti when I go to bed; then I wouldn't wake up in the middle of the night.

Dr. Wilson: [*stimulus control*] You take control of your environment—arrange the things, events, and situations around you. So you will be less likely to get involved in aversive events. We want positives around you.

Jonathan: OK. I suppose I could set up my bedroom to make it possible to go back to sleep—like make sure if I get up I don't smoke and I don't put the TV on.

Dr. Wilson: Sounds good. If you don't have the cigs in the bedroom and you do not go into the TV room, you are more likely to go back to sleep. Also, can you go out for a cup of coffee rather than stay home?

Jonathan: OK. I can try it. I hadn't thought of it. I guess a change of scenery might make the coffee look better.

Session 2

Jonathan: This week I stopped at the sports bar on Monday to keep our contract. Then I went back on Tuesday because it was much better than being alone. So I also had three lunches out this week. And know what? The crying at work stopped.

Dr. Wilson: Great. So you have reduced crying from six times a day to once every other day!

Jonathan: Yes. I also worked on other problems.

Dr. Wilson: OK. How did you do?

Jonathan: I have my plan. When you compare my five-day baseline with what I am doing now, it is pretty good, isn't it?

Dr. Wilson: Absolutely. I am impressed at your progress.

Termination

Jonathan: I think I understand how people who are depressed "lack reinforcement."

Dr.Wilson: Sounds like you have learned the basics of B-mod.

Jonathan: [*laughing*] It is from talking with you that I am coming to this realization. You are pretty reinforcing!

Dr. Wilson: Feel free to drop in anytime.

Jonathan: Yes. Thanks, I will do so if I feel I am slipping back. That book we used that describes the self-modification programs really helps. Once I learned how to do one, then I can use it again each time I need to tackle a new problem. It gives me the basics that I need so I can identify what may be maintaining an undesirable behavior. I am fortunate that I have learned "how to." I have the methods that can help me with most of my problems. But you have really helped me, and I appreciate it.

Case Comment

Jonathan's depressive symptoms were reduced and finally eliminated. His depression was caused by his losses, which resulted in a lack of reinforcement. Tuti and Darren were both sources of social and physical reinforcement to Jonathan. Their abrupt withdrawal left him with no immediate reinforcers. His activity level dropped, he found it punishing to interact with others, and some social situations became classically conditioned to anxiety as pleasurable activities dropped. The more he withdrew and the less he did found Jonathan in a vicious cycle of immobilization and learned helplessness.

Getting him to receive reinforcement was a first step. Contracting with Jonathan was based upon contingency management. His structured behavior therapy provided him with a clear rationale and plan. Jonathan's initial social contact at the sports bar decreased his avoidance of other social contact. Psychoeducation, contingency management, homework assignments, and cognitive methods helped to increase his activity at work, raise his level of self-care at home, enhance his social interaction, reduce his ruminations about losses, and lessen his crying at work. He also improved his problem-solving skills.

✦ RESEARCH DIRECTIONS IN BEHAVIOR THERAPY

Behavior therapy has generated a vast research base of support and has accumulated more empirically supported treatments than any other form of therapy (Emmelkamp, 2004; Kendall, Holmbeck, & Verduin, 2004). A comprehensive summary of the research findings on behavior therapy research would fill volumes (Lambert & Ogles, 2004). This section summarizes and highlights selective information on the evidence base of research for behavior therapies.

Historically, behavior therapists have routinely made research an integral part of practice. To begin with, a behaviorist treats each single case from an empirical perspective. A well-handled behavioral treatment case is not a loose narrative but a scientific study yielding rich empirical information. It tracks and informs the therapist if a particular intervention is effective (Stuart, Treat, & Wade, 2000; Warren & Thomas, 2001).

While sophisticated statistical analyses and complicated factorial designs provide one kind of empirical information, the rigorous experimental designs used by behaviorists, such as the ABA reversal and multiple baselines, provide practical clinical information (Edwards, Dattilio, & Bromley, 2004). For example, small-n studies have validated time-out and contingency management for the developmentally disabled; these interventions are at the heart of the behavioral management of children and have been used reliably over the years (Paul, 2004). The accumulated behavior case studies contain hundreds, perhaps thousands, of single or small-n cases, and are a tremendously rich resource for clinicians. The APA's task force has accepted a number of single-case behavior studies as sufficiently rigorous to show superiority to placebo controls or other bona fide treatment (Chambless & Ollendick, 2001).

The reporting style in behavior journals can be helpful to the therapist because the descriptions of the interventions are so transparent that they are analogous to mini-treatment manuals. Behavior therapists have also published volumes of treatment protocols, manuals, and compendiums of treatments for many clinical conditions such as anxiety, insomnia, and tic disorders (Barlow, 2001; Caballo, 1998). Computer searches allow quick and easy access to this wealth of information. This can assist the therapist in identifying interventions that are likely to help for specific problems (Horner et al., 2005). There is currently a movement to encourage therapists to submit their work to build a coordinated database of case studies, combining both clinical and empirical research (Barlow, 2007; Messer, 2004).

However, critics complain that behavior therapy single-case studies and small-n studies have limited generalizability. In addition, it is not possible to positively conclude that the treatment itself is responsible for the changes in the target behavior. The changes could be attributed to expectancy effects, the attention of the therapist, or some other unidentified confounding variable (Shavelson & Towne, 2002).

Behavior therapy for both adults and children has been included in numerous meta-analyses over the years (Bowers & Clum, 1988; Grawe, Donati, & Bernauer, 1988; Lambert, 2004; Shapiro & Shapiro, 1982; Smith & Glass, 1977; Weisz, 2004; Weisz, Donenburg, Han, & Weiss, 1995; Weisz, Hawley, & Doss, 2004; Weisz & Kazdin, 2003; Weisz, Sandler, Durlak, & Anton, 2005; Weisz, Weiss, Alicke, & Klotz, 1987). The overall conclusions are that behavior therapy recipients, regardless of the specific type of behavior therapy employed, are better off than those who received no treatment.

However, a number of meta-analytic reviewers conclude that behavior and cognitive therapies result in greater improvements than other theoretical orientations, especially psychodynamic therapy (Lambert & Ogles, 2004, p. 161). Of course, the claim of superiority of behavior therapy has generated intense debate (Shapiro & Shapiro, 1982). Critics argue that any advantage behavior therapy has over other forms of therapy can be explained in terms of weak statistical differences, allegiance effects, methodological differences, and lack of representation of other therapies for comparison (Berman, Miller, & Massman, 1985; Miller & Berman, 1983). Critics are also quick to remind behavior therapists that the equivalency effect is well established and applies to behavior therapies as well as to all major psychotherapies, yielding comparable measures of effectiveness (Wampold, 2001). Thus any claims of the overall superiority of behavior therapy remain contested.

When some specific behavioral procedures are used for some specific disorders, the intervention seems to be more efficient than other types of therapies. For example, behavior therapy in the treatment of anxiety disorders—such as agoraphobia, simple phobia, social phobia, generalized anxiety, and obsessive-compulsive—has had clear and consistent positive effects (Anderson et al., 2006; Feske & Chambless, 1995; Taylor, 1996). In addition, operant methods have been shown to be successful in the treatment of depression (Antonuccio, Ward, & Tearnan, 1989; Emmelkamp, 2004; Jarrett, 1990; Rehm, 1984) and sexual dysfunction (Emmelkamp, 1994). Behavior therapies have also been successful in treating substance abuse, with covert sensitization using cue exposure therapy as particularly promising. In addition, other methods with positive outcomes are community programs, aversive conditioning, and relapse prevention (Emmelkamp, 2004, p. 425).

Behavior therapies based on operant and respondent conditioning have been used extensively with children to treat problems such as autism, mental retardation, and attention deficit disorder. For behaviorally disturbed children, behavior therapy was as effective as medication or combined treatment when behavioral interventions were applied (MTA Cooperative Group, 1999). These therapies have been used with institutionalized children who have chronic mental illness and with developmentally delayed children to achieve specific therapeutic goals such as self-care skills (Corrigan, 1991). Such treatments have also effectively helped children with schizophrenia to improve social skills (Diden, Duker, & Korzilius, 1997). Systematic desensitization (for fears), assertive training (for lack of assertiveness), implosive therapy (for fears), and EMDR (for posttraumatic stress) have been widely used although conclusions about the effectiveness of EMDR are controversial (Lohr, Tolin, & Lilienfeld, 1998). Behavioral marital therapy has been shown to be superior to no-treatment controls (Shadish & Baldwin, 2005). Unfortunately, many procedures have become part of pop culture and are touted as being far more effective than can be supported by research data (Kazdin, 2001).

As mentioned above, the APA's Task Force on Promotion and Dissemination of Psychological Procedures recognizes a large number of behavioral treatments as effective (Chambless & Ollendick, 2001). The National Institute for Clinical Excellence (NICE) provides clinical practice guidelines for the appropriate treatment and care of people with various disorders in the United Kingdom. From these resources, we can conclude that many behavioral treatments are well established and empirically supported, including exposure therapy for specific phobias, behavior therapy for depression, relaxation for generalized anxiety, and behavior therapy for rheumatic disease (Chambless & Ollendick, 2001). Students can visit http://www.apa .org/divisions/div12/rev_est/index.html for the most recent updates on empirically supported therapies from APA.

Therapists can explore the constantly changing literature to integrate the information into their own practice when appropriate to remain current. The literature is filled with a large number of single-subject case studies and methodologically sound studies about behavior therapy. These cases studies can be helpful, especially in guiding highly individualized treatment (Shadish & Rindskopf, 2007). To view an excellent example of an evidence-based review, students can look at the treatment for enuresis conducted by the Canadian Pediatric Society (2005) contained in the online Appendix C.

What can the therapist say about behavior therapy to justify using it in treatment? A great deal! Behavior therapy, in general, is as effective as any other therapy and is the best available alternative for many specific conditions. For example, for enuresis, the bell-and-pad method of treating is very effective (see the online Appendix C for an exemplary evidence-based review). There is no doubt that more behavior therapies have been reported as efficacious and effective for specific problems, diagnoses, and populations than for any other type of therapy (Chambless & Ollendick, 2001).

✦ ISSUES OF DIVERSITY

Behavior therapists uphold the belief that behavior therapists must be culturally competent and incorporate a solid understanding of how the client's race, ethnicity, traditions, and value systems interact with treatment planning. However, there are issues pertaining to diversity and behavior therapy that merit serious consideration (Sue, 2003).

Although most behavior therapists claim to be value neutral, this may not be the case overall. Most learning theorists believe classical and operant conditioning work in the same way for all people—even for all species. This conviction has an unintended side effect in that the behavior therapist may be less likely to expect biases and, thus, be less aware of and sensitive to issues of diversity. Endorsing no particular value system can be construed as a silent approval of the status quo, and thus if the society is sexist or racist, the neutral therapist indirectly supports these conditions.

Furthermore, the learning principles underlying behavior therapy may not apply to all clients equally, and they may interact on some level with ethnicity, race, gender, or class. Certainly, studies have not examined any possible differences that can be a function of ethnicity or race of participants. No studies demonstrate that treatments are efficacious for specific ethnic minority populations. Some have proposed creating a research program to assess whether sexist biases affect the delivery of behavior therapy and to answer questions, such as, "Does behavior therapy silently uphold sex-role stereotypes? What kind of social skills training might be considered appropriate for males versus females? Are males or females more likely to be seen as needing assertiveness training and why?" (Atkinson & Hackett, 2004). Some believe that behavior therapists should be more active in promoting positive values that openly advance social justice and equality.

Another concern is that the behavior therapist may endorse objectivity, empiricism, and reductionism, or a worldview that upholds Eurocentric values. Early radical behaviorism left little room for the study of unobservable and mental behaviors. With such a large part of the human experience left unattended, one can speculate it may have affected clients from diverse backgrounds or with clashing values. Numerous cultures endorse nonobjective and holistic principles and stress the importance of spiritual, religious, and intuitive values. Even if the behavior therapist does not discourage the application of these nonobjective qualities, by not incorporating them into therapy, the behavior therapist may inadvertently discount or even "extinguish" them (Shook, 2002). However, behavior therapy is becoming more inclusive.

The criteria by which any behavior is judged as maladaptive or adaptive is a function of its social and cultural context, including class, race, gender, and ethnicity. When the therapist assesses the client's problem through functional analysis, it is important to be mindful of the role that society plays in the formation and maintenance of maladaptive behaviors. For example, if a teacher discusses the "hyperactivity" of a child, the therapist needs to be mindful that boys are more likely to be diagnosed with ADHD than girls. Through pointed questioning, the behavior therapist can assess whether gender bias has influenced the teacher's judgment. These variables must be considered carefully when the behavior therapist designs and implements the intervention program.

Behavior therapy does have specific strengths in relation to multiculturalism. First, the use of functional assessment means the therapist considers the impact of the client's specific life circumstances in treatment planning. Because functional assessment encourages a long, hard look at how the external environment contributes to the client's problems, it must weigh in on the effects of many variables, including social, political, cultural, and gender factors; these external issues help reduce stereotyping of any kind (Dinnel, Kleinknecht, & Tanaka-Matsumi, 2002). Another possible benefit from behavior therapy is that the client from a culture that values authority may find it helpful that the behaviorist acts as an expert and offers specific, concrete, and definitive behavior change plans (Sue, 2003). Future evidence-based research should examine how behavior therapy can be used with culturally diverse clients in a helpful and constructive manner.

✦ MAJOR CRITIQUES OF BEHAVIOR THERAPY

Behaviorism has been criticized for want of a coherent grand theory. Some say it is atheoretical and consists of bits and pieces of interventions supposedly backed by empirical findings strung together in a willy-nilly fashion. Also, because there are many techniques available, how does the behaviorist know how to choose one over another? Other criticisms are that there is such a blending of behavioral theories with cognitive therapies that behavior therapists have lost their identity (Wilson, 2005), and that many of the techniques used by behavior therapists can be explained by alternative models or perspectives.

Critics add that behaviorism's reductionist assumptions are overly simplistic and ignore humanist values. Psychoanalytic therapists and others consider the deterministic and reductionistic perspective of behaviorism to be cold, degrading, and dehumanizing. They argue that the "black box" view of the person neglects the emotional component of human behavior and change. For example, even the language is mechanistic. The terms *stimulus, response,* and *conditioning* make the client feel he or his is being operated upon, rather than an active participant in therapy, although the therapist says he or she is a collaborator. The use of animals to demonstrate the principles of learning can lead humans to the perception of that they are being trained and controlled (Zimring & Raskin, 1992).

Furthermore, critics charge that behavior therapy treats the symptom but not the cause of the client's problem, and as a result, symptom substitution occurs. For example, using cold baths to quell a fever caused by an infection results in a lowered temperature, but the infection remains. An antibiotic, however, treats the cause and ends the fever. Treating a behavior (superficial symptom) may end the behavior, but a new one will appear in its place. Behaviorists argue back that there is no convincing evidence to support the notion that symptom substitution exists; it is merely a fiction of insight-oriented therapists (Lambert & Ogles, 2004). Furthermore, behaviorists claim, the scientific application of operant principles is far more humane than spending endless hours in the unproven procedure of psychoanalysis. The growth of cognitive behavior therapy addresses some of these areas of conflict because more mentalistic processes are now incorporated into behavior therapy.

However, behavior therapy aims at working with very specific, circumscribed problems. Thus these therapists may have blinders on as they concentrate on removing symptoms or defining the problem in a very narrow way. It is neglectful of human emotion and meaning, and not geared to handle big picture problems as the existentialists do. The behavior therapist is hard-pressed to work with clients who are experiencing difficulties that are unclear or nebulous. The behavior therapist would be challenged to perform a functional analysis of "I don't know what is wrong. I am just unhappy with life in general."

Another shortcoming of behaviorists is paying too little attention to the therapeutic process, although it is established empirically that the quality of the therapeutic relationship is influential in the success or failure of behavioral therapies. Well-controlled studies are needed to identify and understand the elements of behavior therapy that account for therapeutic success (Gaston, 1990).

Some also argue that the behavior therapist has too much power in manipulating the actions of clients. Even if clients have given informed consent and behavior therapy is a transparent process, clients may not understand the consequences of allowing a therapist to set up control contingencies for their behavior.

Summary

- Behavior therapy consists of many and varied forms of interventions. It became popular and integrated into psychotherapy practice in the 1970s.
- Behavior therapy—based on classical conditioning, operant conditioning, and modeling—endorses the scientific approach, which includes rigorous, ongoing assessment, active treatment methods, strict evaluation of outcomes, and generalization of learning from treatment to life. Abnormal behavior is maladaptive learning and consists of behavior excesses, deficits, and/or inappropriate stimulus control.
- Models of behavior therapy include exposure therapies, behavior modification therapies, and modeling therapies.
- Exposure therapies provide exposure to the negative stimulus in a safe environment while eliminating escape and avoidance responses. Systematic desensitization is based on reciprocal inhibition, the use of anxiety hierarchies, relaxation training, and desensitization. Assertiveness training counterconditions emotions other than anxiety. Flooding provides exposure to a high-intensity anxiety-provoking stimulus until fear is extinguished. Implosive therapy is based on flooding with psychoanalytic themes. Eye movement desensitization therapy combines imaginal flooding, counterconditioning, and cognitive restructuring.
- Contingency management or behavior modification stresses operant conditioning and includes self-direction and self-control with contingency planning; token economies for groups in institutional settings; aversive conditioning, which is used sparingly due to ethical and practical reasons; physical and covert aversion therapy or counterconditioning a noxious stimulus to the behavior that needs to be eliminated; time-out; and response cost, based on extinction.
- Modeling occurs when an observer imitates a model displaying a behavior. Self-efficacy is the belief that behaviors can be performed. Problem-solving therapy teaches ways to solve problems. Self-instruction and stress inoculation show how to learn to deal with problems and stresses. Social skills training fosters adaptive interaction.
- The practice of behavior therapy involves functional assessment, which includes identifying the problem, defining the target behavior, educating the client, obtaining baseline data, and designing treatment; describing and implementing a program; collecting and analyzing data; and monitoring, reviewing, and revising. The therapist is the expert advisor and consultant to an active client. Therapeutic techniques are tailored to the unique needs of each client.
- Research has routinely been an integral part of behavior therapy. Many behavioral treatments are empirically supported. Claims of the overall superiority of behavior therapy have generated intense debate. Alternative explanations to the claims of superiority include weak statistical differences, allegiance effects, methodological flaws, and lack of representation of other therapies for comparison.

- Diversity issues are that behavior therapy may not be value neutral; learning may interact on some level with ethnicity, race, gender, or class.
- Criticisms of behavior therapy are that it lacks a coherent grand theory, is overly simplistic and deterministic, ignores humanist values, and pays too little attention to the therapeutic process.

RESOURCES

Association for Advancement of Behavior Therapy (AABT)
305 Seventh Avenue
New York, NY 10001-6008
(212) 647-1890
http://www.aabt.org

This organization has 400 members and publishes *Behavior Therapy and Cognitive Behavioral Practice*. The emphasis is on investigation and application of behavioral, cognitive, and other evidence-based principles to assessment, prevention, and treatment.

B. F. Skinner Foundation
12 Arrow Street, Suite 303
Cambridge, MA 02138
(617) 661-9209
http://www.bfskinner.org

The mission of the B. F. Skinner Foundation, established in 1989, is to publish significant literary and scientific works in the analysis of behavior and to educate the public about the science of behavior.

Joseph Wolpe Archive
University of Southern California (USC)
Doheny Memorial Library
3550 Trousdale Parkway
University Park Campus
Los Angeles, CA 90089-0185
(213) 740-2924

Joseph Wolpe's books, papers, and tapes are now housed at USC as a special collection. The Wolpe Archive holds the majority of his original works.

CLASSROOM EXERCISES AND ACTIVITIES

Theory

1. Define behavior therapy. What are the core characteristics all behavior therapies have in common?
2. Explain Little Albert's phobia of rats from a learning theory perspective (in terms of *both* classical and operant conditioning).

3. Break into groups of three to five. Designate one student to play the role of Mary, a woman with a needle phobia. The other students play the roles of members of a treatment team. Explain why Mary's phobia developed. Design a behavioral treatment plan. Decide if contingency management or systematic desensitization is the preferred method of treatment. Back up your choice by conducting an evidence-based review.

Practice

1. Design a self-modification program and describe the component parts of your behavioral plan.
2. Identify a target behavior for yourself and take a baseline to keep track of it for a week. Compare your experiences in one week with three class members. Comment on what you recorded, how you recorded it, and the issues you faced.
3. Fill out the sample treatment plan's in Chapter 1 (Figure 1.2) for Tuti for behavior therapy. (Both Jonathan's and Tuti's case histories are in Appendix A.)

Research

1. Mary (from exercise 3 in the theory section above) asks you, "How do you know this behavior therapy intervention will work?" Select an intervention from among the many available. Provide a rationale for your treatment choice and explain to Mary why you believe it will be helpful.
2. Find a case that you believe is an exemplary single-case design to demonstrate the treatment method that you believe is clinically effective.
3. Conduct a review of a systematic desensitization, contingency management, or EMDR in PubMed and PsycINFO. What did you find? Now modify your search with the therapy the key words: *and randomized control*. What did you find? From an overview of the available articles, describe and discuss the kind of evidence they contain to support their efficacy and effectiveness.

CHAPTER 10

COGNITIVE THERAPY

I concluded that psychoanalysis was a faith-based therapy and that if I was going to practice or teach therapy, it had to be empirically driven.

–Aaron Beck

The goal of this chapter is to present a general overview of cognitive therapy and to describe two major models: rational emotive behavior therapy (REBT) and Beck's cognitive therapy. The chapter looks at biographical information about two cognitive therapists, Albert Ellis and Aaron Beck, the historical context of cognitive therapy, and the theory, practice, and research of these models. Simulated therapists Dr. Rebecca Ellen and Dr. Alex Burnham will present treatment plans and session excerpts for the two models of cognitive therapy for the case of Jonathan. Issues of diversity and major critiques of both models are also included.

✦ HISTORICAL CONTEXT

Modern cognitive therapies arose in the 1950s, as their clinical, theoretical, and empirical approaches to psychotherapy became popular. Many psychotherapists had become dissatisfied with both the dominant models of behaviorism and psychoanalysis and believed neither alone was sufficient to treat clients in a timely or holistic fashion. Psychoanalysis focused upon invisible unconscious forces; it could be viewed as more faith based than scientific and was very time-consuming, expensive, and available only to a limited number of clients. Radical behaviorism, with its emphasis on scientific objectivity and empiricism, excluded mental processes as a legitimate area of study (see Chapter 9).

Because many therapists wanted to broaden the behavioral approach beyond its rigid dimensions, they sought to include a mediational or cognitive component along with behavior therapy, and the result was the growth of cognitive therapy. Some see cognitive therapy as an evolution of behavior therapy, whereas others see it as a revolution resulting in a new point of view (Arnkoff & Glass, 1992).

Albert Ellis (see About Albert Ellis box) was the first clinician to develop a systematized therapeutic approach to cognitive therapy, which he first named *rational emotive therapy* and then *rational emotive behavior therapy.* Ellis's work helped to ignite today's burgeoning cognitive therapy movement.

When Albert Bandura and Richard Walters published *Social Learning and Personality Development* (1963), in which they added mental constructs to the

ABOUT ALBERT ELLIS

Born on September 27, 1913, Ellis grew up in New York City. His parents divorced when he was 12. Suffering from a serious kidney disease and neglected by his parents, he valued being able to care for himself as well as his ability to understand others. With an affinity for philosophy, at age 16 Albert kept a diary in which he recorded his thoughts about well-known philosophers, sometimes challenging their opinions and arguments.

Despite the depression era economy, Ellis worked at a number of jobs, started businesses, and attended City University of New York, graduating in business administration. He aspired to be a writer, but when all of his manuscripts were rejected, he focused on studying human behavior and the sexual revolution. He graduated with a PhD in psychology from Columbia and began practicing in 1952. Although trained in psychoanalysis, Ellis found that therapy was more helpful when he was active and directive with his patients and assigned them homework. Eventually, he abandoned psychoanalysis and introduced his new form of cognitive therapy, establishing the Albert Ellis Institute for Rational Emotive Therapy in 1959 (Sheehy, Chapman, & Conroy, 1997). Ellis, who authored more than 70 books and 200 articles, first called himself a rational therapist, later a rational emotive therapist, and then a rational emotive behavior therapist.

Ellis, who was married and divorced twice when young, never had children. He had a 37-year relationship with the co-director of the Albert Ellis Institute in New York, where he worked for half a century. As president emeritus of the institute, he continued to demonstrate his prowess as a therapist every Friday night, meeting with individuals who walked in and paid a small admission fee. He died on July 24, 2007, in New York City at the age of 93.

Ellis described himself as both the most hated psychologist since B. F. Skinner and one of the best-loved psychologists of all time: "I usually tell it like it is. And I don't give that much of a damn what people think of me for saying it. That's unusual, since the world consists mainly of love slobs who need other people's approval" (Epstein, 2001, p. 1). Ellis summarized his last goals in life in this way: "While I am alive I want to keep doing what I want to do. See people. Give workshops. Write and preach the gospel according to St. Albert" (Hurley, 2004, p. 3).

---

model of radical behaviorism, the study of cognition took on an aura of scientific respectability (Bandura, 1997). By the 1970s, the cognitive revolution was flourishing. Aaron Beck (see About Aaron Beck box) developed his specific form of cognitive therapy with its emphasis on treating depression and anxiety, Donald Meichenbaum developed stress inoculation training and published *Cognitive Behavior Modification* in 1977. Bandura developed modeling and vicarious reinforcement. Other well-known cognitive therapists include Ellis's student Maxie C. Maultsby, who developed rational behavior therapy (National Association of Cognitive Behavior Therapists, 2004) and attributional therapy. Currently, cognitive therapy is the most rapidly growing form of psychotherapy (Dobson, 2000).

Cognitive therapy emphasizes the importance of thinking in human behavior and holds that thinking causes people to feel and act the way they do (Steiman & Dobson, 2002). *Cognitive therapy* (CT) and *cognitive behavior therapy* (CBT) are generic terms for a broad category of psychotherapy used to describe an expanding set of models and approaches that include cognitive and behavioral

ABOUT AARON BECK

Born in 1921 and the youngest of three siblings, Aaron Beck describes his nuclear family as loving and supportive, with Russian immigrant parents who encouraged his scholarship (2001). As a child, he broke his arm and a severe infection resulted that almost required amputation. From this traumatic experience, Beck developed phobias concerning blood, injury, and surgery. In medical school, he forced himself to overcome these fears.

Beck graduated from Yale with an MD in 1946 and joined the faculty at the University of Pennsylvania. In his work with patients, Beck compared the dreams of depressed and nondepressed patients and found the depressed had less hostility. This finding was at odds with the psychoanalytic belief that depression stems from anger turned inward. He also found that so-called masochistic clients wanted positive reinforcement as much controls. This countered the analytic belief that these patients wanted to be punished.

Doubtful of the validity of these analytic concepts, Beck moved away from traditional psychoanalysis.

As he became convinced of the importance of the role of cognition in mental disturbance, Beck became a cognitive therapist and an avid researcher, conducting numerous clinical trials sponsored by the National Institute of Mental Health (NIMH) to validate the clinical efficacy of cognitive therapy for depression and anxiety.

Beck and his wife Phyllis (the first woman to serve as judge for the Pennsylvania Superior Court) have four children: Alice, also a judge in Pennsylvania; Judy, who established the Beck Institute for Cognitive Therapy and Research in Bala Cynwyd, Pennsylvania, in 1994; Roy, an epidemiologist in Florida; and Daniel, a cognitive therapist and researcher in Boston.

In his late 80s now, Beck is an emeritus professor of psychiatry at the University of Pennsylvania. He consults at the Institute for Cognitive Therapy and Research, seeing difficult patients referred to him by other therapists. These recorded sessions are used for clinical training as well (Bloch, 2004).

methods, processes, procedures, and techniques, each with its own developmental history (Dobson & Block, 1988).

Cognitive therapy is also the name of the specific therapy originated by Aaron Beck (Hollon & Beck, 2004). Often these terms are used interchangeably (along with cognitive behavior therapy). To prevent confusion, it is helpful for students to take note of which meaning of the term *cognitive therapy* is intended by any author. This chapter uses *cognitive therapy* (CT) as the umbrella term unless otherwise specified. There are characteristics common to all forms of cognitive therapy, as outlined by the National Association for Cognitive Behavior Therapists (NACBT):

- Cognitions—not external events, people, or situations—cause feelings and behaviors, influence mental health, and play a role in the creation and maintenance of abnormal behaviors.
- Changing thinking is clinically possible and valuable. People who experience aversive and unwanted feelings and behaviors can learn to identify the thoughts that bring about their discomfort and to replace maladaptive thinking with healthier thinking.
- Dysfunctional thinking begins early in life, can dominate feeling and behavior, and varies in content according to the nature of the disorder.

- The Socratic dialogue and inductive reasoning can relieve symptoms and promote good mental health.
- Educational, structured, and directive perspectives and techniques are tools of change. Homework is assigned with the expectation that clients implement learning outside of therapy sessions.
- The therapeutic relationship is collaborative, but it is not the primary focus of therapy.

This chapter describes two of the most mature and well-known models of cognitive therapy: Ellis's rational emotive behavior therapy and Beck's cognitive therapy (Hollon & Beck, 2004).

→ THEORY OF RATIONAL EMOTIVE BEHAVIOR THERAPY

Rational emotive behavior therapy (REBT) deals with the emotional, behavioral, and thinking components of human disturbance. Ellis's theory draws from the core beliefs of the ancient philosophy of stoicism—namely, that it is a belief about an event, not the event itself, that makes people unhappy. REBT emphasizes that people create their own misery due to their unnecessary irrational thinking. Unhappy people can benefit from deep philosophical change if they use rational and scientific thinking to attain good mental health. The key concepts in Ellis's theory include REBT's A-B-C-D-E model, irrational beliefs, irrational processes, disputation, and effective philosophies. Ellis sees healthy, normal behavior exhibited in people who are self-accepting, other accepting, life accepting, and rational.

A-B-C-D-E Model

Ellis uses an *A-B-C-D-E model* to illustrate how humans disturb themselves and can un-disturb themselves.

$$A \text{ (activating event)} \rightarrow B \text{ (belief)} \rightarrow C \text{ (consequence)} \rightarrow$$
$$D \text{ (dispute)} \rightarrow E \text{ (effective philosophy)}$$

A is an activating event (a circumstance, person, place, or thing). *C*, the consequence, can be an emotional, cognitive, or behavioral event. It can be a negative feeling such as depression, rage, anxiety, shame, or guilt; or it can be a neurotic symptom that seems to flow from *A*. *A* is followed by *C*, and people tend to conclude falsely that *A* is the direct cause of *C*. In reality, *B*—a belief about the event—is the mediator between *A* and *C*. Activating events do not cause disturbances; beliefs about the activating event do. The interpretation of an event, not the event itself, creates mental disturbance. Whether an activating event is pleasant or unpleasant depends on how it is interpreted. Holding onto irrational beliefs causes unhealthy, negative emotions such as anxiety, shame, embarrassment, depression, rage, hurt, jealousy, low frustration tolerance, and guilt (Ellis & Harper, 1997).

At point *C*, people make themselves feel angry, guilty, anxious, or depressed by

- making dogmatic demands in the form of musts, shoulds, and oughts, such as "I absolutely must have John's love or I will die!" Or "John should treat me better, and if he doesn't, then he is a horrible human being!"
- "awfulizing" or saying the situation is awful, terrible, horrible.
- thinking that "I cannot stand it," which indicates a low frustration tolerance.
- rating self and others, saying "I am worthless" or "she or he is bad," or caring too much about what others think, thus exaggerating the importance of others' acceptance.
- holding onto absolutist desires to be liked and loved.

Once people upset themselves, they can enter into a vicious cycle and develop secondary symptoms. They become upset about being upset. Their absolutist thinking turns their emotional consequence into another activating event: "Isn't it awful?" which is followed by "I feel upset and depressed," followed by "Isn't it awful to be depressed?" followed by self-criticism for poor performance, guilt for self-condemnation, and yet further self-condemnation for the original self-condemnation. Finally, when they see that they have unsolved problems, they chastise themselves for needing therapy or for not changing quickly enough in therapy. Next, they perseverate in an endless cycle, and they worsen the initial emotional disturbance. This cycle can spin out of control until the person shows extreme self-defeating behaviors (Ellis & MacLaren, 2005).

Irrational Beliefs

Ellis identifies a number of irrational ideas that can cause and maintain self-defeating behavior. Table 10.1 presents a list of common *irrational beliefs* (IrB) described by Ellis. Each is followed by a healthier belief, which, if substituted for the irrational belief, will promote better mental health (Ellis & Dryden, 1997). As a rule of thumb, irrational beliefs tend to contain unqualified shoulds, oughts, musts, commands, and demands, whereas rational beliefs are conditional and are expressed as preferences (Dryden, 2002b). Most irrational beliefs can be reduced to three major core beliefs:

1. I must do well.
2. You must treat me well.
3. The world must be easy.

Irrational Processes

Underlying irrational beliefs are four *irrational processes* that humans frequently utilize (Dryden, DiGiuseppe, & Neenan, 2003):

1. Demandingness is based on a belief in universal musts—also called must-ification, must-urbation, and shoulds.

Table 10.1

Ellis's Irrational Beliefs and Rational Belief Replacements

Irrational Beliefs	Rational Beliefs
• It is an absolute necessity for adults to be loved by significant others for nearly everything they do.	• It is healthy to concentrate on gaining self-respect, winning approval for pragmatic purposes, or on loving rather than being loved.
• Certain actions are awful or wicked, and the people who perform the acts should be severely damned.	• Poor behaviors do not make people rotten. Certain acts are self-defeating or antisocial, and people who perform such acts are behaving stupidly, ignorantly, or neurotically. They could be helped to change.
• It is horrible when things do not turn out the way we want them.	• It is too bad or unfortunate when things are not the way we want. We can try to change circumstances so that they become more satisfactory. If that cannot be done, it is better to temporarily and gracefully accept their existence.
• Human misery is invariably externally caused and is forced on us by outside people and events.	• Neurosis is largely caused by the view we take of unfortunate conditions.
• If something is or may be dangerous or fearsome, we should be terribly upset and endlessly obsess about it.	• It is better to frankly face dangerous or fearsome situations. If it cannot be made safe and nonthreatening, accept the inevitable.
• It is easier to avoid than to face life's difficulties and self-responsibilities.	• The so-called easy way is usually much harder in the long run.
• We absolutely need something stronger or greater than ourselves on which to rely.	• It is better to risk thinking and acting independently.
• We should be thoroughly competent, intelligent, and achieving in all aspects of our lives.	• It is better to do well and to accept ourselves as imperfect human beings with limits and failings.
• If something once strongly affected our life, it should continue to affect it indefinitely.	• We can learn from our past experiences but not be overly attached to or prejudiced by them.
• We must have certainty and control over things.	• The world is full of probability and chance, and we can enjoy life despite this.
• Human happiness can be achieved by inertia and inaction.	• People are most satisfied when they are absorbed in creative pursuits and when they are devoted to people or projects outside themselves.
• We have no control over our emotions, and we cannot stop feeling disturbed about things.	• People have real control over their own destructive emotions if they choose to work at changing the musts, oughts, and shoulds employed to create them.

2. Awfulizing is based on a belief that awful, terrible, and catastrophic events fill the world.
3. Low frustration tolerance is based on a belief that the person cannot stand it when things do not go the way the person wants.
4. Ratings of self-worth and the worth of others are based on the belief that people can be rated either negatively or positively.

Disputation

To develop a healthier philosophy of life, it is necessary to challenge the irrational beliefs that lead to mental disturbances, uprooting them and replacing them with scientifically testable hypotheses about the self and the world. To do this, Ellis emphasizes disputing *D*, to produce an effective new belief, *E*, in the A-B-C-D-E model. He uses empirical, logical, and pragmatic arguments to dispute.

- To dispute empirically, one can ask: "Is there any evidence for this belief? Is it consistent with social reality? Is there any evidence against this belief?"
- To dispute logically, one can ask: "Is my belief logical? Does it follow from my preferences?"
- To question pragmatically, one can ask: "Even if this belief were true, is it really so awful? Can I really not stand it? What is the belief getting me? Is it helpful or self-defeating?"

Effective New Beliefs and Philosophies

New, effective philosophies develop when irrational beliefs are replaced with rational ones. From this, a person begins to acquire a healthier perspective on life and better mental health. Musts, absolutes, and shoulds can be replaced with nondogmatic preferences that are more reasonable. Bad or rotten situations can be seen as unfortunate, impossible circumstances can be viewed as tolerable, miserable situations can be recast as disappointing, and other people can be regarded as human beings with limitations. There are three values that can be used to counteract irrational beliefs (Dryden & Neenan, 2003).

1. *Unconditional self-acceptance:* Accept yourself with all of your flaws and imperfections, and at the same time, do your best to alter your own self-defeating behavior and poor behavior toward others.
2. *Unconditional other acceptance:* Accept others no matter how badly they behave, but try to help them to change unacceptable behavior. It is possible to accept the person but dislike his or her behavior. People are intrinsically valuable because they are human and alive.
3. *Unconditional acceptance of life:* Since life is filled with difficulties, developing a high frustration tolerance helps. The philosophy expressed in the serenity prayer—give me the courage to change the things that can be changed, the ability to accept that which cannot be changed, and the wisdom to know the difference—is helpful in promoting appropriate acceptance.

Normal and Abnormal Behavior

In REBT, the "normal" person is a healthy individual who is self-accepting, other accepting, and life-accepting. He or she adheres to a rational philosophy of life and uses logical self-verbalizations to replace irrational beliefs (Ellis, 1987). Healthy people are mature but constantly work hard to maintain their healthy personalities as they aspire to self-actualization (Ellis, 2004).

A person exhibiting abnormal behavior is a "disturbed" person, one who holds irrational beliefs that result in unhealthy emotions. Clinical symptoms, both neurosis and psychosis, are emotional disturbances that come from inborn tendencies to think irrationally. Disturbed people have low frustration tolerance and tend to make absolutist demands on themselves, others, and the world in the form of musts and shoulds (Ellis & MacLaren, 2005). Such people are disturbed not by things but by their *view* of things. Although it is very easy for people to maintain their disturbances and keep reindoctrinating themselves with irrational beliefs, people are free to choose to identify, challenge, and change irrational thinking (Dryden et al., 2003).

✦ PRACTICE OF RATIONAL EMOTIVE BEHAVIOR THERAPY

Now that we have examined the basic theoretical concepts that underlie rational emotive behavior therapy, we will explore its practice. Dr. Rebecca Ellen, our fictional composite therapist, provides a firsthand perspective of how she integrates theory with practice and applies the techniques of REBT.

Assessment and Diagnosis

Initially, I assess the client's thoughts, feelings, and behaviors to determine the nature and type of emotional disturbance. We immediately begin to work together to identify a specific target problem, and I obtain a recent typical, or vivid, example of a target problem that will allow us to find a clear activating event and a definite consequence (Dryden, 2002b).

I assess the skill deficiencies the client has, such as lack of assertiveness, weak social and communication skills, or vocational skills (Ellis & Dryden, 1997). I choose any assessment tool I believe to be helpful, but I prefer cognitive tests. I may choose to use a standardized clinical instrument such as the Millon Clinical Multiaxial Scale or the Beck Depression Inventory, if necessary (DiGiuseppe, 1991). I use this cautiously because standardized tests may be inaccurate; also, I do not want patients to accept test results as an explanation of what is wrong and falsely conclude that this explanation is helpful, thus deterring them from challenging their absolutist thinking. I avoid projective tests because I do not think they are related to effective treatment. I make *DSM* diagnoses, but they are not as important as identifying the client's core irrational beliefs. The best form of REBT assessment is ongoing therapy. I observe how the client reacts and modify my techniques based on those reactions.

Negotiation of Therapeutic Relationship and Length of Treatment

I am active from the start, but I reinforce independence in the client. I immediately challenge and confront irrational thinking and discuss the necessity of changing basic philosophies and giving up irrational beliefs. I develop a high-quality therapeutic alliance rapidly because I focus on reducing suffering and solving problems. If I assist the client to think rationally, her mood will improve, and this change will enhance rapport and help to cement a positive relationship.

I unconditionally accept the client, and I alter my style to fit each client. I am not overly friendly, overly intellectual, or overly directive. I am not afraid to admit to a client that I do not have the answer to a question, but I am willing to research the information. In this way I model self-acceptance of ignorance and illustrate the importance of an inquiring mind. I call upon the qualities of empathy, respect, concern, caring, concreteness, sense of humor, and the ability to confront the client and to appropriately self-disclose. I use the "reflection process," taking the time to stand back and consider the work that my client and I are doing together at any time during therapy (Dryden & Neenan, 2003).

The client contracts to work together to solve problems. We agree to prioritize goals, work on the most important and self-defeating symptoms first, and then address the others one by one. The client agrees to do the homework, and I check to evaluate its quality and help if the client is stuck.

Clients are generally seen weekly for 50 minutes and can recognize improvement in 1 to 10 sessions; but clients with deep disturbances usually need more—perhaps up to 50 sessions. After some fundamental philosophical change occurs, clients may return for refresher sessions to strengthen what they have learned. All forms of cognitive therapy are considered "time pragmatic"—that is, the work takes as long as it takes to help the patient reach the point of change that is satisfactory. Generally, REBT lasts from 12 to 16 weeks.

My long-range goal is to teach clients to achieve better mental health by adapting the REBT philosophy and applying the principles of rational living on a daily basis. My immediate goals are to educate clients in the use of the A-B-C-D-E model so they can learn how to transform unhealthy thoughts, feelings, and behaviors into healthy ones. My subgoals vary according to the needs of the client, and we decide upon and arrive at goals on a weekly basis.

Therapeutic Techniques

I use a number of techniques to confront irrational beliefs, including disputing and challenging, homework, and various exercises.

Disputing and Challenging
The Socratic method of disputing involves detecting, discriminating, and debating irrational beliefs. The client analyzes the cause of disturbance within the A-B-C-D-E format. For example, if a client says "Jane must love me or I'll be miserable," I query with "Why must she? Where is the evidence? Even if she did not love you, what would be the worst that could happen? What would happen if you gave up this belief? It would be nice if she did, but must she?"

Disputing helps clients replace unhealthy negative emotions (such as depression, anxiety, worry, rage, low frustration tolerance, guilt, shame, embarrassment, hurt, and jealousy) with healthy ones (such as disappointment, concern, annoyance, sadness, regret, and frustration). It also aids clients in substituting unhealthy think-ing with more rational thinking, such as nondogmatic preferences, wishes, wants, and desires, and helps clients to evaluate events as simply unfortunate rather than disastrous. As well, disputation helps clients develop high frustration tolerance so they can say "I do not like it, but I can stand it," and it reduces their tendency to generalize their overall or global ratings of self or others (Ellis & MacLaren, 2005). To reduce clients' tendency to put unrealistic demands on themselves, I use humorous terms (*musturbation, awfulizing,* and *shoulding on oneself*), which helps clients to reframe the situation and stop taking problems so seriously.

Homework

Homework is negotiated at every session, and it is reviewed and evaluated at each subsequent session. Assignments can be cognitive (the client rehearsing rational statements), imaginative (the client visualizing and solving an event), emotive-evocative (the client forcefully questioning irrationalities), or behavioral (the client facing a troubling situation) (Dryden & Neenan, 2003). Homework indicates the client is able to take primary responsibility for change and to integrate the learning from therapy into his or her everyday life. Most of the learning in REBT takes place outside the therapy session.

REBT Self-Help Form

The therapist can use the REBT self-help form during the therapy session (Figure 10.1). The patient can order these forms from the Albert Ellis Institute in New York City and use them as frequently as possible to learn the A-B-C-D-E methodology outside the therapy sessions.

Psychoeducation

A key ingredient of REBT is psychoeducation, which includes using books, videos, and audiotapes. The therapist and the client can draw from the Albert Ellis Institute's large library of educational materials to enable and facilitate self-learning. In addi-tion, I tape each therapy session and instruct the client to review the tape as a homework assignment.

Role Playing and Exercises

I also use role playing and other exercises to give the client practice in appropriate responses to problem situations. Acting out a role allows the client to acquire a repertoire of healthy and appropriate feelings, thoughts, and behaviors that he or she will need to adapt successfully. To decrease negative feelings, I ask the client to purposely act in a way that violates a minor norm, which would bring about slight disapproval from others in a social situation. For example, I ask the client to dress in an outrageous outfit. The technique helps the client to develop tolerance to neg-ative ratings and to be less sensitive to social disapproval.

RATIONAL EMOTIVE BEHAVIOR THERAPY
SELF-HELP FORM

A (Activating Event)

- Briefly summarize the situation you are disturbed about (what would a camera see?).
- An A can be internal or external, real or imagined.
- An A can be an event in the past, present, or future.

C (Consequences)

Major unhealthy negative emotions:
Major self-defeating behaviors:

Unhealthy negative emotions include:
- Anxiety
- Depression
- Low Frustration Tolerance
- Shame/ Embarrassment
- Hurt
- Rage
- Guilt
- Jealousy

IBs (IRRATIONAL BELIEFS)	D (DISPUTING IBs)	RBs (RATIONAL BELIEFS)	E (NEW EFFECT)
• _____ • _____ • _____ • _____	• _____ • _____ • _____ • _____	• _____ • _____ • _____ • _____	New healthy negative behaviors: New constructive behaviors:

To identify IBs, look for:

- **Dogmatic Demands** (musts, absolutes, shoulds)
- **Awfulizing** (It's awful, terrible, horrible)
- **Low Frustration Tolerance** (I can't stand it)
- **Self/Other Rating** (I'm/he/she is bad, worthless)

To dispute, ask yourself:

- Where is holding this belief getting me? Is it *helpful* or *self-defeating*?
- Where is the evidence to support the existence of my irrational belief? Is it consistent with reality?
- Is my belief *logical*? Does it follow from my preferences?
- Is it really *awful* (as bad as it could be)?
- Can I really not stand it?

To think more rationally, strive for:

- **Non-Dogmatic Preferences** (wishes, wants, desires)
- **Evaluating Badness** (It's bad, unfortunate)
- **High Frustration Tolerance** (I don't like it, but I can stand it)
- **Not Globally Rating Self or Others** (I—and others—are fallible human beings)

Healthy negative emotions include:

- Disappointment
- Concern
- Annoyance
- Sadness
- Regret
- Frustration

FIGURE 10.1   *REBT Self-Help Form*

Source: Reprinted with permission of the Albert Ellis Institute.

Another exercise is to ask the client to imagine a situation that is associated with an uncomfortable feeling, to face it directly, and to hold it in his or her mind until it changes from discomfort to a feeling that is neutral, comfortable, or even pleasant. With practice, the client develops better emotional control.

The Process of Therapy

Initially, therapy sessions are devoted to familiarizing clients with basic REBT methods, helping them to identify irrational beliefs and attack self-defeating premises, values, and mistaken views. We begin with the A-C connection, and I then move to the B-C connection as I help clients to fit their presenting problem into the A-B-C-D-E model. Together, we identify each underlying irrational belief and counterpose it with a rational thought, examining how clients feel after thinking rationally.

In the middle stage of therapy, clients deepen their understanding of REBT principles and use them habitually to frame their thinking about problems. We become deeply engaged in the Socratic method for our discussions and use the REBT self-help form frequently. If clients do not perform homework assignments faithfully, we explore why. With practice and exposure, clients become sophisticated practitioners of REBT.

Termination occurs, ideally, when REBT becomes the client's ingrained philosophy and enduring way of life. Since everyone is fallible, few clients achieve this goal entirely. More realistic outcomes are that the client reports symptom remission, there are improvements in the scoring of tests used in assessment, and the client is able to apply the tenets of REBT to his or her everyday functioning (Ellis & MacLaren, 2005).

THERAPY IN ACTION: DR. REBECCA ELLEN AND THE CASE OF JONATHAN

To illustrate the application of REBT, we examine a treatment plan for Jonathan, followed by excerpts from therapy sessions with our fictional therapist, Dr. Ellen. Keep in mind the case excerpts are simulated interviews and represent the ideal of therapy. In reality, clients may take much longer to meet therapeutic goals. Table 10.2 provides a summary of Dr. Ellen's treatment plan.

Case Excerpts

The following excerpts are from sessions based on Dr. Ellen's REBT case formulation.

Session 1

Dr. Ellen: [*after explaining the basics of REBT to the client*] What happens if a particular person does not reciprocate?

Jonathan: I know . . . it's happening now. I wish I were dead.

Dr. Ellen: Is it absolutely essential to have love from one specific person?

Jonathan: Yes. Without her I am nothing. I can't go on.

Table 10.2	
REBT Treatment Plan for Jonathan	
Assessment and Formulation	• Presenting problem: loss of relationship with Tuti and Darren • J. unaware of his underlying irrational beliefs • Avoids contact with friends, creating secondary symptom of fear of criticism and embarrassment (self-critical symptoms)
Therapeutic Relationship	• REBT expert • Build positive relationship using REBT to deal with problems and issues
Contract, Goals, and Treatment Plan	• J. agrees to learn principles of rational living • J. agrees to apply them to daily life to feelings of depression, anger at Tuti and Darren, shame about needing help

Techniques	• Dispute one irrational belief at a time and replace with rational ones; two beliefs J. focuses on are:
	  IrB: It is a dire necessity for adults to be loved by significant others for nearly everything they do.
	  IrB: Certain actions are awful or wicked, and the people who perform the acts should be severely damned.

Process of Therapy	• Immediately teach A-C connection; follow with other connections • Monitor progress • Deepen understanding and ability to apply A-B-C-D-E method • Follow through on action plan
Termination and Outcome	• J. changed his irrational thinking—"it is not Tuti who has upset me; it is what I believe about how Tuti should be that causes my depression" • Decreased symptoms of depression on any outcome measure • Adapted a healthier philosophy of life • Higher frustration tolerance, less awfulizing and shoulding on self and others

Dr. Ellen: Is it healthy to allow a specific person's love to determine your emotional well-being? I can hear Dr. Ellis calling you a "love slob" now!

Jonathan: [*smiles, then frowns*] No, but I need her.

Dr. Ellen: What makes you think that you need her or must have her love in order to survive?

Jonathan: I put everything into this relationship. She threw me away. I hate her.

Dr. Ellen: Do you believe Tuti's actions are so wicked she should be severely damned? Is she a rotten person? Or is it more realistic to say that her behavior has caused you sadness, regret, and frustration? She is a person who behaved badly toward you.

Jonathan: I still don't see how they could do this to me. I'll get even with them.

Dr. Ellen: Doing bad acts does not make a person a horrible human being, only a fallible person who behaved badly.

Jonathan: Maybe I deserved it. I must be a pretty wretched person for them to treat me this way. I am weak.

Dr. Ellen: So, if *they* behave badly, does that mean you are an unworthy worm?

Jonathan: I guess so. I am falling apart to the point where I need therapy. I can't even think rationally, that's how bad off I am.

Dr. Ellen: And then you are disturbed because you have an irrational thought and call them a name. You damn yourself for damning yourself and needing help and so on and so forth. Your thinking can result in a vicious cycle.

Jonathan: Yeah, well what can I do? It is a cycle.

Dr. Ellen: Do you also foolishly believe that the world should be a certain way, and that people must treat you well, and that it is really awful when they don't?

Jonathan: Wait a minute. [*anger in his voice*] Shouldn't the world be pleasant and easy and fun? What's wrong with wanting life to be good—or at least fair?

Dr. Ellen: Should? Where did you learn that life is fair? Where is it written in the universe "Life should be fair to Jonathan!"?

Jonathan: [*smiles*] Well I guess it's not really written anywhere.

Dr. Ellen: What is the evidence to say it must be fair? Look around. There is much more data to show that life is not fair. People are involved in tragedies, live in war zones, and get diseases—just by accident of birth. They did not "deserve" it, did they?

Jonathan: I never thought of it quite this way before.

Dr. Ellen: What does it do to you to hold onto a false belief? Do you think it is awful when things are not the way you want them to be? Do you think that everyone must treat you well and that the world should be an easy place to live? If you just can't stand it when things do not go your way, you will disturb yourself much of your life! You are shoulding on yourself, musturbating, and awfulizing. How does it make your life better to cling to these irrational beliefs?

Jonathan: Are you saying thoughts can cause feelings? If I control my thinking, I can control my feelings?

Dr. Ellen: I have a favorite story. I was on a subway reading the paper. Suddenly, I was poked by a sharp object. Enraged, I bristled. Who the hell was hitting me? I clenched my fists, ready to attack. As I spun around to swing at the s.o.b., I saw the "villain" who "hit" me—an elderly blind man wielding a cane, disoriented, and desperately searching for a place to stand. Did I feel dumb! And just as quickly as my feelings went from calm to rage, my feelings went from rage to pity. Where did the rage go? My emotions were changed by my thoughts. When I assumed malevolent intent, I felt angry, but when I saw a blind man flailing about, I felt pity. That's when it became crystal-clear to me: Activating events do not cause disturbances; beliefs about them do.

Jonathan: Something like that did happen to me. I saw this kid take a piece of gum out of his mouth and put it on the hood of my car. I went after him, ready to kill. I caught up with him, and I saw he was severely mentally retarded. His mother was yelling at him for doing that. I instantly felt sorry for him. I thought, there but for the grace of God go I!

Dr. Ellen: Good. That's it. You've got it. Let's spend the rest of our time today learning the A-B-C-D-E connection. I will give you a homework assignment to fill out the REBT self-help sheets. Here is a copy of the tape of our session so you can review and listen. I think we can agree to meet for at least five or six sessions and then reevaluate.

Session 8

Jonathan: The homework helps, but my mood goes up and down. It hurts so much. I am in such pain all the time.

Dr. Ellen: Is it painful because you are making it painful?. What are you saying to yourself to keep your irrational beliefs alive? Let's work on one irrational belief at a time. But for an overview, I see some specific irrational beliefs at B to replace with more rational beliefs. Let's look at the list on the wall. [*see Table 10.1*] A is the activating event. Tuti left you and is now living with Darren. What beliefs underlie the idea that this is what makes you miserable? You believe that it is a dire necessity, that you must absolutely be loved by Tuti and Darren. Your self-worth seems to be a function of how they treat you—even more important than preserving your self-respect.

Jonathan: Yeah . . . you're right.

Dr. Ellen: Do you see how you are must-urbating? Be aware of your demandingness. You continue to believe that Tuti and Darren are horrible, wicked people who should be severely damned and who should burn in hell forever since they did this to you.

Jonathan: Yeah. I know it isn't true, but I feel it.

Dr. Ellen: You loved both of them at one time. Are they really so vile you want them to suffer in hell, damned for all of eternity? If you replaced your irrational belief and stop insisting they should behave a certain way, how would you feel? See them as fallible human beings who make mistakes and whose behavior has been hurtful to you.

Jonathan: Yeah, you're right. I'd feel better.

Dr. Ellen: Accept yourself, others, and the reality of the world, and you will develop a higher frustration tolerance and a new lifestyle; and you'll be happier. It's not easy to uproot your cherished view.

Jonathan: It's hard, but I am trying not to say "must."

Termination

Jonathan: I think the worst is over. I have changed my view of life in general. It takes practice. I spend an hour a night working on REBT. I can say it would be better if Tuti and Darren were in my life. It is unfortunate they are not, but I can't depend on the love and acceptance of specific people to determine my emotional well-being. I am learning to respect myself. I'll have other relationships in the future. I did not believe that when I first came here.

Dr. Ellen: Of course. You know it. And you can schedule another session whenever you feel you need some support to stay on track or help with those irrational beliefs.

Case Comment

Jonathan's REBT resulted in a remission of his depression. He was able to deal with his sadness and anger, his avoidance of social contacts, and his fear of criticism and embarrassment because he learned, through the Socratic dialogue, to dispute his irrational beliefs. The major beliefs that were keeping Jonathan miserable were "It is a dire necessity for adults to be loved by significant others for nearly everything they do" and "Certain actions are awful or wicked, and the people who perform the acts should be severely damned." Jonathan eventually learned to replace them with rational beliefs. He now knows that he prefers to be loved by Tuti and Darren, but if that cannot be, it will not be the end of the world. Furthermore, they are both simply fallible human beings who behaved badly toward him, but they are not bad people who should be damned in hell. Jonathan adapted a healthier philosophy of life and higher frustration tolerance. As he practiced, he became more sophisticated in the use of REBT and acquired a REBT philosophy toward life.

✦ THEORY OF BECK'S COGNITIVE THERAPY

Beck's cognitive therapy emphasizes the role of cognition in human information processing and how it interfaces with motivation, emotions, and physiology. This therapy consists of highly specific learning experiences that teach clients to transform their maladaptive thinking into more productive thinking. The key theoretical concepts in this system include Beck's view of automatic thoughts, cognitive distortions, and cognitive schemas, systematic biases, and modes. For Beck, abnormal behavior results from cognitive errors.

Automatic Thoughts

When a person is in a negative mood, he or she should be able to identify a corresponding negative thought that preceded the feeling state. This *automatic thought* causes an affective state to arise. Automatic thoughts can become habitual and pass so quickly that people may not be aware of their presence, even though these ingrained habits deeply affect emotions and behaviors.

For example, a person who is awakened out of a sound sleep at 2 A.M. by the phone ringing may be likely to respond with a feeling of dread or anxiety. Without even being aware of it, fleeting thoughts goes through the person's mind before experiencing the anxiety. "Who is calling at this time? It must be an emergency. Something terrible has happened!" When the call turns out to be a wrong number, relief ensues. The preceding thought is likely to be "Thank goodness it's a mistake!" These thoughts are so automatic that few people are aware that they produced both anxiety and relief. In this way, they are similar to Freud's unconscious thoughts. Often, automatic thoughts are distortions of reality, which we discuss next.

Cognitive Distortions

A number of common cognitive distortions can cause and maintain dysfunctional thinking:

- *Arbitrary inference:* The person arrives at a specific conclusion even when lacking relevant evidence to support it and ignores information that contradicts the belief. For example, a man believes he is a failure even though he has a good job, a high income, and a supportive family. *Catastrophizing* is a form of arbitrary inference. An example is the person who fails one test, becomes extremely upset, and tells herself, "If I failed this test, I'll fail the next test, and then I'll fail the course, fail out of school, then I won't be able to get a job, and I won't be able to pay my bills. I'll be out on the street—homeless and starving."
- *Polarized or dichotomous thinking:* The person pigeonholes events in extremes or as dichotomies—either/or, good/bad, black/white—with no shades of gray. For example, the person idealizes the therapist for one session and berates him as worthless one session later. If a situation is less than perfect, it is seen as a complete failure. Unless homework is done

perfectly, everything is ruined. This is also called *all-or-none thinking* or *labeling*, whereby a person is judged to be all bad and labeled the villain, the jerk, the asshole (Burns, 1996, 1990).

- *Magnification and minimization:* The person conceptualizes something as more or less significant than it is in reality. In magnification, people exaggerate the importance of trivial problems. For example, a person is late for work once in a year and assumes that his job must be in jeopardy. When individuals minimize, they dismiss the importance of a real problem. For example, a supervisor tells an employee that if she is tardy one more time, she will be suspended. She laughs over the warning and is surprised when she receives her termination letter. *Discounting the positive* is another example of minimization, such as when the class valedictorian insists the designation does not mean anything valuable. Discounting takes the joy out of life (Burns, 1996, 1990).

- *Personalization:* The person attributes the cause of an external event to her- or himself even though there is no evidence to do so. For example, a friend is in a car accident, and the person assumes that he caused the accident because he was angry at his friend; or a professor has a scowl on her face as she enters the room, and the student assumes she must have done something to cause the professor's bad mood. Thus, the individual holds him- or herself personally responsible for an independent event that may be unrelated (Burns, 1996, 1990).

- *Overgeneralization:* The person makes up a general rule that is based on some isolated incident and applies it inappropriately to other situations. A boyfriend is late for one appointment, and the girlfriend concludes that he is an irresponsible person even though he has always been punctual in the past. A single negative event is interpreted as a never-ending pattern of defeat. Words such as *never* and *always* are used (Burns, 1996, 1990).

- *Selective abstraction:* The person takes the information out of context and ignores other information. He or she makes the assumption that only certain events matter, and they are generally those that are negative. David Burns (1996) calls this *negative mental filter*—where the person picks out a single negative detail and dwells on it exclusively.

Cognitive Schemas, Systematic Biases, and Modes

Humans process incoming information and structure their experiences into an individual schema, a structure that in turn influences the way people feel and behave (J. S. Beck, 2004). Contained in the *cognitive schema* is a person's perceptions of self, others, the world, the future, goals, memories, expectations, and past learning assumptions and beliefs. How people think about their experiences—including people, events, and the environment—and arrange them in their schema is at the core of their personality. If a person consistently distorts information, it can develop into a deep pathology.

A *systematic bias,* also called a *cognitive shift,* in processing information can produce a negative cognitive schema that leads to unhealthy emotions and behaviors such as anxiety, depression, and other mental abnormalities; these can result in further misperceptions, misinterpretations, or otherwise dysfunctional or idiosyncratic interpretations of external events (Burns, 1990). For example, Sara breaks up with Martin, and he concludes that the reason she broke up was because he is an inadequate human being. "I am a defective human being" is the internalized core belief and message and may be experienced as a physiological response, so that Martin feels ill, lethargic, and anhedonic; he may even experience psychomotor retardation. Cognitive schemas are latent until stimulated by a specific stressor or circumstance (Beck & Weishaar, 2008).

There are five types of cognitive schemas: *cognitive-conceptual* (store, interpret, and make meaning of the world, core beliefs); *affective* (positive and negative feelings); *physiological* (perceptions of physical conditions); *behavioral* (actions); and *motivational* (play, eat, study, and desire to avoid pain). Dysfunctions and distortions of reality can develop in any or all of them. When all five types of schemas act together as a system, Beck calls it a *mode* (Clark, Beck, & Alford, 1999). Some modes are primal because they are related to survival needs and include primal thinking processes that are automatic, biased, rigid, absolutist, and stimulated by misperceptions. Maladaptive modes are the basis of various pathologies, particularly those of the personality disorders.

Normal and Abnormal Behavior

A person behaving normally interprets life events accurately, has healthy and functional thoughts, and has positive cognitive schemas. A person behaving abnormally displays faulty thinking, makes logical errors and cognitive distortions, and possesses systematic biases. His or her dysfunctional thinking produces and controls dysfunctional moods and behaviors. In general, cognitive therapy identifies abnormal behavior in a way that is consistent with *DSM* diagnoses and has unique cognitive profiles for many of the individual psychological disorders (Beck & Weishaar, 2008).

Beck believes that people develop abnormal behavior or dysfunctional thinking due to genetic, biological, and environmental factors interacting to compound the pathology. Some people have a cognitive vulnerability or a sensitivity that predisposes them to develop a particular psychological disorder. Although the developing person is particularly vulnerable to unhealthy cognitive schemas, changes can occur at any time, even in later life (Beck & Emery, 1985). Parental negativity can play a role in the development of unhealthy thinking. Caretakers mold a child's early thinking habits. Psychologically healthy parents who reinforce positive basic beliefs and schemas, such as "I am good" and "I am loved and competent," are likely to raise healthy children. Psychologically unhealthy parents who encourage negative basic beliefs, such as "I am bad" and "I am loved only conditionally," are likely to raise emotionally unhealthy children. Trauma or critical incidents occurring at any point in life can activate negative schemas and beliefs (Nietzel, Russell, Hemmings, & Getzer, 1987).

Cognitive therapy makes use of *DSM* diagnoses and recommends specific treatment techniques (J. S. Beck, 2004). For example, the person who is diagnosed with hypomanic tendencies possesses an inflated view of self and the future; the person who is diagnosed with paranoid attributes has a negative bias toward others; the person who is diagnosed with obsessive doubts fears for his or her own safety; the person who is diagnosed with compulsions believes rituals help to ward off a perceived threat. An individual who is diagnosed with anorexia might use her fear of becoming fat to distort information about food or body image; the person who is diagnosed with hypochondriasis has an attribution of serious medical disorder; an individual who is diagnosed with suicidality harbors hopelessness and is deficient in ability to solve problems (Beck, 1991). An individual who is diagnosed with a personality disorder may hold core beliefs that she is helpless, unlovable, or worthless (J. S. Beck, 2004).

Beck's early work in cognitive therapy focused primarily on depression and anxiety, which are the most highly developed and researched cognitive profiles. The *cognitive triad* forms the personality profile of the depressed individual. First, depressed people develop a very negative view of self and see themselves as inadequate. Second, they interpret world experiences negatively. And third, they anticipate failure in the future. Selective abstraction, all-or-none thinking, and generalization tend to permeate their thinking. Their sadness, apathy, and rigid perfectionism bring about painful emotions. The core belief of depressed individuals is that they are inadequate and cannot control or cope with events. A paralysis of the will develops, and negative expectations about life, low energy, fatigue, and inertia prevail (Beck, Rush, Shaw, & Emery, 1979).

People with anxiety disorders distort information from the environment so that they harbor a core belief that there is danger when there is none. They are fearful, think there is a high probability of harm, and fail to recognize safety cues (Beck & Emery, 1985).

✦ PRACTICE OF BECK'S COGNITIVE THERAPY

Now that we have examined the theoretical concepts that underlie Beck's cognitive therapy, we will explore its practice. Dr. Alex Burnham, our fictional, composite therapist, provides a firsthand perspective of how he integrates theory with practice and applies the techniques of Beck's cognitive therapy.

Assessment and Diagnosis

My lengthy initial assessment includes an interview and testing. I administer the Beck Depression Inventory (BDI), a standardized depression questionnaire that can measure progress and provide feedback. The BDI, which has been used in numerous research studies (Beck, Steer, & Brown, 1996), has 21 short items that measure aspects of depression. I may also administer the Scale for Suicide Ideation (SSI) (Beck, 2003; Beck, Kovacs, & Weissman, 1979), the Beck Anxiety Inventory (Beck & Steer, 1990), or the Dysfunctional Attitudes Scale (DAS). I obtain a picture of the background factors that have led up to the patient's distress, current level of functioning, symptoms, and a *DSM* diagnosis. I alert myself to any suicidal risk posed by the client.

In order to assess dysfunctional thinking, I ask specific questions prescribed by Judith Beck (1995): What experiences in childhood contributed to the development and maintenance of the core dysfunctional belief? What is the client's most central core belief about himself or herself? Which positive belief helped the client cope with the core belief, and what is the negative counterpart to this assumption? Which behaviors helped in coping with this core belief? What is the problematic situation? What went through the patient's mind? What did the automatic thought mean to the client? What emotion was associated with the automatic thought? What did the client do then?

Negotiation of Therapeutic Relationship and Length of Treatment

I make the therapy process understandable to the patient, and I work as efficiently as possible to foster a relationship of collaborative empiricism. I actively try to discover and uncover the client's point of view.

The client contracts to provide the thinking, imaging, and beliefs that they experience in life situations as well as the feelings and actions that go along with the thinking. Clients agree to challenge their own assertions about self, experience, and the future. They will experiment with their beliefs by testing them as hypotheses. They work on homework assignments with the understanding that they will progress more quickly if they put effort into changing distorted beliefs outside of the therapeutic relationship and sessions. We generally agree to meet for the necessary number of sessions that will facilitate this cognitive change.

My long-term goals are to make clients into their own cognitive therapists. My immediate goals are to help clients diminish or eliminate symptoms by teaching them specific tools to improve dysfunctional thinking. I teach clients to (a) become aware of and monitor negative automatic thoughts; (b) understand the connections among cognition, affect, behavior, and motivation; (c) examine and challenge evidence for and against distorted thinking; (d) replace distorted and biased thinking with more reality-oriented interpretations; and (e) modify core beliefs and assumptions that bring about emotional distress and behavioral problems.

Therapeutic Techniques

To help the patient acquire healthy cognition, I use a variety of techniques (J. S. Beck, 1995, 2004).

- *Identify, recognize, and question underlying automatic thoughts.* The client may not even be aware of these automatic thoughts and may not understand the significant role they play in mood and behavior. The client needs to learn to critique his or her thoughts for inconsistencies, contradictions, and errors. The therapist helps the patient to learn to test hypotheses and to dispute dysfunctional thoughts.

- *Identify, recognize, and question maladaptive assumptions or themes in automatic thoughts.* Look for inconsistencies, contradictions, and errors within these assumptions. It is more difficult to identify maladaptive assumptions than automatic thoughts because they are more intricate (Beck & Weishaar, 2008).
- *Use logic, hypothesis testing, and Socratic dialogue to challenge automatic thoughts and dysfunctional cognitive distortions.* Use questions to encourage the client to engage in critical thinking and the Socratic dialogue. For example, What is the evidence that my thought is true or not true? What is an alternative explanation or viewpoint? What is the worst thing that could happen? How could I cope with that? What is the best that could happen? What is the most likely outcome? What is the effect of telling myself (this thought)? What could be the effect of changing my thinking? What would I tell (a specific friend or family member) if he or she viewed the situation this way? (Beck & Weishaar, 2008).

Exercises

In addition to these techniques, there are some specific therapeutic exercises that I use.

- *Activity scheduling:* It can be extremely helpful to depressed patients to provide structure for their activities. This helps them balance their time and energy.
- *Decatastrophize:* I encourage the client to face the feared situation. Ask, "What if the worst possible scenario happened?" Then take it to its logical conclusion. This helps to desensitize clients to the fears they are trying to avoid and to adapt problem-solving methods.
- *Decenter:* Clients who think they are the center of attention can be encouraged to observe other people and situations objectively and scientifically. These clients can gain a more realistic understanding of their role in their environment.
- *Redefine:* Clients can be encouraged to rephrase a problem or event in such a way that promotes problem solving. Therapists can help clients to think more creatively and develop new perspectives on problems.
- *Advantages and disadvantages:* With this technique, clients list the pros and cons correlated with different styles of thinking. For example, what are the advantages and disadvantages of thinking "I am a jerk" or "He is a bad person"? When the disadvantages outweigh the advantages, clients are more likely to move toward change.
- *Role playing:* I encourage clients to perform specific behaviors so they can experience the thoughts, feelings, and behaviors that need to be addressed. This practice allows clients to acquire appropriate responses through behavioral rehearsal.
- *Guided discovery:* I guide clients through experiments to help them gain realistic perspectives on life circumstances. Clients can correct maladaptive behaviors and logical errors if they become more obvious through imaging.

- *Coping cards:* With this technique, clients create a "card" upon which they write down problems, thoughts, beliefs, or actions. With my help, clients record alternative responses to help them to cope with the problem. For example, a client can change the automatic thought "I am going to fail at my job" to "My work performance is not perfect, but it is adequate. If my boss fires me, I can find another job and collect unemployment until I do. I will not be out of work forever and I will survive."
- *Group therapy:* Group therapy is an option for clients in Beck's cognitive therapy. Interacting with others with similar issues can be helpful. The client does not feel as alone, isolated, or different, and there are opportunities for positive confrontations to occur among those who know the nature of the problem.

Psychoeducation

Beck has produced a large number of educational materials to enable self-learning.

- *Daily record of dysfunctional thoughts:* By keeping track of personal, automatic, dysfunctional thoughts, the client is better able to identify the problem and to give self-feedback. For example, to find the automatic thought, the client first identifies the problematic situation and asks, "What went through my mind? What does the automatic thought mean to me? What emotion was associated with the thought? What did I do?" (J. S. Beck, 1995).
- *Triple-column technique:* Clients can use this technique to keep track of their moods daily. They first describe the event that upset them and record the negative feeling that accompanies the event, such as sad, anxious, angry, lonely, rating each one from 0 to 100. Next, in the middle column, they identify the distortion that underlies the negative thought in the first column. Clients use the third column to suggest a substitute thought that is more realistic, and they rate those thoughts on the same scale, 1 to 100. By creating three columns, the patient can practice tracking and countering dysfunctional thoughts (Burns, 1990, p. 92).
- *Homework:* Assigning work outside of the therapy session provides an opportunity for practice, self-observation, self-monitoring, and putting learning into practice. People can change their errors in information processing, challenge their distorted and biased beliefs, and contradict the automatic thoughts that fuel dysfunctional thinking by replacing them with valid thoughts (Burns & Spangler, 2000).

Cognitive Mapping for Case Analysis

Beck devised a cognitive conceptualization diagram that therapists can use to map the important elements of their patients' previous experiences, the formation of dysfunctional assumptions, critical incidents, negative automatic thoughts, and symptoms due to behavioral, cognitive, affective, physiological, or motivational schemas. A cognitive map provides an outline to use in analysis of the client's core beliefs, assumptions, coping strategies, situations, automatic thoughts, and reactions (J. S. Beck, 1995).

The Process of Therapy

In the initial phase of therapy, I assess the client. After the assessment meeting, each sessions last 45 minutes. I structure the sessions in the following way: I begin with a brief update, a mood check, a medication check, and a bridge from the last session. Then I set the agenda, review homework, discuss the issues, set up the new homework assignment, summarize, and give feedback. Although the client may feel controlled by the tight structure, he or she will soon appreciate the results (J. S. Beck, 2004).

In the middle phase of therapy, I shift the focus from relieving symptoms to correcting patterns of thinking. I help the client to grasp the connections among cognition, affect, behavior, and motivation. We test hypotheses and challenge evidence for and against distorted thinking. We find themes of automatic thoughts over time and across events. The client becomes increasingly more responsible for what occurs in therapy. We continue to replace dysfunctional thinking with realistic thinking and change unhealthy core beliefs to healthy ones. We modify the client's goals as needed. Termination occurs when the client is much improved or symptom free. The client substitutes unhealthy core beliefs with healthy ones habitually. The change scores on self-monitoring measures and assessment measures (e.g., BDI or SSI) corroborate the verbal reports. The client is now his or her own therapist. We plan on two booster sessions for follow-up and to consolidate gains (Beck & Weishaar, 2008).

THERAPY IN ACTION: DR. ALEX BURNHAM AND THE CASE OF JONATHAN

To illustrate the application of Beck's cognitive therapy, we examine a treatment plan for Jonathan, followed by excerpts from therapy sessions with our fictional cognitive therapist, Dr. Burnham. Keep in mind the case excerpts are simulated interviews and represent the ideal of therapy. In reality, clients may take much longer to meet therapeutic goals. Table 10.3 provides a summary of Dr. Burnham's treatment plan.

Case Excerpts

The following excerpts are from sessions based on Dr. Burnham's cognitive therapy case formulation.

Session 1

Dr. Burnham: Let's get to work immediately so you will feel better. I would like to set an agenda for our first session. I'll suggest some items to work on and then ask you to add to the agenda. Is that all right with you?

Table 10.3

Beck's Cognitive Therapy Treatment Plan for Jonathan

Assessment and Formulation	• Presenting problem: loss of relationship with Tuti and Darren • BDI scores indicate deep depression; SSI shows J. is not at risk for suicide • Schema contains cognitive triad with negative view of self, world, future, and hopelessness as well as paralysis of the will, with low energy, fatigue, inertia • Central core beliefs—"I cannot control events or cope with them, and I am inadequate" • History of early traumatic relationship with father and abandonment motif with mother help development and maintenance of the core dysfunctional belief • Recent loss reactivates this schema and systematic bias
Therapeutic Relationship	• Collaborative empiricism • Good relationship necessary but not sufficient for change • Guide or catalyst to help client learn cognitive therapy • Client attends, learns cognitive therapy method, homework
Contract, Goals, and Treatment Plan	• Lower BDI scores; decrease depression • Eliminate suicidality—scores show little risk • Help increase positive view of self, world, future • Help feel in control of events and cope better • Modify core belief "I cannot control events" to "I can control my life; I am adequate and competent" • Promote more realistic and adaptive thinking • Meet weekly, twice a week at first
Techniques	• Teach J. to identify, observe, monitor own thinking • Socratic disputing of specific distorted beliefs: all-or-none thinking of "I am a failure; loser; inadequate"; I will always be lonely; they are jerks; abstraction or ignoring any past successes; overgeneralization • Activity scheduling • Homework • Problem-solving and coping skills • Deepen understanding and ability to apply
Process of Therapy	• Ongoing assessment for depression and suicidality • Monitor progress • Test thoughts against reality • Teach Jonathan to identify, evaluate, and begin to change dysfunctional thinking
Termination and Outcome	• BDI and DAS scales show improvement • Transform dysfunctional thinking and change negative schemas into healthier ones

Jonathan: I suppose. OK.

Dr. Burnham: Today we begin to know each other. I'd like to know how you are feeling, what brought you here, and what you expect to get, as well as what you already know about cognitive therapy. I'll explain to you what will happen and how homework will help. At the end, I'll summarize our session and ask for feedback from you. Is there anything you would like to put on the agenda today?

Jonathan: Yes. Feeling hopeless.

Dr. Burnham: What part of this situation makes you feel the most hopeless?

Jonathan: Being without Tuti. I feel so alone.

Dr. Burnham: I want you to know there is a very strong link between thinking and feeling. In talking with you for just this short time, I have noticed that you are saying some things to yourself that are upsetting you a great deal. What did you tell yourself just before you began to get tearful and quiet?

Jonathan: I guess nothing will ever change. I will always be miserable. I cannot imagine a future without Tuti.

Dr. Burnham: When this comes into your mind, you obviously get very upset. Let's work together to see why this thought has such an effect on you. Let's try to get at a method to relieve some of your pain.

Jonathan: I guess we can try, but I don't know how anything can help.

Dr. Burnham: The first thing I want you to do is to describe the situations or the actual events that upset you. While we are talking, we can write them down on this flip chart. Also, add in any physical sensations, if you have any.

Jonathan: OK . . . [*writes*] Tuti and my best friend betrayed me. I felt sick and tired.

Dr. Burnham: Now I want to ask you what thoughts and images went through your mind when you thought about this situation?

Jonathan: I don't know. I just feel. I don't think about anything.

Dr. Burnham: You may not be aware of your thoughts at the time. It may seem that the feeling just comes, but tune in to your inner self. Often there is an automatic thought, or one that you are hardly aware of unless you pay attention to it. Let's say you had a fear of closed spaces, and you are waiting for an elevator. You feel afraid and want to run away. You think it is just a feeling, but you had an automatic thought. You told yourself something—like an elevator is a dangerous place: "It can plunge downward and I will be dead!" You may not be aware of these thoughts. Let's try to pinpoint the automatic thought as much as you can.

Jonathan: Well, I guess I thought I was left behind and defective, or worthless. I am a loser, and I hung out with a bunch of jerks who screwed me over.

Dr. Burnham: Now let's estimate how much you actually believe each of these thoughts. Rate them from not at all, or 0 percent, to completely, or 100 percent.

Jonathan: I think at least 90 percent. I feel that no one would ever love me again. And I guess I believe they are jerks just 50 percent.

Dr. Burnham: OK. What emotions did you feel at the time? Rate your negative feelings on a scale of 1 to 100. Make 1 not feeling much at all and 100 the most intense feeling you could ever have. Rate as many feelings as you experience. If you feel anger, rate it from 0 to 100. If you also feel sorrow or guilt, rate it as well.

Jonathan: My anger is a 99. I want to kill them both. And my sorrow is at 99 because I wish I were dead. But I really would not do either, and I feel like a loser at 100 percent.

Dr. Burnham: Can you see the distorted thinking when you call yourself a loser?

Jonathan: I guess it doesn't help to think of yourself as a loser.

Dr. Burnham: So you jumped to a conclusion, didn't you? You drew a specific conclusion with no evidence to support it. You also ignore contradictory information.

Jonathan: I suppose.

Dr. Burnham: Let me challenge your belief now so that in the future hopefully you will learn to challenge your beliefs yourself. Jonathan, what is the evidence to support your automatic thoughts "I am a loser" and "I will always be lonely and miserable"?

Jonathan: The fact that I lost Tuti is absolute proof.

Dr. Burnham: Where is the evidence that you are a total loser? Aren't you generalizing, ignoring the good things that have happened? Can you conclude you do nothing right in any aspect of your life?

Jonathan: I suppose not.

Dr. Burnham: What is the worst that can happen now that Tuti is gone?

Jonathan: I could be alone forever. I could kill myself because of loneliness.

Dr. Burnham: What is the best that can happen?

Jonathan: I suppose Tuti can come back. Or I find someone better than Tuti.

Dr. Burnham: What is the most realistic outcome?

Jonathan: I could meet someone else and have a different relationship.

Dr. Burnham: What is the effect of believing your automatic thoughts "I am a loser" or "I am inadequate" and "I'll never love again"?

Jonathan: It makes me depressed.

Dr. Burnham: What is the effect of changing your thinking to be more realistic?

Jonathan: I'd feel better.

Dr. Burnham: What advice would you give to a good friend in this situation?

Jonathan: I'd tell him hang in there. Get through the worst of it. Your life will get better. If you met Tuti, you will meet someone else. Since you had a good relationship for over 10 years, the chances are you will again. Many people have more than one significant relationship, and often their later ones are better. Also, what about Tuti's role in this? Relationships go two ways. Don't blame her, but no one is perfect, so do critique her role in this as well as Darren's.

Dr. Burnham: Good. Can you see that you need to change the way you think in order to change the way you feel? Seems as if you made your purpose in life to revolve around Tuti. Your automatic thoughts are based on the false assumptions that you need Tuti in order to survive and without her you will be unable to function, or be incapacitated. We all develop schemas, or a kind of cognitive frame. Does yours rely upon Tuti for your self-esteem? Are you saying that unless you have Tuti that you are defective or inadequate and will never have another relationship? Now, if this is your hypothesis, let's test it.

Jonathan: It is, isn't it? It makes me depressed.

Dr. Burnham: Your homework for tonight is to fill out the dysfunctional thought record and bring it back tomorrow.

Session 3

Dr. Burnham: Let's agree on an agenda for today, our third session. I need to check on your mood, how you are feeling, to know how you were after last week's session, and any concerns or problems that may have arisen. Let's review your homework. In the remainder of the session, we'll work together to devise a cognitive conceptualization diagram [*see Figure 10.2*].

Jonathan: I'm feeling better. Doing my homework I identified some automatic thoughts. I say, I really need Tuti, and without her I am nothing. The automatic thoughts that come before it are "I am falling apart, I am a loser, and I will always be alone."

Dr. Burnham: Now, how can you consistently challenge these thoughts so they do not cause the depression? We need to get to the underlying assumptions.

Jonathan: There are some experiences contributing to my core dysfunctional belief. My dad used to say "I'm a loser. I can't even discipline my son!" I think I took it on from him. But I also received a positive belief from my mom, who told me that I should try

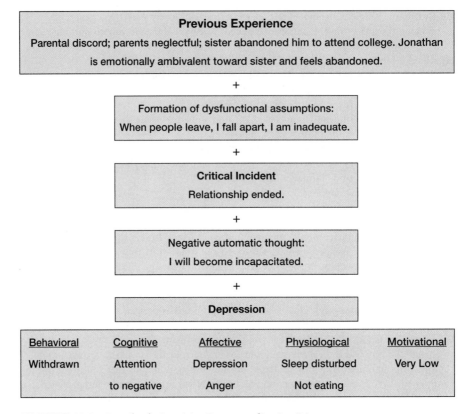

Previous Experience

Parental discord; parents neglectful; sister abandoned him to attend college. Jonathan is emotionally ambivalent toward sister and feels abandoned.

+

Formation of dysfunctional assumptions:

When people leave, I fall apart, I am inadequate.

+

Critical Incident

Relationship ended.

+

Negative automatic thought:

I will become incapacitated.

+

Depression

Behavioral	Cognitive	Affective	Physiological	Motivational
Withdrawn	Attention	Depression	Sleep disturbed	Very Low
	to negative	Anger	Not eating	

FIGURE 10.2   *Jonathan's Cognitive Conceptualization Diagram*

Source: Based on J. S. Beck, 1995.

to understand that my dad was easily discouraged, but I had extra energy, motivation, and would succeed. So is it possible I developed a motivation to work hard and succeed in my studies, and that has helped me to cope with this core belief?

Dr. Burnham: Sure, sounds as if you are discovering what is at the center of your distorted thinking. Let's try something. You have written down the upsetting event and told me you have feelings of panic, sadness, and anger at 100 percent. Let's go through each thought and ask, "If this thought were true, why would it be so upsetting to you?"

Jonathan: Since Tuti left, I am falling apart. I can't go on.

Dr. Burnham: What is so upsetting about that thought?

Jonathan: I'll never find anyone like her.

Dr. Burnham: What is so upsetting about that?

Jonathan: I'll miss her and be hurting for the rest of my life. I will always feel empty and will always wonder where she is and what is she doing.

Dr. Burnham: What is so upsetting about that?

Jonathan: I'll be in emotional pain forever, and I won't be able to function. I think I would want to end my life to stop the pain.

Dr. Burnham: Let's test your hypothesis. What is the evidence to say you will feel this way? And is there any evidence that it is not true?

Jonathan: Well, before I met Tuti, I had several other girlfriends, and we did get along well.

Dr. Burnham: Good. What are the advantages and disadvantages of holding your negative belief that you won't be able to function and that you'll always miss her? Is it helpful or self-defeating?

Jonathan: There aren't many advantages to thinking this thought. I guess on some level I think I'll get her back if I let her know how much I am suffering. And the disadvantages are many, including suffering, feeling bad about myself, and being depressed.

Dr. Burnham: Let's try an experiment. I want you to plan some activities. Let's do a schedule for tomorrow. What are some possible pleasurable activities?

Jonathan: Going to the mall with George. Also taking a walk alone to the reservoir. It is beautiful there.

Dr. Burnham: This will be the homework for this week. And write down what you felt and rate both how empty you felt and how much you enjoyed it.

Session 4

Jonathan: I guess I was surprised at how much I enjoyed the activities from last week's homework. I actually found myself feeling happy and not empty for a while. I was not feeling as if I was falling apart at all. When it ended, though, I felt empty and depressed again.

Dr. Burnham: So, it is possible to enjoy yourself for a short time. Do you think that this could increase?

Jonathan: I guess it could.

Dr. Burnham: You learned you are not totally without enjoyment and that your maladaptive assumptions, that you will fall apart and be empty forever without Tuti, and that you are a loser, are not the case. While you do not like that your relationship ended, it does not make you a total loser and you can function. You can do other things that make you feel good.

Termination

Dr. Burnham: You really have learned how to apply cognitive therapy to yourself and to change depressing thoughts. You have practiced it on a regular basis, and I see you have identified and coped with your problems. Our collaboration has been beneficial, and you are excellent at helping yourself now. You are more optimistic, and you look at yourself more objectively. I have confidence you will continue to do well without coming to see me on a regular basis.

Jonathan: Yes, I agree. I feel much more confident. I know I am not a loser. I can't believe how long I have been telling myself that without realizing it. I feel pretty confident, but what if I slip back?

Dr. Burnham: Feel free to call for an appointment anytime. You might also consider joining one of the groups, or you might just want to check in if you think it will be helpful.

Jonathan: Thanks. I think I'll join one of the groups in about a month. Thanks again.

Case Comment

Jonathan worked through his deep depression in 30 sessions over a 7-month period. Therapy provided Jonathan with a road map to examine the cognitive vulnerabilities that predisposed him to depression and to help himself out of the negative triad with his negative view of himself, the world, and his belief that he will be a failure in the future. He kept a dysfunctional thought record. He learned to identify and examine his distorted thinking and automatic thoughts. He tended to generalize (if Tuti left me I must be a loser, and I will never find anyone else to be with me) and selectively abstract (if I can't function well now, I never will again). He tended to take information out of context and ignore his past successes at work, catastrophizing about his personal and professional future.

As therapy progressed, he was able to look at a problematic situation (e.g., Tuti leaving), and identify what specific automatic thoughts went through his mind, such as I will fall apart, I am a loser, I am inadequate. The automatic thoughts meant to him that he might always be alone, that he would be incapacitated, and the emotions that were associated with the automatic thoughts were panic, hopelessness, and anger. Thinking that Tuti and Darren were jerks fueled his anger. He learned to debate his own distorted thinking through the Socratic method. When he successfully performed homework—increasing his social interactions—he became more assured he could do things differently. With his new cognitive set, he is better able to deal with his issues of depression.

✦ Research Directions in Cognitive Therapy

The evidence base for cognitive therapy, also labeled cognitive behavior therapy, (Beck, 2005), is strong, with a long history. The literature contains over 325 outcome studies on cognitive therapies and cognitive behavioral interventions and numerous meta-analyses (Butler, Chapman, Forman, & Beck, 2006). Various cognitive therapies have been shown to be efficacious and effective for both adult and child populations (Beck, 2005; DeRubeis & Crits-Christoph, 1998; Kazdin & Weis, 1998). The sheer abundance and complexity of empirical research for cognitive therapy is impressive. As is the case for behavior therapy, a summary of the research on cognitive therapy would fill volumes (Hollon & Beck, 2004; Lambert, Garfield, & Bergin, 2004). This section highlights selective and relevant information.

Early research on cognitive therapy is illustrated in the landmark study by the NIMH: Treatment of Depression Collaborative Research Program (TDCRP) (Elkin et al., 1989). With 250 patients in three geographic locations, the longitudinal study with exemplary methodology compared cognitive therapy, interpersonal therapy, pharmacotherapy, and placebo. The design included standardization of research practice, randomized clinical trials, specific diagnostic categories of patients, trained therapists, manualized treatment, adherence checks, and sophisticated data analysis techniques (Elkin, 1994). This study was the prototype for many others that followed, delivering strong support for cognitive therapy. The results showed that clients in all treatments showed significant reduction in depressive symptoms and improvement in functioning. Both psychotherapies—cognitive therapy and interpersonal therapy—were effective. Without regard to initial severity of depression, there was no evidence of greater effectiveness of one of the psychotherapies and no evidence that either of the psychotherapies was significantly less effective than medication and clinical management (Elkin, Gibbons, Shea, & Shaw, 1996). The online Appendix C contains links to the NIMH collaborative study and follow-up studies as well as to the Treatment for Adolescents with Depression (TADS) study, an important current, randomized control trial comparing cognitive therapies and medications in depressed teenagers.

Numerous evidence-based reviews and meta-analyses of cognitive therapies (which are also sometimes called *cognitive behavior therapies* by researchers) have been conducted. A recent meta-analysis of 14 separate meta-analytic studies, encompassing over 9,000 clients, showed that from 68 to 87 percent of patients improved when cognitive therapy was compared to no-treatment, wait list, and placebo controls (DeRubeis & Crits-Cristoph, 1998). Other meta-analyses provide similar support for the efficacy and effectiveness of cognitive behavior therapy (Gloaguen, Cottraux, Cucherat, & Blackburn, 1998; Reinecke, Ryan, & DuBois, 1998; Robinson, Berman, & Neimeyer, 1990). Recent studies show clients who received cognitive therapy had lower relapse rates than those who received antidepressants and had lessened symptoms of depression and anxiety, as well as more enduring effects (DeRubeis et al., 2005; Hollon et al., 2005; Hollon, Stewart, & Strunk, 2006).

Cognitive therapy is effective with clients with a number of specific clinical disorders. In a review of 16 meta-analyses, cognitive therapies had a large effect size not only for unipolar depression, but also for generalized anxiety disorder, panic disorder with or without agoraphobia, social phobia, posttraumatic stress syndrome, childhood depression, and anxiety. Moderate effect sizes were found for marital distress, anger, childhood disorders, and chronic pain (Butler et al., 2006).

Cognitive therapy is also effective for the treatment of bulimia nervosa and binge eating, although its usefulness in treating anorexia is not as well established. Cognitive therapy is effective for the treatment of internalizing disorders in children and adolescents, with potential for the effective treatment of personality disorders and even schizophrenia (Hollon & Beck, 2004).

Research also validates some of the underlying theoretical assumptions of cognitive therapy. The notion that disorders are likely to be based on specific beliefs, known as the *specificity of content hypothesis,* is empirically supported for depression and anxiety disorders (Beck, Freeman, & Associates, 1990). The cognitive triad—or unrealistic negative views about the world, self, and future—can dominate the thinking of a depressed person (Clark, Beck, & Brown, 1989). Those suffering from anxiety conditions tend to see the world as a place filled with harm and danger (Franklin & Foa, 2002). Research has shown that cognitive distortions are associated with specific disorders (Brown, Hammen, Craske, & Wickens, 1995), and more is planned for the future.

Research on cognitive therapy has its critics, who say that the results of the research are not as clear as is being touted by advocates of cognitive therapy. First, they say that the definition of cognitive therapy is very broad. Reviews often blend a variety of techniques and report on hybrid models, which combine behavioral and cognitive techniques. It is advisable to look up any particular study to assess if the form of cognitive therapy that is researched is true to a particular model or uses a generic brand of cognitive therapy. Critics remind cognitive therapists that there is no incontrovertible evidence that cognitive therapy is any more effective than any other type of psychological treatment (Cuijpers & Dekker, 2005). Furthermore, the cognitive therapists must realize that the criteria for empirically based therapies are those which focus on brief treatments for specific disorders and are definitely limited in scope.

In this chapter, we looked at REBT and Beck's cognitive therapy. (A comparison of the two therapies is researched in the online Appendix C.) A look at the research track records for REBT and Beck's cognitive therapy clearly shows Beck's CT had accumulated more high-quality research support for his system of therapy than REBT. While REBT has been the focus of hundreds of studies that offer some empirical support (DiGiuseppe & Miller, 1977; Haaga & Davidson, 1993), no studies of REBT are as comprehensive and well controlled as Beck's NIMH collaborative study. This is understandable since Beck practiced in an academic setting with much research support, and Ellis chose to invest his energy into making REBT well known internationally through clinical work rather than academic research (Dryden, 2002a). Today, members of the Albert Ellis Institute are fostering more critical research (DiGuiseppe, Terjesen, Rose, Doyle, & Vadalakis, 1998).

Overall, therapists can easily justify a choice of cognitive therapy, based on strong research evidence and overall conclusions about the therapy's effectiveness. Cognitive therapy has had superior results to control groups and to minimal treatment, and its results have been at least as strong as pharmacological intervention. Furthermore, the changes in the client who uses cognitive therapy seem to last longer than in patients who receive only medication.

There is strong evidence that, in general, cognitive therapy can be used effectively with a large variety of clients for specific disorders. If a client suffers from depression or anxiety, cognitive therapy is at least as effective as other interventions and also reduces recidivism. It appears to be as effective as medication with respect to the reduction of acute distress, and its effects may last longer. Thus psychotherapists can confidently use cognitive therapy for the treatment of depression, anxiety, and obsessive-compulsive disorders. In addition, cognitive therapy can be useful in treating personality disorders, mania, substance abuse, and hypochondriasis. Finally, the equivalency effect also applies to cognitive therapy.

✦ ISSUES OF DIVERSITY

All forms of cognitive therapy are based upon Western linear thinking. As well, REBT is clearly based on Greek stoicism. The underlying belief system of cognitive therapy strongly emphasizes the importance of thinking, action, independence, autonomy, and individualism (Martell & Land, 2002). Its core value is that thinking is the most powerful force that determines human behavior, including feelings, motivations, and even physiology. Cognition, or thinking, is the target behavior to change therapeutically (Sue & Sue, 2003).

Given this theoretical foundation, when cognitive therapists treat diverse populations, it is highly likely that some values will clash. In particular, what is rational in one culture may be irrational and unacceptable in another. For example, in Western cultures, the values of autonomy and independence are paramount. Social relationships are valued if they contribute to happiness. Marriage partners are chosen by the individual. In non-Western cultures, these ideals may be much less important. In India, for example, arranged marriages may be the norm, with the underlying value that taking care of one's family is paramount. In Western cultures it is common to assert one's individuality against paternalistic authority, whereas individuals from an array of religious, ethnic, and cultural groups contend that parental authority is to be respected and obeyed, not challenged. When there are competing values such as these, the therapist must tread lightly in order to do what is best for the individual client and be sensitive to the cultural issues involved (Sue & Sue, 2003).

Considering these potential pitfalls, the cognitive therapist needs to be culturally competent, and sensitive to issues of inequities associated with gender, class, ethnicity, religion, and sexual orientation. It is important to understand the worldview of the client and to determine whether cognitive therapy is compatible with that belief system. The therapist and client can collaborate and cooperate, adjusting the therapy to make it attuned to the client's core cultural values.

While the majority of clients in cognitive therapy are middle-class, European American adults seeking help for their problems, a few studies indicate that cognitive therapy may be helpful with diverse populations such as Latino Americans and African Americans (Zane, Nagayama Hall, Sue, Young, & Nunez, 2004). However, it is still not clear how effective these techniques are with other populations such as American Indians and Asian Americans or with low-income and minority clients (Satterfield, 2002).

While research supports cognitive therapy for White male Americans with depression, there has been little emphasis on its effectiveness as a function of gender and ethnicity. Issues of depression, particularly in Beck's work, are linked to dysfunctional thinking. Numerous studies show that diagnoses and treatment for depression are more common among women than men, but there has been little empirical exploration of how a woman's experience of cognitive therapy might be different from a man's. Cognitive therapists need to be aware of potential gender differences in behavior, attitude, and social and environmental pressures, as well as differences related to culture, ethnicity, and class. Recently, some studies analyzed gender differences for overall rates of depression and for symptoms such as changes in appetite, tearfulness, thoughts of death, and loss of interest (Wenzel, Steer, & Beck, 2005). Gender differences need to be a priority in research in the future (Sue & Sue, 2003).

Ellis and Beck have both endorsed the values of cultural competence. Both therapists are scientifically minded in that they encourage hypothesis testing for all information. They use dynamic sizing, which is the attempt to know when to generalize to the individual in treatment and when there is a danger of stereotyping based upon class, race, gender, age, or any other quality. Although both therapy-training institutes include a diversity component, neither champions culture-specific expertise as a core component at this time (Atkinson & Hackett, 2004).

→ Major Critiques of Cognitive Therapy

Critics claim that cognitive therapy is nothing more that a philosophy using the scientific mantel of behaviorism. They claim cognitive therapy is only mentalism using the vocabulary of behaviorism to gain scientific respectability. It is simply a modern version of introspectionism. A behavior therapy of the mind is an oxymoron; there is nothing observable, countable, or recordable about thoughts, motives, and intentions.

Ellis's REBT and Beck's cognitive therapy have been criticized for being overly simplistic and lacking depth of understanding of human nature. Both theories assume that thinking is at the root of human pathology and the basis of therapeutic change (Sacks, 2004). These theoretical assumptions have not been proved. Although Beck deals with human emotions on a more clinical level than Ellis, REBT pathologizes strong emotions such as rage and guilt that may play an important and useful role in human adjustment; muting and labeling them as pathological may be inadvisable (Alloy, Riskind, & Manos, 2005).

Whereas Beck stresses the importance of collaborative empiricism with a tendency toward humanistic elements, Ellis's REBT regards the relationship as that of teacher–learner (MacInnes, 2004). Although a good therapy relationship is beneficial in REBT, Ellis contends that the therapeutic methods are the active ingredient of change.

Criticisms have been launched that both therapies use the Socratic method and, thus, may browbeat patients into adapting a belief system, neglect the emotional aspects of therapy, promote intellectual activity to the point of rationalization, and actually diminish some of a client's useful motivation. For example, if a person is outraged over an injustice, his emotional state might prompt him to act in a way that corrects the injustice, unless a cognitive therapist dampens the feelings.

Others claim that Ellis's REBT neglects the past and does not allow the client to use the past to resolve current conflicts. Furthermore, so much responsibility is placed upon the client to change his or her attitude that it may diminish action. By emphasizing an internal process, the client may be looking into herself when she should be changing factors in her external environment.

Proponents of long-term therapies and others complain that the literature is stacked in favor of cognitive therapies because, by their nature, they are easier to research: They are short term (therapy can be conducted in under 20 sessions), they use explicit methods and interventions (obvious outcome measures to demonstrate progress), and the therapy techniques are manualized (methods are easy to replicate, validate, observe, and train). Critics argue that just because the therapy lends itself to a stringent research methodology, it does not necessarily establish its superiority over other forms of psychotherapy. However, there is no doubt that cognitive therapies have a level of support that allows a psychotherapist to use them with confidence and that, if executed correctly, they have a high probability of providing needed help for the client.

SUMMARY

- Cognitive therapy arose in the 1950s, adding a mediational or cognitive dimension to behavior therapy. The underlying theoretical assumption is that cognitions cause feelings and behaviors. Since it is possible for the person to change his or her thinking, he or she can learn to replace irrational and distorted thinking with healthier thinking. *Cognitive therapy* (CT) and *cognitive behavior therapy* (CBT) are generic terms for a broad category of psychotherapy. Cognitive therapy (CT) is also the name of a particular form of therapy developed by Aaron Beck.

- Ellis's rational emotive behavior therapy uses an A-B-C-D-E model to illustrates that *A*, an activating event, does not cause *C*, an emotional, cognitive, or behavioral event; it is *B*, a belief about an event, not the event itself, that causes unhappiness. Disputation (*D*) is used to dispute irrational beliefs through empiricism, logic, and pragmatics. Effective new beliefs (*E*) develop when irrational beliefs are replaced with rational ones. Irrational beliefs can be reduced to three core beliefs—I must do well; you must treat me well; the world must be easy—and four irrational processes—demandingness, awfulizing, low frustration tolerance, and poor ratings of self-worth and others.

- In the practice of rational emotive behavior therapy, assessment is ongoing therapy. The therapist is active, reinforces client independence, and focuses on solving problems with a willing client. Length of treatment is generally no more than 16 weeks. Therapeutic techniques include disputing and challenging, homework, REBT self-help forms, psychoeducation, role playing, and exercises. Termination occurs when the client acquires an REBT philosophy.

- Beck's cognitive therapy posits that an automatic thought can result in an affective state. Automatic thoughts can be cognitive distortions that cause and maintain dysfunctional thinking and feelings. Distorted thinking includes arbitrary inference, polarized or dichotomous thinking, magnification and minimization, personalization, overgeneralization, selective abstraction, and negative mental filter. A person behaving normally interprets life events accurately. A person behaving abnormally possesses cognitive distortions and systematic biases. Systematic bias, also called a cognitive shift, in processing information can produce a negative cognitive schema. A cognitive schema is a person's perceptions of self, others, the world, the future, goals, memories, expectations, and learning assumptions.

- The practice of Beck's cognitive therapy includes an assessment with standardized instruments and identification of the core dysfunctional belief. The therapeutic relationship is one of collaborative empiricism. Length of treatment is individualized. The goals are to make clients into their own cognitive therapists.

- Therapeutic techniques include identification and questioning of underlying automatic thoughts and maladaptive assumptions or themes; hypothesis testing and Socratic dialogue; and many exercises including activity scheduling, decatastrophizing, decentering, redefining advantages and disadvantages, role playing, and guided discovery. Through cognitive mapping, therapists can map the important elements of their patients' experiences.

- The research record for cognitive therapy in general, and for Beck's model in particular, justifies its use. Cognitive therapy has been shown to be superior to control groups and to minimal treatment, and its results have been at least as strong as pharmacological intervention. Changes seem to last longer than in patients who receive only medication. Cognitive therapy can be used effectively with a large variety of clients for specific disorders, specifically for depression and anxiety disorders.

- Cognitive therapists need to be aware of potential gender differences in behavior, attitude, and social and environmental pressures, as well as differences related to culture, ethnicity, and class. Recently, some studies have begun to explore somatic symptoms and women's change in appetite. Gender differences need to be a priority in research in the future.

- Critics claim that cognitive therapy is nothing more that a philosophy using the scientific mantel of behaviorism and that it lacks depth of understanding of human nature. Proponents complain that cognitive therapy has advantages in research because, by its nature (short-term, circumscribed goals, small samples of behavior), its outcomes are easier to assess.

RESOURCES

Albert Ellis Institute (AEI)
45 East 65th Street
New York, NY 10021-6593
(212) 535-0822
http://www.albertellisinstitute.org/aei/index.html

AEI conducts research and continuing education for mental health professionals, self-help workshops for the public, and affordable psychotherapy for adults, couples, children, families, and groups. It was founded in 1959 by Ellis. Also see http://www.rebt.org.

Beck Institute for Cognitive Therapy and Research
One Belmont Avenue, Suite 700
Bala Cynwyd, PA 19004-1610
(610) 664-3020
www.beckinstitute.org

The Beck Institute for Cognitive Therapy and Research was founded in 1994. It grew out of Beck's original Center for Cognitive Therapy at the University of Pennsylvania. Currently, it serves as a training ground for cognitive therapists and cognitive-behavior therapists.

CLASS EXERCISES AND ACTIVITIES

Theory

1. What are the differences and similarities between the theories of Ellis's REBT and Beck's cognitive therapy?
2. Compare and contrast an automatic thought and an irrational belief.
3. Compare each of the following of Beck's distorted beliefs—personalization, overgeneralization, and magnification—with the irrational beliefs from Ellis's REBT that are the most similar.

Practice

1. Describe the A-B-C-D-E method of questioning in REBT.
2. Identify automatic thoughts that might fuel depression, anxiety, and paranoia.
3. Look at the sample treatment plan in Chapter 1 (Figure 1.2). Fill out the plan for Tuti for REBT and Beck's CT. What are the major similarities and differences in these two treatment plans? (Both Jonathan's and Tuti's case histories are in Appendix A.)

Research

1. How do you respond to a patient who asks, "Why are you using cognitive therapy to treat me?"
2. Compare Ellis's model of REBT and Beck's in the area of research. How do these models differ in terms of an evidence base of research?
3. Conduct a review of cognitive therapy by using the following key words in PubMed and PsycINFO: *cognitive therapy.* What did you find? Now use the key words *cognitive behavior therapy and cognitive behaviour therapy.* What did you find? Limit your search to *cognitive behavior therapy and randomized control or to cognitive therapy and randomized control.* What types of articles are available about cognitive behavior therapy and cognitive therapy? Taking a quick overview of the articles, describe the nature of the articles and the kind of evidence they contain.

CHAPTER 11

REALITY THERAPY

And what fun is it to learn anything or achieve anything if we can't share it with others? A friend of mine, a dedicated golfer, shot a hole in one playing by himself. Disaster.

—*William Glasser*

The goal of this chapter is to present a general overview of reality therapy. The chapter looks at biographical information about William Glasser and Robert Wubbolding, the historical context of reality therapy, and the theory, practice, and research of the model. The simulated psychotherapist, Dr. William Lassiter, will present a treatment plan and session excerpts from reality therapy for the case of Jonathan. Issues of diversity and major critiques are also included.

✦ HISTORICAL CONTEXT

William Glasser (see About William Glasser box) created reality therapy around 1965, and it has since become an influential form of psychotherapy (Collins, 1997). It is based on the belief that human misery stems from being unconnected to others, from trying to control others, and from blaming others for the individual's own unhappiness. It emphasizes the belief that good relationships are important to a successful and happy life (Glasser, 1998).

Glasser's work with schizophrenics, juvenile delinquents, unruly adolescents, and hard-core substance abusers led him to believe that psychoanalytic and insight-oriented methods were not very helpful. He became frustrated with the psychoanalytic therapies that were dominant at the time. And he disagreed with the psychoanalytic beliefs that it was essential to unearth the reasons underlying the problems, or to discover why and where a person is fixated on the past, or that insight into the problems was more important than action (Palmatier, 1996). Long-term, seemingly endless discussions of how events in early life were the cause of current misery seemed to Glasser to be a pointless exercise.

Glasser's treatment with delinquent adolescents prompted him to develop a therapeutic approach that allowed him to confront difficult problems related to social issues (Glasser, 1969). He contended that psychology had failed to help people to live better lives because it emphasized external controls on behavior, rather than internal controls (Glasser, 1998). He believed psychology should stress free will and responsibility.

ABOUT WILLIAM GLASSER

Born in 1925, William Glasser was one of three children in a family in Cleveland, Ohio. His father's family had emigrated from Russia to the United States in 1905, leaving behind a life of fabulous wealth that he never regained. His mother, who was self-educated, inspired William to read and to go to museums, parks, and other intellectually stimulating places.

Glasser completed an engineering program and after working as a chemical engineer, began studying psychology at Western Reserve Men's School. There Glasser met a professor who encouraged him to become a psychiatrist and helped him, through a special program for students who did not fit the typical high-achieving profile, to enter Case Western Reserve Medical School. One aspect of medical school that impressed Glasser was that it was a school without failure. He was told that the admission criteria were so stringent that once a student was enrolled he would graduate.

Glasser interned at the Veterans Administration Hospital in West Los Angeles and spent one year at the UCLA Department of Psychiatry, where he was supervised by Dr. G. L. Harrington. Glasser had begun to believe that dwelling on the past, as in traditional Freudian psychoanalysis, was not the best therapeutic method, since the patients he was seeing needed to focus on the problems of the present. When he informed his supervisor, Dr. Harrington, of his beliefs, Harrington shook his hand and said, "Join the club" (Wubbolding, 2000).

After his internship, in 1956 Glasser assumed a position at the Ventura School for Girls, which was a residential facility for delinquent girls. Glasser believed that the best way to help the residents was by encouraging them to develop responsibility by giving them the opportunity to live, learn, work, and socialize in a supportive community. Under his guidance, Ventura became a model of a punishment-free environment in which all members were offered help, friendship, and support. By dealing with the residents without punishment, Glasser believed, patients could be empowered to change.

In 1965 Glasser published *Reality Therapy,* which became a best seller. Although traditional psychiatrists tended to ignore his work, he continued to develop his theory ("no failure, no punishment") in different school settings, particularly in the Watts section of Los Angeles (Glasser, 1990). He named the theory, which is the basis of reality therapy, *control theory* and extended its principles to many different situations, even motivational work for sports (Edens, 1997). When the W. Clement Stone Foundation awarded Glasser a grant, he founded the Institute for Reality Therapy and the Educator Training Center. Glasser also founded Schools Without Failure, an international program that trains teachers to help students to develop a "success identity" rather than a "failure identity."

As he matured, he adapted his therapeutic methods so they could be applied not just to the therapy dyad, but to education, the classroom, the workplace, and institutions, such as military treatment centers, communities, and the clergy (Glasser, 1998). One of his more recent works, begun around 1997, is the Choice Community Project, which he founded for Corning workers in the New York school district. People in the community are taught how to get along well with those who matter the most. Glasser also continues to work at the William Glasser Institute (formerly the Institute for Reality Therapy), a nonprofit charitable foundation (Wubbolding, 2000).

In 1992, Glasser's wife Naomi—who had worked alongside him on reality therapy—died. He has since married Carleen Floyd, who also contributes to the development of reality therapy. In the late 1990s, Glasser decided to change the name of the theory underlying reality therapy from *control theory* to *choice theory,* because he wanted to place more emphasis on the concepts of responsibility and choice (Glasser, 1998, 2000).

In his reality therapy, Glasser incorporated a wide array of ideas, concepts, practice techniques, and research findings from many different theoretical orientations (Glasser, 1965, 1988). Some of his key concepts come from humanism and existentialism. In particular, he adopted the idea that individuals have the freedom to choose and that with freedom comes responsibility; these constructs are also stressed in therapies created by Carl Rogers and Victor Frankl, among others. His theorizing about human behavior and control was influenced by a book entitled *Behavior: The Control of Perception* by William Powers (1973), in which human behavior is seen as regulated through a homeostatic process.

Glasser also used the concepts of survival and belongingness, adapted from Abraham Maslow's hierarchy of needs, and to which he added needs (Glasser, 1985). Glasser argued that needs do not necessarily fall into a hierarchy in which lower needs must be fulfilled before a person moves on to satisfy others; rather, needs can compete with one another, resulting in intra-need conflicts.

Glasser's work also contains elements of other theories: From cognitive therapy, thinking is seen as a powerful component of total behavior; from behavior therapy, action is a powerful way to change total behavior; from biological theory, the old brain and new brain control human needs through a homeostatic mechanism or a tendency to achieve balance; and from constructivism, the quality world plays a vital role in human behavior. It is apparent that Glasser's reality therapy is not easily classified, based on all these threads that combine in its formulation.

Reality therapy is a work in progress. Glasser's theorizing has evolved along several tracks. From *Reality Therapy,* he began working with educational institutions, leading him to apply the ideas of control theory, which he later modified as choice theory, in education settings. *Schools Without Failure,* published in 1969, eventually evolved into *The Quality School,* written in 1990. His book *Control Theory: A New Explanation of How We Control Our Lives,* written in 1985, evolved into *Choice Theory: A New Psychology of Personal Freedom* (1998). Along the way, he also published a best-selling book called *Positive Addiction* (Glasser, 1976). His therapy is now firmly based on choice theory.

A second important figure in the evolution and practice of reality therapy is Robert Wubbolding, Glasser's longtime colleague and close friend. As Glasser developed his theory and practice, Wubbolding wrote *Reality Therapy for the 21st Century* (2000), which presented Glasser's therapy in an accessible format while summarizing relevant research. Wubbolding is now an internationally known teacher, author, and practitioner of reality therapy. He has taught choice theory and reality therapy in the United States, Europe, Asia, and the Middle East, and his contributions to the theory and practice, among others, include the ideas of positive symptoms, the cycle of counseling, and the five levels of commitment. He has also expanded the procedure of evaluation and has published prolifically on reality therapy. His busy professional life includes serving as director of the Center for Reality Therapy and senior faculty at the William Glasser Institute in Los Angeles, as well as professor emeritus at Xavier University in Cincinnati, Ohio. This chapter draws on the works of both Glasser and Wubbolding.

➔ THEORY OF REALITY THERAPY

Glasser's reality therapy is based on his idea of choice theory, which control theory evolved into over time. Glasser (1998) sees choice theory as a new psychology of personal freedom with three basic tenets: (a) all people do is behave, (b) almost all behavior is chosen, and (c) people are driven by genes to satisfy their basic needs.

The basic concepts underlying choice theory include choice and control, needs and intra-need conflict, the quality world, total behavior, and levels of commitment. Normal and abnormal behavior are the result of how well or how poorly a person chooses to act and to think.

Choice and Control

According to Glasser, choice theory has ten axioms:

1. The only person whose behavior we can control is our own.
2. All we can give another person is information.
3. All long-lasting psychological problems are relationship problems.
4. The problem relationship is always part of our present life.
5. What happened in the past has everything to do with what we are today, but we can only satisfy our basic needs right now and plan to continue satisfying them in the future.
6. We can only satisfy our needs by satisfying the pictures in our quality world.
7. All we do is behave.
8. All behavior is total behavior and is made up of four components: acting, thinking, feeling, and physiology.
9. All total behavior is chosen, but we only have direct control over the acting and thinking components. We can only control our feeling and physiology indirectly through how we choose to act and think.
10. All total behavior is designated by verbs and named by the part that is the most recognizable.

For Glasser, choice theory assumes that all human beings possess a motivation to satisfy a set of basic needs. Actions are always a person's choice. When people act, they are choosing to behave in a way to help attain these goals. No external circumstance can force a person to act. People consistently behave in a way that maximizes pleasure and minimizes pain. Whether people experience pleasure or pain is a function of how they fulfill their basic needs: Pleasure comes from fulfilling needs, and pain comes from failing to fulfill them. Overall control over activity is a function of the human brain, which works much like a thermostat on a furnace or air conditioner. It is a self-regulating system; it attempts to maintain homeostasis by altering the world around it (Wubbolding, 2000). When humans effectively satisfy their needs, they gain a sense of control similar to that of the fully functioning or self-actualized person of Carl Rogers (1986). People make choices, both healthy and unhealthy, and the choices they make are behaviors that represent attempts to satisfy their needs.

People tend to use coercion and control when others do not do what they want them to do. The person's desire to control is based on three underlying beliefs:

1. Behavior is a response to an external stimulus (e.g., answering a doorbell).
2. One can make others do what one wants; and others can control how one thinks, acts, and feels.
3. If others do not do what is desired, one must punish, ridicule, or threaten them (Glasser, 1998).

People use different methods of control to meet their needs. One person might manage through wanting money and power, another might aspire to be the top performer in a field, another might seek elected office, and another might desire her family to be perfect. When a person tries to control anyone other than him- or herself, it produces a negative impact, which is manifested in the person's relationships, workplace, or educational setting.

The corollary to this is if people are choosing to behave in a particular way, they are also *responsible* for their behaviors. Since you are the only one in control of your life, you are also the only one responsible for your own behavior. Glasser holds that human behavior—actions, thinking, and feeling—originate inside, not outside, the person. Therefore, the reward and punish system generally used in society is not an effective motivator. People need to make judgments from the inside—using self-evaluation, defining what they want, making plans. Internal motivation is what makes people behave.

Instead of trying to find a way to control others' behavior, the most constructive question that we should ask is, "How can I figure out how to live my life the way I want to live it and still get along with the people I need?" (Glasser, 1998, p.17). To answer this question, it is important to underscore that human beings are free to choose any actions they want to choose, and they are capable of controlling themselves. Thus, at the very heart of choice theory and reality therapy is the core belief that the only person I can really control is myself. Thus, I am the only person who can fulfill my own needs.

Needs and Intra-Need Conflict

People are motivated by five basic, genetically coded needs. These are internal forces that motivate and induce people to act to fulfill these needs:

- *Survival needs* motivate people to obtain appropriate food, air, water, body temperature, and sex. Whereas the old brain keeps the human body functioning physically, the new brain controls psychological needs, some routine needs, and all of our voluntary behaviors.
- *Belonging needs* motivate people to love, cooperate, and share in order to have healthy relationships. When there is a disruption of significant relationships, and belonging and love needs are not met, living is less effective. Belonging is at the heart of good mental health.
- *Power needs* motivate people to achieve, to be competent, to accomplish, to possess inner control, and to feel as if they are in control of their life. If

power is satisfying, it can take the form of achievement. Conflicts arise when people fulfill their own power needs at the expense of others, so that one person's need for power lessens another's ability to fulfill her need. It does not have to be this way. For example, if one person becomes an accomplished poet, it does not necessarily diminish or detract from another person's ability to become an accomplished poet. The need for power is found in families, schools, institutions, and nations.

- *Freedom needs* motivate people to be independent and autonomous. A person always has a choice and always has the option of freely selecting among potential choices. Freedom balances the person's ability to choose with the efforts of others to fulfill their need for power and control. Power and freedom are often connected. It is difficult to have power without freedom.
- *Fun needs* motivate people to enjoy their life. People need to play and to laugh while they are learning and living. Enjoyment is a way to help people to learn more about themselves, and enjoyable experiences help them to differentiate themselves from others as well as to build relationships and fulfill the need for love and belonging. Those who play together increase their level of intimacy, because the mutual investment of time and energy in satisfying their need for fun and pleasure serves as a bonding experience.

These needs are analogous to a five-legged chair, so that each need supports the whole structure in concert with the other needs. They are not hierarchical, as in Maslow's system (Maslow, 1970). In a well-balanced person, all of the needs work together. Needs can overlap, enhance, compete, and conflict with one another. One need may be more intense than another at any given time. For example, the need for survival can compete with the need for love and belongingness. A hungry person might loot a friend's grocery store during a flood. In this case, the need to survive trumped the need to love the friend and respect his property. The CEO of a corporation may have a need to have fun that motivates her to socialize with employees rather than maintain appropriate social distance. The need for power is often connected to the need for freedom, and it is difficult to have power without freedom (Wubbolding, 2000).

Quality World

According to Glasser, the very core of our lives, what we call our "personal Shangrila" is the *quality world* (1998). Each person has his or her unique quality world. And each person develops pictures in their minds related to the five needs described above. Each want produces mental images that form the quality world. The quality world is like a personal picture album containing every person, thing, idea, and ideal that a person believes increases the quality of his or her life.

As people grow, develop, and live their lives, they accumulate this conglomeration of mental images in their mental picture album of things that meet basic needs, and of people to whom they want to relate, things or objects they want to possess or experience, and ideas and beliefs that guide them. While the basic needs are universal and what motivate behavior, the quality world pictures are the means by which people meet these needs. Each person's quality world is unique, diverse, dynamic with pictures that are removable and prioritized, changing and changeable, varying in intensity and attainability, and sometimes in conflict with one another. Thus the quality world contains our core beliefs and our expectations and ways to fulfill needs (Wubbolding, 1985).

People drift back and forth to the images contained in their quality world, accessing the mental pictures that they believe can help them to fill their basic needs. They might see an image of their idea of the perfect mate, the ideal home, the best job, the flawless political candidate, and so on. People behave in a way to match their sensory wants with an image from their mental picture album on a moment-to-moment basis. The majority of the perceptions we store are visual and thus are in our minds like pictures.

The content of this mental picture album is very important in determining the quality of relationships and can help to make them either harmonious or adversarial (Wubbolding, 1985). Conflicts can arise so that the wants from a person's quality world can be in conflict with other wants or with another person's wants. For example, if a husband has a want to take a high-level position that means being away from family for lengthy periods, his power needs are at odds with his need for love and belonging. But since the need for belonging and love is the most dominant need, this need takes priority in the quality world (Wubbolding, 2000).

Ironically, while each person has a unique quality world that contains the knowledge that directs behavior, few people are aware of its existence and of the influence that these mental pictures have in molding their behavior. To determine what images are in her quality world, a woman might ask herself specific questions, such as "What kind of friend do I want? What does it mean to be a friend?" If people were able to gain a greater understanding of how this quality world affected their behavior and their relationships, they would get along much better with others, and the world would be a more peaceful place (Glasser, 1998).

It is impossible to live completely within a personal quality world. On a practical level, the needs within the quality world must be met in the real world. A person may have an image of the most perfect meal in his quality world, but the dream meal may very well be unhealthy and deficient in nutrients. If the dream meal is pizza, it would not be possible to eat only pizza at every meal and remain healthy. People become frustrated, unhappy, and behave ineffectively when their wants in their quality world cannot be matched in the real world.

Total Behavior

Total behavior consists of four inseparable components that comprise how a person conducts him- or herself. These four components—acting, thinking, feeling, and physiology—interact at all times. When a person acts, he also thinks, and when he thinks, he is also acting or doing something; feelings and physiological reactions are also involved with thinking and acting. Because people are often not aware of the connections among thinking, behaving, feeling, and physiology, they do not see how they indirectly choose their feelings and their physiological states (Wubbolding, 2000).

Glasser offers an analogy to illustrate total behavior. Total behavior is like the performance of a car. The steering wheel allows people to drive the car into the quality world. Needs are like the motor of the car and are the source of power. The front wheels of the car represent action and thinking. The back wheels represent feeling and physiology. When the driver of the car turns the steering wheel, she is more aware that she is moving the front wheels and less aware of how the back wheels and the back end of the car are responding. While her attention is on the movement of the front wheels, they appear to be more responsive. However, in actuality all parts of the car are under the control of the driver and are working as a whole. When the driver turns the front wheels with conscious intent, the back wheels eventually follow, and so does the whole car. When a directional change is made, however, there is a slight time lag as the back wheels come along after the front ones. So although the driver is more aware of her control of the front of the car, on some level she takes it for granted that the whole car is under her control.

Imagine if a driver found that the back half of the car was not coordinated with the front part, with the consequence that the back half broke off and traveled in a different direction. How would the driver react? So it is with a person's feelings and physiology. Just as it takes the back wheels of a car time to change as the front wheels shift, when a person behaves and thinks, it takes a bit of time for the person to realize that the feelings and physiology also change. Nevertheless, they are under the person's control, albeit indirectly (Glasser, 1990).

A person who is unhappy does not believe that she is actually choosing unhappiness or misery willfully and voluntarily. It seems illogical that, if given a choice, she would choose to be in a state of discontent, but she *is* choosing to be unhappy. The construct of total behavior makes it easier to understand how people do make a choice to feel a specific emotion. A person often does not *realize* that she has control over her feelings because she does not have *direct* control over emotions in the same way that she has control over thinking and acting. Control over feelings and physiological reactions is less direct.

For example, Ryan is under stress and experiences an anxiety attack. Through therapy, he learns to use self-talk and to think in a constructive manner. His physiological responses may show that these exercises helped to decrease his heart rate and blood pressure. He feels calmer and happier. He has learned that by changing the way he thinks and talks to himself, he is able to control his feelings and physiology. He no longer thinks events are "just happening to him." While it is true that people have the most direct control over the action part of total behavior, choice theory maintains they have control over the other parts of their total behavior as well (Wubbolding, 2000, p. 108).

Total behavior is used to fulfill the quality world and to maneuver the external world so the person can meet wants and needs. Thus the more people understand and practice control over total behavior, the more effective their actions will be.

Level of Commitment

People vary in their level of commitment to their goals, as a function of their motivation. Level of commitment varies along with the level of a person's seriousness, intensity, and willingness to bring about changes. There are five levels of commitment, ranging from least commitment to most commitment:

1. I do not want to be here at all.
2. I want the outcome, but I do not want to exert any effort.
3. I will try. I might change.
4. I could change. I will do my best.
5. I will do whatever it takes to reach my goals.

The more highly committed the client, the more likely the client will implement his or her plan successfully.

Normal and Abnormal Behavior

The healthy person chooses to use effective behavior, balances the five innate needs, gets what she wants from the external world, and still manages to get along and have harmonious relationships with the people she needs (Glasser, 1998; Wubbolding, 1996). Good relationships come with a high level of commitment. The mental pictures of her quality world match some obtainable reality in the external world resulting in her feeling satisfied. She makes life-enhancing choices so that she contributes to society's well-being through behaviors such as volunteerism, meaningful work, or church involvement.

According to Glasser, except for those who are genetically and organically impaired, people who have mental disturbances are not mentally ill. They are unhappy. Reality therapy does not accept the psychiatric medical model of mental illness, and reality therapists do not use *DSM* diagnoses, or accept the definitions of primary problems as traditionally defined as abnormal behavior by psychiatry. According to reality therapy, people who receive labels of mental illness are simply behaving ineffectively for a number of reasons:

- They have failed to develop a satisfying relationship in the present, have not satisfied a need for love and belonging, and do not behave in ways that enable them to love and belong, or to succeed in what they want to do with their lives.
- They blame their problems repeatedly on significant others and spend their time either trying to control these people or trying to escape from efforts to control them.
- They avoid dealing with the real problem in therapy and instead complain, criticize, and focus on suffering, blaming their problems on those who have forced them into therapy (courts, legal system, family, etc.). They avoid taking the responsibility to change their behavior from ineffective to effective in order to satisfy their needs.
- They avoid dealing with the present unhappiness and blame their misery on other people, past events, or what could happen in the future.
- They avoid facing the reality that the only person's behavior they can control is their own and thus avoid facing the fact that, directly or indirectly, they are choosing what they are complaining about.

Abnormal behavior is a person's choice. Symptoms of abnormal behavior are unsuccessful attempts to solve a problem related to meeting one's needs (Wubbolding, 2000, p. 109). The outside observer—such as a traditional mental health professional—who sees the behavior may label it as a symptom of a disease while the person who performs the behavior sees it from the inside as an attempt to fulfill an unsatisfied need. In the medical or traditional model of mental health, if a behavior is effective, it is not labeled as a problem; but if a behavior is ineffective, it is called a symptom.

To describe traditional mental illnesses, Glasser uses verbs instead of nouns to emphasize the role of choice in behaviors and to reinforce the notion that the person is choosing to perform an action rather than becoming a victim at the hands of some external force or uncontrollable internal condition (Glasser, 1998). This clinically useful language reinforces the message that a person can choose to do something about his or her behavior and places the responsibility on the patient to make a change. For example, the diagnosis of major depression is recast as depress-*ing*, because the person is choosing to depress. An individual who is diagnosed with an anxiety disorder is anxietiz-*ing*; phobics are phobic-*ing*; obsessive-compulsives are obsess-*ing*; angry people are anger-*ing*. Relabeling a noun as an action verb underscores the idea that the situation is within the client's realm of choice; it is not an outside event that is happening to her or him.

Depress-ing is a very common presenting problem; it is the most frequent complaint of people who are lonely, and it indicates that the person is complaining about the painful feeling part of his or her total behavior. There are three basic reasons that people choose to depress:

- *To restrain their own anger over the frustration of a deteriorating relationship:* The more the anger is suppressed, the more energy is used, and the greater the depression. Much energy is needed to check the frustration.
- *To ask for help without begging:* A depress-ing person is able to get attention, help, and even therapy, yet is still able to satisfy their power needs by not begging.
- *To avoid doing what they are afraid to do:* Traditionally, a depressed person is not held totally responsible for taking specific actions, and her inertia is accepted as long as she is depressed.

The causes of ineffective behaviors are based in biology and genetics. Human beings simply have a tendency to hold an undying belief in behaviors that do not work. For example, a person who misplaces his keys continues to look for them over and over again in the same places, when it would be far more advantageous to stop and reflect on whether this futile searching was helping (Wubbolding, 2000). Other examples of less-than-effective behavior include giving up, acting out, and unproductive thinking, feeling, and physiological habits (Glasser, 1998).

To explain mental illness such as depression as a neurochemical imbalance is incorrect. The chemical change is not the *cause* of the behavior but rather the *result,* in the same way that perspiring is not caused by running on a hot day but by the choice to run on a hot day. Glasser believes that the term *mental illness* should be reserved for organically based illnesses such as Alzheimer's and epilepsy. Even schizophrenia is a choice to be "crazy" rather than a mental illness. What traditional psychology calls abnormal is a person who Glasser sees as struggling with a relationship in which he wants to connect with a person who is either resisting that connection or forcing the person to do something he or she does not want to do (Glasser, 1998).

✦ PRACTICE OF REALITY THERAPY

Now that we have examined the theoretical concepts that underlie reality therapy, we will explore its practice. Dr. William Lassiter, our fictional composite psychotherapist, provides a firsthand perspective of how he integrates theory with practice and applies the techniques of reality therapy.

Assessment and Diagnosis

In my assessment interview, I initiate a good relationship with my clients so that they will incorporate me into their quality world. I make no formal *DSM* diagnosis. As I interview the client, I search to identify the core problem—a current unsatisfying relationship in his or her life.

Negotiation of Therapeutic Relationship and Length of Treatment

My role as a therapist is to be a strong and active mentor. Our relationship is based on trust, friendliness, firmness, and fairness. To be an adequate reality therapist, I must be my genuine self, but I must possess certain personal characteristics: success in dealing with my own life, a strong personal relationship bond in my own life, the ability to discuss any topic, the ability to connect with and feel at ease with a wide range of people (including those who would not typically be a part of my life), a knowledge of the world (be well-read and culturally aware), and a good sense of humor. The client must see me as someone who cannot be conned or deceived.

I see reality therapy as a time-sensitive therapy. I view each session as a contact with the patient that may be the only one, making the session of some urgency and present-oriented. Thus there is no predetermined length for the course of therapy. Change happens when it happens. The past cannot be changed, and the future is not predictable, thus it is best to focus on the here and now. The therapy will not take any longer than is necessary, and it does not have to be long to be effective.

My immediate goals in reality therapy are to work on the client's core problem, which is either his current unsatisfying relationship or his lack of a relationship; to help the client reconnect with the people with whom he has satisfying relationships; and to teach the client the fundamentals of choice theory. The first order of business is to reach my client in any way that I can, no matter how reluctant he or she may be.

Therapeutic Techniques

There are two distinct parts to successful reality therapy: building the appropriate treatment environment and executing the treatment procedures.

Building the Treatment Environment

It is essential that I build an appropriate and professional environment, which is based on the therapy relationship I described above.

My clients need to know that I care about them, that therapy is safe, that they can confide in me and have a satisfactory relationship with me. I provide the client with an interpersonal environment that is different from the one in which he or she has been living and from which the client has been disconnected for so many years.

Some of the techniques and skills I use include making good eye contact, exhibiting courteous behavior, and listening well. I also use psychoeducation and explain the principles of choice theory. I emphasize that a good outcome can occur if the client works hard and stress that clients can develop effective behaviors. I use empathy and acceptance of the client, without any judgment or criticism, yet I am firm and keep appropriate boundaries that maintain a professional relationship. My questioning is gentle, straightforward, and meant to increase the client's realization that he is responsible for his own behavior, and I tie together what we discuss.

Consequences can be imposed to stress that the client is responsible for his or her own behavior, within reason. And humor can be an invaluable means of building a good therapeutic environment, as is self-disclosing relevant material. Sometimes I use unexpected methods to surprise the client, including reframing, prescribing, and paradoxical techniques. At times I use silence so that the client can think, which also emphasizes the client's responsibility in the treatment.

Executing the Treatment Procedures: WDEP

As I am building the treatment environment, I simultaneously apply the treatment methods or the procedural part of therapy. This is called *WDEP* (wants, direction, evaluation, and plans), which was developed by Wubbolding for use in Glasser's reality therapy.

Wants   To find out what motivates people, find out what they want. I help the client get in touch with the existence of the quality world, explore the mental pictures, and understand which pictures in the mental photo album are healthy and which are unhealthy in order to determine their significance and assess what is in balance and out of balance. I explore the client's unique wants by posing a series of questions about the world, friends, relatives, teachers, spouses, work, school, supervisors, religion, spirituality, and so forth. I help the client to assess his or her level of commitment (from high to low) about wants (Wubbolding, 1996).

Direction   Direction is the behaviors clients use to get what they envision in their quality world. I help clients to describe total behavior and to connect action, thought, feeling, and physiology. I question their overall direction and where their present accumulation of choices is leading.

I specify and keep within a time frame—week, month, year—to help clients increase awareness that they are actively choosing their direction. I look for self-talk that accompanies (not causes) ineffective actions and encourage replacing it, such as substituting "I can control others" with "I am in control of my own behavior, but I cannot control anyone else's" (Wubbolding, 2000, p. 107).

Evaluation   Self-evaluation is the core of the reality therapy delivery system. Clients change only when they decide what they are doing is not helping them to get what they want. Self-evaluation—and the discovery that what they are doing is not helping—is the true basis for change.

I ask my clients to make judgments about their own behavior, wants, levels of commitment, and plans. I use polar words to facilitate the evaluation process— for example, *help/hurt, easy/difficult, important/unimportant, results-centered/futile, to your advantage/not to your advantage, attainable/unattainable* (Wubbolding, 2000, p. 111). By using value-laden words, I help the client to evaluate the effectiveness and progress of current overall behavior. Some of the questions that I can ask to facilitate the client's self-evaluation are listed below (Wubbolding, 2000).

- *Overall behavioral direction and purpose:* Is the overall direction of your life in your best interest? What impact did you expect to have when you chose that behavior? What is the difference between the actual impact, the intended communication, and the message received?
- *Effective or ineffective specific behaviors:* Is your current specific behavior helping or hurting you? Helping you get what you want? Helping or hurting people around you? When you did what you did yesterday, what was the impact on you or others? Does each behavior help you enough? In the long run? Short run?
- *Acceptable or unacceptable specific behaviors:* Is what you did acceptable to your family, friends, society? If you don't know, take a guess. Is acting against reasonable rules to your best advantage? Will such actions get you in trouble with others or the law? How?
- *Self-talk/global evaluation of belief system:* Do your present self-talk and core beliefs help you or hurt you in attaining what you want?
- *Helpful or harmful emotions/feeling behaviors:* Is feeling anger, resentment, guilt, self-pity, or loneliness helping or hurting you? What is to your advantage—to nurse negative feelings of self-pity, depression, and resentment, or let them go? What effect does anger have on your body? What impact do feelings of trust, hope, self-confidence, self-esteem, and positive mental attitude have on your physiology?
- *Long-range interests, high and low quality behavior, and life enhancement:* Does short-term gain equal long-term gain? Are you functioning at the highest level possible? Are you inwardly satisfied with the quality of your work? What effect does your behavior have on the quality of work?

- *Evaluation of wants:* Is what you want attainable? Realistic? Reasonable chance of getting it in the near or far future? Beneficial or harmful to you and others? Clearly defined? Nonnegotiable, highly desirable, or mere wishes? Is it likely the world will change to meet your desires? Is there anyone you want to be closer to?
- *Evaluation of perceptions:* Is it helping or hurting to see yourself, others, things in this way? Where is it getting you to see yourself as inferior?
- *Level of commitment:* Is your present level of commitment the highest you are willing to make? If you work as hard as you are now, will you be able to get what you want? Is "I'll try" enough to accomplish your goals? If you say "probably," "I could," "maybe," or "I might," where will you be in the time frame selected?
- *Evaluation of plan of action:* If you follow through on your plan, how will life be better? Will you be living a more satisfying life? Does the plan have the characteristics of an effective plan?

The client can participate in three levels of self-evaluation, ranging from evaluation with little or no information, to evaluation with knowledge and information, to evaluation based on feedback and a selected, specific standard. I encourage my clients to perform an honest and open self-assessment and to reach level three.

Plans   I help my client to create a workable and successful plan. According to Wubbolding, there are three stages of planning in which the therapist asks "Could you?" "Would you?" and "Will you?" The best plans are those that the client initiates. Plans that are less powerful but still helpful are those that the therapist and client initiate together. Least powerful are plans the therapist initiates. To succeed, the client must be committed to and follow through on the plan. Problems arise when the client desires a particular outcome but is unmotivated and reluctant to put in the necessary effort to make it work. I do everything in my power to encourage the client, such as asking "If you tried this plan for a week, what would you lose?" (Wubbolding, 2000, p. 158).

Helpful plans are those with the following characteristics (Wubbolding, 2000, p. 150). These plans are sometimes referred to by Wubbolding's term SAMI^{2}C^3:

- S—Simple or easy to understand; it is not complicated or confusing.
- A—Attainable, so that the client can realistically do what needs to be done. The plan is not difficult, overwhelming, or overly ambitious.
- M—Measurable, so that the client and therapist know when it has been achieved and exactly what needed to be accomplished.
- I—Immediate, so that the plan is put into place as soon as possible.
- I—Involved, so the therapist helps the client when appropriate, but the client takes responsibility to create and implement the plan.
- C—Controlled by the client and not by anyone else, and not contingent on anyone else (e.g., "If mom changes I will").

- C—Committed, that is, firmly resolved to doing.
- C—Consistent, so the plan is repeated over and over until it becomes habit and part of the client's life.

The four activities, WDEP, are designed to encourage the client to be aware of total behavior. The cycle is repeated over and over in therapy as the client adjusts his or her behavior. Lifelong, ongoing evaluation of progress is absolutely necessary for the therapy to work in the long run.

Ancillary Techniques

I use a number of other treatment methods, including psychoeducation with books on choice therapy and tapes of Dr. Glasser's lectures, physical exercise, relaxation techniques, and meditation. I also ask clients to visualize goal attainment, which brings about changes in behavior and physiology. I encourage positive symptoms or any activity that increases the client's social interest and altruism. Sometimes I use role play for difficult situations to deepen the client's skill levels and increase spontaneity and confidence; I also may use confrontation, paradoxical techniques, and metaphors (Wubbolding, 2000).

The Process of Therapy

Initially, therapy begins with relationship building. The therapy relationship develops over time and the quality of care deepens, but right from the start I continue the same work in the initial session to the termination. I work as quickly as possible.

Because I see therapy as a cycle, my methods throughout treatment do not differ. Depending upon the needs of the patient, I will select any or all of the techniques mentioned above. Termination occurs when the client changes his or her behavior to attain greater need satisfaction and a higher quality of life for him- or herself. The client will know the fundamentals of choice theory and will have or be working toward a satisfying relationship; the client will also be making measurable contributions to the lives of others.

THERAPY IN ACTION: DR. WILLIAM LASSITER AND THE CASE OF JONATHAN

To illustrate the application of reality therapy, we examine a treatment plan for Jonathan, followed by excerpts from therapy sessions with our fictional psychotherapist, Dr. Lassiter. Keep in mind the case excerpts are simulated interviews and represent the ideal of therapy. In real life, clients may take much longer to meet therapeutic goals. Table 11.1 provides a summary of Dr. Lassiter's treatment plan.

Table 11.1	
Reality Therapy Treatment Plan for Jonathan	

Assessment and Formulation	• Presenting problem: loss of relationship with Tuti and Darren in quality world
	• J.'s total behavior is depress-ing and anxietiz-ing:
	  Doing—crying; staying out of work; not performing work duties; isolating; avoiding facing pain
	  Thinking—blaming Tuti and Darren
	  Feeling—angry; helpless; hopeless
	  Physiology—psychomotor slowing; inactivity
	• J. is not able to satisfy his need for love and belonging with Tuti or Darren
	• J.'s attempts to control Tuti's desire for children failed
	• J.'s depress-ing allows him to keep his anger in check, to ask for help, to wait the return of Tuti
	• J. avoids taking responsibility for specific actions

Therapeutic Relationship	• Be part of J.'s quality world • Establish treatment environment • Be empathic, energetic with J. • J. needs hope for his future • J. is highly motivated, highly committed

Contract, Goals, and Treatment Plan	• Help J. to achieve effective total behavior:
	  Doing—challenge depress-ing, noncritically accept pain and responsibility for his part of failed relationship; search for suitable partners and friends; choose meaningful direction
	  Thinking—accept responsibility for relationship with Tuti and Darren; let go of blame
	  Feeling—less angry; more loving; successful
	  Physiology—more energy and active
	• Meet weekly until J. learns choice theory, evaluates problems/moves in more effective direction

Techniques	• Questions for Jonathan:
	  Is J.'s overall direction in his life in his best interest?
	  What makes J. choose to depress?
	  Is this depress-ing, raging, isolating helping or hurting him?
	  What choices are in J.'s best interests?
	  What impact does depress-ing have on J. and others?
	• Encourage J. to develop own specific plan for change and be committed
	• WDEP: discuss mental picture of ideal partner, direction of life for fulfilling that picture, evaluate, plan
	• Find appropriate match: join dating service, interest groups (sailing, hiking), volunteer at church
	• Help sister by interacting with niece and nephew
	• Take a course toward MA in marketing to improve job skills
	• Reconnect with old friends from work and university
	• Exercise

Process of Therapy	• Build relationship and begin to enter into the cycle of counseling • Continue with work from beginning of therapy
Termination and Outcome	• Formulation and follow-through of the action plan • J. changed his ineffective depress-ing to a more active and responsible approach • J.'s verbal report of alleviation of symptoms, achievement of his plan, and performance of activities

Case Excerpts

The following excerpts are from sessions based on Dr. Lassiter's reality therapy case formulation.

Session 1

Dr. Lassiter: I can see that these two important relationships are failing.

Jonathan: Of course. Who else can cause me to feel this upset? I am totally blown away. Why? Why would they do this?

Dr. Lassiter: I can't tell you why, because only Tuti and Darren know why they did what they did. The situation does make me wonder why Tuti was so upset by something that happened. Do you have any idea of what made her change so abruptly?

Jonathan: No, not at all. Well . . .

Dr. Lassiter: We can work more effectively and quickly if you level with me and tell me what has really gone on between the two of you.

Jonathan: I suppose you're right. I just don't feel I know you very well.

Dr. Lassiter: Jonathan, I am on your side. Ask me any question. Ask what I am doing in our sessions and where we are going. You can talk to me about anything and any part of your life you want. I am here to help you to help yourself and not to judge or hurt you. I want to see you improve your relationships or to find new ones. It does not help you to fool me or to avoid embarrassment. I am here to help. Be honest, and we'll go much further much faster.

Jonathan: OK. Maybe I did not handle it well. She wanted to have a child, and I wasn't ready. Perhaps I was selfish. I told her absolutely . . .

Dr. Lassiter: So how long was this going on?

Jonathan: About a year and a half.

Dr. Lassiter: When will you choose to stop depress-ing and either reconcile with Tuti or find a way to have a satisfying relationship?

Jonathan: What do you mean, "choosing to be depress-ing"? I am not choosing. I am feeling this way because of what they did to me. I can't help it.

Dr. Lassiter: Did you choose to come here today?

Jonathan: Yes, because I am desperate, and I don't want to kill myself.

Dr. Lassiter: So you did choose to come here rather than kill yourself?

Jonathan: Well, yes, I did.

Dr. Lassiter: Since Tuti and Darren left, what have you been doing?

Jonathan: Just work, home, TV. I don't want to talk to anyone. The only reason I am here is my supervisor insisted that I come to see you.

Dr. Lassiter: So you have chosen to isolate yourself since Tuti left?

Jonathan: How can you say such a thing? I can't help how I feel, and I am not choosing to be miserable. I have been terribly mistreated. You're not getting it.

Dr. Lassiter: You are right. I don't get it. How can you say that you are not isolating yourself? Has anyone forced you to stay at home and avoid others?

Jonathan: No, I have been so depressed. I haven't chosen anything.

Dr. Lassiter: Did you choose to come to the office for therapy to see me?

Jonathan: That's because my boss told me to. I was forced.

Dr. Lassiter: Or what would happen?

Jonathan: Or he might fire me.

Dr. Lassiter: So you chose to see me rather than be fired?

Jonathan: [*smiling*] I suppose you could say that. It's not much of a choice.

Dr. Lassiter: Your coming to see me is a big step, an excellent starting point. I am glad *you* chose to work on your relationships. And what do you want from this?

Jonathan: I want help getting Tuti back. I want it the way it was.

Dr. Lassiter: And what have you done to help yourself so far?

Jonathan: I don't know.

Dr. Lassiter: What do you want from her?

Jonathan: I want her to love me.

Dr, Lassiter: What do you want for Tuti?

Jonathan: I want her to be happy, but with me again. I want her to want me.

Dr. Lassiter: The only person you can change is you. Looks like you and she may want different worlds. All of us carry around mental picture albums in our heads about our ideal scenarios. Yours has Tuti in it with Darren as your best friend. But Tuti's mental picture album of her ideal relationship seems to have changed. Your quality worlds are in conflict now. Pictures can change, fade, even be removed and new ones developed. Priorities and attractions shift. When people get divorced, the picture of the spouse changes or is even removed. What changed in Tuti's quality world?

Jonathan: I suppose that her picture of being a mother got stronger and stronger. She talked about her biological clock ticking away.

Dr. Lassiter: If your quality worlds are dissimilar, it can be frustrating.

Jonathan: I want Tuti to want me. I want her pictures to be the same as mine.

Dr. Lassiter: Sounds as if you are being held hostage by Tuti, and Darren as well. When we try to control others, we choose to let them hold us hostage.

Jonathan: I guess they do have a hold on me.

Dr. Lassiter: Are you acting like a victim? With no control yourself?

Jonathan: I have been victimized, and I am depressed.

Dr. Lassiter: Are you depressed—or are you depress-ing?

Jonathan: What's the difference?

Dr. Lassiter: Depressed makes it seem as if it happens *to* you from outside, but depress-ing shows that you are in control of your feelings.

Jonathan: Well, I just know I feel bad. And I am not depressed on purpose. I can't help it if I feel this way.

Dr. Lassiter: And how would you like to feel?

Jonathan: I want to feel happy, but I can't if I don't have her.

Dr. Lassiter: People often do not believe they have a choice to control their feelings, but they do. Your total behavior is like a car. What drives your car is your need for love and belongingness. Your quality world has a picture of Tuti as the one who fills that need. There is a discrepancy between what you see as the way to fill the need and the loss of Tuti and Darren. So you are behaving in a way to fill that need, but you need to ask yourself: Is it really an effective way to get what you want? Is it possible that you think your depress-ing will bring Tuti back? Perhaps if you are helpless, it is your way of calling out for them to come back and rescue you from being the victim.

Jonathan: I never thought of it that way. Tuti did always help me out when I got down. And Darren cheered me up. He used to say, "Up and at 'em. You're in the emotional military now. Attention and take orders—cheer up!"

Dr. Lassiter: So, you have used depress-ing in the past. Has it helped?

Jonathan: Guess not. Look at where I am. OK, I'll be honest. I want to kill them both, and that scares me. I really don't want to hurt anyone. But what if I lost control? I can't see them, or I might.

Dr. Lassiter: When we depress, we can be preventing ourselves from acting out our anger and hurting others and ourselves. To depress is to try to stifle the anger we might be afraid of. So does your depress-ing fill a need and stop you from acting out?

Jonathan: That strikes a chord. I can see that. I think you might be right.

Dr. Lassiter: We are responsible for our choices. And let me ask, How is what you are doing now—depress-ing—helping you to get what you want?

Jonathan: It's not.

Dr. Lassiter: How about writing her a letter? Would that let you say what you need to say and give you hope of an answer?

Jonathan: I could try.

Dr. Lassiter: [*remainder of session used to frame things in WDEP*] Do you think your major problem is an unsatisfying relationship with Tuti—and Darren? [*pause*] Your world has suddenly been shaken. Your total behavior consists of obsessing about Tuti. You are depress-ing because you want help; you are stifling your anger. You avoid finding out what went wrong because more rejection would bring more pain. But, if you are depress-ing, it means you take less responsibility for your actions. So, will you be open to learning about choice theory and accept some key notions early in our work—responsibility, quality world, choices? Can you see that as you begin to control your own life more effectively, you will see your choices and be better off?

Jonathan: Yes, I realize this, but let me think more about it.

Session 4

Dr. Lassiter: So it has been over two weeks since you received the reply from Tuti.

Jonathan: She really trashed me. I can't believe she called me insensitive. Well, she is a rotten person who should have a rotten life.

Dr. Lassiter: How is it helping you to get what you want by blaming, criticizing, and complaining about Tuti and Darren?

Jonathan: [*smiles*] I don't know.

Dr. Lassiter: What does your smile mean? What are you doing at this moment?

Jonathan: OK. It is easier to blame them than to own up, I guess.

Dr. Lassiter: Who can you control other than yourself?

Jonathan: No one.

Dr. Lassiter: Do you think these ineffective behaviors will get you what you want? The letter tells me that Tuti's upset-ing is because your quality worlds became different—hers had children as a high priority, yours did not. What choice do you have? To have a family or to not have a family? Which did you make?

Jonathan: I did not make a choice!

Dr. Lassiter: No choice is a choice. How did avoiding the conflict and putting it off help you to get what you want?

Jonathan: It didn't. Tuti decided to fulfill the need for love and belongingness by being with someone who also wants children.

Dr. Lassiter: Why did you choose to avoid a discussion about having a child? Do you think it got you closer to Tuti?

Jonathan: I avoided it because it stems from my childhood. My parents neglected me a great deal. My mom was OK, but Dad was fierce, and he did not give me the kind of role model that I need to be a good father. As a matter of fact, today I am kind of mad at you, and you remind me of him.

Dr. Lassiter: I am not your dad or anyone else but myself. I think taking the discussion in the direction of the past and our parents is a way for both of us to avoid responsibility for what is happening here and now. Do you think it will help you to get what you want?

Jonathan: No, but I thought therapists wanted to hear about childhood.

Dr. Lassiter: Our past influences us, but we can only deal with what is happening now in current relationships. We can't change the past. OK. Now we will look at the WDEP again. It is extremely important for you to *evaluate* yourself—to look at what you are doing and to see if it is effective, if it is helping you or hurting you. Keep asking, Does your present behavior have a reasonable chance of getting you a new relationship, the kind that will bring you where you want to be in life, with no children and a professional career and partner who is willing to travel?

Jonathan: No. I need to behave differently. And I will ask for your help in therapy.

Dr. Lassiter: So we need to come up with a plan. The plan is best if it is simple, attainable, measurable, immediate, involved, and controlled by you. And it must be a plan to which you are committed and perform seriously to gain more control.

Jonathan: Huh? How can I do it? I feel hopeless at times, but I'll work on it. I feel as if Tuti is with me all the time.

Dr. Lassiter: Remember, Tuti is outside of you. Which things are inside of you?

Jonathan: I'll figure it out.

Dr. Lassiter: OK, we'll spend the rest of the session on it, and then you can evaluate how well it worked at the next session.

Session 5

Jonathan: Here's my plan. I'll make at least one social contact a week in order to meet someone. I will have a list of places for singles to meet. I will go out on Thursday, Friday, or Saturday to accomplish this. I've got a little chart and will keep track. I can learn to make better choices.

Dr. Lassiter: Good. You are choosing not to mope and isolate. And I'd like you to give me a call anytime you choose to do something. Leave a message on my answering machine. I want to hear about your successes.

Session 6

Jonathan: I thought a lot this week. I know that she is not coming back. I know I have to make changes, or I will do the same thing over again.

Dr. Lassiter: Yes, you can still choose to have a good life. But if you choose to depress—you will not be happy! Let's be realistic; you choose what you do every moment of the day.

Jonathan: The plan is working. I went out, and I actually met several interesting people who talked to me about their travels. It was great. I was hardly depress-ing at all this week. I chose not to depress—it felt weird. And I exercised three times this week.

Dr. Lassiter: How do you feel as you sit with me and tell me about your successes?

Jonathan: I feel good . . . great!

Dr. Lassiter: I think you're catching on. It is fascinating; when you are depress-ing, you don't feel better, but when you act to help solve the problem, you feel much better. So which is better: acting to solve the problem, or depress-ing and moping?

Jonathan: [*laughing*] I know the answer!

Dr. Lassiter: You are catching on.

Termination

Dr. Lassiter: It's good to see you again. And I am impressed with all that you have done to work on and solve your problems.

Jonathan: Every day I ask myself, "Is what I am doing helping or hurting me get what I want? If I continue in this direction, where will I be in six months?"

Dr. Lassiter: I would like to know what you chose to do differently because you are meeting with me.

Jonathan: I have learned to develop behaviors that get me what I want, and even better, you have helped me to look at myself and see if what I am doing is helpful to me and those that I care about. I have worked hard, but I have learned to be mindful of what I am doing and to see my self-defeating patterns.

Dr. Lassiter: It makes me happy to know you are feeling good.

Jonathan: Thank you. I am driving in the right direction, and I'll fulfill that need for love and belongingness in the near future. But for now, I am happy in the moment taking small steps.

Case Comment

Jonathan benefited from reality therapy in that he was able to understand that his primary problem was an unsatisfying relationship with Tuti and another problem was his broken relationship with Darren. The trauma of the events shook his quality world and his total behavior turned to obsess-ing and depress-ing. Jonathan was stifling his anger and avoiding reality in order to facing psychological and emotional pain. He began to take responsibility for his actions. He saw that he was able to control his own life more effectively and to make choices that brought him happiness. He learned to ask questions of himself: "Is what I am doing helping or hurting me get what I want? If I continue in this direction, where will I be in six months? Where will I go with my life?" Through the use of WDEP analysis, he was able to evaluate and alter his mental picture of his ideal partner as well as the direction of his life for fulfilling his basic needs

✦ RESEARCH DIRECTIONS IN REALITY THERAPY

The evidence base supporting the effectiveness of reality therapy is limited. Currently, no large-scale, randomized control studies comparing reality therapy with other therapies or even with a control group are available. The therapist must turn to the next-best evidence. These research studies range from single-subject case analyses to larger scale studies (Ingram & Hinkle, 1990).

Early published case studies were reported by Glasser (1998) about his original successes at Ventura School for Girls. In 1979, Glasser published findings of rate of discharge from the facility. He reported that when he worked with Dr. Harrington, he discharged 45 patients in his first year, 85 over the next year, and 90 in the following year, a significant increase in discharge rate after clients received reality therapy (Glasser & Zunin, 1979). While this seems impressive clinically, alternative explanations can be made. Success may be attributable to Glasser's charismatic personality, or to a change in the staff or administration, or to a policy change regarding institutionalization. Also, there are no long-term follow-up studies to assess how enduring these changes were after discharge.

Wubbolding devotes an entire chapter of his book *Reality Therapy for the 21st Century* to a summary of research on reality therapy. He describes two types of research—cerebral research and "fire-in-the-belly" research, which he claims is the most persuasive kind of documentation. He argues that people should apply ideas from reality therapy to their own lives, and "If these methods do not work for you, don't apply the techniques to other people. If, on the other hand, they favorably impact your own lives and those of your family, you will become convinced that clients, students, employers, and others will benefit in the same way" (Wubbolding, 2000, p. 203).

Wubbolding outlines a number of conclusions about research into reality therapy, drawing on various studies of drug use, addictions, juvenile offenders, exercise, and locus of control as supporting evidence (Radtke, Sapp, & Farrell, 1997). He points out, for instance, that overall students who feel connected to school and to the teachers increased their effective, assertive, and altruistic behaviors. His interpretations are sensible and intuitive, and the reader can easily follow his logic in support of reality therapy. However, more evidence is needed to confirm that reality therapy is efficacious and effective.

Wubbolding advocates for high quality research in reality therapy, and he argues that reality therapists have an ethical obligation to validate their work through sound scientific studies. However, conducting meaningful research means using genuine reality therapy, controls for the skill level of the practitioner, samples across an appropriate length of therapy of at least 16 weeks, and use of appropriate and objective outcome measures (Sansone, 1998). He also asks that counseling students be trained to use outcome research (Granello & Granello, 1998).

There have been a number of small studies of the effects of reality therapy, as listed here:

- In single-case studies using a baseline design, elementary school students increased on-task behaviors as measured by goal attainment scales when teachers used reality therapy or solution-focused brief counseling (Yarbrough & Thompson, 2002).
- Reality therapy helped 22 participants to increase coping skills and overall need satisfaction in managing chronic pain (Sherman, 2000).
- Choice theory and reality therapy promoted self-management among 29 subjects who were teachers of at-risk students (Holliman, 2000).
- Reality therapy clients showed a decrease in violence in a program of 21 sessions (Rachor, 1995).
- A review of six studies from 1980 to 1995 found that reality therapy shows much potential for increasing school performance and need satisfaction (Murphy, 1997).
- A bullying prevention program derived from reality therapy and choice theory showed significant decreases in bullying as compared to a no-treatment control group (Kim, 2006).

- Researchers have constructed a scale that operationalizes and validates Glasser's five needs (Lafond, 2000).
- Studies have examined to what degree school is part of a student's quality world; students reported that teachers and other people were more highly rated as part of a quality world that studying, exams, and evaluations (Rose, 2003).

In addition to these smaller studies, there are many discussion articles with topics ranging from student perceptions of their schools (Malley, Beck, Tavra, Feric, & Conway, 2003) to how research on the human brain supports choice theory and quality schools and how choice theory interfaces with other topics (Edens, 1997; Law, 2004).

Therapists can explain that their choice of reality therapy for treatment is based on subjective results. It is true that reality therapy has limited scientific data to support it and has not been as well researched as more established therapies, but it is a young therapy, and the subjective reports are positive. Currently reality therapists are attempting to establish its empirical validity and to incorporate accumulated research findings into relevant guidelines that are meaningful for practice. Therapists who perform reality therapy may be working with difficult-to-treat populations. They must be creative, resourceful, and encouraging to people who are facing serious problems.

✦ ISSUES OF DIVERSITY

Reality therapy is a product of Western culture and endorses the values of individualism, autonomy, and self-reliance. In reality therapy, the client's problems are inside the person, not outside in society.

Reality therapists say they respect differences, advocate cultural competence, and adhere to professional ethics in dealing with diversity. Reality therapists have brought reality therapy training to Croatia, Japan, Korea, Singapore, Kuwait, Colombia, Siberia, and Slovenia as well as many European countries with similarities to the United States, such as Ireland. They report that their ideas have been well received by this varied audience, and some research has shown the multicultural efficacy of reality therapy (Wubbolding et al., 1998).

A strength of reality therapists is that they incorporate a systematic worldview that encourages people of all cultures to self-evaluate. Glasser also states that reality therapy can be applied to all cultures and groups because all humans share the genetic endowment of the five basic needs. Satisfying these needs is a universal drive. Therapists adapt treatment to each person, considering the uniqueness of the individual. The client determines the choices he or she will make and what actions to take to improve relationships with others. Thus the reality therapist does not blindly endorse the view that strong individualism is most important but considers the importance of maintaining individual, community, societal, and even global relationships (Wubbolding, 2000).

There are some weak areas in reality therapy's cultural competence, however. For example, it is not specified how the therapist is to adapt the therapy for various cultures. In addition, although the therapy is being used with a broader range of cultures, it was developed and oriented out of Eurocentric values. In addition, feminists have complained that reality therapy lacks an essential feminist perspective, especially if self-evaluation does not weigh the reality of gender oppression and the negative consequences of gender inequality worldwide. How can anyone truly have free choice when dealing with oppression and inequitable access to resources (Ballou, 2006)?

Reality therapy does not take into account the devastating effects of poverty, deprivation, racism, sexism, classism, or discrimination; thus it does not objectively evaluate the effects of social oppression upon human choice. There is little discussion as to whether a person from an impoverished environment is as free to choose as a person from a privileged one. Rather, the belief is that every person in every situation has some choice, and the therapy maximizes the role of choice. But do all genders, races, and classes have the ability to choose equally? Does the billionaire have the same choices as the homeless person? How can we evaluate the effects of chronic oppression on an individual and his or her ability to use the tenets of choice theory? Does the length of the oppression matter? If an individual is the product of generations of oppression, does that affect the individual more than if the oppression is relatively recent (Linnenberg, 1999, 2006)?

→ MAJOR CRITIQUES OF REALITY THERAPY

Critics of reality therapy argue that it lacks theoretical validity. Although it poses as a practical therapy in that it deals with human consciousness and encourages self-awareness and self-evaluation, there is no evidence to back these claims. While it emphasizes how clients can be in control of thinking, feeling, behaving, and even their own physiology, research does not verify this. Glasser's notion of total behavior—the connections among thinking, feeling, behaving, and physiology—rely on unproven assumptions about how one affects the other.

The underlying theoretical basis of the theory is that all human beings are motivated by five genetic instructions: survival or self-preservation, belonging, power or achievement, freedom or independence, fun or enjoyment. But there is no substantive scientific data to support this. Glasser's basic needs are simply a rehash of Maslow's basic needs.

By stressing responsibility and choice, reality therapy implies that once a client adjusts his or her belief system, he or she will be empowered and will be mature, responsible, and self-actualized. In reality, many people are victims of circumstances and need to change their political, social, or economic conditions before they are truly free to choose. The danger of placing so much power in the individual is the tendency to blame the victim when in fact adverse circumstances play a substantial role in mental health conditions. Thus, reality therapy is truly a constructivist approach and does not account for the reality of oppression and how much choice is limited by societal conditions.

Practitioners with a medical orientation are reluctant to use reality therapy because it does not acknowledge *DSM* diagnoses. The idea that schizophrenia is a choice, not a medical condition, is objectionable to many biologically based therapists. Making a diagnosis is essential in order to gain insurance support. That reality therapy discounts transference, the unconscious, and other traditional Freudian concepts may also drive some practitioners away.

With the lack of ongoing, systematic research programs into the effectiveness or efficacy of reality therapy, or any high-quality, well-controlled studies, it may not survive empirical scrutiny. In general, research into reality therapy must occur before clinicians can say definitively that the use of reality therapy is most effective with a particular type of patient in a particular situation. More research with well-designed studies is essential.

Summary

- Reality therapy, created by William Glasser, is based on choice theory (once called control theory), which holds that people can control only their own behavior and no one else's.
- There are five genetically coded basic needs that motivate behavior: survival, belonging, power, freedom, and fun. Every person has a quality world, or mental pictures, that are the means by which people meet these needs. The quality world is a collection of wants related to the five needs. The most important need is that of belonging.
- All behavior is total behavior and is made up of four components: acting, thinking, feeling, and physiology. All behavior is chosen. People have direct control over the acting and thinking components but indirect control of feeling and physiology through how we choose to act and think. All total behavior is designated by verbs and named by the part that is the most recognizable.
- The healthy person chooses to use effective behavior. People who have long-lasting psychological problems have relationship problems; the past is seen from the perspective that we can only satisfy our basic needs right now by satisfying the pictures in our quality world. Abnormal behavior is a choice, not a disease; it represents unsuccessful attempts to meet one's needs.
- In practice, the therapist builds an interpersonal environment of acceptance and is a strong, active mentor who provides an interprersonal environment based on trust, friendliness, firmness, and fairness. Clients learn the principles of choice theory about relationships by being a part of a successful therapeutic one. Length of treatment is individualized.
- Therapeutic techniques include executing the treatment procedures in a method called WDEP or wants, direction, evaluation, and plan. Planning involves these elements: It is simple, attainable, measurable, immediate, involved, controlled, committed, and consistent.
- The evidence base supporting the effectiveness of reality therapy is limited and relies primarily on small studies and case studies. Some studies have reported

favorable results in elementary school students with coping skills and need satisfaction and bullying prevention programs. Wubbolding describes two types of research—cerebral research and "fire-in-the-belly" research, which he claims is the most persuasive kind of documentation.

- Reality therapy has been used successfully in multiple cultures. However, it is criticized for not taking into account the devastating effects of the external effects of poverty, deprivation, racism, sexism, classism, or discrimination on the internal state.

- Critics of reality therapy say it relies on unproven assumptions and generalizations about genetic needs and biology and how one need or person affects the other. Medically oriented practitioners are reluctant to use reality therapy because it does not acknowledge *DSM* diagnoses. The idea that conditions are choices, not medical conditions, is objectionable to many biologically based therapists, especially with a lack of ongoing, systematic research programs into its effectiveness.

RESOURCES

William Glasser Institute
22024 Lassen Street, Suite 118
Chatsworth, CA 91311-3600
(818) 700-8000
http://www.wglasser.com

Founded in 1967 for the purpose of teaching reality therapy, the institute is a non-profit, charitable foundation. It offers training, workshops, networking, educational materials, and certification in reality therapy.

Center for Reality Therapy
Dr. Robert E. Wubbolding
7672 Montgomery Road #383
Cincinnati, OH 45236-4204
(513) 561-1911
http://www.realitytherapywub.com

Affiliated with the William Glasser Institute run by Dr. Robert Wubbolding, this center offers training, workshops, networking, educational materials, and certification in reality therapy as well as consulting about quality schools.

CLASS EXERCISES AND ACTIVITIES

Theory

1. Control is a key issue in the theory of reality therapy. People use control to meet their needs. Give some examples of how we seek control. What are some healthy and unhealthy ways that people use to seek control?

2. A central belief of choice theory is that the only person I can really control is myself. How does this fit with Glasser's concept of choice and responsibility?
3. How does a reality therapist view rewards and punishments as ways to change behaviors?

Practice

1. Jim is a 17-year-old who is in the juvenile detention center. He tells his therapist that his parents are too strict, that the police have some nerve bringing him to this detention center, and that his teachers are picking on him. Describe a WDEP that you could simulate with him.
2. How would you, as a therapist, explain responsibility and choice to a client in a session?
3. Look at the sample treatment plan in Chapter 1 (Figure 1.2). Fill out the treatment plan for Tuti for reality therapy. (Both Jonathan's and Tuti's case histories are in Appendix A.)

Research

1. Critique the research base for reality therapy. How can it be improved in the future? Design a study to support the effectiveness of reality therapy.
2. A patient asks you, "Why are you using reality therapy to treat me? Can you explain your choice of this particular model for me?"
3. Conduct a review of reality therapy by using the following key words in PubMed and PsycINFO: *reality therapy*. What did you find? Limit your search to *reality therapy and randomized control*. What did you find? What kinds of articles are available about reality therapy? Taking a quick overview of the articles, describe the nature of the articles and the kind of evidence they contain to support the efficacy and effectiveness of reality therapy.

CHAPTER 12

❧

FEMINIST THERAPY

*Bid the older women . . . teach what is good, and so train the young women to love
their husbands and children, to be sensible, chaste, domestic, kind and submissive
to their husbands that the word of God may not be discredited.*

–St. Paul's letter to Titus (Titus 2:3–6)

The goal of this chapter is to present an overview of feminist therapy. We look at biographical information about a number of thoughtful feminists who influenced the evolution of this therapy, its historical context, and the theory, practice, and research of feminist therapy. The simulated psychotherapist, Dr. Anita Green, presents a treatment plan and some excerpts from feminist therapy sessions for the case of Jonathan. Issues of diversity and major critiques are also included.

✦ HISTORICAL CONTEXT

Imagine a world in which women are not permitted to own property, to participate in a lawsuit, to serve on a jury, to make a will, to appear in public, or to address an audience in a public space. Picture a civilization in which women who decide to divorce automatically lose custody of their children to the husband. Envision a culture whose members believe that women are, by nature, inferior to men and less competent physically and intellectually. This was the reality for women in the Western world until the 1900s, and it is still a reality for women who live in highly patriarchal societies today (Landrine & Klonoff, 1997).

Feminist therapy emerged as a way to deal with the mental health of women living in sexist societies. A wide range of feminists from many different perspectives created diverse approaches, thus all feminist therapists do not speak with one voice. In its early history, the commonality among all feminist therapists was viewing the impact of gender above all else, but today feminist therapists tend to see the world more broadly, considering how society's treatment of nondominant and oppressed groups influences mental health in general. Among the populations they include in their approach are lesbians, gays, women of color, immigrants, the poor, transnationals, and the disabled (Comas-Diaz & Greene, 1994; Robinson & Howard-Hamilton, 2000).

Feminist therapy creates a "conscious, consistent, and coherent framework" from which the therapist can consider the effects of a multiplicity of social roles on the mental health of women (and men) through the infusion of feminist values into mental health treatment (Enns, 2004, p. 1). With its broadened and expanded scope, feminist therapy has evolved into a multicultural feminist therapy model (Yoder, 2002; Yoder & Kahn, 2003). Before we look at the current state of feminist therapy, let's review the influences that led to this approach (Enns & Sinacore, 2005).

The Waves of Feminism

Feminism is both an ideology and a movement for sociopolitical change (Offen, 2000). It is based on the belief that women and men are inherently equal and, thus, are entitled to equitable treatment in all areas of life. Traditionally, most societies have been structured to give political, social, and economic advantage to men and have systematically subordinated women as a group; this means that women must work to gain equality (Stopler, 2003). Two major beliefs underlie both feminism and feminist therapy: The personal is political, and a person's private life is deeply affected by the sociocultural environment. While feminists generally agree on these beliefs, they differ on what methods are effective in achieving political, social, and economic equality.

What is called the *first wave* of Western feminism, 1800 to 1930, achieved impressive changes in the legal status of women in the United States. The cumulative efforts of suffragettes, Quakers, and abolitionists brought about the passage of "The Declaration of Sentiment" in 1848 in Seneca Falls, New York. This document, an inspiration and guide for feminist activism, advocated equal natural rights for all, and especially women's right to vote. In 1866, the passage of the Fourteenth Amendment ensured that all citizens were equal under the law. And by 1917, the National American Woman Suffrage Association, with over 2 million members, mobilized support for suffrage. In 1920, the Nineteenth Amendment finally awarded American women the vote. The list of women who fought in this first wave of feminism is long but little known. It includes Elizabeth Cady Stanton, Sojourner Truth, Susan B. Anthony, and Margaret Sanger, who fought for women's reproductive rights (Fox & Langley, 1994).

The *second wave* of feminism emerged in the 1960s. The issues that mobilized the movement at this time involved gender equity in the workplace and support for working mothers, such as child care (Anderson, 2005). In 1963, the Kennedy Commission on the Status of Women reported that women were oppressed since they were not treated equally under the law, received less pay for the same work as men, and received insufficient support (that is, child care) to work productively. Activists such as Betty Freidan founded the National Organization for Women (NOW). Margaret Sanger's reproductive rights organization evolved into Planned Parenthood. The U.S. Supreme Court's landmark decision in *Roe v. Wade* affirmed the rights of women to control their own reproduction during the first six months of pregnancy.

Many legislative, judicial, and civil rights gains have advanced and strengthened women's rights and status since the 1960s. However, the second wave did not achieve the goal of total equality between the sexes. Ratified by only 35 of the required 38 states, the Equal Rights Amendment (ERA), a proposed change to the

U.S. Constitution to guarantee equal rights under the law for all citizens regardless of sex, has not passed to date (Fox & Langley, 1994).

In this second wave were four loose and overlapping categories of feminism (Enns, 1992, 1993):

- *Liberal or mainstream feminists* believed legal, economic, and cultural constraints prevented women from equal access to resources. They believed oppression must be countered with political activism and reform of the legal and political systems. A liberal feminist therapist would encourage the client to empower herself through self-fulfillment and to pursue political change.
- *Cultural feminists* argued that violence and aggression could be overcome, and peace could dominate (Donovan, 2000). Women, with the life-affirming values of feminism (harmony, cooperation, gentleness, connectedness, and pacifism), have an obligation to reform the world. A cultural feminist therapist would encourage the client to work toward feminizing the world and to seek support and comfort from other women who understand these principles (group therapies).
- *Radical feminists* argued that that patriarchal, male dominance—with its competition and heterosexism—was oppressive. They emphasized civil rights, antiwar activities, and control over their own bodies and reproductive rights. A radical feminist therapist would encourage the client to be assertive, to be aware of the patriarchal influences on her personality and behaviors, and to campaign for total political and social autonomy (Anderson, 2005).
- *Socialist feminists* believed oppression was a function of the combined impact of all causes of inequities (class, race, nationality, capitalism, economics, control of reproduction and sexuality, and socialization) and that these inequities were enforced in everyday social systems. A socialist feminist therapist would encourage a client to understand the effects of all forms of social injustice on her and to act to achieve universal equality for all. From this standpoint, we can work to change social mechanisms, such as childrearing practices, which reinforce early gender learning.

These categories of feminist therapy are fluid, especially today. For example, a radical feminist may also embrace many of the beliefs of the cultural feminist, so that in therapy the client receives a blend of feminist approaches. Despite internal debates on specific positions within feminism, there are many overlapping and concurrent opinions as well (Contratto & Rossier, 2005).

Today we are at the *third wave* of feminism, which has produced a number of versions, including third wave feminists, postmodern feminists, women of color feminists, lesbian feminists and queer theorists, and global feminists (Ballou & Mulrooney, 2006; Zack, 2005).

Third wave feminists are hybrid feminists with broad concerns (Narayan, 1997). They address issues such as environmentalism, globalization and corporatization of international labor, racism and sexual orientation issues, and immigration from diverse and patriarchal societies (Marecek, 2005). They fight not just the injustices inflicted upon women but all forms of social injustices resulting from oppression by a dominant group (Lotz, 2003). Third wave feminists evolved because women of color, women from Third World cultures, women without power and money, among others, made little progress in the world, while White, Western, middle-class women gained autonomy in the early history of feminism (Braithwaite, 2002; Bruns, 2001).

Postmodern feminists believe all truth is merely a social construction. Knowers of truth are fallible and use truth to mold reality to their advantage. They question all power and how it is attained and maintained. They see things on a continuum, reject bipolar ways of looking at the world such as masculine or feminine, and dismantle dualistic constructs. They see language as a tool to create gender and sex bias, and they emphasize the intersections of oppression and look at the multiplicity of identities.

Women of color feminists often criticize mainstream feminists for inappropriately assuming that White women's experience can be a template for understanding the lives of all women (Donovan, 2000; Espin, 1999). White women have used the unearned advantages of being Caucasian for themselves and have failed to increase the status of women from nondominant groups (Mio, Barker-Hackett, & Tumambing, 2006). All feminists need to question how and what they know about women of color (Kaschak, 2001).

Lesbian feminists hold that the cause of oppression is heterosexualism. They deconstruct rigid categories of heterosexuality. Sex and gender are interdependent categories, best exemplified by the institution of compulsory heterosexuality. Lesbian feminists have been challenged by *queer theorists,* who consider sex and gender to be conceptually distinct. Lesbian feminists and queer theorists may also disagree about the significance of sexual difference and about the importance of what is normative and nonnormative in terms of gender identity (Brown, Riepee, & Coffey, 2005).

Global feminists and transnationalists attribute the cause of oppression to colonialism, nationalism, and multinational corporations. This feminism encourages global cooperation among feminists, stresses worldwide gender quality, and promotes the interconnectedness of women around the world, despite their differences. Global feminism challenges the ethnocentrism of Western feminists as it highlights the importance of implementing global and grassroots efforts by and for women.

Influential Feminists

The impact of a number of key individuals on feminist therapy must be acknowledged before we can discuss the therapy in depth. Some of the following thinkers have been introduced earlier in the book, and others are currently contributing to feminist therapy.

Karen Horney

One of the first feminists to openly object to Freud's psychoanalytic theory was Karen Horney (1885–1952; see About Karen Horney box in Chapter 4). Horney believed that many of Freud's assumptions were detrimental to women's mental health (Horney, 1966; Stopler, 2003). She argued what women really wanted was not the penis, but the social power and privilege associated with it (Offen, 2000).

Horney also pointed out while it was considered normal or even virtuous for a female to expect her life to be fulfilled by serving and nurturing others (husbands or children), attributes associated with males—such as self-sufficiency, independence, and logical reasoning—were more highly regarded by society (Horney, 1968). Many of Horney's ideas were adopted by others but not credited. Her challenges to sexist concepts in psychoanalytic thinking were largely unnoticed until fairly recently.

Alfred Adler

Alfred Adler (1870–1937; see About Alfred Adler box in Chapter 5) was an ardent feminist. He was one of the few European psychoanalysts who believed in women's equality and supported total emancipation. In *Understanding Human Nature* (Adler, 1927), he argued that women need complete equality with men in order to have a fulfilled civilization and an ideal social order. Adler was one of the very few feminist males within the European psychological community.

Jean Baker Miller

Jean Baker Miller (1928–2006), a psychoanalytically oriented psychiatrist, argued that psychoanalytic thinking had lost its way in the hands of men (Miller, 1976/1986, 1991). At Wellesley College, she elucidated power dynamics between males and females and questioned how they were used within psychoanalysis. Her model of relational psychotherapy challenged seminal psychoanalytic ideas. For example, psychoanalysis values the male goal of independence. Miller believed interdependence is a superior goal since it enhances mental development, quality of life, and ability to navigate in the interpersonal world. Miller raised consciousness about the how being members of the dominant and subordinate groups affects personality development. For example, dominants trigger submissives to hide much of their real personality, which blocks them from reaching their full potential.

Nancy Chodorow

Nancy Chodorow has argued that the ideal of mental health and the goals of therapy reflect a male standard (Chodorow, 1989). Girls define their identity by being similar to their mothers—nurturing, caring, and connected. Boys form their identities by breaking away and disconnecting from their mothers. Thus females value interpersonal continuity with the mother, whereas males value separation. Success for a woman is to live in an interdependent fashion, but success for a man is to detach himself interpersonally, to be aggressive and power seeking through identification with a father and his male values.

Carol Gilligan

Carol Gilligan, a developmental psychologist at Harvard University, pointed out the bias in research on moral development (Gilligan, 1982). She objected to Lawrence Kohlberg's theory about moral development, which is based on all-male samples and which gives higher value to moral decision making based on "male" types of reasoning. Gilligan conducted studies that discovered that men make moral judgments based upon principles of justice, while women consider caring to be most important when they make moral decisions; in other words, female morality is based upon caring and not just abstract principles of justice.

Sandra Bem

Sandra Bem, a social psychologist, has researched gender schemas and has demonstrated how society narrowly defines the appropriate behaviors and traits for masculinity and femininity (Bem, 1983, 1993). These organized sets of mental perceptions prescribe that men should be aggressive, and women should be gentle and caring. Both males and females are constrained by these arbitrary distinctions, which have serious implications for development and mental health.

Phyllis Chesler

In 1972, Phyllis Chesler published *Women and Madness,* which created an uproar in the mental health community because she pointed to the blatant sexism of the American mental health system. Her work highlighted sources of bias and sexist practices in assessment, diagnosis, and treatment in the past and insisted that these problems persist. Chesler argued that women were overrepresented, were treated by male-dominated professionals, and were often labeled mentally ill when they could also be viewed as responding to discrimination in an adaptive or predictable fashion. Her book, which has been updated (Chesler, 1997), maintains that the feminist movement has been silenced.

Laura S. Brown

Laura S. Brown, one of the founders of the Feminist Therapy Institute, writes about the fundamentals of feminist therapy and discusses the image of women in her works. In her well-known instructional work *Subversive Dialogues: Theory in Feminist Practice,* Brown (1994, 2005b) describes practical methods for feminist therapists as well as illustrating them in an instructional video series. Brown continues to be an innovator in feminist theory, creating clinical strategies for use in feminist therapy.

Carolyn Zerbe Enns

Carolyn Zerbe Enns, a psychology professor at Cornell College in Iowa, has studied feminism's effects on the therapeutic relationship and therapeutic goals and has looked at these issues historically (Enns, 1997, 2004). She is an advocate of self-analyses of feminism, and her classification of types of feminism (described earlier in the chapter) has helped to clarify the distinct ways of approaching feminist therapy.

Lenore Walker

Lenore Walker is a clinical psychologist who developed a type of survivor therapy, or a practical way to work with women who are suffering from posttraumatic stress

(Walker, 1990). Walker advocates personal responsibility and assertiveness for women, the recognition of detrimental cognitions, and the breaking down of the we–they barrier of traditional therapy relationships.

Olivia Espin

Olivia Espin is a professor of women's studies at San Diego State University and is at the forefront of the third wave of feminism (Espin, 1999). Her work highlights diversity and multiculturalism, as she writes of refugee women and their mental health. Her analysis of the intersections of many forms of oppression and privilege, and how they affect the development of feminist theory, is highly acclaimed. Espin has studied oppression and privilege and how these impact women's identity; recently she has explored women saints from a psychological perspective to uncover what she calls the politics of sainthood.

Lillian Comas-Diaz

Clinical psychologist Lillian Comas-Diaz is the executive director of the Transcultural Mental Health Institute and the former director of the American Psychological Association's Office of Ethnic Minority Affairs. *Ethnocultural psychotherapy* was developed by Comas-Diaz and Frederick M. Jacobsen as a way to integrate human diversity into clinical practice (Comas-Diaz, 2006). This eclectic approach acknowledges the concept of self as an internal ethnocultural representation.

Beverly Greene

Beverly Greene, professor of psychology at St. John's University in New York has produced groundbreaking research on mental health issues of African American lesbians. Her studies have focused on easing the burdens of stigma, stereotype, and ignorance for sexual minorities and people of color. Greene's scholarly contributions to the psychological literature include writings on the psychology of women, on underrepresented groups of women, and on the links among gender, ethnicity, and sexual orientation (Greene & Croom, 2000).

Judith Worell

Clinical psychologist Judith Worell urges therapists to be aware of sexism and its consequences (Worell, 2001). Personality traits traditionally assigned to females (nurturance, kindness, concern for others) are considered to be less typical of the healthy personality than those associated with males (independence, competence); more negative stereotypes are ascribed to women of color and to poor women than to middle-class White women. Normative gender role behaviors for women (such as dependency) are viewed as illnesses, and those who do not conform or who resist these roles are viewed as pathologizing, which is reflected in biased diagnoses.

In addition, a woman's legitimate distress is often diagnosed as having a biological or intrapsychic basis; external causes for this distress, such as power inequities and discrimination in the sociocultural environment, are discounted. The act of labeling a woman's distress as a form of mental illness maintains the prevailing power difference (Worell & Remer, 2003). Worell maintains that the treatment and diagnosis of women in the mental health system is permeated with sexism (Caplan, 1983; Fernando, 2003).

Today's Feminist Issues

There is a wide spectrum of issues concerning feminists today, and these all affect feminist therapy. One recent development in the study of gender roles is a push to identify the psychological effects of gender role expectations on men and on female–male relationships. Ronald Levant (2003) argues for involving men in feminist therapy. Since they are part of the gender identity problem, men need to be part of the solution as well. If men modify their gender roles, a reciprocal change in the way in which women relate to them will inevitably ensue (Evans, Kincaide, Marbley, & Seem, 2005). While some feminists support this exploration, it is not surprising that others argue that males should instead invest their energy advocating for a totally egalitarian relationship between men and women.

Beyond interpersonal issues of concern to feminists are global problems in economic, social, political, and educational realms (European Economic and Social Committee, 2008; Hausmann, Tyson, & Zahidi, 2007; National Organization for Women, 2007; World Health Organization, 2008):

- *Economic:* Women represent two-thirds of the poorest people on the planet. They still earn approximately 78 percent of wages that men receive for the same work, a gap that has not closed even in developed countries. Women's access to the labor market is often restricted to unskilled and low-paying jobs. Feminized professions (e.g., nursing and teaching) are among the lowest paid. Glass ceilings for women ensure that men occupy power positions disproportionately.
- *Political:* Across the world, on average, women occupy 15.6 percent of decision-making positions in political structures; this ranges from 6.8 percent in Arab states to 18.6 percent in the Americas, to 39.7 percent in Nordic regions. These positions are nearly all at the lower levels of the political systems, meaning that women have virtually no impact on important decisions regarding spending priorities for education, the military, and health initiatives.
- *Education:* Women represent two-thirds of the world's illiterate population and are less represented than men in all levels of education.
- *Health:* Over 1,600 women die every day from pregnancy and childbirth-related conditions. Of 46 million abortions worldwide, unsafe procedures are used for 20 million, killing 80,000 women from complications. Erosion of reproductive rights is a challenge to women's health.
- *Violence:* Globally, women and children are often the victims of violence through war, forced marriage, wife battering, and sexual assault, as well as extreme restrictions of rights (Brown, 2004). Abusive attitudes are rampant in Western culture, as well as more patriarchal cultures, as seen in degrading and unrealistic objectifications of women in pornography, TV, movies, music, and video games.

In addition to these concerns, feminists are also involved in lesbian, gay, bisexual, and transsexual (LGBT) rights issues. Feminists consider gay rights to be emblematic of human rights. They demand that the United States speak out against homophobia and take a strong stand for gay rights in the courts (Richards, 2005).

The current trend in the United States is to integrate feminism with multiculturalism. Advocates of this movement argue that women are an oppressed group whose voices have been suppressed in a male-dominated society. Thus they share common characteristics with other oppressed groups. Appreciating their own intersecting identities increases learning and information, as an integrated approach will lead to new ways of knowing from those who have been marginalized (Enns et al., 2005).

However, some see potential problems in this integrated view. The values of a nondominant culture may be at odds with feminist values (Young, 2001). Patriarchal cultures typically oppose individual autonomy for women (Prins, 2006), and many religions object to LGBTs. While some multiculturalists do not want to judge that one culture is superior to another, especially Western to non-Western cultures, there are some tough choices to make. How can a clash of values between the basic rights of women and a culture that subjugates women to the will of men be reconciled (Okin, 1998, 2002)? Often the common ground between feminists and multiculturalists is that both are the voices of less powerful groups wanting to be heard. But many fear that women's rights could pedal backward if the cultural values of a sexist culture are defended (Kukathis, 2001).

✦ THEORY OF FEMINIST THERAPY

Feminist therapy is more of an attitude than a system. Based upon feminist philosophy—the personal is political, and private life is affected by the sociocultural environment—feminist therapists contend the quality of a person's mental health is influenced by social identity (especially gender roles), by social inequities, and by oppression. Most of women's mental health problems stem from living in a sexist society that assigns them an inferior status with less economic and political power than males (Haw, 2000). Feminist therapy helps people to deal with the expectations and constraints of traditional gender role stereotypes and to separate the person's problem from what is disordered in society (APA, 2007; Worell & Remer, 2003).

These assumptions generate some corollaries, specifically that women are vulnerable to the psychological consequences of violence and sexual abuse. Thus gender inequality is not the only social injustice to be addressed; ending other inequities relating to race, class, ethnicity, and sexual orientation as they pertain to women, is also a priority for women's mental health.

Feminist theory rests on a number of key concepts, including social identity, sex and gender, gender role socialization, and sex role stereotyping. Other ideas informing the theory concern broader social problems, such as issues of power, privilege and oppression, and struggles with discrimination and bias.

Social Identity

Social identity is made up of personal and group definitions embedded in social groups and statuses. Social identity is associated with, but not limited to, characteristics such as gender, race, culture, ethnicity, geographic location, intellectual ability, sexual orientation, age, body size, religious affiliation, acculturation status, class, and other sociodemographic characteristics. A complex interaction of these group identities and statuses occurs in the person's social identity, and this identity is influenced by the degree to which these various factors are discernible to others, have situational salience, or are expressions of oppression or privilege (Stewart & McDermotte, 2004).

Sex and Gender

Sex is a person's biological makeup. *Gender* is the combination of psychological, social, and cultural characteristics that are associated with being a specific biological sex. A person incorporates social beliefs, assumptions, expectations, and stereotypes about males and females into his or her gender.

Gender Role Socialization and Conflict

Gender roles are a set of behavioral norms associated with females and males in a given culture; they are part of a person's social identity. Society determines what behavior is appropriate for a person based upon their biological sex and enforces it through rules and values. These gender roles carry certain advantages and disadvantages and thus shape behaviors and destinies. For example, more social, political, and economic power is associated with maleness than with femaleness. Traditional constructions of gender are often patriarchal. Gender expectations vary as a function of other group membership such as ethnicity, class, race, sexual orientation, and disability (Eagly, Diekman, & Aspinwall, 2003).

If the individual finds it difficult to live up to the male/female standards he or she has internalized, a gender role conflict results. This is a psychological state of tension in which socialized gender roles have negative consequences on the individual or on others with whom the individual interacts (Eagly et al., 2003).

Sex Role Stereotyping

Sex role stereotyping is a standardized mental picture of the typical man or woman and his/her personality traits. Current sex role stereotypes define the typical woman as being most concerned with her relationships with others, gentle, kind, emotional, dreamy, modest, fickle, warm, talkative, nervous, and patient. The typical man is most concerned with his own self-interest, self-confident, competitive, active, loud, inventive, greedy, capable, a show off, courageous, and cynical (Anderson, 2005).

Stereotypes can influence behavior in both obvious and subtle ways. They may bring about self-fulfilling prophecies. For example, if a mother believes that boys should be involved in sports and girls should be engaged in ballet, she may overtly or covertly select these behaviors to reinforce and maintain. A father may treat his daughters and sons differently at the dinner table, encouraging the boys to eat so they can be big and strong athletes, but encouraging the girls to be slender, light, and dainty.

Androgyny

Androgyny means possessing both masculine and feminine characteristics. The traditional standard has been to divide the world into a male and female split. An alternative view is for men and women to display both masculine and feminine behaviors when it is appropriate to do so allowing people to have a more flexible lifestyle. However, some object because it does not correct the problem that male characteristics are valued more highly than female traits (Bem, 1983, 1993). These objectors tout gender role transcendence as preferable to androgyny. In this transcendence, the person rises above gender-specific behaviors and does what is personally meaningful and effective (Rebecca, Heffner, & Oleshansky, 1976).

Power Relationships

Power is distributed in any relationship. Relationships can be (a) between equals, (b) between a more powerful or dominant person and a less powerful or subordinate person, or (c) fluctuating between the two (Watzlawick, Beavin, & Jackson, 1967). The ideal relationship is egalitarian. The power balance is symmetrical, and all parties share social, political, and economic equality. In the therapy relationship, although the client expects to benefit from the wisdom and expertise of the therapist, the dyad moves toward equality with an end goal of equal status (APA, 2007).

In dominant–subordinate relationships (traditional and male-led), the dominant is the leader, is more important than the subordinates, is independent, has control of the resources, takes most of the initiative, and makes the final decisions. The subordinate is less important and accommodates to this power differential. In order to survive and to obtain resources from the dominant group, subordinates develop a set of adaptive behaviors, even immature characteristics that allow them to get along with the dominant group such as dependency, passivity, lack of initiative, apparent cooperation, and a motivation to please the dominant group. They perform functions that the dominant group considers to be less important such as forms of manual labor like cleaning, cooking, and child care. While members of the subordinate group pretend to be less than they are, in reality they are playing a role and manipulating situations in order to survive. This lack of honesty blocks all from fully knowing each other and from developing meaningful relationships.

Oppression and Privilege

Oppression is the domination of one group over another. The needs of the less powerful are subordinated to those of the more powerful. The many forms of oppression range from subtle to blatant and include sexism, racism, classism, ageism, and heterosexism (Worell & Remer, 2003).

In contrast, *privilege* is the unwarranted advantage a person has by virtue of being a member of a group. Social status, power, and institutionalized advantage belong to those who are part of a valued social identity. Male privilege is the unearned advantage men have by virtue of a system normed on the experiences, values, and perceptions of males. White privilege automatically confers dominance to Whites, while placing other groups in a descending relational hierarchy (Sue, 2003, p. 137). Privilege is predicated on the false belief that deservedness is a result of hard work, industriousness, strength, family values, and actions other than favoritism. White privilege and male privilege are both deeply embedded in the structure, system, and culture of U.S. society with an invisible veil of unspoken and protected secrecy (McIntosh, 1989).

Internalized Oppression and Other Obstacles

Internalized oppression is the "taking within" of the external message of oppression so that a person thinks, feels, and believes the oppressor's definition of self rather than her own. For example, a well-accepted stereotype is that women are physically weaker than men. This is symbolized through cultural rituals. For example, to be polite, men open the car door for a lady. This reinforces the notion and perpetuates the myth that women are so weak they need a man's help to open a heavy car door.

The glass ceiling is an invisible obstacle faced by women and other oppressed groups when they try to advance to the same level as White males, usually in a business environment. For example, women striving for prestigious positions in corporate settings may find that their progress is inexplicably slow. Although there are no legal impediments to women holding high-ranking positions, the glass ceiling may limit their success.

Discrimination

Discrimination means treating an individual or a group differently simply because of the person's or group's identity. There is a long history of women being treated differently than men (Fiske, 2002). For example, boys are told to follow their dreams and let nothing stand in their way while girls are told they should choose attainable goals such as nursing or secretarial work in Western cultures (Smith & Siegal, 1985). Across the world, women suffer restricted rights and derogatory cultural views (Holmshaw & Hillier, 2000).

Normal and Abnormal Behavior

The feminist definitions of normal and abnormal behavior must include cultural considerations as well as personal ones. To attain ideal mental health, a person needs to live in a nonsexist, diverse society without oppression. Such a society does not exist in this world (Holmshaw & Hillier, 2000). This means that good mental health is a function of how well a person can navigate in a society filled with *isms,* particularly sexism.

A person in good mental health is mature, stable, has a well-integrated self-image, and possesses both agency and communion, or self-assertion and accommodation. She is in charge of her own life within the confines of a flawed society. She is aware that she has been gender socialized, sees the sex role stereotype for what it is, and does not allow it to dictate who she is. Oppression is not used as an excuse to escape her individual responsibilities (Hefner, Rebecca, & Oleshansky, 1975).

She chooses to conform, or not to conform, to the gender role dictates when it is in her best interests. For example, Maria is running for political office; she is also a devoutly religious person, and members of her church strongly believe that women should take care of their husbands. When asked if she intends to continue to cook for her family if she wins the election, she wisely chooses to answer that cooking for her husband and children is one of her greatest delights. It is true Maria enjoys cooking, and she tactfully answers in a way that effectively presents an acceptable image to the traditional churchgoers yet maintains her integrity. What she does not mention is that her egalitarian relationship with her husband has meant that he agreed to take on the cooking since they both understand that her work needs are more pressing than his at this juncture in their lives. The healthy person views the other gender in a realistic, integrated way, with self-assertion, concern, and accommodation (Gerber, 1996).

Feminist theory regards abnormal behavior as the result of mental distress caused by the harmful effects of living in an oppressive society in which the social, political, and cultural mandates subordinate women to men and create negative life circumstances (Butler, Giordano, & Neren, 1985). The culture is one in a world where the dominant group sets the standard of normality, using its members as the yardstick to which all others are compared. Deviations are considered to be inferior, substandard, and pathological (Burn & Ward, 2005). A person, suppressing significant parts of herself is blocked from being her true self.

Role strain may result from a lack of power and control combined with increased social responsibilities such as caring for children and may then lead to depression and anxiety. The mental health system labels it as major depression and treats the coping reaction as if it were a medical pathology. In reality, if the oppressive circumstances changed, the depression and anxiety would dissolve. Thus, differentiating between what is a method of coping with social tyranny and what is a mental health disorder is important (Mio et al., 2006).

A second type of mental distress results from fighting oppression directly. When a woman who has freed herself from the "symptoms" caused by gender roles faces others who have not changed, she may encounter disapproval, rejection, or even ridicule. For example, Paula was seen by a non-feminist therapist for depression and low self-esteem. Not culturally competent, the therapist reinforced sex role stereotypes. She encouraged Paula to lose weight, to get a "make-over," and to be more "feminine" so she could attract the "right kind of man" who would take care of her. When Paula changed to a feminist therapist, her consciousness was raised. Paula realized she was trying to "fit a size 18 body into a size 6 dress." In feminist therapy, Paula became comfortable with her own body, obtained a masters degree, increased her salary and thus her financial independence, and devoted time and energy to satisfying herself rather than everyone else around her. However, her change was not without consequences, and some of them were painful. Many of her friends thought she had become selfish, and her long-time fiancé broke up with her.

Society often places women in a double bind. "To be a healthy woman by society's standards is to be a sick adult. On the other hand, for a woman to aspire to a societal definition of adulthood is to do so at the cost of her womanhood" (Heriot, 1983, p. 12).

Of course, feminist therapists do recognize the existence of organically based mental illnesses that are not caused by social and cultural conditions and that require a medical diagnosis. For example, the prevalence of schizophrenia across all cultures is approximately 1 percent, panic disorder 0.4 to 2.0 percent, and bipolar disorder 0.3 to 1.5 percent. Research indicates there are also genetic components to these conditions (Mio et al., 2006). However, even when the mental disturbance has a physiological basis, such as schizophrenia, the manner in which male and female clients are treated is often different.

Men, as well as women, may suffer negative consequences as they strive to conform to traditional sex role stereotypes (Levant, 2003). Stereotypical beliefs affect how clients view the opposite gender (Gerber, 1996). As a result, they see each other and themselves in a distorted and unrealistic way, reinforcing the self-fulfilling prophecy. When one member of the couple believes the other person is not meeting his or her needs, problems arise, and the quality of the relationship suffers (Yoder & Kahn, 2003). There are delicate balances in adjusting the relationship to changing requirements. When one person changes a self-image, then she will also adjust her image of how she relates to the opposite sex (Yoder & Kahn, 2003).

➔ PRACTICE OF FEMINIST THERAPY

Now that we have examined the theoretical concepts of feminist therapy, we will explore its practice. Dr. Anita Green, our fictional, composite psychotherapist, provides a firsthand perspective of how she integrates theory with practice and applies the techniques of feminist therapy.

Assessment and Diagnosis

I believe that diagnosis is simply a place to begin. I work with my client to give the pain she is suffering a name and I use the label we give it, therapist and client together, as a tool to increase self-knowledge, to decipher the causes of her distress, and to focus on her strengths and skills (Brown, 1994).

I reject using the *DSM* when it locates the source of mental health problems within the client and ignores the sexist culture in which the client lives. *DSM* is harmful to my client when it provides a White, male-centered definition of mental illness. In my view, *DSM* represents "fuzziness masquerading as science and precision" (Brown, 1994, p. 131). The danger of assessing and diagnosing women's distress within the framework of the medical model is that it pressures clients to change when it is society that should change. *DSM* diagnoses, such as personality disorders, force clients to conform to sex role stereotypes.

Any symptom—for example, depression—cannot be considered separate from its sociocultural context. It seems to me that it is only natural that oppressed women who are unable to fulfill themselves feel depressed. Many diagnosis behaviors are legitimate reactions to events in the sociopolitical environment. I assess many of the symptoms my clients present as nonpathological methods of coping with an unjust world, and I do not ever blame the victim (Walker, 1990).

Assessment and treatment overlap as the client and I collaborate to perform a social identity analysis, which may also include a power analysis. We explore how the roles my client plays in her life affect her, as we follow the steps of a social identity analysis (Santos de Barona & Dutton, 1997; Worell & Remer, 2003).

Social Identity Analysis

1. *Identify the gender role messages to which she the client has been exposed:* I must be petite, slender, and beautiful.
2. *Analyze the positive and negative effects of these messages:* It is nice to feel proud of my personal appearance, but I don't fit the profile since I am 5 feet 9 inches, big-boned, and weigh 170 pounds. The goal is impossible.
3. *Identify internalized gender role messages of what the client says to herself:* I must conform to the sex role definition of beauty, or I am not a worthy person.
4. *Identify what messages need to change:* I am a unique individual. I am proud of who I am.

The process helps my client to see the systemic gender biases within her culture. She can then decide if these are helpful, harmful, and if they have played a role in her oppression and/or opportunities. She may question what identities she assumed because she is a woman. She clarifies what *male, female, normal, natural* mean to her. She critically examines whether the authorities from whom she learned about gender, class, race, and ethnicity had any reason to maintain a sexist, racist, classist, heterosexist status quo (Brown, 2005b).

Power Analysis

A power analysis is similar to a social identity analysis with an emphasis on the interaction of power and gender. I educate my client about the nature of power and its effects on every area of life including professional roles, social/governmental structures, and interpersonal relationships. The client can develop her own personal and social power and to seek remedies if she has been wronged and chooses to do so. I reinforce the belief that the political is personal in a world where social change is ongoing (Feminist Therapy Institute, 2000).

With emphasis on the client's strengths and resources, I adapt a framework to provide a map for the course of therapy (Brown, 1994; Worell & Remer, 2003).

Negotiation of Therapeutic Relationship and Length of Treatment

My role as the therapist is to provide an egalitarian relationship that serves as a model for the client in her other relationships and encourages her to assume personal responsibility and expanded alternatives (Walker, 1990). I do not place my client in a subordinate role. If at times I do put myself in a position of authority or expertise, I openly acknowledge this power difference as a temporary inequality. My aim is to "move toward an equality of power" (Brown, 1994, 2005b,c).

I adhere to the Feminist Therapy Code of Ethics and continually evaluate what assumptions underlie my practice, my lifestyle, and my values so that I can understand how these affect my client (Brown, 1994; Feminist Therapy Institute, 2000).

The client's work in therapy is to explore how her role in life has been shaped by gender, to get in touch with feelings including anger at oppression, to identify her own needs (Brabeck & Ting, 2000; Worell & Remer, 2003). The length of treatment is flexible and depends entirely upon my client's estimate of her needs.

The goals of therapy are for the client to be empowered to take charge of her own life and mental health so that she is not depending on me as an expert. This involves valuing feminine characteristics and developing a positive self-image by eliminating negative, damaging, internalized gender stereotypes that cause symptoms; it also involves taking action to foster positive change in her political, social, economic, and ecological environment. She can increase her self-confidence, interdependence, and trust in her own experience, intuition, and way of knowing (Brown & Mueller, 2004).

Therapeutic Techniques

I vary strategies to suit the client and situations, and I draw on many established techniques and adhere to the APA's guidelines for practice with girls and women and the APA's *Guidelines for Psychotherapy with Lesbian, Gay, & Bisexual Clients* as the minimal requirements for successful therapy.

Consciousness-Raising Techniques and Education

Consciousness and education are the mainstays of feminist therapy. Consciousness raising is a simple but effective technique. For example, my depressed client complains that she is ugly and "not beautiful like Jennifer Lopez." I intervene with "Do you think society puts a great deal of pressure on women to look a certain way? Women are almost forced to have a negative self-concept if they don't look like a movie star. The reality is that most women are not! How does it affect a woman when she invests her time and energy in something that is nearly impossible to attain?" I may add, "Can a woman become depressed, even immobilized, if she feels helpless because she can't reach the unreachable? Might she begin to act as if she were inferior?" (Young-Eisendrath & Wiedemann, 1987).

If a client is grappling with issues involving her reproductive rights, I may personalize the political. Drawing on history, I tell a story, such as how Margaret

Sanger was imprisoned for her efforts to circulate information about birth control, and I encourage my client to ponder how her own reproductive rights are at risk with potential changes in Supreme Court decisions.

I assign readings to help clients see the world from a feminist perspective. I discuss these readings in the session. Because there has been a trend toward anti-feminism, I am very selective about the works I assign (Zimmerman, Holm, & Starrels, 2001). I encourage clients to use the readings to replace unhelpful modes of thought with beneficial ones (Walker, 1990).

Group Therapy

Feminist group therapy, popular among feminists in the 1960s, is a consciousness-raising activity. The facilitators are women. Members meet as equals and foster cooperation rather then competitiveness. In such groups today, women explore not only how their status as women affects their social position but also how being women intersects with other parts of identities such as class, race, ethnicity, sexual orientation, and disability, among others. The feminist analysis helps the members to decide how to handle problems that arise. Group members learn to network, to nurture good relationships, and to reinforce one another for showing new sides of themselves and attaining desired goals (Kirsch, 1987).

Women seem to speak more freely when men are not present. Sensing they are not alone in their struggles helps them to develop their strengths (Walker, 1987). I recall one group that began with man-bashing words and attitudes. As the members discussed their relationships over 12 weeks of sessions, they concluded that men were also hurt by the system. Men were unconsciously entrapped in a world of stereotyping and as a result, suffered the consequences of not living up to their own full potential (Levant, 2003).

Empowerment and Political and Social Action

Empowerment occurs within individual and group therapy and is a process by which the powerless person assumes the skills, knowledge, power, and authority to gain control over her life (Smith & Siegal, 1985). Important sources of power are interpersonal and social relationships. Through empowerment the client learns to use power appropriately and effectively (Sprague & Hayes, 2000). Empowerment means the client takes responsibility for coping, adapting to adversity, recovering from mental illness, and becoming a survivor.

I strongly encourage my clients to participate in meaningful social and political activities in order to make a real connection between the personal and the political in their everyday life. The purpose is to give them life experience in taking charge of their own lives, improve relationships with others, and enhance the status of the community. For example, a rape victim who volunteers at a rape crisis center may find that helping other women who experienced similar trauma hastens her own healing.

Assertiveness Training

Assertiveness is perceived to be a male trait. It is the appropriate expression of emotion, whether feelings are negative or positive (Davis, Eshelman, & McKay, 1988).

In assertiveness training, my client learns to stand up for her legitimate rights and express her desires while feeling relaxed in interpersonal situations. She will be able to exercise more power if she chooses to do so. We also deal with the reality that some negative consequences can ensue when a woman asserts herself because she is going against the sex role stereotype and prepare for this pitfall by using self-esteem exercises so women are prepared for it.

Self-Disclosure

I use self-disclosure to communicate ordinarily private information about myself to my clients. My intent is to share information to build a therapy relationship and to remove the we–they barrier. Self-disclosure helps to make our relationship egalitarian and to minimize power differences. The content of what I self-disclose includes my beliefs, what kind of lifestyle I live, my religion, class, sexual orientation, political beliefs, and feelings about the client.

Integrating Feminist Techniques into Other Therapies

I integrate feminist therapy principles into other forms of psychotherapy, while remaining sensitive to the subtle forms of bias built into any therapy model, such as sexist diagnoses, assessments, theoretical constructs, and the use of language (Worell & Remer, 2003).

I am eclectic in that I use the parts of any psychotherapy that are helpful, qualifying my acceptance of the theory by pointing out which parts are sexist and which are useful. For example, although psychoanalytic therapy originated in sexist thinking, Jean Baker Miller's relational theory illustrates the analytic shift in the direction of making interdependency a therapeutic goal (Miller, 1976/1986). Another compatible therapy is Adler's individual psychology. Most recently, feminist therapists have used elements of social constructivism, which emphasizes the interdependence of thinking, feeling, and behavior on individual's construction of reality.

The Process of Therapy

Initially, I help the client to raise her consciousness about how the personal is political and how there is a sociocultural cause of her so-called pathology. The client grasps that sex typing determined her fate and that she has been groomed for second-class status from birth, in a society that ushers its citizens into the world with a statement of gender identification, "It's a boy" or "It's a girl." She often had to endure conditions not tolerated by boys. She was treated differently than males: She was considered to be more fragile and less competent; her success was attributed to luck rather than ability; she was ostracized for performing male behaviors; her ambitions were discounted while those of males were encouraged; and she felt conflicted when she did achieve success.

As the client works through this early phase of therapy, she usually feels a great sense of rage and resentment (Rosewater & Walker, 1985). Since many have multiple identities, particular clients will have different issues. The woman of color will have different content issues to deal with than the LGBT client, yet each will be dealing with the overriding issue of dominance and deprivation and marginalization.

In the middle phase of therapy, the client deals with the anger that emerges in the initial stage. We work together to put her past behavior in perspective and to understand the purposes. For example, dependency within her specific family may have been the best way for her to cope. We assess what she really wanted to do to develop into the kind of person she expected or wanted to be. As she expresses her long-repressed anger and hurt, she becomes stronger and more resilient and is aware of her own power. She is better able to define her own self and choose her own behaviors rather than conform to the pressures of society to be a certain way. By modeling an egalitarian relationship, she is better able to ask for this kind of relationship in her out-of-therapy world.

Termination occurs when the client applies learning from therapy to her everyday life. She takes personal responsibility for her path in life, her actions, and her choices and consciously chooses who she wants to be within the limits of her sociocultural environment (Smith & Siegal, 1985). In the ideal outcome, the client becomes symptom free, feels empowered, and has a positive self-image. She has the strength to take charge of her own mental health in the face of the flawed sexist society and is able to participate in political, social, and economic activism. She looks for egalitarian interpersonal relationships, is more self-confident and independent, and values what is feminine.

THERAPY IN ACTION: DR. ANITA GREEN AND THE CASE OF JONATHAN

To illustrate the application of feminist therapy, we examine a treatment plan for Jonathan, followed by excerpts from therapy sessions with our fictional psychotherapist, Dr. Green. Keep in mind the case excerpts are simulated interviews and represent the ideal of therapy. In real life, clients may take much longer to meet therapeutic goals. Table 12.1 provides a summary of Dr. Green's treatment plan.

Case Excerpts

The following excerpts are from sessions based on Dr. Green's feminist therapy case formulation.

Session 1

[*one-half hour into the session*]

Dr. Green: What does it mean to you that Tuti wants to have children?
Jonathan: I have to bring home a substantial salary, which means I must be successful in my career. And I work in a very competitive environment.
Dr. Green: So, Jonathan, how do you see your role in a family?

Table 12.1

Feminist Therapy Treatment Plan for Jonathan

Assessment and Formulation	• Presenting problem: loss of relationship with Tuti and Darren • Social identity analysis: J.'s beliefs about relationship roles for self and Tuti follow stereotypes of males and females • Sociopolitical and cultural issues • Role strain: J. distressed about fathering with traditional sex role expectations (earner)
Therapeutic Relationship	• Totally egalitarian relationship • Address any discomfort J. has with female therapist
Contract, Goals, and Treatment Plan	• Raise consciousness about social identity: effects on life, lifestyle, and relationship with Tuti • Address social role strain • Examine damaging internalized gender stereotypes • Alter identity (own and couple's) to satisfy own needs • Time: weekly appointments • Assess progress as J. works and re-assesses his goals
Techniques	• Question assumptions: society's role in J.'s relationship with Tuti and Darren • Raise consciousness and identify parts of problem as out there and not in there (externalize); reflect and analyze about the basis of sex role stereotypes • Increase sense of power to change outside world and not see self as problem • Question what happens when gender role stereotypes are changed • Decide upon lifestyle and show how equal partnership can change relationship • Education
Process of Therapy	• Build collaborative and good relationship • Clarify J.'s role, society's influence, etc. • Encourage move in a new direction, take on new lifestyle with decreased stereotyping • J. recognizes source of childhood feelings of maleness/ femaleness • J. learns to share and cooperate, becomes more task and other oriented; helps underprivileged kids and changes his work
Termination and Outcome	• Conscious of how social identity encouraged him to act in controlling/sexist manner and how he manipulated Tuti • Conscious of society's barriers to nurturing form of fathering as cause for avoidance of having own family • Reconnected with Tuti in egalitarian relationship • Lifestyle more in tune with own interests and not dictated by social identity and norms • Better able to share show true feelings and behaviors

Jonathan: Primarily as the breadwinner. But to bring home a good income, I must climb that corporate ladder quickly. In my field a lot of guys want to be promoted and to earn more money. What happens if I can't do it? How will I support a child? Knowing Tuti, she'll want three kids. If I fail at work, I can't afford that. Look at the future—college tuition. Also, if Tuti stops working, there is more pressure on me.

Dr. Green: So how do you see the role of father? [*assess how J. views gender roles and any role stereotyping*]

Jonathan: I like kids. I'd like to spend time with them, but Tuti will forget how stressful it is in the corporate world. She'd put more demands on me, and I'll get stressed out and fail at work. It will be miserable.

Dr. Green: The way in which you are describing this life, this family, this partnership does sound very stressful. Does it *have* to be this way?

Jonathan: Oh yeah. How else can it be? Me killing myself working long hours at work, and not living much of a life for 20 years until the kids are grown up.

Dr. Green: Where did you get this view of Jonathan as the family man? [*ask him to look at the roots of his beliefs*]

Jonathan: It is what it is!

Dr. Green: How did you learn that men and women had to fit into these roles?

Jonathan: I'm not sure. I suppose I saw my mom and dad and my friends' moms and dads. We were a middle-class family. Dad was a hard worker. He wasn't around much. He was just doing what he was supposed to do to take care of the family. My mom liked the fancy stuff. I remember whenever he brought home extra money, my mom glowed. They went off on a trip, and she came back so happy. She boasted of their travels to her friends. Then my dad had some health problems. He was older and had to take a job for less money. Mom was upset. They argued a lot when he was home. After that he spent a lot of time on the golf course. I don't think he liked being with the family, but he always supported us financially. My mom was a housewife, but she did not like being one. She spent a lot of time out of the house when she should have been with us. My sister Annie is the one who really was my surrogate mom.

Dr. Green: Do you think your family was typical?

Jonathan: I think we were traditional. Looking back, my mom really did not want to be a mom. That's why she passed the buck to my sister. I'm not sure she knew what she wanted, but she did know she did not want to be around us kids all of the time.

Dr. Green: How did the way men and women in your family behaved affect your idea of what it is to be a man or a woman?

Jonathan: That's a good question. I need to think about it. I don't want to be like my dad. And I don't want to be with a woman like my mom. I prefer someone more like Annie.

Dr. Green: Let's look at how these images of man and woman influence your behavior today. I am struck by something you said. You want to be the achiever, and you want your partner to be a nurturing woman. Is that right?

Jonathan: I guess so. Well, yes.

Dr. Green: Do you think society plays a role in any of this—what seems right for women and men to do in a marriage?

Jonathan: Yes, I think you have a point. Society does tell us how to be. But men and women have real differences—biologically, naturally.

Dr. Green: Sounds as if you believe that differences between men and women are inborn and have nothing to do with the environment. Do you?

Jonathan: [*smiles*] Well, yeah. I have to act like a man and be tough. Tuti is just being a woman. She is the kind who is very nurturing so her wanting children is very natural.

Dr. Green: Are you saying that you and Tuti are doing what you are doing just because you are a man, and she is a woman?

Jonathan: I guess so.

Dr. Green: What makes it this way?

Jonathan: It is just the way it is.

Dr. Green: Does it have to be this way or could there be other ways?

Jonathan: I don't know. I haven't thought about it before this moment. I guess there could be other ways. I just don't know what they are.

Dr. Green: So you can see that families don't always have to be traditional. Do you know other types of families?

Jonathan: Yes, there are single parents, and they bring the kids up alone. But that's not good for the children.

Dr. Green: How do you know that for certain?

Jonathan: Well, I suppose I don't really know for sure.

Dr. Green: Do you know any single fathers? Or kids that came from homes with single dads?

[*Comment: I encourage Jonathan to recognize differences and to challenge the "rightness" of the stereotype of the traditional family.*]

Jonathan: Hmmm. Actually, I do. As a matter of fact, living in Hawaii and knowing some of Tuti's friends, I saw lots of different things among the native Hawaiians. She came from one of the smaller islands, Kauai, where her family kept up the indigenous lifestyle. The kids were part of a group. They had a practice called hanaii. Children could be given to another set of parents to raise them. They have large extended families there, and everyone pitches in and helps.

Dr. Green: Tell me, what do you think of those families?

Jonathan: [*eyes tearing up*] It was so very open, even loving. I'm remembering how much I liked it. I fell in love with Tuti in that atmosphere. Of course, I always knew she wanted children. She wanted to teach them to be like that, to learn the culture.

Dr. Green: What happened to those plans when you were a couple?

Jonathan: I guess I wanted the good life—I mean, material things. Children get in the way and will be a drain on my career. We have no family members here to take care of them.

Dr. Green: Why? How did you buy into this idea of the "good life"?

Jonathan: Good question. I guess it's like the default drive. But Tuti does not understand how much it costs. Not just money, but time and energy. What would our lives be like?

Dr. Green: Could you arrange your lives any differently?

Jonathan: You have given me some food for thought.

Dr. Green: I wonder what it would be like if you and Tuti were equal partners?

Jonathan: Hmmm.

Dr. Green: What would you call this problem that you have come here about, that has taken over your life? Can you give it a name? [*I help him to externalize the problem so he can see how rigid sex roles are affecting his relationships and his life.*]

Jonathan: I guess I would call it "trapped in the box."

[*Comment: I decide this is a good metaphor to use. I can raise his consciousness about how conforming to some social identity has trapped him into a way of being that is not in his or Tuti's best interest.*]

Dr. Green: Say more.

Jonathan: Well, I suppose I feel as if I am running from corner to corner in this box, and there is no way out except up. And I am too weak to pull the lid open.

Dr. Green: What makes you so weak and unable to open the lid?

Jonathan: Hmmm. I'll have to think about it. No one to help me. It shows how important it is to not depend on anyone. If you are independent and on your own, you are better off and in control of your own life. I figured out that I needed to have some money. So I am trying to get out of the box by making enough money to be free.

Dr. Green: What effect is being in the box having on you now?

Jonathan: [*long pause*] I guess it ended my relationship with Tuti.

Dr. Green: Let me ask you. Are there other ways of living that don't put you in the box?

Jonathan: What do you mean? Other lifestyles?

Dr. Green: Yes. The lifestyle you have now is one where there is pressure on you to be the strong man who takes care of the family with money and power. It's important to you to see yourself as strong, as a macho man with a nurturing woman. That's caused some real problems because Tuti now wants to be the traditional mom. And that is stressful for you?

Jonathan: Sure.

Dr. Green: Is it costing you? Your emotional and family life with Tuti?

Jonathan: Yes, I guess it is.

Dr. Green: What if you didn't subscribe to the traditional way society tells you men and women ought to be? Is there some way that you could live with Tuti in a different life script? One in which love and closeness of you and your partner are priority one? One in which children are not a burden but a shared and joyful responsibility?

[*Comment: I am assessing flexibility. He is tied to the sex role stereotype but seems willing to alter it.*]

Jonathan: I'll think about it. It never occurred to me before this conversation.

Session 4

Dr. Green: Had you ever talked over her idea of motherhood and your idea of fatherhood and familyhood with Tuti?

Jonathan: No, not really. Not like this. I'm not good at communicating. It's a guy thing. You know, men are from Mars and women are from Venus? [*smiles*]

Dr. Green: That implies that women and men are so different they cannot speak each other's language. Do you really believe this myth?

Jonathan: I suppose I do. I know it is easier for Tuti to talk than me. As a matter of fact, sometimes I wish she did not talk so much about our issues. It upsets me.

Dr. Green: What makes you believe you are not capable of communicating to Tuti? You may not like what is being said, but you are in the business of advertising, which is communicating. What makes it hard to communicate to your partner but easy to communicate to the whole world?

Jonathan: [*laughs*] OK. Point taken.

Dr. Green: I once saw a couple who had similar problems. They worked out their differences. They had not really talked to each other about what it would be like to have children. They both had their own ideas, but they were able to compromise and changed their lifestyles. He was worried she would try to control him and nag and nag and nag. But he found out as he put more effort into caring that he was more sensitive to her needs, and she did not want to control him. Their relationship improved tremendously.

The children actually but brought them closer. They realized they had been in a power struggle, and they really did not want to be.

Jonathan: I think I am beginning to understand. We buy what is advertised!

Dr. Green: You know, Jonathan, there is some research to show that people think about relationships in very predictable ways. Sometimes their expectations are based on stereotypes and really do not correspond with real experience. I have a book that I recommend you read. It is helpful homework, and it might help you to see things a bit differently.

Jonathan: OK. I'll read it.

Dr. Green: So what are your homework assignments?

Jonathan: I'll read the book. I'm going to call Tuti. And I'm going to think about how we see our roles in the family.

Session 7

Jonathan: I contacted Tuti. We met at a restaurant and talked for hours. I was surprised. We still have so much in common. You have made me see the problem is more with living up to the stereotypes of an American man and woman. Would you see us in couples therapy?

Case Comment

The couple reunited. In therapy, they were able to communicate honestly and to renegotiate their relationship. Jonathan was able to stop using the yardstick of traditional masculinity that had produced gender role conflict, anxiety, and depression in the relationship with Tuti. He was able to accept Tuti's self-assertion and to let go of his stereotypical male ideals, internalized standards, and problematic behaviors. He became aware that he was suppressing his urge to show concern and accommodation toward Tuti and to be a father. He realized that Tuti did not need to be highly accommodating to him, and he did not have to be highly assertive, successful, and rich. Once Jonathan understood that Tuti did not expect him to be the stereotypical bread winner and she understood the basis of his fears, they agreed to apportion both time and money so that they could have children as a mutual goal.

Jonathan directly confronted his problems, became less defensive, and stopped stonewalling Tuti. His therapy brought him greater personal maturity, and he was able to integrate his ability to assert himself and with accommodating Tuti's needs, as well as his own real needs.

❖ RESEARCH DIRECTIONS IN FEMINIST THERAPY

While there is a substantial amount of information published about feminist therapy, empirical outcome research has been sparse. Reviews and meta-analytic reports seldom mention feminist therapy. Journal publications are dominated by qualitative case studies, anecdotes, discussions and a lack of well-designed large-scale studies that compare the outcomes of clients who received feminist therapy with controls or with those who received other types of therapy (APA, 2006).

While there is general research about gender and mental health, it does not directly pertain to feminist therapy (Matlin, 1996). Since the 1970s, studies have looked at the effects of gender and gender role socialization on mental health (Bem, 1983) and the differential treatment of women and men within the mental health system (Tavris, 1992). The androgynous personality emerged as a possible model for positive mental health (Bem, 1993).

However, the very nature of feminist therapy begs a consideration of the sociocultural context of research. Many feminist values are at odds with those of Western science, which promotes objectivism and reductionism. In this view, the more generalizable the results, the better. The ultimate reason for research in Western science is often knowledge for knowledge's sake with no substantive consideration of the social and moral responsibility for how the results of research are used.

A feminist view of science values interconnectedness, interdependence, "intersubjectivity . . . and context" (Fisher, 2000, p. 138). It urges scientists to take responsibility for the moral and pragmatic impact of science on society, the environment, and human lives. An extreme example can be found in the development of the atomic bomb. By failing to consider the humanitarian implications of their own creation, scientists brought about an enormous destructive potential to humanity (Levy & Richey, 1988).

Feminists argue that "far from being totally objective, those who propose the 'dust bowl objectivity' of logical positivism are unaware of or not concerned with its subjectivity" (Brabeck & Ting, 2000, p. 253). Western science is hardly as objective as it claims. As a matter of fact, biased research has been the norm throughout the history of science. Factors such as gender, race, ethnicity, and power play a role in research. Those who control the agencies that fund research have undue influence in deciding what questions are asked, how they are asked, and how results are published, generalized, and applied (Riger, 1992). For example, until recently, most subjects in social science and medical experiments were White males. The Physicians' Health Study of the effects of aspirin on cardiovascular disease included 22,071 males and not one female. The NIH sponsored the Longitudinal Study of Aging, which excluded women even though they make up more than 60 percent of the over-65 population. Generalizations made to nonmale groups may have put females at risk for incorrect treatment and unnecessary suffering and even death (McKinlay, 1996). Only feminist political action reformed federally funded research, institutionalizing gender equity (Schiebinger, 2003).

There are specific feminist values to consider when discussing research, such as the interdependence of the experimenter and the subject; an awareness of the social and historical context of the subject and the experimenter; an examination of the underlying values; an understanding that facts are not separate from language; and the importance of qualitative information. Feminist research values glean information after the fact and promote the value of uniqueness as much as generalizability. Table 12.2 compares the research values of feminist therapy and evidence-based practice.

Table 12.2		
Comparison of Feminist and EBP Research Values		
	EBP	**Feminist Therapy**
Science	Ultimate perspective	Must be judged within context
Methodology	Quantitative	Qualitative
	Statistical	Oral traditions
	Objective	Subjective
	Randomized control trials	Case study, in-depth
Usefulness	Science for science's sake	Social applications
	Truth	Political and cultural context
	Efficiency	Social justice
	Economics and profit	Better world
	Value free	Ethics and values
Noncontextual	Isolate variables	Context variables important
	Independent or dependent	Cannot isolate variables
	Linear thinking	Nonlinear thinking
Philosophy	Reductionistic	Holistic

Can the clash of values between evidence-based practice and feminist therapy be reconciled (Tiefer, 1996)? On one end of the debate is the argument that "all research that seeks to predict, control, and generalize is sexist and male-oriented" and should be tossed out (Levy & Richey, 1988, p. 422). One the other end is the argument that the basic science paradigm is salvageable provided that it is changed in a way to include feminist principles.

Science should routinely foster a methodology that includes a feminine ethno-methodology. "Doing feminism" in any given situation and "doing feminist research" are the same (Brown, 2006; Stanley & Wise, 1983). For example, some researchers are developing research methods that are compatible with feminist values such as mea-surements of acculturation, assimilation, self-perception, and coping methods in the face of trauma that can satisfy the criteria for good evidence-based research (Moradi, Subich, & Phillips, 2002). Some believe feminist-informed therapists have an "obliga-tion to be accountable for the outcomes of feminist interventions" and to put feminist therapy on a scientific footing (Worell, 2001, p. 335). Feminist research is not a sys-tematized methodology but offers guiding principles—such as research of women, by women, and for women (Worell & Remer, 2003).

Brown (2006) argues that evidence-based mental health and feminist therapy have already found common ground. Conclusions about empirically supported relationships "mirror, echo, and affirm" what feminist therapists already know—the most important ingredient of successful therapy is the egalitarian relationship, which is warm, supportive, and empowering. Other significant factors are patient participation and collaboration with the therapist to contribute jointly to shaping a successful outcome.

What can the therapist say to justify the use of feminist therapy? While it is difficult to show that feminist therapy undoubtedly improves mental health from an evidence-based perspective, keep in mind that it is the male patriarchy that insists on using the criteria of EBM to judge the worthiness of any therapy. These values clash with those of feminist therapy. The best way to know if therapy is effective is if the client feels better intuitively, because the client is the expert on herself. The therapist should use this therapy when it appears to be the best way to alleviate the client's suffering by freeing her from the confines of stereotypes and oppression.

✦ Issues of Diversity

Feminist therapy can serve as a model for all other therapies in terms of handling issues of diversity as it promotes an understanding of the effects of structured inequality and their relationship to race, class, and gender within the therapy dyad (Anderson, 2005). Supporters see it as a model for other oppressed groups. Many professional organizations have adapted ethical standards that fully embrace and incorporate feminist attitudes (Sparks & Park, 2000). It has also prompted the APA's guidelines on multicultural education, training, research, practice, and organizational change for psychologists (2003).

Theory, practice, and research must be all-inclusive, enveloping diverse cultures, races, and political systems as well as gender (Evans et al., 2005). Such a model, if informed and grounded in science, may help to meet the needs of culturally diverse groups. Thus feminist therapists advocate the inclusion of multicultural and gender sensitivity into all mental health treatment and evidence-based therapies (Comas-Diaz, 2006). Therapists need to consider how social and historical context affects treatment. For example, African American cultural feminists have worked toward preserving their unique racial and ethnic roots, particularly those associated with the cultures of their mothers (Enns, 1997; Lotz, 2003).

All mental health professions mandate that therapists learn to be culturally competent, practice culturally sensitive therapy, and attend to issues of gender role socialization, stereotyping, oppression, bias, and social justice. However, much work remains to be done to advance the state of the oppressed (Brown et al., 2005).

✦ Major Critiques of Feminist Therapy

Because it has historically challenged the status quo of male and female relationships, feminism and feminist therapy have met with a wide range of reactions and resistances. Some take up feminism completely and use it as the standard for political correctness. Others reject it and pejoratively label feminists as radical bra burners who would destroy the fabric of the traditional family. Some superficially endorse it, giving it lip service. Others oppose it.

Feminism has prodded us to examine our traditional perspectives, to question our own ethnocentrism and stereotyping, and to look at the effects of oppression on psychological functioning (Fernando, 2003). This can result in feelings of anxiety and discomfort to some (Falludi, 1999).

Critics of feminist therapy are abundant, but many of these detractors hardly understand the tenets of feminist therapy, and they tend to dismiss it, as if it represented only the ranting and raving of a small group of dissatisfied trouble-making women (Caplan, 1983). However, there has been, and still is, an avid, active subculture of women who have invested enormous amounts of time, money, and passion to oppose feminism (Nielson, 2001). Antifeminism arguments, past and current, are that

- Sex role differentiation is not oppressive.
- Patriarchy is universal, natural, and normal.
- Men are dominant by nature; women are compliant by nature.
- The very survival of the family depends upon a division of responsibility in which men assume public duties, and women take on domestic functions.
- Feminism represents opposition to legitimate male authority and results in chaos as well as the need for increased bureaucratic and government control.

Because of the political nature of feminism, the responsible feminist therapist must ascertain if the value systems of antifeminist clients are incompatible with her therapy and deal with the situation according to ethical guidelines. Society has reinforced women to value certain aspects of themselves based upon the true differences between men and women.

Critics further argue that feminist therapists have a worldview that fosters a belief about women as perpetual victims of a vast male conspiracy. Accordingly, principles of feminist therapy have found their way into the arena of domestic violence where, in actuality, women often play a role in inciting conflict in the relationship. Labeling women as passive victims reinforces self-pity and takes away the chance to see how they sabotage themselves, when that understanding of themselves could transform their life (Satel, 1998).

Finally, some critics complain that feminist theory is outdated and has not kept pace with what society is today and the new feminisms have only recently become integrated into mainstream feminist thinking. Other critics claim that, by mixing the psychological and the political, feminist therapy is not really a therapy at all, especially since there is little convincing scientific evidence to show that women's mental health problems come from social and not personal factors and that changing politics will change mental health.

SUMMARY

- Feminist therapy emerged as a way to deal with the mental health of women in sexist societies. Feminism emerged in waves. The first wave, 1800 to 1930, achieved changes in the legal status of women in the United States. The second wave in the 1960s involved gender equity at work and legal and reproductive rights. The third wave, active today, addresses environmentalism and globalization. Current issues important to feminism are women's poor economic conditions, limited political power, inferior education, erosion of health and reproductive rights, and global and domestic violence.

- The theory underlying feminist therapy holds that the personal is political, and private life is affected by the sociocultural environment. Mental health problems are a function of the harmful effects of living in an oppressive society in which social, political, and cultural mandates are reinforced through oppressive gender roles, sex role stereotyping, and role strain. Fighting this oppression creates negative life circumstances. Oppression, the domination of one group over another, takes many forms including sexism, racism, classism, ageism, and heterosexism. Privilege is the unwarranted advantage a person has by virtue of being a member of a group, particularly one with a valued social identity. Harmful oppressive stereotypes can be internalized.

- The practice of feminist therapy includes an assessment and diagnosis that rejects the medical model, uses social identity and power analyses to identify systemic gender biases, and emphasizes the client's strengths and resources. The therapist's role is to provide an egalitarian relationship, and the client's role is to explore how gender shapes her life. Length of treatment is individualized. The goals of therapy are client empowerment; eliminating damaging, internalized gender stereotypes; and increasing self-confidence and trust in the client's own experience.

- Therapeutic techniques include consciousness raising, education, feminist group therapy, empowerment and assertiveness training, and creating an egalitarian relationship. The process of therapy begins with raised consciousness about gender roles, then deals with the rage and resentment about consequences, and ends successfully when the client applies the therapy to her everyday life.

- Empirical outcome research on feminist therapy has been sparse. There is general research about gender, mental health, and the women within the mental health system. The values of feminist therapy are at odds with Western science, pitting intersubjectivity and context against objectivity and logical positivism. One question is whether the clash of values between evidence-based practice and feminist therapy can be reconciled. Specific feminist values should be considered when discussing research. Incorporating these values into research might inspire a paradigm shift.

- Feminist therapy can serve as a model in terms of dealing with current issues of diversity as it promotes an understanding of the effects of structured inequality and their relationship to race, class, and gender within the therapy dyad.
- Feminist therapy challenges the status quo and thus has met with resistance. Major critiques of antifeminism arguments, past and current, focus on the argument that the patriarchy is universal, natural, and beneficial since it promotes the survival of the family.

Resources

Society for the Psychology of Women
Division 35 Central Office
APA 750 First Street, NE
Washington, DC 20002-4242
(202) 336-6013
http://www.apa.org/divisions/div35

Division 35 of the APA promotes feminist scholarship, practice, and advocacy to advance equality and social justice. It provides an organizational base for all feminists who are interested in teaching, research, or practice in the psychology of women.

National Organization for Women (NOW)
1000 16th Street NW, Suite 700
Washington, DC 20036
http://www.now.org

NOW was founded in 1966 and is the largest feminist activist organization in the United States. Its mission is social justice and equality for all women.

Wellesley Centers for Women
Wellesley College
106 Central Street
Wellesley, MA 02481-8203
(781) 283-2500
http://www.wcwonline.org

Grace W. and Robert F. Stone founded the Wellesley Centers for Women in 1981. The mission is to promote education, research, and community outreach emphasizing the experiences of women, children, and families across culturally diverse populations.

Jean Baker Miller Training Institute
Stone Center
Wellesley College
106 Central Street
Wellesley, MA 02481
(781) 283-3800
http://www.wellesley.edu/JBMTI/index.html

The Stone Center is one of the Wellesley Centers; this institute teaches relational cultural theory, based on the work of Jean Baker Miller.

Feminist Majority and Feminist Majority Foundation
1600 Wilson Boulevard, Suite 801
Arlington, VA 22209
(703) 522-2214
433 South Beverly Drive
Beverly Hills, CA 90212
(310)556-2500
http://feminist.org

Founded in 1987, the Feminist Majority is a cutting-edge organization dedicated to women's equality, reproductive health, and nonviolence.

CLASS EXERCISES AND ACTIVITIES

Theory

1. What historical events affected the development of feminist psychotherapy? Find a story about feminism in the psychological literature that would enhance the information contained in this chapter.
2. Describe the sexist elements of Freudian and other analytic psychotherapies.
3. Play the role of a client who has experienced some form of sexism in her personal psychotherapy. Now imagine you are the opposite gender and reverse roles. How would a member of the opposite sex interpret the same information? Are there differences? What are these differences? Are they subtle or obvious?

Practice

1. Break into dyads. One person plays a well-intended but unintentional "sexist" male therapist, and the other plays a feminist therapist. They discuss assessment, diagnosis, and treatment for the case of Jonathan. Describe the dialogue. Switch roles. Discuss your reactions with your partner.
2. Design a homework assignment for a female client that will raise consciousness about sexism and how it has affected her development. Increase awareness of how sexism hurts the quality of her life.
3. Imagine you are a feminist therapist working in a clinic. A nurse from the emergency room calls and asks you to see a woman who has been medically cleared but needs mental health counseling after being beaten by her husband. The nurse tells you she will bring the client "around the back entrance" so "she will not be embarrassed if anyone sees her." The client arrives with two black eyes, a swollen face, and a number of cuts on her face and arm. As she sits in front of you, you feel anger toward the man who beat her and anger at society for hiding such abuse. How do you deal with your own feelings in the situation in order to help your client?
4. Look at the sample treatment plan in Chapter 1 (Figure 1.2). Fill out the sample treatment plan for Tuti for feminist therapy. (Both Jonathan's and Tuti's case histories are in Appendix A.)

Research

1. Conduct a review of feminist therapies using the following key words in PubMed and using PsycINFO: *feminist therapy*. What did you find? Limit your search to *feminist therapy and randomized control*. Taking a quick overview of the articles, describe the nature of the articles and the kinds of evidence they contain to support their efficacy and effectiveness.

2. How can feminist therapists challenge the belief that Western scientific methodology is the only way to conduct research? Can feminist therapy be supported through an evidence-based approach? How can you resolve incompatibilities or conflicts? Comment on how EBM is compatible or not compatible with feminist therapy.

3. A patient asks you why you are using feminist therapy. How can you justify your choice?

CHAPTER 13

BIOPSYCHOSOCIAL THERAPY AND HEALTH PSYCHOLOGY

If we train our breathing, we can control our emotions—that is, we can cope with the happiness and pain in our lives.

–Bhikkhu Bodhi

The goal of this chapter is to present an overview of psychotherapy interventions that are consistent with the biopsychosocial model. These biopsychosocial therapies are currently found in a variety of areas including complementary and alternative medicine (CAM), mind–body therapies, behavioral medicine, psychosomatic medicine, and health psychology. The chapter describes the historical context, theory, practice, and research of the biopsychosocial model and therapies. The simulated psychotherapist, Dr. Laurel Bodmin, presents a treatment plan and some excerpts from therapy sessions with a biopsychosocial emphasis for the case of Jonathan. Issues of diversity and major critiques are also included.

✦ HISTORICAL CONTEXT

Western medicine is transitioning from mind–body dualism to a biopsychosocial perspective. The theory developed by René Descartes (1596–1650) of a mind and body dualism has dominated Western medicine for over a century. A French philosopher, mathematician, and physiologist, Descartes divided the natural world into two distinct components—the mental and the physical. His definitive split provided a blueprint that shaped Western medicine and what is called the biomedical or allopathic model (Damasio, 1994). In this view, the body is seen as a system to be controlled, and disease is seen as an outside enemy to be fought and conquered. Cure is based on producing a condition that is antagonistic to the disease.

The biomedical model views mental disturbances as illnesses with biological bases that are genetic, endocrinological, neurophysiological, or structural. For example, depression is caused by an imbalance in the neurotransmitter serotonin. Diagnoses are based upon from the medically oriented *DSM*. The ideal treatment of mental illness is a physical cure, such as the right psychotropic medication.

However, even the strongest proponents of the medical model acknowledge that social, psychological, and environmental factors contribute to the totality of physical and mental health (Astin, Shapiro, Eisenberg, & Forys, 2003). Thus the medical model has gradually given way to the biopsychosocial model (Astin, Goddard, & Forys, 2005).

The Biopsychosocial Model

Created by the psychiatrist George Engel (1977, 1980), the biopsychosocial model posits that biological, social, and psychological factors all play a significant role in health and illness (Borrell-Carrio, Suchman, & Epstein, 2004). Biopsychosocial therapies are not yet a defined system of treatment but consist of an informal collection of practices or interventions that are consistent with the biopsychosocial model and that share a common set of core values, attitudes, perspectives, and practice tools (Deckert, 1997; Weil, 1998, 2004). The American Surgeon General and the Canadian Minister of National Health and Welfare recognize that more than half of the burden of physical illness is psychological; thus any quality health-care system coordinates and integrates both physical and psychological health needs (Suls & Rothman, 2004). The goal of health care is to promote good personal health habits resulting in a "long and fruitful life, not simply the absence of disease" (Breslow, 2006).

The biopsychosocial model views the person holistically and hierarchically, "through molecular, tissue, organ, and individual levels to two-person, family, community," societal, and even international levels (Rabinowitz, 1999). The case of Marianne (see The Case of Marianne box on the opposite page) illustrates how the biopsychosocial perspective combines general health and mental health treatment. Marianne's chest pains began as a physical reaction in the tissues of her heart but affected every part of her life, including her personal and occupational relationships. Treatment began with an understanding that her denial of her grief and emotional problems led to somatic symptoms. As she opened up and discussed her problems, with the help of her psychotherapist who coordinated treatment with all of her health care providers, she gradually made significant modifications in her life habits. Over a 2-year period, through treatment with a biopsychosocially-oriented therapy, she maintained a lifestyle that attained a high level of mental and physical wellness and deterred her from relapsing into unhealthy behaviors (Hansel & Damour, 2005).

The biopsychosocial approach, at its best, emphasizes values that encourage clients to take charge of their own health, be sensitive to their body's changing patterns, and recognize symptoms of illnesses at an early stage (Weil, 1998). Physical and mental disturbances can even be seen as opportunities for personal growth and transformation. Thus, psychotherapy can play a significant role as a treatment modality within the biopsychosocial approach, as shown in Table 13.1.

The growing acceptance of the biopsychosocial model also paved the way for an appreciation of other areas of health care outside the biomedical model. These include complementary and alternative medicine, behavioral medicine, psychosomatic

THE CASE OF MARIANNE

Marianne arrived in the emergency room with severe chest pains. She is a 42-year-old Wall Street executive with a very successful career. Her husband, Eric, was killed in a car crash on his way to the airport to join her on a trip to Japan in celebration of their 20th anniversary. Devastated over the loss, Marianne decided the best way to cope was to be stoic and to get on with the responsibilities of her life.

She immediately threw herself into her work after Eric's death. A month later, she collapsed in her office. Her staff, thinking Marianne had suffered a heart attack, rushed her to the emergency room. Dr. Morgan, her primary care doctor, met her at the hospital to examine her heart

Tests for any kind of heart involvement were negative. Dr. Morgan asked Marianne about feelings of distress, her living situation, work stresses, and her social support network. He hospitalized her for observation and collaborated with Dr. Sware, a psychotherapist with a biopsychosocial orientation, who began to work with Marianne.

Dr. Sware initially used psychoeducation to teach Marianne about how her sudden and intense loss stressed her physically and mentally. He discussed how her psychological state affected her physically. Marianne told him she had mixed feelings, wished that she could have joined her husband in death, and feared that with a heart condition she would not be around to see her grandchildren born.

Dr. Sware's goal was to reduce her fears that her pain was caused by heart disease. He consulted with and advised her support system—her adult children, close friends, and supportive parents. Upon Marianne's discharge from the hospital, Dr. Sware coordinated her outpatient treatment. She returned to work feeling more assured about her well-being.

Dr. Sware referred her to individual outpatient psychotherapy with a psychodynamic psychotherapist, who also provided psychoeducation. After 12 sessions, Marianne has begun to work through her grief. She has taken time off to handle the unfinished business associated with her husband's death. She decided to sell her house and moved into a condominium.

She attends a stress management group, and has learned meditation and self-soothing techniques, which she uses in her everyday life. Her coping has improved, and her stress level has diminished. She is able to better manage her feelings, thoughts, and behaviors. Although she has exercised all of her life, she has done so inconsistently, so she had an assessment by a personal trainer and a dietician. She has now joined an exercise program and returned to playing tennis with her best friend.

Upon completion of the stress management group, Marianne linked up with a cognitive therapy group for the newly widowed. She tells her psychotherapist and her physician that once she changed her self-defeating thinking and increased her self-awareness of how her body and mind affect each other, she developed a better attitude about her problems and her depression decreased. She is able to trace back how her tenseness, anxiety, and self-pity needed to come under her own control even before the death of her husband. She now works through her guilty feelings that the two of them did not enjoy life and its leisure time more, and now it is too late for her and Eric. But she has decided that she needs to slow down and do something more meaningful with her life. She now believes she has the tools to cope with the constant stressors and to adjust her lifestyle as needed.

medicine, and health psychology, among others. In turn, these have fostered practice methods such as stress management, health promotion, prevention, self-management, and the importance of social support. Health psychology is a manifestation of the biopsychosocial model, in that both fields deal with how biological, behavioral, and social factors influence health and illness and work to promote health through behavior change and disease prevention.

Table 13.1

The Role of Psychotherapy in the Biomedical and Biopsychosocial Models

	Biomedical	Biopsychosocial
Source of Psychological Problem	Mental illness, similar to physical illnesses; organic cause	Interaction among the biological, psychological, and social environment
Psychotherapy	Treatment for diagnosed conditions; pharmacotherapy or medication for a specific condition	Method of solving problems and integrating biological, psychological, and social components of abnormal behavior
Psychotherapist	Mental health specialist	Biopsychosocial therapist/ primary care psychotherapist who coordinates treatment

Complementary and Alternative Medicine

There is a growing appreciation of complementary and alternative medicine (CAM), health areas outside of Western medicine and the allopathic model. The National Institutes of Health now houses the National Center for Complementary and Alternative Medicine (NCCAM). Ignored by Western medicine for years, CAM consists of a "group of diverse medical and health-care systems, practices, and products that are presently not considered to be part of conventional medicine" (American Health, 2005, p. 53). This includes homeopathy, naturopathy, Chinese medicine, and other systems of medicines such as Indian Ayurvedic, Tibetan, African, Native American, and Hawaiian (Rezentes, 1996).

We can see growing support for CAM in dollars spent. Worldwide, over $60 billion per year goes to traditional healing. Sixty-two percent of adults in the United States used CAM in 2004 (American Health, 2005). The American Academy of Pediatrics, Committee on Children with Disabilities (2001) reports that 20 to 40 percent of healthy children and more than 50 percent of chronically ill children use some form of complementary therapies with mainstream care.

CAM considers psychological disorders to be part of a system that is out of balance. Although the cause of a medical disease may be organic, the emotions and behavior that accompany a medical condition can be modified through psychotherapeutic and psychoeducational work that, in turn, influences the course of the medical illness (Damasio, 1994). CAM, medicine's newest, most comprehensive specialty, aims to treat the whole person, to restore balance between the physical and the mental, and to maximize the healing power of the mind–body relationship (Penn & Wilson, 2003).

Psychotherapy interventions consistent with the philosophies of CAM are often referred to as *mind–body therapies*. They encourage positive thinking and create attitudes that empower clients to cope with stress and improve mood, quality of life, and even immune system functioning.

Behavioral Medicine, Psychosomatic Medicine, and Health Psychology

Behavioral medicine, psychosomatic medicine, and health psychology have, until recently, been minor movements within Western medicine. But as the biopsychosocial therapy model grows, their influence and visibility grow as well (Kok & Schaalma, 2004).

✱ *Behavioral medicine* is an interdisciplinary field (drawing from medicine, nursing, psychiatry, psychology, among other disciplines) that supports the integration of mind–body interventions within the context of Western medicine. It draws upon learning principles and techniques from behaviorism to train and alter health behaviors (Sarafino, 2008). Behavioral medicine opened up the field of biofeedback, a method that gives an individual information about his or her internal physiological state and autonomic physical processes. Currently neurofeedback is used to treat various neuropsychological conditions such as attention deficit hyperactivity disorder (Criswell, 1995).

✱ *Psychosomatic medicine*, developed in the 1930s, is a specialty within psychiatry that studies physical health conditions stemming from emotional influences; it views psychological causes as the key to the understanding and treatment of physical symptoms. The field arose from Freud's idea that people often deal with anxiety by converting a repressed emotional conflict into a physical symptom (e.g., hysterical paralysis) and inspired some psychiatrists to search for specific relationships between emotional conflicts and diseases, such as ulcers, hypertension, asthma, colitis, and dermatitis (Nemiah, 2000). Although many of the theories from these early years were not supported by research, they fostered interest in psychosomatic medicine. In 2003, the American Board of Medical Specialties made psychosomatic medicine its seventh psychiatric subspecialty, dealing with the interrelationships among the psychological, social, and biological components of mind and body health (Stone, Colyer, Feltblower, Carson, & Sharpe, 2004).

There is considerable overlap among the models of behavioral medicine and psychosomatic medicine. They can be considered forms of, or under the umbrella term of, *health psychology*, which is in turn part of the biopsychosocial model. Health psychology is a field within psychology with a mission to "understanding the psychological influences on how people stay healthy, why they become ill, and how they respond when they get ill" (Taylor, 2006, p. 4). Emerging in the 1970s, it focuses on health promotion and maintenance, the prevention and treatment of illness, the correlates of health with illness and dysfunction, as well as the study of general health care systems and health policy. Health promotion is the pragmatic arm of health psychology, applying theoretical principles of health psychology to foster mind and body health (Matarazzo, 1982).

Trends in Biopsychosocial Therapy and Health Psychology

The dramatic shift from allopathic medicine to biopsychosocial-oriented models has significant implications for psychotherapists. Given that physiological responses, health behaviors, disease, and psychological factors mutually influence one another, it makes sense for physicians to attend to the mind when they treat the body and for psychotherapists to attend to the body when they treat the mind.

The emphasis on biological treatments and the ready availability of psychotropic drugs makes it convenient for primary care doctors to handle mental health problems, and they are dealing with them more than ever before. Americans made more than 1.1 billion visits to doctors' offices and hospital emergency and outpatient departments in 2004 (National Center for Health Statistics, 2004). A large number of visits to primary care doctors are made by patients with mental health issues (Wang et al., 2005).

The average primary care physician in the United States conducts 120,000 to 160,000 patient interviews in his or her practice lifetime (Frankel & Beckman, 2004, p. 45). But if a significant number of primary care office visits are for mental health treatment, there is an urgent need for collaboration between physicians and mental health professionals (Strosahl, 1996). These practical considerations have encouraged the growth of a new specialty for psychotherapists, utilizing interventions that are compatible with behavioral health care, not only for clinical reasons but for economic ones (Cummings, Cummings, & Johnson, 1997; Victoroff, 2002). (Review Chapter 1 for a discussion of these economic reasons.) More and more, it is acknowledged that there is value in integrating mental and physical health care (Kenkel, DeLeon, Mantell, & Steep, 2005).

As psychotherapy is assimilated into mainstream health care, biopsychosocial interventions are being applied more often. Psychotherapists in a primary care setting can be very helpful, and primary care psychology now represents a significant growth area for psychotherapists (Brody, 2003; Sanderson, 2004). Psychotherapists who embrace the biopsychosocial model can look forward to new roles, duties, and opportunities (Gray, Brody, & Johnson, 2005). They can also expect to work with a wider variety of clients, such as those described in Box 13.1. Psychotherapists practicing in the biopsychosocial model currently have many different labels. For simplicity, this chapter will use the term *biopsychosocial psychotherapist*.

With the growing trend to deliver health care through multidisciplinary teams in collaborative and integrative models of care (see Chapter 1), the biopsychosocial framework encourages consultation between the primary care physician and the biopsychosocial psychotherapist. To work in this primary care model, the biopsychosocial psychotherapist needs to practice forms of therapy that best address the mind–body needs of clients (Vinck & Meganck, 2006).

BOX 13.1   TYPICAL HEALTH PSYCHOLOGY PATIENT ISSUES

- *The somaticizer, whose visits to primary care doctors are a function of psychological issues, or somatization disorders:* For example, the client who is highly anxious visits the primary care doctor repeatedly, complaining of aches and pains. The problem is psychological, but the client translates it into the physical.
- *The acutely medically ill, who develop psychiatric symptoms:* For example, the client with a medical disease, such as cancer, can be more vulnerable to mental illnesses such as depression. Psychotherapy can help to manage symptoms and thus help the physician treat the medical illness.
- *The psychiatrically disturbed, who have medical disorders:* For example, the client with

schizophrenia who develops leukemia is more likely to be noncompliant.
- *The chronically medically ill:* The client suffering from heart disease, cancer, stroke, or chronic obstructive pulmonary diseases, and whose health is impacted by habits and health care, requires psychological and social interventions. For example, the patient with coronary disease needs to manage his lifestyle habits by coping with stress.
- *Family members of the ill:* The client who has been affected by the illness of family members requires therapeutic methods to enhance well-being; these may include prevention (primary, secondary, and tertiary), as well as psychoeducation, self management, and support.

← THEORY OF BIOPSYCHOSOCIAL THERAPY

Biopsychosocial therapy is "an informal collection of attitudes and practices, not a defined system of treatment . . . with an odd assortment of practitioners disaffected with orthodox medicine and committed to alternatives they see as safer and better" (Weil, 1998, p. 181). Although not a single system of treatment, the models within biopsychosocial therapy share a common set of core values, attitudes, perspectives, and practice tools (Deckert, 1997; Weil, 1998, 2004).

The cornerstones of biopsychosocial interventions are

1. Stress management based on relaxation response, learning theory, and cognitive restructuring
2. Health promotion and prevention
3. Self-management
4. Social support

An important construct that interfaces with these interventions is the theory of the stages of change, which can be used to assess the client's motivational state or readiness to change.

Stress Management

The relationship between stress and health is complex; it covers the integration of "behavioral, emotional, cognitive, physical, hormonal, biochemical, cellular,

Table 13.2

Selye's Stress Reaction Pattern

Alarm Stage	Resistance Stage	Exhaustion Stage
Organism meets stressor	Organism adapts to	Coping ceases
Fight-or-flight response	continuation of stress	Adrenal exhaustion
Increased ANS* arousal	Corticosteroids released	Decreased energy,
Increased energy supply	Cortisol suppresses	stress tolerance
to organs to act in	immune system	Suppressed immune system
emergency; decrease	Fatigue, irritability,	Vulnerable to illness
to others	impaired concentration	Collapse/death/exhaustion
Increased adrenaline	for continued stress	of resources

* Autonomic nervous system.

environmental, and even spiritual interconnections" (Boone & Christensen, 1997, p. 265). When a highly stressful event takes place, people respond physically and mentally. If the stressor has a great enough negative impact, people may fall ill.

Pioneering researcher Walter Cannon demonstrated that when an organism faces danger, he reacts by either aggressing or escaping. Energy for this fight-or-flight reaction comes from release of adrenalin and noradrenalin (among other hormones and neurotransmitters) from the sympathetic nervous system and the endocrine system. Hans Selye, a Nobel Prize-winning endocrinologist, expanded on Cannon's work and identified and quantified the biological correlates of the fight flight, or stress reaction, which he called the General Adaptation Syndrome (GAS) (Selye, 1974, 1976a, 1976b). In laboratory experiments (disturbing to many today), he applied environmental stressors such as heat, cold, starvation, drowning, and burning to rats. He discovered a reactivity pattern summarized in Table 13.2.

To meet the stressor initially, animals entered an alarm stage. If the stressor continued, they entered the stage of resistance or a less intense level of arousal in which major body systems continued to be active (e.g., cardiovascular adaptation). If the stress response continued to the point where the vital energy drained from the organism, the animals were exhausted and, as a result, were much more susceptible to illness in the most vulnerable body structure (Blonna, 2005). When autopsied, the rats showed common physical, or nonspecific effects, such as enlarged adrenal glands, swollen lymph glands, ulcers, and a shrinking thymus (Selye, 1976a, 1976b). He extended his theory to humans to show that stress could induce a hormonal system breakdown, which then could produce diseases of adaptation such as coronary heart disease or high blood pressure.

Building on Selye's work, other researchers noted that the stressfulness of an event depends on how a person perceives and judges the stressor and the psychological and social resources he or she has to cope with it (Lazarus & Cohen, 1977; Lazarus & Launier, 1978). Today, stress and stressors are seen as a process. They consist of interchanges between an organism and its environment that involve self-generated or environmentally induced changes. Once the organism perceives these interchanges as exceeding available internal or external resources, homeostatic processes in the organism-environment system are disrupted (Boone & Christensen, 1997).

All living beings are naturally equipped to adapt to the challenges of stress. Some stress is positive, for example, the excitement of getting married. However, some stress is negative, for example, discovering a spouse is physically abusive. How people handle stress is an important factor for maintaining overall physical and mental health. For example, stress and depression are risk factors for serious medical conditions, such as heart disease. We will now look at some of the ways that physical health and stress can interact.

Stress Responses in the Body

The nervous system, the endocrine system, and the immune system play an integrated role in stress and health. The autonomic nervous system (ANS) is an important key to understanding the stress response and its effect on overall health. The ANS is divided into the parasympathetic and the sympathetic systems. The sympathetic nervous system is associated with a response to a stressor. The parasympathetic system is associated with relaxation and with putting the breaks on the sympathetic system.

The stress response begins in the brain and sets the rest of the body into action. When the person detects a threat, the alarm stage begins. Glucocorticoids are secreted by the adrenal cortex, which, in turn, activates a number of brain structures. The hypothalamus, the amygdala, and the pituitary glands communicate with one another through neural and hormonal conduction to prepare the body for flight or fight. The adrenal glands discharge adrenaline, which pumps the heart faster and increases the capacity of the lungs so the body can receive oxygen. Cortisol and other glucocorticoids are released, helping to convert sugar to energy. Digestion and other parasympathetic functions shut down. When the perceived threat is removed, adrenaline and noradrenalin decrease.

However, if dangers continue unrelieved or appear frequently, the organism remains in resistance. The toll is damage to the arteries and, over time, to other structures. Chronic stress can keep the glucocorticoids in the system, which can lead to a weakened immune system and a greater threat of developing mental and physical disease (Greenberg, 2008).

Psychoneuroimmunology (PNI) is the study of the interaction of the mind and the immune system and how the body defends against infection and aberrant cell division. The central nervous system (CNS) influences immune functioning, and, correspondingly, the immune function influences the CNS (Sarafino, 2008). A number of studies have shown the connection among neuronal, psychological, and immunological processes (Ader & Cohen, 1975, 1985). Stressful thoughts and emotions can reach the hypothalamus through the axons, which project from the limbic system and/or the forebrain. This connects with the hypothalamic-pituitary-adrenal (HPA) axis, which leads to the decreased efficiency or down-regulation of the immune system (Salzano, 2003).

Each organ is susceptible to stress and shows it in a different way. The areas that are vulnerable to the effects of stress and thus, vulnerable to disease, include the cardiovascular, gastrointestinal, musculoskeletal, pulmonary, dermatological, neurological, and immune systems. Some of the diseases resulting from stress include coronary heart disease, such as hypertension, atherosclerosis, and arteriosclerosis; gastrointestinal disease, such as inflammatory bowel disease, colon cancer, and digestive disorders; musculoskeletal disease, such as muscle tension and temporomandibular joint pain;) pulmonary disease, such as asthma; and immune diseases, such as rheumatoid arthritis, colitis, lupus, and HIV-AIDS.

Perceptions of Stress

Attitude about stress is a significant element in the person's ability to cope with environmental stressors, and this has been the subject of many research studies, some of which will be discussed.

Thomas Holmes and Richard Rae developed a scale of 43 major life events and rated them according to the amount of readjustment they require for the average individual (Holmes & Rae, 1967). Their scale quantifies changes and finds a consistent relationship between life events and illness patterns. The greater the change in a person's life, the greater the probability he or she can develop a physical or mental disorder (Greenberg, 2008). The most common stressors in adult life include the breakup of intimate relationships, death of a family member or friend, economic hardship, racism and discrimination, poor physical health, and assaults on physical safety (Lazarus & Folkman, 1984). Attitude is a potent force in adjusting the level of stress caused by any given outside event. It is the perception of an event that determines how stressful it is.

Handling Stress

How a person manages stress is fundamental to his or her adjustment. So, an important part of healthy functioning is learning to deal with stress. There are three levels of stress management: primary, secondary, and tertiary (Greenberg, 2008; Sarafino, 2008).

Primary stress management, the most effective way to control stress, means removing the stressor completely. For example, if a person is afraid of her supervisor's aggression, getting out of harm's way by finding another job is the most efficient way to end the stress. However, if it is not realistic to change jobs, then stress management involves secondary and tertiary interventions.

Secondary stress management is reducing stress by increasing resources so a person can effectively manage the demands of the stressors. For example, learning to evoke the relaxation response (see below) upon demand can be an effective stress manager. Learning to act assertively with the bullying boss may prove to be an effective strategy to reducing stress in the workplace.

Tertiary stress management is reducing the negative effects of conditions such as anxiety and depression that are the results of mismanaging stress in the past. If stress was not handled well previously, the person's capacity to handle further stress is reduced. Thus learning to control symptoms can enhance stress management.

Relaxation Response

The relaxation response is the mainstay of stress management. It is a force that counteracts physiological changes of the stress response by moving the stressing factors in the opposite direction. It is like running a film backward so that the body undoes the fight-and-flight reaction (Dolmar & Dreher, 1996). Methods for evoking the relaxation response are detailed in the practice section of the chapter.

Herbert Benson (1975), a Harvard cardiologist, peaked interest in the relaxation response when he systematically studied how integration of mind and body could enhance good health through his studies of Tibetan monks and their ability to control their autonomic responses. The relaxation response represents a conscious effort to calm the mind and relax the body. It involves a well-coordinated series of internal changes that transpire when mind and body become serene and quiet (Dolmar & Dreher, 1996). The quickly beating heart and rapid breathing slows; blood pressure drops; muscles loosen; brain wave patterns shift. To be able to voluntarily relax during a time of stress is a tremendous benefit to one's well-being, and to be able to decrease physiological reactions to negative events can greatly enhance one's health (Dusek et. al., 2006). While there are many ways to teach the client to produce the relaxation response, the resulting physiological changes are the same.

Stress Management Programs

Stress management programs mix and match various methods of dealing with stress. The prototypical program generally includes ways of identifying the stressor and its antecedents, monitoring stress, setting stress reduction goals, and acquiring better coping skills and practicing them (e.g., obtaining social support, rehearsing learned skills through homework, and role playing). After the relaxation response, the second most frequently used intervention in stress management is cognitive restructuring.

One method of cognitive restructuring is Donald Meichenbaum's stress inoculation (1993) (see Chapter 10). Another method is mindfulness-based stress reduction (MBSR), created by Jon Kabat-Zinn (1990) in which clients learn a variety of stress management techniques such as mindfulness and meditation. These techniques are useful for stress-sensitive conditions such as chronic pain and illness, anxiety and panic, GI disturbances, sleep disturbances, fatigue, high blood pressure, and headaches. The goal is to make lasting decreases in physical and psychological symptoms, develop an increased ability to relax, cope with pain, enhance energy and enthusiasm, and cope more effectively with both short- and long-term stressful situations.

Health Promotion and Prevention

Health promotion is both a philosophy and a method to encourage the practice of healthy behaviors (Taylor, 2006, p. 46). Although health promotion is not considered a traditional therapy technique, it can serve as a tool to improve a person's, and a population's, overall health.

Prevention is an important part of health promotion. Prevention means to anticipate, to take precautions against, and to avoid the danger of any disease. The emphasis is on wellness. There are three levels of prevention within health psychology:

- *Primary prevention* is decreasing the incidence of new cases of a psychiatric diagnosis within a population. It stops a disease or condition from occurring and promotes well-being by enhancing the individual's level of positive mental health by increasing his or her ability to deal with crises and by improving the quality of life through education and social engineering (Bloom & Gullotta, 2003).

  The client adapts a healthy style of life, which prevents disease from beginning, especially in a high-risk group. Examples of primary prevention are educating and raising awareness about substance abuse among vulnerable families. For example, the adolescent son of two alcoholic parents is told he is at a high risk for developing alcoholism, and it might be best if he abstains from drinking in order to avoid the possible dangers (Najarian & Werz, 2006).

  Examples of primary prevention in mental health programs are (a) suicide prevention, which teaches people to identify the indicators of suicide and encourages the person involved to seek help; (b) exercise and physical activity to prevent depression; (c) healthy eating with sufficient nutrients to prevent diseases; (d) drug prevention. Information is power; the biopsychosocial psychotherapist can increase the client's state of good health through knowledge of high risk factors (Sarafino, 2008).

- *Secondary prevention* means lowering the prevalence, or number of cases of a disorder, by shortening the length of cases and/or decreasing new ones. The earlier a disease is identified and treated, the fewer the complications (Sarafino, 2008).

  Examples of secondary prevention are early identification of mental health problems, such as the symptoms of depression, followed by rapid treatment. Some useful secondary prevention methods are (a) early identification of symptoms of schizophrenia so medication and respite can prevent hospitalization; (b) use of medication with ADHD to prevent school failure; (c) dietary regulation of phenylketonuria to prevent intellectual deficits; (d) self-monitoring, stimulus control, response substitutions, behavioral contracting, and self-management for clients with alcoholism.

- *Tertiary prevention* means lowering the rate or level of disability or ineffective functioning resulting from a disease. Tertiary prevention is not cure; it is damage control. It is a way to reduce dysfunction by containing or delaying the destruction that comes with a serious disease, or preventing a recurrence. One example of tertiary prevention is treating depression in cancer patients, so their physical state will not be worsened by negative mental states.

An example of a health promotion and prevention program is Healthy America 2000 (now Healthy People 2010), sponsored by the U.S. Department of Health and Human Services. This nationwide program's major goal is to improve the health of every American at the start of the twenty-first century. The program's 467 health objectives include helping people to increase physical activity and exercise, improve their nutrition and the quality of their eating, reduce or eliminate tobacco use, decrease or end alcohol and other drug abuse, and enhance educational and community-based health programs.

To understand how to motivate clients to adopt healthy behaviors, health psychologists have produced theoretical micro-models to explain and predict health behaviors (Weinstein, Rothman, & Sutton, 1998). Some of these predictive models are outlined below.

- *The health promotion/health belief model,* a cognitive perspective, posits that a person's health behavior is caused by his or her beliefs and consideration of the pros and cons of taking a certain action. The threat of an illness is seen as a function of its seriousness and the degree of susceptibility to illness. Cues also influence a person's behavior (e.g., media, public service messages, a loved one developing a disease, appointment reminders, and so on). A person also takes into account barriers to obtaining treatment (e.g., cost, effort, lack of a social support network) and any stigma attached to the condition, such as embarrassment at being diagnosed with a mental disorder or being seen at the mental health clinic (Sarafino, 2008).
- *The theory of planned behavior* sees health behaviors as a function of intention to perform the behavior. Intentions are determined by attitude regarding the behavior (good or bad to do), subjective norms (social pressure or influence), perceived behavioral control (expectations of success in performing the action or self-efficacy) (Sarafino, 2008).
- *Motivation theory* holds that health behavior is motivated by fear and is a function of the degree of the level of noxiousness, the probability of the event, and the efficacy of a protective response of the threatened event (Sarafino, 2008).

Self-Management

Self-management is also called *self-care, self-regulation, self-supervision,* or *self-directed action.* Self management means taking care of a chronic health condition, whether psychiatric or medical. The client and psychotherapist work collaboratively to manage care. The client gains control over cognitive, behavioral, and environmental variables. The components of any self-management program are as follows:

- Goals selection
- Information collection
- Information processing and evaluation
- Decision making
- Action
- Self-reaction

In self-management, the client must be committed to performing goal-oriented skills and must establish his or her preferred outcome. Self-management can be combined with other forms of therapy such as stress management, family support, or behavior therapy.

Social Support

Social support consists of information from others that one is loved and cared for, esteemed and valued, and part of a network of communication and mutual obligation. It consists of contacts such as parents, a spouse, lover, other relatives, friends, and social and community organizations such as churches or clubs (Rietschlin, 1998) or even a beloved pet (Allen, 2003). People who have strong social support have help in assessing threats from stressors, as well as tangible assistance and emotional assurance. Even the perception that one is being supported is helpful. Of course, the psychological health provider is a source of social support, guiding the client to appropriate resources.

Stages of Change

Behavior change is a process. *Stages of change* theory (also called the *transtheoretical model*) is based on data from clients in real situations who were learning to give up the unhealthy behavior of cigarette smoking (Prochaska, DiClemente, & Norcross, 1992). The theory posits that regardless of the specific nature of the problem, patients entering therapy in order to make changes move through a number of predictable phases and "patients do only what they believe in and only what they feel they are able to do" (DiMatteo, 1997). The biopsychosocial therapist can use this model as a guideline to assess a client's readiness to change and to select an appropriate intervention to move the client from one stage to another (Zimmerman, Olsen, & Bosworth, 2000). The stages of change are

1. *Precontemplation:* The client does not acknowledge that a problem exists. He or she avoids and resists discussing it and only comes to therapy at the insistence of others who are affected by the problem. For example, an alcoholic tends to claim his drinking is not a problem for him at all; it is only an issue for his "unreasonable" family.
2. *Contemplation:* The client shows a willingness to think, talk, and consider the pros and cons of what he or she can do about a problem. She may experiment with actions to solve the problem.
3. *Preparation/determination:* The client knows he has a problem and has decided to change but is not yet committed to a specific course of action. He finally chooses it and then figures out how to handle obstacles.
4. *Action:* The client executes a systematic plan of behaviors. She follows a specific action plan and may focus on one day at a time. The patient is committed, resists, slips, and follows a detailed plan.
5. *Maintenance:* The client has attained his goal but may vary in his ability to stick to the plan. In successful cases, clients maintain their changes

and integrate it permanently into a life style. However, most people waver about how much the change has altered the quality of life. His lifestyle might not make it easy to sustain the change, and he finds himself losing ground and vacillating in his resolve to continue the change.

6.   *Relapse:* The client does not resist slips, consistently returns to problem behaviors, and may regress to earlier stages.

Clients can go in and out of various stages of change and often recycle through the stages several times. It is common to relapse a number of times before the change becomes well cemented or well established.

Motivational interviewing is a method that is often used with the stages of change. It is a conversational style in which the psychotherapist emphasizes client strengths. It minimizes resistance and increases engagement between client and psychotherapist, helping the client to identify, explore, and resolve feelings about change (Miller & Rollnick, 2002). Some of the components of motivational interviewing are giving the client objective feedback, strengthening the client's sense of responsibility in changing behavior, and offering the client possible solutions and empathetic support.

Psychotherapists using motivational interviewing try to elicit statements that reflect self-efficacy. For example, if working with precontemplaters, the psychotherapist offers information to increase clients' awareness of the incongruence between where they are and where they want to be. Clients in the contemplation stage usually need help to tip the balance in favor of change. Clients in the preparation stage need to make a commitment to change and to prepare to change their behavior. Clients in the action stage need help to find specific strategies to help them make the changes and then maintain them (Rollnick, Mason, & Butler, 1999).

Normal and Abnormal Behavior

From the biopsychosocial perspective, normal and abnormal are seen in terms of health status. Health is reflected in a person's ability to realize his or her own potential and to cope with the normal stresses of life, work productively, and contribute to the community. Optimal or perfect health (nearly impossible to achieve) is the attainment of a state of complete physical, mental, and social well-being, not just the absence of disease. (World Health Organization, 1964). The healthier the person, the more normal he or she is considered to be.

Health status is a function of "personality factors, coping styles, stressful events and health-related behaviors, such as maintaining good sleep and diet habits" (Nolen-Hoeksama, 2006, p. 176). It is also a function of coping style, which reflects a person's action orientation and intra-psychic efforts to handle stress or minimize environmental and internal demands and conflicts among them (Lazarus & Launier, 1978; Taylor, 2006). The healthy person handles normal environmental pressures adequately to optimally and can adjust to a wide variety of stresses. She takes responsibility for her health status, self-monitors to check for early signs of mental or physical imbalance, and consults with professionals when necessary. Healing is an innate capacity of her body, not an element that comes from outside. In short, the healthy person lives a lifestyle with flexible coping mechanisms, which promote optimal health most of the time (Weil, 1998).

The abnormal or unhealthy person has a less-than-optimal adjustment in which the mind–body interaction is out of balance. She is not always able to handle the normal pressures of the environment and is not flexible in adapting to stress levels. Her lifestyle is one of poor health habits and health-compromising behaviors (e.g., substance abuse, cigarette smoking, or dangerous behaviors). She is not sensitive to her body's patterns and thus is not likely to detect early signs of mental or physical disturbance. Her view of health is passive, and she relies on professionals to deal with health problems. She sees healing as an outside force rather than an innate capacity of the body (Weil, 1998). She is prone to use treatment rather than prevention.

Her personality style makes her more likely to develop illness. For example, she may have a negative outlook or pessimistic style or a personality that is given to multitasking, quick anger, hostility, and is more vulnerable to coronary heart disease (Salzano, 2003; Taylor, 2006). In short, the unhealthy person lives a lifestyle in which her inflexible coping mechanisms do not promote optimal health most of the time. Stress is managed in a way that is harmful to her adjustment.

↢ Practice of Biopsychosocial Therapy

Now that we have examined the major theoretical concepts that underlie biopsychosocial therapy, we will explore its practice. Dr. Laurel Bodmin, our fictional composite biopsychosocial therapist, provides a firsthand perspective of how she integrates theory with practice and applies the techniques of biopsychosocial therapy.

Assessment and Diagnosis

Initially, I assess the client's issues using a biopsychosocial approach. I inquire about any medical, social, psychological, environmental, and cultural factors that may be affecting the client's mental and physical status. I administer a major life events questionnaire such as the Holmes and Rae scale (see page 376). I integrate these variables into the development and implementation of a holistic, unique, and personalized treatment plan. However, I align the plan to be consistent with *DSM*.

I use the stages of change theory in the first three sessions as a concept map to assess my client's readiness to change, and I use a motivational interviewing style. This helps me to estimate my client's compliance with treatment recommendations, as well as allowing me to set realistic expectations and to select appropriate interventions (Brug et al., 2005; O'Connell, 1997).

Negotiation of Therapeutic Relationship and Length of Treatment

I see my role as a biopsychosocial psychotherapist similar to that of the psychological family doctor. I act like a primary care doctor and develop a sustained partnership with my patients (Cummings, 1991). I provide for my client's personal mental health care needs in the context of the family and community (Donaldson, Yordy, Lohr, & Vanselow, 1996). I act as the coordinator of the client's care. I consult with other experts and communicate with everyone involved in the treatment. This includes physician and nonphysician providers, such as nurse practitioners, physician assistants, and clinical pharmacists.

I adapt my role to the particular practice setting. I can function in a general mental health setting, in a medical setting with clients who are chronically ill, in a holistic health center, or in solo practice with consultation with other practitioners in my client's care. Ideally, I prefer to be a member of an integrated health care team.

The client's role is to consider how the psychological factors impact health, such as how depression can result in noncompliance. Also, the client can learn about the impact of physical factors on mental health, such as how exercise and diet affect mood.

The length of therapy varies according to client needs. I see the client on an as-needed basis. I may see a client only once for an emergency or for many sessions over a lifetime of interventions. If a client requires my services, it means his or her health is less than optimal. My goal is to help my client to be mentally and physically healthy, which means making my services obsolete. I help the client to self-induce positive emotions, prevent diseases, and influence the course of an existing disease; this is accomplished by helping the client to choose healthy lifestyles and attitudes about the world (Nolen-Hoeksama, 2006, p. 176).

The general goal for all clients is to adapt their lifestyle to a more optimally healthy one, which, for psychotherapists, means enhancing patient responsibility and participation. For example, the goal of an already healthy client is to help her attain even better health. The goal for a client with acute symptoms is to identify the causes of her unhealthy state and alleviate the symptoms. The goal for a client with chronic illness is to minimize pain and discomfort.

A unique feature of biopsychosocial therapy is that goals of treatment exist for society in general as well as for the individual client. Goals for the society include helping the community to "reduce health disparities, improve health outcomes, decrease unnecessary care, and improve collaboration between various health-care providers" (Boone & Christensen, 1997).

Therapeutic Techniques

I have a toolbox of mind–body interventions from which to choose, including stress management, health promotion, self-management, and social support. But most importantly, my interventions are aimed at helping the client to take charge of his or her own health and to activate the doctor within.

Stress Management: Invoking the Relaxation Response

At the core of my therapy is stress management using the relaxation response. All forms of inducing the relaxation response involve the following four common elements (Benson, 1975):

1. A quiet environment
2. A mental device or focal point, such as repeating a phrase, focusing on a specific object, or attending to inhaling and exhaling
3. A passive attitude, such as not worrying about any distractions or outside stimuli
4. A comfortable position so the individual can relax but not fall asleep

Of the many ways to induce the relaxation response, I choose a method with which the client feels comfortable. These include deep breathing, progressive relaxation, meditation, autogenic training, body scan, yoga, repetitive prayer, guided imagery, biofeedback, hypnosis, and mindfulness to attain a tranquil state of mind and body (Dolmar & Dreher, 1996). Some of these specific techniques are outlined below (Davis, Eshelman, & McKay, 2003).

- *Breathing techniques* include diaphragmatic breathing, which encourages the client to focus on how he or she breathes, consider the shallowness and depth of each breath, expand the stomach like a balloon when breathing in, and compare normal breath to deep abdominal breathing to assess effects.
- *Progressive muscle relaxation* teaches the client to relax muscles over his or her entire body. The client is encouraged to compare the feeling of relaxed and tense muscles, to relax each muscle group in the body from head to toe, and to release mental and physical tensions. The intent is for the client to develop a habit of responding with relaxation when experiencing anxiety. With deep muscle relaxation, a client is counterconditioning an anxiety response with the relaxation response (Greenberg, 2008).
- *Meditation* is a process of gaining control over the mind in which the force of old thought habits diminish and new ones develop (Dalai Lama, 2001). Meditation increases the person's ability to internalize a locus of control (Kabat-Zinn, 1992; Linden, 1973).

  There are many meditation techniques, but they all use a specific focus; the focus can be one of three types: (a) an external object, (b) a geometric form or mandala, or (c) a word or sound with silent repetition. The client learns to assume a comfortable but attentive body position, turn attention inward, focus repetitively on breathing and adjust it to a regular pace. (Dolmar & Dreher, 1996, p. 55; Harp, 1990).
- *Autogenic* (meaning "self-generating") *training* gives the client the tools to control his or her own reactions (Greenberg, 2008; Luthe, 1962; Schultz & Luthe, 1959). In each of the stages of the process, the client focuses on sensations of heaviness in the dominant arm and leg, then on sensations of warmth in the arms and legs, then sensations of warmth and heaviness in the heart, on breathing, on sensations of warmth in the abdomen, and finally on sensations of coolness in the forehead.

- *Body awareness and body scan* are tools to elicit the relaxation response. The client (lying or sitting) begins the scan by focusing on different regions of the body, generally starting with the toes and feet and gradually switching focus to different body regions: leg, pelvis, torso, and so on. Diaphragmatic breathing flows from one end of the body to the other. The result is that clients feel as if their body has dropped away, as if they are "breath flowing freely across all the boundaries of the body" (Kabat-Zinn, 1990, p. 77).

- *Repetitive prayer* can be used to bring about the relaxation response. For example, in the Catholic Church, the Rosary is used as a repetitive form of prayer. Protestant religions use centering prayers. Judaism calls upon pre-davening prayers. With these prayers, the person focuses on a word or phrase, such as "Lord have mercy," "Shalom," "Allah," or "Hail Mary." Similar to meditation, prayer can bring about a state of relaxation.

- *Yoga, massage, and accupressure* are also used to elicit the relaxation response. Yoga, a 3,000-year-old practice, has many different systems: Prana, Brahma, Kriya, Kindalini, Raja, Tantra, and Hatha. In all forms, the purpose is to cleanse and exercise the body using breathing purifications, stretching postures, and meditation (Greenberg, 2008). Students who wish to know more about yoga should refer to the Resources section at the end of the chapter.

    Massage is a technique of manipulating tense muscles in the body. It generally involves applying a lotion and pressing, gliding, or kneading the muscles. Acupressure massage (shiatsu) means pressing down on the body where there are knots or bands of muscle pressure (Greenberg, 2008).

- *Visualizations* are mental sense impressions that the client can create consciously. Three commonly used types of visualization are receptive, programmed, and guided. Receptive visualizations are those in which the client relaxes or empties his mind and creates sketches of vague scenes.

    Programmed visualization occurs when the client creates an image that will help her to accomplish a goal. For example, a skier may imagine herself gracefully navigating a very steep slope. Guided visualization occurs when the biopsychosocial therapist helps the client visualize imagery that induces relaxation and promotes coping skills. Coaching can be either in person or on tape.

- *Hypnosis* is believed by some to be an altered state of consciousness, but others disagree. And hypnotic techniques differ by psychotherapist and by the treatment goals of the client. Procedures traditionally involve suggestions to relax, although relaxation is not necessary for hypnosis, and a wide variety of suggestions to clients can be used, including those to become more alert. Clients can also engage in self-hypnosis, using the hypnotic procedures on themselves (American Psychological Association, 2006).

- *Biofeedback* is simply sending back a biological signal to the person who is producing the signal. These biological signals are recorded by an electronic device, and the person can use the information to change his or her physiology in a desired direction. Generally, physiological signals (e.g., respiration, heart rate, muscle tension) are recorded in real time and shown to the person as they are being recorded. It is a way of teaching clients to recognize and control how their bodies are functioning Among the many uses of biofeedback are for control of anxiety, migraine headaches, ADHD, and muscle pain.

Besides these techniques, I also use cognitive restructuring in stress management, which helps the client examine stress-provoking thoughts and replace them with peaceful, positive, constructive images. To determine if a thought is stress provoking, the client might analyze how the thought contributes to stress and how it helps or hurts. To restructure, the client can confront irrational or illogical thoughts. I draw upon the cognitive models of Albert Ellis and Aaron Beck (see Chapter 10).

Health Promotion, Self-Management, and Social Support

I use information from bona fide health promotion programs and relay it to the client if appropriate. I encourage clients to engage in health-enhancing behaviors through prevention (making treatment unnecessary), through avoidance of health-compromising behaviors, and through ending or decreasing negative health conditions and diseases (Sarafino, 2008).

I attempt to understand what makes the client choose healthy or unhealthy behaviors and use this information to develop specific strategies to motivate my clients toward healthy behaviors. Whereas I prefer primary prevention, I also use secondary activities to maintain or enhance the particular client's health care status. I also use tertiary prevention, or controlling chronic conditions, to optimize compromised health. I must be in command of a more detailed knowledge base of stress-related diseases to help clients sustain the best possible health given serious conditions, such as coronary heart disease and rheumatoid arthritis.

I encourage my client to use self-management techniques (see pages 379–80), especially for his or her health problems or conditions. I educate my client about how social support can reduce risks for physical and mental illness, even for mortality. I urge my client to develop close friendships, interact with people who are positive, and to maximize the help available if the client is sick or disabled. Thus, in my biopsychosocial psychotherapy, I work with my client to make an individualized, integrated treatment plan in which he or she self-manages his or her own health care, integrates stress management and health promotion, and develops ample social support.

The Process of Therapy

Since I act like psychological family doctor, I see the process of biopsychosocial therapy to be a lifelong endeavor. As long as I am in the same practice, I am available to provide necessary services to the clients who need it.

For this reason, biopsychosocial psychotherapy does not have the traditional beginning, middle, and termination. Rather, the process is more likely intermittent therapy across the life span, a series of episodes in which the client contacts me when needed.

I use the stages of change to determine where my client is in the change process and what the best treatment plan for the client may be at any particular time (Brug et al., 2005). This model is particularly helpful with clients who want to stop addictive behaviors, such as cigarette smoking, but I also use it to help clients change other health habits (O'Connell, 1997). I monitor how clients comply with treatment recommendations and whether clients are experiencing difficulties so that I can align my expectations with reality and adjust the treatment accordingly.

THERAPY IN ACTION: DR. LAUREL BODMIN AND THE CASE OF JONATHAN

To illustrate the application of biopsychosocial therapy, we examine a treatment plan for Jonathan, followed by excerpts from therapy sessions with our fictional psychotherapist, Dr. Bodmin. Keep in mind the case excerpts are simulated interviews and represent the ideal of therapy. In real life, clients may take much longer to meet therapeutic goals. Table 13.3 provides a summary of Dr. Bodmin's treatment plan.

Case Excerpts

The following excerpts are from sessions based on Dr. Bodmin's case formulation.

Session 1

[half hour into session]

Dr. Bodmin: Help me to understand the level of your stress and pain. Could you rate how serious your stress level is from 1 to 10? 1 means a mild problem. For example, your car is a little dirty, and the mess dissatisfies you, and a 10 is the worst stress you could ever endure, like being kidnapped or told you have lost everything in a fire.

Jonathan: Ever since Tuti left with Darren, it's been bad, so bad. I give it a 9. It's almost as if I have been held hostage emotionally.

Dr. Bodmin: Tell me more about how you feel both physically and mentally.

Jonathan: I don't sleep well, I don't eat well. I am drinking more than usual.

Dr. Bodmin: How much do you usually drink?

Jonathan: I used to have one or two glasses of wine at night. One when I come home from work with Tuti and one with our dinner. Now I open a bottle, and the whole thing is gone before I go to bed. Sometimes I open a second bottle and have a few more glasses. I don't drink the whole second bottle, though.

Dr. Bodmin: What are your thoughts about the changes in your drinking habits?

Jonathan: I know it's not good. I don't like the fuzzy feeling in my head when I wake up. But it does help me to get in a better mood at night.

Dr. Bodmin: Many people believe alcohol makes them feel better, but it is a common misconception. Alcohol is a depressant. Its effect on mood is not simple. You may feel relaxed and cheerful at first, but overall it is a depressant. Research shows that drinkers who claim they feel better actually behave morosely. Perhaps it is something you'd like to know more about, since it directly affects you at night?

Jonathan: Well, yes, I would.

Dr. Bodmin: I will give you some interesting reading as homework. Do you think you may want to consider a change in your current lifestyle before it becomes habitual.

Table 13.3

Biopsychosocial Treatment Plan for Jonathan

Assessment and Formulation	• Presenting problem: loss of relationship and depression • Biopsychosocial assessment: lifestyle, stress level analysis • Loss as stressful as divorce • Lifestyle factors contributing to depression: decreased physical activity, loss of social activity, increased drinking, disrupted sleep due to smoking • Stage of change: contemplation
Therapeutic Relationship	• Biopsychosocial psychotherapist acts like a psychological primary care doctor • J. reports, discusses openly, makes sincere effort at compliance
Contract, Goals, and Treatment Plan	• Integrated and holistic care: increase physical activity, maintain proper nutrition, establish social support network, stress management • Intermittent therapy schedule after initial crisis is resolved • Cognitive restructuring for depression • Assess for antidepressant medications • Agree to meet weekly and assess goals, lifestyle, and self-management
Techniques	• Stress management with tapes and workbook • Intermittent therapy schedule after initial crisis is resolved and to bring about lifestyle change • Beck and/or Ellis cognitive restructuring therapy for depression • Insight and understanding of role in interpersonal relationships • Holistic approach and health promotion: exercise, consult dietician for nutritional needs, join groups, seek social support, apply stress management program, decrease alcohol and smoking through health promotion and assessment and smoking cessation program • Assess need for antidepressant medications
Process of Therapy	• As stress is managed and coping skills increase, symptoms of depression decline • Appropriate lifestyle changes occur • Moves through stages of change from contemplation to action; therapy sessions for maintenance
Termination and Outcome	• Healthier lifestyle achieved • Remission of depression; symptoms controlled

[*Comment: I am using psychoeducation through early identification of alcohol misuse in hopes of preventing alcohol problems. The earlier J. understands the potential problem, the more likely complications can be prevented.*]

Jonathan: If I don't drink, how do I cope?

Dr. Bodmin: There are many other ways to cope, and I am here to help you to learn these ways. How have you coped with stress in the past?

Jonathan: I try to get rid of it. If something is bothering me, I get away from it.

Dr. Bodmin: How can you get away from your current problems?

Jonathan: I can't. I am angry with them for doing what they did to me. [*long silence*] I am upset all of the time. I can't stay like this. I need to work.

Dr. Bodmin: What have been your most successful ways of coping in the past?

[*Comment: I tap into resources as quickly as possible. Jonathan seems to be stuck in Selye's stage of resistance and beginning to move toward exhaustion.*]

Jonathan: I guess I throw myself into my work and exercise.

Dr. Bodmin: When is the last time you worked off stress with exercise?

Jonathan: Don't remember!

Dr. Bodmin: Can that change?

Jonathan: I suppose. I always manage to pull myself together, but now it's different. I am so down I don't feel like doing anything at all.

Dr. Bodmin: Would you say your loss is very similar to that of a divorce?

Jonathan: Yes. It absolutely feels like it.

Dr. Bodmin: Divorce is a tough stressor. It's a huge lifestyle change. It's best to counter it with a healthy lifestyle change and easy to fall into one that is unhealthy. Experiencing great sadness does not *have* to lead to depression. We need to work together to minimize your risk of greater depression. For example, drinking alcohol is contributing to depression. Smoking when you can't sleep makes you less likely to sleep! And sleep disturbance can contribute to depression. Plus, giving up your usual exercise is also part of a lifestyle that contributes to your depression. Do you think this is true?

Jonathan: Yes, I think you are right.

[*Comment: I see if Jonathan is willing to take actions to enhance his lifestyle and optimize his ability to deal with the depression.*]

Jonathan: I guess if I had a healthier lifestyle I might feel better.

Dr. Bodmin: I suppose you could think about it like the chicken or the egg. When Tuti left, you were upset. You tried to cope with drinking and working, and when that did not help, you felt even worse.

Jonathan: I can't seem to get out of it. I'd like to find the cause of why I am doing this.

Dr. Bodmin: Does finding the cause seem as important to you as changing to a healthier lifestyle?

Jonathan: Well, when you say it like that, no.

Dr. Bodmin: Let's work to help you find ways to handle stress. Once you do, it will be easier to try to understand.

Jonathan: I have read a bit about stress. When I was on the college football team, we had a sports psychologist who worked with us every other week.

Dr. Bodmin: What did you learn that was helpful?

Jonathan: Quite a bit. I liked the visualization training. He'd get us relaxed, and then he'd help us go through a script with various scenes, envisioning ourselves as winners.

Dr. Bodmin: Can any of this apply to your current situation?

Jonathan: Well, I guess some could. [*suddenly, tears roll down his cheeks*] I don't know if it's worth it. Why do I care about my ability to cope? She wanted children. I could not do it. I do not want a family. Not at all. I didn't want to talk about it. It's not doing me much good to talk about it again.

[*Comment: I wait until Jonathan has time to experience the intense emotion.*]

Dr. Bodmin: [*long pause*] Sometimes when we avoid facing emotional issues in the short run, it makes it harder to deal with them in the long run. Isn't it interesting that people can look at the same event and see it so differently? What you consider to be stress, Tuti thought was meaningful. Not having children would have been stressful to her. Your stress was her dis-stress. So you and Tuti saw a family lifestyle with children in very different ways. You had very different visions for your respective life plans.

Jonathan: Good point.

Dr. Bodmin: Looking at what the sports psychologist told you, what is a healthy way to deal with stress or loss when you suffer defeat?

Jonathan: You must keep on trying. Don't feel sorry or guilty. That will cause you even more pain.

Dr. Bodmin: It's possible that you can see this situation like winning a game. You've been defeated, but do you want to give up the season when you have lost only one game?

Jonathan: No.

Dr. Bodmin: Let's look at the tools, and you decide which ways are most helpful for you personally.

Jonathan: Having Tuti with me—that was having a supportive partner.

Dr. Bodmin: Social support is very important. We know that people who have social support feel better than those who feel alone or cut off. Now that your social support is temporarily gone, you are acting as if you can't stand it. I know you just can't replace people, but you can try to find some substitutes for the support you received from Tuti and your best friend. You were standing on stable ground, and the rug was pulled out from under you. Let's break it down into small parts. What were some of the supports they gave you on a daily basis? Like when you came home, what was it like to have Tuti and Darren in your life?

Jonathan: It made everything OK. They made me feel like I could handle the bad days. And now I can't. I just want to hide from the world.

Dr. Bodmin: Please consider that. What if a friend of yours told you this is how he is coping with a great loss? What would you say?

Jonathan: I'd say you need to do things—to be more active, to get out of yourself.

Dr. Bodmin: What kinds of things did you do with Darren?

Jonathan: We would play racquetball every Thursday night and Saturday morning. We had a good workout together.

Dr. Bodmin: What effect does playing sports have on you?

Jonathan: I would be out, meeting friends, getting exercise, figuring out what I had done. figuring out my plans for the future. When I'm physically active, I seem to be better at thinking things over. I would even explore new job possibilities.

Dr. Bodmin: Can we work out a plan for you to involve yourself in these activities?

Jonathan: Yes.

Termination

Dr. Bodmin: How do you judge your progress in therapy?

Jonathan: I am much better now. I have completely stopped smoking, and my sleep patterns are normal. Most important, I am coming to grips with my loss of Tuti, and I know now that the relationship was too stressful for both of us. I'm no longer angry, just disappointed. I understand what we have talked about. I continue to use the practices I have learned and the stress management tools you taught me. I like the visualization best.

Dr. Bodmin: Let me encourage you to continue.

Jonathan: Yes. I see. I want to be sure I don't slip back into depression—or not exercising any longer.

Dr. Bodmin: Let me know whenever you need to come to see me. Think of me as your mind–body coach, available to help you out whenever you need it so you can continue to maintain the changes you have accomplished.

Case Comment

Jonathan entered therapy in the stage of contemplation and leaves it after having achieved action. He is executing a systematic plan of behavior and focusing on one day at a time. He is committed to his change, sometimes resists it and slips, but has a plan to prevent relapse. He reduced his drinking and smoking and adapted a healthy exercise regime, restructured his thinking about his loss, and increased his social support network. His self-management skills improved.

He chose not to take antidepressants after being offered the option, and he performed his homework assignments. His lifestyle change seems firm. He will return to therapy intermittently for maintenance of his gains.

✦ Research Directions in Biopsychosocial Therapy and Health Psychology

There is considerable evidence that mind–body interventions have positive effects on psychological functioning and quality of life. The National Institute of Mental Health (NIMH) states many mind–body interventions have become extensively researched since the 1960s and are considered to be evidence-based practices. Particularly helpful are therapies for people who are coping with chronic illness or who are in need of palliative care. The National Center for Complementary and Alternative Medicine (NCCAM) evidence-based review of mind–body therapies can be easily accessed through the website. Emphasizing randomized controlled trials and systematic reviews of the literature, NCCAM came to the following conclusions:

- Increased understanding exists about the interaction among central and autonomic nervous system, immune, and endocrine functioning, which impacts upon a person's health status.
- Neurochemical and anatomical bases for some of the effects of biopsychosocial (mind–body) therapies are being discovered, defined, and confirmed.
- Psychological factors can play a significant role in a number of health-related areas, such as the development and progression of disease, pain management, mood, quality of life, and coping skills. They can also help alleviate treatment-related symptoms, such as chemotherapy reactions.
- Biopsychosocial therapy—using combined interventions of relaxation therapy, stress management, coping skills training, and cognitive behavior training—seem to be an effective adjunctive treatment for coronary artery disease and some pain-related disorders, such as arthritis.

- Biopsychosocial therapy using multiple interventions such as cognitive behavior therapy can be effective in the management of various chronic conditions, particularly when combined with informational materials.
- Imagery, hypnosis, and relaxation applied to presurgical clients can reduce pain and shorten postsurgery recovery time.
- Evidence for the effectiveness of biofeedback, cognitive behavior therapy (CBT), and hypnosis is quite solid; there is less research to support the use of CAM approaches like meditation and yoga. Meditators may be less anxious and better able to control their feelings and oxygen levels (Kabat-Zinn, 1992; Linden, 1973; Miller, Fletcher, & Kabat-Zinn, 1995).

A number of reviews of biopsychosocial therapy can be found under the headings of behavioral medicine, health psychology, and integrated behavioral health care, among others (Creer, Holroyd, Glasgow, & Smith, 2004; U.S. Department of Health and Human Services, 1999). See the online Appendix C for summaries of reviews and links to such research.

Research on health promotion and prevention programs demonstrates conclusively that these efforts are effective. For example, cigarette smoking is the single most preventable cause of death and disease in the United States. Worldwide programs to reduce smoking show the percentage of people who smoke has dropped dramatically since 1964, when the education and health promotion programs began. In the United States in 1964, 40 percent of Americans smoked. In 1988, only 25 percent smoked. In the United Kingdom, annual use declined from 150 billion to 80 billion cigarettes from 1965 to 1995. Norway's ban on smoking advertisements was followed by decreased tobacco sales particularly among the young. Estimates are that the rate of smoking there would be 80 percent higher without the program. Thailand experienced a 4 percent drop in total smoking prevalence among males and a 3 percent drop in 15- to 19-year-olds after smoking prevention efforts.

In the United States, the Florida Pilot Program on Tobacco Control, a primary prevention program, showed a reduction over a 2-year period among students (Creer et al., 2004). Secondary prevention programs have also been effective in reducing lung cancer, irreversible chronic respiratory disease, and coronary heart disease inked to tobacco use. From 1988 to 1997, per capita cigarette smoking in California declined more than twice as fast as in the rest of the country after introducing the California Tobacco Control Program (Creer et al., 2004).

Tertiary prevention incorporates traditional therapy techniques—in particular, behavioral, cognitive, and self-management methods that are adapted and personalized for each unique condition, person, group, program, or community's needs—have also proved effective in dealing with a variety of conditions. Health promotion and prevention programs are highly likely to assist clients in making changes and good choices regarding behavior.

Research on the self-management of chronic diseases (type of chronic condition, mode of instruction, the assessment of needs and changes, and cost-benefits) show that self-management techniques are helpful for a number of chronic conditions (Dusseldorp, van Elderen, Maes, Meulman, & Kraaij, 1996). Self-management also helped to increase health status in a number of conditions. Cognitive techniques (see Chapter 10) can be used to help the client self-manage in the treatment of chronic diseases (Andersen, 2003).

Stress management interventions have also been found to be effective (Ellis, Gordon, Neenan, & Palmer, 1997). A comprehensive review showed triple the number of studies on work sites and stress management from 1984 to 1996 (Murphy, 1996). Stress management programs helped clients to increase resources to help them to handle stress (O'Connell, 1997). The most frequently used stress management technique was relaxation training, followed by cognitive reframing, but combinations of stress management methods were used about twice as frequently. The positive findings must be tempered by methodological limitations, such as low numbers of subjects and insufficient follow-up (Evers, et al., 2006; Fleming, 1997; O'Connell, 1997).

Some controversy has developed in association with the stages of change. This intuitively appealing theory has been adapted by psychotherapists for many purposes, including dealing with exercise, weight control, and addiction. However, some claim there is a relative paucity of strong evidence for the changes of stage model (Riemsma et al., 2003; Whitelaw, Baldwin, & Bunton, 2000). Others argue that there can be difficulties applying the stages of change construct to complex health behaviors (Brug et al., 2005; Sutton, 2006).

An exciting new area of evidence-based research is brain imaging, a technology that has confirmed that mental states are linked to physical states and vice versa. The scanning technologies show what parts of the brain are involved in mental functioning and what is happening between mind and body. In the 1990s, functional magnetic resonance (fMRI) imaging showed oxygen use and blood flow to areas of the brain. Most recently, fMRI has shown a relationship between patterns in nerve firings and activities, such as the specific brain regions that are active during meditation. Research shows that meditation produced "significant increases in left-sided anterior brain activity, which is associated with positive emotional states," which is also connected to improved immune function (National Center for Complementary and Alternative Medicine, 2008).

What can the psychotherapist tell the client about research into the effectiveness and efficacy of biopsychosocial therapy? Proponents point to the impressive strides in developing and applying techniques for a wide variety of physical disorders, as well as helping patients cope with physical conditions and illness (Creer et al., 2004). Evidence is accumulating that many forms of mind–body techniques have positive effects on psychological functioning, increase quality of life, help people cope with chronic illness, and provide palliative care (Luborsky et al., 2004). However, each model or technique can be researched individually before making a decision about using it.

✦ ISSUES OF DIVERSITY

Many variables affecting health care including racism, sexism, ageism, classism, and ethnicity were not understood or adequately researched in relationship to health status. Disease prevalence varies among these groups, and it is important to discover the reasons for that variation. Factors such as access to health care, genetic predisposition, motivation to care for oneself, early education and training, and educational opportunities affect a person's health status and need to be studied.

For example, stress and hypertension are higher among lower income African American males than other groups. Research shows that a number of factors may account for that finding, including high stress due to discrimination, suppressed hostility, and minority status. Factors such as dietary patterns and socioeconomic status may play a significant role in this health finding.

Specific women's health issues were neglected in health psychology until the 1980s (see Chapter 14). Research has shown that there are important differences between males and females in their health behaviors. For example, women differ from men in their reactions to stress and in their tobacco and alcohol use.

Many sociocultural differences affect health behaviors. Recent immigrants to the United States have very different notions of what adequate health care may be. Religious beliefs can also influence the forms of treatment individuals find acceptable. For example, Christian Scientists are opposed to many biomedical treatments. Considering all of the inequities in population health, health care, and health promotion must be part of a political agenda (O'Neil, 2004).

✦ MAJOR CRITIQUES OF BIOPSYCHOSOCIAL THERAPY AND HEALTH PSYCHOLOGY

Critics argue that the biopsychosocial model is in its infancy. It explains healthy adjustment and unhealthy adjustment in terms of the interaction of biology, society, and environment, but it does not identify what the precise interactions are that can explain maladaptive functioning. It lacks the specificity of a good theory. We do not know, and cannot predict, how these interactions will occur. Thus it is difficult to implement it in practice. While much research has been conducted on biopsychosocial interventions, many researchers have come to very different conclusions.

Critics of mind–body therapies say that the problem is not with biomedical, Western health care but with the delivery system. In essence, people who are dissatisfied with their health care providers are willing to turn to alternative health care for a good relationship with a caregiver. Many clients are discouraged with the health care system in the United States today; these clients are seeking more personal care with a more human connection. However, critics of biopsychosocial therapy maintain that the problem is with the economics of the system, not the medicine. The danger is that these dissatisfied patients may choose practitioners who are not qualified and undergo procedures that are not clinically safe.

Some say that biopsychosocial therapy has not attained the status of a full discipline, since it borrows theoretical and methodological approaches from many other established disciplines (McQueen, 2002; McQueen & Anderson, 2004). The assumption that how we think and feel alters the disease process may be true, but we may question the strength and the extent of this mind–body connection. Understanding research into the effectiveness and efficacy of mind–body therapy *is* complicated. Extensive research is available on the psychosocial factors that cause and influence the progression and the treatment of many stress-related illnesses, and psychotherapists want to apply the promotion of healthy lifestyles to clients (Fotheringham & Owen, 1999, p. 501). But searching for specific evidence is necessary considering the multidimensional nature of the theory underlying the biopsychosocial model (Wong, 2002).

SUMMARY

- Western medicine currently embraces a biomedical model, but it is transitioning into a biopsychosocial perspective that assumes that biological, social, and psychological factors interact to play a significant role in health and illness.
- Biopsychosocial interventions are an informal collection of attitudes and practices, not a single system of treatment, which share core values, attitudes, perspectives, and practice tools with health psychology. The many therapeutic interventions consistent with the values of the biopsychosocial model are called biopsychosocial therapy in this chapter.
- The biopsychosocial model draws not only from health psychology but from complementary and alternative medicine, often referred to as mind–body therapies, behavioral medicine, and psychosomatic medicine.
- Psychotherapists who embrace the biopsychosocial perspective can look forward to new roles as the trend grows to deliver health care through multidisciplinary teams in collaborative and integrative models of care.
- Major types of biopsychosocial interventions include stress management (primary, secondary, or tertiary) with the relaxation response as its mainstay, health promotion and prevention, self-management, and social support.
- The theory of the stages of change assesses a client's readiness to change along with motivational interviewing. Normal and abnormal behavior are seen in terms of health status.
- The practice of biopsychosocial therapy includes assessment and diagnosis of factors that affect the client's mental and physical health status. The ideal role for the psychotherapist in this model is similar to that of a psychological family doctor with integrated behavioral health services. The client's role is to consider the psychological impact on health. The timing of therapy is intermittent, on an as-needed basis. The goal is to adapt an optimally healthy lifestyle and to look for ways to reduce health disparities within society.
- Therapeutic techniques, in addition to all of the traditional methods, consist of stress management—including deep breathing, progressive relaxation, meditation, guided imagery, autogenic training, biofeedback, and hypnosis; other useful techniques are yoga, massage, accupressure, repetitive prayer, and cognitive restructuring. In addition to relaxation response techniques, health promotion, self-management, and social support are important.
- Research shows that mind–body interventions have positive effects on psychological functioning and quality of life. Evidence for the effectiveness of biofeedback, cognitive behavior therapy (CBT), and hypnosis is solid; there is less research to support the use of CAM. Research shows that health promotion and prevention programs are effective, and stress management and self-management

for chronic diseases looks promising. Research on stages of change theory is controversial. Brain imaging has confirmed that mental states are linked to physical states and vice versa.

- Issues of diversity affect health and are obvious in areas such as access to health care, motivation to care for oneself, early education and training, and educational opportunities.

- Critics argue that the biopsychosocial model is in its infancy and has not yet reached the status of a fully recognized discipline; it lacks the specificity of a strong theory and does not identify the precise interactions that explain maladaptive functioning. Unqualified practitioners abound and promote procedures that are not clinically safe.

RESOURCES

National Center for Complementary and Alternative Medicine (NCCAM)
NCCAM Clearinghouse
P.O. Box 7923
Gaithersburg, MD 20898
(888) 644-6226
http://nccam.nih.gov

This center, part of the National Institutes of Health, provides information on training, research, published results, and education in alternative medicine.

World Health Organization (WHO)
World Health Organization
Avenue Appia 20
CH-1211 Geneva 27
Switzerland
http://www.who.int/en

WHO oversees health issues throughout the world. It helps guide research, sets priorities for health agendas, and addresses global health trends.

U.S. Department of Health and Human Services (HHS)
200 Independence Avenue, S.W.
Washington, DC 20201
(202) 619-0257 or (877) 696-6775
http://www.hhs.gov

HHS is the U.S. government's principal agency for protecting the health of all Americans and for providing essential human services, especially for those who are least able to help themselves.

Health Psychology, Division 38 of the American Psychological Association
Barbara A. Keeton
P.O. Box 1838
APA Division 38

Ashland, VA 23005-2544
(804) 752-4987
http://www.health-psych.org

Division 38 of the APA, health psychology, promotes collaboration among psychologists and other health professionals, particularly those interested in the psychological and behavioral aspects of physical and mental health.

CLASS EXERCISES AND ACTIVITIES

Theory

1. Describe the theory of stress and illness. Conceptualize some of the *DSM's* diagnoses (schizophrenia, depression, borderline personality disorder) from the stress–illness perspective.
2. Discuss how motivational interviewing and the stages of change can be helpful in working in a health care setting with clients who have diabetes, coronary heart disease, and asthma.
3. How can biopsychosocial theory be integrated into forms of psychotherapy? Write a theoretical statement discussing how mind and body are interdependent and how theory, research, and practice can come together in biopsychosocial therapy.

Practice

1. How can a psychotherapist use information from primary prevention programs to help an individual client in a one-to-one session? Find a successful prevention program, describe it, condense its results, and apply it to a case.
2. How can a psychotherapist interface with a primary care physician? Is it useful? How can it enhance practice? How useful is it to be a primary care psychotherapist? How does being located in the same clinic or practice with primary care physicians affect mental health and psychotherapy practice?
3. Look at the sample treatment plan in Chapter 1 (Figure 1.2) and fill it out for Tuti for biopsychosocial therapy, particularly using stress management. (Both Jonathan's and Tuti's case histories are in Appendix A.)

Research

1. A patient asks you "Why are you using biopsychosocial therapy to treat me? How did you choose this particular therapy model for me?" How can you justify your choice?
2. Conduct a review of the relaxation response in PubMed and using PsychINFO. Limit your search to: *relaxation therapy and randomized control*. What kinds of articles did you find? What kinds of research articles are available on stress management as a treatment? Taking an overview of the articles, describe the kind of evidence they contain. Is there any support for the efficacy and effectiveness of any particular stress management package?
3. How would you defend biopsychosocial therapy against the claim that the research that support it is not based on a single discipline or unifying theory?

CHAPTER 14

PSYCHOPHARMACOLOGY

The greatest mistake in the treatment of diseases is that there are physicians for the body and physicians for the soul, although the two cannot be separated.

–Plato

The goal of this chapter is to help the student to gain basic information about psychopharmacology that is useful to a nonprescribing psychotherapist. The chapter discusses the historical background of psychotropic medications and psychotherapy, associated controversies, and the theory, practice, and research of psychopharmacology. It provides an overview of basic pharmacology, including information about pharmacodynamics, pharmacokinetics, how and which neurotransmitters are involved in mental disorders, and the major types of psychotropic medications prescribed today. The simulated nonprescribing psychotherapist, Dr. Christa Perry, will present a treatment plan and therapy excerpts for the case of Jonathan. Issues of diversity and major critiques are also included.

✦ HISTORICAL CONTEXT

In today's health care environment, all nonprescribing mental health providers should acquire a basic knowledge of psychopharmacology and the use of psychotropic medications, their limitations, their side effects, and their benefits to clients (Lange & Julien, 1998). Until recently, nonprescribing psychotherapists and prescribing practitioners belonged to two distinct camps: the psychological or the biological. Each side argued about whether mental disturbance was caused by psychology or biology. Although these perspectives are not necessarily incompatible, they emphasize very different treatment philosophies (Gelenberg & Keith, 1997; Preston & Johnson, 2002; Preston, O'Neal, & Talaga, 2005). To the greatest extent possible, psychotherapists today must seek the most effective treatments for their clients, regardless of their personal philosophy (Feldman & Keltner, 2005). The box on the opposite page presents two cases of patients treated with psychotropic medications.

Psychological Perspective

The psychological perspective maintains that mental disorders are based primarily in the mind. Emotional stressors, early traumas, and intrapsychic conflicts are at the root of neurosis, psychosis, and other forms of mental disturbances. Psychotherapy is the major treatment of choice. If the use of medication is judged to be appropriate, it is seen

TWO CASE STUDIES

The two following cases illustrate how medications can enhance the ability of some patients to handle serious crises, maintain autonomy, and benefit from psychotherapy. These patients may have taken much longer to improve, or they may not have ever achieved better mental health, without medication.

Angela

Angela was in a state of utter despair, despondency, and desperation. The mother of three small children, her husband had been sentenced to two years in prison for selling drugs. Losing him abruptly resulted in her feeling hopeless, overwhelmed, and suicidal. She told me "my heart is broken into a million pieces, and life without him is too much to bear." I wanted to hospitalize her for her own safety, but she begged me not to. Promising me she would not hurt herself because her children could not tolerate the loss of both parents, she vowed to struggle on.

I set up a social support system. Her mother and sister stayed with her and her children every waking moment. Needing to quickly begin a program of therapy and medication, I consulted with Angela's primary care doctor, and she prescribed antidepressants, which Angela began immediately. Her response was miraculous; Angela told me that within one day many symptoms had lifted like a veil. Although still miserable, she was able to go to work and care for the children.

Over the next six months, psychotherapy focused on her issues of dependency, and she became a healthier, more self-assured person. After her husband's return from prison following an early release, he remained drug free and rejoined the family.

Angela's case is exceptional in that antidepressants generally do not have as rapid an effect as that reported here. But regardless of whether it was the placebo effect or just that Angela was a rapid responder, receiving the medication allowed her to quickly gain control of her symptoms. She was able to become fully involved in therapy to cope with her difficult situation.

Kevin

Kevin was a 23-year-old who came to see me because he was having graphic visions of his parents having sex. Alarmed and disturbed by these images, he was embarrassed to discuss them and confused about what to do. Discussion with his family revealed that Kevin had shown signs of mental disturbance during his teens in the form of withdrawal and strange thinking.

After consulting with his primary care physician and a psychiatrist, Kevin began antipsychotic medications. I saw him on a daily basis for 30-minute appointments. After a month, the visions decreased in frequency, and Kevin was coping well. Through psychoeducation, Kevin was able to grasp what being diagnosed as a schizophrenic meant to his life.

With symptoms in remission, Kevin dropped out of therapy. After six months, his symptoms reappeared, and Kevin returned to see me. Our previous work had laid the groundwork for effective interventions for the reoccurrence, and he immediately went back on his medications. Within three weeks again, he was ready for more therapy. He stayed on his meds longer this time and remained in control of his symptoms for a full year.

Kevin, like many others in his situation, learned experientially. He was the typical "noncompliant" client who descends back into symptoms, which in turn motivates him to seek treatment. Medications make it possible for patients like Kevin to stay out of the hospital. This is not the ideal treatment, but it is the treatment that frequently occurs in the real world of mental health.

as an ancillary aid to psychotherapy. The arguments that support the use of psychotherapy as the treatment of choice are as follows (Julien, 2001; Thase & Jindal, 2004):

- Psychotherapy treats the whole person and the psyche, not just symptoms.
- Medications give the message the person is "sick" or "ill"; they imply the person cannot help him- or herself to the degree possible if a disease model were not used.

- Medication fosters reliance on external solutions to problems and thus reduces a client's motivation to look internally for resources to help.
- Psychotherapy moves the client toward independence and self-reliance, and away from fostering dependency on medications.
- Medication does not teach the client problem-solving skills.
- Medications do not cure or produce permanent change; they are a temporary treatment.
- There are potential dangers with drugs, such as side effects, drug overdose, addiction, dependency, and abuse.
- Not enough is known about many medications over long-term use. There may be many untoward effects that have not yet been discovered.
- In the past, medications have been used as chemical straightjackets.
- Psychotherapists must use great caution when endorsing the use of medications and must be careful not to lose the client's trust.
- Providers can make errors in prescribing and do not always adopt the philosophy that the less medication for the shortest period of time should be the rule.
- Even standardized treatment such as medication is affected by and dependent on the interpersonal skills of the psychotherapist.

Biological Perspective

The biological viewpoint argues that mental disorders are forms of mental illness that are organically based and that they will eventually be cured through organic interventions. Historically, evidence exists to support this idea. In the late 1800s, scientists found that the physical diseases syphilis and pellagra caused symptoms of mental disorders. In the 1920s, biological treatments such as electric shock therapy, insulin shock, psychosurgery, and lobotomy were helpful in controlling agitated mental patients and psychotics.

The 1950s marked a revolution in the treatment of mental illness when researchers discovered drugs that altered brain function. These were chlorpromazine, imipramine, chlordiazepoxide, and meprobamate, the prototypes of modern psychotropic medications (Spiegal, 1989). Each drug has a chemical, or generic name, and a brand name. Chlorpromazine, the first antipsychotic (brand name Thorazine), decreased symptoms of paranoia, mania, and other psychoses. Since then, numerous antipsychotics have been developed. Today there are new generations of these drugs, all of which help to control the symptoms of the seriously disturbed.

Once researchers saw the effectiveness of these chemicals in changing psychotic states and moods, they searched for other mind-altering drugs. In the 1950s, a number of prototypical drugs were produced. The first class of antidepressants was the monoamine oxidase inhibitor (brand names Nardil, Parnate, Marplan), which had serious side effects such as hypertension when mixed with high levels of a substance commonly found in the human diet called tyrosine. Further prototypes of antidepressants were the cyclic antidepressants (imipramine, brand name Tofranil), mood stabilizers (lithium carbonate, brand name Eskalith), and anti-anxiety agents (chlordiazepoxide, brand name Librium). Meprobamate, with the brand name Miltown, was produced as a tranquilizer but had addictive properties. Over the years, more drugs that modified psychotic thinking and mood were synthesized and found to be useful in the management of mental disorders.

Advocates of the biological model believe medications should be the major treatment of choice for mental disorders; in this view, psychotherapy is the ancillary treatment. The arguments to use medications as the primary mode of treatment are as follows (Julien, 2001; Thase & Jindal, 2004):

- History illustrates that research will produce even better, more effective drugs in the future. Every day, more medications are being created to target and improve symptoms of mental disorders.
- Once the correct medications are found and applied, they act quickly to reduce symptoms.
- Medications improve the client's ability to respond to other treatments such as psychotherapy; they work quickly to make the client more hopeful and enhance the course of treatment.
- Medications are more cost effective than longer, expensive forms of psychotherapy.
- In areas where there are few mental health resources, at least medications can be readily available. Some treatment is better than none.
- Some conditions, such as schizophrenia, respond only to or primarily to medication.
- Medication fosters less dependency on the prescribing provider than psychotherapy.
- Research and outcome studies of medication are easier to control than those of psychotherapy.
- Advances in research demonstrate the efficaciousness and efficacy of many medications through the use of well-controlled clinical drug trials, neuro-imaging research, and neural transmission studies.
- Many abnormal behaviors have organic causes such as defects in structures of the brain, genetics, metabolic aberrations, and malfunctions in neurotransmission (e.g., misshapen ventricles and aberrant neurochemicals in schizophrenia).
- Some outcome studies confirm that psychotherapy can make a client worse (have *iatrogenic* effects).

Trends in Psychopharmacology

Today, the relatively sharp divide between those who practice psychotherapy and those who prescribe medications is narrowing. The importance of the interplay of psychosocial, psychobiological, and psychopharmacological in the treatment of mental disorders is acknowledged through the growing popularity of the biopsychosocial model (Borrell-Carrio, Suchman, & Epstein, 2004; Busch & Malin, 1998). The view that treatment must be either medication or psychotherapy is diminishing (Schatzberg & Nemeroff, 2004). Today, practitioners are more concerned with the *extent* to which a disorder is due to psychological factors or biological factors, which leads to a treatment combination of psychotherapy and medication that is most beneficial to the client (Preston & Johnson, 2002). The current thinking about psychopharmacology is as follows:

- Psychotherapists must be able to make the most effective, high-quality treatment resources available to the client. A number of conditions are most effectively treated with medications, including schizophrenia and psychosis. The medications for these clients are the standard for care within the mental health profession (Bassuk, Schoonover, & Gelenberg, 1988).
- Clients who have not taken psychotropics but who have a medication-responsive condition should be referred for a medication assessment by a well-informed nonprescribing provider who knows when and how to refer appropriately.
- Some clients come to therapy with a history of treatment with medications. Many currently receive medications from primary care doctors and psychiatrists. The nonprescribing psychotherapist is better able to help a client if he or she understands how a particular drug works.
- Diagnosis can be more accurate and errors can be prevented if psychotherapists have a basic knowledge about medication effects. Some untoward medication reactions mimic mental health problems. For example, the elderly person who uses over-the-counter medications such as bromides (e.g., Alka Seltzer) may hallucinate or have delusions. A psychotherapist must be able to accurately identify substance abuses, misuses, and interactions.
- Clients are generally curious about medications and frequently ask questions about the appropriateness and usefulness of specific drugs. Knowledgeable psychotherapists provide a meaningful service when they address these inquiries and discuss the potential advantages, limitations, side effects, and contraindications with their clients (Stambor, 2006).
- Effective consultation is vital for quality mental health care. The nonprescribing psychotherapist who communicates well with the client's medical provider is a benefit to the patient. It is not acceptable for a psychotherapist to be uninformed, or to claim ignorance about medications, or to tell the client that only the psychiatrist knows about medications (Stratyner, 2004).
- There are increasing opportunities for nonprescribing psychotherapists to work with a greater variety of prescribing professionals as the use of psychotropic medication grows and the number of providers who prescribe increases (Doran, 2003). More professions are gaining prescription privileges (Dittman, 2003).

When a client takes a medication, a series of reactions takes place. Although the nonprescribing psychotherapist is not expected to attain the depth of knowledge of a prescribing provider, he or she can help her client better if conversant about the fundamentals of medications (Pettus, 2006).

The nonprescribing psychotherapist can help the prescribing therapist to demystify psychopharmacology for clients. For example, a depressed client wants symptom relief. The psychotherapist explains that one cause of depression is a low level of serotonin, or of norepinephrine, or of both. The prescribing provider orders one type of antidepressant, the serotonin selective reuptake inhibitor (SSRI), which increases the chemical serotonin specifically by preventing it from being taken back up into the nerve cell. This medication requires several weeks of consistent use before it is effective. If the client's symptoms are not relieved within this predetermined time, then the prescribing provider may change to another class of antidepressants, such as bupropion, a drug that works by increasing the chemical norepinephrine rather than serotonin. The nonprescribing provider knows when one medication has been given enough time to reach its maximum effect, and it is obvious it is not working for this particular patient, the prescribing clinician can order another trial of a different medication to try to find a better fit between medication and client.

Furthermore, a client's complaint that a medication is "not working" will be handled differently depending upon the type of drug. If the medication is designed to decrease anxiety (an anti-anxiety drug), and it does not relieve symptoms within an hour, the dosage of the same medication may need to be increased. However, if a drug is one for alleviating depression (an antidepressant), and the client complains that the medication is not effective within an hour, it is no surprise since it takes several weeks before an antidepressant sufficiently builds up in the body to bring about a therapeutic change. The client needs to give the drug trial at least three weeks before expecting a change. A client may complain she does not like the way the antidepressant makes her feel, since the side effects are dry mouth or nausea. After consulting with the prescribing provider, the psychotherapist may either encourage the client to adapt to the unpleasant side effects since they are short-lived or to switch to a medication with fewer side effects.

Another benefit of the knowledgeable nonprescribing psychotherapist is that prescribing errors are more likely to be detected. For example, Andrea Yates, a woman who fatally drowned her five children in the bathtub in Texas in 2002, was suffering from a psychotic disorder. In hindsight, she appears to have been misdiagnosed with depression and prescribed antidepressants, when she needed antipsychotics. Had Yates been monitored by a nonprescribing psychotherapist with the knowledge that an antipsychotic (not an antidepressant) would be the standard of care for this client, precious lives may have been saved (Cummings, 2007).

✦ THEORY OF PSYCHOPHARMACOLOGY

This section presents fundamental and selective information about how psychotropic drugs work. It contains some very technical information which is not intended to overwhelm the student, but to introduce him or her to the vocabulary and basic information that prescribers use when they choose a medication. I recommend that every psychotherapist learn about these topics in greater depth and take a basic drugs and behavior course. The student needs to think about medications from a micro-level perspective first to understand how they change a person's mood or behavior. Which neurotransmitters are thought to be involved in mental disorders? What are the target symptoms that would lead to a particular drug being prescribed? What are the possible side effects? How does the drug work at the cellular level? How is the drug terminated? Overall, how does the drug affect the body and how does the body affect the drug? Finally, how does the diagnosis of mental illness interface with prescribing?

The terms *drug* and *medication* are used interchangeably. *Drug* refers to a substance that changes bodily functioning, and *medication* refers to the use of a drug to prevent, treat, or alleviate the symptoms of a disease. Medication is usually produced by a drug company.

Overview of the Nervous System and the Brain

The human nervous system is divided into the peripheral nervous system (PNS) and the central nervous system (CNS). The peripheral nervous system contains the somatic and the autonomic nervous system (ANS). The ANS controls functions such as heart rate, breathing, sweating, pupil dilation, and so on (Spiegal, 1989). The central nervous system contains the spinal cord and the brain, which controls higher human functions such as cognition. It is helpful to differentiate between the CNS and the ANS conceptually because as a rule of thumb, the therapeutic, or intended, effects of psychotropic medications generally occur in the central nervous system, and the side effects, the unintended effects that occur in addition to the therapeutic effects, tend to occur in the autonomic nervous system. For example, an antidepressant may work on structures in the CNS that mediate thinking, feeling, and behaving, but its unwanted side effects, such as increased sweating, increased heart rate, or dry mouth, occur primarily in the autonomic system.

Nerve Cells

Many drugs act similarly to or effect changes to neurotransmitters, so if the student wants to understand how psychotropic medications act it helps to know how neurotransmitters act. Psychotropic medications act on a molecular level within a single nerve cell. While they work on one cell at a time, they affect large numbers of cells in groups, clusters, and patterns of connectedness until regulation in the CNS is adjusted, modified, and corrected. Understanding how the nerve cell, or neuron, functions is essential to understanding how medications act (Keltner & Folks, 2005).

The human brain is home to over 100 billion neurons, and they are communicators. They converse with one another through an electrochemical process. Each has the potential to provide many connections and, thus, to bring about an astonishing number of complex transmissions within the brain.

The "typical" nerve cell (there are many sizes and shapes) consists of a cell body, dendrites, axons, and terminal endings. The *axon* is the part of the nerve cell that sends messages. The *dendrites* are the parts of the nerve cell that receive messages. A neuron may have one axon but a number of dendrites and dendritic receptors (depending on the type of nerve cell). A space called the *synaptic gap* exists between the axon of one cell and the dendrites of another cell (also called *presynaptic* and *postsynaptic* cells). Neurons communicate across that synaptic gap through neurotransmitters. *Neurotransmitters* are chemicals, such as acetylcholine or norepinephrine, manufactured within the cell and then stored in the terminal endings of the axon. These chemicals are released at the appropriate times in order for one cell to communicate with another.

When a drop of neurotransmitter from one cell is released, it travels across the synaptic gap and lands on or binds to the receptors on the dendrites of another cell. The neurotransmitter and the receptor site work like a lock and key (Sue, Sue, & Sue, 2006). Each molecule of neurotransmitter has a specific shape that fits onto a specific receptor much like the piece of a puzzle. The miniscule dendrites have *receptors,* or dendritic spikes, on their surface that recognize the neurotransmitter (or the medication), receive the message, and thus respond to the arriving transmitter (Schatzberg & Nemeroff, 2004). While the process underlying neural transmission is a complex electrochemical reaction (beyond the scope of this text), communication among cells is largely due to the activity of neurotransmitters (Preston et al., 2005).

Pharmacodynamics

Pharmacodynamics is the study of how drugs affect the body and how drugs and receptors interact (Julien, 2001; Meyer & Quenzer, 2005). We know that neurotransmitters are molecules that selectively bind to a specific nerve cell receptor and either enhance or reduce the neuron's normal functioning. A drug can mimic the action of the neurotransmitter. A drug that activates the cell's natural response is called an *agonist.* A drug that prevents or blocks the neurotransmitter that regularly activates the cell and inhibits the cell's natural response is called an *antagonist* (Dale & Hallett, 2004).

The nature of a drug reaction depends on if it is an agonist or antagonist and the number of receptors a drug occupies, usually several thousand per cell. Receptors located on the surface of the cell can be *ephemeral,* with a life span of several days. A drug can stimulate a change in the number of receptors serving to adjust to the reaction. The neuron tries to adapt to environmental circumstances by regulating the amount of neurotransmitters. This is called *down-regulation* if the number of receptors decreases to compensate for prolonged stimulation, or *up-regulation* if the number of receptors increases to compensate for the absence of receptor stimulation. One of the reasons it may take several weeks for a drug to have maximum effect is that it takes some time for the neuron to increase or decrease its number of receptors.

Mental disorders are thought to be caused by too much, too little, or an error in neural transmission. Of course, this occurs in some particular area of the CNS. There can be multiple causes for these aberrations. Medications can moderate these irregularities by changing synaptic transmission in some way (Meyer & Quenzer, 2005). If we think about how the drug acts, we can imagine how it can change the neuron's level of neurotransmitter. A medication might

- correct a situation where too little neurotransmitter is being produced and act as a chemical building block or precursor to a neurotransmitter so more is made.
- correct a situation where too much neurotransmitter is being produced by inhibiting the synthesis of a neurotransmitter so less is made.

- correct a situation where too little neurotransmitter is in the synaptic gap, so more will be available.
- correct a situation where too much neurotransmitter is in the synaptic gap, by preventing the neurotransmitter from being stored in the synaptic vesicles, so less will be available.

Neurotransmitters

Of special interest to psychotherapists are the major neurotransmitters that appear to be involved in the cause and treatment of mental disorders. They are called *catecholamines* (norepinephrine and dopamine), *serotonin, acetylcholine,* and *gamma amino butyric acid* (GABA). It is useful for the nonprescribing psychotherapist to not only know their names, but to know if they are *excitatory,* meaning the neurotransmitter tells the cell to act, or *inhibitory,* meaning the neurotransmitter tells the cell to not act.

It is also vital to know the disorders with which they are associated and how they are *released* and *deactivated,* which can happen in several ways. Deactivation means the neurotransmitter can be diffused (neurotransmitter drifts away), removed (taken away by cells), degraded (destroyed or transformed into another chemical; it can also be metabolized into a substance different enough so it is no longer recognized by that cell receptor, or reuptake can occur (the neuron acts like a vacuum cleaner, sweeps up the neurotransmitter, and takes it back up into the synaptic vesicle). This information is useful because different types of malfunctions can occur in any of the above processes. The result is altered levels of neurotransmitters.

According to the catecholamine hypothesis, some mental disturbances, especially schizophrenia and depression, are caused by an imbalance of these neurotransmitter substances, catecholamines. Prescribing the right drug with the right action can adjust these imbalances and end the symptoms of these disturbances. For example, if a client is depressed, the catecholamine hypothesis says that his depression is caused by lowered levels of catecholamines. If he takes an antidepressant, it will increase levels of catecholamines in the brain, and the symptoms of depression will disappear.

Catecholamines: Norepinephrine and Dopamine

The major catecholamines in the brain are *dopamine* (DA) and *norepinephrine* (NE). They are excitatory neurotransmitters. Behaviorally, they increase alertness, produce high energy levels, and enhance positive emotions. In short, high levels make a person feel good and low levels make a person feel bad (Salamone, Cousins, & Snyder, 1997).

The positive symptoms of schizophrenia, which are excesses in behavior such as hallucinations, delusions, and thought disorders, are associated with changes in dopamine—excesses in some parts of the brain, and perhaps with other neurotransmitters as well (Dale & Hallett, 2004). The symptoms of depression are associated with imbalances either in norephinephrine or in serotonin (see below), or both. The symptoms of mania are associated with an increased level of norepinephrine or serotonin, or both (Dale & Hallett, 2004; Meyer & Quenzer, 2005, p. 137).

Medications adjust supplies of dopamine and norepinephrine through complicated processes that alter synthesis, release, or termination of the neurotransmitter action. Methods of termination include being taken back up into the cell (reuptake), being degraded or broken down, (usually by enzymes or chemicals like monoamine oxidase), and being carried off (diffusion) (Julien, 2001).

Antipsychotic drugs decrease the symptoms of schizophrenia by adjusting levels of dopamine in specific areas of the brain. Antidepresssant medications increase levels of catecholamines in the synaptic gap in a number of ways such as blocking reuptake or adding *monoamine oxidase inhibitors* (MAOIs), which are chemicals that break down the substances that break down norepinephrine.

Some significant harmful side effects may be produced at the cellular level by drugs that work on catecholamines. For example, some antipsychotics produce side effects such as motor problems, slowed heart beat, muscle weakness and cramps, convulsions, weak breathing, and nausea and vomiting among others, which are called *cholinergic effects*. Triciyclic antidepressants produce side effects such as dry mouth, blurred vision, urinary difficulties, and so on. In order to counteract and diminish these unwanted cholinergic side effects, another drug called an anticholinergic medication can be prescribed. The newer antidepressant medications are replacing the tricyclics as the first choice because they are thought to have fewer side effects and are less toxic.

Serotonin

Serotonin is a very versatile and complicated neurotransmitter. Just to illustrate how complex it is, there are at least 15 different types of receptors for serotonin, and its specific function depends on the receptor to which it binds.

Serotonin can either be excitatory or inhibitory. In the CNS, behaviorally, serotonin is involved in mood, depression, bipolar disorder, anxiety, sleeping, eating and drinking, and vomiting (Keltner & Folks, 2005). Some antidepressants increase levels of serotonin by keeping serotonin available in the synaptic gap. SSRIs (selective serotonin reuptake inhibitors) prevent serotonin from being taken back up by the cell. One of the ways serotonin is terminated is by reuptake where it is vacuumed up in the synaptic gap by the terminals at the end of the cells from which it came. Some of the side effects of SSRIs include gastrointestinal effects such as nausea, sleeping problems, and loss of sexual desire.

Gamma Amino Butyric Acid (GABA)

GABA is the chief inhibitory neurotransmitter in the central nervous system. This is a complicated neurotransmitter since there are approximately 10 subtypes of GABA receptors. (Meyer & Quenzer, 2005). GABA seems to be correlated with decreased subjective feelings of anxiety and increased feelings of relaxation and calm. Anti-anxiety medications act as agonists and bind onto GABA sites, which in turn increases available GABA. Some of the side effects of GABA are sedation, amnesia, tolerance development, and abuse potential; there is also the possibility of alcohol and barbiturates effects (Teuber, Watjens, & Jensen, 1999).

The Cholinergic System

Acetylcholine (Ach) is an excitatory transmitter involved in cognitive functioning, particularly learning and memory, pain, and sensory reception; it is also involved in sleep. (In the peripheral nervous system, it makes muscles contract.) Damage to acetylcholine neurons may result in dementia. Alzheimer is one dementia that is associated with the selective destruction of cholinergic neurons.

Many of the subjectively felt unpleasant side effects associated with drugs (especially tricyclics and antipsychotics) are attributable to the blocking of Ach in the peripheral nervous system. The block is called an anticholinergic effect. These include, in the peripheral nervous system, dry mouth, constipation, and urinary retention, and in the central nervous system, dizziness, confusion, impaired memory, and blurred vision.

Medications that enhance acetylcholine are used to diminish the side effects of drugs that block acetylcholine (antipsychotics); acetylcholine drugs are also used for the treatment of dementia (Julien, 2001; Meyer & Quenzer, 2005).

Now that we can identify and describe these neurotransmitters—those that the psychotropic medications affect and modify—we will examine pharmacokinetics. This will help us envision what happens when the client ingests the medications.

Pharmacokinetics

Drugs are expected to have predictable effects on the body, and the body is expected to have predictable effects on drugs as well. The psychotherapist who understands the process from the time the client ingests the drug until it leaves the body is better able to help his client know what to expect. *Pharmacokinetics* is the study of how the drug is taken in, absorbed, distributed, biotransformed, and excreted (Preston et al., 2005). It shows how the body is handling the medication once ingested and when it reaches its highest concentration in the targeted organs. *Bioavailability* is the portion of any drug that reaches the circulation, which is important to consider when calculating the dose of a drug.

The first factor to take into account is how, or in what form, the client will take the drug. The possible routes are orally (by mouth), intravenously (in the veins), intramuscularly (in the muscle), intraperitoneally (in the stomach cavity), subcutaneously (under the skin), inhaled (breathing it in), topically or transdermally (on the surface of the skin), or epidurally (in the space around the spinal cord). These routes make a difference in how and where the drug is available. The most efficient route is intravenous. It brings about the most complete absorption. Once in the body, the drug is absorbed into the bloodstream. Most psychiatric drugs are administered orally, but a few are given as injectables, or transdermals, with a time release component. For example, the intramuscular (IM) haloperidol (brand name Haldol) has a slow and sustained release that helps the noncompliant client to keep enough drug in his system to remain free of psychotic symptoms.

The *absorption* of a drug regulates its bioavailability. The initial way in which the drug is taken has an effect on the amount of the drug that is metabolized before it reaches the bloodstream, which is called the *first-pass effect*. *Distribution* is how the drug transports itself to all of the cells in the body and how it is spread to the organs or the sites of action. In phase one, the drug is dispersed into organs that have a rich blood supply. In phase two, the drug reaches body structures that have less circulation such as muscle, fat, and bone. *Binding* is the way in which the drug attaches itself to receptors and/or is stored in bone and fat as an inactive substance. Through *biotransformation* the drug is transformed into substances that are excreted by the kidneys, inactivated by the liver and its enzymes, and produces metabolites that can be helpful or toxic (Preston et al., 2005).

After a drug is metabolized, it is excreted, which means it is eliminated from the body. This occurs primarily through the kidneys via the urine and through the gastrointestinal tract (also through respiration, salivation, sweat, and breast milk). Factors such as health status can have an effect upon how well any drug is eliminated from the body. For example, a client with failing kidneys would need to be monitored very closely.

The prescribing practitioner must determine a dose level for every medication. There are four important questions to ask about dosage (Preston et al., 2005):

1. What is the most effective dose to achieve a therapeutic effect?
2. What dose is harmful or toxic?
3. What doses constitutes a safety margin?
4. At what point might adverse reactions occur?

The *dose response curve* is a graph illustrating how a drug acts and the biological change occurring in relationship to a given dose. There is a point at which the body shows the strongest therapeutic effect. When a client takes a drug, there is an individual dose- and time-related wait (Julien, 2001). The *half life* indicates the time it takes to remove half of a drug dose from the blood. This is important to know in order to calculate the best dose for a client and the time between doses (Ksir, Hart, & Ray, 2008).

Bioavailability (absorption, distribution, metabolism, biotransformation, and excretion) can be affected by other drugs in the body. In complicated cases, patients are often prescribed multiple medications, so drug interactions must be carefully monitored. Psychotropic medications are able to move across the blood–brain barrier, a membrane structure that protects the brain by preventing many harmful substances from crossing into the brain tissues (Ksir et al., 2008). Knowing this information allows the psychotherapist to understand if a particular drug is acting as predicted and when to take note of unusual events and address concerns with the prescribing provider.

Psychotropic Medications

Drugs are classified in a variety of ways, for example, according to psychiatric use, chemical structure, neurochemical effects, abuse status, legal status, and behavioral effects (Meyer & Quenzer, 2005). However, for our purposes as mental health caregivers, it is most useful to categorize these drugs according to their effects on diagnosed conditions.

Diagnosis and prescribing go hand in hand, and an accurate diagnosis is essential for successful drug treatment. The *DSM* attempts to describe discrete diagnostic categories that are responsive to specific drugs. To choose the right medication to treat specific symptoms, it is important for the diagnosis to be reliable. Matching a *DSM* diagnosis with the treatment works only about 60 percent of the time (Bassuk et al., 1988). Many clients do not neatly fit into one particular diagnostic group, meaning there is overlap among diagnostic categories. It can be useful to match a given treatment with clusters of symptoms rather than with an overall diagnostic category. But many individuals do not respond as predicted to a drug, and sometimes the side effects are greater than the therapeutic effects (Feldman & Keltner, 2005).

The major types of medications for diagnosed mental conditions are as follows:

- Antidepressants and mood stabilizers
- Antipsychotics
- Anti-anxiety agents
- Stimulants
- Cholinase inhibitors for dementia
- Drugs for treatment of substance abuse

Antidepressants and Mood Stabilizers

Depression is characterized by disturbances of mood. Major depression has the following symptoms: depressed mood, anhedonia, neurovegetative functioning (such as excessive or inadequate sleeping, eating, and psychomotor activity), loss of energy, fatigue, difficulties concentrating and attending, feelings of guilt and worthlessness, suicidal ideation, and impaired or distressed functioning (*DSM*). The purpose of antidepressants is to treat serious depression by elevating mood, increasing motor activity, and improving sleeping, eating, and motor activity. They are also prescribed for milder forms of depression. Antidepressants are taken orally and have a relatively long half life.

Since depression seems to be related to decreased catecholamines, norepeinephrine (and possibly dopamine), and/or serotonin, then drugs that increase these neurotransmitters can decrease the symptoms of depression. The antidepressants are divided into several types or classes, each with differing actions. Antidepressants can work in some of the following ways, among others: (a) blocking reuptake, which results in a down-regulation or a decrease in the number of postsynaptic receptors; and (b) blocking monoamine oxidase (MAO), which is a substance that breaks down the chemical that metabolizes the neurotransmitter stored in the nerve ending. Types include SSRIs, tricyclics (cyclics), and SNRIs and MAOIs.

The *SSRIs* (selective serotonin reuptake inhibitors) are currently the first line of treatment for depression. For the most part, they are safer than the tricyclic antidepressants (TCAs) since they are seldom lethal when taken in an overdose. The SSRIs also have fewer side effects than the TCAs (discussed below) such as lowered sexual appetite, headache, anxiety and jitteriness, and gastrointestinal problems or nausea.

The most commonly prescribed SSRIs sold in the United States are fluoxetine (Prozac), fluvaoxamine (Luvox), paroxetine (Paxil), sertraline (Zoloft), citalopram (Celexa), and escitalopram (Lexapro).

Tricyclic antidepressants (TCAs) (also called *heterocyclics* or just *cyclics*), named because of their ringed chemical structure, were widely used prior to the arrival of the SSRIs. TCAs block the reuptake of neurotransmitters, increasing their availability in the synapse resulting in a down-regulation. The TCAs can take as long as eight or more weeks to reach maximum therapeutic effectiveness (Meyer & Quenzer, 2005). TCAs also block acetylcholine, which can lead to unpleasant side effects, such as dry mouth, blurred vision, and sedation, among others. Patients can be noncompliant, especially since the side effects occur before the therapeutic effects, so they may be in danger of giving up treatment before experiencing any benefits.

An overdose of TCAs can be lethal. If a depressed client stored up a 30-day supply of many of the TCAs, he or she has the means to do serious harm to herself. Some of the commonly used TCAs include imipramine (Tofranil) and amitriptyline (Elavil), among others.

Other antidepressants, with different chemical structures, were developed to eliminate the undesirable side effects of the tricyclics and include maprotaline (Ludiomil), amoxapine (Asendin), trazodone (Desyrel), bupropion (Wellbutrin), nefazodone (Serzone), venlafaxine (Effexor), and duloxetine (Cymbalta).

Monoamine oxidase inhibitors (MAOIs) were introduced in the 1950s. Monoamine (MAO) is a substance in the brain that typically breaks down the neurotransmitters—serotonin, norepinephrine, and dopamine. If MAO becomes overly active and breaks down too much of the catecholamines, too little of these neurotransmitters is left in the synaptic gap. The person becomes depressed due to lowered levels of catecholamines. The solution to this dysfunction is to slow down the activity of the MAO so there will be more catecholamines and serotonin available. Medications called monoamine oxidase inhibitors (MAOIs) work by inhibiting the activity of monoamine oxidase, preventing the breakdown of and increasing the available stores of serotonin, norepinephrine, and dopamine. Since depression may be associated with low stores of the neurotransmitters, increasing them may help to alleviate depressive symptoms. MAOI medications are tranylcypromine (Parnate) and phenelzine (Nardil) (Preston, 2007).

MAOIs are generally the least favored treatment choice and are used when other antidepressants have not succeeded. This is because they have very serious side effects if the client does not comply with the strict dietary restrictions that accompany their use. If MAOIs interact with certain foods that contain tyrosine or certain medications, it can increase blood pressure and result in stroke. MAOIs are safe as long as the patient follows the dietary regimen, which includes avoiding beer, red wine, aged cheeses, sausage, fava and green beans, brewers yeast, and smoked fish. Foods that can only be consumed in small quantities include alcohol, ripe avocado, yogurt, bananas, and soy sauce. Other foods to be careful of include chocolate, figs, meat tenderizers, caffeine, and raisins (Schatzberg, Cole, & De Battista, 1997).

A person with bipolar disorder has cyclical mood changes ranging from mania to depression. In the manic mood, the person has a great deal of energy, is overly active and talkative, needs less sleep, is easily distracted, has flights of ideas and cannot get thoughts out fast enough; the person can also be irritable and have an inflated idea of his or her importance in the world. Manics show poor judgment and can be impulsive, involving themselves in foolish business schemes or spending sprees or other destructive behaviors. A manic state is thought to be caused by an excess of catecholamines; medication is needed to decrease their levels. At the other end of the spectrum, the client can be depressed, sad, and have feelings of hopelessness. All the other symptoms of depression as discussed above also apply.

People with bipolar disorder are treated with lithium, which is a naturally occurring substance in some mineral spring waters. Lithium carbonate is what is used in clinical treatment. Some of the commercial products are Eskalith and Lithobid. The term *lithium* is not officially recognized by the U.S. Food and Drug Administration, but it is commonly used in clinical practice. Although the precise biochemical interaction of lithium in treatment is not clear, it is known that lithium alters the metabolism of catecholamines and is especially effective for the manic portion of bipolar disorder.

Lithium has a very narrow therapeutic dose range, and its use must be closely monitored by taking blood levels. If there is too little lithium in the blood, the drug will not be effective, but if the lithium level is too high, toxicity occurs with a reaction that ranges from slight to fatal. The side effects are gastrointestinal symptoms such as nausea and vomiting; tremors, such as in the hand: headache; muscle weakness; confusion and slurred speech; endocrine changes; kidney dysfunction; white blood cell elevation; cardiac changes; skin rashes; and weight gain.

There are some alternatives to lithium. Some anticonvulsants, such as carbamazepine and divalproex, which are typically used for seizure disorders, can be effective with bipolar disorder. These drugs (Tegretol, Depakote) have their own side effects, though, including sedation, dizziness, loss of coordination, nausea, vomiting, diarrhea, cramps, blurred vision, and increased white blood cells. Blood monitoring is also necessary to identify potential toxicity (Preston et al., 2005).

Antipsychotics

Psychotic disorders are conditions in which a person's sense of reality is grossly impaired. The underlying cause of psychosis can be functional or organic. Antipsychotic drugs treat the positive, acute symptoms of psychosis in schizophrenia such as delusions, hallucinations, thought disturbances, and agitated and aggressive conduct; they also help treat brief psychotic disorders, paranoid disorders, and schizoaffective disorders. These drugs help to control assaultive behavior, organic mental disease, and difficult personality disorders (Gelenberg & Keith, 1997).

Antipsychotics are also called neuroleptics, major tranquilizers, or antischizophrenics. Antipsychotic drugs block specific dopamine receptors in specific places in the brain. There are several types of antipsychotics with differing actions.

Traditional, Standard, or Classical Antipsychotics   Chlorpromazine (sold as Thorazine) is the prototype of the traditional antipsychotic. This drug blocks certain types of dopamine receptors. Troublesome side effects of the drug are called *extrapyramidal effects* (EPS), a result of the blocking of dopamine receptors in one particular area of the brain that is involved in controlling motor movement, the basal ganglia. This is the same area that when damaged causes Parkinson's disease. There are four types of EPS: (a) acute dystonic reactions, which are involuntary spasmodic muscle contractions and twitching, rhythmical movements; (b) akathisia, which is an inability to sit with subjective feelings of restlessness; (c) akinesia, which are Parkinsonian symptoms of slowed movement, masklike face, rigidity, and hypersalivation; and (d) tardive dyskinesia, which is involuntary motor movements of the face, tongue, trunk, and limbs and choreoathetoid movements of the fingers, arms, trunk, and legs with no awareness of these movements. Anticholinergic drugs are prescribed to decrease these extrapyramidal side effects (Stanilla & Simpson, 2004).

New Generation Antipsychotics   The atypical antipsychotics work on multiple neurotransmitters and block a subtype of dopamine receptor called *DA4,* which is a different area than those blocked by traditional antipsychotics. Some also block serotonin. These new drugs lower the incidence of extrapyramidal side effects and seem to reduce the negative symptoms of schizophrenia. Some of these new drugs are molindone (Moban), loxapine (Loxitane), pimozide (Orap), clozapine (Clozaril), olanzapine (Zyprexa), and rispiridone (Risperdal).

Anti-Anxiety Agents

The *DSM* describes a number of anxiety disorders including generalized anxiety disorder, panic disorder with and without agoraphobia, phobias, social phobia, obsessive-compulsive disorder, posttraumatic stress, and anxiety disorders that accompany a general medical disorder. The symptom profile is unique for each of these disorders, but they all share symptoms of anxiety. Anxiety can also be a part of another disorder, such as depression.

Anti-anxiety drugs are also called *anxiolytics, benzodiazepines, sedative-hypnotics,* and *minor tranquilizers.* Anti-anxiety drugs are short-acting and rapidly relieve anxiety by causing.

There are side effects with anti-anxiety drugs, including sedation, sleepiness, fatigue, depression, coordination problems, and memory impairment. Long-term use can lead to physical and psychological dependence, especially at high doses. For this reason, they are best used for only short periods of time or when symptoms are acute.

The first benzodiazepine was developed in 1957 with Librium. Today, some of the most common ones are clonazepam (Klonopin), alprazolam (Xanax), diazepam (Valium), and lorazepam (Ativan). Buspirone (Buspar) is the only drug given for anxiety conditions other than the benzodiazepines because the likelihood of developing dependency is low. The newer benzodiazepines and/or hypnotics include estazolam (ProSom), quazepam (Doral), zolpidem (Ambien), atenolol (Tenormin), guanfacine (Tenex), and clonidine (Catapres). Anxiety is also treated with some of the antidepressant drugs already mentioned because they also have anxiety-reducing effects. These are Anafanil, Prozac, Zoloft, Luvox, Paxil, and Effexor.

Sometimes propranolol (Inderal), a drug used to lower blood pressure, is used for acute anxiety events, such as for giving a public speech. For obsessive-compulsive disorders, a number of antidepressants with anti-anxiety effects are used to reduce the symptoms rather than the anti-anxiety drugs. These drugs, already mentioned, include Prozac, Zoloft, and clomipramine (Anafranil), among others.

There are also two other kinds of drugs that treat anxiety but that are not generally prescribed because of their addictive properties. These are barbituates (Amobarbital, Phenobarbital) and propanediols (Meprobamate, Tybamate). Sometimes, alternative drugs are used for anxiety such as antihistamines (Carlton, 1983).

Stimulants for Attention Deficit Hyperactivity Disorder (ADHD)

ADHD is characterized by short attention span, hyperactivity, impulsivity, noncompliance, and excessive motor activity. Children and adults with ADHD respond to stimulant therapy (Klein & Rowland, 1996). These drugs are thought to increase the release of norepinephrine and dopamine.

The main stimulant drugs are D-amphetamines methylohenidate and methylphenidate (Ritalin, Metadate, Methylin, Concerta), dextroamphetamine (Dexedrine), amphetamine (Adderall), and methamphetamine (Desoxyn). There are also extended release amphetamines (Kaplan, Grados, & Reiss, 1998). There are side effects of stimulants, including loss of appetite, nausea, vomiting, fatigue, emotional liability, insomnia, increased pulse rate and blood pressure, among others. Physical and psychological dependence can occur especially at higher doses (40mg per day). Overdosing on stimulants can be fatal, and at high levels, these drugs can induce psychosis.

Cholinase Inhibitors for Dementia

There are many forms of dementia; these are generally associated with vascular disease, alcoholism, and Alzheimer's. The specific causes of cognitive impairment are often not fully understood, so it is difficult to choose the best match for these conditions. Most of the drugs that are used to manage dementia are based on information from studies of Alzheimer's disease.

The cholinergic hypothesis is that acetylcholine neurotransmission is broken down in the cortex of those suffering from Alzheimer's disease. Cognitive loss can be slowed down by using drugs that increase acetylcholine. Drugs to enhance acetylcholine are tacrine (Cognex), donezipil (Aricept), rivastigmine (Exelon), and galantamine (Razadyne). These drugs specifically target the acetylcholine esterase, the enzyme that breaks down acetylcholine. The possible side effects of these dementia drugs are nausea, vomiting, diarrhea, facial flushing, muscle cramps, slowed heart rate, and mucus discharge from nose.

Drugs for Treatment of Substance Abuse

Clients with dual diagnoses make up 30 to 50 percent of psychiatric patients. Persons with mood disorders, schizophrenia, anxiety disorders, attention deficit hyperactivity disorder, conduct disorders, and personality disorders sometimes abuse alcohol and drugs. Furthermore, substance use can exacerbate or suppress the symptoms of these disorders.

Most of the drugs that are used to manage drug abuse are of three types. First, drugs are prescribed that have the same effect as the drug of abuse to alleviate withdrawal symptoms. For example, drugs that help with withdrawal from alcohol and other CNS depressants are the benzodiazepines and, in some limited cases, the sedative-hypnotics. The basic idea is to treat withdrawal symptoms by quickly substituting sufficient doses to suppress withdrawal and then to taper off the dose over several days. Drugs generally used for this purpose are Librium, Valium, and Klonopin.

Second, drugs are prescribed that have the same effect as the abused substance, but have less toxicity. The most common example of this type of treatment is using methadone to treat heroin addiction.

Third, drugs are prescribed that aversively condition the client by making the experience of taking the abused substance unpleasant. For example, a person taking Antabuse will experience nausea, dizziness, confusion, sweatiness, vomiting, chest pain, and so on if he or she drinks alcohol. The chemical agent in Antabuse is disulfiram. It can be very dangerous in interaction with other drugs. Also, the person may be unaware that there is a small amount of alcohol in many household products, and the reaction can be serious. For example, there is some alcohol in cough syrup, shaving lotion, mouthwash, and cooking products. Table 14.1 contains a useful list of psychotropic medications.

Alternative Treatments

Sixty-two percent of adults used alternative medicine in 2004, and the number is growing. Women are more likely than men to use these treatments, and the likelihood of use rises with age (Keltner & Folks, 2005). The popularity of dietary supplements is growing, and there is an increasing public demand for holistic approaches in medicine. Many are choosing to use complementary or alternative medicine and to use mind-altering herbals and botanical products. The psychotherapist needs to be informed about these herbal and dietary treatments as well.

Herbs are complex compounds and have variable potency. Drugs approved by the FDA are single-substance, potency-standardized, dose-established, and patentable products. Herbal remedies do not have FDA approval; nonetheless, herbs are used to treat psychiatric symptoms and may interact with the drugs prescribed for these disorders. Some well-known herbs used for their psychotropic effects are St. John's wort, valerian, kava, lemon balm, and black cohash.

← PRACTICE OF PSYCHOPHARMACOLOGY

Now that we have examined the basic theoretical concepts that underlie psychopharmacology, we will explore its practice. Dr. Christa Perry, our fictional composite nonprescribing psychotherapist, provides a firsthand perspective on how she integrates theory with practice and applies the techniques of psychopharmacology.

Table 14.1

Alphabetical List of Medications by Trade Name

Trade Name	Generic Name	Usual daily Dose Range*
Antipsychotic Medications		
Abilify	aripiprazole	15-30 mg
Clozaril	clozapine	300-900 mg
Geodon	ziprasidone	60-160 mg
Haldol	haloperidol	2-40 mg
Lidone	molindone	20-225 mg
Loxitane	loxapine	50-250 mg
Mellaril	thioridazine	150-800 mg
Moban	molindone	20-225 mg
Navane	thiothixene	10-60 mg
Orap (for Tourette's syndrome)	pimozide	1-10 mg
Prolixin	fluphenazine	2.5 to 20 mg
Risperdal	risperidone	4-16 mg
Serentil	mesoridazine	50-500 mg
Seroquel	quetiapine	150-600 mg
Stelazine	trifluoperazine	2-40 mg
Taractan	chlorprothixene	100-200 mg
Thorazine	chlorpromazine	50-800 mg
Trilafon	perphenazine	8-60 mg
Vesprin	trifluopromazine	25-50 mg
Zyprexa	olanzapine	5-20 mg
Antimanic Medications or Mood Stabilizers		
Depakote	valproic acid, divalproex sodium	750-1500 mg
Eskalith, Lithane, Lithobid	lithium carbonate	600-2400 mg
Lamictal	lamotrigine	50-500 mg
Neurontin	gabapentin	300-2400 mg
Tegretol	carbamazepine	600-1600 mg
Topamax	topiramate	50-300 mg
Antidepressant Medications		
Adapin, sinneqan	doxepin	150-300 mg
Anafranil	clomipramine	150-250 mg
Asendin	amoxapine	150-400 mg
Aventyl	nortriptyline	75-125 mg
Celexa (SSRI)	citalopram	10-60 mg
Desyrel	trazodone	150-400 mg
Effexor	venlafaxine	75-350 mg
Elavil	amitriptyline	150-300 mg
Lexapro (SSRI)	escitalopram	5-20 mg
Ludiomil	maprotiline	150-225 mg
Luvox (SSRI)	fluvoxamine	50-300 mg
Marplan (MAOI)	isocarboxazid	20-60 mg
Nardil (MAOI)	phenelzine	30-90 mg
Norpramin	desipramine	150-300 mg
Pamelor	nortriptyline	75-125 mg
Parnate (MAOI)	tranylcypromine	20-60 mg
Paxil (SSRI)	paroxetine	20-50 mg
Pertofrane	desipramine	150-300 mg
Prozac (SSRI)	fluoxetine	20-80 mg
Remeron	mirtazapine	15-45 mg

Serzone	nefazodone	300-600 mg
Sinequan	doxepin	150-300 mg
Surmontil	trimipramine	100-300 mg
Tofranil	imipramine	150-300 mg
Vivactil	protriptyline	15-40 mg
Wellbutrin	bupropion	150-400 mg
Zoloft (SSRI)	sertraline	50-200 mg

Anti-anxiety Medications (All of these anti-anxiety medications except BuSpar are benzodiazepines.)

Ativan	lorazepam	0.5-2.0 mg
Azene, Tranxene	clorazepate	3.75-15 mg
BuSpar	buspirone	5-20 mg
Centrax	prazepam	5-30 mg
Librax, Libritabs, Librium	chlordiazepoxide	10-50 mg
Klonopin	clonazepam	0.5-2.0 mg
Serax	oxazepam	10-30 mg
Tranxene	clorazepate	3.75-15 mg
Valium	diazepam	2-10 mg
Xanax	alprazolam	0.25-2.0 mg

Hypnotic Medications

Ambien	zolpiden	5-10 mg.
Benadryl	dipohenhydramine	25-100 mg
Dalmane	flurazepam	15-30 mg
Doral	quazepam	7.5-15 mg
Halcion	triazolam	0.25-0.5 mg
Lunesta	eszopiclone	1-3 mg
ProSom	estazolam	1.0-2.0 mg
Restoril	temazepam	15-30 mg
Rozerem	ramelteon	4-16 mg

Psychostimulant Medications (typically used for ADHD)

Adderall	Amphetamine	5-40 mg
Concerta	methylphenidate (long acting)	8-52 mg
Cylert	Pemoline	37.5-112.5 mg
Dexedrine	Dextroamphetamine	5-40 mg
Dextrostat	Dextroamphetamine	5-40 mg
Focalin	Dexmethylphenidate	5-40 mg
Metadate -ER	Methylphenidate (extended release)	5-40 mg
Ritalin	Methylphenidate	5-50 mg
Strattera	Atomoxetine	60-120 mg

Common Side Effects:

These are common side effects, but all medications can produce unique side effects:

Anticholinergic effects (block acetylcholine)—dry mouth, constipation, blurred vision, memory impairment, confusional states, urinary retention

Extrapyramidal effects—Parkinson-like effects including rigidity, shuffling gait, tremor, and other motor dysfunctioning

Autonomic effects—dizziness, imbalance, especially in elderly

Sedation—drowsiness, impaired concentration and reaction time

Source: Quick reference Medication Chart at www.Psyd-fx.com and NIMH http://www.nimh.nih.gov/health/publications/medications/complete-publication.shtml#pub11. The student can obtain more complete and detailed information about these medications by accessing these websites.

Assessment and Diagnosis

As a nonprescribing psychotherapist, I am well informed about what conditions respond to medication. Diagnosis and prescribing go together, and I use the *DSM* to diagnose. When I conclude that a client is medication responsive, I refer him or her to a prescribing practitioner with whom I have developed a good professional, collaborative relationship. I know that my client will be assessed by my collaborative prescriber. He or she will perform a routine medication interview/psychopharmacological assessment that includes

- a traditional interview: chief complaint, history of current problem, past history, previous episodes and treatment, medical history, substance use and abuse history, mental status exam.
- a valid and reliable *DSM* diagnosis of the client's condition and identification of target symptoms to be treated; coordination of the diagnosis with the particular potential medications.
- scheduling and obtaining results of a medical work-up.
- prescribing medication after considering which of the psychopharmacological agents seem to be most appropriate or the major types and classes of medications for the client's particular diagnosis or condition.
- communication of the diagnosis and treatment plan to referring clinician and other providers if necessary.

Negotiation of Therapeutic Relationship and Length of Treatment

My role is to provide psychotherapy and to act as a coordinator of the psychopharmacological treatment process. If I believe my client can benefit from medication, my role is to collaborate with the client and the prescribing provider about all aspects of my client's medications in order to integrate the judicious use of psychopharmacological treatment into the overall psychotherapy strategy. If the client agrees to psychopharmacological treatment, the role of the client is to be compliant with treatment recommendations and to report any reactions to the medications.

The length of psychopharmacological treatment depends on the severity of the client's symptoms, and it varies as a function of the individual client's needs and rate of improvement. For example, a client with a diagnosis of schizophrenia might expect to take antipsychotic medication over his or her life span. A client suffering from panic disorder might expect to use anti-anxiety medication for a short time until he can train himself to use behavioral methods of coping.

The goal of prescribing is to find the medication that most effectively alleviates the client's symptoms and makes the client feel most comfortable psychologically and physically. The goal is of psychopharmacology is to alleviate, decrease, or manage the symptoms of a mental disorder, such as psychotic thinking, or an affective state, such as depression or anxiety. To do so, the prescribing provider

- chooses the specific medication.
- considers side effects.

- provides the patient with a clear assessment and explanation of treatment with medication in layperson's terms.
- initiates a trial of psychotherapeutic medication.
- may try another drug within the same class if the first one does not work.
- may choose a drug from another class if several drugs from the first class do not work.
- manages the side effects of medications in the most helpful way possible.
- considers and calculates dose level to achieve maximum effect.

Therapeutic Techniques

Both the prescribing and nonprescribing psychotherapist closely monitor the client taking medications. The same medication can affect people differently. The client's individual nervous system undoubtedly has a tremendous impact on thinking, feeling, and behaving (Keltner & Folks, 2005). The client's subjective reports about his or her unique reaction should be taken seriously so that individual reactions to drugs can be monitored.

Along with the therapeutic effects of a drug come unwanted side effects. For example, the antipsychotic medication may alleviate psychotic symptoms but also cause involuntary motor movements called *tardive dyskinesia*. Side effects are best handled by using the drugs as constructively as possible. For example, if an antidepressant makes a client drowsy for the first couple of hours after taking it, the medication should be ingested at bedtime rather than in the morning.

Drugs can also cause allergic reactions, ranging from rashes to death. Idiosyncratic effects can also occur, though very rare, which are specific to certain people or groups (Preston et al., 2005). Serious reactions are unusual because the drugs have been tested and approved by the Federal Drug Administration (FDA), but they do sometimes occur. In addition, some drugs can produce dependence, so that when the drug is stopped abruptly, the person experiences withdrawal reactions and psychological and physical distress. Box 14.1 presents some practical information for nonprescribing psychotherapists.

The Process of Therapy

In the initial stages of the nonprescribing psychotherapist dealing with psychopharmacology, the nonprescribing psychotherapist assesses that client is suffering from symptoms that may be helped by medication. She asks the client to participate in a consultation with a prescribing provider. If the prescribing provider assesses that the client has a condition that makes him a good candidate for psychopharmacological treatment, the prescriber will initiate a trial of medications.

The nonprescribing psychotherapist is in ongoing collaboration with the prescribing provider and monitors the client's reactions to the medication. Psychopharmacological treatment is either terminated when the symptoms for which the client is being treated end, or it is decided that it is best to use medication over an indefinite, extended time.

BOX 14.1   PRACTICAL INFORMATION FOR NONPRESCRIBING PSYCHOTHERAPISTS

- Drugs have a generic name and a brand name. The generic name is the chemical name. The brand name is what the particular drug company calls it.
- Know what a particular drug looks like. Look at pictures in the *Physicians' Desk Reference (PDR)*. The same generic drug can look very different produced by different companies.
- Know the range of dose levels for various medications.
- Know that potency makes a difference. Thus, 1mg of Haldol is equivalent to 100mg of Thorazine. A client will say, "I am on a small dose of anxiolytics (0.5mg of Xanax)." Explain to the client that 0.5mg does not mean the same for all drugs.

- Know the side effect of medications so the client can be aware of any harmful actions.
- Know which other drugs or dietary substances interact so the client does not either negate the effects of the drug (antagonists) or potentiate them (agonists).
- Know the length of time to achieve therapeutic effectiveness so the client will be able to wait out some unpleasant side effects to reach therapeutic effectiveness.
- Know the potential lethality of any medication.
- Know the symbols used on prescriptions. They are Latin abbreviations. For example, *qh* means "every hour" so *qhs* means "at hour of sleep," *q1h* means "every 1 hour," *qid* means "four times a day."

THERAPY IN ACTION: DR. CHRISTA PERRY AND THE CASE OF JONATHAN

To illustrate the application of psychopharmacology, we examine a treatment plan for Jonathan, followed by excerpts from therapy sessions with our fictional nonprescribing psychotherapist, Dr. Christa Perry. Keep in mind the case excerpts are simulated interviews and represent the ideal of therapy. In real life, clients may take much longer to meet therapeutic goals. Table 14.2 provides a summary of Dr. Perry's treatment plan.

Case Excerpts

The following excerpts are from sessions based on Dr. Perry's psychopharmacological case formulation.

Session 3

[*Comment: I discuss the option of antidepressant medication with Jonathan.*]

Dr. Perry: Now that we have had two sessions, I have some ideas about how to help you to feel more comfortable as quickly as possible. If you agree, I would like to send you to Dr. Michelle Lambert for a medication consultation. Dr. Lambert can assess whether medications might be helpful as part of your treatment and our work together. You and I have been talking about your life situation and ways to change your thinking. I am sure we will make excellent gains in our therapy. However, I can see that from the

Table 14.2	
Psychopharmacology Treatment Plan for Jonathan	
Assessment and Formulation	• Presenting problem: loss of relationship with Tuti and Darren; major depression • Dr. Perry, nonprescribing psychotherapist, makes accurate diagnosis and assesses need for pharmacological intervention • Depression is responsive to antidepressants • Refer J. to prescribing provider for psychopharmacological assessment
Therapeutic Relationship	• Dr. Perry collaborates with and coordinates with prescriber; performs psychotherapy • Prescribing therapist prescribes and maintains J. on medications • J. reports honestly and complies with medication regime
Contract, Goals, and Treatment Plan	• Seeks consultation for antidepressant through referral • Agrees to accept medication if judged appropriate • Medication checks are regularly performed • Medicates biochemical imbalance to decrease and then eliminate symptoms of depression
Techniques	• Antidepressant prescribed: SSRI
Process of Therapy	• Medication management
Termination and Outcome	• Free of significant symptoms • Depression episode resolved

length of time that you have had your symptoms, it might be helpful for you to speak with someone who can specifically assess if medication can help you more than psychotherapy alone.

Jonathan: I don't know. I like the idea of doing it on my own. What symptoms are you talking about?

Dr. Perry: You have told me about your low energy level and your sleeplessness. In my experience, people with your symptoms have benefited greatly by taking antidepressant medications. How do you feel about that?

Jonathan: Like I'd like you to give me the medication.

Dr. Perry: In order to obtain medication that can help, we need a licensed professional who can legally prescribe. My training is in psychotherapy and not in medication or pharmacology. But I have been educated to recognize who might benefit from receiving medication and when to refer to a provider who can prescribe. This person will not spend the appointment time talking about the life issues we speak about, but will focus on your symptoms to see if medication will help you, and which medication can be most helpful, and prescribe it for you. This can help your progress in psychotherapy. How does that sound?

Jonathan: I don't know. I feel a bit reluctant to do this.

Dr. Perry: Making an appointment for medication assessment is not always easy, but I think it could be a wise decision. You are not obligated to take any medications, just to listen to an expert and to decide if you want to try the medication she suggests.

Jonathan: So what will happen? What will she do?

Dr. Perry: Dr. Lambert will ask you to describe the major problem. She'll then look at past history, any prior problems, any previous mental health treatment. She'll discuss your medical history and ask you about drinking and drugs. Then she will make up a plan that she thinks will help you. She'll share her thoughts with you. We already know you are depressed. She'll suggest specific medications if needed. She and I will consult and discuss this plan and continue to collaborate to make sure that you are receiving the very best coordinated care. She will also have some follow-up appointments with you on a regular basis to see how you are adjusting to the medication.

Jonathan: Well, if you think it will help, I'll give it a try.

Dr. Perry: I know how important it is for you to be able to function at work, so I think this may help.

Session 5

[two weeks after the medication consultation]

Jonathan: You were right. It is important for me to be able to do well at work. I think the antidepressant is helping me do this. And I am sleeping a bit better and feel less tired. So far, so good. I do feel as if the situation is manageable. But I am concerned that my personality is changing. Will this drug affect me this way?

Dr. Perry: I can see that you are not experiencing some of those problems that were getting in the way of you functioning daily. But I don't think any medication can stop us from being who we are, do you?

Jonathan: Yes, you have a point. True.

Dr. Perry: Aren't you still confronting your issues and dealing with the disappointment and losses in your life?

Jonathan: Yes, I am.

Dr. Perry: Are you taking the medication every day, as prescribed?

Jonathan: Yes. She told me to be sure that I did take it the way she prescribed. Also, not to stop taking the medication just because I am beginning to feel better—and not to stop taking it without contacting her.

Dr. Perry: Yes, I know you can experience some benefits from taking medications immediately, but it takes several weeks for the antidepressant to accumulate in your body so that the medication levels are high enough for you to really feel better.

Jonathan: Yes, I can see that now. But there is one thing—I feel a little nauseous from time to time. Could it be the medications?

Dr. Perry: It is possible. Sometimes these types of medication do have some side effects such as nausea. These problems usually disappear after you have been taking the medication for a while. However, I 'd like to set up another appointment with Dr. Lambert right away, just to be sure it is only a common side effect. Is that agreeable to you?

Jonathan: Sure. I'll do that.

Dr. Perry: Also, I generally recommend clients to educate themselves about the medications they are taking. I know you are computer literate, so I have a few recommendations for some websites you can access.

Jonathan: Thanks. I'll do that. I do like to know what I am putting in my body.

Dr. Lambert has consulted with Dr. Perry. They discussed the effect of the SSRI antidepressant on the symptoms of sleeplessness, fatigue, and anhedonia and have monitored the side effects; the nausea has disappeared. The symptoms of depression are decreasing. The dose and drug seem to be effective. Jonathan is complying with the medication and is no longer experiencing any troublesome side effects.

Session 18

[*three months later*]

Jonathan: It seems as if the medication is doing its job.

Dr. Perry: OK. Can you rate how you feel? Let's look at a 1 to 10 scale with 1 being the worst you have ever been depressed and 10 representing the best you have ever felt. Tell me where you were when you began the medication and where you are now.

Jonathan: OK. I was at 5 when I started the meds. Now I'd say I am at 7.

Dr. Perry: OK. What will it take for you to reach a 9?

Jonathan: To get there, I don't think I need the drugs. I need to figure out some solutions to problems in my relationships.

Case Comment

Jonathan responded well to the combination of antidepressant medication and individual therapy. He showed a favorable response to the antidepressant with no problematic side effects. The intensity of his symptoms diminished. After a symptom-free six months, we will discuss discontinuing the medication. If the medication is stopped and no symptoms recur, the treatment is successful and the temporary depression is over. If the symptoms come back or worsen, Jonathan will return to taking the medication.

↰ RESEARCH DIRECTIONS IN PSYCHOPHARMACOLOGY

The evidence base for pharmacological treatments for mental disorders is huge. Numerous well-controlled studies—including randomized, placebo-controlled, and double blind—demonstrate that psychotropic medications are efficacious and effective for treating many severe mental disorders such as schizophrenia, bipolar disorder, obsessive-compulsive disorder, and depression (Thase & Jindal, 2004; Thase, Jindal, & Howland, 2002). The evidence is less clear when it attempts to establish which specific medication is most effective for a specific condition. It is beyond the scope of this chapter to summarize the vast literature on psychopharmacology efficacy studies. Students can access the drug trials at the National Institute of Mental Health (NIMH) (http://www.nimh.nih.gov/health/publications/index .shtml), and they can find criticism of the studies in professional journals. In this chapter, we will examine research into medications in general to gain an understanding of the basic type of research and development that accompanies any drug that is sold in the United States, which has to adhere to the requirements of the FDA.

The U.S. Food and Drug Administration (FDA) is the government agency dedicated to ensuring that drugs sold in this country are safe and effective. Before any medication is approved for use in the United States, the FDA requires that basic research be conducted that follows the FDA-specified protocol before testing in humans can begin. The first step is to perform extensive preclinical or laboratory research and animal testing in order to assess toxicity, which usually involves years of extensive testing with animal and human cells. If this is successful, the creator provides this data to the FDA and asks to begin testing the drug in humans. At this stage, it is called an investigational new drug (IND) application. A plan for human testing is devised, with three phases of research. Each successive phase involves a larger number of people.

Phase I determines the safety and dose level of the medication. This initial phase is done with a small number of healthy volunteers (20 to 100), who are usually paid for their participation. The focus is to determine what happens to the drug in the human body. It identifies how it is absorbed, metabolized, and excreted. It also investigates side effects that occur as dosage levels are increased. This phase of the research focuses on safely administering the drug, establishing safe dose levels, and discovering any toxicity. This initial phase of testing typically takes several months. About 70 percent of experimental drugs pass this initial phase.

In Phase II, trials use much more sophisticated methodology. They are generally randomized trials with a control group. One group of patients receives the experimental drug, and a control group receives standard treatment or placebo. Usually the studies are "blinded"—neither the patients nor the researchers know who is getting the experimental drug. This provides information about the relative safety of the new drug and its effectiveness. The focus is on testing the effectiveness of the drug over a range of doses as well as searching for common side effects. Once shown to be safe, the focus shifts to efficacy. Phase II of testing may last from several months to 2 years and involves up to several hundred patients. Only about one-third of experimental drugs successfully complete both Phase I and Phase II studies.

In Phase III, a drug is tested in several hundred with several thousand patients. The focus is on gaining an understanding of the drug's efficacy, benefits, and the range of possible adverse reactions. Most studies are randomized, blinded trials. Several hundred to several thousand subjects serve in these trials to establish efficacy of the drug for a particular use. The drug is compared with a placebo control and at least one comparison drug. There must be at least two positive placebo-controlled studies before approval of the psychotropic medication is granted (Martinez, 2000). Once this phase is successfully completed, the FDA can approve the drug for marketing. Phase III studies typically last several years. Seventy to 90 percent of drugs that enter Phase III complete this phase of testing.

For each drug study, there is a specific design. The protocol describes the participant pool, tests, procedures, medications, dosages, and the length of the study. The FDA requires these specific criteria for the safety of a drug. However, acceptable effect sizes need only be relatively modest. While this research requirement means the drug has achieved a certain level of safety and efficacy, many questions can still be posed about the superiority of one medication over another.

Another issue is the off-label use of a medication. Drugs that have been accepted for one purpose can be used for other reasons, without adequate clinical trials to assess the effectiveness and efficacy of the medication for that particular use.

The findings of many studies support the status of psychotropic medications as first-line treatments and long-term treatments. However, there are considerable gaps in the evidence base. More studies are needed to determine when medications alone are sufficient or when they should be combined with psychotherapy for optimal results.

Finally, studies are needed to determine whether psychotherapy alone is more effective than medication. Four major studies of severely depressed patients have shown that cognitive behavior therapy (CBT) is at least as effective as psychotropic treatment and that the effects of CBT are longer lasting (DeRubeis, Gelfand, Tang, & Simons, 1999).

A number of practice guidelines have been developed to help clinicians make psychopharmacological decisions (Doran, 2003). These guidelines—based on recommendations, comprehensive treatment options, medication algorithms, and expert consensus—are useful for both prescribing and nonprescribing providers (Mellman et al., 2001). They can be used as standards of comparison and in decision trees.

Practice guidelines have been created by professional organizations such as the American Psychological Association (APA, 2002, 2005). The American Psychiatric Association has also published a quick reference guide for clinicians (Fochtmann, McIntyre, & Hart, 2003). Guidelines specifically addressed to ADHD are also available for pediatricians (Rushton, Fant, & Clark, 2004).

← ISSUES OF DIVERSITY

Interest is growing in assessing psychopharmacology with a diverse population of patients. Psychotherapists need to understand the various factors that can influence a patient's compliance and attitude regarding medication. Because Americans are a culturally diverse group, we need to develop culturally sensitive interventions (Feldman & Keltner, 2005).

It is important to be aware that differences can affect how people respond to any given medication (Pavlovich-Danis, 1999). The prescribing provider can factor these considerations into selecting the most appropriate drug for a given client (Burroughs, Maxey, & Levy, 2002). Of course, each client must be considered individually; no assumptions should be made about how a client would react based on membership in a minority group.

When considering using medications with clients, it is important to take into account the person's cultural values, especially regarding health beliefs and mental health treatment (Schnittker, 2003). While many White Americans believe in the efficacy of drugs and expect a prescription from their doctor, members of other ethnic and cultural groups may have different expectations regarding the type of drug prescribed, dosages, and tolerance of side effects that could affect a client's ability to adhere to medication requirements. Sometimes religious customs, such as ritual fasting, can affect medication schedules and interfere with drug absorption.

← MAJOR CRITIQUES OF PSYCHOPHARMACOLOGY

Many people, both mental health professionals and others, are concerned that the widespread use of psychotropic medications today is harmful. Some believe that economic rather than clinical considerations may be fueling this practice. Drug manufacturers have undue influence within the political system, which they use to advance their own profit:

> In the last ten years, drug companies have steered 44 million dollars in contributions to the major [American] political parties and candidates. What this means is that the FDA is effectively financed by the pharmaceutical industry. (Greek & Greek, 2002, pp.115–116)

Others look at the influence the pharmaceutical industry exerts on the public. Drug companies have increased their advertising about the usefulness of drugs and have aimed advertising directly at consumers, which in turn influences physician behavior and increases the likelihood of prescribing medications. For example, total spending on direct-to-consumer advertising increased from $11.4 billion in 1996 to $29.9 billion in 2005 (Donohue, Cevasco, & Rosenthal, 2007).

Others are concerned about the relationship of diagnosis and medications. Inflating and expanding diagnoses, so that normal forms of emotional and mental suffering are medicalized, means more and more people with simple problems in living are eligible to be treated with medication (Kleinman, 2006). For example, social phobia is now the third most frequently diagnosed mental disorder. Is a fear of speaking out in public a true mental disorder, or are some people simply shy and feel uncomfortable being judged?

Others are concerned about how drug research is funded. With economic pressures upon the universities and research centers to generate funding, the drug companies are willing to provide huge sums to test their medications. Critics need to ask who is doing the research, who is funding it, and what possible biases may be involved.

On the other hand, the popularization of medication for the treatment of mental disorders—both through advertising for psychotropic drugs and through increasing awareness of mental disorders—can help to reduce the stigma associated with mental health problems and encourage people to seek treatment (Pettus, 2006). Some researchers claim that about half of all Americans will meet the criteria for a *DSM* diagnosis at some time in their life and will need treatment (Kessler et al., 2005).

Box 14.2 summarizes some of the major controversies associated with psychopharmacology. Mental health professionals need to keep a critical eye on pharmacological practice and research. It is a multibillion-dollar industry with the potential for great good and great harm.

SUMMARY

- The 1950s marked a revolution in the treatment of mental disorders with the development of psychotropic drugs. Initially there were opposing camps. The psychological camp said mental disorders are based in the mind, and

BOX 14.2 CONTROVERSIES IN PSYCHOPHARMACOLOGY

- Many drugs have associated risks and have been linked with dangerous medical conditions.
- There has been such a growth in the prescription of stimulant medications for ADHD that it has outpaced the increase in the research necessary to justify their use (Bhatara, Feil, Hoagwood, Vitiello, & Zima, 2004).
- There have been serious warnings about ADHD medications. The FDA has made it mandatory for all ADHD stimulant drug labels to warn users about risks of cardiovascular symptoms and adverse psychiatric symptoms associated with the use of these drugs.
- SSRIs were named in a number of lawsuits as increasing the risk of suicidality and aggression.
- Risperdal, Seroquel, and Zyproxa are thought to increase the risk of diabetes.
- There are serious questions that pharmaceutical companies are dictating how we define mental illnesses.

psychotherapy is the treatment of choice. The biological camp said mental illness is organic, and medication is the treatment of choice. Today, nonprescribing psychotherapists need to grasp the fundamentals of psychopharmacology in order to practice competently.

- Pharmacodynamics reveals how drugs affect the body. Psychotropic drugs work on a molecular level and adjust neurotransmitter levels. Agonists activate the cell's natural response, and antagonists inhibit this response. Mental disorders are thought to be caused by defects in neural transmission particularly in catecholamines (norepinephrine and dopamine), serotonin, acetylcholine, and gamma amino butyric acid (GABA). Pharmacokinetics reveals how a drug is ingested, absorbed, distributed, biotransformed, and excreted; these are vital factors to consider in using medications safely.

- The major types of medications are antidepressants for depression (SSRIs, tricyclics, MAOIs). The mood stabilizer lithium treats bipolar disorder. Antipsychotic drugs treat psychosis and assaultive behavior; traditional antipsychotics have troublesome side effects, but a new generation of antipsychotics has reduced these side effects. Anti-anxiety drugs relieve anxiety by causing central nervous system depression; however, long-term use can lead to increased tolerance and withdrawal symptoms. Stimulants treat ADHD in children and adults. Physical and psychological dependence can occur. Cholinase inhibitors treat dementia. Drugs for treatment of substance abuse help with withdrawal from other CNS depressants. Alternative treatments such as herbal and dietary treatments are increasing in use.

- The practice of psychopharmacology for nonprescribing providers means referring clients to a collaborating prescribing practitioner in order to assess the need for medication and prescribe it. The nonprescribing psychotherapist provides psychotherapy and acts as collaborator-coordinator with the prescriber. Length of treatment is individualized. The goal of prescribing is to find the optimal medication and dose to decrease symptoms and provide the most comfort. Therapeutic techniques include monitoring by both providers. The process of pharmacotherapy begins with assessment and ends with either termination of the drug or its long-term use.

- Research shows a solid evidence base for pharmacological treatments with well-controlled studies showing psychotropic medications are efficacious and effective for treating severe mental disorders such as schizophrenia, bipolar disorder, obsessive-compulsive disorder, and depression. The evidence is less clear concerning which specific medication is most effective for specific conditions.

- The FDA regulates drugs in the United States to ensure they are safe and effective. The basic research protocol consists of three phases of well-controlled research studies. A number of professional practice guidelines have been developed to help clinicians make decisions.

- Americans are a culturally diverse group, so it is important to be aware that differences can affect how people respond to any given medication.

- Critiques of psychopharmacology are that it is based on a multibillion-dollar industry with the potential for great good and great harm. Drug manufacturers have undue political influence. Direct advertising influences client and physician behavior, increasing the likelihood of prescribing medications. Thus economics rather than clinical considerations may be fueling practice. Biases may be present in research based on who is funding the research. A positive to marketing is that it encourages people to seek treatment and may even reduce the stigma associated with mental health problems.

RESOURCES

Quick Reference Psychiatric Medication Chart
John Preston, PsyD
425 University Avenue #201
Sacramento, CA 95825
(916) 558-0282
www.Psyd-fx.com

This website provides a thorough and current reference guide to psychotropic medications.

National Institute of Mental Health
6001 Executive Boulevard
Room 8184, MSC 9663
Bethesda, MD 20892-9663
(301) 443-4513
www.nimh.nih.gov

The student will find this website to be a valuable source of information. Once the home page is accessed, the student can go to any number of well-prepared pages. In relationship to psychopharmacology, the student can access links to information about drugs with up-to-date details about ongoing clinical trials, scientific meetings, and career opportunities.

U.S. Food and Drug Administration
Center for Drug Evaluation and Research
5600 Fishers Lane
Rockville, MD 20857-0498
(888) INFO-FDA
http://www.fda.gov/cder/drug
www.nimh.nih.gov

This website is a link to the FDA and is a source of information about all of the drugs that the FDA has approved over the years. It contains detailed information about drug safety for both the professional and the consumer or client. The non-prescribing psychotherapist can recommend that clients access the information as well in order to be well informed about treatment.

Physicians' Desk Reference
http://www.pdr.net/login/Login.aspx

The Physicians' Desk Reference, called the PDR, provides drug and clinical information to physicians and other health providers. It is in book form and also has a website that contains consumer-friendly information about prescription and non-prescription medications.

Maudsley Prescribing Guidelines
Institute of Psychiatry
King's College London
De Crespigny Park London
United Kingdom, SE5 8AF
(020) 7017-6000
http://www.iop.kcl.ac.uk/departments/?locator=379

This resource contains practical advice for common clinical situations. It is used by prescribers, nursing staff, pharmacists, general practitioners, and those in related professions who treat patients with mental disorders in the United Kingdom. It also provides information about mental health and about the research at the Institute of Psychiatry and South London and Maudsley NHS trust.

CLASS EXERCISES AND ACTIVITIES

Theory

1. Define *pharmacodynamics* and *pharmacokinetics*. Explain the differences between them.
2. Describe how neurotransmitters are related to mental health. Which are the major neurotransmitters that are related to mental disorders?
3. Discuss the biological theory of mental illness.

Practice

1. What is the role of the nonprescribing psychotherapist regarding psychotropic medications?
2. Break into two groups and argue the pros and cons of prescribing medications to psychotherapy clients.
3. Devise a referral for Tuti for a prescribing provider. Devise a treatment plan for her as the nonprescribing psychotherapist using Figure 1.2.

Research

1. Describe the process of developing and releasing a new drug to the public in the United States.
2. Do you believe that the method required for releasing a new psychotropic medication is adequate to ensure that a drug is safe? Why or why not? What suggestions do you have to change or improve the process? What can you tell a client who asks your opinion about whether a drug is truly safe?
3. Find one study testing a psychotropic medication using randomized control trials. Critique the methodology and discuss how the randomized control group is an essential part of all modern drug studies.

CHAPTER 15

ECLECTIC AND OTHER PSYCHOTHERAPIES

The risk inherent in eclecticism is that therapists will fall into idiosyncratic approaches, as they did in the pre-empirical past.

–J. C. Markowitz

The goal of this chapter is to present information about several models of psychotherapy. These therapies are representative of various trends in the development of psychotherapy and have achieved growing interest from psychotherapists. The chapter will introduce therapeutic models in three major areas: eclectic and integrationist (multimodal therapy), postmodern and constructivist (solution-focused brief therapy and narrative therapy), and models for specific problems and diagnoses (interpersonal psychotherapy and dialectical behavior therapy).

✦ ECLECTIC AND INTEGRATIONIST THERAPIES

Eclecticism is the use of procedures from differing theoretical orientations, and *integrationism* is the joining of two or more theoretical positions into a more consistent approach (Lambert, Bergin, & Garfield, 2004). Adding to that definition, others have described integrationism as an "openness to understanding the convergences and commonalities amongst the vast array of sectarian psychotherapies" (Stricker & Gold, 2003, p. 317). In this view, integrationism allows the therapist to learn from all perspectives rather than having to maintain one exclusive approach. Others see eclecticism and integrationism as slightly different, with eclecticism regarded as more theoretical and integrationism as more idealistic (Prochaska & Norcross, 2007; Safran & Messer, 1997).

Whether we see eclecticism and integrationism as different or eclecticism as a subcategory of integrationism, both emphasize not restricting the therapist to a single theoretical orientation. And both agree that no single psychotherapeutic approach is comprehensive enough to deal with the wide variety of psychotherapy issues (Garfield, 1994).

Historical Context

Many psychotherapists do not rely on a single model of psychotherapy. Rather, they see themselves as integrative or eclectic and draw on a number of theories and practices that they find useful in working with their clients. This practice has grown over the past 35 years. In a recent survey, 30 percent of psychologists, 34 percent of social workers, and 37 percent of counselors say that their practice is eclectic or integrative (Prochaska & Norcross, 2007). Other studies show that one half to two thirds of therapists choose to use a variety of techniques from major theoretical models of psychotherapy (Lambert et al., 2004).

It is no wonder that eclecticism/integrationism is the dominant trend in psychotherapeutic practice today. As discussed in Chapter 1, a confluence of factors has created a favorable environment for the trend, including the growing diversity of clients and problems being treated and empirical findings that effective psychotherapy involves common factors and that no single model is superior to the others. Thus eclecticism/integrationism allow therapists to use their expertise and clinical judgment to choose what they believe to be the best from a variety of approaches and to combine them in a way that they judge to be most helpful to the specific needs of clients (Beutler, Consoli, & Lane, 2005; Lambert et al., 2004). The four generally accepted ways to practice eclecticism are technical eclecticism, theoretical integration, common factors, and assimilative integration (Stricker & Gold, 2003, pp. 321–322).

First, in *technical eclecticism,* the psychotherapist combines or sequentially applies clinical strategies, methods, and interventions. The therapist chooses the specific techniques he believes will be the best match to help the client (Lazarus, 1997). The therapist who practices technical eclecticism combines these various treatment interventions without adhering to any theoretical beliefs associated with the psychotherapy and thus does not have a comprehensive model from which to view human behavior and psychopathology. This moves the therapist away from a theoretically based psychotherapy to the use of interventions that are empirically based (Stricker & Gold, 2003). Some examples of technical eclecticism are Arnold Lazarus's multimodal therapy and Larry Beutler's prescriptive matching.

Second, in *theoretical integration,* the psychotherapist expands the conceptual framework of psychotherapy beyond technical eclecticism by integrating theoretical constructs. For example, she may combine ideas about the causes of psychopathology or synthesize ideas about personality from two or more traditional models. An example of integrationism is Paul Wachtel's model, which combines psychodynamic and behavior therapy (Wachtel, 1987).

Third, the psychotherapist who uses the *common factors approach* identifies common ingredients within any group of therapies and tries to use the ones that are most important in the treatment of a particular individual. The therapist reviews the interventions to find those that promote the change needed for a particular client.

Fourth, *assimilative integration* is a combination of both theoretical integration and technical eclecticism (Messer, 1992). In this approach the therapist uses a standard method and guidelines from one psychotherapy but brings in methods from other therapies when called for in order to advance therapeutic goals. For example, the therapist may use a psychodynamic approach to treat a phobia and then use behavioral interventions to increase the efficiency of the psychodynamic treatment (Stricker & Gold, 2003).

There are some daunting challenges for therapists who use eclectic and integrative psychotherapy (Lazarus & Messer, 1991). They need to avoid being labeled lazy for describing treatment that is willy-nilly and without a well-planned strategy. In addition, they must have a good command over the approaches and interventions they choose to use with their clients. Ethical therapists must not practice outside of the scope of their expertise. Also, they must be capable of generating a careful and helpful treatment plan, with appropriate goals, strategies, structure, and direction to the psychotherapy, as well as posttreatment evaluations to show that the treatment was effective (Seligman, 1998, 2004). (See Table 15.1 for an example of a well-organized treatment plan designed by a multimodel psychotherapist.)

Some of the most prominent integrationists practicing today are Arnold Lazarus, Paul Wachtel, and Larry Beutler. Beutler developed an integrated system called prescriptive psychotherapy, which matches forms of eclectic psychotherapy to specific interventions for specific problems (Beutler & Harwood, 2000). Wachtel's integrative psychodynamic behavior therapy is a method of integrating and accommodating elements of both psychoanalysis and behavior therapy (Wachtel, 1987). For our example of eclectic and integrationist therapies in this chapter, we will take a closer look at Lazarus's multimodal therapy.

Multimodal Therapy

The best-known proponent of eclectic psychotherapy is Arnold Lazarus. Born in Johannesburg, South Africa, in 1932, he obtained a doctorate from the University of Witwaterstrand in 1960, and he has worked with Joseph Wolpe and other well-known behaviorists in South Africa. He has been on the faculty at several universities, including Stanford, Temple, and Rutgers, where he is now professor emeritus.

Lazarus (1993) claims that the empirical stance of behavior therapy has always impressed him and convinced him that he needed to apply more behavioral techniques in his therapy. In his multimodal therapy, he combines the techniques that he believes to be most effective and necessary.

Multimodal therapy is a systematic and comprehensive psychotherapeutic approach that grew out of Lazarus's research into short-term yet comprehensive psychotherapy strategies. It is concerned with three questions: What works? For whom? Under what conditions? (Lazarus, 1976). It transcends behavior therapy by including other variables, such as affective and interpersonal ones, but it still adheres to the scientific basis of psychology (Lazarus, 2005).

One of Lazarus's fundamental assumptions is that people use seven dimensions, or modalities, to experience themselves and their world. Clients who present for treatment are usually troubled by at least several specific problems, which calls for a correspondingly wide range of specific interventions. Treatment is a function of the client–therapist work across seven dimensions of personality. These seven interactive dimensions (what Lazarus calls *modalities*) are represented by the acronym BASIC ID (Lazarus & Abramovitz, 2004):

- *Behavior:* What is the client doing that gets in the way of her happiness or personal fulfillment? Identify the self-defeating and maladaptive behaviors.

What does she need to increase and/or decrease? What should she stop doing and start doing?

- *Affect:* What emotions are predominant? What affective reactions are present—such as anger, anxiety, depression, or combinations of these affects like profound melancholy and sadness or irritation and rage? What seems to generate these negative affects—such as specific cognitions, images, interpersonal conflicts? How does the client control his emotions?
- *Sensation:* What is the client sensing? Or, what is she seeing or hearing, touching, tasting, and smelling? What negative sensations is the client experiencing? For example is she experiencing headaches, numbness, dizziness, gastrointestinal problems, hallucinations, sexual disturbances?
- *Imagery:* What fantasies, mental pictures, images, or dreams might the client be experiencing? Do the images counteract auditory, visual, or other sensations? What is the client's body image and self-image like?
- *Cognition:* What kinds of thoughts and ideas, values and opinions, does the client have? Does the client experience any negative thoughts about himself, such as being worthless, unattractive, crazy, stupid, or undesirable? Does the client experience any positive thoughts, such as being intelligent or honest or fair?
- *Interpersonal relationships:* What kind of interpersonal relationships does the client have? How does the client interact with family, friends, associates, colleagues, or authority figures and others? Does the client have difficulties in relationships with others and especially in marriage, intimate relationships, and sexual relationships?
- *Drugs and biology:* What is the client's general state of physiological functioning? What health and medical concerns may the client have? What is the state of her physiological functioning? Does the client take any prescription or nonprescription drugs?

Each individual has a priority system for these modalities (dimensions), called a *firing order*. The therapist will need to address several of them, but only very complex cases involve all seven facets and the associated interventions.

Practice of Multimodal Therapy

Multimodal therapy draws from the practice interventions and techniques of behavior therapy, rational emotive behavior therapy, and cognitive therapy, as well as social learning theory, general systems theory, and communications theory (Lazarus, 2005).

The therapist assesses each client systematically, precisely, and accurately. The major question to be answered is, "Who or what is best for this particular client?" (Lazarus, 2005). The therapist uses the BASIC ID to guide the assessment, along with several other methods. First, the therapist interviews the client in a face-to-face session, and the client fills out questionnaires outside of sessions. The structural profile inventory assists the client and therapist to clarify the client's preferred modalities and their level of importance. The multimodal life history, which was created by Lazarus and his son Clifford (Lazarus & Lazarus, 2005), provide background information. While assessment is emphasized in the first session, it is ongoing and the therapist continually evaluates and reevaluates throughout the client's psychotherapy.

The multimodal therapist tailors the relationship to address the unique needs of each client and adjusts the psychotherapy relationship according to the reaction of the client. Lazarus recommends that the therapeutic relationship should not be bound by rigid, inflexible rules, but the real work of the client lies in the BASIC ID, not only in the experience of a warm, caring therapeutic relationship.

The overriding goal of multimodal therapy is to help each client make the changes he or she desires as quickly as possible by using the best methods or interventions available. The specific goals of multimodal therapy for each individual client are reflected in the specific seven BASIC ID dimensions. For example, Table 15.1 illustrates a multimodal profile for Jonathan.

Tracking is the method Lazarus uses to carefully scrutinize the firing order of the client's modalities. For example, Jonathan typically reacted to his losses, or to a discouraging situation, by generating negative emotions by dwelling on sensations (not sleeping, loss of appetite), immediately followed by aversive images (Tuti leaving him), followed by maladaptive behavior (avoidance of people, smoking, drinking). This is his current firing order, and tracking it helps the therapist to select the most effective interventions. For example, medication for depression might enhance Jonathan's ability to cope in the other modalities.

Bridging is a procedure in which the therapist deliberately responds to the client in his or her dominant modality before moving into another modality. Thus the therapist first deals with his preferred modality of affect and lets the client express his feelings for a while before switching to the imagery modality. Then the therapist might ask, "Can you describe the vivid image that you conjure up in your mind when you think about your losses? And how do they affect your sleep patterns?" The therapist works with one mode at a time before moving onto the next. In this way, the therapist bridges to the next modality when the timing is appropriate.

Research Directions in Eclectic and Integrationist Therapies

There are a limited number of studies that have examined outcomes in eclectic therapy, and there are a few controlled studies that concentrate on multimodal therapy alone. Lazarus himself has conducted studies in which he has followed up a number of clients who receive multimodal treatment. There is some evidence suggesting that the more modalities that are addressed, the more permanent and lasting the changes. However, there is not a definitive body of empirical support specifically for multimodal therapy, so it does not qualify as an evidence-based therapy.

In general, the research literature on eclectic therapies is minimal (Lambert et al., 2004). Eclectic therapists have not kept up with the growing theoretical and clinical interest in the psychotherapy field. Eclectic therapists do not agree about which techniques are most helpful, and since eclecticism does not represent any

Table 15.1

Multimodal Profile for the Case of Jonathan

Modality	Problem	Proposed Treatment
Behavior	Fear of rejection and abandonment Avoidance of social situations	Desensitization with imagery
Affect	Depression, sadness Anxiety Loneliness Fear of rejection Anger and guilt	Discuss possible use of medication Anxiety management training Relationship building, social skills training, and role play Corrective self-talk Empty chair and role play
Sensation	Somatic complaints, sleeplessness	Relaxation training Deep breathing exercises Consultation with primary care doctor
Imagery	Disturbing images of Tuti and Darren	Positive imagery Empty chair technique Corrective self-talk
Cognition	Distorted beliefs that fuel anxiety and depression (e.g., catastrophizing, negative mental filter, etc.) Irrational beliefs and oughts, musts, shoulds	Beck's cognitive therapy Ellis's REBT
Interpersonal Relationships	Loss and disappointment are overwhelming	Interpersonal therapy (IPT) techniques to improve relationships
Drugs and Biology	Sleep disturbance Poor appetite Cigarette smoking Lack of exercise Drinking alcohol to excess	Consult with primary care physician about health and medication Nutritional consult Smoking cessation program Exercise program Monitor and decrease drinking, psychoeducation

specific systematic approach, it is difficult to replicate studies that do exist. However, since eclectic or integrationist therapists use interventions from a variety of therapies that have been supported by research evidence, they assume that these interventions will also be effective when used in an eclectic model (Glass, Arnkoff, & Rodriguez, 1998). As well, it is reasonable to assume that the equivalency effect applies to multimodal therapy. More research is needed to confirm that these assumptions are accurate.

✦ POSTMODERN AND CONSTRUCTIVIST THERAPIES

Historical Context

Postmodernism is an intellectual trend, a questioning of the old ways of knowing, such as objectivism and empiricism, that offers alternative perspectives such as subjectivism and relativism. Typically, social historians mark the postmodern era as beginning in the 1950s with advances in technology that significantly changed the world. For example, postmodernism encourages pluralistic thinking and multicultural perspectives. Instead of relying on objective truth to know something, postmodernism encourages intuition, relationships, and spirituality (Blatner, 1997). Within the field of psychotherapy, a variety of therapies have emerged that represent postmodern thinking. Examples are solution-focused, solution-oriented, and constructivist therapies.

Constructivist therapies have the following common beliefs and assumptions (Hoyt, 1994). Truth is not objective; rather, truth is constructed. The truth is not out there, it is within. Any and all human realities are personal, cultural, and linguistic constructs. People create institutions that define their lives and often unknowingly accept the roles they have been handed without questioning. Individuals and political groups make up the dominant ideology of the day, and these constructs are no truer than any other; they are just established by those in power. In a social relationship, there are hidden ways in which power is constructed, and the therapist's role is to deconstruct the authority constructs that limit the client's potential (Blatner, 1997).

The precursor to today's constructivist psychotherapy was George Kelly, who created a theory called *constructive alternativism* and developed *fixed role psychotherapy* (Kelly, 1955). Kelly, a pioneering therapist, worked out of a rural clinic in a farming community in Kansas in the 1930s and 40s. His work has strongly influenced today's constructivist psychotherapy.

Kelly believed reality is constructed by the person, and there is not just one true reality, there are many—as many as there are people to construct them. There are an infinite number of alternative constructions that people can make up about the world. A corollary to this thinking is that if a person's construction of the world is not helpful to him, he can change it; since a person is his own creation, he can re-create himself.

Kelly's fixed role psychotherapy is a unique method in which the client, in collaboration with the therapist, writes a very detailed self-characterization sketch in the third person. The therapist, having discussed the changes the client wants to make, then writes a sketch of a fictional character very different from the client but possessing the characteristics that the client wants to acquire. The client assumes and plays the role of that character in everyday life for two or three weeks, which encourages the client to live life from a different perspective for this period of time. The client often can make a rapid and meaningful change as a result.

Postmodern therapists, including constructivist therapists, do not adhere to any particular grand theory but use training and experience to tailor the psychotherapy to the client and the moment. These therapists analyze and deconstruct those factors (constructs) that limit the possibilities for a given person or community. The work of the psychotherapy is to deconstruct features of the constructed truth that inhibit the person's potential. Clients learn to consider alternative ways of defining and constructing their own life, and the therapist tailors the psychotherapy to the individual client and to the moment in the evolving therapeutic process. Many consider feminist therapy (see Chapter 12) to be a postmodern psychotherapy, as it also deconstructs limitations in the client's experience. In this chapter, we will look at two constructivist psychotherapies: solution-focused brief therapy and narrative therapy.

Solution-Focused Brief Therapy

One form of short-term or brief psychotherapy emphasizes seeking solutions to problems rather than focusing on the problems themselves. In *solution-focused brief therapy*, the process examines previous solutions and exceptions to the problem and then, through a series of interventions, encourages clients to do more of those successful behaviors. With a focus on client strengths and resiliencies, the psychotherapy emphasizes the clients' ability to know what is best for them and to plan how to get there. The "why" of the problems and the past are deemphasized so that people can use their strengths to achieve the desired state of being (de Shazer, 1985, 1988, 1991, 1994; Trepper, Dolan, McCollum, & Nelson, 2006).

Therapists who emphasize solution-focused brief therapy are growing in number and include William O'Hanlon and Weiner Davis. The names most frequently associated with solution-focused brief therapy are Steve de Shazer and Insoo Kim Berg, who co-founded the Brief Family Center in Milwaukee, Wisconsin, a not-for-profit training and research institution formed in 1978; the term *solution-focused brief therapy* (SFBT) was first coined in 1982 (de Shazer, 1982).

Steve de Shazer, born in Milwaukee in 1940, studied under Milton Erickson and at the Mental Research Institute in Palo Alto, California, which specialized in brief psychotherapy, communications, and understanding systems of human interaction based on direct observation. Insoo Kim Berg, born and raised in Korea, came to the United States in 1957. After earning a masters in social work at the University of Wisconsin, she trained at the Mental Research Institute in Palo Alto, where she first met de Shazer. After they married, they were the primary developers of solution-focused brief therapy, an approach that gained in popularity in the 1970s. Both Steve and Insoo Kim died within 15 months of each other. De Shazer had presented a workshop in London, flown to Vienna, and died of a blood disorder and pneumonia within a few days (Iveson, 2005). A few months later Insoo Kim died suddenly (Dolan, 2007).

The theory underlying solution-oriented therapy is quite straightforward. Solution-oriented therapists believe that many mental health professionals spend too much time and effort thinking, talking, and analyzing a client's problems, while the client continues to suffer. They believe that if the therapist helps the client to arrive at solutions, relief from their suffering will occur as quickly as possible. Rather than using energy to look for explanations, solution-oriented therapists believe that clients are better helped by taking action to change troubled patterns of behavior. They need to construct solutions for their problems.

Solution-oriented therapists observe that there are times when even the most chronic problems are less intense or even absent. When these times are examined, it is apparent that the client, possibly unknowingly, performs many positive actions. If the therapist raises the client's awareness about such small successes, it can make it more likely the client will repeat these successful actions at other times. In turn, the client builds up more confidence, and life becomes better. When the client experiences small successes, it increases hopefulness about self and life. Once the client begins to solve problems, empowerment follows, and there is more interest in achieving a better life for self and others in the future.

Because these solutions are found in the exceptions, they are already part of the client's sporadic behavioral repertoire. Thus repeating these particular successful behaviors is easier than learning a whole new set of behaviors. Duplicating an already existing action takes less effort than learning new solutions used by others that may not work as well for a client. Some basic assumptions of solution-focused brief therapy follow (Berg & Miller, 1992):

- Focus on the positive, on the solution.
- Change is inevitable and occurs all the time.
- Emphasis should be on the client's strengths and resources and not on weaknesses.
- There are exceptions to every problem, and they can be used to help build solutions.
- Use parsimonious interventions because small changes lead to larger changes so that even the slightest intervention can bring about dramatic changes.
- Look to the client's particular complaint to find a solution for the individual rather than searching for a universal solution to a universal problem.
- The client is the expert; work within the client's frame of reference with the goal of helping the client to discover his or her own solution to the problem.

Solution-focused brief therapy has continually evolved over the last 30 years. It emphasizes solutions rather than problems and looks at the client's desired outcome rather than the history and frequency of symptoms. Solutions are created by the psychotherapist and client in collaboration to match specific problems. In these ways, SFBT is a constructive and not a prescriptive psychotherapy (Berg, 2005).

Practice of Solution-Focused Brief Therapy

Assessment is a collaborative and ongoing process. There are a number of important questions the psychotherapist can ask the client. For example: What and who is important to the client? What does the client want? Is the client able and willing to do what it takes? How can the therapist and client together negotiate small, simple, easy steps that client knows how to do? How can they determine if the client truly carries out the agreed-to plan? How can they review and reassess the next small step? How can they help the client to repeat the steps until the client reaches a level where he or she is improved enough to stop? (Berg, 2005).

The therapeutic relationship is collaborative, with a respectful, nonblaming, and cooperative stance. The psychotherapist and client are both working toward the client's goals from the client's frame of reference. The therapist is active, shifting the focus from problems to solutions. The therapist emphasizes the strengths of the patient rather than any weaknesses and solicits solutions from the client. All therapeutic success is attributed to the client.

The psychotherapist regards every session as important and treats it as if it were the last session. He or she works to negotiate realistic solutions and to assist the client in assessing progress toward attaining the goals. The client is encouraged to solve current problems by focusing on solutions and actions that will bring about a happier and healthier life.

Solution-focused brief therapy uses questions and comments to help the psychotherapist and client identify exceptions, create solutions, and measure progress toward goals.

- *Goal questions:* From the beginning of therapy, the therapist focuses on ways to help the client begin to focus on solutions. The therapists asks, "What has to be different as a result of your coming and talking to me today? What is the first small thing I can do to be of help to you? What needs to be different in regard to _____ (complaints)? What do you know about your _____ that tells you that this can happen? Whose idea was it that you come to see me? What will convince _____ that you don't need to see me?"
- *The miracle question:* The miracle question, asked in the first session, begins the goal negotiation. The miracle question is, "Suppose that one night while you were asleep, a miracle happened, and the problem that brought you here is solved. What would you be doing differently? Who would be the first to notice you are doing things differently? What would he/she notice that is different about you then? If you were to pretend, even for a little while, that a small portion of the miracle had occurred, what one or two things would you be doing differently?" The client's answers to the miracle question help the therapist and client clarify the solution to the presenting problem.
- *Exception questions:* These are times when the client's problem is absent or occurs less frequently. These situations draw on the client's strengths. The therapist asks questions that identify and clarify exceptions: "When was the last time you did this, even a little bit, or for even a short time? How did you do this? What would your best friend say about how you did this? What would it take you to do this again? When was the most recent time when this happened?" Exceptions show that much is under the client's own

control and indicate that there are ways to increase how these events can occur. By focusing on an environment in which the problem is absent, the therapist encourages a change in behavior and helps keep the work in the present, avoiding getting stuck in the past.

- *Scaling questions:* Scaling questions help the client to determine what he or she can do to repeat the exceptions. The therapist asks the client to rate her status. For example, "On a scale of 1 to 10 (1 being the worst, 10 the best) where would you rate yourself at this time? Where would _____ rate you on the same scale? Where would like you to be at? How important is it for you to make these changes (scale of 1 to 10)? How willing are you to work at it? What needs to happen to move up a single point on the scale? How close to your goals have you moved so far? At what number would you be able to live with how things are? How confident are you that you can maintain the level of success achieved so far (scale of 1 to 10)?" Questions can also be asked about how significant others would scale the client's progress toward the goals.

- *Language questions:* The therapist uses linguistic techniques to help formulate treatment goals that the client finds meaningful, useful, and attainable. The therapist also uses solution-focused words and phrases. For example, "Suppose _____. What difference would it make? Was it different for you? What would you do instead? What should they do instead? You must have some good reasons to do what you do." The therapist can also use metaphors or stories to create hope and change, reframing and relabeling, emphasizing strengths, and making suggestions about being unstuck.

- *Compliments:* The therapist uses language to shape desirable behaviors and compliments the client whenever possible. Berg (2005) discusses how she used the word *wow* over 25 times in a session to express her amazement and respect for a deeply depressed mother who managed to get out of bed to take care of her children. Responding in an awestruck manner helps the client see himself in a different perspective and underscores how ordinary behavior can represent extraordinary efforts. Using words to give credit to a client who deserves it positively reinforces the behavior.

In addition to language techniques and questioning methods, SFBT uses homework to reinforce the client's responsibility for finding solutions. The psychotherapy begins a process that the client can continue to implement throughout daily life in the outside world.

Research Directions in Solution-Focused Brief Therapy

Until recently, research for SFBT consisted only of anecdotal reports of success, with scanty controlled empirical research to support it. Though case reports and subjective follow-up studies have provided preliminary encouragement, there is a lack of well-controlled clinical trials validating SFBT's effectiveness.

De Shazer spearheaded follow-up studies at the Brief Therapy Center using clients' assessment of their own progress, and he found that clients benefited from the psychotherapy (de Shazer, 1985; de Shazer et al., 2007). A recent review of the outcome research literature on SFBT found more than 15 studies of varying quality (Gingerich & Eisengart, 2000). We can conclude that SFBT is more effective than no treatment, is at least as effective as current psychosocial treatments, and in some cases may be more effective than problem-focused treatments. Furthermore, some psychotherapy models that are very similar to SFBT have been shown to be effective in controlled studies. Given this preliminary support, more extensive research would be valuable and is planned for the future in hopes of SFBT achieving the status of an evidence-based psychotherapy (de Shazer et al, 1986; Trepper et al., 2006).

Narrative Therapy

Narrative therapy is a constructivist psychotherapy in which the therapist and client explore the client's life stories and their meanings and context (Morgan, 2008; White & Epston, 1989). By telling and retelling a story from different perspectives, or by looking at different parts of the story, a client can work on solving various problems in his or her life.

Australian Michael White developed his model of narrative therapy with New Zealander David Epston (Epston & White, 1992; White & Epston, 1989). White, the founding editor of the *Australian Journal of Family Therapy*, has written a number of publications on narrative and family therapy. He is at the Dulwich Centre in Adelaide, Australia. The mission of the Dulwich Centre is to support social action, to understand personal issues within wider social forums, and to assist those who have experienced trauma such as survivors of the Rwanda genocide.

Narrative therapists believe that people make up stories about their own lives and as a result create their own selves. As people make up their world through stories, in turn, the stories also become a part of the self. People give their own personal meanings to experiences that shape the plot of their story. They link specific events together in a particular chronological sequence in order to explain them. There are dominant and alternative stories and dominant and alternative plots. Events that are linked together over time have implications for past, present, and future actions.

People ascribe meaning to events during stressful times, and they may use *thin descriptions* that allow little room for explanation or movement. A thin description is a superficial description in which the person has unexamined social and cultural beliefs. For example, a psychotherapist diagnoses a client with major depression. Calling him a "depressive" is a superficial way of summarizing the client's experience and detracts from the whole process of how this human being came to be the way he is. *Thick* stories represent the actuality and the complexity of a person's life and his understanding of experience.

The person may buy into thin truths and superficial explanations, given by powerful figures, which replace the rich actuality of the person's life experience in the story (Payne, 2006). These thin descriptions decrease a person's choices and potential. If a story is saturated with problems that seem unsolvable, the person telling the story has decreased his power. If a story emphasizes inadequacies and failings, the person has limited her ability. An example of a thin description could be, "I come from a very disturbed and dysfunctional family. As a result, I am embarrassed and feel unworthy." This person has concluded that she is unworthy based on her own description of her family and their problems. An alternative description would result in other possibilities: "I come from a family that has endured some hardship and survived admirably. The strength of my family is commendable." Here she has framed the story from the perspective of strength, concluding that she has the ability to handle tough situations.

Practice of Narrative Therapy

Clients come in with problem-saturated stories that get in the way of having satisfactory life experiences. The key question for the therapist to ask is: How can we assist people to re-author new and preferred stories for their lives and relationships? The therapist begins with the client's subjective view of the problem and how he or she hopes the situation will change. Together the client and the therapist talk about how to bring about the desired successes. Homework is assigned to reinforce the change process. The length of psychotherapy varies depending on client need but can take months or even longer (Epston & White, 1992).

The psychotherapist acts as a collaborator and consultant to the client. The client is the expert on him- or herself and the only requirement is that the client wants to discuss the situation. A number of professionals can be part of the process, as well as family or friends (Freedman & Combs, 1996).

The goal of narrative therapy is to involve the client in re-authoring or re-storying and thus to allow him or her to live out new self-images, new possibilities for relationships, and new futures (Walter & Peller, 1994). Just as various thin descriptions and conclusions can support and sustain problems, alternative stories can reduce the influence of problems and create new possibilities for living (Morgan, 2008). Stories can also be used for conflict management (Winslade & Monk, 2000).

Narrative therapists, when initially faced with problem stories and thin conclusions, want to engage their clients in conversations that seek out alternative stories allowing clients to live the life they would choose. Through conversation, the psychotherapist wants to help clients create stories of identity that will help them to break free of the problems they are facing, assisting people in re-authoring their preferred stories for their lives and their relationships. Curiosity and a willingness to ask questions to which we genuinely do not know the answers are important principles of this work (Freedman & Combs, 1996).

However, it is not enough to simply be freed from problematic stories through re-authoring alternative versions (Morgan, 2008). Narrative therapists want to find ways in which people can richly describe these alternative stories. Through *rich description* clients can provide fine detail of the story lines of their life and can interconnect their story with others. Narrative therapy has a positive view of people and their strengths in coping with problems. The following are some of techniques used in narrative therapy.

- *Deconstruct stories:* Ask the client to extend the stories into the future and about neglected aspects of the stories. Have clients tell stories in which they are more powerful than their problems.
- *Externalize the problem:* Place the problem outside of the client, making it different and not a part of the client's identity. For example, if a client says that he is incapable of controlling his drinking, have him say, "Not drinking is difficult for me." This externalizing allows him to see that he can change the story.
- *Create alternative narratives:* Revising and re-authoring allow clients to make changes to their own stories. While the therapist can offer alternative viewpoints and encourage the client to make up a story that is helpful, clients who revise their own stories make changes in their views of themselves (Payne, 2006).
- *Change thin descriptions and conclusions:* By substituting rich descriptions and conclusions for thin ones, clients can replace problems with detailed solutions and clear steps to take to improving their situation.
- *Write therapeutic documents:* These documents, prepared by both the therapist and the client, reinforce evidence of the client's accomplishments (White & Epston, 1989).

Narrative therapists help people to re-create life stories that re-create their lives. The therapy can also challenge sociopolitical conditions that contribute to human suffering. For example, the woman who has been raped or abused can author a positive and life-affirming life story to help others who have been victimized. Narrative therapy can also be a respectful way to understand people from diverse cultural backgrounds, giving them the opportunity to tell the story of their lives with the values and beliefs of their cultures (Seligman, 2006, p. 250).

Research Directions in Narrative Therapy

There is little research for individual narrative therapy. There are some interesting anecdotal accounts about how narrative therapy helped resolve issues among members of traumatized communities, such as in Rwanda after the 1994 genocide of over a million Tutsis. In general, however, constructivist therapists do not endorse traditional research, viewing it as more concerned with maintaining the power and prestige of the psychotherapy profession than with the well-being of the clients.

✦ PSYCHOTHERAPY MODELS FOR SPECIFIC PROBLEMS AND DIAGNOSES

Recently, there has been a trend toward developing psychotherapies to treat specific, circumscribed conditions (diagnoses) or problems. Two such therapies are interpersonal psychotherapy (IPT) for depression and dialectical behavior therapy (DBT) for the treatment of borderline personality disorder. These therapies are designed with very specific clinical conditions in mind. They include manuals so a student can readily train in the treatment philosophy, theory, and practice of the psychotherapy. Such training also makes it easier to conduct research with controlled clinical trials.

Since the therapies are so circumscribed and training is standardized, these therapies have the added advantage of being research friendly, making it easier to acquire a solid evidence base. They are live examples of how both research and practice can contribute to the knowledge base of psychotherapy to provide information to improve the quality of client care. These models are bridging the gap between clinical research and practice (Kazdin, 2008). Of course, they are not without critics who say that evidence from studies conducted in highly controlled conditions does not accurately reflect the reality of the clinical encounter and can be misleading about the true nature of psychotherapy. Nevertheless, it is important for the student to know and understand these types of psychotherapies.

Interpersonal Psychotherapy

Interpersonal psychotherapy (IPT) is a structured, manual-based form of brief psychotherapy for depression. A unique feature of interpersonal psychotherapy is that from its beginning, it was founded in research. It has been tested in randomized controlled trials and been shown to be efficacious and effective. It is truly an evidence-based psychotherapy.

IPT draws from theoretical concepts of Harry Stack Sullivan and John Bowlby. Sullivan's psychotherapy was based on the concept that a personality could never be isolated from the context of interpersonal relationships in which the person exists (see Chapter 3). Bowlby brought up the notion of the experience of loss and theorized about disordered attachment as the cause of a great deal of human psychopathology. Interpersonal psychotherapy indirectly addresses these topics within the therapeutic framework because it views depression, and the symptoms of depression, as associated with the client's experiences in early relationships and in attachment issues.

Gerald Klerman (1928–1992) and Myrna Weissman are the major developers of interpersonal psychotherapy. Their book, *Interpersonal Psychotherapy of Depression*, clearly describes this successful psychotherapy (Klerman, Weissman, Rounsaville, & Chevron, 1984). Klerman, who taught at Yale, Harvard, and Cornell, achieved a reputation for developing multi-site studies of affective and anxiety disorders and for developing and researching treatments; he believed that any treatment method, including psychotherapy and psychopharmacology, should be thoroughly researched and tested before being used. His wife Myrna Weissman and one of his more recent collaborators, John Markowitz, continued to develop and research IPT after Klerman's death in 1992. Weissman, who is a professor of epidemiology and psychiatry, has published a comprehensive guide to interpersonal psychotherapy (Weissman, Markowitz, & Klerman, 2000).

Interpersonal psychotherapy was developed to address the relationships and roles that are frequently affected by depression. The focus of the psychotherapy is on interpersonal events that seem to be significant in the onset and the maintenance of the depression, which can be seen as clustering into four areas: (a) interpersonal disputes, (b) role transitions, (c) interpersonal deficits, and (d) grief that extends beyond the normal bereavement period.

Interpersonal disputes—disagreements, arguments, and struggles with other individuals who are important in the person's life—can bring about depression especially if they occur regularly and frequently. These disputes tend to occur in marital, family, social, or work settings. Interpersonal psychotherapy assesses the level of intractability of the dispute, identifies sources of misunderstanding, checks for faulty communication, and looks for invalid or unreasonable expectations. The aim is to intervene with communication training, problem solving, or other techniques to facilitate change.

Role transitions are situations in which the patient must adapt to a change in life circumstances. Some are normal developmental transitions such as going to high school or college, marrying, having children, leaving the home, or retiring. Other role transitions may be unexpected or atypical such as participating in war, being kidnapped, or being the victim of a disaster. Those prone to depression may experience these as traumatic and feel as though they have suffered a loss or that their lives are out of control, resulting in the development of symptoms. Interpersonal psychotherapy helps the client to identify sources of difficulty in the new role, clarify inconsistencies, and correct cognitive errors as well as solve problems and encourage appropriate affect.

Interpersonal deficits are a lack of social skills that results in difficulty in interpersonal relationships. The interpersonal therapist considers the client's impoverished relationships in terms of both number and quality. In psychotherapy, the focus will be on both old relationships and on the relationship that the client has with the therapist.

Grief can be normal or abnormal. Interpersonal psychotherapy deals with the depression that results when the client fails to progress through the phases of normal mourning. Abnormal grief can be evident when the client has endured multiple losses, has inadequately grieved, has avoided or denied a significant death, has feared the illness that caused a death, or has a lack of social support during bereavement. The interpersonal psychotherapist helps the client to reconstruct the patient's relationship with the deceased, which facilitates the mourning process.

Practice of Interpersonal Psychotherapy

In interpersonal psychotherapy, the therapist is warm and collaborative, while strictly adhering to the manual. There is constant focus on termination from the outset, so regression and other more analytic processes are avoided as much as possible. While transference and countertransference are not interpreted, they are utilized as a tool for identifying problematic processes within the IPT process. Common themes in transference are identified and linked to current circumstances.

In using the therapeutic relationship, the therapist aims to identify problematic processes, such as excessive dependency or hostility, and modifies these within the therapeutic framework. In this way the therapeutic relationship can serve as a template for further relationships that the therapist will help the patient create. This group of problems is common in the more chronic affective disorders, such a dysthymia, in which significant degrees of social impoverishment have occurred either before or after the illness.

The goal of IPT is to improve interpersonal relationships and reduce and relieve the symptoms of depression. Generally, the therapist, in collaboration with the client, sets two or three specific treatment goals, such as improved eating or sleeping. The therapist may ask the client to rate goals on a goal attainment scale for each problem area. The therapist is very clear about the hoped-for outcomes at the beginning of psychotherapy, which aids clients in accurately seeing their progress throughout psychotherapy and at termination (Klerman et al., 1984).

Up to three sessions are spent gathering information, assessing symptoms and interpersonal experience, diagnosing, and evaluating the client's level of depression. The therapist reviews the client's current relationships and social functioning and decides upon the framework for the focus of treatment as interpersonal disputes, role transition, grief, or interpersonal deficits (Feijo de Mello, de Jesus Mari, Bacaltchuk, Verdeli, & Neugebauer, 2005). The client's illness is formulated and explained in interpersonal terms, as are the nature and structure of the psycho-therapy sessions. This phase of treatment concludes with the composition of the *interpersonal inventory,* a register of all the key relationships in the client's life.

The final sessions focus on termination. Termination is usually formulated as a loss experience from which clients can learn a great deal about their own responses to loss and how well the modifications attempted in the therapeutic process have evolved. Some of the techniques used in IPT techniques are listed here.

- *Exploratory techniques:* These consist of nondirective exploration (using general open-ended questions) to facilitate free discussion of a client's material. Nondirective techniques are also used to encourage the client to continue talking, such as supportive acknowledgments (nodding or saying "please continue"), extension of the topic discussed (encouraging the patient to continue or repeating key charged words), and receptive silence (maintaining an interested attentive attitude).
- *Encouragement of affect:* This is intended to help the patient express, understand, and manage feelings. Therapists may help patients to acknowledge and accept painful feelings (affects) that cannot be changed.
- *Questioning:* There are several questioning styles and techniques that can be used in ITP, including clarification, supportive listening, role playing, and communication analysis.

Table 15.2 presents an outline of interpersonal psychotherapy, with a review of the therapeutic process.

Research Directions in Interpersonal Psychotherapy
IPT has been an evidence-based psychotherapy with empirical research findings from its inception and continues to be researched as it evolves. A number of large-scale

Table 15.2

Outline of Interpersonal Psychotherapy

I. *The initial session*

A. Dealing with depression

1. Review depressive symptoms
2. Give the syndrome a name
3. Explain depression as a medical illness and explain the treatment
4. Give the patient the sick role
5. Evaluate the need for medication

B. Relation of depression to interpersonal context

1. Review current and past interpersonal relationship as they relate to current depressive symptoms. Determine with the patient the following:
    a. Nature of interaction with significant persons
    b. Expectations of patient and significant persons from one another and whether these were fulfilled
    c. Satisfying and unsatisfying aspects of the relationships
    d. Changes the patient wants in the relationship

C. Identification of major problem areas

1. Determine the problem area related to current depression and set the treatment goals
2. Determine which relationship or aspect of the relationship is related to the depression and what might change in it

D. Explain the IPT concepts and contract

1. Outline your understanding of the problem
2. Agree on treatment goals, determining which problem area will be the focus
3. Describe procedures of IPT: here and now focus, need for patient to discuss important concerns; review of current interpersonal relations; discussion of practical aspects of treatment—length, frequency, times, fees, policy for missed appointments

II. *Intermediate sessions: the problem areas*

A. Grief

1. Goals
    a. Facilitate the mourning process
    b. Help the patient re-establish interest in relationships to substitute for what has been lost
2. Strategies
    a. Review depressive symptoms
    b. Relate symptom onset to death of a significant other
    c. Reconstruct the patient's relationship with the deceased
    d. Describe the sequence and consequences of events just prior to, during, and after the death
    e. Explore associated feelings (negative as well as positive)
    f. Consider possible ways of becoming involved with others

B. Interpersonal disputes

1. Goals
    a. Identify dispute
    b. Choose plan of action
    c. Modify expectations are faulty communication to bring about a satisfactory resolution
2. Strategies
    a. Review depressive symptoms
    b. Relate symptom onset to overt or covert dispute with significant other with whom patient is currently involved
    c. Determine the stage of dispute
        i. Renegotiate (calm down participants to facilitate resolution)
        ii. Impasse (increase disharmony in order to reopen negotiation)
        iii. Dissolution (assist mourning)
    d. Understand how nonreciprocal role expectations relate to dispute
        i. What are the issues in the dispute
        ii. What are differences in expectations and value

        iii. What are the options

        iv. What is the likelihood of finding alternatives

        v. What resources are available to bring about changes in the relationship

    e. Are there parallels in all the relationships

        i. What is the patient gaining

        ii. What unspoken assumptions lie behind the patient's behavior

    f. How is the dispute perpetuated

C. Role transitions

    1. Goals

      a. Mourning and acceptance of the loss of the old role

      b. Help the patient to regard the new role as more positive

      c. Restore self-esteem by developing a sense of mastery regarding demands of new roles

    2. Strategies

      a. Review depressive symptoms

      b. Relate depressive symptoms to difficulty in coping with some recent life change

      c. Review positive and negative aspects of old and new roles

      d. Explore feelings about what is lost

      e. Explore feelings about the change itself

      f. Explore opportunities in new role

      g. Realistically evaluate what is lost

      h. Encourage appropriate release of affect

      i. Encourage development of social support system and of new skills called for in a new role

D. Interpersonal deficits

    1. Goals

      a. Reduce the patient's social isolation

      b. Encourage formation of new relationships

    2. Strategies

      a. Review depressive symptoms

      b. Relate depressive symptoms to problems of social isolation or unfulfillment

      c. Review past significant relationships including their negative and positive aspects

      d. Explore repetitive patterns in relationships

      e. Discuss patient's positive and negative feelings about therapist and seek parallels in other relationships

III. *Termination*

A. Explicit discussion of termination

B. Acknowledgement that termination is time of grieving

C. Moves toward recognition of independent competence

IV. *Specific techniques*

A. Exploratory

B. Encouragement of affect

C. Clarification

D. Communication analysis

E. Use of therapeutic relationship

F. Behavior change technique

G. Adjunctive techniques

V. *Therapist role*

A. Patient advocate, not neutral

B. Active, not passive

C. Not interpreted as transference

D. Not friendship

Source: Adapted from *A Comprehensive Guide to Interpersonal Psychotherapy* by M. M. Weissman, J. C. Markowitz, & G. L. Klerman, pp. 22–25. New York: Basic Books, 2000. Reprinted by permission of Basic Books, a member of Perseus Books Group.

randomized control trials support its efficacy for the treatment of depression. Overall, IPT is as effective as antidepressant medications and cognitive behavior therapy for the treatment of depressive symptoms (Markowitz et al., 2005). Recent systematic review of research findings on the efficacy of interpersonal psychotherapy for depressive disorders shows that IPT is an efficacious psychotherapy for depressive spectrum disorders and may be superior to other manualized psychotherapies or some forms of cognitive behavior therapies. See the online Appendix C for some examples.

However, interpersonal psychotherapy may not be effective with every client. The decision to use IPT and medication for depression is based on a number of factors, such as the severity of the depression, past treatment history, and patient preferences (Feijo de Mello et al., 2005). IPT is being modified, tested, and used for a variety of other conditions. It shows potential for the treatment of bulimia nervosa, acute adolescent depression, dysthymic disorder, bipolar disorder, and postpartum depression.

Even with its impressive research base, interpersonal psychotherapy is not without critics. Some maintain that IPT remains a psychotherapy conducted primarily in research settings rather than in the real-life world of clients.

Dialectical Behavior Therapy

Dialectical behavior therapy (DBT) is a psychotherapy developed specifically to treat borderline personality disorder (BPD). It makes use of a broad array of cognitive and behavior therapy strategies and applies them to the problems of those with BPD, especially those who are suicidal and self-destructive. Some of the procedures of dialectical behavior therapy are problem solving, exposure techniques, skills training, contingency management, and cognitive modification. Its overriding characteristic is an emphasis on dialectics, or the reconciliation of opposites, in a continual process of synthesis. While DBT was designed for borderline personality disorder, it has also been used for clients with other diagnoses.

One of the key figures in the development of DBT is Marsha M. Linehan, professor of psychology and psychiatry and behavioral sciences at the University of Washington. Linehan's philosophy, which underlies dialectical behavior therapy, is that the therapist's attitude toward the treatment and the client is critical. The psychotherapist's attitude is significant in forming the therapist's relationship with the client, which is fundamental to the effects of treatment with suicidal and borderline personality individuals (Linehan, 1993a, 1993b).

Dialectical behavior therapy is based on biosocial theory, the concept of the invalidating environment, and dialectical philosophy. We will look at each of these concepts in more detail here.

The core assumption of *biosocial theory* is that borderline personality disorder (BPD) is a dysfunction of emotional regulation. The person with BPD has an emotional response system that is overly sensitive and overly reactive, with an inability to modulate the resulting strong emotions and actions associated with them. The person with BPD lacks the ability to inhibit inappropriate behaviors related to strong negative or positive emotions, to coordinate action in the service of an external goal, or to self-soothe the physiological arousal that accompanies the strong emotion. These deficits are the result of a biologically based emotional vulnerability.

The *invalidating environment* plays a pivotal role in the development and maintenance of BPD. The invalidating environment consists of the caretakers' punishing, ignoring, or trivializing the communications, thoughts, emotions, and self-initiating behaviors of the person with BPD. It may involve sexual, physical, and emotional abuse. For a child with high emotional vulnerability, such an environment is very damaging in early life. In turn, the emotionally vulnerable and reactive child acts in a way that elicits more invalidation from an environment that could be supportive to another personality type. The child fails to learn to label and modulate arousal, to tolerate stress, and to trust in his or her own emotional responses as valid interpretations of the world. The end result is behavioral, intrapersonal, self, and cognitive instability. Symptoms such as self-defeating behaviors, suicidal ideation and behavior, self injury, and eating disorders represent attempts to regulate responses.

The *dialectic* is a process by which a phenomenon is transformed. There are three stages to the dialectic—thesis, antithesis, and synthesis. The thesis is the initial proposition or statement. The antithesis is the second stage of the dialectic, and it consists of the negation of the initial proposition. Tension develops between the thesis and the antithesis in order for the synthesis to occur. This process is repeated over and over again. The dialectic is a way to reconcile opposites through a continual process of synthesis.

Understanding the philosophical concepts of dialectics helps the therapist to conceptualize and make sense of the behavior of a person with borderline personality disorder. It also allows the therapist to teach the client a dialectical method of reasoning, moving the patient toward a more balanced and integrative response to life situations. Much of dialectical behavior therapy is based on the Buddhist idea of walking the middle path.

In the dialectical, there is no absolute truth, so that when polarities arise, people seek synthesis rather than search for the truth. To reason dialectically is to let go of logic and intellectual analysis as the only way to the truth and to tap into more experiential knowledge and for generating meanings and new relationships.

The most fundamental dialectic in this psychotherapy is accepting the client for who he or she is while at same time attempting to teach the client to change. Other specific dialectical tensions common in borderline personality disorder include skill enhancement versus self-acceptance, problem solving versus problem acceptance, affect regulation versus affect tolerance, self-focusing versus other focusing, needing from others versus giving to others, attending and watching versus participating, controlling versus observing, emotional control versus emotional tolerance, trust versus suspicion, independence versus dependence, self-efficacy versus help seeking (Linehan, 1993a, 1993b). The dialectic stresses interrelatedness and wholeness and helps to explain the internal reality of the client.

Practice of Dialectical Behavior Therapy

Dialectical behavior therapy emphasizes ongoing assessment and data collection on current behaviors, as well as clear and precise definition of treatment targets. Linehan has devised a number of assessment questionnaires (see Resources at the end of the chapter). For example, the borderline symptom list is to be filled out before individual sessions. Other examples include the diary card, the parasuicidal count (Linehan, 1993).

The therapeutic relationship has a dual role in DBT. First, it *is* the therapy, and second, it is used as the vehicle through which the therapist can effect the psychotherapy. The whole of treatment emphasizes building and maintaining a positive, interpersonal, collaborative relationship between client and therapist.

The therapist must facilitate both acceptance of the client as she is, as well as acceptance of the client's development. To do this, the therapist uses validation. Therapists must promote balance between the poles of a number of dimensions and be able to synthesize acceptance and change within the client. As well, therapists treating borderline personality disorder must synthesize unwavering centeredness versus compassionate flexibility, and benevolent demanding versus nurturing.

The therapist uses a problem-solving focus, which requires addressing all problematic client behaviors both in and out of psychotherapy in a systematic manner. This includes conducting a collaborative behavior analysis, formulating hypotheses about possible variables influencing the problem, generating possible changes (behavioral solutions), and trying out and evaluating the solutions (Linehan, 1993b, p. 5).

The client and the therapist have a reciprocal influence on each other. The primary role of the therapist is as consultant to the client, consistently being on the side of the client, and maintaining a constant belief in the client's essential desire to progress, as well as a belief in her inherent capability to change. The therapist's validation also involves frequent sympathetic responses to acknowledge the client's emotional desperation. The goals of DBT are to reduce ineffective action tendencies associated with dysregulated emotions and to increase adaptive behavioral skills. Specific techniques of the psychotherapy focus on skills training, behavior change, and validation of capabilities and behaviors. Much of DBT is devoted to teaching the client skills to increase interpersonal effectiveness in conflict situations and to tolerate emotional distress.

Dialectical behavior therapy has both individual and group components. The individual component deals with issues that come up during the client's week. Issues are discussed in the following order of priorities: suicidal and self-injurious behaviors, therapy-interfering behaviors, quality of life, and working to improve life. In the group psychotherapy, which meets once weekly for approximately 2½ hours, clients learn to deal with four modalities: core mindfulness, interpersonal effectiveness, emotion regulation, and distress tolerance (Linehan, 1993).

- *Core mindfulness* is a method to increase conscious control over attention, attain a wise integration of emotional and rational thinking, and experience a sense of unity with self, others, and the universe. It is the quality of awareness, keeping consciousness alive to the present reality, letting go of attachment, becoming one with the current experience, suspending judgment, or doing and being what is. It helps the client to find the middle path between extremes or polarities. Core mindfulness skills are observe, describe, and participate. DBT teaches the client there is a reasonable mind and an emotion mind.

- *Interpersonal effectiveness* involves skills similar to those taught in traditional assertiveness and interpersonal problem-solving training. These include strategies for saying no, asking for what one needs, and dealing with interpersonal conflict. The emphasis is on maximizing meeting needs in a specific situation, but not damaging either the relationship or the person's self-respect. People with borderline personality disorders often have good interpersonal skills but poor intrapersonal skills. They may be able to describe effective behavioral sequences when discussing another person but be incapable of carrying out such a sequence for themselves.

- *Emotional regulation* is particularly difficult for people with borderline personality disorder. They have intense and unstable emotions and are frequently angry, frustrated, depressed, and anxious. People with borderline personality disorder believe that these painful feelings are the problems to be solved, but dialectical behavior therapy sees these feelings as the way the person with BPD copes with problems. Therapy teaches the regulation of emotions through identifying and labeling emotions, identifying obstacles to changing emotions, reducing vulnerability to "emotion mind," increasing positive emotional events, increasing mindfulness to current emotions, and taking opposite action. Emotional regulation requires the application of mindfulness skills, especially nonjudgmental observation and description of the person's current emotional responses.

- *Distress tolerance* is taught in psychotherapy so that the person can bear pain more skillfully. Distress tolerance skills naturally evolve from mindfulness skills. They encourage acceptance of both oneself and the current situation in a nonjudgmental fashion. This does not mean that distress is approved, just that it is tolerated.

These methods help clients learn to tolerate and survive crises, accepting life as it is in the moment.

Research Directions in Dialectical Behavior Therapy

Dialectical behavior therapy has considerable evidence to support its efficacy in treating borderline personality disordered clients. A number of studies have validated its efficaciousness using randomized control trial studies and independent investigators. It has been found to be effective in reducing problems associated with BPD such as self-injurious behavior and suicidality, including depression and bulimia. It has been designated as a well-established treatment in APA guidelines (Chambless & Hollon, 1998). Therapists can be comfortable with its evidence base for the treatment of borderline personality disordered clients.

SUMMARY

- The chapter describes a variety of psychotherapy models including eclectic/integrationist (multimodal therapy), postmodern and constructivist (solution-focused brief therapy and narrative therapy), and psychotherapy models for specific problems and diagnoses (interpersonal psychotherapy and dialectical behavior therapy).
- Many psychotherapists today do not rely on a single model of psychotherapy and use eclecticism and integrationism. Multimodal therapy is an eclectic therapy using the BASIC ID dimensions, tracking, and bridging. Research on eclectic therapies has not kept up with the growing interest in eclecticism and integrationism.
- Constructivist psychotherapies assume truth is formed by personal, cultural, and linguistic constructs. Individuals and political groups make up the dominant ideology established by the powerful. Solution-focused brief therapy emphasizes solutions to problems, focuses on client strengths, therapist–client collaboration, and small, simple steps to solve problems. Goal questions include the miracle question, exception questions, scaling questions, and language questions. The evidence base is scanty and varied, with more extensive research planned for the future.
- In narrative therapy the therapist and client explore the client's life stories with an eye to deconstructing unfavorable and thin stories and reconstructing favorable and thick stories. The therapist acts as a collaborator and consultant to help the client to find new life possibilities. Techniques include deconstructing stories, externalizing the problem, creating alternative narratives, changing thin to thick stories, and writing a therapeutic document. Little research supports narrative therapy; narrative therapists do not endorse traditional research since it maintains the status quo.
- Models of psychotherapy for specific problems and diagnoses include interpersonal psychotherapy, a structured, manual-based form of brief therapy for depression, founded in research and tested in randomized controlled trials. IPT deals with four areas: interpersonal disputes, role transitions, interpersonal deficits, and extended grief. A warm, collaborative therapy relationship is a template for further relationships so that the client learns to improve interpersonal relationships, which decreases depression. Techniques include exploration, encouragement of affect, and questioning.
- Dialectical behavior therapy is used to treat borderline personality disorder. Procedures include problem solving, behavioral techniques, cognitive modification, an emphasis on dialectics, and an examination of the invalidating environment. The client and therapist have a reciprocal influence on each other with goals to increase adaptive behavioral skills. The therapist facilitates the synthesis of acceptance and change within the client. DBT has both individual and group components and teaches the techniques of core mindfulness, interpersonal effectiveness, emotional regulation, and distress tolerance. Considerable research evidence supports its efficacy in treating borderline personality disordered clients.

Resources

Multimodal Therapy
APA Systems of Psychotherapy, Multimodal Therapy
APA Service Center
750 First Street, NE
Washington, DC 20002-4242
(800) 374-2721; (202) 336-5510; (202) 336-6123
http://www.apa.org/videos/4310210.html

There is an excellent demonstration video in multimodal therapy showing Dr. Arnold Lazarus in action. An summary of the therapy is available is the book *The Practice of Multimodal Therapy* by Arnold Lazarus, Johns Hopkins University Press, 1989.

European Brief Therapy Association (EBTA)
http://www.ebta.nu

The EBTA encourages and sponsors research into brief therapies. The student therapist will find a summary of the essential elements of SFBT in a manualized format that puts forth the minimal essential elements to include in a study and includes measurement tools such as the Progress Scale Question.

Narrative Therapy
Dulwich Centre
ACN: 087 569 579
Hutt St PO Box 7192
Adelaide, South Australia 5000
(61-8) 8223-3966
http://www.dulwichcentre.com.au/homepage.html

The Dulwich Centre is an excellent resource for the student to obtain information about narrative therapy. The Centre, in Adelaide, Australia, provides training in narrative therapy and in community work. It also publishes books and articles about narrative therapy that are downloadable; many are free or can be obtained at a nominal fee.

Dialectical Behavior Therapy
Behavioral Tech, LLC
2133 Third Avenue, Suite 205
Seattle, WA 98121
(206) 675-8588
www.behavioraltech.org

Dr. Marsha Linehan has founded a company that trains mental health providers in dialectical behavior therapy to work with severely disturbed clients. The website allows the student to access many types of training tools for DBT. There are workshops, online training, consultations, books, and audiovisual materials available. There are also links to free materials.

Interpersonal Therapy
http://www.apa.org/videos/4310210.html

Dr. Myrna Weissman is interviewed on the topic of IPT, available at the website.

CLASS EXERCISES AND ACTIVITIES

Theory

1. Describe the theory underlying the five models discussed in this chapter. Concisely compare the major theoretical assumptions of each of the five models.
2. Solution-oriented therapists believe that clients are better helped by acting to change troubled patterns of behavior and constructing solutions for their problems rather than trying to explain behaviors. Do you agree or disagree? Explain your reasoning.
3. How can telling a story about ourselves be integrated into other forms of therapy besides narrative therapy? What is the theoretical assumption about storytelling that underlies narrative therapy? Do you think that all forms of psychotherapy involve storytelling? If so, explain how.

Practice

1. Look at the sample treatment plan in Chapter 1 (Figure 1.2). Fill out the plan for Jonathan for each of the five therapies described in this chapter. Fill out the treatment plan for Tuti for each of the five therapies described in this chapter. What are the similarities and differences in how each of these clients is treated in these models?
2. Break into discussion groups of three to five. Each person should take 10 minutes to tell his or her story. After all members have told their stories, discuss the themes found in the stories. What did you learn about yourself and the others through storytelling?
3. First describe the role of the therapist in each of the five therapies by writing it on a piece of paper. Then break up into groups (or continue to write the exercise). Imagine you are the therapist in each of these five types of therapy. Compare and contrast the similarities and differences as you take on these differing assignments. What are some of the interventions you would use?

Research

1. How do the interpersonal psychotherapy model and the dialectical behavior therapy model compare to the other psychotherapies in this chapter when we look for supporting research evidence?

2. Search for the research that supports IPT. How many studies can you find that have been conducted over the past two years? Do you think that IPT has a strong evidence base? Why?

3. What types of measures would you use to assess the outcomes for IPT, DBT, and multimodal therapy? Compare them with the types of outcome measures you might use for narrative therapy and solution-based brief therapy. Are these measures similar or different? What might a narrative psychotherapist and an IPT psychotherapist say about randomized controlled trials to test the efficacy of forms of psychotherapy?

Appendix A
Case Studies

To provide students with a concrete learning experience, two case studies (also called case histories) are presented here. These cases will be referred to throughout the book, allowing students to compare treatment modalities with the same two individuals. After both case studies are presented, students will have the opportunity to fill out sample treatment plans for Tuti.

THE CASE OF JONATHAN

Current Situation

Jonathan, well dressed but slightly unkempt, enters the therapy room. He is a tall, handsome, dark-haired male. His blue eyes are ringed with dark circles. Looking down at the floor, he speaks in a slow, low monotone.

> My boss insisted that I see someone. I am not functioning well at work. That is unusual because I have always been a very ambitious person. Usually, I am motivated and efficient, but lately I just don't care. I can't finish anything I start. I can't concentrate. I know my job is in jeopardy, but I can't seem to get it together. I ask myself, "What is the point in going on?" I have tried so hard, but everything seems so useless now.

Jonathan is a 30-year-old, single White male living in Washington, DC. For the past four years he has worked in an advertising firm. He describes his job as demanding but challenging. He earns $62,000 per year with good medical benefits. He graduated with honors from the University of Hawaii six years ago with a major in marketing and a minor in computer science.

At this time, Jonathan is not functioning well in any aspect of his life. He struggles to get through the day at work, and when he returns home, he feels hopeless and despondent. He cannot bring himself to answer the phone or leave his house. His appetite is poor, and he has lost 10 pounds over the past month. He has stopped socializing. He stares at the TV in the evening but can hardly remember what programs he watched. He falls asleep in the living room and wakes up at 2 A.M., goes to bed, tosses and turns, and cannot get back to sleep. At 6 A.M. when he must get up for work, he is tired. He finds it difficult to concentrate and to attend to what he has to do. He often feels jittery and on edge.

Precipitating Event

One month prior to the onset of these symptoms, Jonathan experienced the breakup of his 11-year relationship with Tuti. They met in college and had been together since he was 19.

About a year ago, Jonathan sensed there was a change in their relationship. He felt that he was losing Tuti—that they were becoming more distant and remote. Tuti wanted to get pregnant, but Jonathan did not feel ready for the responsibilities of fatherhood. Although he knew there were problems in his relationship, he ignored them, figuring they would iron themselves out. Tuti repeatedly asked him to go to therapy, but Jonathan put it off, making excuses and minimizing the seriousness of the problems. Tuti also told Jonathan she was homesick. Tuti, a native Hawaiian, had been active in the Hawaiian independence movement. She missed her Hawaiian friends and her extended family.

A month ago, Jonathan came home to his apartment to find Tuti had moved out. She left a long letter that explained why she could no longer tolerate their relationship. Jonathan said at first he was numb, but then he fell to pieces shortly after facing the reality that she was really gone. To make the situation even worse, he found out that Tuti had moved in with one of his best friends, Darren. He feels foolish, betrayed, unworthy, and jerked around.

Background

Both Jonathan's parents are deceased. His father died 10 years ago of stomach cancer. His mother died six years ago of a heart attack. He describes his relationship with his parents while growing up as "basically OK. Not terrific, but tolerable." Jonathan's sister Annie (age 39) lives in California. They were very close growing up and got along well. Their relationship is still friendly, but they seldom see each other due to the long distances.

Jonathan has had no psychological counseling in the past and no significant medical problems. Although he has had some passing thoughts of suicide in the past month, he does not have suicidal intentions at this time.

THE CASE OF TUTI

Current Situation

Tuti, meticulously dressed, enters the therapy room. She is 5 feet 6 inches, average build, with dark eyes, long dark hair, and an aura of dignity and grace. Her gaze is steady and direct, and her voice is firm but gentle. She appears to be sincere and concerned.

Tuti is a 32-year-old indigenous Hawaiian female living in Washington, DC. For the past four years, Tuti has worked as a seventh-grade teacher. She describes her job as "meaningful but difficult." She loves kids and teaching, but the behavior problems of the students in the DC area often overwhelm her. She earns $52,000 a year with good medical benefits.

She graduated with honors from the University of Hawaii six years before with a major in education and a teaching certificate. She left Hawaii with Jonathan when she was 26. After dating him as an undergraduate for several years, she decided to move in with him and travel to Washington where he received a job offer in an advertising firm.

She enjoyed the change at first, but over the past three years, she became very homesick for Hawaii. Tuti says that she did not realize just how happy she was in Hawaii until she left. She also wants to become more politically active in the Hawaiian independent movement, which is a group of people who believe that Hawaii should go back to nation status. She has made a firm resolve to teach in the Hawaiian schools in order to preserve and advance the cause of her native Hawaiian culture by educating the children in Hawaiian language and customs.

Precipitating Event

In a calm but emotional voice, Tuti relates her situation.

> I came to see you because I am very upset, even depressed, over my life situation. I was involved in a relationship with a man. It was good in the beginning, but we grew apart slowly. I tried to do everything I could to save the relationship, but it got to the point where I knew it was not going in the direction that I wanted. The biggest problem was that I am 32, and I really want to have children soon. Jonathan, my ex-partner, would not really make a commitment to have them. He would never say absolutely no, but he kept saying that he was not ready. It drove me crazy that he would not give me a direct yes or no.
>
> Then last year I found my soul mate. He and I became more and more attracted to each other. I turned to Darren when things went wrong with Jonathan. Darren and I knew we belonged together. I tried to tell Jonathan, but he would not hear me. Finally, I decided I only have one life to live and I left Jonathan.
>
> The problem is that Darren is also a close friend of Jonathan's. Now, I feel guilty—not so much about what I did, but how I did it. I was so frustrated I finally packed up and left him a note. I just couldn't face him. I know he is very upset. I'm worried about him. I care for him after all of these years, but I can't go back.

Tuti says she is functioning well at work and is happy to be with Darren, but her guilt over hurting Jonathan is placing a pall over her current happiness. She can not bring himself to contact Jonathan, and she cannot stop herself from thinking about him.

She wakes up in the middle of the night and ruminates about her hurtful behavior. She feels she will be punished for her evil deed and that she will not have normal children because of what she did to Jonathan. She also feels jittery and on edge.

> Why did he ignore our problems? Did he think they would just go away? Why wouldn't he go to therapy? He made excuses, and he brushed off my concerns. He knew I was homesick and that I missed my Hawaiian friends. Also, if I were to have children, I would want them to grow up in the Hawaiian culture with my extended family there to help.
>
> I had no choice but to move into Darren's, who is being really great about this and very patient with me. I feel angry, upset, and mistreated.

He has been a jerk to me! After all I did for him, he wouldn't even support us in having a child. So why do I feel so bad about what I did? It is really his fault.

Background

Both Tuti's parents are living. Her father is currently working as a supervisor for the highway department in Honolulu. Her mother works as a nursing assistant. Tuti describes her relationship with her parents while growing up as "warm and loving and spiritual." Tuti has two brothers and two sisters, ranging in age from 26 to 40. Growing up, they stuck together and got along well. Their relationship is close, and all of them except Tuti live in Hawaii—either on Oahu or Kauai. She stays in frequent contact with them through e-mail and phone.

Tuti has never had psychological counseling and has no significant medical problems. She is not at risk for suicide at this time.

WORKSHEET AND TREATMENT PLAN

Use Table A.1 to describe the treatment plan and the research support you would use for Tuti.

Table A.1
Worksheet of Treatment Plan
Presenting Problem
Assessment and Formulation
Therapeutic Relationship
Contract, Goals, and Treatment Plan
Techniques
Process of Therapy
Termination and Outcome
Research Support for Therapy Model

Use Table A.2 to make out a therapy plan for each of the major models we have discussed. How would Tuti be treated under these differing models?

Table A.2
Treatment Plans for Tuti
Psychoanalytic
Post-Freudian and Psychodynamic
Individual Psychology
Client Centered
Existential: Logotherapy
Gestalt
Behavior
Cognitive: REBT and Beck's CT
Reality
Feminist
Biopsychosocial Therapy
Psychopharmacology
Eclectic: Multimodal
Constructivist: Solution-Focused and Narrative
Interpersonal
Dialectical

APPENDIX B
Comparison of Psychotherapies

The content of this book furnishes the student with fundamental information about the theory underlying the major models of psychotherapy and the basics of how these theories are put into practice. Students are encouraged to think about how current research evidence can be used to support therapeutic choices. Furthermore, the text contends that psychotherapy should be considered within a sociocultural context. The variables that affect practice include the health care system, economics, multiculturalism and diversity, business, technology, and even politics.

At this point, you most likely have a preference for a therapy model and may soon begin your own practice. You may be asked about the therapy models you choose. A client may ask you, "What do you think would be most effective for my specific problem?" Or you might be asked, "What model of therapy are you most interested in? What do you think would be most helpful for your clients?" Although there is a strong trend toward eclecticism and integrationism today, it is wise for the beginning therapist to obtain training and gain expertise in at least two or three theoretical orientations.

The purpose of Appendix B is to help students to review and integrate this basic information. Each of the major psychotherapies is summarized and compared in tabular form. Having the information organized in one place makes it easier to compare and contrast these therapies.

BASIC CONCEPTS OF PSYCHOTHERAPY

Each psychotherapy model possesses unique concepts. These are highlighted in Table B.1.

Table B.1
Basic Psychotherapy Concepts

Model of Psychotherapy	Basic Concepts
Psychoanalysis	Focus on libidinal energy, character structure, and intrapsychic conflicts that originate in early childhood and generate anxiety; emphasize uncovering and resolving unconscious conflicts in analysis.

Post-Freudian and Psychodynamic	Used Freud's basic concepts and altered them in unique ways. • Jung: viewed people as moving toward wholeness and integration. • Horney: reformulated female sexuality and claimed basic anxiety was human motivation for neurosis. • Sullivan: viewed the person within an interpersonal context. • Ego psychology, self psychology, and object relations: differed from Freud in how psychic personality structures, developmental stages, and conflicts are formed. • Davanloo, Malan, Mann, Sifneos: altered the time course and limited the goals in short-term (brief) psychodynamic therapy • Relational psychoanalysis: emphasized interpersonal relationship in the therapeutic dyad.
Individual Psychology	Striving for significance is primary human motivation; social interest is key to happiness; human behavior is purposeful; family constellations influence personality.
Client Centered	Humans possess an innate goodness and potential for growth; the human ideal is the fully functioning person.
Existential: Logotherapy	Death, freedom, responsibility, isolation are issues to deal with as humans struggle with being in the world, authenticity, and self-transcendence. Logotherapy stresses meaningfulness and the inevitability of suffering. Awareness is important to living fully.
Gestalt	Existential values are incorporated into theory, and awareness is important to human functioning. The person is embedded in context, and the whole is greater than the sum of its parts.
Behavior	People are their behaviors. All behaviors, adaptive and maladaptive, are acquired through the scientific principles of learning. Forms or models of behavior therapy are based solidly on learning theory.
Cognitive: REBT and Beck's CT	Thoughts are covert behaviors subject to similar learning conditions as overt behaviors with similar results. REBT: adapts universal core irrational beliefs. Beck's CT: adapts more specific beliefs depending upon specific disorders such as depression and anxiety.
Reality	Based on choice theory, which claims humans choose and are responsible for their total behavior—doing, thinking, feeling, and physiological responses. People are motivated by the psychological needs of belonging, power, freedom, and fun, with belonging as the most important.
Feminist	Sociocultural environment and social structures affect private life. The personal is political. The status of women (and other nondominant oppressed groups) affects women's quality of life and mental health.
Biopsychosocial/ Health Psychology	An interaction among the biological, sociocultural, and psychological occur to affect mental health. Psychopharmacology, health psychology, stress management, and integrated health care are components of this perspective.

Psychopharmacology	Biological factors such as chemical imbalances, structural defects, and or/faulty genes produce physical and psychological symptoms. Medications can adjust dysfunctioning physical processes and imbalances.
Eclectic: Multimodal	Theory and practice methods from diverse systems of psychotherapy judged to be helpful are adapted to treat the individual. Lazarus's BASIC ID (behavior, affect, sensation, imagery, cognition, interpersonal relationships, drugs/biology) is eclectic.
Constructivist: Solution-Focused Brief and Narrative	The person creates his or her own view of reality. The focus is on the meaning people attribute to the world and the way it shapes their view of self, interpersonal relationships, and events in their lives.
Interpersonal	Views depression as associated with the client's experiences in early relationships or as a result of attachment issues; the therapy focuses on interpersonal issues of disputes, interpersonal deficits, role transitions, and complicated grief in relationship to the depressed individual.
Dialectical Behavior	Borderline personality and suicidal and self-destructive behaviors are addressed by using a broad eclectic approach including cognitive and behavior therapy strategies.

GOALS OF PSYCHOTHERAPY

Each model of therapy stresses different goals. These are highlighted in Table B.2.

Table B.2	
Goals of Psychotherapy	
Model of Psychotherapy	**Goals**
Psychoanalysis	Increase capacity to live an active and enjoyable life by freeing self from neurotic tendencies. Resolve the conflicts that are causing symptoms, inhibitions, or self-punishment. Character reconstruction by strengthening the functioning of the ego so it can control the unconscious libidinal drives.
Post-Freudian and Psychodynamic	Jung: individuate and develop self, wholeness, unity, balance, and heal the psyche. Horney: resolve central inner conflicts, escape from the vicious cycle, free self from search for glory, and acquire self-confidence. Sullivan: deal with anxiety, correct harmful perceptions, and understand self within a consensually validated view. Ego analysis: develop ego strength in a conflict-free zone. Object relations: develop mature interpersonal relations and modify inner mental objects. Self psychology: achieve healthy narcissism and develop a cohesive self and adequate self-esteem. Davanloo, Malan, Mann, Sifneos: insight into conflicts, symptom relief, improved relationships, problem-solving, self-esteem, and adaptive skills. Relational psychoanalysis: improve interpersonal functioning.

Individual Psychology	Increase social interest, feelings of community, and interconnectedness with others; alter lifestyle to meet the tasks of life—community, work, and love. Contribute to human social evolution.
Client Centered	Client chooses specific goals; self-actualization; facilitation of the inherent growth principle in all living things; clarification of inner experience and inner wisdom.
Existential: Logotherapy	Be authentic, experiencing, and responsible; grapple with moral, ethical, and spiritual issues; cope with alienation and isolation; acquire helpful attitudes, decisions, behaviors. Logotherapy: find meaning in life, transcend suffering.
Gestalt	Increase awareness of what I am doing, how I am doing it, and how I can change while simultaneously assuming responsibility, accepting, and valuing the self.
Behavior	Change maladaptive behavior and increase adaptive behaviors; decrease and/or eliminate maladaptive behaviors through scientifically established learning principles.
Cognitive: REBT and Beck's CT	Change maladaptive thinking to healthy, rational, logical thinking. REBT: adapt the philosophy of rational living and apply principles daily. Beck's CT: adapt rational thinking to change distorted thinking.
Reality	Satisfaction of five genetically coded human need; attain satisfactory relationship, adapt effective total behaviors, attain individual responsibility, achieve better decision making, and remediate personal deficits.
Feminist	Raise consciousness, empower clients, relieve symptoms, become educated about the effects of gender inequities and oppression on mental health; develop a positive self-image, eliminate negative, damaging, internalized gender stereotypes.
Biopsychosocial/ Health Psychology	Optimize health and wellness, develop and maintain a healthy lifestyle, engage in health-enhancing behaviors, change poor health habits, decrease/end health-compromising behaviors.
Psychopharmacology	Alleviate symptoms of mental dysfunction, illness, and discomfort; increase psychological level of comfort.
Eclectic: Multimodal Therapy	Client makes desired changes by using the best methods or interventions as quickly as possible. Multimodal therapy goals are defined for each individual client in parameters of specific seven BASIC ID modalities.
Constructivist: Solution-Focused Brief and Narrative	Construct new view of self, environment, and interactions. Solution-focused brief: solve current problems; focus on goals, solutions, and actions; be responsible for taking action. Narrative: deconstruct old stories and author more favorable ones; live out new self-images, new possibilities for relationships, new futures.
Interpersonal	Improve interpersonal relationships associated with depression; reduce or eliminate symptoms of depression; set two or three specific treatment goals such as eating or sleeping.
Dialectical Behavior	Reduce ineffective action, dysregulated emotions; increase adaptive behavioral skills; modulate extreme emotionality; reduce maladaptive mood-dependent behaviors; trust and validate own emotions.

CAUSES OF ABNORMAL BEHAVIOR

A particularly significant part of any model of psychotherapy is its definition of abnormal behavior and it causes. This theory guides the therapeutic process and determines the nature of the intervention chosen by the therapist. Table B.3 displays these ideas.

Table B.3	
Abnormal Behavior and Its Causes	
Model of Psychotherapy	**Abnormal Behavior**
Psychoanalysis	Childhood trauma causes arrests and fixations at specific developmental stages (e.g., unresolved oral, anal, Oedipal issues); libido is cathected in a way that produces an imbalance among ego, id, superego; unconscious material breaks into consciousness resulting in the ego protecting itself, which causes unhealthy, faulty, rigid adaptations that distort reality. The continuum of abnormal behavior is from neurosis to psychosis.
Post-Freudian and Psychodynamic	Jung: lack of balance, integration, and individuation. Horney: parental mistreatment, basic anxiety and hostility, feelings of helplessness, vicious circle, and search for glory. Sullivan: anxiety transmitted from primary caretaker influences personality development. Ego psychology: weak, nonautonomous ego and a lack of a conflict-free sphere of functioning. Object relations: splitting of objects into good and bad aspects. Self psychology: parts of self split off and projected onto others. Relational psychoanalysis: poor interpersonal relationships.
Individual Psychology	Discouragement due to insufficiently developed feelings of community and exaggerated inferiority feelings.
Client Centered	Lack of unconditional positive regard; conditions of worth block self-actualization, negate experience, cause incongruence and perceptual distortions; clash between self and reality.
Existential: Logotherapy	Inauthentic life, dampening of true potential, and unwise choices; there is existential anxiety due to failure to confront reality of death, freedom, isolation, and meaninglessness. Logotherapy: lack of meaning results in alienation, spiritual death, noogenic neuroses, and existential vacuum.
Gestalt	Disrupted awareness, poor contact with boundary disturbance, failure at creative adjustment, and an inability to identify with the in-the-moment experience.
Behavior	Maladaptive learning is due to faulty classical conditioning, operant conditioning, and/or modeling; this faulty learning is expressed in the form of behavioral excesses, deficiencies, or inappropriate stimulus control.
Cognitive: REBT and Beck's CT	Maladaptive mental processes and covert cognitions follow similar learning principles as overt behavioral processes.

REBT: irrational beliefs cause pathology. *B*, belief or internal process, causes *C*, negative consequence, and not *A*, the activating external event.

Beck's CT: specific patterns of faulty thinking such as magnification, overgeneralization, and selective abstraction result in cognitive distortions that cause specific disorders.

Reality Deficits result from not fulfilling human needs of belonging, power, freedom, and fun, with the need to belong being most important. This disconnection from relationships is at the root of most problems. Humans have a genetic tendency to repeat behaviors that do not work Abnormal behavior is a choice.

Feminist The power structure of male-dominated societies is the problem, not the oppressed woman. Damaging gender role stereotypes are internalized, coupled with a lack of empowerment and the accompanying stresses, which cause mental distress.

Biopsychosocial/
Health Psychology Interactions among mind, body, and environmental variables are out of balance, with less-than-optimal adjustment; this causes the inability to adapt to stress without damage, poor health habits, and health-compromising behaviors. The view of health is passive, using treatment rather than prevention.

Psychopharmacology Organic, biological basis to mental illness; biological dysfunctions and imbalances in physiological systems—such as neurotransmitter, endocrinological, and autonomic—cause excesses, deficits, or irregularities, which produces abnormal behavior and disease states.

Eclectic: Multimodal Different ideas depending on theory. Lazarus's multimodal therapy says cause of abnormal behavior can be found in one or more of the seven specific modalities (behavior, affect, sensation, imagery, cognition, interpersonal relationships, drugs/biology) and in the unique pattern of use or firing order for each individual.

Constructivist:
Solution-Focused
and Narrative Solution-focused: deemphasizes the why and the past of the problem and looks at the present, how to solve problems, and achieve desired state of being.
Narrative: person has narrative with deficient view of skills, competencies, beliefs, values, commitments, and coping mechanisms; this is called a thin description.

Interpersonal Interpersonal events cause and maintain depression, including interpersonal disputes, interpersonal deficits, role transitions, and complicated grief.

Dialectical Behavior There is dysfunction of emotional regulation, with overreactive emotional response system, failure to inhibit inappropriate behaviors, and inability to self-soothe strong emotions; there is biologically based emotional vulnerability, compounded by an invalidating environment.

ASSESSMENT

Each therapy has unique techniques to help gather detailed, in-depth information to guide the psychotherapist in diagnosis, determine client level of functioning, and provide treatment. Assessment is a method that cues the therapist to look for the issues with which he or she and the client will be dealing. Table B.4 displays the assessment issues for each therapy.

Table B.4	
Assessment	
Psychoanalysis	Is client a suitable candidate for analysis? Determines if client has ego strength to tolerate anxiety, length of treatment, intensity, pain, and expense of therapy. Determines whether client can use interpretations to make the unconscious conscious, can fully participate.
Post-Freudian and Psychodynamic	Assessment looks at client's symptoms, anxiety, self-control, and levels of consciousness. Consider stages of development—id, ego, superego. Ego analysis: assess maturity and sphere of autonomous ego functioning. Object relations: assess nature and quality of the mother–child relationship and self–object formation. Self psychology: assess relations with significant others, narcissism, damage to self-structures. Relational psychoanalysis: assess quality of relationship.
Individual Psychology	Lifestyle analysis uses general formal assessment, questionnaires, standardized interviews, projectives, and/or an Adlerian client questionnaire. Early recollections are assessed, as are family constellations and dynamics, genogram, and strengths.
Client Centered	Assessment is part of ongoing relationship of client and therapist to reach the client's phenomenological field. The client is expert on own self; Q-Sort is used as is enhanced relationship and empathic understanding and process diagnoses.
Existential: Logotherapy	Assessment is part of ongoing relationship between client and therapist; involves moment to moment interaction, awareness of themes affecting authenticity, body movement, feelings, and sensations. Also involves level of awareness, dreams, and projective devices.
Gestalt	Similar to existential, assessment looks for disturbances of sensation, awareness, mobilization, contact, resolution/closures, and withdrawal.
Behavior	Functional assessment identifies problem behavior, antecedents, and consequents; involves defining the target behaviors and terminal goals clearly, specifying the nature and the desired levels of behavior change. Uses overt behavior observations, ratings, tests, physiological measures, and functional analysis.
Cognitive: REBT and Beck's CT	Tracks client's thoughts, feelings, and behaviors in order to determine the nature and type of emotional disturbance; identifies a specific target problem with questionnaires and forms. REBT: finds a clear activating event and a definite consequence. Beck's CT: identifies cognitive distortions.
Reality	Identifies current unsatisfying relationship in client's life, looks at total behavior (doing, thinking, feeling, physiology), and need fulfillment, and what client wants.
Feminist	Deciphers causes of distress, focuses on strengths and skills, sees how specific symptoms or problems are a coping strategy in an oppressive sexist culture; does not see problem from the medical model viewpoint (White and male); begins to name the pain with increasing self-knowledge.

Biopsychosocial/ Health Psychology	Determine interactions of biological, psychological, social, and environmental stressors affecting the client's mental and physical status, consistent with *DSM*; uses motivational interviewing.
Psychopharmacology	The nonprescribing therapist recognizes need for assessment with prescribing provider for psychopharmacological needs.
Eclectic: Multimodal	Assessment is based on adapted model. Categories for dysfunctioning in various modalities. Multimodal uses the structural profile inventory, the multimodal life history, and other tests.
Constructivist: Solution-Focused and Narrative	Solution-focused: Assessment is a collaborative and ongoing process; therapist asks client a number of important questions. Narrative: Assessment begins with asking the client to re-author new and preferred stories for their lives and relationships.
Interpersonal	Assess quality and types of interpersonal relationships for disputes, deficits, role transitions, and losses.
Dialectical Behavior	Identify ineffective action, dysregulated emotions, maladaptive behavioral skills, extreme emotionality, mood-dependent behaviors, lack of trust and legitimacy of own emotions.

TREATMENT TECHNIQUES

Each therapy stresses its unique techniques, yet there is considerable overlap among many therapies. All of the therapies accept that the therapeutic relationship itself is important. It must be satisfactory in order for the client to accept the other techniques. The therapeutic techniques of each model are presented in Table B.5.

Table B.5

Therapeutic Techniques

Model of Psychotherapy	Techniques
Psychoanalysis	Unconscious made conscious, free association, analysis of transference and resistance, interpretation, dream interpretation, awareness, countertransference.
Post-Freudian and Psychodynamic	Similar to psychoanalysis but limited in scope; unconscious made conscious, interpretation, analysis of transference and resistance, dream interpretation, countertransference.
Individual Psychology	Encouragement, increase social interest, ask "the question," spitting in client's soup, collaboration, acting "as if," early memory recollection, interpretation, task setting, Socratic dialogue, dream analysis.
Client Centered	Emphasis on therapy relationship, in the moment, necessary and sufficient conditions for inner exploration/change; genuine, unconditional regard; empathy communicated; psychological contact; move toward experiencing and self-disclosure; reflection; phenomenological approach.

Existential: *Logotherapy*	No specific techniques; any method to enhance therapy, I–Thou dialogic, authentic therapy relationship; phenomenological approach. Examines existential themes to cultivate presence and responsibility to presence. Logotherapy: do a deed, experience a value, endure suffering, Socratic dialogue, dereflection, paradoxical intention, appealing, confrontation, deal with specific problems.
Gestalt	I–Thou dialogic authentic therapy relationship. Uses phenomenological approach and experiments to increase awareness, focusing, language patterns, nonverbal behavior, here and now, enactment, role playing, role reversal, empty chair, confrontation, finishing unfinished business, dream analysis, getting in touch with feelings.
Behavior	Exposure therapies: systematic desensitization, assertiveness training, implosion, eye movement desensitization, and reprocessing. Contingency management therapies: self-direction, self-control, token economies, aversive conditioning. Modeling: stress inoculation, problem solving, social skill training.
Cognitive: REBT and *Beck's CT*	REBT: replace irrational thinking with REBT philosophy, A-B-C-D dispute, psychoeducation, exercises such as self-help form, role play, and homework. Beck's CT: question automatic thoughts, maladaptive assumptions, themes, hypothesis testing, Socratic dialogue, exercises such as activity scheduling, decatastrophize, decenter, redefine, advantages and disadvantages, role playing, guided discovery.
Reality	Build appropriate treatment environment (clients know therapist cares, safe) and execute the treatment procedures of wants, direction, evaluation, and plans that are simple, attainable, measurable, immediate, involved, controlled, committed, and consistent.
Feminist	Gender role and power analyses, assertiveness training, group therapies, political involvement, self-image interventions, egalitarian therapy relationship.
Biopsychosocial/ *Health Psychology*	Stress management, relaxation therapies, mindfulness, visualization, hypnosis, biofeedback, repetitive prayer, yoga, massage, cognitive restructuring, health promotion and prevention, appropriate medical interventions for specific conditions.
Psychopharmacology	Consultation between nonprescribing and prescribing clinicians, psychotropic medications to correct biochemical imbalances in neurotransmitters, matching of particular drugs with particular diagnostic conditions, managing side effects and adverse reactions.
Eclectic: Multimodal	Uses any effective techniques from other models; specific interventions for each individual problem within the seven modalities; also uses tracking and bridging.
Constructivist: *Solution-Focused* *and Narrative*	Solution-focused: miracle question, find exceptions, stress solutions, specify goal, scaling. Narrative: change story with deficient view of skills, competencies, beliefs, values, commitments, and abilities to story with successful view.
Interpersonal	Change way of dealing with interpersonal events related to depression; identify and change interpersonal disputes, deficits, role transitions, and complicated grief; relate symptoms to events; facilitate acceptance of loss of the old role; restore self-esteem; encourage development of social support system, new skills, new role.
Dialectical Behavior	Skills training in individual and group settings, core mindfulness, interpersonal effectiveness skills, emotion regulation skills, distress tolerance.

RESEARCH

The book has emphasized the research status for various psychotherapeutic models. Table B.6 summarizes these research standings.

Table B.6

Research: Past, Current, and Evidence Based

Model of Psychotherapy	Research
Psychoanalysis	Past evidence base consisted of primarily case studies, research on unconscious and defenses; currently, proponents interested in conducting studies of outcome research.
Post-Freudian and Psychodynamic	Jung, Horney, Sullivan, ego analysis, object relations, self psychology, and relational psychoanalysis theories have limited research evidence base—primarily case studies. There is research in related areas, such as attachment behavior. Brief psychodynamic models have more outcome research than traditional analyses or other post-Freudian models. Cochrane Reviews are available. There is current interest and investment in conducting outcome research.
Individual Psychology	Limited research evidence base, based primarily on case studies. There is research in related areas such as birth order, social interest, early memories, and family constellation. Proponents encourage current research.
Client Centered	Rogers encouraged both process and outcome research and pioneered the recording of actual interviews. Quantity of past research is substantial, but Roger's methodology, devised in the 1960s, has been criticized with the advent of current methodologies and evidence-based practice. Current qualitative methods used for studying experiential research show promise.
Existential: Logotherapy	Limited research evidence base, primarily case studies. The therapy questions the value of traditional Western research, but values qualitative research that is compatible with perspective of existential therapy. Specific interventions (e.g., paradoxical intervention) have some evidence-based research support.
Gestalt	Same as existential research. Specific interventions (e.g., empty chair) have research support.
Behavior	High-quality, high-quantity evidence base of research, including randomized controlled studies, single-case research (ABA) demonstrating efficacy and effectiveness. Many forms of interventions classified as empirically supported treatments.
Cognitive: REBT and Beck's CT	High-quality, high-quantity evidence base of research, including large-scale randomized controlled studies. Compared with medication, cognitive therapy fares well. Studies focus on depression and anxiety. A number of interventions classified as empirically supported treatments.
Reality	Limited research but some available in area of substance abuse and offenders. Agrees that future research is important and encourages studies.

Feminist	Limited research evidence base, primarily case studies.
	Philosophically and politically opposed to research consistent with male patriarchy and in favor of research that is consistent with feminist ways of knowing that do not support the status quo.
Biopsychosocial/ Health Psychology	Much research on many forms of intervention, but information is across various disciplines and overlaps within disciplines with other models. Research is encouraged and in need of coordination.
Psychopharmacology	Evidence base is large. Much past research, with randomized controlled trials. Current state of the art research conducted at NIMH.
Eclectic: Multimodal	Limited evidence base of research, with a few controlled studies specifically for multimodal therapy. Eclecticism represents multiple approaches. Not certain that methods selected from effective therapies continue to be effective when applied within the eclectic approach.
Constructivist: Solution-Focused Brief and Narrative	Limited evidence base of research, but these are relatively new therapies. Anecdotal reports of success, but a lack of well-controlled clinical trials; some follow-up studies. Preliminary support implies potential success. Proponents in favor of research into brief therapies and manual for minimal essential elements to include in a study.
Interpersonal	Large evidence base of research available to show effectiveness of IPT from its inception; large-scale randomized control trials. IPT as effective as antidepressants and cognitive behavior therapy. As part of NIMH Collaborative Treatment Study of Depression, IPT may be superior to other psychotherapies. Has been designated as a well-established, empirically supported treatment.
Dialectical Behavior	Evidence to support its efficacy in treating clients with borderline personality disorder including RCTs and independent investigators; effective in reducing problems associated with BPD; designated as a well-established, empirically supported treatment.

REFERENCES

Aanstoos, C., Serlin, I., & Greening, T. (2000). History of Division 32 (Humanistic Psychology) of the American Psychological Association. In D. Dewsbury (Ed.), *Unification through Division: Histories of the divisions of the American Psychological Association,* Vol. V. Washington, DC: American Psychological Association.

Abbass, A. A. (2006). Intensive short-term dynamic psychotherapy of treatment-resistant depression: A pilot study. *Depression and Anxiety, 23*(7), 449–452.

Abbass, A. A., Hancock, J. T., Henderson, J., & Kisely, S. (2006). Short-term psychodynamic psychotherapies for common mental disorders. *Cochrane Database of Systematic Reviews* (online). http://www.cochrane.org/index.htm. Accessed February 2, 2008.

Ablon, J. S. (2004). An open door review of outcome studies in psychoanalysis. *Journal of the American Psychoanalytic Association, 52*(2), 605–609.

Ader, R., & Cohen, N. (1975). Behaviorally conditioned immunosuppression. *Psychosomatic Medicine, 37,* 333–340.

Ader, R., & Cohen, N. (1985). CNS immune system interactions. *Behavioral and Brain Sciences, 8,* 379–384.

Adler, A. (1927) *Understanding human nature.* W. B. Wolfe (trans.). London and New York: Allen & Unwin, Garden City/Star Books.

Adler, A. (1929). *Problems of neurosis.* London: Kegan Paul.

Adler, A. (1930). Individual psychology. In C. Murchison (Ed.), *Psychologies of the 1930s* (pp. 395–406). Worcester, MA: Clark University Press.

Adler, A. (1933). First childhood recollection. *International Journal of Individual Psychology, 11,* 81–90.

Adler, A. (1935). The structure of neurosis. *International Journal for Individual Psychology, 1*(1), 3–12.

Adler, A. (1937). Significance of earliest recollections. *International Journal of Individual Psychology, 3,* 6–11.

Adler, A. (1980). *Cooperation between the sexes: Writings on women, love, and marriage.* H. L. Ansbacher & R. R. Ansbacher (Ed. and Trans.). New York: Aronson.

Adler, A. (1992). *Understanding human nature.* C. Brett (Trans.) from the 1927 ed. Oxford: Oneworld Publications.

Ainsworth, M. D. (1962). The effects of maternal deprivation: A review of findings and controversy in the context of research strategy. In M. D. Ainsworth & R. G. Andry (Eds.), *Deprivation of maternal care.* Geneva: World Health Organization.

Ainsworth, M. D., Blehar, M. C., Waters, E., & Wall, S. (1978). *Patterns of attachment: A psychological study of the strange situation.* Hillsdale, NJ: Erlbaum.

Alexander, F. (1956). Two forms of regression and their therapeutic implications. *Psychoanalytic Quarterly, 23,* 178–198.

Alexander, F., & French, T. (1946). *Psychoanalytic therapy.* New York: Ronald Press.

Alfred Adler Institute. (2007). *Basic principles of classical Adlerian psychology.* http://ourworld.compuserve.com/homepages/HStein/principl.htm. Accessed October 19, 2007.

Allen, K. (2003). Are pets a healthy pleasure? The influence of pets on blood pressure. *Current Directions in Psychological Science, 12*(6), 236–239.

Allen, M. S. (1995). Sullivan's closet: A reappraisal of Harry Stack Sullivan's life and his pioneering role in American psychiatry. *Journal of Homosexuality, 29*(1): 1–18.

Alloy, L. B., Riskind, J. H., & Manos, M. J. (2004). *Abnormal psychology.* New York: McGraw-Hill.

Almond, R. (2006). How do we bridge the gap. Commentary on Luyten, Blatt, and Corveleyn. *Journal of the American Psychoanalytic Association, 54*(2), 611–618.

American Academy of Pediatrics, Committee on Children with Disabilities. (2001). Counseling families who choose complementary and alternative medicine for their child with chronic illness or disability. *Pediatrics, 107*(3), 598–601.

American Health. (2005). *Demographics and spending of health care consumers.* New York: New Strategist's Publications.

American Psychiatric Association. (1994). *Diagnostic and statistical manual of mental disorders* (4th ed.). Washington, DC: Author.

American Psychiatric Nurses Association. (2008). http://www.apna.org/i4a/pages/index.cfm?pageid=3343. Accessed February 19, 2008.

American Psychoanalytic Association. (2007). http://www.apsa.org/ABOUTAPSAA/tabid/55/Default.aspx. Accessed March 8, 2007.

American Psychological Association, Board of Ethnic Minority Affairs. (1988). Task Force on the Delivery of Services to Ethnic Minority Populations. http://www.apa.org/pi/oema/guide.html. Accessed February 1, 2008.

American Psychological Association. (2002). Criteria for evaluating treatment guidelines. *American Psychologist, 57*(12), 1052–1059.

American Psychological Association. (2003). Guidelines on multicultural education, training, research, practice, and organizational change for psychologists. *American Psychologist, 58*(5), 377–402.

American Psychological Association. (2005). *Determination and documentation of the need for practical guidelines.* Washington, DC: Author.

American Psychological Association. (2006). Evidence-based practice in psychology: APA presidential task force on evidence based practice. *American Psychologist, 61*(4), 271–281.

American Psychological Association. (2006). http://www.apa.org/divisions/div30. Accessed January 23, 2008.

American Psychological Association. (2007). *Guidelines for psychological practice with girls and women: A joint task force of APA division 17 and 35.* http://www.apa.org/about/division/girlsandwomen.pdf. Accessed January 31, 2008.

American Psychological Association. (2008). Dissemination Subcommittee of the Committee on Science and Practice. http://www.apa.org/divisions/div12/rev_est/committee.html. Accessed February 2, 2008.

American Psychological Association. (2008). *Guidelines for psychotherapy with lesbian, gay, & bisexual clients.* http://www.apa.org/pi/lgbc/guidelines. html#a. Accessed January 31, 2008.

American Psychological Association. (2008). Society of Clinical Psychology. http://www.apa.org/divisions/div12/homepage.html. Accessed February 2, 2008.

Andersen, B. L. (2003). Biobehavioral outcomes following psychological interventions for cancer patients. *Journal of Consulting and Clinical Psychology, 70,* 481.

Anderson, E. M., & Lambert, M. J. (1995). Short-term dynamically oriented psychotherapy: A review and meta-analysis. *Clinical Psychology Review, 15,* 503–514.

Anderson, E. M., & Lambert, M. J. (2001). A survival analysis of clinically significant change in outpatient psychotherapy. *Journal of Clinical Psychology, 57,* 875–878.

Anderson, G., Carlbring, P., Holmstrong, A., Sparthan, E., Furmark, T., Nilsson, I., Buhrman, M., & Ekselious, L. (2006). Internet based self-help with therapist feedback and in vivo group exposure for special phobia: A randomized controlled trial. *Journal of Consulting and Clinical Psychology, 74*(4), 677–686.

Anderson, M. (2005). Thinking about women: A quarter century's. *Gender and Society, 14,* 437–455.

Anderson, T. (2000). Integrating research and practice in psychotherapy. In S. Soldz & L. McCullogh (Eds.), *Reconciling empirical knowledge and clinical experience* (pp. 83–99). Washington, DC: American Psychological Association.

Ansbacher, H. L. (1990). Alfred Adler, pioneer in prevention of mental disorders. *Journal of Primary Prevention, 11*(1), 37–68.

Ansbacher, H. L., & Ansbacher, R. R. (Eds.). (1956). *The individual psychology of Alfred Adler.* New York: Basic Books.

Ansbacher, H. L., & Ansbacher, R. R. (1967). *The individual psychology of Alfred Adler: A systematic presentation in selections from his writings.* New York: Harper & Row.

Antonuccio, D. O., Ward, C. H., & Tearnan, B. H. (1989). The behavioral treatment of unipolar depression in adult outpatients. In M. Hersen, R. Eisler, & P. M. Miller (Eds.), *Progress in behavior modification* (pp. 152–191). Newbury Park, CA: Sage.

Antony, M., & Roemer, L. (2003). Behavior therapy. In A. Gurman & S. Messer (Eds.), *Essential psychotherapies: Theory and practice* (pp. 182–223). New York: Guilford.

Antony, M. M., & Barlow, D. H. (2002). Specific phobia. In D. H. Barlow (Ed.), *Anxiety and its disorders: The nature and treatment of anxiety and panic* (2nd ed., pp. 380–417). New York: Guilford.

Arlington National Cemetery. (2008). http://www.arlingtoncemetery.net/hssullivan.htm. Accessed March 1, 2008.

Arlow, J. (2005). Psychoanalysis. In R. J. Corsini & D. Wedding (Eds.), *Current psychotherapies* (7th ed., pp. 15–51). Belmont, CA: Brooks/Cole.

Arnkoff, D. B., & Glass, C. R. (1992). Cognitive therapy and psychotherapy integration. In D. Freedheim (Ed.), *History of psychotherapy* (pp. 657–694). Washington, DC: American Psychological Association.

Association for Humanistic Psychology. (2005). http://www.ahpweb.org/aboutahp/whatis.html. Accessed February 2, 2008.

Astin, J. A., Goddard, T. G., & Forys, K. L. (2005). Barriers to the integration of mind–body medicine's perceptions of physicians, residents, and medical students. *Explore, 1*(4), 278–283.

Astin, J. A., Shapiro, S. L., Eisenberg, D. M., & Forys, K. L. (2003). Mind–body medicine: State of science, implications for practice. *Journal of the American Board of Family Practice, 16* (2), 131–147.

Atkinson, D. R., & Hackett, G. (2004). *Counseling diverse populations.* New York: McGraw-Hill.

Austad, C. (1996). *Is long-term psychotherapy unethical in an era of managed health care?* San Francisco: Jossey-Bass.

Austad, C. S., & Hoyt, M. (1992). The managed care movement and the future of psychotherapy. *Psychotherapy, 29*(1), 109–118.

Aveline, M. (2005). Clinical case studies: Their place in evidence-based practice. *Psychodynamic Practice: Individuals, Groups, and Organizations, 11*(2), 133–152.

Ayllon, T., & Azrin, N. H. (1965). The measurement and reinforcement of the behavior of psychotics. *Journal of the Experimental Analysis of Behavior, 8,* 357–383.

Bachrach, J., Galatzer-Levy, R., Skolinoff, A., & Waldron, S. (1991). On the efficacy of psychoanalysis. *Journal of the American Psychoanalytic Association, 39*(4), 871–916.

Ballou, M. (2006). Critical self-reflection necessary but not sufficient. *International Journal of Reality Therapy, 26*(1), 27–28.

Ballou, M., & Mulrooney, C. (2006). Categories and intersections: What feminists should be questioning. *Psychology of Women Quarterly, 30*(3), 323–332.

Bandura, A. (1977). *Social learning theory.* Englewood Cliffs, NJ: Prentice-Hall.

Bandura, A. (1997). *Self efficacy: The exercise of self-control.* New York: Freeman.

Bandura, A. (2000). Social cognitive theory: An agentic perspective. *Annual Review of Psychology, 52,* 1–26.

Bandura, A., & Walters, R. H. (1963). *Social learning and personality development.* New York: Holt, Rinehart & Winston.

Bandura, A., & Walters, R. H. (1969). *Principles of behavior modification.* New York: Holt, Rinehart & Winston.

Barlow, D. H. (Ed). (2001). *Clinical handbook of psychological disorders* (3rd ed.). New York: Guilford.

Barlow, D. H. (2007). *The case of Hope: "Evidence-Based Practice" (EBT) in action. Pragmatic case studies in psychotherapy* [online].

Barlowe, A. R. (1981). Gestalt-antecedent influence or historical accident. *The Gestalt Journal, 4*(2), 35–54.

Basch, C. A. (1982). *Revista de Psicoanálisis, 39*(6), 1001–1008.

Bassuk, E., Schoonover, S., & Gelenberg, A. (1988). *The practitioner's guide to psychoactive drugs* (2nd ed.). New York: Plenum.

Bauman, S., & Waldo, M. (1998). Existential theory and mental health counseling. If it were a snake it would have bitten. *Journal of Mental Health Counseling, 20,* 13–27.

Beahrs, J. O., & Guthrie, T. G. (2001). Informed consent in psychotherapy. *American Journal of Psychiatry, 158,* 4–10.

Bechtoldt, H., Norcross, J. C., Wyckoff, L. A., & Pokrywa, M. L. (2001). Theoretical orientations and employment settings of clinical and counseling psychologists. *The Clinical Psychologist, 5*(1), 3–7.

Beck, A. T. (1991). Cognitive therapy: A 30-year retrospective. *American Psychologist, 46,* 368–375.

Beck, A. T. (2001). Biography of Aaron T. Beck, M. D. In *The Corsini encyclopedia of psychology and behavioral science* (3rd ed., pp. 177–178). New York: Wiley.

Beck, A. T. (2003). Beck Scale for Suicide Ideation. http://mail.med.upenn.edu/~abeck/scaleintro.htm. Accessed February 3, 2008

Beck, A. T. (2005). The current state of cognitive therapy: A 40 year retrospective. *Archives of General Psychiatry, 62*(9), 953–959.

Beck, A. T., & Emery, G. (1985) *Anxiety disorders and phobias: A cognitive perspective.* New York: Basic Books.

Beck, A. T., & Steer, R. A. (1990). *The Beck Anxiety Inventory Manual.* San Antonio: Psychological Corporation.

Beck, A. T., & Weishaar, M. E. (2008). Cognitive therapy. In R. J. Corsini & D. Wedding (Eds.), *Current psychotherapies* (8th ed., pp. 263–294). Belmont, CA: Thomson, Brooks/Cole.

Beck, A. T., Freeman, A., & Associates. (1990). *Cognitive therapy of personality disorders.* New York: Guilford.

Beck, A. T., Kovacs, M., & Weissman, A. (1979). Assessment of suicidal intention: The Scale for Suicide Ideation. *Journal of Consultation and Clinical Psychology, 47,* 343–352.

Beck, A. T., Rush, A. J., Shaw, B. F., & Emery, G. (1979). *Cognitive therapy of depression.* New York: Guilford.

Beck, A. T., Steer, R. A., & Brown, G. K. (1996). The Beck Depression Inventory manual (2nd ed.). San Antonio: Psychological Corporation.

Beck, J. S. (1995). *Cognitive therapy: Basics and beyond.* New York: Guilford.

Beck, J. S. (2004, December 10). *Cognitive therapy for personality disorders.* UCONN Master Therapist Series. Farmington, CT.

Beisser, A. (1970). Paradoxical theory of change. In J. Fagan & I. Sheperd's *Gestalt therapy now.* New York: HarperCollins.

Bellack, A. S., & Hersen, M. (Eds.). (1985). *Dictionary of behavior therapy techniques* New York: Pergamon.

Bem, S. (1983). Gender schema theory and its implications for child development. *Signs, 8*(4), 598–616.

Bem, S. (1993). *The lenses of gender.* New Haven, CT: Yale University Press.

Benson, H. (1975). *The relaxation response.* New York. Morrow.

Berens, M. J. (2006, April 30). Gregoire pledges to reform health-care licensing. *Seattle Times.*

Berg, I. K. (2005).http://www.brief-therapy.org/insoo_handouts.htm. Accessed February 4, 2008.

Berg, I. K., & Miller, S. D. (1992). *Working with the problem drinker: A solution-focused approach.* New York: Norton.

Bergin, A., & Garfield, S. (1986). *Handbook of psychotherapy and behavior change* (3rd ed.). New York: Wiley.

Berman, J. S., Miller, R. C., & Massman, P. J. (1985). Cognitive therapy versus systematic desensitization: Is one treatment superior? *Psychological Bulletin, 97*(33), 451–461.

Bernstein, B., & Hartsell, T. (2000). *The portable ethicist.* New York: Wiley.

Beutler, L. E. (2002). It isn't the size, but the fit: Commentary. *Clinical Psychology: Science and Practice, 9*(4), 434–438.

Beutler, L. E., Consoli, A. J., & Lane, G. (2005). Systematic treatment selection and prescriptive psychotherapy. In J. Norcross & M. Goldfried (Eds.), *Handbook of psychotherapy integration* (2nd ed.). New York: Oxford University Press.

Beutler, L. E., Crago, M., & Arezmendi, T. (1986). Research on therapist variables in psychotherapy. In S. L. Garfield & A. E. Bergin (Eds.), *Handbook of psychotherapy and behavior change* (3rd ed., pp. 257–310). New York: Wiley.

Beutler, L. E., & Harwood, T. M. (2000). *A prescriptive psychotherapy: A practical* guide to *systematic treatment selection.* New York: Oxford University Press.

Beutler, L. E., Malik, M., Alimohamed, S., Harwood, T. M., Talebi, H., Noble, S., & Wong, E. (2004). Therapist variables. In M. J. Lambert (Ed.), *Bergin and Garfield's handbook of psychotherapy and behavior change* (5th ed., pp. 227–307). New York: Wiley.

Bhatara, V., Feil, M., Hoagwood, K., Vitiello, B., & Zima, B. (2004). National trends in concomitant psychotropic medication with stimulants in pediatric visits: Practice versus knowledge. *Journal of Attention Disorders, 7*(4), 217–226.

Binswanger, L. (1958). The case of Ellen West. In R. May, E. Anger, & H. Ellenberger (Eds.), *Existence* (pp. 237–298). New York: Basic Books.

Binswanger, L. (1963). *Being in the world: Selected papers of Ludwig Binswanger.* New York: Basic Books.

Bird, B. (2005). Understanding dream and dreamer: An Adlerian perspective. *Journal of Individual Psychology, 61*(3), 200–216.

Black, R. (2005). Intersections of care: Culturally competent care: Client centered care and the feminist ethic of care. *Work, 24,* 409–422.

Blanck, R., & Blanck, G. (1986). *Beyond ego psychology: Developmental object relations theory.* New York: Columbia University Press.

Blatner, A. (1997). The implications of postmodernism for psychotherapy today. *Journal of individual psychology, 53*(4), 476–482.

Bloch, S. (2004, May 4). An interview with Aaron (Tim) Beck. http://www.acadcmyofct.org/Library/InfoManage/Guide.asp?FolderID-1169. Accessed January 2, 2008.

Blonna, R. (2005). *Coping with stress in a changing world.* New York: McGraw-Hill.

Bloom, B. (1997). *Planned short-term psychotherapy: A clinical handbook.* Boston: Allyn & Bacon.

Bloom, M., & Gullotta, T. P. (2003). Evolving definition of primary prevention. In T. P. Gullotta & M. Bloom (Eds.), *Encyclopedia of primary health care and prevention* (p. 9). New York: Springer.

Blount, A. (1998). *Integrated primary care: The future of medical and mental health collaboration.* New York: Norton.

Bobbitt, B. L. (2006). The importance of professional psychology: A view from managed care. *Professional Psychology: Research and Practice, 37*(6), 590–597.

Bohart, A. C. (1996). The active client: Therapy as self-help. *Journal of Humanistic Psychology, 36*(3), 7–30.

Bohart, A. C. (2003). Person-centered psychotherapy and related experiential approaches. In A. S. Gurman & S. B. Messer (Eds.), *Essential psychotherapies* (pp. 107–149). New York: Guilford.

Bohart, A. C., & Greenberg, L. S. (Eds.). (1997). *Empathy reconsidered: New directions in psychotherapy.* Washington, DC: American Psychological Association.

Bohart, A. C., & Greening, T. (2001). Humanistic psychology and positive psychology. *American Psychologist, 56i*(1), 81–82.

Bohart, A. C., Elliott, R., Greenberg, L. S., & Watson, J. C. (2002). Empathy redux: The efficacy of therapist empathy. In J. Norcross (Ed.), *Psychotherapy relationships that work.* New York: Oxford University Press.

Bohart, A. C., O'Hara, M., & Leitner, L. M. (1998). Empirically violated treatments: Disenfranchisement of humanistic and other psychotherapies. *Psychotherapy Research, 8,* 141–157.

Boone, J. L., & Christensen, J. F. (1997). Stress and disease. In R. E. Feinstein & A. A. Brewer (Eds.), *Primary care psychiatry and behavioral medicine:*

Brief office treatment and management pathways (pp. 265–283). New York: Springer.

Borckardt, J. J., Nash, M. R., Murphy, M. D., Moore, M., Shaw, D., & O'Neil, P. (2008). Clinical practice as natural laboratory for psychotherapy research: A guide to case-based time-series analysis. *American Psychologist, 63*(2), 77–95.

Bornstein, R. (2001). The impending death of psychoanalysis. *Psychoanalytic Psychology, 18,* 3–20.

Bornstein, R. (2005). Reconnecting psychoanalysis to mainstream psychology: Challenges and opportunities. *Psychoanalytic Psychology, 22*(3), 323–340.

Borrell-Carrio, F., Suchman, A. L., & Epstein, R. M. (2004). The biopsychosocial model 25 years later: Principles, practice, and scientific inquiry. *Annals of Family Medicine, 2,* 576–582.

Boss, M. (1962). Anxiety, guilt and psychotherapeutic liberation. *Review of Existential Psychology and Psychiatry, 11*(3), 173–207.

Boss, M. (1963). *Daseinanalysis and psychoanalysis.* New York: Basic Books.

Bowers, T., & Clum, G. A. (1988). Relative contribution of specific and non specific treatment effects: Meta-analysis of placebo controlled behavior therapy research. *Psychological Bulletin, 103,* 315–323.

Bowlby, J. (1973). *Loss.* London: Hogarth Press and the Institute for Psychoanalysis.

Bozarth, J. (1997). Empathy from the framework of client-centered theory and the Rogerian hypothesis. In A. C. Bohart & L. S. Greenberg (Eds.), *Empathy reconsidered: New directions in psychotherapy* (pp. 81–102). Washington, DC: American Psychological Association.

Bozarth, J. (1998). Playing the probabilities of psychotherapy. *Person Centered Practice, 6,* 33–37.

Bozarth, J. (1999). *Person centered therapy: A revolutionary paradigm.* Ross-on-Wye, England: PCCS books.

Bozarth, J. (2001). The art of being in psychotherapy. *Humanistic Psychologist, 29*(1–3), 167–203.

Brabeck, M., & Ting, K. (2000). Feminist ethics: Lenses for examining ethical psychological practice. In M. Brabeck (Ed.), *Practicing feminist ethics in psychology* (pp. 17–37). Washington, DC: American Psychological Association.

Bracke, P. E., & Bugental, J. F. T. (2002). Existential/humanistic psychotherapy. In F. W. Kaslow,

R. F. Massey, & S. D. Massey (Eds.), *Comprehensive handbook of psychotherapy. Volume 3: Interpersonal/ humanistic/existential* (pp. 255–277). Hoboken, NJ: Wiley.

Braithwaite, A. (2002). The personal, the political, third-wave, and postfeminisms. *Feminist Theory, 3*(3), 335–344.

Breitbart, W., Gibson, C., Poppito, S. R., & Berg, A. (2004). Psychotherapeutic interventions at the end of life: A focus on meaning and spirituality. *Canadian Journal of Psychiatry, 49*(6), 366–372.

Breslow, L. (2006). Health measurement I: The third era of health. *American Journal of Public Health, 96*(1), 17–19.

Britzman, M., & Henkin, A. (1992). Wellness and personality priorities: The utilization of Adlerian encouragement strategies. *Individual Psychology: Journal of Adlerian Theory, Research & Practice, 48*(2), 194–202.

Brodly, B. (2006). Client initiated homework and client centered therapy. *Journal of Psychotherapy Integration, 16*(2), 140–161.

Brody, D. S. (2003). Improving the management of depression in primary care: Recent accomplishments and ongoing challenges. *Disease Management Outcomes, 11,* 21–31.

Brown, G. (1988). The farther reaches of Gestalt therapy: A conversation with George Brown. *The Gestalt Journal, 15,* 61–94.

Brown, G. P., Hammen, C. L., Craske, M. G., & Wickens, T. D. (1995). Dimensions of dysfunctional attitudes as vulnerabilities to depressive symptoms. *Journal of Abnormal Psychology, 104,* 431–435.

Brown, L. S. (1994). *Subversive dialogues: Theory in feminist therapy.* New York: Basic Books.

Brown, L. S. (2004). Memories of childhood abuse: Recovered, discovered, and otherwise. In B. J. Cling (Ed.), *Sexualized violence against women and children: A psychology and law perspective.* New York, Guilford.

Brown, L. S. (2005a). Don't be a sheep: How this eldest daughter became a feminist therapist. *Journal of Clinical Psychology: In Session, 61,* 949–956.

Brown, L. S. (2005b). Feminist therapy with psychotherapists. In J. Geller, R Orlinsky, & J. Norcross (Eds.), *Psychotherapy with psycho-therapists.* New York: Oxford University Press.

Brown, L. S. (2005c). Outwit, out-last, out-flirt? The women of reality TV. In E. Cole & J. H. Daniel (Eds.), *Featuring females: Feminist analyses of media.* Washington, DC: American Psychological Association.

Brown, L. S. (2006). Still subversive after all these years: The relevance of feminist therapy in the age of evidence-based practice. *Psychology of Women Quarterly, 30*(1), 15–24.

Brown, L. S., & Mueller, F. A. (2004). Guidelines for treating women in psychotherapy. In G. P. Koocher, J. C. Norcross, & S. S. Hill III (Eds.), *Psychologist's desk reference* (2nd ed., pp. 295–298). New York: Oxford University Press.

Brown, L. S., Riepee, L. E., & Coffey, R. (2005). Beyond color and culture: Feminist contributions to paradigms of human difference. *Women and Therapy, 28*(3-4), 63–92.

Brown, S. R. (1996). Q methodology and qualitative research. *Qualitative Health Research, 6*(4), 561–567.

Brug, J., Conner, M., Harré, N., Kremers, S., McKellar, S., & Whitelaw, S. (2005). The transtheoretical model and stages of change: A critique: Observations by five commentators on the paper by Adams, J. and White, M. (2004). Why don't stage-based activity promotion interventions work? *Health Education Research, 20*(2), 244–258.

Bruns, C. M. (2001). Rising tide: Taking our place as young feminist psychologists. *Women and Therapy, 23*(2), 19–36.

Budman, S. (Ed). (1981). *Forms of brief therapy.* New York: Guilford.

Budman, S. H., & Gurman, A. (1988). *Theory and practice of brief therapy.* New York: Guilford.

Bugental, J. F. T. (1964). The third force in psychology. *Journal of Humanistic Psychology, 4*(1), 19–25.

Bugental, J. F. T. (1965). *The search for authenticity.* New York: Holt, Rinehart & Winston.

Bugental, J. F. T. (1987). *The art of the psychotherapist.* New York: Norton.

Bugental, J. F. T. (1990). Existential–humanistic psychotherapy. In J. K. Zeig & W. M. Munion (Eds.), *What is psychotherapy? Contemporary perspectives* (pp. 189–193). San Francisco: Jossey-Bass.

Bugental, J. F. T., & Kleiner, R. (1993). Existential psychotherapies. In G. Stricker and J. Gold (Eds.), *Comprehensive handbook of psychotherapy integration* (pp. 101–112). New York: Plenum.

Burn, S. M., & Ward, A. Z. (2005). Men's conformity to traditional masculinity and relationship satisfaction. *Psychology of Men & Masculinity, 6*(4), 254–263.

Burns, D. (1990). *The feeling good handbook.* New York. Plume.

Burns, D. (1996). *Feeling good: The new mood therapy.* New York: Guilford.

Burns, D. D., & Spangler, D. L. (2000). Does psychotherapy homework lead to improvements in cognitive-behavioral therapy or does improvement lead to increased compliance? *Journal of Consulting and Clinical Psychology, 68,* 46–56.

Burroughs, V. J., Maxey, R. W., & Levy, R. A. (2002). Racial and ethnic differences in response to medicines: Towards individualized pharmaceutical treatment. *Journal of the National Medical Association, 94*(4), 1–26.

Busch, F. N., & Malin, B. D. (1998). Combining psychopharmacology, psychotherapy, and psychoanalysis. *Psychiatric Times, 19*(5), 5.

Butler, A. C., Chapman, J. E., Forman, E. M., & Beck, A. T. (2006). The empirical status of cognitive behavioral therapy: A review of meta-analyses. *Clinical Psychology Review, 26*(1), 17–31.

Butler, T., Giordano, S., & Neren, S. (1985). Gender and sex-role attributes as predictors of utilization of natural support systems during personal stress events. *Sex Roles, 13*(9-10), 515–524.

Caballo, V. E. (Ed.). (1998). *International handbook of cognitive and behavioral treatments for psychological disorders.* Oxford, England: Pergamon.

Cain, D. J., & Seeman, J. (Eds.). (2001). *Humanistic psychotherapies: Handbook of research and practice.* Washington, DC: American Psychological Association.

Canadian Pediatric Society, Community Pediatric Committee (2005). Management of primary nocturnal enuresis. *Paediatrics and Child Health, 10,* 611–614.

Cannon, W. B. (1932). *The wisdom of the body.* New York: Norton.

Caplan, P. (1983). Woman's issues: New assessments. In J. Robbins & R. J. Siegal. (Eds.), *Women changing therapy* (pp. 51–79). New York: Haworth.

Carich, M. S., & Willingham, W. (1987). Individual psychology. *Individual Psychology: Journal of Adlerian Theory, Research & Practice, 43*(1), 71–78.

Carlson, J. M., & Carlson, J. D. (2000). The application of Adlerian psychotherapy with Asian-Americans. *Journal of Individual Psychology, 56*(2), 214–225.

Carlson, J., Watts, R. E., & Maniacci, M. (2005). *Adlerian therapy: Theory and practice.* Washington, DC: APA Books.

Carlton, P. L. (1983). A primer of behavioral pharmacology. New York: Freeman.

Carroll, L. (1898). *Alice's adventures in wonderland.* London: Macmillan.

Cartwright, D. (2004) The psychoanalytic research interview: Preliminary suggestions. *Journal of the American Psychoanalytic Association, 52*(1), 1–30.

Cashdan, S. (1988). *Object relations therapy: Using the relationship.* New York: Norton.

Cautela, J. R. (1967). Covert sensitization. *Psychological Reports, 20,* 459–468.

Centre for Clinical Effectiveness. (2006). Monash University. http://www.mihsr.monash.org/cce. Accessed October 14, 2007.

Chambless, D. L. (1996). In defense of dissemination of empirically supported psychological interventions. *Clinical Psychology: Science and Practice, 3*(3), 230–235.

Chambless, D. L., & Hollon, S. D. (1998). Defining empirically supported therapies. *Journal of Consulting and Clinical Psychology, 66*(1), 7–18.

Chambless, D. L., & Ollendick, T. H. (2001). Empirically supported psychological interventions: Controversies and evidence. *Annual Review of Psychology, 52,* 685–716.

Champoux, M., Byrne, E., DeLizio, R., & Suomi, S. J. (1992). Motherless mothers revisited: Rhesus maternal behavior and rearing history. *Primates, 33*(2), 251–255.

Chantler, K. (2005). From disconnection to connection: Race, gender, and the politics of therapy. *British Journal of Guidance and Counseling, 33*(2), 239–256.

Chantler, K. (2006). Pittu Laungani in conversation with William West. *British Journal of Guidance and Counseling, 34*(3), 385–389.

Chapman, A. H. (1978). *The treatment techniques of Harry Stack Sullivan.* New York: Brunner/Mazel.

Chesler, P. (1972). *Women and madness.* Garden City, NY: Doubleday.

Chesler, P. (1997). *Women and madness.* New York: Four Walls Eight Windows.

Chodorow, N. (1989). *Feminism and psychoanalytic theory.* New Haven, CT: Yale University Press.

Clark, D. A., Beck, A. T., & Alford, B. A. (1999). *Scientific foundations of cognitive theory and therapy of depression.* New York: Wiley.

Clark, D., Beck, A., & Brown, G. (1989). Cognitive mediation in general psychiatric outpatients: A test of the content-specificity hypothesis. *Journal of Personality and Social Psychology, 56,* 958–964.

Cochrane Collaboration. (2007). The Cochrane library: An introduction. http://www.cochrane.org/reviews. Accessed February 2, 2008.

Cohen, P., & Cohen, J. (1984). The clinician's illusion. *Archives of General Psychiatry, 41,* 1178–1182.

Collins, J. (1976). Applying the Mowrer conditioning device to nocturnal enuresis. *Journal of Pediatric Psychology, 1,* 27–30.

Collins, P. L. (1997). The historical development of reality therapy. *Texas Counseling Association Journal, 25*(2), 50–57.

Comas-Diaz, L. (2006). Cultural variation in the therapeutic relationship. In C. Goodheart, A. Kazdin, & R. J. Sternberg (Eds.), *Evidence-based psychotherapy* (pp. 81–99). Washington, DC: American Psychological Association.

Comas-Diaz, L., & Greene, B. (1994). *Women of color: Integrating ethnic and gender identities in psychotherapy.* New York: Guilford.

Comas-Diaz, L., & Griffith, E. H. (1988). *Clinical guidelines in cross-cultural mental health.* New York: Wiley.

Committee on Bioethics. (1995). Informed consent, parental permission, and assent in pediatric practice: Committee on Bioethics. *Pediatrics, 95*(2), 314–317

Compass, B. E., & Gotlib, I. H. (2002). *Introduction to clinical psychology.* New York: McGraw-Hill.

Cone, J. D. (2001). *Evaluating outcomes: Empirical tools for effective practice.* Washington, DC: American Psychological Association.

Connecticut General Statutes. (2006). State of Connecticut: Chapter 383, Psychologists: Section 20-186.

Contratto, S., & Rossier, J. (2005). Early trends in feminist therapy, theory, and practice. *Private Practice, Women and Therapy, 28*(3-4), 7–26.

Cooper, J. O., Heron, T. E., & Heward, W. L. (2007). *Applied behavior analysis* (2nd ed). Upper Saddle River, NJ: Pearson, Merrill Prentice-Hall.

Corey, G., Corey, M. S., & Callanan, P. (2003). *Issues and ethics in the helping professions* (6th ed.). New York: Brooks/Cole.

Cormier, S., & Nurius, P. S. (2003). *Interviewing and change strategies for helpers: Fundamental skills and cognitive behavioral interventions* (5th ed.). Pacific Grove, CA: Brooks/Cole.

Corrie, S., & Callanan, M. (2002). Therapists beliefs about research and the scientist-practitioner model in an evidence-based health-care climate: A qualitative study. *British Journal of Medical Psychology, 74,* 135–149.

Corrigan, P. W. (1991). Social skills training in adult psychiatric populations: A meta-analysis. *Journal of Behaviour Therapy and Experimental Psychiatry, 22,* 203–210.

Creer, T. L., Holroyd, K. A., Glasgow, R. E., & Smith, T. W. (2004). Health psychology. In A. Bergin & S. Garfield (Eds.), *Handbook of psychotherapy and behavior change* (4th ed.). New York: Wiley.

Creer, T. L., Holroyd, K., Glasgow, R. E., & Smith, T. W. (2004). Health psychology. In M. Lambert (Ed.), Bergin and Garfield's handbook of psychotherapy and behavior change (5th ed., pp. 697–742). New York: Wiley.

Crick, F., & Koch, C. (2002). The problem of consciousness [special issue]. *Scientific American, 12*(1), 10–17.

Criswell, E. (1995). *Biofeedback and somatics.* Novato, CA: Freeperson Press.

Crits-Christoph, P. (1992). The efficacy of brief dynamic psychotherapy: A meta-analysis. *American Journal of Psychiatry, 149,* 151–158.

Crits-Cristoph, P., & Barber, J. (1990). Psychological treatments of personality disorders. In P. E. Nathan & J. M. German (Eds.), *A guide to treatments that work* (2nd ed., pp. 611–623). New York: Oxford University Press.

Cuijpers, P., & Dekker, J. (2005). Psychological treatment of depression: A systematic review of meta-analyses. *Ned Tijdschr, 149*(34), 1892–1897.

Cummings, N. (2007). Personal communication.

Cummings, N. A. (1991). Intermittent therapy throughout the life cycle. In C. S. Austad & W. H. Berman (Eds.), *Psychotherapy in managed health care: The optimal use of time and resources* (pp. 35–46). Washington, DC: American Psychological Association.

Cummings, N. A. (1991). The somaticizing patient. In C. S. Austad & W. Berman (Eds.), *Psychotherapy in managed care: The optimal use of time and resources* (pp. 234–248). Washington, DC: American Psychological Association.

Cummings, N. A. (1995). Impact of managed care on employment and training: A primer for survival. *Professional Psychology: Research and Practice, 26*(1), 10–15.

Cummings, N. A. (2006). Psychology, the stalwart profession, faces new challenges and opportunities. *Professional Psychology, Research, and Practice, 37*(6), 598–605.

Cummings, N. A., Cummings, J. L., & Johnson, J. N. (Eds.). (1997). *Behavioral health care in primary care: A guide for clinical integration* (pp. 3–21). Madison, CT: Psychosocial Press.

Cummings, N., & Cummings, J. (2005). Behavioral interventions for somaticizers within the primary care setting. In N. A. Cummings, W. O'Donohue, & E. Naylor (Eds.), *Psychological approaches to chronic disease management* (pp. 78–97). Reno, NV: Context Press.

Cushman, P. (1992). Psychotherapy to 1992: A historically situated interpretation. In D. Friedheim (Ed.), *History of psychotherapy* (pp. 21–64). Washington, DC: American Psychological Association.

Dalai Lama, (2001). *An open heart.* Boston: Little, Brown.

Dale, M. M., & Hallett, D. G. (2004). *Pharmacology condensed.* Edinburgh: Churchill Livingstone.

Damasio, A. R. (1994). *Descartes' error.* New York: Putnam.

Davanloo, H. (1990). *Intensive short-term dynamic psychotherapy.* New York: Wiley.

Davanloo, H. (2001). *Unlocking the unconscious.* New York: Wiley.

Davis, D. M. (1990). Resistance and transference in intensive short-term dynamic psychotherapy (IS-TDP) and classical psychoanalysis: Similarities and differences—Part II. *International Journal of Intensive Short-Term Dynamic Psychotherapy, 14*(4), 1–24.

Davis, M., Eshelman, E. R., & Mckay, M. (2000). *The relaxation and stress reduction workbook* (5th ed.). Oakland, CA: New Harbinger.

Davis, M., Eshelman, E. R., & McKay, M. (2003). *The relaxation and stress reduction workbook* (5th ed.). Oakland: New Harbinger.

de Shazer, S. (1982). *Patterns of brief family therapy: An ecosystemic approach.* New York: Guilford.

de Shazer, S. (1985). *Keys to solution in brief therapy.* New York: Norton.

de Shazer, S. (1988). *Clues: Investigating solutions in brief therapy.* New York: Norton.

de Shazer, S. (1991). *Putting difference to work.* New York: Norton.

de Shazer, S. (1994). *Words were originally magic.* New York: Norton.

de Shazer, S., Berg, I. K., Lipchik, E., Nunnally, E., Molnar, A., Gingerich, W., et al. (1986). Brief therapy: Focused solution development. *Family Process, 25,* 207–221.

de Shazer, S., Dolan, Y., Korman, H., Trepper, T. S., McCollum, E. E., & Berg, I. K. (2007). More than miracles: The state of the art in solution focused brief therapy. New York: Haworth Press.

Deckert, E. D. (1997). *Psychiatry and behavioral medicine.* Philadelphia: Lippincott-Raven.

DeRubeis, R. J., & Crits-Christoph, P. (1998). Empirically supported individual and group psychological treatments for adult mental disorders. *Journal of Consulting and Clinical Psychology, 57,* 414–419.

DeRubeis, R. J., Gelfand, L. A., Tang, T. Z., & Simons, A. D. (1999). Medications versus cognitive behavior therapy for severely depressed outpatients: Mega-analysis of four randomized comparisons. *American Journal of Psychiatry, 156*(July), 1007–1013.

DeRubeis, R. J., Hollon, S. D., Amsterdam, J. D., Shelton, R. C., Young, P., Saloman, R. M., O'Reardon, J. P., Lovett, M. L., Gladis, M. M., Brown, L., Gallop, R. (2005). Cognitive therapy vs. medication in the treatment of moderate to severe depression. *Archives of General Psychiatry, 62,* 409–416.

Diden, R., Duker, P. C., & Korzilius, H. (1997). Meta-analytic study on treatment effectiveness for problem behaviors with individuals who have mental retardation. *American Journal of Mental Retardation, 101,* 387–399.

DiGiuseppe, R. (1991). A rational emotive model of assessment. In M. E. Barnard (Ed.), *Using rational-emotive therapy effectively: A practitioner's guide* (pp. 151–172). New York: Plenum.

DiGiuseppe, R., & Miller, N. J. (1977). A review of outcome studies on rational emotive therapy. In A. Ellis & R. Grieger (Eds.), *Handbook of rational emotive therapy* (pp. 72–95). New York: Springer.

DiGuiseppe, R. A., Terjesen, M., Rose, R., Doyle, K., & Vadalakis, N. (1998). *Selective abstractions errors in reviewing REBT outcome studies: A review of reviews.* Poster presented at the 106th Annual Convention of the American Psychological Association, San Francisco.

DiMatteo, R. M. (1997). Adherence. In M. D. Feldman & J. F. Christensen (Eds.), *Behavioral medicine in primary care* (pp. 136–140). New York: Lange Medical Book, McGraw-Hill.

Dinnel, D. L., Kleinknecht, R. A., & Tanaka-Matsumi, J. (2002). A cross-cultural comparison of social phobia symptoms. *Journal of Psychopathology and Behavioral Assessment, 24,* 2, 75–84.

Dittman, M. (2003). Psychology's first prescribers. *Monitor on Psychology, 34*(2), 36.

Dobson, K. S. (Ed), (2000). *Handbook of cognitive behavioral therapies* (2nd ed). New York: Guilford.

Dobson, K. S., & Block, L. (1988). Historical and philosophical basis of the cognitive behavioral therapies. In K. Dobson (Ed.), *Handbook of cognitive behavior therapies* (2nd ed., pp. 3–35). New York: Guilford.

Dolan, Y. (2007). Tribute to Insoo Kim Berg, *Journal of Marital and Family Therapy, 33*(2), 129–131.

Dollard, J., & Miller, N. E. (1950). *Personality and psychotherapy: An analysis in terms of learning, thinking, and culture.* New York: McGraw-Hill.

Dolmar, A., & Dreher, H. (1996). *Healing mind, healthy woman.* New York: Henry Holt.

Donaldson, M. S., Yordy, K. D., Lohr, K. N., & Vanselow, N. A. (1996). *Primary care: America's health in a new era.* Washington, DC: National Academy Press.

Donohue, J. M., Cevasco, M., & Rosenthal, M. B. (2007). A decade of direct-to-consumer advertising of prescription drugs. *New England Journal of Medicine, 357*(7), 673–681.

Donovan, J. (2000). *Feminist therapy: The intellectual traditions.* New York: Continuum.

Doran, C. (2003). *Prescribing mental health medication.* New York: Routledge.

Douglas, C. (2005). Analytic psychotherapy. In R. J. Corsini & D. Wedding (Eds.), *Current psychotherapies* (7th ed., pp. 96–129). Belmont, CA: Thomson.

Dreikurs, R., & Grey, L. (1968). *A new approach to discipline: Logical consequences.* New York: Hawthorne.

Dreikurs, R. & Soltz, V. (1964). *Children: The challenge.* New York: Hawthorne/Dutton.

Dreikurs, R., & Soltz, V. (2005). *Children: The challenge.* New York: Putnam-Penguin.

Dreikurs, R., Cassel, P., & Ferguson, E. D. (2004). *Discipline without tears.* Toronto: Wiley.

Dreikurs, R., Grey, L., & Oxford, E. (1968). *Logical consequences: A new approach of discipline.* New York: Meredith.

Dryden, W. (2002a). Rational emotive group therapy. In F. W. Kaslow & T. Patterson, *Comprehensive handbook of psychotherapy: Volume II: Cognitive-behavioral approaches* (pp. 471–493). Hoboken, NJ: Wiley.

Dryden, W. (2002b). *Fundamentals of rational emotive behavior therapy: A training handbook.* London: Whurr.

Dryden, W., & Neenan, M. (2003). *The REBT therapist's pocket companion.* New York: Albert Ellis Institute.

Dryden, W., DiGiuseppe, R., & Neenan, M. (2003). *A primer on rational emotive therapy* (2nd ed.). Champaign, IL: Research Press.

Dubois, J. M. (2006). Frankl's theory of mental disorders. *International Forum for Logotherapy, 29*(2), 81–92.

Dusek, J., Chang, B. H., Zaki, J., Lazar, S. W., Deykin, A., Stefano, G. B., Wohlhueter, A., Hibberd, P., & Benson, H. (2006). Association between oxygen consumption and nitric oxide production during the relaxation response. *Medical Science Monitor, 12*(1), 1–10.

Dusseldorp, E., van Elderen, T., Maes, S., Meulman, J., & Kraaij, V. (1996). A meta-analysis of psychoeducational programs for coronary heart disease patients. *Health Psychology, 18*(5), 41–48.

Eagle, M., & Wolitzky, D. L. (1992). Psychoanalytic theories of psychotherapy. In D. Freedheim (Ed.), *History of psychotherapy: A century of change* (pp. 109–158). Washington, DC: American Psychological Association.

Eagly, A., Diekman, A., & Aspinwall, L. (2003). The malleability of sex differences in response to changing social roles. In L. G. Aspinwall & U. M. Staudinger (Eds.), *A psychology of human strengths: Fundamental questions and future directions for a positive psychology* (pp. 103–115). Washington, DC: American Psychological Association.

Edens, R. M. (1997). The application of choice theory/reality therapy in sports psychology. *International Journal of Reality Therapy, 17*(1), 34–36.

Edwards, D. A., Dattilio, F. M., & Bromley, D. B. (2004). Developing evidence based practice: The role of case-based research. *Professional Psychology: Research and Practice, 35*(6), 589–597.

Edwards, D. L., & Gfroerer, K. P. (2001). Adlerian school-based interventions for children with attention-deficit/hyperactivity disorder. *Journal of Individual Psychology, 57*(3), 210–214.

Elkin, I. (1994). The NIMH treatment of depression, collaborative research program: Where we began and where we are. In A. E. Bergin & S. L. Garfield (Eds.), *Handbook of psychotherapy and behavior change* (4th ed., pp. 114–139). New York: Wiley.

Elkin, I., Gibbons, R. D., Shea, M. T., & Shaw, B. F. (1996). Science is not a trial (but sometimes it can be a tribulation). *Journal of Consulting and Clinical Psychology, 64,* 92–103.

Elkin, I., Shea, M. T., Watkins, J. T., Imber, S. D., Sotsky, S. M., Collins, J. F., Glass, D. R, Pilkonis, P. A., Leber, W. R., Docherty, J. P., Fiester, S. J., & Parloff, M. B. (1989). National Institute of Mental Health Treatment of Depression Collaborative Research Program: General effectiveness of treatments. *Archives of General Psychiatry, 46,* 971–982.

Ellenberger, H. (1970). *The discovery of the unconscious: The history and evolution of dynamic psychiatry.* New York: Basic Books.

Elliott, R. (2000a). *Proposed criteria for demonstrating empirical support for humanistic and other therapies: Working draft.* http://www.experiential-researchers .org/methodology/humanist.html. Accessed October 27, 2007.

Elliott, R. (2000b). Origins of process-experiential therapy: A personal case study in practice-research orientations. In S. Soldz & L. McCullough (Eds.), *Reconciling empirical knowledge and clinical experience* (pp. 17–32). Washington, DC: American Psychological Association.

Elliott, R. (2000c). *Proposed criteria for demonstrating empirical support for humanistic and other therapies.* http://64.233.169.104/search?q=cache: bNf93gizCBAJ:www.experiential-researchers.org/ methodology/Humanist.DOC+Elliott+Proposed+ criteria+for+demonstrating+empirical+support+ for+humanistic+and+other+therapies:+Working+ draft&hl=en&ct=clnk&cd=1&gl=us&ie= UTF-8&client= firefox-a. Accessed February 2, 2008.

Elliott, R. (2001). Hermeneutic single-case efficacy design: An overview. In K. J. Schneider, J. F. T. Bugental, & J. F. Pierson (Eds.), *The handbook of humanistic psychology* (pp. 315–324). Thousand Oaks, CA. Sage.

Elliott, R. (2002). Hermeneutic single case efficacy design. *Psychotherapy Research, 12,* 1–20.

Elliott, R., & Greenberg, L. S. (2002). Process-experiential psychotherapy. In D. J. Cain & J. Seeman (Eds.), *Humanistic psychotherapies: Handbook of research and process* (pp. 57–81). Washington, DC: American Psychological Association.

Elliott, R., Greenberg, L., & Lietaer, G. (2004). Research on experiential therapies. In M. J. Lambert (Ed.), *Bergin and Garfield's handbook of psychotherapy and behavior change* (5th ed., pp. 493–539). New York: Wiley.

Ellis, A. (1987). The impossibility of achieving consistently good mental health. *American Psychologist, 42,* 364–375.

Ellis, A. (2004). *Rational emotive behavior therapy: It works for me. It can work for you.* Amherst, NY: Prometheus.

Ellis, A., & Dryden, W. (1997) *Practice of rational emotive behavior therapy.* New York: Springer.

Ellis, A., & Harper, R. (1997). *A guide to rational living.* New York: Albert Ellis Institute.

Ellis, A., & MacLaren, C. (2005). *Rational emotive behavior therapy: A therapist's guide* (2nd ed.). Atascadero, CA: Impact.

Ellis, A., Gordon, J., Neenan, M., & Palmer, S. (1997). *Stress counseling: A rational emotive approach.* London: Cassell.

Emmelkamp, P. (1994). Behavior therapy with adults. In A. Bergin & S. Garfield (Eds.), *Handbook of psychotherapy and behavior change* (4th ed., pp. 385–442). New York: Wiley.

Emmelkamp, P. (2004). Behavior therapy with adults. In M. J. Lambert (Ed.), *Bergin and Garfield's handbook of psychotherapy and behavior change* (5th ed., pp. 393–446). New York: Wiley.

Engel, G. L. (1977). The clinical application of the biopsychosocial model: A challenge for biomedicine. *American Journal of Psychiatry, 137,* 535–544.

Engel, G. L. (1980). The need for a new new medical model: A challenge for biomedicine. *Science, 196,* 129–136.

Enns, C. Z. (1992). Toward integrating feminist psychotherapy and feminist philosophy. *Professional Psychology: Research and Practice, 23*(6), 453–466.

Enns, C. Z. (1993). Twenty years of feminist counseling and therapy: From naming biases to implementing multifaceted practice. *The Counseling Psychologist, 21,* 3–87.

Enns, C. Z. (1997). *Feminist theories and feminist psychotherapies: Origins, themes, and variations.* New York: Haworth.

Enns, C. Z. (2004). *Feminist theories and feminist psychotherapies: Origins, themes, and diversity* (2nd ed.). New York: Haworth.

Enns, C. Z., & Sinacore, A. L. (Eds.). (2005). *Teaching and social justice.* Washington, DC: American Psychological Association.

Enns, C. Z., Sinacore, A. L, Acevedo, V., Ozge, A., Saba, R., Julier, A. T., Anctil, T. M., Boatwright, K. J., Boyer, M., Byars-Winston, A., Fassinger, R. E., Forrest, L. M., Hensler, N. F., Fassinger, H., Larson, H., Nepomuchno, C. A., & Tao, K. (2005). Integrating multicultural and feminist pedagogies: Personal perspectives on positionality, challenges, and benefits. In C. Z. Enns & A. L. Sinacore (Eds.), *Teaching and social justice.* Washington, DC: American Psychological Association.

Epstein, R. (2001). An interview with Albert Ellis. *Psychology Today,* (January/February), 1–8. http:// psychologytoday.com/articles/pto-20010101-000035 .html. Accessed February 3, 2008.

Epston, D., & White, M. (1992). *Experience, contradiction, narrative & imagination: Selected papers of David Epston & Michael White 1989–1991.* Adelaide, South Australia: Dulwich Centre Publications.

Erikson, E. (1950). *Childhood and society.* New York: Norton.

Erikson, E. (1968). *Identity, youth and crisis.* New York: Norton.

Erikson, E. (1974) *Dimension of a new identity.* New York. Norton, 1974.

Espín, O. M. (1997). *Essays on healing, migration, and sexuality.* Boulder, CO: Westview.

Espin, O. M. (1999). *Women crossing boundaries: A psychology of immigration and the transformation of sexuality.* New York: Routledge.

European Economic and Social Committee, the Committee of the Regions on Equality between Women and Men. (2008). *Report from the Commission to the Council, the European Parliament.* http://ec.europa.eu/employment_social/gender_ equality/docs/2007/com_2007_49_en.pdf. Accessed January 3, 2008.

Evans, K. M., Kincaide, E. A., Marbley, A. F., & Seem, S. R. (2005). Feminism and feminist therapy: Lessons from the past: Hope for the future. *Journal of Counseling Development, 83,* 269–277.

Evers, K. E., Prochaska, J. O., Johnson, J. L., Mauriello, L. M., Padula, J. A., & Prochaska, J. M. (2006). A randomized clinical trial of a population and transtheoretical model–based stress-management intervention. *Health Psychology, 25*(4), 521–529.

Fagan, T. K., & Wise, P. S. (2000). *School psychology: Past, present, and future.* Bethesda, MD: National Association of School Psychologists.

Fairbairn, W. R. D. (1952a). *An object-relations theory of the personality.* New York: Basic Books.

Fairbairn, W. R. D. (1952b). *Endopsychic structure considered in terms of object relationships.* London: Routledge.

Falludi, S. (1999). *Backlash.* New York: Crown.

Feijo de Mello, M., de Jesus Mari, J., Bacaltchuk, J., Verdeli, H., & Neugebauer, R. (2005). A systematic review of research findings on the efficacy of interpersonal therapy for depressive disorders. *European Archives of Psychiatry and Clinical Neuroscience, 255,* 75–82.

Feldman, J. M., & Keltner, N. L. (2005). In N. L. Keltner & D. G. Folks (Eds.), *Psychotropic drugs* (4th ed., pp. 87–93). St. Louis: Elsevier Mosby.

Feldman, R. S. (2005). *Essentials of psychology.* New York: McGraw-Hill.

Feminist Therapy Institute. (2000). *Feminist therapy code of ethics.* Georgetown. ME: Author.

Ferguson, E. D. (1989). Adler's motivational theory: An historical perspective on belonging and the fundamental human striving. *Individual Psychology: Journal of Adlerian Theory, Research & Practice, 45,* 354–361.

Ferguson, E. D. (2001). Adler and Dreikurs: Cognitive-social dynamic innovators. *Journal of Individual Psychology, 57*(4), 324–341.

Fernando, S. (2003). *Cultural diversity: Mental health and psychiatry: The study against racism.* Hove, United Kingdom: Brunner/Routledge.

Feske, U., & Chambless, D. L. (1995). Cognitive behavioral versus exposure only treatment for social phobia: A meta-analysis. *Behavior Therapy, 26,* 695–720.

Fiebert, M. S. (1983). *Ways of growth* (3rd ed.). Lexington, MA: Ginn.

Fisher, C. (2000). Relational ethics in psychological research: One feminist's journey. In M. Brabeck (Ed.), *Practicing feminist ethics in psychology* (pp. 125–139). Washington, DC: American Psychological Association.

Fisher, M. A. (2008). Protecting confidentiality rights: The need for an ethical practice model. *American Psychologist, 63*(1), 1–13.

Fishman, D. B., & Franks, C. M. (1992). *Evolution and differentiation within behavior therapy: A theoretical and epistemological review.* In D. Freedheim (Ed.), *History of psychotherapy* (pp. 159–196). Washington, DC: American Psychological Association.

Fiske, S. T. (2002). What we know about bias and intergroup conflict: The problem of the century. *Current Directions in Psychological Science, 11,* 123–128.

Fleming, M. (1997). Alcohol and substance abuse. In M. D. Feldman & J. F. Christensen (Eds.), *Behavioral Medicine in Primary Care,* (pp. 125–135). New York: Lange Medical Book, McGraw-Hill.

Fochtmann, L. J., McIntyre, S. J., & Hart, C. (2003). Quick reference guides for APA practice guidelines. *Psychiatry Services, 54,* 252.

Follette, W. C., & Beitz, K. (2003). Adding a more rigorous scientific agenda to the empirically supported treatment movement. *Behavior Modification, 27*(3), 369–386.

Follette, W. C., & Houts, A. C. (1996). Models of scientific progress and the role of theory in taxonomy development: A case study of the DSM. *Journal of Consulting and Clinical Psychology, 64,* 1120–1132.

Fotheringham, M. J., & Owen, N. (1999). Applying psychological theories to promote healthy lifestyles. In J. M. Rippe (Ed.), *Lifestyle medicine* (pp. 501–510). Shrewsbury, MA: Blackwell Science.

Fox, V. C., & Langley, W. C. (1994). *Womens's rights in the United States: A documentary history.* New York: Praeger.

Frager, R., & Fadiman, J. (1984). *Personality and personal growth.* New York: Harper & Row.

Frank, J. D., & Frank, J. B. (1991). *Persuasion and healing* (3rd ed.). Baltimore: Johns Hopkins University Press.

Frank, R., McDaniel, S. H., Bray, J. H., & Heldring, M. (Eds.). (2004). *Primary care psychology.* Washington, DC: American Psychological Association.

Frankel, R., & Beckman, H. (2004). The physician-patient relationship. In R. G. Frank, S. H. McDaniel, J. H. Bray, & M. Heldring (Eds.), *Primary care psychology* (pp. 45–61). Washington, DC: American Psychological Association.

Frankl, V. (1959). *Man's search for meaning.* Boston: Beacon.

Frankl, V. (1963). Existential dynamics and neurotic escapism. *Journal of Existential Psychiatry, 4,* 27–42.

Frankl, V. (1965). *The doctor and the soul* (2nd ed.). New York: Knopf.

Frankl, V. (1972). *Man's search for meaning: An introduction to logotherapy.* New York: Beacon.

Frankl, V. (1978). *The unheard cry for meaning.* New York: Simon & Schuster.

Frankl, V. (1992). Preface to the 1972 edition. In V. Frankl, *Man's search for meaning: An introduction to logotherapy* (pp. 11–13). Cutchogue, NY: Buccaneer Books.

Franklin, M. E., & Foa, E. B. (2002). Cognitive behavioral treatments for obsessive compulsive disorder. In P. Nathan & J. M. Gorman (Eds.), *A guide to treatments that work* (pp. 367–386). New York: Oxford University Press.

Freedheim, D. (1992). *History of psychotherapy.* Washington, DC: American Psychological Association.

Freedman, J., & Combs, G. (1996). *Narrative therapy: The social construction of preferred realities.* New York: Norton.

Freese, J., Powell, B., & Steelman, L. L. (1999). Rebel without a cause or effect: Birth order and social attitudes. *American Sociological Review, 64*(2), 207–231.

Freud, A. (1936). *The ego and the mechanisms of defense.* New York: International Universities Press.

Freud, S. (1905). Three essays on sexuality. In J. Strachey et al. (Eds.), *The standard edition of the complete psychological works of Sigmund Freud,* Vol. 7. London: Hogarth.

Freud, S. (1910). Five lectures on psychoanalysis. In J. Strachey et al. (Eds.), *The standard edition of the complete psychological works of Sigmund Freud,* Vol. 11. London: Hogarth.

Freud, S. (1913). On beginning the treatment. In J. Strachey et al. (Eds.), *The standard edition of the complete psychological works of Sigmund Freud,* Vol. 12. London: Hogarth.

Freud, S. (1914). On narcissism. In J. Strachey et al. (Eds.), *The standard edition of the complete psychological works of Sigmund Freud,* Vol. 14. London: Hogarth.

Freud, S. (1914). On the history of the psycho-analytic movement. In J. Strachey et al. (Eds.), The *standard edition of the complete psychological works of Sigmund Freud,* Vol. 14 (pp. 1–66). London: Hogarth.

Freud, S. (1914/1917). *The history of the psychoanalytic movement.* A. A. Brill (Trans.). Translation first published in the *Nervous and Mental Disease Monograph Series* (No. 25). New York: Nervous and Mental Disease Publishing Co.

Friedman, M. (1985). *The healing dialogue in psychotherapy.* New York: Aronson.

Friedman, R. C., Bucci, W., Christian, C., Drucker, P., & Garrison, W. B., III. (1998). Private psychotherapy patients of psychiatrist psychoanalysts. *American Journal of Psychiatry, 155*(12), 1772–1774.

Fukuyama, M. A., & Sevig, T. D. (1999). *Integrating spirituality into multicultural counseling.* Thousand Oaks, CA: Sage.

Gabbard, G. O., Gunderson, J. G., & Fonagy, P. (2002). The place of psychoanalytic treatments within psychiatry. *Archives of General Psychiatry, 59*(6), 505–510.

Garcia–Shelton, L. (2006). Meeting U.S. health care needs: A challenge to psychology. *Professional Psychology: Research and Practice, 37*(6), 676–682.

Garfield, S. (1994). Eclecticism and integration and psychotherapy: Developments and issues. *Clinical Psychology: Science and Practice, 1*(2), 123–137.

Garfield, S. L. (1996). Some problems associated with "validated" forms of therapy. *Clinical Psychology: Science and Practice, 3*(3), 218–229.

Garfield, S. L. (1998). The future and the scientist-practitioner split. *American Psychologist, 53*(11), 1231–1232.

Garfield, S. L., & Bergin, A. E. (1994). Introduction and historical overview. In A. E. Bergin & S. L. Garfield (Eds.), *Handbook of psychotherapy and behavior change* (pp. 3–18). New York: Wiley.

Gaston, L. (1990). The concept of the alliance and its role in psychotherapy: Theoretical and empirical considerations. *Psychotherapy, 27,* 143–153.

Gay, P. (1988). *Freud: A life for our time.* New York: Norton.

Gelenberg, A. J., & Keith, S. (1997). Psychosis. In A. Gelenberg & E. Bassuk (Eds.), *The practitioner's guide to psychoactive drugs* (4th ed., pp. 153–211). New York: Plenum.

Gendlin, E. (2002). Foreword. *Carl Rogers: The quiet revolutionary, an oral history. Carl Rogers and David E. Russell.* Roseville, CA: Penmarin.

Gerber, G. (1996). Gender stereotypes and the change toward greater personal maturity in psychotherapy. In J. C. Chrisler & D. Howard (Eds.), *New direction in feminist psychology: Practice, theory, and research* (pp. 46–58). New York: Springer.

Gilligan, C. (1982). *In a different voice.* Cambridge, MA: Harvard University Press.

Gilman, S. L. (2001). Karen Horney, M. D.: 1885–1952. *American Journal of Psychiatry, 158,* 1205.

Gingerich, W. J., & Eisengart, S. (2000). Solution-focused brief therapy: A review of the outcome research. *Family Process, 39*(4), 477–498.

Glass, C. R., & Arnkoff, D. B. (1992). Behavior therapy. In D. Freedheim (Ed.), *History of psychotherapy* (pp. 587–628). Washington, DC: American Psychological Association.

Glass, C. R., Arnkoff, D. B., & Rodriguez, B. F. (1998). An overview of directions in psychotherapy integration research. *Journal of Psychotherapy Integration, 8*(4), 187–209.

Glasser, W. (1965). *Reality therapy: A new approach to psychiatry.* New York: Harper & Row.

Glasser, W. (1969). *Schools without failure.* New York: Harper & Row.

Glasser, W. (1976). *Positive addiction.* New York: Harper & Row.

Glasser, W. (1985). *Control theory: A new explanation for how we control our lives.* New York: HarperCollins.

Glasser, W. (1988). *Using reality therapy.* New York: Harper & Row.

Glasser, W. (1990). *The quality school.* New York: Harper & Row.

Glasser, W. (1998). *Choice theory: A new psychology of personal freedom.* New York: HarperCollins.

Glasser, W. (2000). *Counseling with choice theory.* New York: HarperCollins.

Glasser, W., & Zunin, L. M. (1979). Reality therapy. In R. Corsini (Ed.), *Current psychotherapies* (2nd ed., pp. 302–339). Itasca, IL: Peacock.

Glines, C. V. (2005). Top secret WWII bat and bird bomber program. *Aviation History, 15*(5), 38–44.

Glinnwater, J. T. (2000). Gestalt therapy: Treatment of the affective self. *The Gestalt Journal, 23*(2), 81–87.

Gloaguen, V., Cottraux, J., Cucherat, M., & Blackburn, I. (1998). A meta-analysis of the effects of cognitive therapy in depressed patients. *Journal of Affective Disorders, 49,* 59–72.

Goin, M. K. (2005). Practical psychotherapy: A current perspective on the psychotherapies. *Psychiatric Services, 56,* 255–257.

Goldfried, M. R., & Davison, G. C. (1994). *Clinical behavior therapy* (exp.). New York: Wiley.

Goleman, D. (1995). *Emotional intelligence.* New York: Bantam.

Goleman, D. (2003). *Destructive emotions: How can we overcome them? A scientific dialogue with the Dalai Lama.* New York: Bantam.

Gordon, N. S. (2000). Researching psychotherapy: The importance of the client's view: A methodological challenge. *The Qualitative Report, 4*(3, 4). http://www. nova.edu/sss/QR/QR4–3/gordon.html.

Gotham, H. J. (2006). Advancing the implementation of evidence-based practices into clinical practice: How do we get there from here? *Professional Psychology, Research and Practice, 37*(6), 606–613.

Gottdiener, W. H. (2007). What psychoanalytic institutes must do to effectively recruit academic clinical psychology researchers to become psychoanalytic candidates. *Psychoanalytic Psychology, 24*(3), 496–502.

Granello, P. F., & Granello, D. H. (1998). Training counseling students to use outcome research. *Counselor Education and Supervision, 37,* 224–237.

Grawe, K., Donati, R., & Bernauer, F. (1998). *Psychotherapy in transition.* Seattle: Hogrefe & Huber.

Gray, G. V., Brody, D. S., & Johnson, D. (2005). The evolution of behavioral primary care. *Professional Psychology, Research and Practice, 36*(2), 123–129.

Gray, S. (1996). Developing practice guidelines for psychoanalysis. *Journal of Psychotherapy, Practice and Research, 5*(3), 213–227.

Gray, S. (2002). Evidence-based psychotherapies. *Journal of the American Academy of Psychoanalysis and Dynamic Therapy, 30*, 3–16.

Greek, R., & Greek, J. (2002). *Specious science*. New York, London: Continuum.

Green, C. (2007). The history of the psychoanalytic movement. In *Classics in the history of psychology: An internet resource*. Toronto, Ontario: York University. http://psychclassics.yorku.ca. Accessed February 2, 2008.

Greenberg, J. (2008). *Comprehensive stress management*. New York: McGraw-Hill.

Greenberg, J. R. (2001). The analyst's participation: A new look. *Journal of the American Psychoanalytic Association, 49*, 417–426.

Greenberg, J. R., & Mitchell, S. A. (1983). *Object relations and psychoanalytic theory*. Cambridge, MA: Harvard University Press.

Greenberg, L., & Paivio, S. C. (1997). *Working with emotions in psychotherapy*. New York: Guilford.

Greenberg, L., & Pascual-Leone, A. (2006). Emotion in psychotherapy: A practice-friendly research review. *Journal of Clinical Psychology: In Session, 62*(5), 611–630.

Greenberg, L., Elliott, R., & Lietaer, G. (1994). Research on experiential therapies. In S. L. Garfield & A. L. Bergin (Eds.), *Handbook of psychotherapy and behavior change* (4th ed., pp. 509–539). New York: Wiley.

Greenberg, L., Rice, L., & Elliott, R. (1993). *Facilitating emotional change: The moment by moment process*. New York: Guilford.

Greenberg, L. S., Watson, J. C., & Lietaer, G. (Eds.). (1998). *Handbook of experiential psychotherapy*. New York: Guilford.

Greene, B., & Croom, G. L. (Eds.). (2000). *Psychological perspectives on lesbian, gay, and bisexual issues*. Thousand Oaks, CA: Sage.

Greenson, R. R. (1965). The working alliance and the transference neurosis. *Psychoanalytic Quarterly, 34*, 155–181.

Greenson, R. R. (1967). *The technique and practice of psychoanalysis*. New York: International Universities Press.

Grey, L. (1998). *Adler: The forgotten prophet*. New York: Praeger.

Grinfeld, M. J. (1999). Texas Supreme Court says there is no duty to warn. *Psychiatric Times, 16*(12), 1.

Gurman, A. S., & Messer, S. B. (2003). Contemporary issues in the theory and practice of psychotherapy: A framework for comparative study. In A. S. Gurman & S. B. Messer (Eds.), *Essential psychotherapies: Theory and practice* (2nd ed., pp. 1–24). New York: Guilford.

Guyatt, G. H., Haynes, R. B., Jaeschke, R. Z., Cook, D. J., Green, L., Naylor, C. D., Wilson, M. C., & Richardson, W. S. (2000a). Users guide to the medical literature: XXV. Evidence-based medicine: Principles for applying users guides to patient care. Evidence Based Medicine Working Group. *JAMA, 284*(10), 1290–1296.

Guyatt, G. H., Meade, M. O., Jaeschke, R. Z., Cook, D. J., & Haynes, R. B. (2000b). Practitioners of evidence-based care. Not all clinicians need to appraise evidence from scratch but all need some skills. *British Medical Journal, 320*(7240), 954–955.

Haaga, D. A., & Davidson, G. C. (1993). An appraisal of rational emotive therapy. *Journal of Consulting and Clinical Psychology, 61*, 215–220.

Habben, C. J. (2005). Life after graduate school in psychology. In R. D. Morgan, T. L. Kuther, & J. Corey, *Insider's advice from new psychologists* (pp. 97–112). New York: Psychology Press.

Hale, N. (2000). American psychoanalysis since World War II. In R. Meninger & J. C. Nemiah, *American psychiatry after World War II* (pp. 73–102). Washington, DC: American Psychiatric Press.

Hale, N. G. (2000). Lay analysis: *Life inside the controversy*: Robert S. Wallerstein. Hillsdale, NJ: Analytic Press, 1988. *Psychoanalytic Psychology, 17*, 414–419.

Hall, C. S., & Lindzey, G. (1985). *Introduction to theories of personality*. New York: Wiley.

Hampton, B. R., & Hulgus, Y. F. (1993). The efficacy of paradoxical strategies: A quantitative review of the research. *Psychotherapy in Private Practice, 12*, 53–72.

Hansel, J., & Damour, L. (2005). *Abnormal psychology*. New York: Wiley.

Harp, D. (1990). *The three minute meditator*. San Francisco: Mind's I Press.

Hartmann, H. (1939). *Ego psychology and the problems of adaptation*. New York: International Universities Press.

Hartmann, H., Kris, E., & Loewenstein, R. M. (1964). *Papers on psychoanalytic psychology*. New York: International Universities Press.

Hauser, S. T. (2006). Studying psychoanalysis. Asking and answering the hard questions. *Journal of the Psychoanalytic Association, 54,* 561–570

Hausmann, R., Tyson, L. D., & Zahidi, S. (2007). *The global gender gap report.* World Economic Forum. http://www.weforum.org/pdf/gendergap/report2007.pdf.

Haw, C. (2000). Psychological perspectives on women's vulnerability to mental illness. In D. Kohen (Ed.), *Women and mental health* (pp. 64–105). London: Routledge.

Haynes, S. N., Leisen, M. B., & Blaine, D. D. (1997). Design of individualized behavioral treatment programs using functional analytic clinical cases. *Psychological Assessment, 9*(4), 334–348.

Health Insurance Portability and Accountability Act (HIPAA). (2006). HIPAA advisory. www.hipaadvisory. com/REGS/HIPAAprimer. htm. Accessed December 18, 2006.

Hefner, R., Rebecca, M., & Oleshansky, B. (1975). Development of sex role transcendence. *Human Development, 18*(3), 143–158.

Heidegger, M. (1927/1975). *The basic problems of phenomenology.* Indianapolis: Indiana University Press.

Heidegger, M. (1996). *Being and time.* J. Stambaugh (Trans.). Albany: SUNY Press.

Hender, K. (2001). *Is gestalt therapy more effective than other therapeutic approaches?* Melbourne: Monash Centre for Clinical Effectiveness: Southern Health, Monash Institute of Health Services Research. http://www.med.monash.edu.au/publichealth/cce; and http://www.gestaltbodymind.co.uk/Gestalt%20therapy%20effectiveness%20comparisons.pdf

Henle, M. (1975). Gestalt psychology and gestalt therapy. *Journal of the History of the Behavioral Sciences, 14,* 23–32.

Heppner, P. P. (2006). The benefits and challenges of becoming cross-culturally competent counseling psychologists. *Counseling Psychologist, 34*(1), 147–172.

Heriot, J. (1983). The double bind: The healing split. In J. H. Robbins & R. J. Siegal (Eds.), *Women changing therapy* (pp. 11–29). New York: Haworth.

Hill, C. E., & Lambert, M. J. (2004). Methodological issues in studying psychotherapy processes and outcomes. In M. J. Lambert (Ed.), *Bergin and Garfield's handbook of psychotherapy and behavior change* (5th ed., pp. 84–135). New York: Wiley.

Hill, C. E. & Nakayama, E. Y. (2000). Client-centered therapy: Where has it been and where is it going?

Special issue: Advances in clinical psychology *Journal of Clinical Psychology, 56(7),* 861–875.

Hill, K. A. (1987). Meta analysis of paradoxical interventions. *Psychotherapy, 24,* 266–270.

Hing, E., Cherry, D. K., & Woodwell, D. A. (2006). *National ambulatory medical care survey: (2004) Summary.* Advance data from vital and health statistics; No. 374. Hyattsville, MD: National Center for Health Statistics. http://www.cdc.gov/nchs.htm.

Hitchcock, S. T. (2004). *Karen Horney: Pioneer of feminine psychology.* New York: Chelsea House.

Hixson, R. (2007). Balancing ethics in an unethical marketplace. *Annals of the American Psychotherapy Association, 10*(2), 43–45.

Hoffman, E. (1996). *The drive for self: Alfred Adler and the founding of individual psychology.* New York: Addison Wesley.

Hoglend, P. (1999). Psychotherapy research: New findings and implications for training and practice. *Journal of Psychotherapy Practice & Research, 8*(4), 257–263.

Holliman, E. C. (2000). Self-management: Instruction and training in choice theory and reality therapy as measured by the Adult Nowicki-Strickland Locus of Control Scale. *Dissertation Abstracts International Section A: Humanities and Social Sciences, 61*(6-A), 2184.

Hollon, S. D. (1999). Allegiance effects in treatment research: A commentary. *Clinical Psychology: Science and Practice, 6,* 107–112.

Hollon, S. D. (1999). Psychotherapy and pharmacotherapy: Efficacy, generalizability, and cost-effectiveness. In N. E. Miller & K. M. Magruder (Eds.), *Cost-effectiveness of psychotherapy: A guide for practitioners, researchers, and policymakers* (pp. 14–25). New York: Oxford University Press.

Hollon, S. D., & Beck, A. (2004). Cognitive behavioral therapies. In M. J. Lambert (Ed.), *Bergin and Garfield's handbook of psychotherapy and behavior change* (5th ed., pp. 447–493). New York: Wiley.

Hollon, S. D., DeRubeis, R. J., Shelton, R. C., Amsterdam, J. D., Saloman, R. M., O'Reardon, J. P., Lovett, M. L., Young, P. R., Haman, K. L., Freemon, B. B., & Gallop, R. (2005). Prevention of relapse following cognitive therapy vs. medication in moderate to severe depression. *Archives of General Psychiatry, 62,* 417–422.

Hollon, S. D., Stewart, M. O., & Strunk, D. (2006). Enduring effects for cognitive behavior therapy in the treatment of depression and anxiety. *Annual Review of Psychology, 57,* 285–315.

Holmer, A. F. (1999). Direct-to-consumer prescription drug advertising builds bridges between patients and physicians. *JAMA, 281*(4), 380–382.

Holmes, T. H., & Rae, R. H. (1967). The social readjustment rating scale. *Journal of Psychosomatic Research, 11,* 213–218.

Holmshaw, J., & Hillier, S. (2000). Gender and culture: A sociological perspective to mental health problems in women. In D. Kohen (Ed.), *Women and mental health* (pp. 39–64). London: Routledge.

Holt, R. R. (1989). *Freud reappraised: A fresh look at psychoanalytic theory.* New York: Guilford.

Horner, R. H., Carr, E. G., Halle, J., McGee, G., Odom, S., & Wolery, M. (2005). The use of single-subject research to identify evidence-based practice in special education. *Exceptional Children, 71*(2), 165–179.

Horney, K. (1937). *The neurotic personality of our time.* New York: Norton.

Horney, K. (1939). *New ways in psychoanalysis.* New York: Norton.

Horney, K. (1942). *Self-analysis.* New York: Norton.

Horney, K. (1945). *Our inner conflicts.* New York: Norton.

Horney, K. (1950). *Neurosis and human growth.* New York: Norton.

Horney, K. (1966). *New ways in psychoanalysis.* New York: Norton.

Horney, K. (1968). *Self-analysis.* New York: Norton.

Horrigan, B., & LeTourneau, M. (2003). News briefs. *Alternative Therapies, 9*(5), 20–21.

Houts, A. C., Liebert, R. M., & Padawer, W. (1983). A delivery system for the treatment of primary enuresis. *Journal of Abnormal Child Psychology, 11*(4), 513–519.

Howard, K. I., Kopta, S. M., Krause, M. S., & Orlinsky, D. E. (1986). The dose-effect relationship in psychotherapy [Special issue]. *American Psychologist, 41,* 159–164.

Howard, K. I., Moras, K., Brill, P. L., Martinovich, Z., & Lutz, W. (1996). Evaluation of psychotherapy: Efficacy, effectiveness, and patient progress. *American Psychologist, 51,* 1059–1064.

Hoyt, M. (1988). On time in brief therapy. In R. Wells & V. Ginaetti (Eds.), *Handbook of the brief psychotherapies* (pp. 115–143). New York: Plenum.

Hoyt, M. (1994). *Constructive therapies.* New York: Guilford. http://www.nova.edu/sss/QR/QR4-3/gordon.html.

Humanist manifesto I. (1933). http://www.americanhumanist.org. Accessed February 2. 2008.

Humanist manifesto II. (1973). http://www.americanhumanist.org. Accessed February 2, 2008.

Hunt, M. (1993). *The story of psychology.* New York: Doubleday.

Hurley, D. (2004). *Get over it! Stop whining.* http://www.nytimes.com/2004/05/04/health/psychology/04PROF. html.

Hutchinson, G. (2005). A logotherapy enhanced our EBT: An integration of discovery and reason. *Journal of Contemporary Psychotherapy, 35*(2), 145 155.

Hyatt, R. (1977). Karen Horney (1885–1952): A tribute. *Journal of Marital and Family Therapy, 3*(4), 39–43.

Ingram, J. K., & Hinkle, J. S. (1990). Reality therapy and the scientist practitioner approach: A case study. *Journal of Reality Therapy, 10,* 54–58.

Institute of Medicine. (2001). *Crossing the quality chasm: A new health care system for the 21st century.* Washington, DC: National Academy Press.

International Psychoanalytic Association. (2008). http://www.ipa.org.uk. Accessed February 2, 2008.

Iveson, C. (2005, October 13). Obituary: Steve de Shazer. *The Guardian.*

Ivker, R. S., Anderson, R. A., & Trivieri, L. (1999). *The complete self-care guide to holistic medicine.* East Rutherford, NJ: Tarcher/Putnam.

Jacobs, L. (1996). Shame in the therapeutic dialogue. In R. Lee & G. Wheeler (Eds.), *The voice of shame.* San Francisco: Jossey-Bass.

Jacobs, L. (1998). *Dialogue and paradox: In training with Lynne Jacobs, the dialogue maven.* http://www.g-gej.org/2-1/jacobs. html. Accessed February 2, 2008.

Jacobson, E. (1938). *Progressive relaxation.* Chicago: University of Chicago Press.

Jahoda, M. (1977). *Freud and the dilemmas of psychology.* Lincoln: University of Nebraska Press.

Jarrett, R. B. (1990). Psychosocial aspects of depression and the role of psychotherapy. *Journal of Clinical Psychiatry, 51*(6, Suppl.), 26–25.

Johnson, P., Smith, A. J., & Nelson, M. D. (2003). Predictors of social interest in young adults. *Journal of Individual Psychology, 59,* 281–292.

Jones, E. (1953). *The life and work of Sigmund Freud. Vol. One: The formative years.* New York: Basic Books.

Julien, R. M. (2001). *A primer of drug action* (9th ed.). New York: Freeman.

Kabat-Zinn, J. (1990). *Full catastrophe living.* New York. Delacorte.

Kabat-Zinn, J. (1992). *Full catastrophe living: Using the wisdom of your body and mind to face stress, pain, and illness.* New York: Dell.

Kaiser, C. (1995). An interview with Kurt Adler on his 90th birthday at the Adler Institute of Zurich, Winterthur, Switzerland. http://ourworld. compuserve.com/homepages/hstein/adler. htm.

Kalin, N. (2002). The neurobiology of fear [special issue]. *Scientific American, 12*(1), 72–81.

Kaplan, D. M., Grados, M. A., & Reiss, A. L. (1998). Attention deficit and developmental disorders. In S. J. Enna & J. T. Coyle (Eds.), *Pharmacological management of neurological and psychotic disorders* (pp. 137–176). New York: McGraw-Hill.

Kaschak, E. (Ed.). (2001). *The next generation: Third wave feminist psychotherapy*. Binghamton, NY: Haworth.

Katz, D., Williams, A., Girard, C., Goodman, J., Comerford, B., Behrman, A., & Bracken, M. (2003). The evidence base for complementary and alternative medicine: Methods of evidence mapping with application to CAM. *Alternative Therapies, 9*(4), 22–30.

Kazdin, A. (2002). Psychosocial treatments for conduct disorder in children and adolescents. In P. E. Nathan & J. M. Gorman (Eds.), *A guide to treatments that work* (2nd ed., pp. 57–87). New York: Oxford University Press.

Kazdin, A. (2003). *Evidence based psychotherapies for children and adolescents*. New York: Guilford.

Kazdin, A. E. (1977). *The token economy*. New York: Plenum.

Kazdin, A. E. (1994). Psychotherapy for children and adolescents. In A. E. Bergin & S. L. Garfield (Eds.), *Handbook of psychotherapy and behavior change* (4th ed., pp. 543–594). New York: Wiley.

Kazdin, A. E. (2001). *Behavior modification in applied settings* (6th ed.). Pacific Grove, CA: Brooks/Cole.

Kazdin, A. E. (2008). Evidence-based treatment and practice: New opportunities to bridge clinical research and practice, enhance the knowledge base, and improve patient care. *American Psychologist, 63*(3), 146–159.

Kazdin, A. E., & Weis, J. R. (1998). Identifying and developing empirically supported child and adolescent treatments. *Journal of Consulting and Clinical Psychology, 66,* 19–36.

Kellogg, S. (2004). Dialogical encounters: Contemporary perspectives on "chairwork" in psychotherapy. *Psychotherapy: Theory, Research, Practice and Training, 42,* 310–320.

Kelly, G. (1955). *The psychology of personal constructs*. New York: Norton.

Keltner, N. L., & Folks, D. G. (2005). *Psychotropic drugs* (4th ed.). St. Louis: Elsevier Mosby.

Kendall, P. C., Holmbeck, G., & Verduin, T. (2004). Methodology, design, and evaluation in psychotherapy research. In M. J. Lambert (Ed.), *Bergin and Garfield's handbook of psychotherapy and behavior change* (5th ed., pp. 16–43). New York: Wiley.

Kenkel, M. B. (2006). Professional psychology: Expanding its discoveries, reach, and impact. Professional Psychology: Research and Practice, *37*(6), 587–589.

Kenkel, M. B., DeLeon, P. H., Mantell, E. O., & Steep, A. E. (2005). Divided no more: Psychology's role in integrated health care. *Canadian Psychology, 46*(4), 189–202.

Kepner, J. I. (1987). *Body process: A gestalt approach to working with body in psychotherapy*. New York: Gestalt Institute of Cleveland Press.

Kernberg, O. (2004). Rewards, dangers, findings, and attitudes in psychoanalytic research. *Canadian Journal of Psychoanalysis, 12*(2), 178–194.

Kernberg, O. (2006). The pressing need to increase research in and on psychoanalysis. *International Journal of Psychoanalysis, 87*(4), 919–926.

Kernberg, O. F. (1976). *Object relations theory and clinical psychoanalysis*. New York: Aronson.

Keshen, A. (2006). A new look at existential psychotherapy. *American Journal of Psychotherapy, 60*(3), 285–298.

Kessler, R. C., Berglund, P., Demler, O., Jin, R., Merikangas, K., & Walters, A. E. (2005). Lifetime prevalence and age of onset distributions of DSM-IV disorders in the national comorbidity survey replication. *Archives of General Psychiatry, 62,* 593–602.

Khan, N., Bower, P., & Rogers, A. (2007). Meta-synthesis of qualitative studies of patient experience. *British Journal of Psychiatry, 191,* 206–211.

Kim, J. U. (2006). The effect of bullying prevention program on responsibility and victimization of bullied children in Korea. *International Journal of Reality Therapy, 26*(1), 4–8.

King, M., Sibbald, B., Ward, E., Bower, P., Lloyd, M., Gabbay, M., & Byford, S. (2000). Randomized controlled trial of non-directive counseling, cognitive-behavior therapy and usual general practitioner care in the management of depression as well as mixed anxiety and depression in primary care. *Health Technology Assessment, 4*(19).

Kirchner, M. (2000). Gestalt therapy: An overview. *Gestalt, 4*(3). http://www.g-gej.org.

Kirk, S. A., & Kutchins, H. (1996). The selling of DSM: The rhetoric of science in psychiatry. *Social Problems and Social Issues, 3*(2), 168–171.

Kirsch, B. (1987). Evolution of consciousness raising groups. In C. M. Brody (Ed.), *Women's therapy groups* (pp. 43–66). New York: Springer.

Kirschenbaum, H. (2004). Carl Rogers' life and work: An assessment on the hundredth anniversary of his birth. *Journal of Counseling and Development,* (winter), 116.

Kirschenbaum, H., & Jourdan, A. (2005). The current status of Carl Rogers and the person-centered approach. *Psychotherapy, 42,* 37–51.

Klein, D. F., & Rowland, L. P. (1996). *Current psychotherapeutic drugs.* New York: Bruner/Mazel.

Klein, M. (1975). *Envy and gratitude and other works.* New York: Delta.

Klein, M. J., & Elliott, R. (2006). Client accounts of personal change in process—experiential psychotherapy: A methodologically pluralistic approach. *Psychotherapy Research, 16*(1), 91–105.

Kleinke, C. L. (1994). *Common principles of psychotherapy.* Pacific Grove, CA: Brooks.

Kleinman, C. S. (2006). Ethical drift: When good people do bad things. *JONA's Healthcare Law, Ethics, and Regulation, 8*(3), 72–76.

Klerman, G., Weissman, M. M., Rounsaville, B., & Chevron, E. (1984). *Interpersonal psychotherapy of depression.* New York: Basic Books.

Knight, R. P. (1941). Evaluation of the results of psychoanalytic therapy. *American Journal of Psychiatry, 98,* 434–447.

Kohut, H. (1971). *The analysis of the self: A systematic approach to the psychological treatment of narcissistic personality disorders.* New York: International Universities Press.

Kohut, H., & Wolf, E. S. (1978). The disorders of the self in their treatment: An outline. *International Journal of Psychoanalysis, 59,* 413–425.

Kok, G., & Schaalma, H. (2004). Using theory in psychological interventions. In S. Michie & C. Abraham (Eds.), *Health psychology in practice* (pp. 20–229). Malden, MA: Blackwell.

Kopp, R. R. (2003). Toward a developmental theory of lifestyle and social interest in the first three years of life. *Journal of Individual Psychology, 59*(4), 437–451.

Koss, M., & Shiang, J. (1994). Research on brief psychotherapy. In A. Bergin & S. Garfield (Eds.), *Handbook of psychotherapy and behavior change* (4th ed., pp. 664–700). New York: Wiley.

Krasner, L. (1971). Behavior therapy. *Annual Review of Psychology, 22,* 483–532.

Krasner, L. (1990). History of behavior modification. In A. S. Bellack, M. Hersen, & A. E. Kazdin (Eds.), *International handbook of behavior modification and therapy* (2nd ed., pp. 3–26). New York: Plenum.

Krupnick, J. L. Sotsky, S. M., Elkin, I., Simmens, S., Moyer, J., Watkins, J., & Pilkonis, P. A. (1996). The role of the therapeutic alliance in psychotherapy and pharmacotherapy outcome: Findings in the National Institute of Mental Health treatment of depression collaborative research program *Journal of Consulting and Clinical Psychology, 64,* 532–539.

Ksir, C., Hart, C. L., & Ray, O. (2008). *Drugs, society, and human behavior.* New York: McGraw-Hill.

Kukathis, C. (2002). Is feminism bad for multiculturalism? *Public Affairs Quarterly, 5*(2), 83–98.

Lachman, F. M. (1993). Self psychology: Origins and overview. *British Journal of Psychotherapy, 10,* 226–231.

Lafond, B. (2000). Glasser's reality therapy approach to relationships: Validation of a choice theory basic needs scale. *Dissertation Abstracts International Section B: The Sciences and Engineering, 60*(7-B), 3615.

Lambert, M. J. (2001). Psychotherapy outcome and quality improvement: Introduction to the special section on client assessment. *Journal of Consulting and Clinical Psychology, 67,* 285–289.

Lambert, M. J. (Ed.). (2004). *Bergin and Garfield's handbook of psychotherapy and behavior change* (5th ed.). New York: Wiley.

Lambert, M. J., & Bergin, A. E. (1994). The effectiveness of psychotherapy. In A. E. Bergin & S. L. Garfield (Eds.), *Handbook of psychotherapy and behavior change* (4th ed., pp. 143–189). New York: Wiley.

Lambert, M. J., Bergin, A. E., & Garfield, S. L. (2004). Introduction and historical overview. In M. J. Lambert (Ed.), *Bergin and Garfield's handbook of psychotherapy and behavior change* (5th ed., pp. 3–15). New York: Wiley.

Lambert, M. J., Garfield, S. A., & Bergin, A. E. (2004). Overview, trends and future issues. In M. J. Lambert (Ed.), *Bergin and Garfield's handbook of psychotherapy and behavior change* (5th ed., pp. 805–821). New York: Wiley.

Lambert, P., & Ogles, B. M. (2004). The efficacy and effectiveness of psychotherapy. In M. J. Lambert (Ed.), *Bergin and Garfield's handbook of psychotherapy and behavior change* (5th ed., pp. 139–193). New York: Wiley.

Lampert, R. (2006). The case for going gentle. http://www .gestalt.org/gentle.htm. Accessed February 2, 2008.

Landrine, H., & Klonoff, E. A. (1997). *Discrimination against women: Prevalence, consequences, remedies.* Thousand Oaks, CA: Sage.

Lange, D. E., & Julien, R. M. (1998). Integration of drugs and psychological therapies in treating mental and behavior disorders. In R. M. Julien (Ed.), *A primer of drug action* (pp. 429–465). New York: Freeman.

Längle, A., & Sykes, B. M. (2006). Viktor Frankl—advocate for humanity: On his 100th birthday. *Journal of Humanistic Psychology, 46*(1), 36–47.

Lantz, J. (2006). *Existential family therapy: Using the concepts of Victor Frankel:* New York: Aaronson.

Latner, J. (1992). The theory of gestalt therapy. In E. C. Nevis (Ed.), *Gestalt therapy perspectives* (pp. 253–262). Cleveland: Gestalt Institute of Cleveland Press.

Latner, J. (2005a). *Boundary disturbances.* http://pgti. org/gestalt/dream_theroy. html.

Latner, J. (2005b). *Character, psychopathology and development.* http://pgti.org/gestalt/dream_ theroy. html.

Latner, J. (2005c). *Dream theory.* http://pgti.org/gestalt/ dream_theroy. html.

Law, D. R. (2004). A choice theory perspective on Taekwondo. *International Journal of Reality Therapy, 24* (1), 13–18.

Lazarus, A. (1973). On assertive behavior: A brief note. *Behavior Therapy, 4,* 697–699.

Lazarus, A. (1976). *Multimodal behavior therapy.* New York: Springer.

Lazarus, A. (1993). Tailoring the therapeutic relationship, or being an authentic chameleon. *Psychotherapy, 30,* 404–407.

Lazarus, A. (1997). *Brief but comprehensive psychotherapy: The multimodal way.* New York: Springer.

Lazarus, A. (2005). Multimodal therapy. In J. Norcross & M. Goldfried (Eds.), *Handbook of psychotherapy integration* (2nd ed.). New York: Oxford University Press.

Lazarus, A. A. (1963). The results of 126 cases of severe neurosis. *Behavior Research and Therapy, 1,* 69–79.

Lazarus, A. A. (1971). *Behavior therapy and beyond.* New York: McGraw-Hill.

Lazarus, A., & Abramovitz, A. (2004). A multimodal behavioral approach to performance anxiety. *Journal of Clinical and Psychology/In Session, 60*(8), 831–840.

Lazarus, A., & Lazarus, C. (2005). The multimodal life history inventory. In P. E. Koocher & J. C. Norcross

(Eds.), *Psychologist's desk reference* (2nd ed.). New York: Oxford University Press.

Lazarus, A., & Messer, S. B. (1991). Does chaos prevail? An exchange on technical eclecticism and integration. *Journal of psychotherapy integration, 1,* 143–158.

Lazarus, R. S., & Cohen, J. B. (1977). Environmental stress. In I. Altman & J. F. Wohlwill (Eds.), *Human behavior and the environment: Current theory and research.* New York: Plenum.

Lazarus, R. S., & Folkman, S. (1984). *Stress, appraisal, and coping.* New York: Springer.

Lazarus, R. S., & Launier, R. (1978). Stress related transactions between person and environment. In. L. A. Pervin & M. Lewis (Eds.), *Internal and external determinants of behavior* (pp. 287–321). New York: Plenum.

Leichsenring, F., & Leibing, E. (2003). The effectiveness of psychodynamic psychotherapy and cognitive behavior therapy in the treatment of personality disorders: A meta-analysis. *American Journal of Psychiatry, 160,* 1223–1231.

Leichsenring, F., Biskup, J., & Kreische, R. (2005). The Göttingen study of psychoanalytic therapy: First results. *International Journal of Psychoanalysis, 86*(2), 433–455.

Leichsenring, F., Rabung, S., & Leibing, E. (2004). The efficacy of short-term psychodynamic psychotherapy and specific psychiatric disorders: A meta-analysis. *Archives of General Psychiatry, 61,* 1208–1216.

Levant, R.F. (2003). The new psychology of men. *Professional Psychology: Research and Practice, 27*(3), 259–265.

Levant, R. F. (2005). Graduate education in clinical psychology for the twenty-first century: Educating psychological health care providers. *Journal of Clinical Psychology, 61*(9), 1087–1090.

Levinsky, N. (1998). Truth or consequences. *New England Journal of Medicine, 338*(13), 913–915.

Levy, R. L., & Richey, C. A. (1988). Measurement and research design. In E. A. Blechman & K. D. Brownell (Eds.), *Handbook of behavioral medicine for women* (pp. 421–438). New York: Pergamon.

Liff, Z. A. (1992). Psychoanalysis and dynamic techniques. In D. Freedheim (Ed.), *History of psychotherapy: A century of change* (pp. 571–586). Washington, DC: American Psychological Association.

Linden, W. (1973, August). Practicing of meditation by school children and their levels of field independence—dependence, test anxiety, and reading achievement. *Journal of Consulting and Clinical Psychology, 41*(1), 139–143.

Lindsley, O. R. (1956). Operant conditioning methods applied to research in chronic schizophrenia. *Psychiatric Research Reports, 5,* 118–139.

Lindsley, O. R., Skinner, B. F., & Solomon, H. C. (1953). *Studies in behavior therapy.* Waltham, MA: Metropolitan State Hospital.

Linehan, M. (1999). Borderline personality disorder: Costs, course, and treatment outcomes. In N. E. Miller & K. M. Magruder (Eds.), *Cost-effectiveness of psychotherapy: A guide for practitioners, researchers, and policymakers* (pp. 291–305). New York: Oxford University Press.

Linehan, M. M. (1993a). *Cognitive-behavioral treatment of borderline personality disorder.* New York: Guilford.

Linehan, M. M. (1993b). Skills training manual for treatment of borderline personality disorder. New York: Guilford.

Linnenberg, D. (1999). Moral education and choice theory/reality therapy: An initial examination. *International Journal of Reality Therapy, 19*(1), 52–55.

Linnenberg, D. (2006). Thoughts on reality therapy from a pro-feminist perspective. *International Journal of Reality Therapy, 26* (1), 23–26.

Lipsitt, D. R. (2001). Consultation-liaison psychiatry and psychosomatic medicine: The company they keep. *Psychosomatic Medicine, 63*(6), 896–909.

Lo, H.-T., & Fung, K. P. (2003). Culturally competent psychotherapy: Transcultural psychiatry [special issue]. *Canadian Journal of Psychiatry, 48*(3), 161–170.

Lochman, J. E., & Wells, K. C. (2002). The coping power program at the middle school transition: Universal and indicated prevention effects. *Psychology of Addictive Behaviors, 16,* 540–554.

Lohr, J. M., Tolin, D. F., & Lilienfeld, S. O. (1998). Efficacy of eye movement desensitization and reprocessing: Implications for behavior therapy. *Behavior Therapy, 29*(1), 123–156.

London, P. (1964). Group for the advancement of psychiatry. *Psychological Critiques, 9*(11), 442–443, 446–448.

London, P. (1964). *Modes and morals of psychotherapy.* New York: Holt, Rinehart & Winston.

Lotz, A. (2003). Communicating third-wave feminism and new social movements: Challenges for the next century of feminist endeavor. *Women and Language, 26*(1), 2.

Luborsky, L., Diguer, L. Seligman, D. A., Rosenthal, R., Krause, E. D., Johnson, S., Halperin, G., Bishop, M., Berman, J., & Schweizer, E. (1999). The researchers own therapy allegiances: A "wild card" in comparisons of treatment efficacy. *Clinical Psychology: Science and Practice, 6,* 95–106.

Luborsky, L., German, R. E., Diguer, L., Berman, J. S., Kirk, D., Barrett, M. S., & Luborsky, E. (2004). Is psychotherapy good for your health? *American Journal of Psychotherapy, 58*(4), 386–405.

Lukas, E., & Hirsch, B. Z. (2002). Logotherapy. In F. W. Kaslow, R. F. Massey, & S. D. Massey (Eds.), *Comprehensive handbook of psychotherapy. Vol. 3. Interpersonal/humanistic/existential* (pp. 333–356). Hoboken, NJ: Wiley.

Luthe, W. (1962). Method, research, application of autogenic training. *American Journal of Clinical Hypnosis, 5,* 17–23.

MacInnes, D. (2004). The theories underpinning rational emotive behavior therapy: Where's the supportive evidence? *International Journal of Nursing Studies, 41*(6), 685–695.

Magnavita, J. (2002). Psychodynamic approaches to psychotherapy: A century of innovations. In F. Kaslow & J. Magnavita, *Comprehensive handbook of psychotherapy: Psychodynamic/object relations* (pp. 1–12). New York: Wiley.

Mahler, M. (1968). *On the human symbiosis of the vicissitudes of individuation.* New York: International Universities Press.

Mahoney, M. J. (1988). Constructive metatheory: Basic features and historical foundations. *International Journal of Personal Construct Psychology,* (1), 1–35.

Mahrer, A. R. (1996). *The complete guide to experiential psychotherapy.* New York: Wiley.

Mahrer, A. R. (2005). Experiential psychotherapy. In R. Corsini & D. Wedding, (Eds.), *Current psychotherapies* (pp. 439–474). Belmont, CA: Brooks/Cole.

Malan, D. (1976). *The frontiers of brief therapy.* New York: Plenum.

Malin, A. (1966). Predictive identification of the therapeutic process. *International Journal of Psychoanalysis, 47,* 26–31.

Malley, J., Beck, M., Tavra, V. K., Feric, M., & Conway, J. (2003). Student perception of their schools: An international perspective. *International Journal of Reality Therapy, 223* (1), 4–11.

Mallott, R. L., Whalley, D., & Mallott, M. (1997). *Elementary principles of behavior.* Englewood Cliffs, NJ: Prentice-Hall.

Maniacci, M. P., & Sackett-Maniacci, L. A. (2002). The use of *DSM-IV* in treatment planning: An Adlerian view. *The Journal of Individual Psychology, 58*(4), 389–397.

Mann, J. (1973). *Time limited psychotherapy.* Cambridge, MA: Harvard University Press.

March, J. S. (2002). Combining medication and psychosocial treatments: An evidence-based medicine approach. *International Review of Psychiatry, 14,* 155–163.

Marcus, P. (1998). Classical Adlerian theory and practice. In P. Marcus & A. Rosenberg (Eds.), *Psychoanalytic versions of the human condition: Philosophies of life and their impact on practice.* New York: New York University Press.

Marecek, J. (2005). Female violence against intimate partners [special issue]. *Psychology of Women Quarterly, 29*(3), 339–340.

Markowitz, J. C. (2005, May). Letter to the editor. *Psychotherapy and Eclecticism Psychiatric Service, 56,* 612.

Markowitz, J. C., Leon, A. C., Miller, N. L., Cherry, S., Clougherty, K. F., & Villalobos, L. (2005). Rater agreement on interpersonal psychotherapy problem areas. *Psychotherapy Practice and Research, 9,* 131–135.

Martell, C. R., & Land, T. (2002). Cognitive-behavioral therapy with gay and lesbian couples. In F. W. Kaslow & T. Patterson (Eds.), *Comprehensive handbook of psychotherapy, Volume II: Cognitive-behavioral approaches* (pp. 451–468). Hoboken, NJ: Wiley.

Martin, G. M., & Pear, J. (2007). *Behavior modification* (8th ed.). Englewood Cliffs, NJ: Prentice-Hall.

Martinez, J. (2000). *An overview of the drug approval process: FDA overview.* http//findarticles.com/p/articles/mi_m0EXV/is_8_/ai_9010882.

Masling, J. (2003). Stephen A. Mitchell, relational psychoanalysis, and empirical data. *Psychoanalytic Psychology, 20,* 587–608.

Maslow, A. (1969). *Motivation and personality* (2nd ed.) New York: Harper & Row.

Maslow, A. H. (1970). New introduction: Religions, values, and peak-experiences. *Journal of Transpersonal Psychology, 2*(2), 83–90.

Masson, J. M. (1990). *The final analysis: The making and the unmaking of a psychoanalyst.* New York: Addison Wesley.

Masson, J. M. (1992). *The assault on truth: Freud's suppression of the of the seduction theory.* New York: HarperCollins.

Matarazzo, J. D. (1982). Behavioral health's challenge to academic, scientific, and professional psychology. *American Psychologist, 37,* 1–14.

Matlin, M. (1996). *The psychology of women* (3rd. ed.). New York: Harcourt Brace College.

Mattes, R. (2005). Spiritual need one: Spiritual development: The aging process: A journey of lifelong spiritual formation. *Journal of Religion, Spirituality and Aging, 17*(3–4), 55–72.

May, R. (1951). *The meaning of anxiety.* New York: Ronald Press.

May, R. (1953). *Man's search for himself.* New York: Dell.

May, R. (1955). *The meaning of anxiety.* New York: Ronald.

May, R. (1967). *Psychology and the human dilemma.* Princeton, NJ: Van Nostrand.

May, R., & Yalom, I. (2005). Existential psychotherapy. In R. J. Corsini & D. Wedding (Eds), *Current psychotherapies* (7th ed., pp. 269–298). Belmont, CA: Brooks/Cole.

May, R., Angel, E., & Ellenberger, H. (Eds.). (1958). *Existence.* New York: Basic Books.

McCall, R. (1983). *Phenomenological psychology.* Madison: University of Wisconsin Press.

McIntosh, P. (1989). White privilege: Unpacking the invisible knapsack. *Peace and Freedom,* (July/August), 10–12.

McKinlay, J. B. (1996). Some contributions from the social system to gender inequalities in heart disease. *Journal of health and Social Behavior, 37*(March), 1–26.

McQueen, D. V. (2002). Strengthening the evidence bias for health promotion. *Health Promotion International, 16* (3), 262–268.

McQueen, D. V., & Anderson, L. M. (2004). Using evidence to assess the effectiveness of health promotion programs: A few fundamental issues. *Promotion and Education,* (1), 11–6, 49.

Meichenbaum, D. (1974). Stress instructional training: A cognitive prosthesis for the aged. *Human Development, 17,* 273–280.

Meichenbaum, D. (1977). *Cognitive behavior modification: An integrative approach.* New York: Plenum.

Meichenbaum, D. (1985). *Stress inoculation training.* New York: Pergamon.

Meichenbaum, D. (1993). Stress inoculation training: A 20 year update. In P. M. Lehrer & R. L. Woolfool

(Eds.), *Principles and practice of stress management* (2nd ed., pp. 373–406). New York: Guilford.

Meichenbaum, D. H., & Deffenbacher, J. L. (1988). Stress inoculation training. *Counseling Psychologist, 16,* 69–90.

Meichenbaum, D. H., & Goodman, J. (1971). Training impulsive children to talk to themselves: A means of developing self-control. *Journal of Abnormal Psychology,* 77(2), 115–126.

Mellman, T. A., Miller, A. L., Weissman, E. M., Crismon, M. L., Essock, S. L., & Marder, S. R. (2001). Evidence-based pharmacologic treatment for people with severe mental illness: A focus on guidelines and algorithms. *Psychiatric Services, 52*(5), 619–625.

Mendelowitz, E., & Schneider, K. (2008). Existential therapy. In R. J. Corsini & D. Wedding (Eds.), *Current psychotherapies* (pp. 295–328). Belmont, CA: Thomson, Brooks/Cole.

Meninger, R. W., & Nemiah, J. C. (2000). *American psychiatry after World War II (1944–1994).* Washington, DC: American Psychiatric Press.

Messer, S. B. (2004). Evidence based practice: Beyond empirically supported treatments. *Professional Psychology: Research and Practice, 35,* 580–588.

Messer, S. B. (2005). A critical examination of belief structures in integrative and eclectic psychotherapy. In J. C. Norcross, & M. R. Goldfried (Eds.), *Handbook of psychotherapy integration* (pp. 130–165). New York: Basic Books.

Messer, S. B., & Warren, C. S. (1995). *Models of brief psychodynamic therapy: A comparative approach.* New York: Guilford.

Meyer, J. S., & Quenzer, L. F. (2005). *Psychopharmacology: Drugs, the brain, and behavior.* Sunderland, MA: Sinauer.

Meyers, L. (2006). Psychologists and psychotropic medications. *Monitor on Psychology,* 37(6), 46–47.

Miklowitz, D. J. (2001). Bipolar disorder. In D. H. Barlow (Ed.), *Clinical handbook of psychological disorders* (3rd ed., pp. 523–561). New York: Guilford.

Miller, J. B. (1976/1986). *Toward a new psychology of women.* Boston: Beacon.

Miller, J. B. (1979). *Toward a new psychology of women.* Boston: Beacon.

Miller, J. B. (1991). How psychoanalytic thinking lost its way in the hands of men: The case for feminist psychotherapy. *British Journal of Guidance & Counseling,* 19(1), 93–103.

Miller, J. J., Fletcher, K., & Kabat-Zinn, J. (1995). Three-year follow-up and clinical implications of a mindfulness meditation-based stress reduction intervention in the treatment of anxiety disorders. *General Hospital Psychiatry, 17*(3), 192–200.

Miller, R. C., & Berman, J. S. (1983). The efficacy of cognitive behavior therapies: A quantitative review of the research evidence. *Psychological Bulletin, 94*(1), 39–53.

Miller, W. R., & Rollnick, S. (2002) *Motivational interviewing: Preparing people for change* (2nd ed.). New York: Guilford.

Mio, S., Barker-Hackett, L., & Tumambing, J. (2006) *Multicultural society: Understanding our diverse communities.* New York: McGraw-Hill.

Monte, C. E. (1987). *Beneath the mask: An introduction to theories of personality.* New York, Holt, Rinehart & Winston.

Moradi, B., Subich, J. C., & Phillips, J. C. (2002). Revisiting feminist identity development: Theory, research, and practice. *The Counseling Psychologist, 30*(1), 6–43.

Morgan, A. (2008). *What is narrative therapy?* From Dulwich Centre Narrative Therapy Library and Bookshop: http://www.dulwichcentre.com.au/alicearticle.html. Accessed February 3, 2008.

Mosak, H. (1989). Adlerian psychotherapy. In R. J. Corsini (Ed.), *Current psychotherapies* (pp. 65–116). Itasca, IL: Peacock.

Mosak, H. (2005). Adlerian psychotherapy. In R. Corsini & D. Wedding (Eds.), *Current psychotherapies* (7th ed., pp. 53–95). Belmont, CA: Thomson, Brooks/Cole.

Mosak, H., & Dreikurs, R. (1967). The life tasks III. The fifth life task. *Journal of Individual Psychology, 5,* 16–22.

Mosak, H., & Maniacci, M. (1999). *A primer of Adlerian psychology.* Philadelphia: Brunner/Mazel.

Moss, D. (1999). Carl Rogers, the person centered approach, and experiential therapy. In D. Moss (Ed.), *The humanistic and transpersonal psychology: A historical and biographical sourcebook* (pp. 41–48). Westport, CT: Greenwood.

Mowrer, O., & Mowrer, W. (1938). Enuresis: A method for its study and treatment. *American Journal of Orthopsychiatry, 8,* 436–459.

MTA Cooperative Group. (1999). Moderators and mediators of treatment response for children with attention-deficit/ hyperactivity disorder. *Archive of General Psychiatry, 56,* 1088–1096.

Murphy, L. (1997). Efficacy of reality therapy in the schools: A review of the research from 1980–1995. *Journal of Reality Therapy, 16*(2), 12–20.

Murphy, L. R. (1996). Stress management in work settings: A critical review of the health effects. *American Journal of Health Promotion, 11*(2), 112–135.

Najarian, D., & Werz, H. (2006). Alcohol and the law in Connecticut: A practical guide for parents. Department of Mental Health and Addiction Services, State of Connecticut. www.prevention.works.ct.com.

Narayan, U. (1997). *Dislocating cultures: Identities, traditions, and third-world feminism.* New York: Routledge.

National Association of Cognitive Behavior Therapists. (NACBT). (2004). http://www.nacbt.org/whatiscbt.htm.

National Center for Complementary and Alternative Medicine. (2008). http://nccam.nih.gov/health/whatiscam. Accessed April 20, 2008

National Center for Health Statistics. (2004). http://www.cdc.gov/nchs/howto/w2w/w2welcom.htm. Accessed January 20, 2008.

National Organization for Women. (2007). http://www.now.org. Accessed May 4, 2007.

Neimeyer, R. A., & Bridges, S. (2003). Postmodern approaches to psychotherapy. In A. Gurman & S. Messer (Eds.), *Essential psychotherapies* (2nd ed., pp. 272–316). New York: Guilford.

Nelson, R. O., & Hayes, S. C. (1986). The nature of behavioral assessment. In R. O. Nelson & S. C. Hayes (Eds.), *Conceptual foundations of behavioral assessment* (pp. 3–41). New York: Guilford.

Nemiah, J. C. (2000). A psychodynamic view of psychosomatic medicine. *Psychosomatic Medicine, 62,* 299–303.

Nezu, A. M. (1986). Efficacy of a social problem solving therapy approach for unipolar depression. *Journal of Consulting and Clinical Psychology, 54,* 196–202.

Nielson, K. (2001) *Un-American womanhood: Antiradicalism, antifeminism, and the first red scare.* Columbus: Ohio State University Press.

Nietzel, M. T., Russell, R. L. Hemmings, K. A., & Getzer, M. L. (1987). The clinical significance of psychotherapy for unipolar depression: A meta-analytic approach to social comparison. *Journal of Consulting and Clinical Psychology, 55,* 156–161.

Nolen-Hoeksama, L. (2006). *Abnormal psychology* (4th ed.). New York: McGraw-Hill.

Norcross, J. C. (Ed.). (2001). Empirically supported therapy relationships: Summary report of the Division 29 Task Force. *Psychotherapy, 38*(4).

Norcross, J. C. (Ed.). (2002). *Psychotherapy relationships that work: Therapist contributions and responsiveness to patient needs.* New York: Oxford University Press.

Norcross, J. C., & Goldfried, M. R. (Eds.). (2005). *Handbook of psychotherapy integration* (2nd ed.) New York: Oxford University Press.

Norcross, J. C., Beutler, L. E., & Levant, R. F. (Eds.). (2005). *Evidence based practice in mental health: Debate and dialogue on the fundamental questions.* Washington, DC: American Psychological Association.

Norcross, J. C., Karpiak, C. P., & Lister, K. M. (2005). What's an integrationist? Self identified and (occasionally) eclectic psychologists. *Journal of Clinical Psychology, 61,* 1587–1594.

Oberst, U. E., & Stewart, A. E. (2002). *Adlerian psychotherapy: An advanced approach to individual psychology.* London: Routledge.

O'Connell, D. (1997). Behavior change. In M. D. Feldman & J. F. Christensen (Eds.), *Behavioral medicine in primary care* (pp. 12–135). New York: Lange Medical Book, McGraw-Hill.

O'Leary, K. D., & Wilson, G. T. (1987). *Behavior therapy: Application and outcome* (2nd ed.). Englewood Cliffs, NJ: Prentice-Hall.

O'Neil, M. (2004). The international debate on the importance of the effectiveness of health promotion: Where does it come from? *Promotion and Education,* (1), 6–10, 49.

Offen, K. (2000). *European feminism: 1700–1950.* Stanford, CA: Stanford University Press.

Okin, S. M. (1998). Feminism and multiculturalism: Some tensions. *Ethics, 108,* 661–684.

Okin, S. M. (2002). Mistresses of their own destiny: Group rights, gender, and realistic rights of exit. *Ethics, 112,* 205–230.

Orlinsky, D. E., & Howard, K. I. (1986). Process and outcome research in psychotherapy. In S. L. Garfield & A. E. Bergin (Eds.), *Handbook of psychotherapy and behavior change* (3rd ed.). New York: Wiley.

Orlinsky, D. E., Ronnestad, M. H., & Willutzki, U. (2004). Fifty years of psychotherapy process-outcome research: Continuity and change. In M. J. Lambert (Ed.), *Bergin and Garfield's handbook of psychotherapy and behavior change* (5th ed., pp. 307–389). New York: Wiley.

Pagoto, S. L., Spring, B., Elliott, J. C., Mulvaney, S., Coutu, M. F., & Ozakinci, G. (2007). Barriers and facilitators of evidence-based practice perceived by behavioral science health professionals. *Journal of Clinical Psychology, 63*(7), 695–705.

Paivio, S. C., & Greenberg, L. S. (1995). Resolving unfinished business: Efficacy of experiential psychotherapy using the empty-chair dialogue. *Journal of Consulting and Clinical Psychology, 63,* 419–425.

Palmatier, L. (1996). Freud defrauded while Glasser defrauded: From pathologizing to talking solutions. *Journal of Reality Therapy, 16*(1), 75–94.

Paris, J. (2005). *The fall of an icon: Psychoanalysis and academic psychiatry.* Toronto: University of Toronto Press.

Passer, M. W., & Smith, R. E. (2004). *Psychology: The science of mind and behavior* (3rd ed.). New York: McGraw-Hill.

Patterson, C. H. (1984). Empathy, warmth, and genuineness in psychotherapy: A review of reviews. *Psychotherapy, 21*(4), 431–438.

Patterson, C. H. (1986). *Theories of counseling and psychotherapy* (4th ed.). New York: Harper & Row.

Patterson, C. H. (2000). Winds of change for client centered counseling. In C. H. Patterson (Ed.), *Understanding psychotherapy: Fifty years of client-centered theory and practice.* Ross-on-Wye, England: PCCS Books.

Paul, H. A. (2004). Issues and controversies that surround recent texts on empirically supported and empirically based treatments. *Child and Family Behavior Therapy, 26*(3), 37–51.

Pavlovich-Danis, S. (1999, October 4). Ethnicity and culture vary medicinal effects. *Nursing Spectator,* 18–19.

Payne, M. (2006). *Narrative therapy: An introduction for counselors* (2nd ed.). London: Sage.

Penn, M. L., & Wilson, L. (2003). Mind, medicine and metaphysics: Reflections on the reclamation of the human spirit. *American Journal of Psychotherapy, 57*(1), 18–31.

Perls, F. (1970). Four lectures. In J. Fagan & I. Shepherd (Eds.), *Gestalt therapy now.* Palo Alto, CA: Science and Behavior Books.

Perls, F. S. (1942/1992). *Ego, hunger and aggression: The beginning of gestalt therapy.* New York: Gestalt Journal Press.

Perls, F. S. (1969a). *Gestalt therapy verbatim.* Highland, NY: Gestalt Journal Press.

Perls, F. S. (1969b). *In and out of the garbage pail.* Lafayette, CA: Real People Press.

Perls, F. S. (1973/1976). *The gestalt approach and eyewitness to psychotherapy.* Palo Alto, CA: Science and Behavior Books.

Perls, F. S., Hefferline, R. F., & Goodman, P. (1951/1994). *Gestalt therapy: Excitement and growth in the human personality.* New York: Julian.

Perls, L. (1976). Comments on new directions. In E. W. L. Smith (Ed.), *The growing edge of gestalt psychology.* New York: Brunner/Mazel.

Perls, S. (1993). Frederick Perls: A son's recollections. Talk given at celebration of the centennial of the birth of Frederick Perls, Fifteenth Annual Conference on the Theory and Practice of Gestalt Therapy. April 23, 1993, at the Hotel du Parc in Montreal. Quebec, Canada and published in the Gestalt Journal on line http://www.gestalt.org/Stephen.htm.

Perry, H. S. (1982). *Psychiatrist of America: The life of Harry Stack Sullivan.* Cambridge: Belknap.

Peterson, D. (1992). The doctor of psychology degree. In D. Friedham, *History of psychotherapy: A century of change* (pp. 829–849). Washington, DC: American Psychological Association.

Pettus, A. (2006). Psychiatry by prescription. *Harvard Magazine,* (July–August), 37–38.

Phillips, J. (2003). Philosophical and ethical issues in psychiatry. *Current Opinion in Psychiatry, 16*(6), 685–689.

Phillips, L. (1985a). *A guide for therapists and patients to short-term psychotherapy.* Springfield, IL: Thomas.

Phillips, L. (1985b). *Psychotherapy revised: New frontiers in research and practice.* Hillsdale, NJ: Erlbaum.

Piper, W. E. (2004). Implications of psychotherapy research for psychotherapy training. *Canadian Journal of Psychiatry, 49*(4), 221–228.

Polster, M. (1987). Gestalt therapy. In J. K. Zeig (Ed.), *The evolution of psychotherapy* (pp. 312–325). New York: Brunner/Mazel.

Polster, M., & Polster, E. (1973). *Gestalt therapy integrated.* New York: Brunner/Mazel.

Polster, M., & Polster, E. (1990). Gestalt therapy. In J. K. Zeig & W. M. Munion (Eds.), *What is psychotherapy? Contemporary perspectives* (pp. 103–107). San Francisco: Jossey-Bass.

Pomerantz, A. M. (2005). Increasing informed consent: Discussing distinct aspects of psychotherapy at different points in time. *Ethics and Behavior, 15*(4), 351–360.

Poppen, R. (1998). Joseph Wolpe 1915–1997. *Journal of Behavior Therapy and Experimental Psychiatry, 29*(3), 189–191.

Powers. W. (1973). *Behavior: The control of perception.* Hawthorne, NY: Aldine.

Poyrazli, S. (2003). Validation of Rogerian therapy in the Turkish culture: A cross cultural perspective. *Journal of Humanistic Counseling, Education & Development, 42*(1), 107–115.

Preston, J. (2007). *Quick reference guide to psychotropic medications.* www.PsyD-fx.com. Accessed July 15, 2007.

Preston, J., & Johnson, J. (2002). *Clinical psychopharmacology made ridiculously simple.* Miami: Medmaster.

Preston, J., O'Neal, J. H., & Talaga, M. C. (2005) *Handbook of clinical psychopharmacology for therapists.* Oakland: New Harbinger.

Prilleltensky, I. (1992). Humanistic psychology, human welfare and the social order. *Journal of Mind and Behaviour, 13*(4), 315–327.

Prins, B. (2006). Mothers and Muslims, Sisters and sojourners: The contested boundaries of feminine citizenship. In . K. Davis, M. Evans, & J. Lorber (Eds.), *Handbook of gender and women's studies* (pp. 234–251). Thousand Oaks, CA: Sage.

Prochaska, J. O., & DiClemente, C. C. (1984). *The transtheoretical approach: Crossing the traditional boundaries of therapy.* Homewood, IL: Dow Jones-Irwin.

Prochaska, J. O., & Norcross, J. C. (2003). *Systems of psychotherapy: A transtheoretical analysis* (5th ed.). Pacific Grove, CA: Brooks/Cole.

Prochaska, J. O., & Norcross, J. C. (2007). *Systems of psychotherapy: A transtheoretical approach* (6th ed.). Belmont, CA: Brooks/Cole.

Prochaska, J. O., DiClemente, C. C., & Norcross, J. C. (1992). In search of how people change: Applications to addictive behaviors. *American Psychologist, 47,* 1102.

Prochaska, J. O., DiClemente, C. C., & Norcross, J. C. (2003). *Social psychology of health.* New York: Psychology Press.

Purton, C. (2002). Person-centered therapy without the core conditions. *Counseling and Psychotherapy Journal, 12*(2), 6–9.

Puskar, K. R. (2007). The nurse practitioner role in psychiatric nursing. *Online Journal of Issues in Nursing.* http://www.nursingworld.org/MainMenuCategories/ANAMarketplace/ANAPeriodicals/OJIN/TableofContents/Volume/No1aJune/NursePractitionerRole. aspx.

Quinn, S. (1987). *A mind of her own: The life of Karen Horney.* New York: Summit Books.

Quintana, S., & Minami, T. (2006). Guidelines for meta-analyses of counseling psychology research. *The Counseling Psychologist, 34*(6), 839–877.

Rabinowitz, P. M. (1999). Psychosocial aspects of primary care: Theoretical models of practice. In R. E. Feinstein & A. A. Brewer (Eds.), *Primary care psychiatry and behavioral medicine: Brief office treatment and management pathways* (pp. 1–13). New York: Springer.

Rachman, S. (2000). Obituary: Joseph Wolpe. *American Psychologist, 55*(4), 431–432.

Rachor, R. E. (1995). An evaluation of the First Step PASSAGES domestic violence program. *Journal of Reality Therapy, 14*(2), 29–36.

Radtke, L., Sapp, M., & Farrell, W. (1997). Reality therapy: A meta-analysis. *International Journal of Reality Therapy, 17*(1), 4–9.

Raskin, N. J. (1952). An objective study of the locus-of-evaluation factor in psychotherapy. In W. Wolfe & J. A. Pecker (Eds.), *Success in psychotherapy* (pp. 143–162). New York: Grune & Stratton.

Raskin, N. J., & Rogers, C. R. (1989). Person-centered therapy. In R. Corsini & D. Wedding (Eds.), *Current psychotherapies* (4th ed.). Itasca, IL: Peacock.

Raskin, N. J., & Rogers, C. R. (2005). Person-centered therapy. In R. Corsini & D. Wedding (Eds.), *Current psychotherapies* (7th ed., pp. 141–186). Belmont, CA: Thomson, Brooks/Cole.

Raskin, N. J., Rogers, C. R., & Witty, M. C. (2008). Client-centered psychotherapy. In R. J. Corsini & D. Wedding (Eds.), *Current psychotherapies* (8th ed., pp. 141–182). Belmont, CA: Thomson, Brooks/Cole.

Rebecca, M., Heffner, R., & Oleshansky, B. (1976). A model of sex-role transcendence. In A. G. Kaplan & J. P. Bean (Eds), *Beyond sex role stereotypes: Readings toward a psychology of androgyny* (pp. 90–97). Boston: Little, Brown.

Regestein, Q. R. (2000). Psychiatrists view of managed care and the future of psychiatry. *General Hospital Psychiatry, 22*(2), 97–106.

Rehm, L. P. (1984). Self-management therapy for depression. *Advances in Behavior Research and Therapy, 6*(2), 83–98.

Reinecke, M. A., Ryan, N. E., & DuBois, D. L. (1998). Cognitive-behavioral therapy of depression and depressive symptoms during adolescence: A review and meta-analysis. *Journal of the American Academy of Child and Adolescent Psychiatry, 37,* 1006–1007.

Rennison, N. (2001). *Freud and psychoanalysis.* Manchester, England: Pocket Essentials.

Reynolds, S., & Richardson, P. (2000). Evidence based practice and psychotherapy research. *Journal of Mental Health, 9*(3), 257–267.

Rezentes, W. (1996). *Ka lama kukui: Hawaiian psychology: An introduction.* Honolulu: AAlii Books.

Rice, L., & Greenberg, L. S. (1992). Humanistic approaches to therapy. In D. K. Freedheim (Ed.), *History of psychotherapy* (pp. 197–224). Washington, DC: American Psychological Association.

Richards, D. A. J. (2005). *The case for gay rights: From Bowers to Lawrence and beyond.* Lawrence: University Press of Kansas.

Richards, G. (1997). *Race, racism and psychology: Towards a reflexive history.* London: Routledge.

Riemsma, R. P., Pattenden, J., Bridle, C., Snowden, A., Mather, L., Watt, I. S., & Walker, A. (2003). Systematic review of the effectiveness of stage based interventions to promote smoking cessation. *British Medical Journal, 326*(31 May), 1175–1177.

Rietschlin, J. (1998). Voluntary association membership and psychological distress. *Journal of Health and Social Behavior, 39*(4), 348–355.

Riger, S. (1992). Epistemological debates, feminist voices. *American Psychologist, 47*(6), 730–740.

Rioch, M. J. (1986). Fifty years at the Washington School of Psychiatry. *Psychiatry, 49,* 33–44.

Riordan, R. J., & Wilson, L. S. (1989). Bibliotherapy: Does it work? *Journal of Counseling and Development, 67*(9), 292.

Robbins, A. D. (1989). Harry Stack Sullivan: Neo-Freudian or not? *Contemporary Psychoanalysis, 25,* 624–640.

Roberts, L. W., & Dyer, A. R. (2004). *Concise guide to ethics in mental health care.* Arlington, VA: American Psychiatric Publishing.

Robertson, B. M., & Perry, C. (2004). Prologue to the special issue on psychoanalytic research. *Canadian Journal of Psychoanalysis, 12*(2), 173–177.

Robinson, L. A., Berman, J. S., & Niemeyer, R. A. (1990). Psychotherapy for the treatment of depression: A comprehensive review of controlled outcome research. *Psychological Bulletin, 108,* 30–49.

Robinson, T. L., & Howard-Hamilton, M. F. (2000). *The convergence of race, ethnicity, and gender: Multiple identities in counseling.* Upper Saddle River, NJ: Merrill.

Roger, P., & Stone, G. (2006). What is the difference between a clinical psychologist and a counseling psychologist? Counseling Psychology, Division 17 of the American Psychological Association. http://www.div17.org/Students/difference. htm. Accessed December 16, 2006.

Rogers, C. (2000). Interview with Carl Rogers on the use of the self and therapy. In M. Baldwin (Ed.), *The use of self and therapy* (2nd ed., pp. 29–38). Binghamton, NY: Haworth.

Rogers, C., & Skinner, B. F. (1956). Some issues concerning the control of human behavior. *Science, 124,* 1057–1065.

Rogers, C. R. (1947). Some observations on the organization of personality. *American Psychologist, 2,* 358–368.

Rogers, C. R. (1951). *Client centered therapy.* Boston: Houghton Mifflin.

Rogers, C. R. (1957). The necessary and sufficient conditions of therapeutic personality change. *Journal of Consulting Psychology, 21,* 95–103.

Rogers, C. R. (1959). A theory of therapy, personality and interpersonal relationships as developed in the client centered framework. In S. Koch (Ed.), *Psychology: A study of science* (pp. 184–256). New York: McGraw-Hill.

Rogers, C. R. (1961). *On becoming a person.* Boston: Houghton Mifflin.

Rogers, C. R. (1977). *Carl Rogers on personal power.* New York: Delacorte.

Rogers, C. R. (1986a). Carl Rogers on the development of the person-centered approach. *Person Centered Review, 1,* 257–259.

Rogers, C. R. (1986b). The Rust workshop: A personal overview. *Journal of Humanistic Psychology, 26,* 23–45.

Rogers, C. R., & Dymond, R. F. (1954). *Psychotherapy and personality change.* Chicago: University of Chicago Press.

Rogers, C. R., Gendlin, G. T., Kiesler, D. V., & Truax, C. (1967). *The therapeutic relationship and its impact: A study of psychotherapy with schizophrenics.* Madison: University of Wisconsin Press.

Rokke, P. D., & Rehm, L. P. (2001). Self management therapies. In K. S. Dobson (Ed.), *Handbook of cognitive behavioral therapies* (2nd ed., pp. 173–210). New York: Guilford.

Rollnick, S., Mason, P., & Butler, C. (1999). *Health behavior change: A guide for practitioners.* London: Churchill Livingstone.

Root, M. P. P. (1985). Guidelines for facilitating therapy with Asian American clients. *Psychotherapy, 22*(2s), 349–356.

Rose, S. W. (2003). The relationship between Glasser's quality school concept and brain-based theory. *International Journal of Reality Therapy, 22*(2), 52–56.

Rosenfeld, E. (1977). An oral history of Gestalt therapy: Part One: A conversation with Laura Perls. *The Gestalt Journal,* May.

Rosewater, L. B., & Walker, L. E. A. (1985). Introduction—feminist therapy coming of age. In L. B. Rosewater & L. E. A. Walker (Eds.), *Handbook of feminist therapy* (pp. ix–xix). New York: Springer.

Rosner, R., Beutler, L. E., & Daldrup, R. J. (2000). Vicarious emotional experience and emotional expression in group psychotherapy. *Journal of Clinical Psychology, 56*(1), 1–10.

Rowan, J. (2001). *Ordinary ecstasy: The dialectics of humanistic psychology.* Hove, United Kingdom: Brunner-Routledge.

Rushton, J. L., Fant, K. E., & Clark, S. J. (2004). Use of practice guidelines in the primary care office with attention-deficit/hyperactivity disorder. *Pediatrics, 114*(1), e23–e28.

Russo, N. F., & O'Connell, A. E. (1992). Women in psychotherapy: Selected contributions. In D. Freedheim (Ed.), *History of psychotherapy: A century of change* (pp. 493–527). Washington, DC: American Psychological Association.

Rychik, A. M., & Lowenkopf, E. M. (2000, August). Reviewing medical malpractice and risk management issues. *Psychiatric Times, 17*(8).

Sackett, D. L., Rosenberg, J. L., Gray, J. L., Haynes, R. B., & Richardson, W. S. (1996). Evidence based medicine: What it is and isn't. *British Medical Journal, 312,* 71–72.

Sacks, S. B. (2004). Rational emotive behavior therapy: Disputing irrational philosophies. *Journal of Psychosocial Nursing Mental Health Services, 42*(5), 22–31.

Safran, J. D. (2001). When worlds collide: Psychoanalysis and the empirically supported treatment movement. *Psychoanalytic Dialogues, 11*(4), 659–681.

Safran, J. D., & Messer, S. B. (1997). Psychotherapy integration: A postmodern critique. *Clinical Psychology: Science and Practice, 4*(2), 140–152.

Salamone, J. D., Cousins, M. S., & Snyder, B. J. (1997). Behavioral functions of nucleus accumbens dopamine: Empirical and conceptual problems with the anhedonia hypothesis. *Neuroscience, 21*(3), 341–359.

Salzano, J. (2003). Taming stress. *Scientific American, 289,* 88–98.

Sandell, R. (2001). Can psychoanalysis become empirically supported? *International Forum of Psychoanalysis, 10*(3–4), 184–190.

Sanderson, C. A. (2004). *Health psychology.* New York: Wiley.

Sandler, A. (1996). The psychoanalytic legacy of Anna Freud. *Psychoanalytic Study of the Child, 51,* 270–284.

Sansone, D. (1998). Research, internal control and choice theory: Where's the beef? *International Journal of Reality Therapy, 17*(2), 39–43.

Santiago-Rivera, A. L., & Altarriba, J. (2002). The role of language in therapy with the Spanish-English bilingual client. *Professional Psychology: Research and Practice, 33*(1), 30–38.

Santos de Barona, M., & Dutton, M. (1997). Feminist perspectives on assessment. In J. Worell & N. Johnson (Eds.), *Feminist visions in psychology: Education, research and practice* (pp. 37–56). Washington, DC: American Psychological Association.

Sarafino, J. (2008). *Health psychology: Biopsychosocial interactions.* New York: Wiley.

Satel, S. (1998). The patriarchy made me do it. *Women's Freedom Network Newsletter, 5*(5), September/October.

Satterfield, J. (2002). Culturally sensitive-cognitive behavioral therapy for depression with low-income and minority clients. In F. W. Kaslow & T. Patterson (Eds.), *Comprehensive handbook of psychotherapy. Volume II: Cognitive-behavioral approaches* (pp. 519–545). Hoboken, NJ: Wiley.

Schacter, J., & Luborsky, L. (1998). Who's afraid of psychoanalytic research? Analysts' attitudes toward reading clinical versus empirical research papers. *International Journal of Psychoanalysis, 79,* 965–969.

Schatzberg, A. F., Cole, J. O., & De Battista, C. (1997). *Manual of clinical psychopharmacology* (3rd ed.). Washington, DC: American Psychiatric Association.

Schatzberg, A. F., & Nemeroff, C. B. (2004). *Textbook of psychopharmacology* (3rd ed.). Washington, DC: American Psychiatric Association.

Schiebinger, L. (2003). Women's health and clinical trials. *Journal of Clinical Investigation, 112,* 937–977.

Schlesinger, M. J., Gray, B. H., & Perriera, K. (1997). Medical professionalism under managed care: The pros and cons of utilization review. *Health Affairs, 16*(1), 106–124.

Schlesinger, M., Wynia, M., & Cummins, D. (2000). Some distinctive features of the impact of managed care on psychiatry. *Harvard Review of Psychiatry, 8*(5), 216–230.

Schneider, K. J. (1998). Toward a science of the heart: Romanticism and the revival of psychology. *American Psychologist, 53*(3), 277–289.

Schneider, K. J. (2001). Multiple case depth research: Bringing experience near closer. In K. J. Schneider, J. F. T. Bugental, & J. F. Pierson (Eds.), *The handbook of humanistic psychology* (pp. 305–314). Thousand Oaks, CA: Sage.

Schneider, K. J. (2003). Existential-humanistic psychotherapies. In A. S. Gurman & S. B. Messer (Eds.), *Essential psychotherapies*(149–182). New York: Guilford.

Schneider-Berti, A. (2004). Inner transformation and existential crises: Renancer groups for bereaved parents. *International forum for logotherapy, 27*(2), 65–76.

Schnittker, J. (2003). Misgivings of medicine? African Americans' skepticism of psychiatric medications. *Journal of Health and Social Behavior, 44*(4), 506–524.

Schubmehl, J. Q. (1996). Technique and metapsychology of the early working through phase of Davanloo's intensive short-term dynamic psychotherapy. *International Journal of Short-Term Psychotherapy, 11*, 225–251.

Schultz, J., & Luthe, W. (1959). *Autogenic training: A psychophysiological approach to psychotherapy.* New York: Grune & Stratton.

Schulz, W. (2002). *Making the manifesto: The birth of religious humanism.* Boston: Skinner House.

Scully, M. (1995). Viktor Frankl at ninety: An interview. *First Things, 52,* 39–43.

Seligman, L. (1998). *Selecting effective treatments.* San Francisco: Jossey-Bass.

Seligman, L. (2004). *Diagnosis and treatment planning in counseling* (3rd ed.). New York: Springer

Seligman, L. (2005). *Theories of counseling and psychotherapy: Systems, strategies, and skills* (2nd ed.). Englewood Cliffs, NJ: Prentice-Hall.

Seligman, L. (2006). *Theories of counseling and psychotherapy* (2nd ed.). Hoboken, NJ: Pearson.

Seligman, M. E. P. (1995). The effectiveness of psychotherapy: The consumer reports study. *American Psychologist, 50,* 965–974.

Selye, H. (1974). *Stress without distress.* New York: Lippincott.

Selye, H. (1976a). *Stress in health and disease.* Reading, MA: Butterworths.

Selye, H. (1976b). *The stress of life.* New York: McGraw-Hill.

Sexton, H. (1996). Process, life events, and symptomatic change in brief eclectic psychotherapy. *Journal of Consulting and Clinical Psychology, 64*(6), 1358–1365.

Sexton, T. L. (1996). The relevance of counseling outcome research: Current trends and practical implications. *Journal of Counseling and Development, 74,* 590–600.

Shadish, W. R., & Baldwin, S. A. (2005.) Effects of behavioral marital therapy: A meta-analysis of randomized controlled trials. *Journal of Consulting and Clinical Psychology, 73,* 6–14.

Shadish, W. R., & Rindskopf, D. M. (2007). Methods for evidence-based practice: Quantitative synthesis of single-subject designs. *New Directions for Evaluation* [online]. http://www3.interscience.wiley.com/journal/85512890/home.

Shapiro, D. A., & Shapiro, D. (1982) Meta-analysis of comparative psychotherapy studies: A replication and refinement. *Psychological Bulletin, 92,* 581–604.

Shapiro, F. (1999). Eye movement desensitization and reprocessing (EMDR): Evaluation of controlled PTSD research. *Journal of Behavior Therapy and Experimental Psychiatry, 27,* 209–218.

Shapiro, F. (2001). *Eye movement desensitization and reprocessing: Basic principles, protocols, and procedures* (2nd ed.). New York: Guilford.

Shapiro, F., Snyker, E., & Maxfield, L. (2002). EMDR: Eye movement desensitization and reprocessing. In F. Kaslow & T. Patterson (Eds.), *Comprehensive handbook of psychotherapy* (pp. 241–272). New York: Wiley.

Sharf, R. S. (2004). *Theories of psychotherapy and counseling: Concepts and cases* (3rd ed.). Pacific Grove, CA: Brooks/Cole.

Shavelson, R., & Towne, L. (2002). *Scientific research in education.* Washington, DC: National Academy Press.

Sheehy, N., Chapman, A. J., & Conroy, W. (Eds). (1997). *Biographical dictionary of psychology.* London: Routledge.

Sherman, K. C. (2000). CT/RT in chronic pain management: Using choice/reality therapy as a cognitive behavioral intervention for chronic pain management: A pilot study. *International Journal of Reality Therapy, 19*(2), 10–14.

Sherrill, R. E. (1986). Gestalt therapy and gestalt psychology. *The Gestalt Journal,* Fall.

Shoham-Saloman, V., & Rosenthal, R. (1987). Paradoxical interventions: A meta-analysis. *Journal of Consulting and Clinical Psychology, 55,* 22–28.

Shook, V. (2002). *Ho' oponopono: Contemporary uses of Hawaiian problem-solving process.* Honolulu: University of Hawai'i Press.

Sifneos, P. E. (1992). *Short-term anxiety-provoking psychotherapy.* New York: Basic Books.

Skinner, B. F. (1938) *The behavior of organisms.* New York: Appleton-Century-Crofts.

Skinner, B. F. (1953). *Science and human behavior.* New York: Macmillan.

Skinner, B. F. (1974). *About behaviorism.* New York: Knopf.

Skinner, B. F. (1976). *The particulars of my life.* New York: McGraw-Hill.

Skinner, B. F. (1990). *Keynote address: Lifetime scientific contributions.* American Psychological Association, Boston, August 10.

Slavik, S., & Carlson, J. (Eds.). (2005). *Readings in the theory of individual psychology.* London: Routledge.

Slavik, S., Carlson, J., & Sperry, L. (1995). Individual psychology. *Journal of Adlerian Theory, Research & Practice, 51*(4), 358–374.

Sloane, R. B., Staples, F. R., Cristol, A. H., Yorkston, N. J., & Whipple, K. (1975). *Psychotherapy vs. behavior therapy.* Cambridge, MA: Harvard University Press.

Smith, A. J., & Siegal, R. F. (1985). Feminist therapy: Redefining power for the powerless. In L. B. Rosewater & L. E. A. Walker (Eds.), *Handbook of feminist therapy* (pp. 13–21). New York: Springer.

Smith, M. L., & Glass, G. V. (1977). Meta-analysis of psychotherapy outcome studies. *American Psychologist, 32,* 752–760.

Smith, M. L., Glass G. V., & Miller, T. I. (1980). *The benefits of psychotherapy.* Baltimore: Johns Hopkins University Press.

Sochurek, H. (1988). *Medicine's new vision.* Easton, PA: Mack.

Soderlund, J. (2007). Integral EMDR: An exclusive interview with Francine Shapiro, the originator of Eye Movement Desensitization and Reprocessing, on why it's a protypically integrative approach. *New Therapist,* 9. http://www.newtherapist.com/shapiro9. html. Accessed March 25, 2007.

Soldz, S., & McCullogh, L. (2000). *Reconciling empirical knowledge and clinical experience.* Washington, DC: American Psychological Association.

Spagnuolo Lobb, M. (2006). *What's gestalt therapy?* http://www.gestalt.it/inglese/get-e.htm.

Spagnuolo Lobb, M., & Amendt-Lyon, N. (2003). *Creative license: The art of gestalt therapy.* New York: Springer Wein.

Sparks, E. E., & Park, A. (2000). The integration of feminism and multiculturalism: Ethical dilemmas at the border. In M. Brabeck (Ed.), *Practicing feminist ethics in psychology* (pp. 203–224). Washington, DC: American Psychological Association.

Spiegal, R. (1989). *Psychopharmacology: An Introduction.* New York: Wiley.

Spiegler, M. D., & Guevremont, D. C. (1993). *Contemporary behavior therapy* (2nd ed.). Pacific Grove, CA: Brooks/Cole.

Spiegler, M. D., & Guevremont, D. C. (2003). *Contemporary behavior therapy* (4th ed.). Pacific Grove, CA: Brooks/Cole.

Sprague, J., & Hayes, J. (2000). Self-determination and empowerment: A feminist standpoint analysis of talk about disability. *American Journal of Community Psychology, 28*(5), 671–697.

St. Clair, M., with Wigren, J. (2004). *Object relations and self psychology: An introduction* (4th ed.). Boston: Thomson.

Stambor, Z. (2006). Psychology's prescribing pioneers. *Monitor on Psychology, 37*(7), 30–32.

Stampfl, T. G., & Levis, D. J. (1967). Essentials of implosive therapy: A learning based psychodynamic approach. *Journal of Abnormal Psychology, 72,* 496–503.

Stanilla, J. K., & Simpson, G. M. (2004). Drugs to treat extrapyramidal side effects. In A. F. Schatzberg & C. B. Nemeroff (Eds.), *Textbook of psychopharmacology* (3rd ed., pp. 519–544). Washington, DC: American Psychiatric Publishing.

Stanley, L., & Wise, S. (1983). *Breaking out: Feminist consciousness and feminist research.* London: Routledge & Kegan Paul.

Steiman, M., & Dobson S. (2002). Cognitive-behavioral approaches to depression. In F. W. Kaslow & T. Patterson (Eds.), *Comprehensive handbook of psychotherapy: Volume II,* (pp. 296–319). Hoboken, NJ: Wiley.

Stein, H. T. (1988). Twelve stages of creative Adlerian psychotherapy. *Individual Psychology, 44*(2), 138–143.

Stein, H. T. (1990). *Classical Adlerian depth psychotherapy: A Socratic approach.* San Francisco: Alfred Adler Institute of San Francisco.

Stein, H. T. (1991). Adler and Socrates: Similarities and differences. *Individual Psychology, 47*(2), 123–127.

Stein, H. T. (2006). Personal communication.

Stein, H. T., & Edwards, M. E. (1998). Classical Adlerian theory and practice. In P. Marcus & A. Rosenberg (Eds.), *Psychoanalytic versions of the human condition: Philosophies of life and their impact on practice.* New York: New York University Press.

Stein, H. T., & Edwards, M. E. (2003). Classical Adlerian therapy. In M. Hersen & W. H. Sledge (Eds.), *The encyclopedia of psychotherapy* (Vol. 1, pp. 23–31). Elsevier Science.

Stewart, A. J., & McDermott, C. (2004). Gender in psychology. A*nnual Review of Psychology, 55,* 519–544.

Stone, J., Colyer, M., Feltblower, S., Carson, A., & Sharpe, M. (2004). Psychosomatic: A systematic review of its meaning in newspaper articles. *Psychosomatics, 45,* 287–290.

Stopler, G. (2003). Countenancing the oppression of women: How liberals tolerate religious and cultural practices that discriminate against women. *Columbia Journal of Gender and Law, 12*(1), 154 ff.

Stout, C. E., & Hayes, R. A. (2005). *The evidence-based practice: Methods, models, and tools for mental health professionals.* New York: Wiley.

Stratyner, H. (2004). Foreword. In *PDR: Drug guide for mental health professionals* (pp. v–vi). Montvale, NJ: Thomson.

Stricker, G., & Gold, J. (2003). Integrative approaches to psychotherapy. Essential psychotherapies: Theory and practice (2nd ed., pp. 317–349). New York: Guilford.

Stricker, G., & Gold, J. (Eds.). (1996). *Comprehensive handbook of psychotherapy integration.* New York: Plenum.

Strosahl, K. (1996). Confessions of a behavior therapist in primary care: The odyssey and the ecstasy. *Cognitive and Behavioral Practice, 3*(1), 1–28.

Strosahl, K. (1996). Mind and body primary mental health career: New model for integrated services. *Behavioral Healthcare Tomorrow, 5,* 93–96.

Strozier, C. B. (2001). *Heinz Kohut: The making of a psychoanalyst.* New York: Farrar, Straus & Giroux.

Strumpfel, U. (2006). *Therapie Der Gefubile: Forschungsbefunde zur Gestalttherapie.* Cologne, Germany: Edition Humansistiche Psychologie. http://therapie-der-gefuehle.de/summary. html (some English translation).

Strumpfel, U., & Goldman, R. (2002). Contacting Gestalt therapy. In D. J. Cain & J. Seeman (Eds.), *Humanistic psychotherapies: Handbook of research and practice* (pp. 189–219). Washington, DC: American Psychological Association.

Strupp, H. (1995). The psychotherapist's skill revisited. *Clinical Psychology: Science and Practice, 2,* 70–74.

Stuart, G. L., Treat, T. A., & Wade, W. A. (2000). Effectiveness of an empirically based treatment for panic disorder delivered in a clinic setting: One year follow up. *Journal of Consulting and Clinical Psychology, 68,* 506–512.

Sturmey, P., & Gaubatz, M. (2003). *Clinical and counseling practice.* Boston: Pearson.

Sue, D. (2003). *Overcoming our racism.* San Francisco: Jossey-Bass.

Sue, D. W. (2001). Multidimensional facets of cultural competence. *The Counseling Psychologist, 29*(6), 790–821.

Sue, D. W., & Sue, D. (2003). *Counseling the culturally diverse: Theory and practice* (4th ed.). New York: Wiley.

Sue, D. W., & Sue, S. (1987). Cultural factors in the clinical assessment of Asian Americans. *Journal of Consulting and Clinical Psychology,* 55(4), 479–487.

Suc, D., & Suc, D. (2003). *Counseling the diverse: Theory and practice* (4th ed.). New York: Wiley.

Sue, D., Sue, D., & Sue, S. (2006). *Abnormal psychology.* Boston: Houghton Mifflin.

Sue, S. (1988). Psychotherapeutic services for ethnic minorities: Two decades of research findings. *American Psychologist, 43,* 301–308.

Sue, S. (1998). In search of cultural competence in psychotherapy and counseling. *American Psychologist, 53*(4).

Sue, S. W. (2003). *Overcoming our racism: The journey to liberation.* San Francisco: Jossey-Bass.

Sue, S., & Chu, J. (2003). The mental health of ethnic minority groups: Challenges posed by the U. S. Surgeon General. *Culture, Medicine and Psychiatry, 27,* 447–465.

Sullivan, H. S. (1953) The interpersonal theory of psychiatry. New York, Norton

Sulloway, F. (1996). *Born to rebel: Birth order, family dynamics, and creative lives.* New York: Pantheon.

Suls, J., & Rothman, A. (2004). Evolution of the biopsychosocial model: Prospects and challenges for health psychology. *Health Psychology, 23,* 119–125.

Summers, F. L. (1999). *Transcending the self: An object relations model of psychoanalytic therapy.* Hillsdale, NJ: Analytic Press.

Sutton., S. (2006). Commentaries on Dijkstra et al. Needed: More match-mismatch studies of well-specified stage theories. *Addiction, 101*(7), 915.

Szasz, T. (2005). What is existential therapy not? *Existential Analysis, 16*(1), 127–130.

Tavris, C. (1992). *The mismeasure of woman.* New York, Simon & Schuster.

Taylor, S. (1996). Meta-analysis of cognitive-behavioral treatment for school phobia. *Journal of Behavior Therapy and Experimental Psychiatry, 27,* 1–9.

Taylor, S. E. (2006). *Health psychology* (6th ed.). New York: McGraw-Hill.

Teuber, L., Watjens, F., & Jensen, L. H. (1999). Ligands for the benzodiazepine binding site—a survey. *Current Pharmacy, 5*(5), 317–343.

Thase, M. E., & Jindal, R. D. (2004). Combining psychotherapy and psychopharmacology treatment of mental disorders. In M. Lambert (Ed.), *Bergin and Garfield's handbook of psychotherapy and behavior changes* (5th ed., pp. 743–766). New York: Wiley.

Thase, M. E., Jindal, R., & Howland, R. (2002). In I. H. Gotlib & C. L. Hammen (Eds.), *Biological aspects of depression: Handbook of depression* (pp. 192–218). New York: Guilford.

Tiefer, L. (1996). Feminism and sex research: Ten years' reminiscences and appraisal. In J. C. Chrisler & D. Howard (Eds.), *New direction in feminist psychology: Practice, theory, and research.* New York: Springer.

Todman, J., & Dugard, P. (2001). *Single-case and small-n experimental design: A practical guide to randomization tests.* Mahwah, NJ: Erlbaum.

Trepper, T. S., Dolan, Y., McCollum, E. E., & Nelson, T. (2006). Steve de Shazer and the future of solution-focused therapy. *Journal of Marital and Family Therapy, 32*(2), 133–139.

Trull, T. J., & Phares, J. (2001). *Clinical psychology.* Belmont, CA: Wadsworth.

U. S. Census Bureau. (2001). *Population division and housing and household economic statistics division.* Washington, DC: Author.

U. S. Department of Health and Human Services. (1999). *Mental health: A report of the Surgeon General—Executive summary.* Rockville, MD: Author.

U. S. Department of Health and Human Services. (2000). *A report of a Surgeon General's working meeting on the integration of mental health services and primary health care.* Rockville, MD: Author.

U. S. Department of Labor, Bureau of Labor Statistics. (2004). *Occupational outlook handbook.* www. bls. gov.

U. S. Department of Labor, Bureau of Labor Statistics. (2006). *Occupational outlook handbook.* http://www .bls.gov.

Vaihinger, H. (1952). *The philosophy of "as if."* C. K. Ogden (Trans.). London: Routledge.

van Deurzen-Smith, E. (1988). *Existential counselling in practice* (2nd ed.). London: Sage.

van Deurzen-Smith, E. (1990a). What is existential analysis? *Journal of the Society for Existential Analysis, 1,* 6–14.

van Deurzen-Smith, E. (1990b). Existential therapy. In W. Dryden (Ed.), *Individual therapy* (pp. 149–174). Philadelphia: Open University Press.

van Deurzen-Smith, E. (1998). *Paradox and passion in psychotherapy: An existential approach to therapy and counseling.* Chichester, United Kingdom: Wiley.

van Deurzen, E. (2007). *Introduction: Existentialism and existential psychotherapy.* http://www.nspc.org.uk/ docs/papers/exist_EVanD. pdf. Accessed May 30, 2007.

Vande Kemp, V. (2003). *The Feminist Psychologist, 30*(2).

Vaughan, S. C., Marshall, R. D., Mackinnon, R. A., Vaughan, R., Mellman, L., & Roose, S. P. (2000). Can we do psychoanalytic outcome research? A feasibility study. *International Journal of Psychoanalysis, 81*(Pt. 3), 513–527.

Victoroff, J. (2002). A warm welcome to 21st century psychiatry. *Psychiatric Times, XIX* (8).

Vinck, J., & Meganck, J. (2006). Do we need critical health psychology or rather critical health psychologists? *Journal of Health Psychology, 11*(3), 391–393.

Vitz, P. C. (1977). *Psychology as religion: The cult of self-worship.* Grand Rapids, MI: Eerdmans.

Von Sassen, H. W. (1967). Adler's and Freud's concepts of man: A phenomenological comparison. *Journal of Individual Psychology, 23*(3), 10.

Vontress, C. (2003). On becoming an existential cross-cultural counselor. In F. D. Harper & J. McFadden (Eds.), *Culture and counseling* (pp. 20–30). Boston: Allyn & Bacon.

Wachtel, P. (1982). *Resistance: Psychodynamic and behavior approaches.* New York, Plenum.

Wachtel, P. (1987). *Action and insight.* New York: Guilford.

Wake, N. (2007). The military, psychiatry, and "unfit" soldiers, 1939–1942. *Journal of History of Medical Allied Science, 62*(4), 461–494.

Walker, L. (1987). Women's groups are different. In C. M. Brody (Ed.), *Women's therapy groups* (pp. 1–11). New York: Springer.

Walker, L. (1990). A feminist therapist views the case. In D. W. Cantor (Ed.), *Women as therapists* (pp. 78–79). New York: Springer.

Walker, L. (1994) *Abused women and survivor therapy: A practical guide for the psychotherapist.* Washington, DC: American Psychological Association.

Wallerstein, R. S. (1988). Assessment of structural change in psychoanalytic therapy and research. *Journal of the American Psychoanalytic Association, 36*(Suppl.), 241–261.

Wallerstein, R. S. (1989). The psychotherapy research project of the Meninger Foundation: An overview. *Journal of Consulting and Clinical Psychology, 57,* 195–205.

Wallerstein, R. S. (2002). The place of psychoanalytic treatments within psychiatry. Commentary to: The place of psychoanalytic treatments within psychiatry. *Archives of General Psychiatry, 59*(16), 528.

Walter, J., & Peller, J. (1994). On track in brief therapy. In M. Hoyt (Ed.), *Constructive therapies* (pp. 111–125). New York: Guilford.

Wampold, B. E. (2001). *The great psychotherapy debate: Models, methods, and findings.* Mahwah, NJ: Erlbaum.

Wampold, B. E. (2006). Not a scintilla of evidence to support empirically supported treatments as more effective than other treatments. In J. C. Norcross, L. E. Beutler, & R. F. Levant (Eds.), *Evidence-based practice in mental health: Debate and dialogue on the fundamental questions* (pp. 299–307). Washington, DC: American Psychological Association.

Wampold, B. E., Mondin, G. W., Moody, M., Stich, F., Benson, K., & Ahn, H. (1997). A meta-analysis of outcome studies comparing bona fide psychotherapies: Empirically, "All must have prizes." *Psychological Bulletin, 122*(3), 203–215.

Wang, P. S., Lane, M., Olfson, M., Pincus, H. A., Wells, K. B., & Kessler, R. B. (2005). Twelve month use of mental health services in the United States. *Archives of General Psychiatry, 62,* 629–640.

Warmoth, A. (1998). Humanistic psychology and humanistic social science. *Humanity and Society, 22*(3), 2–7.

Warren, R., & Thomas, C. J. (2001). Cognitive behavior therapy of an obsessive compulsive disorder in private practice: An effectiveness study. *Journal of Anxiety Disorder, 15,* 277–285.

Watson, D. L., & Tharp, R. G. (2002). *Self-directed behavior modification: Self-modification for personal adjustment* (8th ed.). Pacific Grove, CA: Brooks/Cole.

Watson, J. (1913). Psychology as a behaviorist views it. *Psychological Review, 20,* 158–177.

Watson, J., & Rayner, R. (1920). Conditioned emotional reactions. *Journal of Experimental Psychology, 3,* 1–14.

Watts, R. E. (1998). The remarkable similarity between Rogers' core conditions and Adler's social interest. *Journal of Individual Psychology, 54,* 4–9.

Watts, R. E. (2000). Is individual psychology still relevant? *Journal of Individual Psychology, 56,* 21–30.

Watts, R. E. (2003). Adlerian therapy as a relational constructivist approach. *Counseling and Therapy for Couples and Families, 11*(2), 139–147.

Watts, R. E., & Pietrzak, D. R. (2000). Adlerian encouragement and the therapeutic process of solution based brief therapy. *Journal of Counseling and Development, 78,* 442–447.

Watzlawick, P., Beavin, J. H., & Jackson, D. D. (1967). *Pragmatics of human communication: A study of interactional patterns, pathologies, and paradoxes.* New York: Norton.

Weil, A. (2004). *Natural health, natural medicine: A comprehensive manual for wellness and self-care.* Boston: Houghton Mifflin.

Weil, A. W. (2004). *Health and healing.* Boston: Houghton Mifflin.

Weil, A. W. (1998). *Health and healing.* New York: Houghton Mifflin.

Weinberger, J. (1995). Common factors aren't so common: The common factors dilemma. *Clinical Psychology: Science and Practice, 2,* 45–69.

Weinstein, N. D., Rothman, A. J., & Sutton, S. R. (1998). Stage theories of health behavior: Conceptual and methodological issues. *Health Psychology, 17,* 290–299.

Weissman, M. M., Markowitz, J. C., & Klerman, G. L. (2000). *A comprehensive guide to interpersonal therapy.* New York: Basic Books.

Weisz, J. R. (2004). *Psychotherapy for children and adolescents: Evidence-based treatments and case examples.* Cambridge, England: Cambridge University Press.

Weisz, J. R., & Kazdin, A. E. (2003). Context and background of evidence-based psychotherapies for children and adolescents. In J. R. Weisz & A. E. Kazdin (Eds.), *Evidence based psychotherapies for children and adolescents* (pp. 3–21). New York: Guilford.

Weisz, J. R., & Kazdin, A. E. (2003). Present and future of evidence based psychotherapies for children and adolescents. In J. R. Weisz & A. E. Kazdin (Eds.), *Evidence based psychotherapies for children and adolescents* (pp. 439–451). New York: Guilford.

Weisz, J. R., Donenburg, G. R., Han, S. S., & Weiss, B. (1995). Bridging the gap between laboratory and clinic in child and adolescent psychiatry. *Journal of Consulting and Clinical Psychotherapy, 63,* 688–701.

Weisz, J. R., Hawley, K. M., & Doss, A. J. (2004). Empirically tested psychotherapies for youth internalizing and externalizing problems and disorders. *Child and Adolescent Psychiatric Clinics of North America, 13,* 729–815.

Weisz, J. R., Sandler, I. N., Durlak, J. A., & Anton, B. S. (2005). Promoting and protecting youth mental health through evidence-based prevention and treatment. *American Psychologist, 60,* 628–648.

Weisz, J. R., Weiss, B., Alicke, M. D., & Klotz, M. L. (1987). Effectiveness of psychotherapy with children and adolescents: A meta-analysis for clinicians. *Journal of Consulting and Clinical Psychology, 55,* 542–549.

Wenar, C., & Kerig, P. (2000). *Developmental psychopathology.* New York: McGraw-Hill.

Wenzel, A., Steer, R. A., & Beck, A. T. (2005). Are there any gender differences in frequency of self reported somatic symptoms of depression? *Journal of Affective Disorders, 89,* 177–181.

Westen, D. (1998). The scientific legacy of Sigmund Freud: Toward a psychodynamically informed psychological science. *Psychological Bulletin, 124*(3), 333–371.

Western, D. (2001). A multidimensional meta-analysis of treatment for depression, panic, and generalized anxiety disorder: An empirical examination of the status of empirically supported therapies. *Journal of Consulting and Clinical Psychology, 69*(6), 875–899.

Western, D., Novotny, C. M., & Thompson-Brenner, H. (2004). The empirical status of empirically supported psychotherapies: Assumptions, finding, and reporting in controlled clinical trials. *Psychological Bulletin, 130*(4), 631–663.

White, M., & Epston, D. (1989). *Literate means to therapeutic ends.* Adelaide, South Australia: Dulwich Centre Publications.

Whitelaw, S., Baldwin, S., & Bunton, R. (2000). The status of evidence and outcomes in stages of change research. *Health Education Research, 15,* 707–718.

Wierzbicki, M. (1993). *Issues in clinical psychology.* Needham Heights, MA: Allyn & Bacon.

Wilson, E. H. (1995). *The genesis of a humanist manifesto.* Amherst, NY: Humanist Press.

Wilson, T. (2005). Behavior therapy. In R. J. Corsini & D. Wedding (Eds.), *Current psychotherapies* (7th ed., pp. 202–237). Belmont, CA: Brooks/Cole.

Winslade, J., & Monk, G. (2000). *Narrative mediation: A new approach to conflict resolution.* San Francisco: Jossey-Bass.

Wohl, J. (1995). Traditional individual psychotherapy and ethnic minorities. In J. F. Aponte, R. Y. Rivers, & J. Wohl (Eds.), *Psychological interventions and cultural diversity* (pp. 74–91). Boston: Allyn & Bacon.

Woldt, A. S., & Toman, S. M. (Eds.). (2005). *Gestalt therapy: History, theory, practice.* Newbury, CA: Sage.

Wolf, E. S. (1995). How to supervise without doing harm. *Psychoanalytic Inquiry, 5*(2), 271.

Wolitzsky, D. L. (2003). The theory and practice of traditional psychoanalytic treatment. In A. S. Gurman & S. B. Messer (Eds.), *Essential psychotherapies: Theory and practice* (pp. 24–68). New York: Guilford.

Wolpe, J. (1958). *Psychotherapy by reciprocal inhibition.* Stanford, CA: Stanford University Press.

Wolpe, J. (1973) *The practice of behavior therapy* (2nd. ed.) Elmsford, NY: Pergamon.

Wolpe, J. (1987). Destigmatization of behavior therapy. *American Psychologist, 42*(1), 100–101.

Wolpe, J. (1990). *The practice of behavior therapy* (4th ed.). New York: Pergamon.

Wolpe, J. (1997). Pavlov's contribution to behavior therapy: The obvious and the not so obvious. *American Psychologist, 52*(91), 966–972.

Wong, E. C. (2003). An aptitude by treatment interaction approach to developing culturally sensitive therapy: Relying on client characteristics to guide the selection of treatment. *Dissertation Abstracts International: Section B: The Sciences and Engineering, 64*(6-B), 2964.

Wong, M. L. (2002). Evidence-based health promotion: Applying it in practice. *Annals, Academy of Medicine, Singapore, 5,* 656–662.

Wong, P. T. (2004) Existential psychology for the 21st century. *International Journal of Existential Psychology and Psychotherapy, 1*(1, July), 1–2.

Woody, S. R., Weisz, J., & McLean, C. (2005). Empirically supported treatments: 10 years later. *The Clinical Psychologist, 58*(4), 5–11.

Worell, J. (2001). Feminist interventions: Accountability beyond symptom reduction. *Psychology of Women Quarterly, 25,* 335–343.

Worell, J., & Remer, P. (Eds.). (2003). *Feminist perspective in therapy: Empowering diverse women.* New York: Wiley.

World Health Organization, Department of Gender, Women, and Health. (2008). http://www.who.int/gender/en.

World Health Organization. (1964). *Basic documents* (15th ed., p. 1). Geneva: Author.

Wubbolding, R. E. (1985). Characteristics of the inner picture album. *Journal of Reality Therapy, 5*(1), 28–30.

Wubbolding, R. E. (1996). Professional issues: The use of questioning in reality therapy. *Journal of Reality Therapy, 16*(1), 122–127.

Wubbolding, R. E. (2000). *Reality therapy for the 21st century.* Philadelphia: Brunner/Routledge.

Wubbolding, R., Al-Rashidi, B., Brickell, J., Kakitani, M., Kim, R. I., Lennon, B., Lojik, L., Ong, K. H., Honey, I., Stijacic, D., & Tham, E. (1998). Multicultural awareness: Implications for reality therapy and choice theory. *International Journal of Reality Therapy, 17*(2), 4–6.

Wulf, R. (1996). The historical roots of gestalt therapy. *Gestalt dialogue: Newsletter for the Integrative Gestalt Centre,* Aoteroa, New Zealand. prj@chc.planet.org.nz.

Yalom, I. (1980). *Existential psychotherapy.* New York: Basic Books.

Yalom, I. (1989). *Love's executioner and other tales of psychotherapy.* London: Bloomsbury.

Yalom, I. (1996) *Lying on the couch.* New York: Basic Books.

Yarbrough, J., & Thompson, C. L. (2002). Using single participant research to assess counseling approaches to children's off task behavior. *Professional School Counseling, 5,* 308–314.

Yoder, J. D. (2002). 2001 division 35 presidential address: Context matters: Understanding tokenism processes and their impact on women's work. *Psychology of Women Quarterly, 26*(1), 1–8.

Yoder, J. D., & Kahn, A. S. (2003). Making gender comparisons more meaningful: A call for more attention to social context. *Psychology of Women Quarterly, 27*(4), 281–290.

Yontef, G. M. (1993). Introduction to field theory. In G. Yontef (Ed.), *Awareness, dialogue and process: Essays on gestalt therapy* (pp. 285–325). New York: Gestalt Journal Press.

Yontef, G. M. (1995). Gestalt therapy. In A. Gurman & S. Messer (Eds.), *Essential psychotherapies* (pp. 261–303). New York: Guilford.

Yontef, G. M. (1998). Dialogic gestalt therapy. In L. S. Greenberg, J. C. Watson, & G. Lietaer (Eds.), *Handbook of experiential psychotherapy* (pp. 82–102). New York: Guilford.

Yontef, G. M. (1999). *Los Angeles Pacific Gestalt Institute.* http://www.gestalttherapy.org/publications/index.html. Acccessed March 4, 2007.

Yontef, G. M., & Jacobs, L. (2008) Gestalt therapy. In R. J. Corsini & D. Wedding (Eds.), *Current psychotherapies* (8th ed., pp. 328–367). Belmont, CA: Thomson, Brooks/Cole.

Yontef, G. M., & Simkin, J. S. (1989). Gestalt therapy. In R. J. Corsini & D. Wedding (Eds.), *Current psychotherapies* (pp. 323–362). Itasca, IL: Peacock.

Young, C. (2001, October 18). Multiculturalism and feminism. *Reason Magazine.*

Young-Eisendrath, P., & Wiedemann, F. L. (1987). *Female authority: Empowering women through psychotherapy.* New York: Guilford.

Zack, N. (2005). *Inclusive feminism: A third wave theory of women's commonality.* Lanham, MD: Rowman & Littlefield.

Zane, N., Hall, G. C., Sue, S., Young, K., & Nunez, J. (2004). Research on psychotherapy with culturally diverse populations. In M. J. Lambert (Ed.), *Bergin and Garfield's handbook of psychotherapy and behavior change* (5th ed., pp. 767–804). New York: Wiley.

Zaser, R. (2006). Viktor E. Frankl as a pioneer of the modern philosophical practice. *International Forum for Logotherapy, 29*(2), 69–72.

Zimmerman, G. L., Olsen, C. G., & Bosworth, M. F. (2000). A stages of change approach to patient change. *American Family Physician, 61* (5), 1409–1416.

Zimmerman, T. S., Holm, K. E., & Starrels, M. E. (2001). A feminist analysis of self-help bestsellers for improving relationships: A decade review.

Journal of Marital and Family Therapy, 27, 165–175.

Zimring, F. M., & Raskin, N. J. (1992). Carl Rogers and client/person centered therapy. In D. K. Freedheim (Ed.), *History of psychotherapy* (pp. 629–656). Washington, DC: American Psychological Association.

Zinker, J. (1977). *Creative process in gestalt therapy.* New York: Brunner/Mazel.

Zur, O. (2007). Dual relationships. *Boundaries in psychotherapy: Ethical and clinical explorations* (pp. 21–46). Washington, DC: American Psychological Association.

Name Index

SUBJECT INDEX